CHANGING INTERPRETATIONS
AND NEW SOURCES
IN NAVAL HISTORY

CHANGING INTERPRETATIONS AND NEW SOURCES IN NAVAL HISTORY

Papers from the Third
United States Naval Academy
History Symposium

edited by
Robert William Love, Jr.

co-editors:
P. Robert Artigiani
Merrill L. Bartlett
William M. Belote
James C. Bradford
Carroll M. Gillmore
Kenneth J. Hagan
Frederick S. Harrod
Jack Sweetman
Craig Symonds
James P. Thomas, Jr.
Larry V. Thompson
Philip W. Warken

GARLAND PUBLISHING, INC. • NEW YORK & LONDON
1980

Library of Congress Cataloging in Publication Data

United States Naval Academy History Symposium,
3rd, 1977.
Changing interpretations and new sources in
naval history.

1. Naval history—Congresses. I. Love,
Robert William, 1944–   II. United States.
Naval Academy, Annapolis.   III. Title.
D27.U63   1977   359'.009   80-5
ISBN 0-8240-9517-0

Printed on acid-free, 250-year-life paper
Manufactured in the United States of America

Contents

D 27 .U63 1977

Preface

It is not an unreasonable speculation that, when Stone Age men in the eighth millennium B.C. organized water craft to combat enemies, a history, probably in the form of tribal legend, was maintained of their victories and defeats. From those earliest days to the present, the disciples of the muse Clio have recorded the ways of naval men and their leaders, the characteristics of boats and ships, the relationship of navies to societies, and the features that set navies apart from other social units. In this endeavor, past naval historians often tried to explain greater truths about their own or other civilizations.

The body of literature which they wrote is our naval history. It is rich in narrative prose, relentless in its pursuit of the reasons for triumph or loss in battle, and sturdy in its assertion that the study of warfare at sea is the highest form of the art. The intellectual father of modern naval historians, Alfred Thayer Mahan, wrote ninety years ago that "the history of sea power, while embracing in its broad sweep all that tends to make a people great upon the sea or by the sea, is largely a military history." Although Mahan recognized and enumerated "conditions affecting the sea power of nations," the study of these matters was mostly beyond the scope of his definition of "a military history." However, the most recent historical literature on navies indicates that contemporary scholars have rejected Mahan's definition and hold instead that more attention needs to be paid to those "conditions" which define navies—and which themselves may dictate military victory or loss at sea. This suggests that a tendency to over-emphasize the epics of warfare has for too long meant that we have forfeited a more complex, and more satisfying, appreciation of the history of navies.

It was in part to test this last assertion that the Third Naval History Symposium was organized. Held at the United States Naval Academy on 27 and 28 October 1977, the conference sought to gauge the state of current research on and thought about naval history, and perhaps to suggest new areas of study for members of the fraternity. The following articles, selected from those presented at the Symposium, are perhaps a rough benchmark of the current state of this unique field of scholarship. In a modest way, they testify to its present character and suggest realms for future growth. As David Trask concluded, naval history "may not yet be a school, but it is at least a kindergarten."

Acknowledgments ⎯⎯⎯⎯⎯

Many kind and intelligent people made this book possible. Dr. Bruce M. Davidson, Academic Dean of the United States Naval Academy, and Dr. Richard D. Mathieu, Director of Research, provided unstinting support both for the Third Naval History Symposium and especially for publication of this volume. Colonel Frank Zimolzak, USMC, Director of the Division of English and History, was invariably helpful and enthusiastic. Professor Larry V. Thompson, Chairman of the History Department, provided thoughtful direction for the Symposium and practical help with this book. Captain William T. Bowers, USA; Lieutenant Richard G. Gilbert, USN; Lieutenant Commander Dennis Glass, USN; Lieutenant, j.g., Leslie Knowlton, USN; Major Donald W. Nelson, USAF; Lieutenant Larry Robinson, USN; and Lieutenant Commander Steven Vanderbosch, USN, assured that the arrangements for the conference were executed with great professionalism. My other colleagues in the History Department gave constantly and unflinchingly of their time to ensure that the conference was a success and they are due my warmest appreciation. To my fellow editors, on whose expertise and learning I relied in editing these papers, I extend my sincere thanks. Finally, to Assistant Professor Craig Symonds, who devoted himself to the Symposium and to whom I ran when I needed sound advice during the preparation of this book, I owe a pleasant debt. My wife, Rose, supported me with affection and good humor throughout this enterprise and has my gratitude.

Annapolis, Maryland   Robert William Love, Jr.
31 July 1979

CHAPTER 1

The Greek Ship: New Evidence through Nautical Archaeology

J. Richard Steffy

Texas & M University

Much of our present knowledge of ancient Greek maritime activities comes from writings and representations. Historians have leaned heavily on the literary works of Homer and later authors. Athenian dockyard documents, carved in stone, have been extremely helpful in determining the sizes and chandlering of warships. Vase paintings and other representations have provided at least some idea of the appearance of classical traders and men-of-war.

As early as 1894, Cecil Torr wrote an excellent book describing the construction and handling of ancient ships.[1] Much of the evidence we are using today in our study of Hellenistic shipbuilding and seafaring was already familiar in the early years of this century. There have been subsequent definitive works on the subject—one by Morrison and Williams[2] and another by Casson,[3] to name only two—and some notable new discoveries to support or refute past theories, but many of the studies conducted in recent years have been re-evaluations or expanded research of information from earlier years.

Important questions still remain unanswered. Although a number of interesting arguments concerning the arrangement of oarsmen on large warships have been published, all can be challenged from historical or technological points of view. Similar situations exist relative to the structuring and maneuvering of multi-banked rowing vessels, the handling of all types of sailing gear, and numerous details of shipwrightery.

Many sources upon which ancient Greek maritime research is based are either fallible or secondary in nature. Vase paintings, regardless of the confidence with which they were accepted by certain classicists, cannot be considered to be totally reliable. The style of the artist is often such that

1

interpretation of the painting is controversial and inconclusive; actually, one can never be certain that authenticity was the intent of the creator. Decorated cups, vases, and walls may be expected to provide generalities, but the arguments concerning minute technical details on many of these representations are pointless at best.

Accounts of battles and expeditions must also be questioned. Certainly, the position of the author should be analyzed. Was he opinionated or nationalistic, or was he intent on furthering his own cause? Even accounts which were intended to be factual can sometimes be biased or misleading. Homeric literature, an important reference, is essentially a series of adventure stories. As such, deeds of the characters stand foremost, and investigators must ponder to what degree details have been altered to emphasize those deeds.

One cannot deny that there is some valid information in all of these sources. Indeed, the above-mentioned scholars have all done a masterful job in their interpretations and evaluations. But there remain a number of questions concerning ancient Greek maritime activities which, because of areas of doubt surrounding them, may never be answered by representations, documents, or literary works. Some historians have expressed the hope that archaeology will provide additional discoveries of this type, but that is merely wishing for more secondary evidence and, perhaps, more controversy and uncertainty. Better discoveries would be the ships themselves, or at least some of the weapons, supplies, or artifacts connected with maritime activity. Such finds are primary evidence; they are original subject matter and can be handled and studied directly by many scholars. This paper will briefly outline some discoveries resulting from nautical archaeology and suggest or describe new research methodology.

NAUTICAL ARCHAEOLOGY

Nautical archaeology is still in its infancy, yet it has made impressive strides during its short existence. Within nautical archaeology, certain research disciplines promise to greatly increase knowledge of maritime activities in all periods of history. Granted, there has not yet been an excavation of a classical Greek warship, yet one merchant ship from that era has been preserved and reconstructed, while a variety of other projects have provided additional limited information.

Most excavated shipwrecks owe their state of preservation to the fact that they were silted over in a comparatively short time after sinking, and thus they were protected from further decomposition. The majority of ancient wrecks recovered to date have been merchant hulls laden with ingots, pottery, stoneware, or other dense cargo which soon after sinking flattened the hull sides onto the seabed and protected them until the silting process was completed. Those timbers which were not so protected usually disappeared. Warships, lacking such a protective cargo, stood less of a chance of good preservation. That is not to say that well-preserved warships will never be discovered. The Punic Wreck discovered off Sicily a few years ago was apparently a warship or support vessel and had no such protective cargo.[4] It is quite possible that a naval ship may have been protected by another settling directly on top of it, or that a violent storm may have covered it with overburden shortly after it sank. Accessories, such as rams, anchors, and armor stand a good chance of survival, even when hull timbers have completely disappeared.

The Institute of Nautical Archaeology, headquartered at Texas A & M University's Research Annex, has been developing an investigative program designed to obtain the maximum possible amount of information from shipwreck excavations, regardless of their state of preservation. The work is continuously being expanded and improved, and older projects are occasionally reviewed for new information. Although this research program is intended to benefit all areas of nautical archaeology, it is primarily designed to study ships, crews, builders, and cargoes. Briefly, it is conducted over a period beginning with excavation and ending with the publication of the final report. All timbers and fragments of the subject ship's hull are photographed, sketched, recorded in regard to details, and often reproduced in model form if the function of the member is unknown. When the hull is well enough preserved to reconstruct, this is always done graphically and three-dimensionally in the form of large scale models. In three cases, ships have been, or are being, physically preserved and restored.

Recording and inspection processes note every discernable detail, no matter how minute. Tool marks, graffiti, caulking, paints and other coatings—the list goes on and on—are cataloged by description, photograph, and drawing. Conservation, where applicable, insures permanence for future scholarly study. Reconstruction provides an even greater scope. Special types of projection methods, combined with architectural drafting, determine hull lines of extant areas as well as some portions which have disappeared. Construction models, built to scales of either one-fifth or one-tenth full size, duplicate every nail, timber, and joint; such models unlock construction secrets and reveal technological details not ordinarily recognizable. Other models are built for testing tanks, where hydrostatic and other physical properties are determined. In one case, a sailing model large enough to be manned by a crew of two revealed sailing and handling techniques not previously brought to light. Even full-size replicas are made of anchors, fittings, or hull sections to provide a better understanding of their function. Such replicas continue their usefulness as museum displays or teaching aids after they have fulfilled their original purpose.

3

Members of the Institute of Nautical Archaeology have directed three shipwreck excavations which are applicable to our study—at Porticello, Kyrenia, and Secca de Capistello. Several Greco-Roman shipwrecks, slightly later in date but showing similar structural properties, have also been investigated for contributory material.

THE SHIPS

The Porticello wreck[5] dates to the fifth centry B.C. It sank in the Straits of Messina with a cargo that included amphorae and statuary. Although hull remains were extremely sparse, comparative studies of their features and those of the other two INA ships revealed their importance as historical evidence. Fittings, fastenings, tools, and anchor stocks increased the historical importance of this discovery.

The Kyrenia ship[6] sank around 300 B.C. off Kyrenia, Cyprus. This merchantman was carrying more than 20 tons of cargo, most of it in amphorae. It was somewhat smaller than the other wrecks, having a length on deck of 16 meters, a beam slightly more than 5 meters, and a cargo capacity of about 30 tons. Nearly three-fourths of its hull survived; it was completely preserved in polyethylene glycol, was entirely reconstructed, and is now on display in Crusader Castle in Kyrenia. This little trader was so complete in surviving structure and artifacts that all of the aforementioned research methods could be applied in its evaluation. In fact, it was the Kyrenia ship which first revealed so much of the ancient technology, the knowledge of which now forms the basis of all our ancient ship investigations.

The La Secca de Capistello wreck[7] is still in the excavation stage at this writing, but a wreck plan and catalog of construction details have already yielded enough information to permit preliminary evaluation. It sank in 65 meters of water near Lipari, Sicily, with a cargo of black glazed pottery dated to about 375 B.C. Too deep for standard SCUBA excavation, this project is the first serious attempt at deepwater archaeology.

Information from these three wrecks, combined with published information on other relevant hull remains, cargoes, and artifacts, can be applied to the study of maritime activities of ancient Greece. In some cases, they can be used in conjuncton with previously mentioned representations and translations to solve problems. A few examples of such application are listed below.

HULL CONSTRUCTION

There is already an abundance of information regarding this subject for merchant ships, although resource material for ships of war is still limited. In better known periods of history, there has always been a similarity between the construction methods used in merchant and war vessels. But in most of those periods, there was also a similarity in hull form and

4

shiphandling. There never was a greater difference between merchantmen and warships than that seen during the classical periods. Naval vessels were primarily oar-driven craft with ratios of length to beam of about ten to one. Merchantmen, at least the bulk carriers, were primarily sailing ships with length to beam ratios of three to one. One was light, fast, maneuverable, and expensive to operate; the other was slow, clumsy, great in displacement, but economical even on long voyages.

In spite of these differences, certain characteristics were common to both types. Both were displacement vessels constructed of wood. The same metals must have been available for fastenings and fittings in both kinds of vessel. The fact that the excavated merchantmen were carrying cargoes indicates that they were competitive; operating economy must have demanded an effort on the part of owners and builders to acquire shipbuilding expertise approaching that of the warship builders. In fact, commercial ventures may have necessitated a higher degree of technology than that employed in naval ships where rigidity and strength were concerned. Warship builders may have become merchant ship builders when the need demanded, interchanging techniques where applicable.

The construction methods used in the various excavated merchantmen of the period were found to be strikingly similar. Construction was light and weak by latter-day wooden ship standards. Keels and posts were comparatively small and poorly connected. Frames were widely spaced and internal structure was sparse. Pine was the predominant material, some ships being made entirely from this light wood, while heavier woods were used sparingly. In all cases the ships were shell-built; i.e., the planking shell was erected before the framework. To accomplish this, mortises were cut into the edges of adjoining planks at intervals of 8 to 15 centimeters and oak tenons were inserted into the mortises to align and connect the adjacent planks. Small oak pegs were driven laterally through both plank and tenon to lock the joint. The mortise-and-tenon joints stiffened and aligned the planking so that frames were not necessary in order to erect the planking shell. A ship 20 meters long would have had 5,000 or more of these mortise-and-tenon joints cut into edges of planking only 3.5 or 4 centimeters thick. Individual mortises were cut as deep as 10 centimeters; the labor involved in this method was considerably greater than that involved in latter-day methods of hull construction.

Frames were fastened to the inside of the completed planking shell. Usually, the shipwrights completed about half of the hull planking before erecting the first lower frames. They were fastened together with long copper spikes which were clenched over on the inside of the frames. Frame spacing was so great, and internal structure so sparse, that ancient Greek merchant hulls weighed little more than half the weight of an eighteenth century trader of comparable size. Yet a ship 16 meters long could carry 30 tons of cargo.

5

Why were these ships constructed so lightly? Partly, it was due to availability of materials and quality of tools. Pine was abundant and easy to work. Its lighter weight must have been an asset in the eyes of the shipowner, for it permitted an increased cargo weight for the same displacement. It was more easily bent and worked, an important feature because of all the mortises cut into planking edges. Pine was also more compatible with the copper and bronze tools used during at least part of this era. Certainly, these shipwrights were aware of the relative strengths of different kinds of wood because hardwoods were used for keel shoes, tenons, mast steps, and other members where strength or hardness was absolutely essential.

There were other reasons for lighter construction. Ancients reportedly sailed only during the spring, summer, and early fall when the Mediterranean was relatively kind to sailing ships. Demand for strong fabrication was not nearly so great as it was in the case of later trans-Atlantic ships. Another very important factor seems to have determined the lighter construction. These ships were almost certainly structured to the technological limits of their shipwrights' abilities. Framing was widely spaced; longitudinal members, such as keelsons, ceiling, and clamps, were either missing or primitive. We see these members improving in other excavated ships from Roman, Byzantine, medieval, and later periods. In most cases, there is a steady evolution of these timbers, each period displaying improvements in strength, application, or economy.

One other feature eliminated the need for closer framing, stronger beams, and more longitudinal structure—the mortise-and-tenon-joined planking. Considerable additional strength was achieved through the use of this joinery, perhaps enough to offset weaknesses elsewhere. With such strong edge-fastening of the planks, builders were not required to provide better internal members. As hulls and cargoes increased in size and construction time became an important factor, shipwrights were forced to develop stronger inner hull timbers. With improved internal structure, mortise-and-tenon joints became smaller and more widely spaced. By the seventh century A.D., these joints were only half the size of the Greek versions, and only one-fourth as many were used.[8] Four hundred years later, they had disappeared entirely.[9]

At INA, we have performed an elaborate series of experiments with shell-first construction. For the most part, our work has confirmed what ship historians suspected for years—that mortise-and-tenon construction was used because ancients had not yet developed the expertise first to erect the frames onto the keel and then to fasten the outer planking to them. Shell-first construction does not lend itself to ship draughts as we know them. If there had been any pre-planning of construction in any of the ancient hulls we have studied, our experiments and inspections have not brought it to light.

OARED SHIPS

To this point we have dealt only with merchant hulls, which at best could serve as transports or supply ships for naval operations. There are, however, certain clues derived from our research which can be applied to warships. It seems unlikely, for instance, that edge-joinery would have been used on the planking of merchant ships if a more satisfactory method of construction had been employed on warships. The light construction found in the merchantmen would have been even more desirable in rowing vessels intended for speed and maneuverability. It is the lack of good longitudinal structure that does not seem applicable to rowing vessels. If the accounts of the various Greek naval engagements and the sizes of vessels involved are to be taken seriously, then other means of bracing these long, narrow hulls must have been used. So far, nothing has been found on the wrecks to suggest how such bracing was erected.

Whatever structural system was used, it had to be light, rigid, and strong. Within the recognizable limits of technology found on the merchant ships, a few suggestions can be offered concerning the construction of oared warships. Whenever it was available, pine or another low density wood was probably used throughout the hull in order to keep weight to a minimum. The only exceptions would have been the use of live oak for the tenons used in planking joinery, and oak or other hardwoods for any bearing surfaces upon which the oars rested, for the mast step, and for an easily replaceable false keel whose hardness was a necessity during beaching and dry-docking operations. Ships over 25 meters in length might have had a keelson; it is doubtful that proper keelsons existed at all before the classical period. A perfectly straight keel, at least 20 centimeters high and 10 centimeters wide for every 20 meters of hull length, would have been scarphed into a gracefully curving sternpost of diminishing cross-section. At the bow, the straight and perpendicular stempost would have been mortised into the top of the keel. A large knee, extending nearly to the top of the stempost and two meters aft along the top of the keel, braced the junction of these two members. The ram was attached to the forward end of the keel, but may also have been fastened to the stem. Because the structure of the hull was interconnected by knees, bracing, stringers, and various forms of joinery, the force produced during ramming would have been absorbed by virtually the entire hull.

I estimate that the planking thickness averaged 2.5 centimeters for the first 15 meters of hull length and 1 additional centimeter thickness for each successive 15 meters. Mortise-and-tenon joints connecting the edges of the planking would have been spaced at intervals no greater than 10 centimeters, perhaps slightly closer in the bow and along the sides. The hull probably possessed medium deadrise in the bottom, a softly curving bilge, and flat sides—experience must have dictated a very efficient rowing form by the time of the Geometric period.

7

Wales at least twice the thickness of the planking were installed just below the level of the oars; multi-banked vessels would have required additional wales between each bank of oars. A clamp, or stringer, also may have girded the interior of the hull directly opposite each wale. Perhaps another pair of stringers along the bottom of the hull and some lightly nailed ceiling planking would have completed the longitudinal structure below decks.

Framing was probably the same combination of small, widely spaced floors and futtocks found in the merchantmen. High in the hull, however, construction differed in order to afford the required additional longitudinal strength. Stout crossbeams were probably mounted 2 to 4 meters from stem and sternpost, depending on the size of the ship. They extended a meter or more beyond the sides of the hull, in the stern to double as supports for steering oars and in the bow to act as catheads and mounts for possible armament. These through-beams were connected to bow, stern, and each other by belts of four to six heavy planks; a number of conventional deck beams would have supported these planks and further strengthened the upper part of the hull. Such gangway-type belts would have provided the additional longitudinal strength needed at the top of the hull to prevent hogging. Perhaps this platform, a meter or two wide, was all the deck these warships carried amidships.

CONCLUSIONS

I have indicated a very basic construction procedure, and it has been formed from our studies of one well-preserved ship and the fragmentary remains of a few others. It suggests a lightly constructed hull, much more sparsely timbered than those indicated by the drawings, models, and descriptions offered by prior investigators who have based their theories on paintings and literary evidence. And that was precisely what we marveled at when we reconstructed the Kyrenia ship— the high strength in relation to weight, made possible by the thousands of mortise-and-tenon joints gripping the outer shell of planking. If the merchant ship builders invested so much extra time and meticulous joinery work in achieving a lighter hull with little sacrifice in strength, then certainly the warship builders must also have taken advantage of this feature which was even more important to them. Conversely, if all the extra effort expended on the merchant ships had been due to a lack of advanced structural technology, a fact I believe to be true, then it must be supposed that the shipwrights who constructed oared warships also lacked that degree of expertise.

With its varied forms of research, there is no doubt that nautical archaeology will contribute greatly to our knowledge of ancient maritime activities in the future. The construction study outlined above can and will be expanded to include rigging, handling, and a host of other associated subjects. Field archaeologists continue their search for all types of vessels, and are especially eager to discover a great oared warship. But much more can be done with the evidence already at hand by striving to combine the results of our ship finds with information gleaned from paintings, literary works, and the like.

FOOTNOTES

[1] Cecil Torr, *Ancient Ships* (London: Cambridge University Press, 1894; reprint ed. Chicago: Argonaut, 1964).

[2] J. S. Morrison and R. T. Williams, *Greek Oared Ships, 900-322 B.C.* (London: Cambridge University Press, 1968).

[3] Lionel Casson, *Ships and Seamanship in the Ancient World* (Princeton, N.J.: Princeton University Press, 1971).

[4] Honor Frost, "The Punic Wreck in Sicily." *International Journal of Nautical Archaeology* 3 (March, 1974): 35-54.

[5] Cynthia J. Eiseman, "The Porticello Shipwreck." *AINA Newsletter* 2 (Spring, 1975).

   This excavation was sponsored by University Museum, Philadelphia, and directed by Dr. David I. Owen. Various other articles have been published on the project and artifacts, and a final excavation report is being prepared.

[6] S.W. and M.L. Katzev, "Last Harbor for the Oldest Ship," *National Geographic*, November, 1974, pp. 618-25.

   The excavation was directed by Michael L. Katzev under the sponsorship of University Museum. Reconstruction was sponsored by the Institute of Nautical Archaeology, College Station, Texas, under the same director. Numerous reports of the excavation and artifacts have been published by Mr. Katzev. A complete report of all phases of the expedition will soon be published.

[7] Donald A. Frey, "La Secca de Capistello, Lipari," *AINA Newsletter* 3 (Winter, 1977).

[8] George F. Bass, "A Byzantine Trading Venture," *Scientific American*, August, 1971, pp. 23-33.

[9] A medieval ship, which INA has just begun excavating in Turkey under the direction of Dr. George F. Bass, has no mortise-and-tenon joints and appears to be built frame-first. Reports will be published at the end of the first season of excavation.

CHAPTER 2

Food, Transport, and Policy: Roman Maritime Logistics

Laurence Evans

State University of New York at Binghamton

The historical significance of the great sea battles of the ancient and classical world needs no emphasis. The history of the military developments at sea in the great imperial wars of the Phoenicians, the Egyptians, the Persians, the Greeks, and the Romans are almost commonplaces of history. But there was another dimension to the naval history of those days that I believe has not received the attention it warrants, the role played in ancient naval history by supply. I do not mean merely economic history or trading patterns in the Mediterranean, for example. Great progress has been made in these fields. I am not concerned here with how Trimalchio got rich, or the price of fish gizzard sauce in Pompeii in 90 B.C., or the net returns to Athens of olive oil exports. I am interested rather in supply when it becomes a factor in state policy, the role of supply in the two world wars of this century, for example.

At first glance, it might seem difficult to establish any correlation between the war at sea in 1917 or 1943, and conditions in the Mediterranean world two thousand years ago. Let me mention only the consequences of the Athenian defeat at Aegospotami and the cutting of the routes of the Athenian grain supply through the Bosphorus and from Sicily, and then turn to an exploration and analysis of the conditions under which the mundane world of the shipper and trader becomes the focus of statesmen and military leaders. This is the region where politics and economics are distinguished. If economics is concerned with the production, transportation, and consumption of goods as directed by choice between different goods or advantages, politics is concerned with manipulating necessity, with that which one must obtain or cease to exist, as a state or as an individual. By the intensive analysis of existing sources and new material recent studies enable us to identify the historical circumstances when necessity directed action in the world of Rome, and by extrapolation new light may be thrown on ancient history generally.[1] The hypothesis presented here is that the grain supply of the ancient cities and civilizations was not merely an economic phenomenon but was a crucial factor in the high strategy and politics of these states, and that much of their history cannot be understood except in terms of the problems of assuring adequate grain. A corollary of this hypothesis is that only water transport could move the quantities of grain required for the maintenance of the populations of the cities on which these civilizations and Empires were based. For Rome, and also for the Greek city states, water transport meant seaborne transport.

To investigate the viability of this hypothesis we set up a theoretical model of the City of Rome and begin by measuring the demand for grain and its supply. The basic datum is the food requirements of humans, or, put in another form, the energy requirements of humans. Modern nutritional studies have accurately measured the relationship between energy intake and output in humans, as well as the nutritional requirements to maintain a healthy body.[2] For a regime of moderate activity a man requires about 3000 calories, a woman about two-thirds of this, a child about a half, an adolescent from a half to two-thirds. For heavy labor the calorie needs of a man increase to about 5000, for sedentary work they are reduced to 2500; 3000 is a figure generally adopted as an average. The calorie intake is basic. Food is a fuel and it is burned in the production of work just as truly as gasoline is burned in a tractor. Even in authoritarian societies and slave-owning societies adequate nutrition must be maintained.

Grain foods provide most of the calories in the majority of societies, in the present and in ancient times, and the favored grain is wheat; in addition to being rich in energy foods it provides many other nutritional needs including substantial amounts of protein and it can be stored for considerable lengths of time. In the ancient world, as in the undeveloped areas of the world today, the average man obtained from 75 to 90 percent of his calories from grain. White enriched bread today gives 270 calories per 100 grams or 2700 per kilogram of 2.2 pounds. The calorie yields of the grains of the Roman world were less per unit of weight, though apparently they had more protein according to measurements made of modern versions of Roman wheat varieties.[3] These modern findings correspond closely with the data from the Roman world. Cato gives the monthly rations of slaves on his estate as from five to six modii (of twenty Roman pounds or fifteen pounds avoirdupois) of grain for the heavy workers in the chain gang; unchained field slaves got from four to four-and-a-half modii of grain; slaves doing light work got three modii; in addition the slaves got poor quality wines, olives, cheese, oil, and salt on a regular basis and from time to time meat

11

and fruits, etc. Duncan-Jones estimates that one modius of wheat a month would give a daily ration of 700 calories. Thus we get 3500 to 4000 a day of bread plus another 700 for heavy workers, 3360 total for moderate work, and 2520 for light workers, very close to modern figures.[4] If we take our present average of 3000 for a male, this would seem to be a reasonable average for Rome. In terms of wheat grains, four modii a month would provide a generous allowance for a working man.

This we may take as our norm, fifty modii a year per man, and this is close to the wheat dole in Rome for much of the period it was given; for an active man it provided a basic diet and one less active could keep his wife on it also. For a working family, the monthly wheat requirements would be four modii for a man, two-thirds of that for his wife, and a half for each dependent child less than twelve. A man with a wife and two children then would need about 130 modii or 2500 pounds of wheat a year as their basic food requirement, plus additional food in the form of olives, very important in the Mediterranean diet; wine; vegetables such as peas, beans, turnips, and cabbage; and a very moderate amount of animal protein from goat milk and cheese and pork, the most common meat of the Roman diet.[5] Farmers were engaged in heavy work only for a hundred days a year, so this ration may be overly generous in calculating the annual calorie intake; it would be less inaccurate for women and children, however.

The next datum is the supply of food. From the expulsion of the Kings to the first major expansion of Rome in 396 B.C. with the conquest of Veii, the territory of Rome, the Roman Ager, amounted to about 300 square miles, of which about two-thirds was suitable for wheat.[6] The standard Roman measure of land area was the iugerum, about two-thirds of an acre. If 200 square miles were suited to wheat farming, this gives 166,400 iugera. The practice at this time was to let the land lie fallow every other year; this was not universal and was not practiced for all crops, only for grain, but as a rule little more than a half of the land would be producing food in any given year.[7] This gives about 83,200 iugera sown to wheat per year. The invariable rule was, it seems, that five modii of twenty Roman pounds would be sown to each iugerum. The average yield varied from a fourfold return, less than which meant that the land was not worth sowing, to tenfold on the best land in the Roman Ager of the time; the norm was about sevenfold.[8] In Sicily it was about tenfold and in the Po Valley up to fifteenfold.[9]

The normal yield per iugerum was 35 modii, or about three-quarters of the wheat requirements of an adult male. In a normal year, then, the wheat grown in Rome would amount to 2.9 million modii, enough to feed 60,000 adult males, or, assuming families of a male, a wife, and two children together equaling two-and-two-thirds shares, about 21,500 families or 86,000 people all living at the same level. Population figures recorded in the classic writers give 130,000 free in 508 B.C. at the time of the expulsion of the Kings, 151,000 in 498; 110,000 in 493; 103,000 in 474; and 117,000 in 459; Pliny gives 152,573 in 392.[10] Taking the figures from food production and assuming that not everyone lived at this standard of consumption, that there were also in the population infants who did not eat their full share, as well as the elderly who also consumed below average, and that the levels of individual consumption we have assumed would be held to for working males only during the seasons of heavy work, at least an additional 25 percent could be maintained by the wheat production of Rome, or a total of 107,500.

The men who produced this food were the farmer citizens of Rome, the men who left the plough in the field and became generals leading the Roman legions to victory, Cincinnatus and his compatriots who became the exemplars of the Roman citizen in the days of the Empire when he and his like had disappeared forever from the Roman world. They were not myths. The Roman Army, according to Servius' classification of citizens by wealth for service in the army and for voting weight, consisted of four legions of 4,200 men with auxiliary and support troops and cavalry to a total of 19,300 men. They were drawn from all males seventeen and over and included older men. These figures for the army are probably accurate. This would not be an unreasonable number of fighting men out of a total male population of half a hundred thousand or so inhabitants. The Servian classification grouped men according to their wealth, this being the measure of their stake in the community and also of their ability to purchase weapons and armor. There were six classes including knights. The largest class was the first class below the knights. In this class there were eighty centuries, up to 8,000 men, owning up to 100,000 asses. The second, third, and fourth classes each contained twenty centuries and owned up to 75,000, 50,000, and 25,000 asses respectively. The fifth class owned 12,500 asses and numbered thirty centuries. There were eighteen centuries of knights.[11]

Of course the population figures from the classical writers cannot be taken at their face value; in the same way the question of the real significance of the figures of the Servian classification cannot be answered here, quite apart from the question of their historical reality in fact and time; in addition, the figures derived from the food production and the food consumption of ancient Rome are speculative. Nevertheless, it must be remarked how closely all three hypothetical population indicators correlate. This correlation is perhaps justification enough to speculate a little further: first, that if the population figures are even approximately reliable, then the Servian classification represents a real historical fact and more importantly reflects the actual economic structure of the Roman population; second, that in such a society under normal conditions there is no place for slaves for there isn't enough food for them with the population pressing constantly against the upper limits of the food supply.

From the classic writers it has been estimated that one man could farm seven iugera or so of ordinary arable land sown to wheat or other similar crop. This corresponds to the modern concept of "five acres and a cow" being enough to provide a basic living to a laborer using intensive hand cultivation with perhaps the use of a plough (though the modern worker would not have sown wheat but potatoes for his major source of calories).[12] The Roman would have sown only three or four iugera to wheat in any one year, the rest being left fallow; it would have to be ploughed or hoed, however. From three-and-a-half iugera he would get on the average 125 modii, or two-and-a-half full annual rations, close to his requirements for his family of himself, his wife, and two weaned living children.[13]

The acquisition of large quantities of food adds nothing to the stability of human institutions or to the prolongation of human existence itself unless the food can be stored; otherwise one would merely assemble mounds of rotting vegetation or flesh. And before men can break out of the village settlement and create towns and cities, food must also be transportable. After consumption and production, the third and fourth data are thus storage and transportation. As for storage, it is enough to note that, of all foods, grains are perhaps the most suited for prolonged storage. Grain retains its food value for many seasons if it receives rudimentary care. Transportation, the fourth datum, is more complicated and requires a detailed analysis.

Studies of the cost of transportation in its various modes have a long history. One of the earliest was that made for the Edict of Diocletian in 302 A.D. setting prices for the Empire. It was readily recognized that the cost of transportation was an essential element in any price system, and, along with regulation prices for cabbages, chestnuts, wheat, and lamb, the prices for transportation by donkey back, ox-cart, barge, and ship were set.[14] During the great canal boom in England after the 1760's, studies were made to show the desirability of canal transportation and its great savings over carriage by wagon.[15] In 1816, the United States Senate conducted a survey of transportation costs in the United States and of freight costs across the Atlantic. The Committee found that it cost $9 per ton for freight from Liverpool to Philadelphia, and the same $9 to carry the same ton thirty miles inland.[16] A research project of great importance and with revolutionary consequences was that begun by the National Academy of Sciences-National Research Council in 1956 at the request of the Defense Department to study costs of supplying the American forces in Germany. Out of this project came Roll-on/Roll-off ships, containerization, and LASH ships, changing the entire character of ocean freight.

From all these studies one outstanding fact appears: the enormous disparity between the costs of land transport and sea transport. In Roman times and in the nineteenth century, the ratio of cost was about twenty-five to one; a special case was the one hundred to one ratio between the cost of shipping from Liverpool to Philadelphia against the cost of wagon transport from the port inland. Diocletian's Edict set transportation costs at two denarii per mile for a man, four for an ass, eight for a camel load of 600 pounds, and twenty for an ox-cart of 1200 pounds; at this time it cost sixteen denarii to ship one modius of wheat the 1200 miles from Alexandria to Rome.[17] These costs are of course artificial; compared to the price of wheat and other goods set in the Edict, transportation would appear to be undervalued by two-thirds when measured by costs recorded elsewhere in the Roman world. The costs of transportation are generally taken to double the cost of wheat in a hundred miles. However, land transportation was used only for short distances for wheat and other foodstuffs and there are no actual cases to compare with sea transportation. It is significant, though, that the twenty-five to one ratio between the most efficient land transport, the ox cart, and sea transport holds up in Diocletian's Edict.

Measuring actual costs of transportation in its various modes can be misleading if modern concepts of prices are used. Assessing monetary costs tells only part of the story. The great seldom recognized fact about premachine era land transportation of food is that the fuel used was itself food, and the transportation of food from one place to another consumed part of the land, in fact or by consumption of equivalent quantities from the supplies of the localities along the way.[18] This food, animal or human, had to be subtracted from the finite quantity available in a society, and land used for the production of animal foodstuff (and animals must also be fed on nutritious food) could not be used to grow human foods. Another factor overlooked is that the wagon or vessel had to return to the point of origin and in food shipments this usually meant that it travelled empty. Costs were much the same either way, and thus the costs of transport of food were usually nearly twice the apparent cost in the absence of return freight. This was probably the source of the unrealistic costs assessed in Diocletian's Edict.

Time consumed in transportation is an economic factor in terms of the freight carried and the vessel itself, not to mention the cost of the humans involved. There are accurate figures for speed and time of journeys in the literature and records of Rome and the ancient world. Twenty miles a day or less was normal for long range transportation on land by caravan, though the Imperial Post averaged 50 Roman miles or 75 kilometers a day; special couriers made twice that and the maximum was 240 kilometers a day including stops.[19] Ox-carts as a rule did not make more than 15 to 17 kilometers a day; more was difficult to achieve and, in any case, was considered injurious to the animals.[20]

Speeds of ship transport are given by Casson for the classical period after careful calculation as four to six knots (from five to seven miles an

15

hour) with a favorable wind, one to two knots in an unfavorable wind, and a probable overall average of three knots (three-and-a-half to four miles an hour).[21] Long distance shipping travelling day and night would thus make about 75 miles every twenty-four hours, or four times the average speed of land transport, and, under favorable conditions, 150 miles a day; even if the vessel anchored every night it would make twice the distance of land transport. Thus the journey of about 1200 miles from Alexandria to Rome would take about 400 hours or 17 days by sea, but 60 days by land for an equivalent journey.

Putting together the four data, food requirements, food production, food storage, and food transportation, we can establish certain basic facts about early Rome (and by extension about the early history of city states generally in the Mediterranean area). First, of course, that the populatuion was directly proportional to the food supply, and, by assessing the food supply, we can establish the population. Second, that there are absolute limits to the importation of food by land, and that even if an area has a surplus it cannot be exported beyond a certain distance. Third, this means that local production is the measure of the local food supply. Fourth, that in early Rome and other Mediterranean states, almost all the land was used for grain production, because this produced the maximum calorie supply coupled with essential nutriments. Fifth, that almost all the population must be engaged in food production, transportation, or processing, and that the numbers of people who were not so engaged, apart from the very young and old, could not have been more than about 10 percent of the population.[22]

What all this means is that land transportation cannot support a city as we think of the meaning of the word. If the population of Rome within the walls was 40,000, 30,000 of them would have to be farmers working the land five miles in radius around the City[23] with the rest being 10,000 supernumeraries, the rich, artisans, priests and so forth living on the surplus of the whole Ager. Merely to add 10,000 inhabitants to this number would take the surplus of an area as great as the Ager of Rome (these new inhabitants could not have produced their own food since all the arable land was in use). The Roman Ager was about twenty miles in diameter, ten miles from the boundary to the City. A city of 100,000 would require a territory fifty miles in diameter of first class farm land, an extensive road system and no geographical barriers. Every other town and city in the area would have to be eliminated so that all surplus grain could be sent to the City. Everyone would be living at subsistence level. And if we suppose that the rural towns were not destroyed and that half the supernumerary consumers lived in them, and if we add the workers and animals required to transport, store, and process food, and if some of the state's resources must be exported to provide imports, and some people lived in comfort and perhaps luxury, then a city of 50,000 or 60,000 inhabitants would represent the maximum that the most favorable conditions would allow, no matter what the size of the territory of the state was, with 25,000 the maximum under actual conditions in the ancient world.

Once we add water transportation to the situation, an entirely different picture emerges. Water transport has three great advantages: it is cheap; it is fast; and transport using sails or a current does not consume any food as fuel. In consequence, a wider area can be tapped for food supplies. We note that all the great civilizations grew up around cities built on rivers, cities that owed their existence to the availability of water transport. In the western world, the empires of Babylon and Egypt are demonstrations of the necessity of water transport, and the profound effect it has on the structure of states is demonstrated by their different patterns of river transportation. Mesopotamia and Egypt could draw on the surplus of their entire respective river basins. Transport in Mesopotamia could run efficiently only down to the mouth of the river; the City in its several manifestations grew, therefore, near the mouths of the twin rivers. In Egypt, the river could be used up stream and down stream by vessels floating with the current going northwards and using the prevailing north wind to sail against the current going southwards.[24] The rulers of Egypt could locate their capital anywhere along the river; the whole of the Nile Basin was a long string of villages with temples and towns along most of its length. The limits of the Tigris-Euphrates system in comparison is shown by the history of Nineveh built by the Assyrians far to the north; its food supply had to be hauled against the current or carried by land. The development of sea-going vessels made possible the growth of cities in areas beyond the river basins, on the coasts of the Mediterranean; this represents the next stage in the history of western civilization.

Up to the Second Punic War, the population of the Roman state, taking into account its increase in size with its steady domination of its neighbors, was apparently in direct proportion to its domestic grain supply. From time to time, and in increasing quantities, Rome purchased sea-borne grain from Sicily and other sources in time of shortage; this grain came to the City up the Tiber either directly or after off-loading at the mouth of the river, later at Puteoli. With the defeat of the Carthaginians, and the political and economic ties established during the First and Second Punic Wars with non-Carthaginian Sicily, particularly with respect to grain supplies for the military, the necessary conditions for a food supply based on imports rather than domestic production were achieved: guaranteed access to the surplus production of other regions, and secure means of transportation of the grain supply. The opening up of Sicily and also North Africa as sources of grain and the elimination of the Carthaginian naval forces assured these conditions.

The economic and social impact of new supplies of grain was felt

17

immediately.[25] Sicilian wheat and also that from the former Carthaginian possessions and supply regions in North Africa could be bought and shipped to Rome, FOB the trading dock of the city on the Tiber, for about three-quarters of the current price charged for home-grown wheat.[26] Much of the economic and political history of Rome in the second and first centuries B.C. is the history of the impact of imported grain. The small landholders and those with marginal land could not compete with imported grain and either left their ancestral land or had it taken from them. They migrated to the City where they formed a growing proletariat, no longer independent citizens and masters of their own destiny, but dependents, working for other men. Their lands under the new masters were turned into olive groves and vineyards; close to the city truck farms were developed to supply vegetables and other case crops, for it was soon apparent that even the best grain land would produce more money in crops grown for cash than if it were left in wheat. The social upheavals and civil wars, the denunciation of the overplanting of vineyards, the reversion of large tracts of Roman Ager to waste and swamps, the attempts to settle the landless in newly acquired territory, the disruption in other words of the old way of life of the Roman people, are evidence of the impact of imported grain.[27]

Rome had now passed the Point of No Return. The supply of grain no longer limited the population of the city, which soon far surpassed its own food supply, and in any case the land was now used to grow cucumbers and olives for cash. The City was totally dependent on imported grain; in other words it was hostage to its sea-borne trade. This went far beyond the vulnerability of any city to a siege; it was a long-term or permanent state of affairs.[28] The Athenian Empire may have been built and maintained for many reasons including all the traditional ones, but control of the grain routes through the Straits and the Archipelago would be sufficient cause alone.[29] And while Rome acquired the extra-Italian Empire for a variety of political and strategic reasons, once acquired it had to be held and then extended to protect the grain supply and to deny it to other states. The conquest of Egypt not only gave Rome the most reliable grain supply in the ancient world, it also gave her the power to deny it to the states of the eastern Mediterranean and western Asia.

If we turn now from the domestic implications of imported grain to its significance in the international policies of Rome, we see that at the beginning of this phase of her history and for some centuries thereafter, Rome reaped only benefits from this new development. Unlimited supplies of grain meant, for one thing, that her manpower, no longer needed for essential food production, could be used at will for military purposes; there was bread for the legions and for the City. For much of the grain Rome paid nothing. It was part of the tribute of the new territories or was produced on land directly or indirectly controlled by the City. There was no power capable of challenging Roman control, of the new provinces or of inter-dicting the sea-borne supply of grain.

On the other hand, it was at first difficult for Rome to exploit fully the vulnerability of the states of the rest of the Mediterranean world which were also dependent on sea-borne grain. Roman sea-power was an ad hoc weapon of war and its use was imperfectly understood by the leaders of Rome. The supplies of the Greek city states, for example, now came, after Sicily and the western Mediterranean fell under Roman control, primarily from Egypt and the Black Sea. To a modern naval commander the blockade of Alexandria and the Straits would present almost no problem at all. But here we hit one reason why the aspect of sea-power presented in this essay has had little attention from modern naval historians, bred in the pattern of modern naval history and the concept of the storm-beaten ships that ultimately defeated Napoleon. The type of sea-war practiced by Britain was impossible in the Mediterranean in the days of Rome. The ships of the day could not in fact patrol and therefore they could not blockade, except in a fashion that was merely an extension on the water of a land siege. But, if one had a base close enough to a sea route to keep a constant watch on traffic and a squadron ready to intercept it, then an effective local blockade could be established. The cities of the Archipelago, including Athens, felt the truth of this. Rome established control of the grain supply of the states of the eastern Mediterranean and generally of the whole territory of the Empire by dominating sea routes from sea bases; by destroying naval power that might challenge this control, as the Rhodian fleet was destroyed; and, most effectively, by controlling grain-producing areas, such as Egypt.

Once the independent states of the Mediterranean world were under Roman control, Roman control of the source and supply routes of the grain trade produced its greatest dividend: no further means of control were re-quired to maintain Imperial domination, no armies of occupation, no Imperial garrisons, no punitive expeditions (though it is instructive that the last hold-outs were those states that had large grain-producing areas under their control). The campaigns against the Jews are the exceptions that prove the rule; they are notable because they are exceptional. The legions were kept on the borders of the Empire; with the exception of Egypt and Rome itself, only police forces and patrols in the rural areas maintained order and the authority of the Imperial Government in the enormous area of the Empire. For the conquered, obedience assured the supply of grain, diso-bedience meant starvation.

For the next two hundred years or so after the establishment of the Imperial system, which really is merely a way of describing the rationalisa-tion of Roman Imperial policy by Augustus after nearly two hundred years of improvisation from the end of the Second Punic War, only the intrinsic problems of the huge task of shipping a quarter of a million tons of wheat every year to the City troubled the officials charged with the grain supply;[30] these were, in the main: first, the normal problems of shipping—the development, supply, and maintenance of efficient vessels at costs satisfactory to the city and to the ship owners—and second, the silting up of the Tiber. This last was serious, for shipment overland from Ostia to Rome could cost almost as much as the entire journey from Alexandria.[31] Shipbuilding techniques developed fruitfully to meet the demands of the trade. Where cargos could be concentrated for loading as at Alexandria, the focus of the river-borne grain trade of Egypt, great ships were built; where cargos were collected piecemeal in small ports or across beaches, appropriate types of smaller craft were developed.[32]

In sum, the authority of Rome was based on control of the surplus grain production of the Mediterranean basin and control of the means of distribution as much as it was on military force. Rome simply did not dispose of the numbers of men required to control the Empire by military force alone. This distribution system was based in turn on water transportation of necessity, for only water transportation could handle the quantities and distances involved. This system controlled even when the Empire expanded beyond the Mediterranean basin, into Gaul and beyond and into the Danubian provinces. The Rhine and the Danube were essential water routes for the supply of the Roman forces along the boundaries of the Empire. In Britain, the centers of Roman control, London, York, Chester, Caerleon, and Lincoln, were all supplied by sea.

This happy state of affairs began to break down in the third century A.D. The historical record is, of course, far from complete, but certain themes recur over and over in those sources that are available. The economic burden of maintaining Rome told heavily on the Empire. The growing inadequacy of economic motivation in the supply of grain, the physical problems of transporting the grain inland from the coast to the City, the demands of other cities, and the deterioration of the general economic position of Italy and of Rome in particular, all were reflected in the extreme measures taken to ensure direct control by the Government of the grain supply and transport. Confiscations, commandeering, and price control are commonplaces of the economic history of this period; it is worth considering whether the enormous economic burden of maintaining the essentially parasitic City of Rome was not a major factor in the economic problems of the Empire.[33] The parallels with Peking are striking.[34]

These problems added to the strategic vulnerability of the City. The administrative and military capitol in the west was moved from Rome to Trier, Milan, or wherever the Emperor established his headquarters and, though there were good military reasons for this, the increasing difficulties of getting food to Rome must have told heavily in the decision, for not only did the location of the court add to the problems of supply but the Government itself might now become a hostage to whatever military force might gain control over a major source of the Roman grain supply. The supply problem was doubled when Egyptian grain was diverted to the new City, Constantinopolis. The fate of Rome was now sealed. Byzantium was ideally situated for bulk supply by sea. It was directly on the sea and it could tap the resources of the whole Black Sea litoral as well as the eastern Mediterranean, Egypt, and Africa. Rome, and Italy too for that matter, were no longer politically functional, were deteriorating economically, and were becoming more and more irrelevant to the life of the Empire. When control of Spain and North Africa was lost, Rome was lost, and the cost of maintaining the City made it not worth regaining. Belisarius' recapture of the City was merely an incident in the reconquest of Italy, and that campaign itself followed upon the reconquest of North Africa and Sicily.

The loss by the central government of strategic control of African and Sicilian grain supply to insurgents and barbarians in the third, fourth, and fifth centuries turned what had been one of its principal sources of strength into a lethal weapon at the throat of the Empire in the West. Rome (and the other cities of the West) were at the mercy of whoever controlled the grain supply. But loss of strategic control resulted not only from the loss of physical control of traditional grain regions and routes, but also from the development in Gaul and Britain of wheat production in quantities adequate for the supply of substantial bodies of men.[35] Here wheat had been a staple before the Romans appeared and Britain had actually exported wheat before the conquest; in the two hundred years or so after the Roman occupation wheat production had reached levels that made it possible to maintain substantial military forces independent of the Mediterranean and Black Sea supplies under the control of the metropolitan authorities. Hence came the succession of usurpers, and hence came also the succession of barbarian war bands. The authority of the central government now ended in much of the western world when the traditional method of control broke down, based as it was only in part on military force and for the rest on control of food surpluses. But in the East these traditional methods still prevailed and the Eastern Empire survived and, when Islam burst out of the desert, external pressure and the threat of alien conquest by Muslims and barbarians helped to keep the remnant of the Empire in existence for another six hundred years and kept the new Rome Christian for two hundred more.

FOOTNOTES

[1] In particular Richard Duncan-Jones, *The Economy of the Roman Empire: Quantitative Studies* (London: Cambridge University Press, 1974); K. D. White, *Roman Farming* (Ithaca, N.Y.: Cornell University Press, 1970), the standard work; R. J. Forbes, *Studies in Ancient Technology*, 9 vols. (Leiden: E. J. Brill, 1955) 2; for ships and shipbuilding, Lionel Casson, *Ships and Seamanship in the Ancient World* (Princeton, N.J.: Princeton University Press, 1971); and the essential work for its period, A. H. M. Jones, *The Later Roman Empire, 284-602; A Social Economic and Administrative Survey*, 1st American ed., 2 vols. (Norman: University of Oklahoma Press, 1964). There is much valuable material in the collected essays of the same author, *The Roman Economy; Studies in Ancient and Administrative History*, ed. by P. A. Blunt (Totowa, N.J.: Rowman and Littlefield, 1974). This is not to slight such standard works as Tenney Frank, *An Economic Survey of Ancient Rome*, vol. 1: *Rome and Italy of the Republic* (Baltimore: The Johns Hopkins Press, 1933) and vol. 5: *Rome and Italy of the Empire* (Baltimore: The Johns Hopkins Press, 1940); M. Heichelheim, *An Ancient Economic History From the Palaeolithic Age to the Migrations of the Germanic, Slavic, and Arabic Nations*, trans. Joyce Stevens, rev. and complete English ed., 3 vols. (Leiden: A. W. Sijthoff, 1958-1970); and M. Rostovtzeff, *The Social and Economic History of the Roman Empire*, 2nd ed., rev. P. M. Fraser, 2 vols. (Oxford: The Clarendon Press, 1957).

[2] H. S. Mitchell *et al.*, eds., *Cooper's Nutrition in Health and Disease*, 15th ed. (Philadelphia: J. B. Lippincott Co., 1968) is a standard text for the nonspecialist.

[3] *Cf.* L. A. Moritz, *Grain Mills and Flour in Classical Antiquity* (London: Oxford University Press, 1958) pp. 145 ff.

[4] *De Agricultura*, cited in Duncan-Jones, *op. cit.*, p. 146, and Frank, *op. cit.*, 1:166. On the condition of slaves generally including diet, see White, *op. cit.*, chap. XI. The standard ration for Chinese laborers was two catties of rice (2.66 pounds) per day; see footnote 17 below.

[5] Duncan-Jones, *op. cit.*, p. 146.

[6] The boundaries were the sea on the West, Lavinia, Ardes, Lanuvinium, Aricia, and Tusculum on the South, Tibur on the East, and Etruria on the North with a small strip of Roman territory north of the Tiber; *cf.* Frank, *op. cit.*, 1:9-10.

[7] *Cf.* White, *op. cit.*, chapter IV, citing Varro, Columella, and Cato; also Duncan-Jones, p. 49.

[8] *Ibid.*, citing Varro, Columella and Pliny. The classical writers often refer to a fourfold return as standard in many areas, but this was for slave cultivation; intensive hand-cultivation by the owner would account for the discrepancy; *cf.* White, *op. cit.*, pp. 335 ff. and p. 370.

[9] Duncan-Jones, *op. cit.*, pp. 50-51, p. 145. Prices give some indication of relative productivity in the classical period. In Italy wheat cost 4 sesterces a modius, (in Rome itself it was rather higher), in Sicily 2 to 3 sesterces, in Asia 2.25, and in Africa 2.5. In the early principiate the price in Egypt was less than 2 sesterces a modius; in A.D. 70 it was again from 2 to 3 in Sicily; the controlled price in Rome after the fire of A.D. 65 was 3 sesterces.

[10] Cited in Frank, *op. cit.*, 1:21-22.

[11] Frank estimates that in modern gold values (of 1932), the first four classes were worth respectively, $2,000, $1,500, $1,000, and $500. He states that a citizen with twenty iugera of land (about thirteen acres) with a two-room hut, two oxen, some sheep, and his crop of wheat for the year would qualify for the first class, *ibid.*, p. 22.

[12] White, *op. cit.*, pp. 335 ff., p. 345. He would also have a pig, some sheep or goats on the common land for milk and cheese, and a garden for vegetables. Some of his land might be sown to peas or beans, the food value of which was close to wheat and could take its place

pound for pound as a source of calories, adding some variety in nutriments and protein as well as in taste. Seven iugera, representing the middle of the fourth Servian class, was the minimum holding on which a man could live in moderate comfort according to the standards of the day; the lowest level of the fourth Servian class, about five iugera, was probably the absolute minimum on which a man might eke out an independent living. Socially and politically it may represent the lower limit of economic independence and may have been chosen as the lower limit of the Servian classes specifically for that reason.

[13] *Ibid.*, p. 345.

[14] The text of the Edict is in Frank, *op. cit.*, 5:305-421, appendix by E. R. Graser.

[15] L. T. C. Rolt, *Navigable Waterways* (London and Harlow: Longmans, Green and Co., 1969), p. 1., summarizes the findings of the engineers of the relative efficiency of various modes of transport according to the loads a horse can draw: pack horse–300 pounds; wagon (soft road)–1,500 pounds; wagon (macadam road)–4,500 pounds; wagon (iron rails)–8 tons; barge (canal)–50 tons; citing A. W. Skempton, "The Engineers of the English River Navigations, 1620-1760", Newcomen Society, *Transactions* 29 (1953):25. Duncan-Jones, *op. cit.*, appendix 17, notes that relative costs in the Edict are: sea, 1, inland waterway, 4.9, land, 28, and that in England in the eighteenth century they were 1, 4.17, and 22.16. He cites an Egyptian papyrus giving the cost of river transport of wheat in A.D. 42 as 6.8% per 100 miles.

[16] *American State Papers: Miscellaneous II* (1834), 287, cited in Henry David *et al.*, eds., *The Economic History of the United States*, 10 vols. (New York: Holt, Rinehart and Winston, 1951), vol. 4: *The Transportation Revolution, 1815-1860*, by George Rogers Taylor, p. 132.

[17] Jones, *op. cit.*, p. 37.

[18] A dramatic example of this fact is given in W. H. Mallory, *China: Land of Famine* (New York: American Geographical Society, 1926), citing a study by the Chinese Minister of Mines, J. E. Baker. He notes that in many regions of China, most transport is on human backs or at best on wheelbarrows. If there is a famine in one area and a surplus of rice in the neighboring province, the absolute limit on the emergency transportation of rice to the famine zone is about 250 miles, and 500 if wheelbarrows are used (which assumes that roads exist over the mountains). This is because the porter would consume the entire load of one-half picul of 66 pounds in 25 days, or 12½ there and 12½ back. Adding in the food requirements of the porter's family reduces this by two-fifths and 100 miles. As a practical matter the effective maxima would be not more than two-thirds of these theoretical maxima. Baker's estimates are twice this rate; he assumes that a porter could carry one picul of 133 pounds on a long journey. This could be carried for short trips within a town perhaps, as the hammals of today can still be seen in Stambul bowed under the weight of a refrigerator, but this is very different from carrying such a load all day for two or three weeks. Military experience indicates that fifty or sixty pounds is a maximum for cross country portage. The Roman legionaries carried a standard issue of twenty days' field rations on campaigns. If this was biscuit it would weigh about thirty-five pounds. He would also be carrying his weapons and the rest of his equipment, of course. The porters of the long distance traders in the Maya world carried about fifty pounds; Anne C. Chapman, "Port of Trade Enclaves in Aztec and Mayan Civilizations", in *Trade and Market in the Early Empires; Economies in History and Theory*, ed. Karl Polanyi *et al.* (New York: Free Press, 1957).

[19] A. W. Ramsay, "A Roman Postal Service Under the Republic", *Journal of Roman Studies* 10 (1920) and "The Speed of the Imperial Post", *ibid.*, 15 (1925). Some documented times for particular journeys are: Jericho to Petra, three to four days; Jerusalem to Edessa, twenty-five days; Antioch to Babylon, seventy days; Jerusalem to Alexandria, fifteen to

sixteen days: M. P. Charlesworth, *Trade Routes and Commerce of the Roman Empire* (London: Cambridge University Press, 1924), p. 43. The author also cites Josephus' account of a journey by Titus from Alexandria to Palestine along the coast, averaging sixteen to twenty miles a day. Such journeys are closer to us than one might imagine. The present writer was the guest in Damascus not many years ago of the son of the Commander, the Amir al-Hajj, of the last Pilgrim Caravan before the opening of the Pilgrim Railway. In the early part of this century a loyal subject of Sultan Abdul-Hamid wrote a defense of the Sultan's proposal to build a railway to serve the Pilgrimage from Damascus to Mecca; it had been denounced by the pious as sacreligious. In the course of explaining the great value of the railway the author, a certain Muhammad Arif, describes the actual journey followed by the great pilgrim caravan that left each year from Damascus. The caravan took 332 hours of travel in thirty-two stages to cover 684 miles to Medina at an average speed of two miles an hour. From Damascus to Ma'an took 103 hours, thence to Aquaba 127 hours, and the final stage to Medina took 102 hours. Muhammad Arif's account was translated and annotated in Jacob M. Landau, ed., *The Hejaz Railway and the Muslim Pilgrimage; A case of Ottoman Propaganda* (Detroit: Wayne State University Press, 1971).

[20] Forbes, *op. cit.*, pp. 154-155.

[21] Casson, *op. cit.*, p. 270.

[22] Two exceptions test these generalizations as they apply to Rome. The Tiber was used to a limited extent to float cargoes of grain down to the City. Pliny describes how he sent his grain down the river when the river was high and mentions the primitive canalization of the river through the use of simple flash locks. Also, farm animals, oxen and asses, would be available for local transport of farm produce when they were not needed on the farm, at a cost only of a slight increase in fodder requirements.

[23] It would not be practical to work land much further than five miles from the farmer's dwelling. This requires a ten-mile or four-hour walk, a third of the working day. From this circumstance come the small towns and villages spread throughout the Ager, and characteristic today of Italian agriculture.

[24] It may be noted here that the tidal rivers of the Atlantic coasts of Europe provide the same advantage of two-way travel as the Nile. Going with the tide upstream and down and anchoring when the current is unfavorable makes possible the full exploitation of waterborne traffic to cities far inland; thus Paris and London, to mention only the outstanding examples, could grow and flourish in the heart of extensive territory at the head of tidewater. Examples of the importance of the tides to sailing vessels in our own recent past are given in Basil Greenhill, *The Merchant Schooners*, new rev. ed., 2 vols. (New York: Augustus M. Kelley, 1968). Without the tides only traffic with the current would be possible, as is the case, of course, in the Mediterranean.

[25] We are dealing here with long-term effects, but the short-term effects of the war were extremely damaging to the Roman farmer. The defeat of Carthage left the Roman Government with huge quantities of wheat accumulated for the army, and these were simply thrown on the market. This oversupply, augmented by the continuing shipment of grain by dealers with contracts, smashed prices in Rome to the point where dealers were giving their wheat to the ship masters in payment for the freight. The citizen farmers were left with a crop almost worthless on the market, and many of them with absolutely no means of paying their debts. Barely had the farmer recovered when at the end of the Macedonian War precisely the same policy of the Government repeated the disaster. This situation was temporary, but it did adumbrate the long-term effects of imported grain. Frank, *op. cit.*, 1:97-98, 158.

[26] On wheat prices in Rome *cf.* Duncan-Jones, *op. cit.*, pp. 50-51, p. 111, p. 145; Frank, *op. cit.*, 1: 97-98, 192, 196, 197, where Frank gives the price of wheat at the loading point in coastal Spain as one denarius for five modii. He quotes Cicero for wheat prices in Sicily compared to prices in Rome.

[27] White, *op. cit.*, pp. 50-51; White cites Strabo and Livy for the depopulation of Latium, with sheep grazing right up to the city walls, (as they did up to World War II), the growth of vineyards, etc., but these are common themes of all the writers. We are familiar with this phenomenon from our own history and the impact of western wheat on New England's farmers in the nineteenth century.

[28] The early Emperors were very conscious of this danger. Augustus, Tiberius and Claudius all expressed great concern about the impact on Rome of a breakdown in overseas supplies of grain, and all attempted without much success to encourage local production of wheat, gave bonuses to grain producers, and strongly opposed the conversion of grain fields to vineyards. This vulnerability was brought home to the rulers of Rome when the recrudescence of piracy after Rome had put down the maritime states actually threatened ship-borne trade to Rome. Pompey was forced to organize practically the whole maritime forces of the state and its allies in a short but intensive and successful sweep of all the pirate strongholds. A more dangerous threat was the naval warfare against Roman shipping carried out by Pompey's son after Caesar's triumph, when from bases in Sardinia and Sicily he attacked the grain ships moving north along the coast to Rome and almost strangled the city. These threats were soon overcome but both took major military efforts before they were mastered, though the actual numbers of men and ships were small.

[29] Recent work of significance on the Athenian Empire is incorporated in Russell Meiggs, *The Athenian Empire* (Oxford: The Clarendon Press, 1972). While it does not make a point of the positive role of the grain supply in the expansion of Athens, there can be no doubt of the importance of loss of control of the supply routes in the end of the Empire. But see the very interesting study of the Athenian campaign against Syracuse, Peter Green, *Armada from Athens* (London: Hodder and Stoughton, 1970), the hypothesis of which is that Athenian policy was based on the necessity of gaining control of Sicilian grain production.

[30] Twenty-five barges with 2,500 modii of wheat were hauled every day by oxen up the Tiber from Ostia, plus of course all the other imported goods and foodstuffs. Frank, *op. cit.*, 5:219.

[31] Cf. Russell Meiggs, *Roman Ostia*, 2d ed., (London: Oxford University Press, 1973), *passim*, especially chapters 3 and 4.

[32] Cf. Casson, *op. cit.*, pp. 169 ff. for accounts of the various types of freighter and their development.

[33] For accounts of this phase, cf. Jones, *The Later Roman Empire*, pp. 84-89; *The Roman Economy*, chapter 9, "Inflation under the Roman Empire"; Frank, *op. cit.*, pp. 296-304; Heichelheim, *op. cit.*, 3:208-337; Rostovtzeff, *op. cit.*, pp. 106 ff.

[34] For an account of the provisioning of Peking as capital of the Chinese Empire and its economic and social cost see Hoshi Ayao, *Mindai soun no Kenkyu*, Tokyo, 1963, published as *The Ming Tribute Grain System*, trans. Mark Elvin, Michigan Abstracts of Chinese and Japanese Works on Chinese History (Ann Arbor: University of Michigan Press, 1969).

[35] For a general account of trade with western and northern provinces in this period see Frank, *op. cit.*, 5:287-295.

CHAPTER 3

New Evidence Concerning Developments in Anchor and Hull Construction Technology during the Roman and Byzantine Periods

Frederick H. van Doorninck

Texas A & M University

Until such time as substantial remains of one or more Roman or Byzantine period warships are brought to light in the Mediterranean, we must rely primarily on excavations of the wrecks of merchant ships for new evidence on developments in naval architecture during those times. The number of such wrecks that have been properly excavated remains rather small but is now increasing at a steady rate. As a result, comparative studies of these wrecks have begun to yield much in the way of new information. The present paper will confine itself to outlining recent new information concerning developments in the design and use of anchors and in hull construction during the Roman and Byzantine periods.

The iron anchor came to replace the wooden anchor with lead or stone stock during the course of the Roman period. The Greeks had employed iron anchors with lead stocks on their warships as early as the fourth century B.C. in order to cut down on anchor dimensions. That the iron in these anchors weighed no more than 50 pounds presumably was due to a limited iron-making technology. By the third century B.C., however, some slightly heavier iron anchors were being used on merchantmen.

The Punta Scalleta ship, a large, roughly 30-meter-long vessel dating to the middle of the second century B.C., was carrying seven anchors in the bow when she sank off the island of Giannutri near the coast of Italy opposite Corsica. Only four of the anchors were of wood with lead stocks;

the other three were of iron. The iron anchors were very thin, had small dimensions, and must have had but a limited use. The best-preserved one had a shank only 1.6 meters long. As was the case with the Greco-Roman wooden anchor, the arms of these and other late Hellenistic period iron anchors were straight and formed an acute angle with the shank.

It proved possible to increase the scope of use for iron anchors by increasing the number that were employed as a compensation for their lightness. This did pose a stowage problem, which was solved by the invention of the anchor with removable stock, the so-called admiralty anchor. The best-preserved iron anchor from the Punta Scalleta ship presents us with the earliest securely-dated example of an anchor of this type. Wooden anchors with removable lead stocks also came into use during the late Hellenistic period, and the fixed lead stock was already becoming obsolete in the first century of our era.

The Imperial period saw further increases in the weight of iron anchors. The heaviest Roman iron anchor known weighed just over 900 pounds. This anchor, however, belonged to one of the great imperial barges at Lake Nemi dating to the middle of the first century and appears to have been an iron anchor of extraordinary weight even for Roman times. The practical maximum weight of iron anchors was certainly much less. Consequently, the larger Roman merchantmen, whose capacities in some cases were as much as perhaps 1300 tons, continued to rely on wooden anchors with heavy lead stocks. On the largest merchantmen, lead stocks weighed as much as 1600 pounds. It was not until merchantmen of over some 300 tons burden disappeared from the Mediterranean at the end of the Roman period that the wooden anchor with lead stock went out of use.

Iron anchors underwent considerable change in configuration during the course of the Roman period. Since iron can undergo greater stress than wood, the angle between the arms and shank of iron anchors was soon increased to permit deeper sea-bed penetration. Anchors with radius, or crescent-shaped, arms became the standard design in the first century, but these gave way to the cruciform anchor by the fourth century, perhaps in the wake of Christianity's triumph. The cruciform anchor continued in use through the Byzantine period.

Iron anchors and stocks were rectangular in section in late Hellenistic and early Imperial times. The larger dimension of shank and arms was in the direction of the anchor's flection when in use. As iron anchors became somewhat more robust during the Roman period, shanks and stocks became circular in cross-section and continued so during the Byzantine period.

Two shipwrecks excavated within the last decade at Cape Dramont on the southern coast of France have yielded some good information concerning the design and use of iron anchors during the Roman period.

The Dramont D ship was a roughly 20-meter-long vessel dating to the middle of the first century. Three iron bower anchors were found on the wreck. Two had been on the port bulwark; one on the starboard bulwark. All three had been ready for use with iron removable stock mounted in place. The anchors have crescent-shaped arms with chisel-shaped flukes, and the stocks are rectangular in section. Judging from published dimensions and drawings of these anchors, none of them would have weighed more than about 150 pounds when complete with iron stock. A lead stock was observed on the wreck site. Thus it is possible that the ship also carried one or more heavier wooden anchors with lead stocks.

The Dramont F ship, a coastal freighter dating to the latter part of the fourth century, had an overall length of only 10 to 12 meters. Despite its small size, this vessel gives us what is presently our earliest clear evidence of how spare iron anchors were stowed on shipboard. Four anchors were uncovered on the wreck. They had been neatly stacked in a single pile, all facing the same direction, one on top of the other. Since they did not have stocks mounted in place, it is clear that they had been spares piled on the deck. Apparently, the ship's bower anchors had been cast before she went down. The largest spare anchor, located at the bottom of the pile, had crescent-shaped arms and chisel-shaped flukes. The other three anchors were cruciform with pointed flukes. The shanks of all four anchors were rectangular in section but had apertures for stocks round in section. One judges from the dimensions and configuration of the largest anchor that it could not have weighed much more than 60 pounds. Its shank measured only 6 by 2 to 6 by 3 centimeters in section. Such anchors could easily have been broken. It is little wonder that four spares were considered desirable even though the ship was so small.

A seventh century ship excavated off the Turkish coastal island of Yassi Ada within sight of the Greek island of Cos has been unusually informative regarding the design and use of anchors during the Byzantine period. This vessel, 20 meters long, had a capacity of 60 tons and was carrying eleven anchors when she sank. Three bower anchors, each weighing about 173 pounds, and a best bower, weighing about 243 pounds, were on the forward bulwarks. Three spare bowers and a spare best bower lay piled on the deck nearby. At the bottom of the pile of spare anchors lay three heavier sheet anchors, each weighing about 312 pounds. Remnants of iron stocks were not found with the bower anchors ready for use on the bulwarks. Their stocks must have been of wood. However, two or perhaps three iron stocks were stowed with the spare anchors on the deck. These stocks would have been used with anchors when on relatively short cable. Details in the stocks' design suggest that they were sheathed in wood when used.

The flukes of the anchors, poorly developed as are those of other Byzantine and most Roman anchors, were chisel-shaped. In order to learn how

28

well one of these anchors would have performed, J. Richard Steffy has tested a half-sized model against a model of an eighteenth century anchor of equal weight. Surprisingly, the Yassi Ada Byzantine anchor appeared to work a bit better on hard bottoms, but the eighteenth century anchor was clearly better for soft bottoms.

A number of "Y"-shaped iron anchors, which as a group are thought to date to the latter part of the Byzantine period, have been found off the islands of Cyprus and Sicily. These anchors have straight arms, which form an obtuse angle with the shank, and flukes set at right angles to the arms.

A ship dating to about A.D. 1000 and equipped with such anchors is presently being excavated by the American Institute of Nautical Archaeology at Serce Liman on the south coast of Turkey opposite Rhodes. The ship was carrying a cargo of Islamic glass. Perhaps "Y"-shaped anchors were used primarily by Islamic ships.

The Serce Liman ship was about 17 meters long and carried eight anchors. Two of these were bower anchors mounted on the forward bulwarks. The remaining six were spares stacked within the hold just forward of midships. Detailed measurements of the anchors have not yet been made, but they were quite small, probably weighing somewhere between 100 and 150 pounds.

Toward the end of the first millennium of our era, the maximum size of Mediterranean ships began to increase, and by the thirteenth century the largest vessels afloat had capacities of around 500 tons. These vessels were required to carry as many as twenty-eight anchors on long voyages, a situation which was quickly rectified, however, by a then rapidly improving iron-making technology. Large vessels were carrying far fewer anchors of a much greater weight by the fourteenth century. At the same time, the removable stock went out of general use.

More economical methods of ship construction evolved in the Mediterranean during the first millennium of our era. The disappearance of state subsidies for shipbuilding at the end of the Roman period may have been an important factor. Greco-Roman shipwrights shell-built their hulls. They assembled the outer shell of the hull by edge-joining the planking with mortise-and-tenon joints, imparting to the hull the shape desired as each strake was fitted to the preceding one. The work of framing the hull was begun only after most of the shell had been completed. From the fourth century onward, however, the role played by edge-joining was gradually diminished, and we now have evidence that Mediterranean shipbuilders already were capable of entirely dispensing with the technique by the end of the first millennium. The counterpart of this evolutionary development was a gradual increase in the strength and independent structural integrity of skeletal frameworks and in the role played by skeletal building in hull construction.

A just under 20-meter-long fourth century ship excavated at Yassi Ada, Turkey, will serve to illustrate some of the more important developments in Mediterranean hull construction that occurred during the Roman period. A number of other contemporaneous ships that have been brought to light affirm that the construction techniques employed in the building of this ship are by no means atypical for late Roman times.

The hull's framing pattern was essentially a traditional one like that found in the much earlier Kyrenia ship. Floors alternated with half-frames, and floors and futtocks were not scarfed or fastened together in any way. Nor were most frames fastened to the keel. Even so, we find, in comparing the vessel to pre-Roman period ships, some movement toward a stronger, more integrated skeletal framework. The half-frames extended all the way in to the keel. Moreover, roughly every third floor was fastened to the keel by an iron bolt. Iron bolts were also employed to fasten to stem and sternpost the ends of four pairs of wales girding the hull sides between waterline and deck. Remnants of a mast step or keelson did not survive on the fourth century Yassi Ada hull, but recent excavations, particularly of three hulls of late Roman date in southern France, have revealed that the short mast step of the Greek and Hellenistic periods developed during the Roman period into a true keelson.

These improvements in the strength and integrity of the skeletal framework made it possible for late Roman period shipwrights to rely somewhat less on the outer shell of edge-joined planking for hull strength. The fourth century Yassi Ada hull represents an early phase in a trend toward reducing both the number of mortise-and-tenon joints employed in edge-joining the outer shell and the time and effort involved in fashioning and assembling these joints, thereby cutting construction costs. The joints are markedly smaller and more widely spaced than in merchantmen of earlier periods, including even the much smaller Kyrenia ship. The most frequent center-to-center interval was from 25 to 32 centimeters. A further departure from earlier practice is the fact that the tenons were made to fit loosely within their mortises. Time and manpower required in cutting mortises and tenons and in fitting and joining one planking strake to another were in this way significantly reduced. A further saving of time was made by fastening the extremities of the outer shell planking strakes to stem and sternpost with iron nails rather than with mortise-and-tenon joints as was done in earlier times.

Some evidence was found that appears to indicate that the shipwright who built the fourth century Yassi Ada ship installed a pair of half-frames at midships after perhaps only five strakes of outer hull planking had been assembled to either side of the keel. Perhaps he was using his midship frame as a guide in achieving the hull shape desired. Evidence of a possible erection of one or more frames at an early stage in the construction of any other extant late Roman hulls has not, however, been reported to date.

We must at present rely on the relatively poorly preserved hulls of only two ships for evidence concerning hull construction methods employed during early Byzantine times. One of these, an unusually large, roughly 30-meter-long vessel dating to the sixth or seventh century, has been excavated at Pantano Longarini, located near the south-eastern corner of Sicily. The other is the much smaller seventh century Yassi Ada ship. The basic construction techniques employed in either ship are quite similar and would seem, therefore, to be representative of the period.

The framing pattern of the Pantano Longarini ship appears to have been a traditional one in which floors alternated with half-frames and floors and futtocks were not fastened together. However, floors were fastened to the keel, as were one of each pair of half-frames in alternating fashion. Furthermore, five pairs of wales girding the hull sides above the waterline were fastened to frames with iron bolts. Quite regularly, they were bolted to each successive frame. The ship's bow is not preserved, but at the stern the wale ends were bolted to a transom, which may have supported a large after cabin. The wales were half logs, as were many of the ceiling strakes inside the hull. Whole logs were used for through-beams tying the hull sides together. The through-beams were braced on either side by a rider. The major hull timbers, often massive and rigidly connected, formed a strong skeletal framework.

The builder of the Pantano Longarini ship, unlike earlier Greco-Roman shipwrights, relied primarily on his framework rather than on edge-joined shell planking for hull strength. His outer shell of planking was edge-joined only up to the waterline wale. Furthermore, the tenons were very small, fitted loosely in mortises set at intervals of about 1 meter, and were not fixed in place by a pair of wooden pegs after joint assembly as was done in earlier periods. The joints were designed to facilitate as much as possible the shaping and assembly of bottom planking prior to the installation of overlying frames but made only a minimal contribution to hull strength.

Above the waterline wale, where hull curvatures were relatively simple, the builder of the Pantano Longarini ship was able to dispense with edge-joining altogether through skeletal building. After erecting some of the side framing, he bent and fastened certain of the wales to it. More frames were installed, and the remaining wales were fastened in place. The planking and framing of the sides was then completed.

The builder of the smaller seventh century Yassi Ada ship also relied primarily on his framework for hull strength. About one-quarter of the frames were fastened to the keel, each by an iron bolt; the rest, each by an iron nail. The hull sides were girded by four pairs of half-log wales. Each wale was bolted on the average to every fourth frame, only one wale being bolted to any particular frame. The bolts passed through wale and frame and then through a large ceiling strake, or clamp. Most ceiling strakes were half logs which contributed greatly toward stiffening the hull internally. Through-beams were quite large, and knees were employed to brace deck beams.

Here again, mortise-and-tenon joints like those of the Pantano Longarini ship were employed only below the waterline wale. These joints had center-to-center intervals of from 30 to 40 centimeters in the stern area and intervals not normally exceeding 90 centimeters in the hull's middle body.

The frames were very poorly preserved in the seventh century Yassi Ada ship. Consequently, we do not have a great deal of direct evidence concerning the hull's framing pattern and the role played by the frames in the step-by-step process of building the hull. However, J. Richard Steffy has reached some tentative conclusions concerning these matters after making a series of test models of the hull. The unpegged joints in the bottom planking were so small and widely spaced that they would not by themselves have held together all of the planking up to the waterline. After considering all possibilities in the light of available evidence, Mr. Steffy believes that the hull most probably was constructed in much the following way. The hull's bottom planking, temporarily held together by the joints, was first assembled. The bottom planking once completed was permanently fastened in place through installation of short floors to which the planking was fastened with iron nails. The shell was then continued up through the turn of the bilge, and long floors were installed and nailed. The shell was now continued to the waterline, after which half-frames and futtocks were installed. The sequence followed in then completing the hull was much like that followed by the Pantano Longarini builder. Indeed, the step-by-step procedure in building both hulls must have been rather similar throughout.

It remained for Mediterranean shipwrights to learn how to extend their skeletal-building techniques to the hull below the waterline with its more complex curvatures. The Serce Liman ship has revealed that they had already learned to do so by the end of the first millenium. Skeletal-building was employed in all stages of the hull's construction.

The hull bottom had a deadrise that was extremely flat. The simplicity of the bottom lines facilitated skeletal-building in this part of the hull. An as yet undetermined number of frame floors were erected before the planking of the hull was begun. All of the frames along the length of the hull had long floors, naturally curved timbers with a short arm extending out to the turn of the bilge on one side and a long arm extending up through the bilge turn on the other. Long and short arms alternated on either side throughout the main body of the hull. Futtocks were laterally scarfed and fastened to the short arms.

A pre-erection of some of this framing obviated the need for any edge-joining of planking strakes. Interestingly, the garboards were not even fastened to the keel, but rather were narrow strakes apparently installed only after neighboring strakes were already in place.

Skeletal, non edge-joined construction permits a greater variety of hull shapes and makes it economically practical to build much larger ships. Basil Greenhill, the Director of the National Maritime Museum at Greenwich, has recently written: "The development of the non edge-joined, skeleton-built ship is one of the technical factors which made possible the exploration of the world by western European man and the development of the commerce which gave him predominance."[1] Mediterranean shipwrights over the course of many generations may have made a substantial contribution to this historically important technical development.

FOOTNOTE

[1]   Basil Greenhill, *Archæology of the Boat: A New Introductory Study* (Middletown, Conn.: Wesleyan University Press, 1976), p. 72

CHAPTER 4

Admiralties and Warships of Europe and the Mediterranean, 1000-1500 _____

Richard W. Unger

University of British Columbia

While a great deal has been and is still being learned about European warships of the Middle Ages from archaeology, iconography and government documents, the history of the admiralty as a government office in medieval Europe is still something of a mystery. No author has ever tried a general survey of the evolution of the institution. The word admiral is merely a corruption of the Arabic term 'emir'. When the Normans conquered Sicily in the late eleventh century they simply retained the office for the town of Palermo. Over time the *amiratus Palermi* became an important figure in the administration of government income and also expenditure, particularly for the navy. There were a number of admirals in twelfth century Sicily, but one became preeminent and usually he combined executive duties in fiscal administration with military command.

By the late twelfth century the admiral was a naval commander who had nothing to do with fiscal administration. That man was Margaritus of Brindisi, a Greek who led the Sicilian fleet to victory in Spain, Africa, Greece, and Syria while also defeating the Pisans and Genoese all in the short space of the ten years before 1194. Margaritus' fame led Italian maritime republics to imitation, Venice having an admiral as early as 1208, Pisa in 1210 and Genoa in 1226. The office spread north from Italy to France, in 1246, and to England at the end of the thirteenth century.[1] In those cases the admiral was a military commander, expected to lead the fleet in battle. The office was temporary and could disappear in peace time, at least in northern Europe in the thirteenth century. In Sicily the admiral retained administrative duties and by 1239 was also responsible for jurisdiction over many criminal attacks carried out at sea. In the fourteenth century jurisdiction was added to the tasks of admirals in France and England.

That gave the office permanence and, more important, income from the fines and fees paid in litigation. Kings favoured an increase in the competence of admirals because it meant in fact an expansion of their own claims of sovereignty, including the sea as well as traders and ports and coastal districts. The office of admiral was thus made into another royal tool to undermine the power of their mighty subjects.[2] At least in fourteenth century northern Europe it became one of the great offices of state and was held by men from the highest social stratum, men not necessarily recognized for their fighting ability.

By about 1500 most admiralties had three functions: naval command, jurisdiction over maritime affairs and provision of a fleet.[3] The last, the administrative function was attached to the office of admiral as part of his job as naval commander. The administration of military forces at sea, the size, extent and complexity of government offices responsible for that task, their functioning and funding, while usually treated as part of naval history, is rather normally taken as just the pre-history of the administrative structures which emerged in the sixteenth century. It is certainly true that from then on the administration of the navy was typically associated with the office of admiral and naval administration did generate highly complex organizations in the following two centuries. But construction and care of the fleet was never fully integrated with the other two functions of the admiral's office since these required different skills and different organizational forms. To some degree then even though the task of administering the fleet was placed in the hands of the naval commander, the admiral, that function still had a distinct history after 1500 just as it did in the Middle Ages.[4]

It was not just the states of early modern Europe which developed offices for administering their military forces at sea. The Byzantine Empire in the course of the seventh century established a series of 'themes' with both military and administrative positions. This system was extended to include the navy by the end of the ninth century, with commanders in charge of leading ships in battle, building and maintaining ships and collecting taxes for their support.[5] The growth in naval administration, the establishment of permanent government departments to deal with fighting ships in sixteenth century Europe can just be attributed to the introduction of artillery on board ship. The guns made the job of preparing a fleet more difficult hence the expansion of bureaucracy responsible for the task. A similar claim could be made for Byzantine organization since that fleet relied heavily on artillery for offensive action, and not just Greek fire used both at a distance and at close range, but also stone-throwing machines, relying on the principle of balanced weights and on tension.[6] Certainly the use of artillery is a partial explanation of the scale of naval administration. Other systems of naval administration existed—extensive, complex and continuing—with navies where artillery was not used. For example, Scandinavian monarchies in the tenth and eleventh centuries had a system of muster ships. Districts were responsible for supplying on short notice a specified number of ships and crews when called on by the king. These *leidangen,* the muster fleets, also had to be stored in yards and kept ready for sea.[7] Italian maritime republics, Iberian and French monarchs in the thirteenth and fourteenth centuries built and expanded government-owned shipbuilding facilities which were the exterior representation of a fixed, permanent organization for support of the navy. For those vessels as with the earlier Norse naval units, though to a lesser degree, artillery was of minor importance both for offense and defense. Artillery on board then was only one feature of changes in ship design which explain the evolution of naval administrations.

In the second half of the Middle Ages, from 1000 to 1500 permanent departments of government to deal with naval administration appeared and disappeared. There was a decline in the establishments of about 1000 and then a gradual re-emergence of offices for supplying and supporting fighting ships, but there were also variations and fluctuations within that long term trend. The changes can in large part be explained by technological developments in ship design.

Simply the contention here is that the existence of a permanent naval administration within governments was a function of the extent to which navies were made up of ships which could be used as cargo vessels in peace time. The composition of naval forces depended on what ship type available at any point in time was most effective for doing violence at sea. That in turn dictated what governments did to their navies. There are a number of other reasons for the level of naval administration, that is, for the size and scope of the 'admiralty.' The naval ambitions of the government, the perceived and the real threat to the kingdom or state from hostile naval forces, the degree to which fiscal or police powers were combined with naval administration, the general level of administrative competence of the government of the day, the ability of the government to afford a navy, and simply the stability of government all contributed to decisions on the number of men and quantity of resources which could be devoted to administering military forces at sea. But all those considerations were political and above all they were short term, often very short term. The list contains explanations which are known and often mentioned by naval and administrative historians.[8] Over the long term it was rather the advances in ship design which was the principal force in dictating the pattern of development in naval administration. It is an explanation generally ignored when dealing with one state or one period of time. Here it is only possible to sketch briefly the general tendencies and suggest some of the more obvious connections between changes in ships and naval organization.

The Byzantine navy was made up of both regional, territorial fleets and a central fleet based at Constantinople. For all the fleets there was a body of permanent officers responsible for having the ships manned and ready when needed. The fleets contained a variety of different ships. The major fighting vessel was the dromon, a large oared ship equipped with a ram and carrying up to 300 men. In the larger forms these descendants of Roman war galleys were not fast compared to smaller oared vessels. Byzantine fleets even included transport vessels (*chelandia*) of basically the same design. Certainly Byzantine dromons had more commercial potential simply because of their size than did the smaller galleys. Those were little more than rowing shells having extremely shallow draught.[9] With the relatively large complement of rowers, about 70, those ships could never be effective cargo ships, that is except for moving luxuries, goods light in weight relative to value. Instead relatively small coasters probably carried most cargoes. The difference was obvious from the relative length of the two types, the oared vessels having length-to-breadth ratios of 5:1 and usually higher while the ratio for cargo ships was typically under 4:1.

This distinction between warships and cargo ships was well established in the Mediterranean in Roman times and before. Historians have always acknowledged the two ship designs, but they have failed to recognize a similar contemporary variation in northern Europe, especially in Scandinavia. The warships are much better known thanks to excavations of ninth century Viking long ships. Even by that date however there were two separate designs within the Scandinavian tradition: the cargo carrier, more heavily built, a small number of oars, say six, at the bow leaving a deep, open hold amidships and a length-to-breadth ratio of from 2:1 to 5:1, and the warship, a personnel carrier with 15 to 20 oars to a side, shallow draught and low freeboard, a full deck and a length-to-breadth ratio ranging from 4.5:1 up to and over 7:1.[10] The warships, like contemporary Mediterranean oared ships, were of little value for carrying freight, that is, with the exceptions of luxuries and people. In the eleventh through the fourteenth centuries the cargo ship developed into an even larger vessel, highly seaworthy and able to maintain regular trading between Scandinavia and Iceland and Greenland.[11] Evolution in the design of the warship further differentiated it from that cargo vessel. Draught remained relatively shallow but the lines became even sharper. Oared ships were built longer, reaching more than 50 oars to a side. But warships of about 25 oars per side proved the most consistently effective. The muster system was generated to guarantee Scandinavian kings a supply of vessels of precisely that size and design. The kings went even further to assure themselves of a fleet of warships which could be deployed immediately. In the eleventh century Danish monarchs built at least four sizeable naval bases in their kingdom complete with earthworks, landing area for the ships and buildings to house crews.[12]

By the fourteenth century the naval bases were gone and the muster system had been abandoned. The indirect cause for those changes in naval organization was the development in the design of the cog. Used as a coaster in the Low Countries in the early Middle Ages, the cog was significantly changed by the addition of a keel, that some time in the eleventh century. The new cog then was capable of sailing in the open sea. A sailing ship carrying a single square sail with straight post, high freeboard, a low length-to-breadth ratio rarely exceeding 3:1, the cog could carry more goods for each unit of length than any of its predecessors. Moreover the cog could be built bigger than its predecessors with no significant loss in handling qualities. By about 1200 the cog was the dominant cargo vessel in northern Europe as well as the most sought after warship. Because the cog rode so high in the water it served as an excellent platform for hurling missiles down on an enemy as well as a good base from which to launch an attack on another ship lying alongside. The addition of castles at bow and stern increased that height above an opponent. Cog hulls were thick and there was no contemporary vessel which could be used to sink it. Fighting at sea was done between cogs at close range with victories won by boarding enemy ships. That in turn meant that as many men as possible had to be put on board. The job of naval forces became armed transport, moving troops on these large cogs. It took only a few minor changes to make a trading cog into a warship. The biggest change was the increase in the complement of fighting men.

The effectiveness of the cog in northern fleets led to significant changes in government and naval policies. In Denmark in 1304 the *leidang* system was dropped. Instead of supplying long ships the districts had to send the king a much smaller number of cogs. In some cases this was just converted to a cash payment to the crown which in turn arranged for the supply of cogs.[13] In England in the twelfth and early thirteenth centuries the king relied on the Cinque Ports for naval forces. Those ports along the southeast coast received privileges from the crown in exchange for supplying a fixed number of ships for a definite number of days per year, when called on to do so. The vessels were sailing ships, related in design to Scandinavian cargo ships. By the mid-thirteenth century the king used other sources for fighting ships. The contract with the Cinque Ports had the two disadvantages of creating a semi-independent political force within the kingdom which might prove uncontrollable—it did on more than one occasion—and of not giving the king the most reliable fighting ships of the period: cogs. By the reign of Henry III (1216-1272) the king owned cogs himself. They served as armed transports carrying troops to France. In peacetime the crown leased them to merchants. The English navy was made up largely of impressed ships since all vessels were required to serve in something like a naval militia. At times orders for the general arrest of ships set a minimum tonnage for impressed vessels. Obviously the crown was interested in getting just bigger ships, especially cogs. By the late thirteenth century the English king was able to administer his fleet with a warden to oversee the Cinque Ports, a bookkeeper to keep track of who had his own ships and to see that correct payments were made to owners of impressed ships and also a small number of specially appointed temporary commissioners responsible for impressing ships at the start of a war.[14] The king of France relied on a similar levy of all ships, especially from Norman ports. The French crown had a simple system of naval administration very much like the English one. Even naval commanders were impermanent, the crown importing them from Italy, especially Genoa, for the duration of wars with England.

Both England and France expanded their naval administrations on occasion in the thirteenth and fourteenth centuries. Such growth was not incidentally associated with the building and maintaining of galleys. Such vessels were not suited to the heavy weather and the roll in the Atlantic and the North Sea, but they were useful for raiding in the Channel. The possession of a galley fleet by one king obliged his royal competitor to do the same. In England, King John (1199-1216) established shelters for his galleys at different ports and appointed permanent officers to see to their maintenance. The practice continued in the reign of Henry III. Apparently the plan was to use the galleys for police work in peace time as well. At the end of the thirteenth century King Edward I (1272-1307) built a fleet of 30 galleys, ordering certain ports to construct fixed numbers of vessels. The development of the galley fleet to fight the French came at the same time as the appointment of England's first admiral and at the time when the royal office of Clerk of the King's Ships became permanent.[15] Edward I was reacting to the French king's opening in 1294 of a permanent shipbuilding yard in Rouen, the *Clos des Galées*. These smaller yards were also built at Boulogne and Abbéville. They were to construct and maintain galleys and sailing barges. Taxes for their support led to some resentment including in one case a tax revolt in Rouen (1382). The royal yards in Normandy had permanent staffs including salaried shipbuilders, some of them brought in from Italy.[16] To those royal officers were added the administrators of tax money used to support the establishments. In both France and England, then, the presence of warships with no commercial use, that is, galleys, meant a drain on royal treasuries and led to comparable expansion in naval administrations.

The *Clos des Galées* at Rouen was based on a Castilian model which in turn had been copied from the Venetian arsenal. The word is Arabic meaning 'house of work' but in Romance languages it came to mean a naval shipyard. Those buildings and slipways were an obvious representation of a continuing naval administration. The most famous, the Venetian arsenal, was just a warehouse for some naval stores until about 1300 when it got the job of building and maintaining a galley fleet. That change coincided with the development of similar arsenals elsewhere in southern Europe, for example at Seville and Barcelona. The arsenals and the concomitant growth in naval administration were the result of a change in naval warfare in the Mediterranean. It was no longer possible to rely on merchant ships for fighting and states like Venice had to support two fleets, one for peace and one for war.[17] The latter was made up of light galleys, vessels of no value as cargo carriers. Galleys lost their limited role as cargo ships in the thirteenth century because of improvements in sailing ships. Those vessels could carry heavy goods in the hold, and lighter cargoes, those traditionally reserved for galleys, between decks. Sailing ships became more defensible because of the increasing use of the crossbow, a weapon which could be used more effectively from the higher sailing ship which also had high gunwales to offer protection for archers. Valuable cargoes, luxury goods could then be carried on sailing ships with greater security. Improved navigation techniques lengthened the season for sailing ships and gave them an advantage over galleys. The introduction of the cog to the Mediterranean in the thirteenth century provided southern European merchants with a big sailing ship, not vulnerable to galleys and capable of carrying bulky goods.[18] That made it possible to design Mediterranean cargo ships more for speed and that in turn formed a threat to the traditional shipping markets for galleys. The general displacement of galleys from trade led to the development of the great galley, first built at the Venetian arsenal in the last years of the thirteenth century. The great galley was a large Mediterranean sailing ship equipped with oars for occasional use. It was valuable in certain special trades, such as carrying pilgrims to the Holy Land, which in turn helped displace smaller galleys from trade.[19]

The construction and expansion of arsenals was a result of the same developments that led to the building of the great galley. By the fourteenth century small galleys were almost exclusively fighting ships. Shipwrights made them even lighter and with shallower draught. Governments had to build those vessels themselves. No private builder would. The arsenals and all the personnel that went with them had to operate continuously if states were to have galley fleets when war came. By the fifteenth century, in Venice for example, the government arsenal had a monopoly of the construction of galleys. Private builders, the few that were left, worked exclusively on sailing ships.

The full-rigged ship, developed in the fifteenth century, combined the advantages of square and lateen sails. That and other features made for a major improvement in sailing ships. The full-rigged ship was more maneuverable than its predecessors and so captains were better able to get away from attackers. It was hard enough to catch an opponent using cogs and so there were few battles in the open sea, at least in northern Europe. The full-rigged ship made engaging an enemy ship even more difficult and that in turn made reprisals, privateering and piracy less useful as part of naval policy. Governments commonly in the Middle Ages relied on seamen's traditions of greed and violence to allow them to inflict losses on an enemy. With full-rigged ships more of the task fell to governments themselves. The larger a full-rigged ship the greater were the advantages gleaned from the new design. Moreover size was still at a premium because it made ships more defensible. As before fighting in the fifteenth century was done at close quarters and ships usually ended up grappled together as crews fought across the decks. Governments began a policy of granting subsidies for the construction of larger merchant vessels. Though probably started in Italy, by the mid-fifteenth century subsidies were being granted in Spain, France and England.[20] It could be that governments were also trying to counteract a general tendency toward smaller ships which resulted from a fall in the volume of trade in the second half of the fourteenth century. Subsidies had the added advantage of being easily paid and requiring no permanent staff. The larger cargo vessels were impressed into service in wartime just as cogs were in the thirteenth century.

The introduction of heavy guns on board ship made it difficult to convert merchant ships to warships. The use of guns on board pre-dated the development of the full-rigged ship, but they were originally only anti-personnel weapons mounted on the castles or the masts. In the early sixteenth century heavy siege guns were placed on the lower decks and that gave sailing ships the ability to sink other sailing ships and at a distance. The combination of full-rig and heavy guns meant that sailing ships used tactics in battle, something reserved for galleys to that time. Big guns gave big ships even more of an advantage and so governments enlarged the subsidy programmes. They also expanded their own shipbuilding yards, both in number and in size. Ships with heavy guns could be used for trade but less easily over time as the guns took up more space and the vessels had to be specially designed to carry the extra weight. By the second quarter of the sixteenth century northern European monarchs had to have ships of their own, built by them and for them, used only for fighting. They also had galley fleets with the same limitations.

The result of changes in ship design in the fifteenth and sixteenth centuries was a marked growth in admiralty organizations. Permanent departments of state took on the task of administering the fleets, in peacetime as well as wartime. The best-known example is the establishment of the Navy Board in England in the 1540's.[21] Admiralties extended their competence as well. Those government departments were certainly the products of earlier institutions. Organizations and officers for the administration of naval forces came and went through the Middle Ages, and the sixteenth century departments were based to some degree on the older patterns. More important, those permanent bodies for administering European navies were a product of changes in ship design which by that time had made it extremely difficult if not impossible to use warships economically as cargo carriers.

Of course it is only possible to offer a quick survey of changes between 1000 and 1500, changes in ship design, in the economics of shipping and especially superficial of changes in naval administration. The final conclusion of the survey may be almost banal and obvious on reflection, that governments did not need an extensive organization to administer their navies if the ships could be used to carry cargo in peace time. Fortunately the obvious is in this case given strong support by the evidence of changes in ship design. The development of admiralties in Europe in the second half of the Middle Ages did not follow a straight line. Certainly they did emerge with the general and long term increase in the scope of government activity in the high and late Middle Ages. But the growth of government offers neither a complete nor a specific explanation for the pattern of change in naval administration in the second half of the Middle Ages. Certainly there can be no single or unique reason for the ways governments chose to implement naval policies. On the other hand it seems clear that changes in the technology of shipbuilding, changes in the design of ships made a difference to the way wars were fought at sea. War was one of the principal functions of government if not the most important one, so it is not surprising to find a connection between the technology of warfare, in this case war at sea, and the level, character and scope of at least one set of public institutions: the admiralties.

FOOTNOTES

[1] Evelyn Jamison, *Admiral Eugenius of Sicily* (London, 1957), 33-55; Fredric L. Cheyette, "The Sovereign and the Pirates, 1332," *Speculum*, 45 (1970), 50.

[2] Fredric L. Cheyette, "The Sovereign and the Pirates, 1332," 40-68; Armand le Hénaff, *Étude sur l'Organisation Administrative de la Marine sous l'Ancien Regime at la Revolution* (Paris, 1913), 27-36.

[3] Michael Lewis, *The Navy of Britain* (London, 1948), 337-341, on the functions of the admiral and the office of admiral in the Middle Ages.

[4] See for example, J. R. Bruijn, *De Admiraliteit van Amsterdam in Rustige Jaren, 1713-1751* (Amsterdam/Haarlem, 1970); Daniel A. Baugh, *British Naval Administration in the Age of Walpole* (Princeton, New Jersey, 1965).

[5] Hélène Ahrweiler, *Byzance et la Mer* (Paris, 1966), 21-117; Hélène Antoniadis-Bibicou, *Études d'histoire maritime de Byzance* (Paris, 1966), 53-58, 99-116.

[6] See for example, F. W. Brooks, *The English Naval Forces, 1199-1272* (London, 1962²), 54-63.

[7] Edv. Bull, *Leding Militær-og Finansforfatning i Norge i Ældre Tid* (Christiana, 1920); G. P. Harbitz, "Leidangen og det Gamle Norske Samfunn," in G. P. Harbitz, S. Oppegard and R. Scheen, *Den Norske Leidangen* (Oslo, 1951), 11-160; A. Schück, "Ledung och Konunghamm," *Sjöhistorisk Arsbok* (1950), 97-128.

[8] The most obvious example is the expansion of the English navy after King John lost Normandy to the King of France. F. W. Brooks, *The English Naval Forces, 1199-1272*, 87-89; Michael Lewis, *The History of the British Navy* (Harmondsworth, 1957), 16-17.

[9] R. H. Dolley, "The Warships of the Later Roman Empire," *"The Journal of Roman Studies*, 38 (1948), 47-53; Louis Bréhier, "La Marine de Byzance du VIIIᵉ au XIᵉ Siècle," *Byzantion*, 19 (1949), 10-14; Lionel Casson, *Ships and Seamanship in the Ancient World* (Princeton, New Jersey, 1971), 146-168.

[10] Detlev Ellmers, *Frühmittelalterliche Handelsschiffahrt in Mittel-und Nordeuropa* (Neumünster, 1972), 30-45, 118-119; Olaf Olsen and Ole Crumlin-Pedersen, "The Skuldelev Ships (II)," *Acta Archaeologica*, 38 (1967), 106-118; A. W. Brøgger and Haakon Shetelig, *The Viking Ships* (Oslo, 1971²), 76-90, 106-112.

[11] G. J. Marcus, "The Evolution of the *Knörr*," *The Mariner's Mirror*, 41 (1955), 115-122.

[12] For a summary of information on the military camps see, Johannes Brønstad, *The Vikings* (Harmondsworth, 1965), 173-185.

[13] Detlev Ellmers, *Frühmittelalterliche Handelsschiffahrt*, 63-75, 258-259. Paul Heinsius, *Das Schiff der Hansischen Frühzeit* (Weimar, 1956), 69-93 for discussions of the development of the cog design in the high Middle Ages; Ole Crumlin-Pedersen, "The Vikings and the Hanseatic merchants: 900-1450," in *A History of Seafaring Based on Underwater Archaeology*, G. Bass, ed. (London, 1972), 190-191.

[14] F. W. Brooks, *The English Naval Forces, 1199-1272*, 64-68, 79-140, 168-195; F. W. Brooks, "William de Wrotham and the Office of Keeper of the King's Ports and Galleys," *English Historical Review*, 40 (1925), 570-579; H. J. Hewitt, *The Black Prince's Expedition of 1355-1357* (Manchester, 1958), 33-42. Ships smaller than cogs were used in war, barges and balingers for example. But they like cogs could be and were used as cargo ships in peacetime, the greatest distinction between those used for trading and those used for fighting being crew size. J. W. Sherborne, "English Barges and Balingers of the Late Fourteenth Century," *The Mariner's Mirror*, 63 (1977), 109-114.

[15] R. C. Anderson, "English Galleys in 1295," *The Mariner's Mirror*, 14 (1928), 220-241; J. T. Tinniswood, "English Galleys, 1272-1377," *The Mariner's Mirror*, 35 (1949), 276-292; Michael Prestwich, *War, Politics and Finance under Edward I* (London, 1972), 137-140; F. W. Brooks, *The English Naval Forces, 1199-1272*, 147-158.

[16] Charles de la Roncière, *Histoire de la Marine Francaise* (Paris, 1909-1920²), volume I, 399-407, volume II, 70-72; H. A. Miskimin, "The Last Act of Charles V: The Background of the Revolts of 1382," *Speculum*, 38 (1963), 437.

[17] Louis Nicolas, *Histoire de la Marine Francaise* (Paris, 1961²), 6; F. C. Lane, *Navires et Constructeurs à Venise pendant la Renaissance* (Paris, 1965), 126-135; Florentino Perez-Embid, "Navigation et commerce dans le porte de Séville au bas Moyen âge," *Le Moyen Age*, 1 (1969), 269. The Seville arsenal dates from 1252 while the Barcelona Atarazanas date from the first half of the thirteenth century.

[18] Hilmar C. Krueger, "The Routine of Commerce between Genoa and North-West Africa during the late Twelfth Century," *The Mariner's Mirror*, 19 (1933), 430-431; F. C. Lane, "The Crossbow in the Nautical Revolution of the Middle Ages," in *Economy, Society and Government in Medieval Italy* D. Herlihy *et al.*, eds. (Kent, 1969), 161-166; F. C. Lane, "Progrès technologiques et productivité dans les transports maritimes de la fin du Moyen Age au début des Temps modernes," *Reveue Historique*, 251 (1974), 287-297.

[19] F. C. Lane, *Navires et Constructeurs à Venise* 2-24; R. C. Anderson, "Italian Naval Architecture about 1445," *The Mariner's Mirror*, 11 (1925), 144-145.

[20] *Inter alia*, Charles de la Roncière, *Histoire de la Marine Francaise*, volume II, 152-153, 363-365, 462-465; Michael Oppenheim, *A History of the Administration of the Royal Navy* (London, 1896), 25-26, 37-38; F. C. Lane, *Navires et Constructeurs à Venise* 97-100.

[21] C. S. L. Davies, "The Administration of the Royal Navy under Henry VIII: the Origins of the Navy Board," *English Historical Review*, 80 (1965), 268-288; Michael Lewis, *The History of the British Navy*, 39-44.

CHAPTER 5

Combined Arms Operations and the Latin Conquest of Constantinople

Donald E. Queller

University of Illinois at Urbana

In early 1201 the leaders of the new Fourth Crusade entered into an alliance with the Venetians, who were to supply transportation and a force of fifty galleys for the expedition. For the purpose of gaining additional forces and finances, the allies later agreed to install the refugee Byzantine prince Alexius upon the throne of his usurping uncle, Alexius III, in Constantinople. In July 1203 and again in April 1204 the combined forces of the crusaders and the Venetians took the capital city of Eastern Christendom.

According to the terms of the crusader-Venetian treaty the crusaders were to number 33,500 men, but only about one-third of that number appeared in Venice and some of them were lost to defection en route to Constantinople.[1] At least as many Venetians manned the fleet.[2] The armada numbered two hundred vessels or slightly more, approximately half of which were horse transports and very roughly one-quarter transports and the other quarter galleys.[3]

In early July of 1203 the combined forces had positioned themselves at Scutari across the Bosporus above Constantinople. They had observed that the towered walls of Constantinople facing the sea of Marmara and the Bosporus rose almost immediately out of the water, leaving practically no space for attackers to gain a foothold. Any assault upon these walls would also be endangered by the strong current sweeping the ships southward. On the northern shore of the Golden Horn, however, there was a larger beach defended only by the strong tower of Galata. The leaders agreed that their first objective must be to gain a foothold on this northern shore and control of the Golden Horn.[4] After much discussion they agreed upon an order of battle with the army grouped into seven battalions. The advance guard was given to Count Baldwin of Flanders, since he had under his command the most skilled and numerous archers.[5] A feudal army, while it relied upon the charge of heavily armed knights for the blow giving victory, customarily tried to shelter that mounted mass behind a screen of infantry until the critical moment.

Just after sunrise on the fine morning of July 5 the Venetian galleys moved forward in order of battle, each towing behind it one of the more un- wieldy sailing ships in order to cross over more securely.[6] Near the northern shore of the entrance to the harbor, less than a mile from Scutari, Emperor Alexius III disposed his forces to meet the attack. The crusaders sent barks packed with crossbowmen and archers ahead of the galleys to attempt to clear the shore for landing. As missiles cast by mangonels and petraries on the walls of Constantinople splashed in the water about them the vessels made their way across the treacherous Bosporus without mishap. When they ran aground, the ports in the sides of the horse transports were quickly lowered to form bridges down which the fully armored knights rode into the water up to their waists, lances in hand. The archers followed the knights, and then other foot-soldiers. As these lesser men clambered to shore they drew up in front of the battalions of knights in the accustomed formation.[7]

The Greeks made only a feeble pretense of contesting the landing. Some volleys of arrows were fired from a distance at the knights with their long lances poised for the thunderous mounted charge. But when Count Baldwin set in motion his vanguard, and the other battalions began to move forward after the Flemings, the Greeks quickly showed their heels in precipitous flight. The knights chased their fleeing quarry all along the northern shore of the harbor as far as the fortified bridge beyond the northwest extremity of Constantinople. Over this bridge the frightened Greeks escaped to the other shore. Without the loss of a man the crusaders had gained the whole northern shore of the Golden Horn except for the suburb of Galata and the critical tower.[8]

The Venetians urged that they should make an assault upon the tower on the following day, for it was essential to get the fleet out of the un- sheltered straits and into the safety of the Golden Horn, and the council of war agreed with the Venetian proposal.[9] The tower was the key to the harbor, for to it was fastened one end of the great chain which barred the mouth. On the next day the crusaders set up their siege equipment, while the ships bearing petraries drew within range. The defenders made several sorties, inflicting some damage. In response to the last of these, however, the crusaders successfully counterattacked, dividing the enemy force and demolishing it. The crusaders pressed so hard after those seeking to regain the shelter of the tower that it was impossible to close the gate, so the pursuers crowded in and the tower was captured.[10]

Now the attackers set about the destruction of the chain which extended, supported by wooden floats, across the mouth of the Golden Horn. The greatest ship in the armada, the *Eagle*, gaining a full head of sail before the wind and the current, ran with its reinforced and iron-cased prow upon the chain, and the chain broke.[11] The galleys and the other transports and horse-transports followed the Eagle into the harbor, falling upon and destroying the few and dilapidated Byzantine galleys, barges and light craft drawn up behind the chain.[12]

A council of war now determined to follow up the advantage with an attack before Alexius III would have time to improve his defensive position. The northern knights and the Venetians, however, disagreed upon tactics. The Venetians favored a water-borne assault across the harbor against the enemies' weaker fortifications. On the harbor side the city was protected by a single wall about thirty feet high, flanked, of course, with many projecting towers. The Venetians proposed to attack the heights of these fortifications from bridges mounted on their ships. The knights preferred to attack the land walls, despite their greater strength. The disagreement was settled by a compromise: the crusaders would attack the land walls near the Blachernae Palace at the northern apex of the triangle of Constantinople; the Venetians in their ships would assault the nearby harbor walls.[13]

On July 10 the crusaders marched along the northern shore of the Golden Horn, intending to pass over the stone bridge across the Barbysis river where it enters the harbor. When they arrived they discovered that the Greeks had prudently demolished it. The crusaders therefore set men to work through the night to repair the bridge, the next day it was ready. The Byzantines ought to have defended the crossing vigorously. The Greeks, however, had no heart for battle, and they offered little or no opposition to the crossing. The crusaders thus passed over and set up camp facing the wall in front of a hill within the city which had the Blachernae Palace at the base of its northern slope. The fleet anchored nearby.[14] This was a corner of the city where the army and the fleet could attack almost side by side. The besiegers set about fortifying their camp with earthworks and a palisade. They set up their petraries and mangonels and other siege machinery to pound the walls and the palace, which was seriously damaged.[15]

The Venetians also made ready for the attack. Dandolo ordered the construction of flying bridges on the transports. These bridges of planks with rope railings were suspended from the masts and supported by lashed yards. They hung high above the water before the vessels. They could be maneuvered onto the tops of the walls, making the vessels fast and forming a passage by which as many as three soldiers abreast could advance from their ships to the ramparts.[16] Siege weapons were readied on the prow of each vessel to batter the walls and threaten the defenders. From cages aloft crossbowmen could soften the defenses for the swordsmen on the bridges.[17]

47

From within the beleaguered city the emperor had the crusaders' camp pelted by archers and by whatever artillery the defenders could muster. He also ordered sorties from the gates as many as six or seven times a day.[18] Even at night there was no respite for the crusaders, for the whole camp had to be called to arms whenever one of these sorties occurred.[19] Villehardouin tells us that it was impossible to venture in search of supplies more than four bowshots from the fortified camp. Since foraging parties could not function freely, provisions became painfully short, although there was a sufficient store of flour and salt meat. Because of their lack of provisions the leaders knew that they could not sustain the siege beyond two or three weeks.[20]

So on July 17 they began their attack upon the walls of Constantinople. From the landward side the crossbowmen opened fire upon the defenders and the crusaders drew up a ram in an effort to smash a hole in the fortifications, which were not so strong as the wall stretching to the south.[21] Three battalions of knights were assigned to protect the camp, while the other four hurled themselves at the wall with scaling ladders.[22] In spite of fierce resistance they planted two of these ladders against a barbican close to the sea. Two knights and two sergeants scaled the ladders and with their swords forced their way in spite of the blows rained upon them onto the parapet. They held their foothold tenaciously, while a handful of others succeeded in following them, for a total of about fifteen men. Here they fought bloodily, the swords of the crusaders against the dread doubleheaded axes of the elite Varangian Guard. The savagery of the latter before long drove the attackers off the wall, and two of them were captured. The assault from the landward side was a failure, and the crusaders retreated behind their protecting palisade, greatly upset by their defeat.[23]

The Venetians had more success in attacking the harbor walls. Although the defenders showered upon the attacking fleet a torrent of stones from the artillery mounted on the towers, no ships were lost. The mangonels from the fleet returned the Greek bombardment, and as the ships drew within range of crossbowmen and archers, bolts and arrows filled the air. The flying bridges of some vessels came so close to the walls that the attackers, suspended precariously in the air above sea and shore, exchanged pike thrusts and sword blows with the defenders.[24]

At first the galleys remained behind the larger vessels, but then the oarsmen drove them forward in their characteristic short and choppy rhythm in a series of leaps. Dandolo's vermilion galley was the first to run aground on the narrow strip between the walls and the water, and the men leaped ashore, bearing the ensign of the winged lion before the doge. When those on the other galleys saw their banner beneath the walls, they too piled ashore. Under fire on the narrow beach they raised scaling ladders against the walls. After a time, amidst the confusion of the fray, they saw their winged lion banner flying from one of the towers.[25] Meanwhile the

Venetians also perhaps breached the wall with a battering ram near the imperial landing dock and gained a foothold within the city.[26]

Some of the roundships in the meantime had maneuvered their bridges onto the tops of the towers. The attackers on the bridges, once these were made fast, had the advantage of height, and the Venetians fought fiercely to claw their way onto the ramparts. When a large number of them had gained a footing the defenders fled, and the Venetians were able to open gates for their companions on the shore. These rushed in, and soon the attackers were in possession of twenty-five or thirty towers fronting the quarter called the Petrion.[27] Since the wall facing the Golden Horn had a hundred ten towers the Venetians held something like one-fourth of the entire harbor wall.[28] They tried to penetrate into the city, but met ferocious resistance from the Varangians. Many Venetians were wounded and they fell back to the wall. The defenders of the city rallied to attempt to retake the captured towers, but even the axe-wielding Varangians were beaten off. The Venetians, however, did not dare again advance beyond their section of the wall into the city.[29]

In order to protect their position the doge's men set fire to the houses that were built against the wall. The wind blowing across the harbor fanned the flames and spread fiery destruction into the interior of Constantinople.[30] Dandolo meanwhile had received word from the crusaders that they needed help.[31]

Under pressure the indecisive Alexius III was persuaded to try to relieve the danger from the stronger foes, the Venetians, by threatening the crusaders, whom his forces had already repelled from the land walls.[32] From three gates Alexius led the best troops he could muster in an apparent effort to catch the crusaders in the right flank. His force was so large—although it was grossly exaggerated by most Western sources—that it threatened to envelop them and their camp.[33] It appeared so overwhelming, in fact, that the magnates sent a plea for reinforcement to the doge, who ordered his Venetians to abandon their hard-won towers and go to live or die in an effort to rescue their allies.[34]

One battalion of the crusaders had remained outside the palisade as usual on guard. Now the other six moved out and drew up in front of their fortifications facing the enemy to the south, so that they could not be attacked on the flank.[35] Three battalions were assigned to attack under Baldwin of Flanders, who was given the vanguard again, Hugh of St. Pol and Henry, Baldwin's brother. The Count of Flanders rode forward with his battalion, with Henry of Hainaut and Hugh of St. Pol following. When Baldwin's battalion was two bowshots from the camp, it turned back, not wishing to go beyond the help of the reserves before the palisades. The battalion of the Count of St. Pol, however, would not follow this example, and proceeded to seize the vanguard. Baldwin, shamed, resumed the attack, and pulled even with Hugh's battalion. On top of a ridge beyond which they would be concealed from the battalions on guard, and separated from the enemy by a ditch (perhaps the Lycus), they halted.[36]

While the crusaders were considering what to do, the emperor also had a decision to make. According to our Latin sources, he was overcome with fear of the courage, size and strength of the Latins, and it is true that the Greeks had an acute awareness of the "irresistible first shock" of the feudal charge of the Western knights.[37] So Alexius III declined battle and turned his forces back into the city.[38] It was not only the determined advance of the crusaders, however, but the imminent arrival of Venetian reinforcements, which caused the emperor to retreat. Above all, the sortie was probably from the beginning merely a tactical maneuver to draw the Venetians away from the harbor walls, and the emperor had never had the intention of joining battle. By threatening the crusaders and their camp he compelled the Venetians, who had won a considerable stretch of the harbor walls, to withdraw.[39] In spite of temporary successes the attack upon the city was a failure.

During the night, however, Emperor Alexius III fled his capital. The Greeks of Constantinople accepted young Alexius and his deposed father, Isaac II, as joint emperors. The restored rulers were unable to fulfill their obligations to the crusaders and the Venetians, however, and soon skirmishing resumed. Alexius IV and Isaac II were deposed by the virulently anti-Latin Alexius V, called Mourtzouphlus.

In the late winter and early spring of 1204, therefore, the crusaders and the Venetians, who had withdrawn to the northern shore of the Golden Horn at the request of the joint emperors, busied themselves with preparations for another assault upon the imperial city. The army's experience in attacking Constantinople in July of 1203 had revealed the very great difficulty of scaling the land walls, whereas the Venetians had been more successful in their assault across the harbor, so it was now agreed to concentrate all their forces against the walls fronting the Golden Horn, as from the outset the Venetians had advised.[40] The northerners set up mangonels and petraries on the shore before the Blachernae Palace to harass the defenders and to raise the threat of another attack from that quarter. The assault bridges which the Venetians were accustomed to suspend from the superstructures of the transports were raised even higher to compensate for Alexius V's heightening of the walls.[41]

Within the city Mourtzouphlus also made ready for the coming battle. Along the land curtain to the west he ordered many of the gates walled up with bricks.[42] Along the harbor curtain he had built of stout beams towers of several stories between the permanent stone towers and also had the latter raised by several stories of wood. These hoardings overhung the stone wall, and each story overhung the one below, so that stones, missiles, hot sand and boiling oil could be poured upon the attackers at the wall's base. Mangonels and petraries were mounted along the wall to fire upon the enemy ships. Mourtzouphlus ordered a double ditch dug between the curtain and the water, so that the attackers on foot would find it difficult to drag or push their wheeled machines to the foot of the fortifications.[43] Despite the crusaders' attempt to patrol the land wall the new emperor was able to bring into the city many additional troops. With these he amply garrisoned the towers along the harbor.[44]

On Thursday, April 8,[45] the Venetian vessels were drawn up side by side, transports alternating with galleys and horse transports, loaded with men and horses.[46] With the first light of dawn the ships moved forward along a front of a good mile.[47] The galleys and horse transports were to discharge their troops ashore to attempt to break through, undermine or scale the fortifications. The transports would try to effect a foothold on the walls with their flying bridges.[48] They approached the same part of the wall that the Venetians had assaulted in July, 1203.[49]

As the ships neared the walls they attempted to establish a cover for the assault forces with volleys of stones, bolts, and arrows. The defenders showered the fleet with return fire, which smashed some of the equipment and made it dangerous for those exposed on the decks.[50] The galleys and horse transports drew as near the shore as they could, some beaching and others of deeper draft running aground farther out, so that their troops had to splash ashore burdened with scaling ladders, pickaxes and other gear. The protective wheeled shells were carefully unloaded. These troops attacked the walls from the narrow strip of land between the fortifications and the harbor. The defenders hurled great stones from above upon the equipment for breaching the wall, smashing their protective roofs and forcing the engineers to flee.[51] While some crusaders attacked the shore, the transports with their flying bridges flung out and burdened with brave men assaulted the heights of the walls.[52] One vessel had been assigned to a tower,[53] and each pushed forward to attempt to anchor its bridge to the top of the fortifications. An unusual south wind hampered operations, driving the ships back from the walls. None succeeded in affixing its assault bridge.[54] For a good part of the day the battle raged in more than a hundred places,[55] but those who had landed on the shore were driven back and took to their vessels.[56] Abandoning their equipment, the leaders of the crusade were constrained to give the order to retreat.[57] The attack was a complete failure, and the pilgrims had lost nearly a hundred dead.[58] We do not have a figure for the Greek losses, but they seem to have been very slight.

Toward six o'clock, shortly after their retreat to the north side of the harbor, the magnates and the doge gathered in a church to decide what they should do. Some of the barons wanted to try a new attack on another side of the city, along the Bosporus or the Sea of Marmara, where the defenses

51

had not been so strongly reinforced. The doge pointed out that the strong current running down the Bosporus and the almost continual wind from the north-north-east would carry their vessles away from the walls and into the open sea.[59] As they were accustomed to do, the crusaders deferred to the wisdom of Dandolo. They decided to allocate two days to rest, refitting the ships, and repairing the equipment, before making another assault on the same walls on Monday. This time they determined to bind the transports together two by two, so that a greater force could be brought to bear against each point of attack.[60] At sunrise on Monday, April 12, every available crusader and Venetian was in his place, ready to resume the assault. Forty of the large roundships had been tied together in pairs, so that each pair might attack a single tower. The fleet approached the same section of wall from Blachernae to Euergetes which they had unsuccessfully assailed on Friday.[61] Greek stonethrowers hammered the fleet with boulders so large that a single man could not lift one, but the Venetians had protected their ships with timbers and grapevines, so that no serious damage was done. The roundships came as near the walls as they could, then cast anchor and rained arrows, stones and Greek fire upon the defenders, but the towers also were protected with hides, and would not burn.[62] Until about middday the defenders stood firm and the scale of battle remained in precarious balance.[63]

Toward noon there arose a north wind, which blew the ships toward the shore. Robert of Clari tells us that only four or five of the greatest vessels could reach with their assault bridges the tops of the wooden towers erected by Mourtzouphlus.[64] A gust of wind and a surge of water drove a pair of these, the *Paradise* and the *Pilgrim*, forward, so that for an instant the end of the flying bridge of the *Pilgrim* banged against a tower. A Venetian managed to pull himself onto the tower, but he was quite alone, and was promptly killed.[65] Tossed by wave and wind, the ship once more bumped the tower and a knight named Andrew d'Ureboise followed the example of the Venetian, and his armor protected him enough so that he was able to draw his sword and drive the defenders to a lower level. Some of his comrades followed after him, and they secured the ship with ropes to the tower, allowing still more crusaders to join them. The surge of the sea, however, pulled at the ships so strongly that the whole tower trembled, so the ships had to cast off for fear of pulling down the timbered superstructure with their own men upon it. Those who crossed, however, were enough to take the tower, and soon another, and then several more were in the crusaders' hands.[66] Mourtzouphlus, of course, sent reinforcements to the threatened sector, and the Latins did not care to venture beyond their captured towers.[67]

Robert of Clari was one of a party, about ten knights and sixty sergeants, who landed on a narrow strip of ground betwen the walls and the shore and discovered a walled-up postern. They fell upon it with picks, axes, crowbars, and even swords, while some tried to protect them with their shields from the hail of stones, boiling pitch and Greek fire. They succeeded in making a small hole, through which they could see a crowd of Greeks inside the city. Robert's brother, Aleaumes, a courageous priest in hauberk, crawled through, and drove back the defenders, so that others could follow him. The emperor made a show of spurring his horse upon the invaders, but the small band of crusaders outfaced him, and he returned to his command post.[68]

The crusaders then opened the gates, the Venetians brought the transports to shore, and the Latins swarmed into the city. When the heavily armed knights began their charge against the emperor's command post, the Greeks fled.[69] The crusaders camped for the night near the walls, ready for continued fighting in the morning.[70] They knew that the troops defending the imperial city had not been destroyed. During the night, however, the Greeks were not able to organize a defense, Mourtzouphlus fled, and on the morrow the crusaders found no resistance. The city was theirs.

FOOTNOTES

[1] Geoffroi de Villehardouin, *La Conquête de Constantinople*, ed. Edmond Faral, 2 vols. (Paris, 1938-1939), sec. 56, I, 58. Benjamin Hendrickx has recently examined the question of the number of troops gathered in Venice. "À propos du nombre des troupes de la quatrième croisade et de l'empereur Baudouin I," *Byzantina (Thessalonica)*, III (1971), 29-40. He gives a minimum figure of 11,167 (Villehardouin's one-third) and a maximum of 21,750 (p. 34). I see no reason to accept the assumption upon which the latter is based, that one-half of the crusaders in Venice paid two marks each of the 83,000 or 85,000 marks owed. Moreover, 21,750 must be a mistake for 21,250 (p. 33). Edgar H. McNeal and Robert Lee Wolff estimate 10,000-12,000. "The Fourth Crusade," in *A History of the Crusades*, ed. Kenneth M. Setton, *et al.*, (Madison, Wisc., 1969) II, 166-167. Robert of Clari says that there were not more than a thousand knights. *La Conquête de Constantinople*, ed. Philippe Lauer (Paris, 1924), sec. XI, 9-10. We know, however, how unreliable his numbers are. If he is correct, though, in stating that 50,000 marks remained to be paid (*ibid.*), which seems reasonable and in line with Villehardouin's statement that less than half had been paid (*Conquête de Constantinople*, sec. 58, I, 60), and if those present had paid at the contracted rate, this would indicate about 13,000 crusaders. I do not have much faith in Antonio Carile's elaborate attempt to quantify the crusading army. "Alle origini dell'impero latino d'Oriente: Analisi quantitative dell'esercito crociato e repartizione dei feudi," *Nuova rivista storica*, LVI, (1972), 288-314. See my specific criticisms: Donald E. Queller, Thomas K, Compton and Donald A. Campbell, "The Fourth Crusade: The Neglected Majority," *Speculum*, XLIX (1974), 446-447, n. 24.

[2] Robert of Clari reports a conscription of Venetians to go with the fleet. Pairs of waxed balls were prepared, one of each two containing a summons to service. They were blessed by a priest and drawn by him, giving one ball to each eligible male. *Conquête*, sec. XI, 9. Carile estimates that a fleet of this size required a complement of 17,264 men. "Alle origini dell'impero d'Oriente," 287-288. Probably overestimated.

[3] *Devastatio Constantinopolitana*, in *Annales Herbipolenses, M.G.H., SS.*, XVI, 10 (also in *Chroniques Gréco-Romanes*, ed. Charles Hopf (Berlin, 1873), 87; Hugh of St. Pol, *Epistola*, in *Annales Coloniensis maximi, M.G.H., SS.*, XVII, 813. (The letter is also found in *Urkunden zur älteren Handels- und Staatsgeschichte der Republik Venedig*, ed. G. L. Fr. Tafel and G. M. Thomas, 3 vols, 1st ed., 1856-1857, reprinted (Amsterdam, 1967), I, 304-311, and in *Rec. hist. Gaules*, XVIII, 517-519.) Nicetas Choniates, *Historia*, ed. Aloysius van Dieten, 2 vols. (vol. II, index) (Berlin and New York, 1975), 539. (Also in the 1835 Bonn ed., 714.) Carile's statement that among the thirteenth century sources only the *Devastatio* gives a figure for the size of the fleet is incorrect. "Alle origini dell'impero d'oriente," 287-288.

[4] Leopoldo Usseglio, *I marchesi di Monferrato in Italia ed in Oriente durante i secoli XII e XIII*, vol. II (Turin, 1926), 221.

[5] Villehardouin, *Conquête de Constantinople*, sec. 147, I, 148.

[6] Robert of Clari, *Conquête*, sec. XLI, 42; Villehardouin, *Conquête*, secs. 155-156, I, 154-156.

[7] Robert of Clari, *Conquête*, secs. XLII-XLIII, 42; Villehardouin, *Conquête de Constantinople*, sec. 156, I, 156; Hugh of St. Pol, *Epistola*, 813. Clari makes it clear that the knights issued mounted from the transports. Probably lesser men led the horses down the bridge into the water.

[8] Robert of Clari, *Conquête*, sec. XLIII, 42-43; Villehardouin, *Conquête de Constantinople*, secs. 157-158, I, 156-158; Hugh of St. Pol, *Epistola*, 813. This Tower of Galata, located on the shore, must not be confused with the fourteenth century tower, which still stands on the hillside at a considerable distance from the shore.

[9] Robert of Clari, *Conquête*, sec. XLIII, 43; Villehardouin, *Conquête de Constantinople*, sec. 159, I. 158.

[10] Robert of Clari, *Conquête*, sec. XLIV, 43; Villehardouin, *Conquête de Constantinople*, secs. 160-161, I, 158-160; Hugh of St. Pol, *Epistola*, 813; Nicetas, *Historia*, 542-543.

[11] Andrea Dandulo, *Chronica*, ed. E. Pastorello, in *R.I.S.*[2], XII, i, 322. The *Historia ducum Veneticorum*, ed. by H. Simonsfeld, *M.G.H., SS.*, XIV, 93, mentions a bridge over the chain by means of which men passed back and forth between Constantinople and Galata. It was supposedly struck and broken by the *Eagle*. This is wrong.

[12] Robert of Clari, *Conquête*, sec. XLIV, 43; Nicetas, *Historia*, 543.

[13] Villehardouin, *Conquête de Constantinople*, sec. 162, I, 160-162; Robert of Clari, *Conquête*, sec. XLIV, 43-44. Martino da Canale puts into the mouth of Dandolo in 1204 a remark concerning the French lack of experience in fighting from the flying bridges mounted on ships. *Les estoires de Venise; Cronaca veneziana in lingua francese dalle origini al 1275*, ed. Alberto Limentani (Florence, 1972), Part I, sec. LI, 57. (An older ed. by Filippo-Luigi Polidori, with Ital. trans. Conte Giovanni Galvani, in *Archivio Storico Italiano*, ser. 1, VIII (1845), 332.)

[14] Villehardouin, *Conquête de Constantinople*, sec. 163, I, 162-164; Robert of Clari, *Conquête*, sec. XLIV, 44; Hugh of St. Pol, *Epistola*, 813. Charles M. Brand ignores the demolition of the bridge by the Greeks. *Byzantium Confronts the West, 1180-1204* (Cambridge, Mass., 1968), 238.

[15] Villehardouin, *Conquête de Constantinople*, sec. 166, I, 168; Hugh of St. Pol, *Epistola*, 813; Nicetas, *Historia*, 544-545.

[16] Perhaps these bridges operated by a pulley system similar to that used on a land-based siege tower in the Fifth Crusade at Damietta and described by Hans Eberhard Mayer, *The Crusades*, trans. from the 1st Germ. ed., 1965, by John Gillingham and rev. by the author (New York and Oxford, 1972), 211.

[17] Robert of Clari, *Conquête*, sec. XLIV, 44; Alethea Wiel, *The Navy of Venice* (London, 1910), 412.

[18] Villehardouin, *Conquête de Constantinople*, sec. 165, I, 166.

[19] *Ibid.*, secs. 165-166, 168, I, 166-170.

[20] *Ibid.*, sec. 165, I, 166. The marshal estimates that they could maintain the siege for three weeks. In the letter of the crusading leaders to Innocent III, they estimate only fifteen days. Innocent III, *Epistolae*, in Migne, *PL*, CCXV, 239.

[21] Nicetas, *Historia*, 545. Although very strong, the walls in this area lacked a ditch or moat and a second wall. R. Janin, *Constantinople byzantine*, 1st ed., 1950, 2nd ed. rev. (Paris, 1964), 283.

[22] Villehardouin, *Conquête de Constantinople*, sec. 170, I, 170-172.

[23] *Ibid.*, sec. 171, I, 172-174.

[24] *Ibid.*, sec. 172, I, 174.

[25] *Ibid.*, secs. 173-174, I, 174-176.

[26] Nicetas, *Historia*, pp. 544-545. Western chroniclers make no mention of a breach caused by a ram, and Raimbaut says specifically "the wall breached in many places without the battering ram. . ." Raimbaut de Vaqueiras, *The Poems of the Troubador Raimbaut de Vaqueiras*, ed. Joseph Linskill (The Hague, 1964), 305, 310, and 332, note to line 42.

[27] Villehardouin, *Conquête de Constantinople*, sec. 175, I, 176, lists twenty-five towers, but Hugh of St. Pol. *Epistola*, 814, says thirty.

[28] Michael Maclagen, *The City of Constantinople* (New York and Washington, 1968), 35-36.

[29] Nicetas, *Historia*, 544-545 Villehardouin, *Conquête de Constantinople*, secs. 175-176, I, 178.

[30] Nicetas, *Historia*, 545; Villehardouin, *Conquête de Constantinople*, sec. 176, I, 178; Robert of Clari, *Conquête*, sec. XLVI, 47.

[31] Villehardouin, *Conquête de Constantinople*, sec. 179, I, 180-182.

[32] Ernoul and Bernard le Tresorier, *Chronique*, ed. Louis de Mas Latrie (Paris, 1871), 364-365.

[33] Linskill in Raimbaut de Vaqueiras, *Poems*, 332, note to lines 43-45. Robert of Clari, *Conquête*, sec. XLIV, 45; Nicetas, *Historia*, 546; Hugh of St. Pol, *Epistola*, 814.

[34] Villehardouin, *Conquête de Constantinople*, sec. 179, I, 180-182.

[35] *Ibid.*, secs. 177-179, I, 178-180.

[36] Robert of Clari, *Conquête*, secs. XLVII-XLVIII, 47-51. The identification of Robert's canal was made by Brand, *Byzantium Confronts the West*, 240. He also reverses the numbers of the attacking and guarding battalions. *Ibid.*, 239-240.

[37] Anna Comnena had written long ago that a Frank on horseback "would make a hole through the walls of Babylon." *The Alexiad*, trans. by Elizabeth A. S. Dawes (London, 1928; reissued, 1967), 342. R. C. Smail, *Crusading Warfare (1097-1193)* (Cambridge, Eng., 1956), 115, n. 1.

[38] Villehardouin has the emperor retreat to the Philopatrion, which was a palace outside the walls. *Conquête de Constantinople*, sec. 180, I, 182. Other sources, however, have him withdrawing into the city. Robert of Clari, *Conquête*, sec. XLVIII, 51; Nicetas, *Historia*, 546; Innocent III, *Epistolae*, VI, 211; Migne, *PL*, CCXV, 239.

[39] Brand, on the other hand, arranges the chronology differently. He believes that it might have been the news of the Venetian success against the harbor wall that caused Alexius III to return to the city. *Byzantium Confronts the West*, 240. I do not think that this is quite as acceptable an interpretation, since the crusaders summoned the Venetians to rescue them, presumably when they learned that the emperor had come out of the city in force. The Venetian success had been achieved already at that time.

[40] Villehardouin, *Conquête de Constantinople*, sec. 162, I, 162.

[41] Robert of Clari, *Conquête*, sec. LXIX, 69; C. Manfroni, *Storia della marina italiana dalle invasioni barbariche alla caduta di Costantinopoli* (Leghorn, 1899), i, 335.

[42] Nicetas, *Historia*, 567.

[43] *Ibid.*; Villehardouin, *Conquête de Constantinople*, sec. 233, II, 32-34; Baldwin of Flanders, in Innocent III, *Epistolae*, VII, 152, in Migne, *PL*, CCXV, 448-449; Robert of Clari, *Conquête*, sec. LXI, pp. 60-61, and sec. LXIX, p. 69.

[44] Gunther of Paris, *Historia Constantinopolitana*, ed. Comte Paul Riant, *Exuviae*, I, pp. 92-93.

[45] Carile has confused the dating: "Il 9 aprile, *joesdi aprés mi quaresme,* i crociati lanciarono l'attacco alle mura della città e dopo paracchie ore di lotta dovettero riparare al campo . . ." Antonio Carile, "Partitio Terrarum Imperii Romanie," *Studi Veneziani*, VII (1965), 131. They *boarded* their vessels on April 8, Thursday, and attacked at break of day on Friday, April 9. Villehardouin, *Conquête de Constantinople*, secs. 236-237, II, 36-38. Inexplicably Sir Steven Runciman fixes the attack on April 6. *A History of the Crusades*, 3 vols. (Cambridge, Eng., 1954), III, 122.

[46] Villehardouin, *Conquête de Constantinople*, sec. 236, II, 36-38; Robert of Clari, *Conquête*, sec. LXX, 69-70.

[47] Villehardouin, *Conquête de Constantinople*, secs. 236-267, II, 36-38. Edwin Pears conjectured that the galleys and horse transports formed a first line and the transports a second. *The Fall of Constantinople* (London, 1885), 347. Some MSS. support this interpretation, but Faral rejects it. In Villehardouin, *Conquête de Constantinople*, II, 39, no. 1.

[48] Villehardouin, *Conquête de Constantinople*, sec. 237, II, 38.

[49] Nicetas, *Historia*, 568. From the Palace of Blachernae to the monastery of Euergetes.

[50] *Ibid.*, 568-569.

[51] Robert of Clari, *Conquête*, sec. LXXI, 70.

[52] Villehardouin, *Conquête de Constantinople*, sec. 237, II, 38.

[53] *Ibid.*, sec. 240, II, 42.

[54] Robert of Clari, *Conquête*, sec. LXXI, 70.

[55] Villehardouin, *Conquête de Constantinople*, sec. 237, II, 38.

[56] *Ibid.*, sec. 238, II, 38.

[57] Baldwin of Flanders, in Innocent III, *Epistolae*, VII, 152, Migne, *PL, XXCV*, 450.

[58] *The Chronicle of Novgorod, 1016-1471*, trans. Robert Michell and Nevill Forbes, in Camden Third Series, vol. XXV (London, 1914), 46. The *Devastatio Constantinopolitana, M.G.H., SS.*, XVI, 12 (Hopf ed., 92), says that the losses were heavy on both sides. Baldwin of Flanders seems to say that the defeat occurred without much loss of Latin blood. In Innocent III, *Epistolae*, VII, 152, Migne, *PL*, CCXV, 450. The version addressed to the archbishop of Cologne does have a "non", but no other version has it. *De oorkonden der graven van Vlaanderen (1191-aanvang 1206)*, ed. W. Prevenier, 3 vols. (Brussels, 1964), II, 57), 581 (Cologne version), 588 and 598. Villehardouin confesses that the Latins lost more men than did the Greeks. *Conquête de Constantinople*, sec. 238, II, 38-40.

[59] Villehardouin, *Conquête de Constantinople*, sec. 239, II, 40. Janin, *Constantinople byzantine*, 2 reports that the current, due to the overflow of the Black Sea, runs at 3-5 Km. For an appreciation of Dandolo's role in the crusade, see Manfroni, *Storia della marina italiana*, I, 334-335.

[60] Villehardouin, *Conquête de Constantinople*, sec. 240, II, 240-242.

[61] *Chronicle of Novgorod*, 46.

[62] Robert of Clari, *Conquête*, sec. LXXIV, 73. Greek fire, it seems, was not a secret weapon of the Greeks.

[63] Villehardouin, *Conquête de Constantinople*, sec. 241, II, 42; Nicetas, *Historia*, 569.

[64] Robert of Clari, Conquête, sec. LXXIV, 73.

[65] Venetian tradition named him Pietro Alberti. See Zorzi Dolfin, *Chronica*, Biblioteca Marciana, cl. ital. VII, cod. 794 (8503). Dolfin and the Venetian tradition generally, however, are not very reliable on the Fourth Crusade. Dolfin also has him bearing the standard of St. Mark.

[66] Robert of Clari, *Conquête*, sec. LXXIV, 73-74; Villehardouin, *Conquête de Constantinople*, secs. 242-243, II, 42-44; Baldwin of Flanders, in Innocent III, *Epistolae*, II, 152, in Migne, *PL*, CCXV, 450; Nicetas, *Historia*, 568-569; Ernoul-Bernard, *Chronique*, 372; Anonymous of Soissons, *De terra Iherosolimitana*, 6-7. On the identity of Andrew, see *Exuviae sacrae Constantinopolitanae*, ed. Comte Paul Riant, 3 vols (Paris, 1877-1904), I, 1v.

[67] Robert of Clari, *Conquête*, sec. LXXIV, 74-75.

[68] *Ibid.*, secs. LXXV-LXXVIII, pp. 75-77. In another position beneath the walls the poet-companion of Boniface of Montferrat, Raimbaut de Vaqueiras, was wounded. Linskill, in Raimbaut de Vaqueiras, *Poems*, 305 and 310, and notes. This gives a slight indication of the place of Boniface and his followers in the battle.

[69] Robert of Clari, *Conquête*, sec. LXXVIII, 77; Villehardouin, *Conquête de Constantinople*, sec. 243, II, 44-46.

[70] Villehardouin, *Conquête de Constantinople*, secs. 243-244, II, 46; Robert of Clari, *Conquête*, sec. LXXVII, 78-79.

CHAPTER 6

Wooden Walls: the English Navy in the Reign of Edward I

A. Z. Freeman
College of William and Mary

No one would deny that the English—the Celts before them and the Norman-Angevins after them—were sea-going. Even without specific data, geography provides indirect evidence. After all, no part of England lies more than sixty miles from the sea, and most land-locked areas are watered by brimming rivers rolling without falls to the sea. A glance at the map lets us presume that the inhabitants of Britain were acquainted with the sea: how could they not have been when great estuaries like Severn, Thames, Humber, Southampton Water, and the Wash led them to it? Well, we know by now that the inferences of a latter day do not always lead back to fact. Italy and Japan should surely have produced races of mariners, but the Romans had to learn from the Carthaginians how to build and sail ships, while the Japanese did not navigate the open ocean until after the Meiji Restoration.

From the 13th century, evidence of many kinds has accumulated to support the premises suggested by geography. The litigious Normans and the bureaucratic Angevins left an extensive mass of unsystematized documents which were finally put into order by their 19th century descendants. From these letters, writs, charters, official rolls, relics, and from relics and sphragistic depictions, we can know for certain that the English who might be presumed pelagic, were indeed so. The records proliferate from the time of John, showing him to have been an innovator in setting England's naval defense. They show that the navy of Edward I did not spring full-formed from the mind and dockyards of that energetic king. Neither did it sail in unbroken line from the days of Alfred. Although Alfred may be the legendary founder of the navy, John was the practical one.

From the Conquest to the loss of Normandy, English kings had controlled both shores of the Channel. Well within a great empire, the Channel floated no enemy except for rebels, whose rebellions died young, and Danes, whose threat vanished after 1070. The Channel functioned as a riverine, not a pelagic binder which was active with the commerce of peoples living under a common suzerain and lord. When Philip Augustus took Normandy, he changed a peaceful internal waterway into a hostile frontier. Except for Gascony, John's continental ports were now Philip's ports. Now Philip could muster the Norman-Breton antagonism for their neighbors north of the Channel into a naval vendetta that led to raids on shipping and even threatened sporadic invasions. From 1204 on, English kings faced the new strategic requirement of a fleet to protect England from attack and to carry them and their armies across the water in support of their own aggressive actions. English sailors now had to protect the island against invasion from lands of their recent fellow subjects.

War between England and the Continent, one part or another, had become continuous before Edward I's reign. Whether to defend the shore from invasion—as in 1205—or to carry king and his army to the Continent—as in 1242—English seamen had worked into the habit of serving as a navy by the time Edward returned from Outremer in 1274.

Within two years of his return he added a new burden to the responsibilities of his ports and portmen, requiring naval support for the conquest of the whole island. From 1276 to his death, off and on, Edward I engaged the Welsh and the Scots as well as the French. The Channel dictated naval needs in French campaigns, but Edward's strategic sense led him to use the sea to help subdue the Welsh and Scots. Neither insular enemy launched a fleet to dispute control of the sea, so Edward needed only to move men and supplies to the theater of operations and to blockade his enemies, cutting them off from allies overseas and interdicting their internal supply lines. When the war with France expanded, after 1294, Edward faced vastly more complicated naval requirements than those dictated by the Welsh and Scotch wars. His principal enemy, Philip IV, had allied with the Scots and with of all people, the Norwegians. Under the terms of the alliance the Scots would move against Edward when the French, in their Norwegian ships, embarked on an invasion of England. Even the Welsh would move against the English, so the king of France was told.[1]

The French invasion never came, the Scots merely raided the northern counties, and the Welsh rose and promptly fell. Even so, Edward I had to analyze and balance his strategic requirements in terms of three major enemies, two of them sharing the island with him. He finished the Welsh, putting down what turned out to be their last rising of his reign, in 1295. That left the Scots and the French. When he was fighting one he had to obtain protection from incursions by the other; he needed a band of castles against the Scots, secure and as far north as possible to protect England from raids and to provide a forward line of departure for operations in Scotland. He also required a shield of ships to protect his coasts, east and west, and even more so as to give him transport of men and provisions to the theater of operations. He need not have worried about a hostile Scottish fleet.

Edward based his French strategy on several considerations. Eventually it produced no greater success than did the simpler strategy against the Scots. In France he had Gascony to defend, and in Flanders he had a vital commercial link to maintain. Between these territories lay the North Sea, the Channel, and the Bay of Biscay—to be contested with Philip the Fair. English communications with Flanders and Gascony involved not only the passage of troops but the vital wool and wine trades. But the winds blow both ways in those stretches of water and the French could arrive almost as easily as the English could depart, so Edward defended his coasts of England and Gascony with ships, on station and in port, and with coastal defense forces, from the Wash to Land's End.[2]

Fleets of ships formed the key to his defenses, and, like his father and grandfather, Edward formed his fleets out of three elements. First were ships arrested for royal service. Everyone of his subjects owed him help in preserving the realm—*comites et barones, milites et rustici, senes et juvenes, fereque omnis populus simul*—so denizens of the ports met their obligation by serving as naval personnel in their own ships, fully paid for their service.[3] Landsmen owed similar service at this time, service whose outlines formed in the time of Henry II, John, and Henry III, and whose details became set by frequent use in the Welsh and Scotch wars of Edward I. All men from ages fifteen to sixty owed service with weapons appropriate to their station and occupation. Simple rustics owed service with bow and arrows, grander men with knightly arms, whether they were knights or not. The obligation that encompassed landsmen included shipmen as well. Just as the former gathered by the king's orders to stand inspection and selection by his arrayers—to be elected from the most able and vigorous—so the shipmen were liable to "arrest" of their ships and crews under the same obligation.[4]

The second element from which Edward formed his navy were the ships and men of the Cinque Ports. By this time the confederation of Dover, Hastings, Sandwich, Romney, and Winchelsea had become a unit, juridical as well as naval. It had also become a confederation of more than five ports, since most of the originals had acquired satellites which shared the privileges and obligations of the principals. Edward, at the end of the Barons' Wars, had subdued the Ports, fighting a pitched battle against them at Winchelsea and being inclined to hang their leader at its conclusion. Instead, he granted the Cinque Ports a free pardon and confirmed their liberties.[5] He recognized the need for reconciliation at the end of a civil war, and he also appreciated the importance of the Cinque Ports, for he became warden at this time, with his good friend Roger Leyburn, a Kentishman, as his lieutenant.[6]

Whatever the origins of the Ports and the antiquity of their privileges, what led the lord Edward to assume jurisdiction in 1266 surely must have been tied to the fact that they were the closest ports to France; with prevailing winds out of the northwest and ships at their best running, the Ports could dominate the Channel, so Edward dominated the Ports. Their ships ruled the waters from the Thames to Southampton Water, and sometimes beyond, and could be dealt with as a unit. This convenient arrangement served to enhance royal authority. By custom the Ports owed the king fifty-seven ships, manned by 1254 men, for fifteen days each year.[7] By summoning the Portsmen to their obligation the king had a sizeable fleet on short notice. Moreover, the fleet of the Cinque Ports would sail under the command of one of its own—it would have a certain cohesiveness, at least more than the ships arrested from all the other ports.

Unity of command stands close to the top among the military virtues. It existed most nearly in the third element of the royal navy, the king's own ships and galleys. English kings had owned ships from time out of mind, of course. Alfred built the first recorded royal fleet, starting in 897. His ships were superior to the Danish craft because they were longer, faster, steadier, and of a better basic design, according to the Anglo-Saxon Chronicle.[8] At least as important, Alfred used them with a clear sense of naval strategy. From Alfred to the Conqueror royal ships formed part of England's naval force, but after the Conquest the need for a royal squadron disappeared with the transformation of the Channel into a Norman river. It was after 1204 that the need to defend and dominate the Channel became insistent once again, and not merely because John wished to regain the lost lands, but because the French threatened invasion. John equipped a fleet—really four fleets—of some fifty-one ships to guard the east, southeast, south, and west, each under its own commander.[9] The vessels were all galleys, not merchant ships. Henry III continued the custom of John, keeping merchantmen and galleys of his own and building dockyards to maintain them.[10] By the time of Edward I, the three methods of gathering ships and sailors had become usual: impressment under the general obligation owed by all subjects, the Cinque Ports, and the king's own ships. While the obligation fell on all to defend the realm, it was by no means unrestricted. To be invoked the king must make clear that service would, in fact, defend the realm from some clear and present danger. To be continued, the men serving—ashore or afloat—would have to receive wages.

Danger to the realm threatened from late 1295, as it was to do throughout the remainder of Edward's reign, with time out for truces. At such times of military emergency the king could call upon his subjects to help him defend the realm, appropriately justifying the service. Generally, Edward cited the perils they all faced, but in any case the reason for calling upon his people, ashore or afloat, was made clear—"*en la sauvacion de notre Roiaume e de notre peuple; e de eux garder e defendre de mal e de damage."* [11]

A confusing variety of merchant ships and galleys comprised Edward's naval squadrons. It is clear that the basic vessel of the time, in English waters, continued to be the clinker-built double-ended longship, propelled by a single square sail and oars. Roundships sailed the seas at this time, but rarely as the king's naval vessels. They served exclusively as private merchant ships, only occasionally being arrested for the king's service.

The king's galleys—so Mediterranean a name, but completely northern vessels—formed one part of Edward's fleet. He ordered a fleet of 120-oar galleys to be built, in a writ of 16 November 1294, by the men of twenty-six English towns. [12] He required them against the French and he ordered them finished by Christmas. Needless to say, they were not. Time-lags and cost-overruns of government orders are not new to our times. How many eventually did sail and when is not known to us, but records for eight of them do exist, to give us a great deal of detail about the longship of the time. [13] Pictures and seals of galleys are very scarce, but the accounts allow a close look. One thing is clear: English longships owed little in their design to southern models, neither in construction, rigging, power source, nor fitments. Whatever the relations between Bayonne and England, little that characterized Mediterranean and Gascon ships came north. Northern seas and the northern littoral had their own requirements. English galleys were clinker-built, with strakes swelling out and up from the keel. Ribs and stringers fitted into the hull so formed to provide added strength and platforms for decks. The single northern mast, stepped 8-10% of the distance forward of the mid-point of the keel, possessed a single square sail lofted by a one-piece spar. [14] For naval purposes, the English galley carried temporary fore and stern castles and a fighting top built forward the mast. She was probably a sailer first, with oar-power when needed. In contrast, the Mediterranean galley was carvel-built, a planked frame, with two or three masts, lateen-rigged with two-piece spars, integral fore and stern castles, and fighting tops atop the masts. Edward, it will be remembered, had in mind to build a formidable fleet of twenty galleys to aid in his war with Philip the Fair. Bristol, Winchelsea, and Shoreham-Seaford received orders for two galleys each, Newcastle, Southampton, London, Yarmouth, Lynn, York, Scarborough, Ipswich-Gosford, Dunwich-Oxford, Lyme-Weymouth, Romney-Hythe, Dartmouth-Plymouth, Sandwich-Dover, and Grimsby-Ravensey-Hull orders for one each. [15] Not all these galleys were built, but the orders he issued show Edward's plan for one part of a royal navy.

Besides galleys, the king had at his disposal vessels of other kinds. Barges appear in the documents, obviously more than towed boats of burden. When shipwrights made galleys for Edward I, they also made barges, apparently as tenders for the galleys. The documents show, for example, Dunwich men building a 100-oared galley and a 40-oared barge, at Ipswich a 100-oared galley and a 30-oared barge.[16] The barge served as a tender; it carried its own sail and oar power and could sail on its own as a small galley. When descriptions of naval activity refer to galleys, ships, and barges, they are concerned with three types of vessels capable of independent free sailing on the open sea. Barges functioned as auxiliaries to the galleys, but they also performed as patrol boats, escorts, passenger vessels and for the general work not suitable for larger ships. Boats, of course, are different. Boats are carried by ships or towed behind them. Since galleys needed considerable space between the rakes for oarsmen, boat-stowage on deck would be unlikely; stowed boats would certainly have been the answer.

Building ships solved only part of the problem of maintaining a navy. Ships arrested from private owners were maintained by these owners; the king's galleys had to be maintained at his cost and in his dockyards. John had created a dockyard at Portsmouth in 1212—"for the preservation of the king's ships and galley"—with a wall for general protection.[17] During his son's reign similar yards appeared at Rye, Shoreham, and Winchelsea. Every port of any consequence had its yards to build, repair, and outfit its own ships, so when the king took them into royal service he, in effect, could make use of their dockyards. As an example, when Edward I ordered the men of Bayonne to build and outfit twelve ships and twenty-four galleys, in May 1275, he effectively took over the yards there for his navy. In this case, he wanted to aid his brother-in-law, Alfonso of Castile, against the Moors.[19] The size of the fleet he ordered built would have cost a considerable sum—£37,330/16/8, so the king's official William de Montegauger said—more than Edward could pay. William urged the king to order construction to start right away (May, 1276) because dockyard workers were paid by the day, and the long days of summer would give the king greater value than if he waited for the days to shorten. The builders wanted half their money by Midsummer Day and the rest by 1 August.[20] Crews were to hire for a year, not less, to receive an indulgence as for a crusade, and could expect half of all prizes taken, except cities, towns, castles, or lands. At the end of the year, the ships were to become the property of the builders, while the galley remained the king's. The vessels the Bayonne men contracted to build were six ships of 180 tons or more, to carry sixty men each, and twelve galleys, four of 120 oars, four of 100, and four of 80, each carrying twenty, twenty, and fifteen crossbowmen respectively besides their crews.[21]

The matter of money plagued Edward I throughout his reign; it was a crushing legacy for his son. To pay for ships and galleys he had to find some other way than cash. Like the method adopted in Gascony, he paid English builders partly in cash and partly by turning over to them the vessels they built after he had finished with them. Thus when, in 1301, the men of York had not received payment for the galley (97 oars), barge (30 oars), and small ship they had built for the king, he allowed them any profit out of the three they could make.[24] For the remainder of Edward I's reign no records tell of the building of ships for the king.

The Channel war followed upon an ancient tradition of rivalry, raids, and spoliation between the Normans and south-coast English. By the spring of 1293 the friction ignited seafaring populations conditioned by generations of enmity and now ranged into opposition by contesting kings. The English, with Irish and Dutch allies, met the Normans, with French, Flemish, and Genoese allies, in a set battle, anchored in the Channel. That one the English won.[23]

When the war really started—and it was to last sporadically for more than a century—the two adversaries commenced with their navies. Edward sent out three squadrons, the largest of 53 sail of ships from Yarmouth and east coast ports under John Botetourt. William Leyburn commanded the southern squadron based in Portsmouth, and an Irishman commanded the western squadron of ships from western ports and Ireland.[24] Philip's actions gave good cause for this shield of ships, for he had planned an invasion. Rumors fed fears of an imminent descent upon the south coast, in the summer of 1295.

While the event failed to justify the rumors, Edward could not avoid preparing the land for defense, using the information about enemy intentions that disclosed the enormity of their plans. An alliance among the French, the Scots, and the Norwegians made invasion a real threat.[25] In some cases the rumors came true—the French landed at Dover on August 1295 at midday and burned some of the town. At about the same time they attacked other ports—Winchelsea, Yarmouth, Hythe[26]—and the French threatened, as Edward warned, to invade England and extirpate the English tongue from the earth.[27]

Edward had sent out three squadrons to guard the coasts in the summer of 1294. Besides this mission, the southern squadron had the duty of transporting horses and men to Gascony, for Edward rarely remained on the defensive long. These transports and warships carried hurdles for making horse-transports of them. The conversion probably consisted of placing simple frames in the well of a round-bodied cog so that planking could then be laid on them to form a flat deck. The navy protecting England from 1295, then, consisted of three squadrons, of some 139 ships and galleys of all kinds.[28] Of the ships impressed, 114 came from England and 25 from Bayonne. At the time this fleet was forming, Edward ordered the aforementioned twenty galleys. While most of them never shipped into salt water, the king's intentions were clear. He placed the eastern squadron under two commands. That responsible for security of the coast from Berwick to Lynn sailed under Osbert de Spaldington, a tried and proven military commander who had served Eward well in Wales.[29] Protection of the sector from Lynn to the mouth of the Thames came under a combined Yarmouth-Harwich squadron, some thirty Yarmouth ships having been recalled from their previous station at Winchelsea and Portsmouth.[30]

Naval forces covered the south coast from Winchelsea, Southampton, Portsmouth, and Plymouth, where they gathered from the additional purpose of carrying an invasion force. Once the coasts were secure, Edward went immediately to the offensive, preparing invasions of both Gascony and Scotland. Fleets alone could not secure his coasts, and Edward had created a land-guard to back up his cruising squadrons. All along the coast, from Lynn to Land's End, the king's officers had set coast-watchers, had arrayed foot to answer alarms, and had provided mounted officers to lead them, all directed by the practical military administrators of the king.[31] With squadrons afloat, a screen of guards on the shore, and mobile reserves of horse and foot on call inland, Edward could well feel ready to move against his enemies, so the first Scotch campaign proceeded in March, 1296, in spite of an enemy threat to attack Yarmouth. Edward sailed north with thirty-three ships, having dispatched John Botetourt with his squadron to cover East Anglia.[32]

Such was Edward's navy, an arm with marked similarities to his armies, Sailors, their captains and their admirals came from those of the king's subjects best qualified for naval service. Ashore, common soldiers performed their duties under commissioners of array. Afloat, seamen served with their ships when the king arrested them, and both took the king's penny for their service. In both cases, men who mustered at the king's order campaigned in theaters of operations nearest their homes. Most of the men mobilized for Scotland, for example, came from the northern counties. The fleets patrolling England's coasts, in most cases, remained based in home ports.

Just as the king expanded his household in time of war to include more men, for combat, support, and service duties, he bought or leased ships and crews to augment his navy. Household officers served as commanders of major troop formations on land, the same sort of men served as admirals at sea.

A universal obligation to serve and a standard administration of this service allowed Edward advantages of unified control. Coast guards at sea coordinated with detachments ashore; supply depots were stocked with provisions and equipment for troops when they needed them. Amphibious operations found ships and boats ready for troops when the troops were ready to move. Not to say that all went smoothly—at least one campaign aborted because supplies failed. But the navy was ready to haul the supplies even if the supplies failed to appear. Combined operations were not only possible, in Edward's campaigns, they were frequent. Naval-military cooperation characterized his campaigns.

That Edward failed to subdue Scotland cannot be blamed on either army or navy. The Scots simply were not subduable at the time. That the Welsh fell to Edward is attributable to unity of command. The groundwork done by Edward I did not survive him long. Under his son all fell apart, the center could not hold, but under the first Edward an English navy prospered.

FOOTNOTES

[1] Joseph Stevenson, *Documents Illustrative of the History of Scotland,* 2 vols. (Edinburgh, 1870), II, 8-12; Bartholomaeus de Cotton, *Historia Anglicana* (Rolls Series, no. 16), 438. J. G. Edwards, "The Treason of Thomas Turberville, 1295," *Studies in Medieval History Presented to Frederick Maurice Powicke,* eds. R. W. Hunt, W. A. Pantin, R. W. Southern (Oxford, 1948), 296-309.

[2] See my article, "A Moat Defensive: the Coast Defense Scheme of 1295," *Speculum,* 42 (1967), 442-462.

[3] Continuatio Chronici Willelmi de Novoburgo (Rolls Series no. 82), 514.

[4] M. R. Powicke, *Military Obligation in Medieval England* (Oxford, 1962), passim; C. W. Hollister, *The Military Organization of Norman England* (Oxford, 1965), chs. 8, 9; Michael Prestwich, *War, Politics, and Finance under Edward I* (New York, 1972), chs. 3, 4, 6.

[5] J. H. Ramsay, *The Dawn of the Constitution* (London, 1908), 253.

[6] F. M. Powicke, *The Thirteenth Century* (Oxford, 1953), 207.

[7] F. W. Brooks, *The English Naval Forces 1199-1272* (London, n.d.), 92.

[8] Anglo-Saxon Chronicle (Rolls Series no. 23), I, 176, 177.

[9] N. H. Nicolas, *A History of the Royal Navy,* 2 vols. (London, 1847); F. W. Brooks, "The King's Ships and Galleys mainly under John and Henry III," *Mariner's Mirror,* 15 (1929), 27.

[10] F. W. Brooks, ibid., 37-38.

[11] *Parliamentary Writs and Writs of Military Summons,* etc., ed. Sir Francis Palgrave, 2 vols (Record Commission, 1827-34), II, 328/11, 5 January 1300.

[12] R. C. Anderson, "English Galleys in 1295," *Mariner's Mirror,* 14 (1928), 221.

[13] The principal source of information on longships comes from J. T. Tinniswood, "English Galleys, 1272-1377," *Mariner's Mirror,* 35 (1949), 276-315.

[14] Ibid., 301.

[15] Anderson, 221.

[16] Tinniswood, 284.

[17] Nicolas, *History of the Royal Navy,* I, 147.

[18] Ibid., 226.

[19] Rymer's *Foedera* (Record Commission, 1816-1830), I, 531, 552, 580.

[20] Nicolas, *History of the Royal Navy,* I, 284.

[21] Ibid.

[22] Ibid., 301.

[23] Ibid., 268.

[24] Ibid., 270; Nicholas Trivet, *Annales sex regum Angliae, etc.* (English Historical Society, 1845), 279.

[25] Stevenson, *Documents*, II, 8-12; B. Cotton, 438, 439.

[26] B. Cotton, 296.

[27] Rymer's *Foedera*, I, 827.

[28] A ship inventory, probably of this time, lists 444 ships in the king's ports of England, from Lynn around to Haverford, Wales, and Bayonne. Public Record Office, Exchequer Account E 101/684/54/4.

[29] *Lord's Report on the Dignity of a Peer*, III, 66.

[30] E. B. Fryde, ed. *The Book of Prests of the King's Wardrobe for 1294-95* (Oxford, 1962), 106, 114, 87-88.

[31] Freeman, "A Moat Defensive. . .", 454.

[32] Nicolas, *History of the Royal Navy*, I, 277-8.

CHAPTER 7

Rationality and Expedience in the Growth of Elizabethan Naval Administration

Ronald Pollitt

University of Cincinnati

Few would deny Robert Bolt's stature as one of the most accomplished playwrights of our era. His use of langauge and his skill at character analysis are often brilliant. Yet in what many think is his greatest work, *A Man for All Seasons*, Bolt portrays Tudor governmental administration as the soul of cynical expedience. Bolt's Cromwell, recruiting Richard Rich for his service, asserts that the "normal" aim of administration is to make everything "convenient," and by logical extension the job of administrators is to make things as convenient as they can.[1] In short, the playwright portrays the architect of the "Tudor Revolution in Government" as a man who made expedience the cornerstone of the foundation for England's modern bureaucratic state. Making allowances for poetic license, there is a large grain of truth in Bolt's depiction, for cynicism and expedience are two of the more easily discernible characteristics of bureaucracies.

Bolt's picture is, however, a false and hollow one, for he ignores the force of rationality in the structure and procedure of administrative units, and thus he gives us a one dimensional perspective that deceives while it informs. In truth, bureaucracies are forged in rationality and tempered with expedience, and anyone who would understand administrators and their organizations would do well to bear in mind the organic nature of bureaucracy. Of the many areas of Tudor administration that bear witness to that observation, none provides better evidence than the bureaucracy of the Royal Navy, which was created and shaped by the forces of rationality and expedience in the last half of the sixteenth century.

Most of the administrative organizations that were formed in European states during the early modern period were not the result of careful consideration and planning. Novel bureaucratic units were founded and grew rather like Topsy, ordinarily by the process of an already existing department of state having its powers and duties expanded to cover the multiplying responsibilities of the prince. The Admiralty or Navy Board of Tudor England proved to be no exception to this trend.

From the time of King John to the reign of Henry VIII, the administrative needs of England's navy were satisfied by a single Crown servant, the Clerk of the Ships. He saw to the safe keeping of the ships, supervised the purchase of materials and the construction of new vessels, hired and paid the wages of workmen, and kept the accounts of the navy.[2] The Clerk and his tiny staff were, quite simply, the naval bureaucracy. But with the succession of the second Tudor monarch, the administrative organization of the navy began to change dramatically, largely because of King Henry's aggressive foreign policy and the strains it placed on the navy.

Henry VIII's first Clerk of the Ships was Robert Brigandine, an able servant who, in addition to running the navy effectively and establishing new storehouses and anchorages at Deptford and Erith, provided a solid base for the King's expansion of the naval bureaucracy. By 1513, for instance, the King had created a new administrative post, that of "keeper of the King's new storehouse at Erith and Deptford," and granted the post to John Hopton. Over the succeeding fifteen years changes in the naval administration accelerated, producing a long and unsettled transitory period that in many ways marks the change from medieval to modern in the navy. Brigandine's authority seemed to wane while that of Hopton expanded in scope and even in title, until by 1518 the Clerk of the Storehouse was being referred to as "Comptroller of the King's Ships." There were, moreover, new faces appearing in the naval offices, having as yet no official status but wielding some power. Men such as Thomas Spert, William Gonson and John Ysham began acting in what were clearly administrative capacities for the navy, and as the years passed their positions were more clearly delineated by the Crown. By the 1530's there were several naval administrators, some with clear designations such as the Clerk of the Ships and the Clerk of the Storehouse, and others with less precise titles such as the "clerk comptroller of ships" and the "clerk of the King's ships."

The result of this largely undisciplined expansion of the naval bureaucracy was that by 1541 the administration of the fleet was directed by a number of officers whose powers and responsibilities were ill-defined. William Gonson was officially Clerk of the Storehouse and unofficially Vice Admiral as well as Treasurer of Marine Causes. Thomas Spert was officially Controller of the Ships and unofficially Surveyor of the Ships. Finally, Edward Water was officially Clerk of the Ships and in charge of the Portsmouth yard. All that was needed for the creation of a formal Admiralty was for the King to assess the overall needs of the navy, delineate departments with responsibility for meeting those needs, and appoint men to supervise those departments. In short, all Henry VIII had to do was to organize rationally the administrative units of his navy. This he did in 1545, and the naval bureaucracy that resulted appears for the first time in the documents in patents issued in April 1546.

The Admiralty that was established by King Henry on April 24, 1546, was a good example of how governmental administrative organizations were structured under the influence of the Cromwellian "revolution." It was assumed that the Lord Admiral would not be a true administrator in the sense that he supervised the daily work of the unit, so while he was in theory in charge of the Navy Board his main functions were to protect the interests of the navy at Court and command fleets in time of war. The real administrative control of the Admiralty was vested in the Lieutenant of the Admiralty, who was to be the executive officer and form a link between the government and the naval officials through his position as immediate subordinate to the Lord Admiral. Sir Thomas Clere was given the Lieutenant's Office. Under his direction were established the offices of: Treasurer of Marine Causes; Master of Naval Ordnance; Controller of the Navy; Surveyor of the Navy; Clerk of the Ships; and Clerk of the Storehouse.[4] Each office was assigned a salary and in the absence of further direction by the Crown it was assumed that all officers would be equal in status and authority and subordinate to the Lieutenant.

Henry VIII's founding of the Admiralty in the last year of his life was, to be sure, an innovation of great significance for English naval history. It was not, however, very much more than the rational structuring of an organization that existed *de facto* as early as 1541; and there was a great deal wrong with the Admiralty forged by King Henry. There were, for example, neither specific ordinances for the conduct of naval business nor specification of channels of administrative control. There was not accepted and normal procedure of accounting for expenditures. Moreover, there was no procedure for appointing department heads and staffing units except patronage, which could just as easily find places for fools as it could for competent officials. The Navy Board created by Henry VIII had the form of a modern bureaucracy with its Weberian hierarchy and centralized control, but it lacked all of the other elements noted by Weber in his criteria for the existence of a "bureaucracy." There were hardly fixed and agreed upon areas of operation, there was precious little regulation, the Admiralty's reliance on written records was at best sporadic, and there was certainly no sense of professionalism involved in seeking and holding a Navy Board office.[5] The Admiralty of 1546 was, quite simply, a skeletal structure that was through trial and error as much as by human intent to be shaped into a permanent and vital department of government during the remaining decades of the Tudor century.

There was administrative evolution at the Navy Board during the years of the "little Tudors," but the changes were more of form than of substance.

It was not until the accession of Elizabeth that the rational process that had founded the Navy Board was applied once again to the organization with notable effect. Although it is difficult to prove conclusively that the changes at the Admiralty during the first few years of Elizabeth's reign were the product of Sir William Cecil's genius, there is much in his career to indicate that he authored the changes. Cecil was, after all, very organization conscious, tidy in work habits, extremely reliant on documents, and a strong advocate of naval strength, so it should come as no surprise that he directed the rationalization of the Admiralty in the early 1560's.

Cecil's refinement of the naval administration encompassed several aspects of Admiralty function, and it seems sensible to deal only with the more important elements and to do so in chronological order. The first of the instances, or in a sense harbingers of innovation, came barely four months after Elizabeth's succession, at the end of Easter Term 1559. It took the form of several documents dealing with the navy and its governance that not only made it evident that the new monarch and her servants intended to regulate the navy more closely, but also that such regulation promised intensification for the future.

These documents deal both with the strategic handling of the fleet as well as with its care by the naval administrators.[6] One memorandum, for example, lists the vessels owned by the Crown, discusses their condition and need of repair, and suggests that some ships be sold and the remainder be refurbished. Two other documents deal with naval costs, one providing information about extraordinary expenditures stemming from the war of Queen Mary's last year and the other relating the ordinary costs of ship maintenance in harbor. Another memorandum, and in many ways the most interesting one, was concerned with the care of the navy in peace time. Specifically, this paper addressed the issue of where the Queen's ships should be kept in harbor, which raised the question of a permanent dockyard for the fleet. It was suggested that what later was called Chatham was the best location for the ships, and eventually most of the apparatus of the naval administration was established there as well. Finally, one other of these documents seems especially worthy of mention, for it established a rough formula for the number of warships and their tonnage that the Crown should maintain. Twenty-four ships totalling 8200 tons were listed as the ideal number, and until the fleet expansion in the mid-1580's this formula provided the naval bureaucrats with a reliable guide for projections in budgeting, purchasing and staffing. These papers of March 1559, set the tone of the government's concern for the navy and served notice that the Queen and her advisors intended to tighten their control over that branch of government. One year later the Crown made another important move in its systematization of the navy and its administration.

Taking the form of a series of ordinances entitled "For the office of our Admiralty and marine affairs," the Crown action of 1560 was perhaps the

71

most important step in the rational construction of the Navy Board as an administrative unit.[7] In the preamble of the document the government noted that while King Henry VIII established the Admiralty, he did not draw up regulations for its orderly operation. That oversight Queen Elizabeth intended to rectify immediately. The ordinances of 1560 list all of the offices of the Navy Board authorized by King Henry, and include one that was omitted in the patents of 1546; the office of Surveyor of the Victuals. The document's significance, however, lies in the detailed way it decreed the administrative procedures of the Admiralty. The Navy Board officers were to meet together at least once a week to consult upon the condition of the navy, and no less than once a month they were to submit reports on their work to either the Lord Admiral or the Lieutenant in his absence. Additionally, the behavior of each administrator was carefully regulated by ordinance. The orders pertaining to the Navy Treasurer are typical of those governing all of the offices. He was, for instance, required to submit weekly reports to the Vice Admiral of his expenditures and receipts, and he was forbidden to make payments without the authorization of at least two other officers, one of whom had to be either the Lieutenant, the Surveyor or the Comptroller. The Treasurer was, moreover, required to prepare his books for a quarterly audit by at least two other department heads, and he was also charged with informing either the Lord Admiral or the Lieutenant at least monthly of the state of his particular office. The other Admiralty department heads were subject to virtually identical requirements.

The ordinances of 1560 did not, however, stop at a detailed regulation of each Admiralty office. All of the officers were required to consult on matters affecting the navy at large and to reach agreement on such issues. The orders resulting from these consultations were to be entered in a ledger book which was to become part of the written record of the Navy Board. Furthermore, the assistants in the various departments were not to be viewed by the government as equivalents to department heads, but they were nonetheless to have the power of Admiralty officers when they travelled or otherwise transacted naval business. From the standpoint of rational construction of a bureaucracy, none of the ordinances rivals the one that required "that every of our said officers shall see into their fellow's offices, to the intent that when God shall dispose his will upon any of them, they living may be able, if we shall prefer any of them to receive the same." Finally, the Crown ordered that all of the ordinances be read at least once a quarter by the Admiralty officers, and it concluded by neatly explaining the purpose of the regulations: to help each of the officers "better understand his duty."

This document of 1560 is quite unusual, for it was one of the few attempts by a Tudor government to specify the structure of an administrative unit and establish performance regulations for Crown servants. Yet it was only one of several efforts in the early years of Elizabeth to establish the naval bureaucracy both in structure and function on a rational foundation. Another very important step taken by the Crown at about the same time as the 1560 ordinances was aimed at regularizing the accounting processes of the Navy Board.

It is difficult for anyone who works in the financial records of the Tudor navy not to notice the irregularity of record keeping until the reign of Edward VI, when the Pipe Office accounts exhibit some concern for regularity in naval accounting.[8] It was not, however, until the first full calendar year of Elizabeth that naval accounts were declared systematically before the Audit Office and approved after thorough examination by the Lord Treasurer and the Chancellor of the Exchequer. Accustomed as we are to an excess of accountancy, it is difficult for the modern mind to comprehend the importance of adopting this practice for the Elizabethan navy. These accounts, meticulously prepared, obviously based on a great store of data, and aimed at providing the government with a summary of the navy's financial position as well as its general activity, are noteworthy enough in the rationalization of the Elizabethan Admiralty to merit some discussion.

A typical example of one of these accounts is that of Benjamin Gonson for 1569.[9] In order of presentation, the account first displayed a detailed description of the office of Treasurer of Marine Causes and explained when Gonson assumed the office. It then discussed the state of Gonson's account from the previous year, which incidentally had a surplus, and listed the amounts of money Gonson received, totalling £17,015 15s 7d, and when he received them. The real substance of the account then followed in the list of Gonson's allowances for expenditures, which included all items from over £1500 for sail making material to £18 for "reeds, broom rushes and straw." Wages of workmen and ship's crews were, of course, a major item in the recounting of Gonson's expenditures. The account then concluded with a summary of all receipts and expenditures that told the Queen's councillors all they needed to know about the activity of the navy to be reasonably well informed about naval affairs. On one page of the roll, for instance, the Lord Treasurer could readily see that it cost £17,802 18 s 4d to maintain the navy in 1569, and of that sum about £13,000 were spent on ordinary harbor charges, equipping the ships for sea duty, and paying the wages of captains, mariners, gunners and workmen. The Treasurer or any other official could also easily see that the Admiralty spent £24 10d making rafters into oars if they chose to do so, and it is likely that they did, for the summary pages of all Audit Office Declared Accounts are signed by the Treasurer and the Chancellor. Understandably, these men would much rather have read a one page synopsis of naval activity than have to study several pages of what can be dull material.

The practice of declaring naval accounts in the Audit Office was a vitally important part of the Elizabethan restructuring of the Admiralty for two fundamental reasons. On the one hand it made it possible for the Queen's advisors to learn with ease the scope and nature of naval activity and to evaluate the fitness of the navy to meet its responsibilities. On the other hand, it forced on the navy, and especially on the Navy Treasurer, who emerged as the chief Admiralty officer, a careful record keeping system, which tended to keep peculation under a semblance of control while it gave the Navy Board officers a readily available data base for making administrative decisions. Thus the accounting changes that accompanied the accession of Elizabeth I worked toward the same end as the ordinances of 1560; they made the Admiralty more orderly in its procedures while keeping it firmly under the control of the Crown.

Rationality, then, loomed large in forging the Admiralty into a reliable unit of government, but rational planning and careful structuring through ordinance and procedure was only partly responsible for shaping Elizabethan naval administration. Another vital force in the evolution of the Admiralty was expedience, and to a very great extent it was not so much bureaucratic expedience but rather that of the political and personal variety.

Throughout the last half of the Tudor era no one knew more about or was more deeply involved in the political life of England than Sir Wiliam Cecil, who, probably because of the prominence of his position, was the principal author of expedience as it applied to the naval administration. Cecil was one of the foremost advocates of the navy as England's first line of defense, and that attitude combined with his well developed sense of drawing as many units of government under his control as possible led him to make changes at the Admiralty that frequently contravened the rational structure of which he was probably the major architect. One of the earliest of these changes came in Cecil's tampering with the chain of command at the Navy Board.

Both at the creation of the Navy Board in 1546 and in the ordinances of 1560, the hierarchy that governed the naval administration began with the monarch, passed to the Council, descended to the Lord Admiral and then on to the Lieutenant of the Admiralty, and finally ended with the department heads. Because of his desire to control what he thought was an important department of state, one likely to become more significant as international tensions deepened, and also because of his interest in the financial aspect of government, Cecil apparently decided to alter his chain of command at two key points. One was where the Lord Admiral acted as the Council's agent in directing the naval bureaucracy, and the other was where the Lieutenant of the Admiralty acted as chief executive officer in the organization. Superficially, it would seem no mean task to usurp the power of these two officials, but because of circumstances and his own skill Cecil accomplished it with ease.

Steering the Lord Admiral's interest away from the administrative side of naval affairs was a simple matter. The Lord Admiral, Lord Clinton and Saye, was throughout a long career of serving the Crown a staunch ally and friend of Cecil.[10] He was not one to quibble about the implications of the Secretary's suggestions that he concentrate his interest on matters of broad naval strategy, protection of his maritime prerogatives, and supporting naval programs in the Council. Concern with such matters would, of course, largely preclude the Admiral's paying very much attention to the tedious daily functions of the Navy Board. Because of friendship and a certain amount of political naivete, the Lord Admiral largely surrendered his administrative power to Cecil. In fact, this situation became *de jure* when the Admiral went to sea, for on several occasions he deputized the Secretary as Lord Admiral to exercise his powers and protect his privileges in England.

Disposing of the Lieutenant of the Admiralty was not quite so easy. The original Lieutenant, Sir Thomas Clere, had been succeeded by Sir William Woodhouse, a prominent man at Court who had considerable experience in sea commands. Cecil could not simply dismiss Woodhouse, so he elected to wait until the Lieutenant either died or an opportunity arose to remove him from office gracefully. Meanwhile, he solidified his relationship with Benjamin Gonson, the Navy Treasurer, who Cecil intended to make the head of the Admiralty without promoting him to the Lieutenancy.

In 1564, Sir William Woodhouse died, and Cecil moved deftly to secure control of the Navy Board. Pointing out to Elizabeth that the Lieutenant's office really was superfluous inasmuch as the Treasury already did most of the work, and also that an abolition of the office would save the Crown over £323 a year, the Secretary persuaded the Queen to leave the office vacant.[11] It remained so from 1564 until 1604, opening the way for Secretary Cecil to make the Treasurer head of the Admiralty, which made possible Cecil's close supervision of the navy through financial channels. The Secretary's connection with the Navy Board only intensified with his appointment as Lord Treasurer early in the 1570's.

The political expedients necessary to secure Cecil's control over the Admiralty and thus the navy had some notable effects on the administration. For one, it removed from the position of overseer an officer who did not have direct departmental responsibilities and was in a position to know what each of the departmental needs were and how they were functioning. For another, it changed the structure of the Navy Board without securing sanction for such change in an alteration of the ordinances of 1560. But above all in terms of the effect of this expedient, it sowed the seeds of dissension among the Principal Officers of the Navy by making one of them more equal than the others, which produced serious personnel problems in the years after 1564.

Perhaps the most noteworthy of these personnel problems stemmed directly from the elevation of the Treasurer to primacy by Cecil, for the Treasurer was Benjamin Gonson. Son of a former Treasurer and a London merchant of substance, Gonson was not an especially fiery personality and hence not the source of tension at the Admiralty. His son-in-law, John Hawkins, was however, quite a different sort of individual, and when he secured from Cecil a reversion of Gonson's office it assured a clash of wills at the Navy Board that eventually required another expedient to correct the situation.[12]

Hawkins had some very definite ideas about naval affairs, and when he became Treasurer in 1578 he displayed little reticence about making his opinions known. Well aware of Cecil's elevation of the Treasurer, Hawkins proved both aggressive in taking command of the organization and obnoxious in his criticisms of earlier administrative procedures at the Admiralty. This approach particularly offended Sir William Wynter, who had extensive experience at the Navy Board and also had his full share of Elizabethan haughty pride. The two men quarreled virtually from the moment Hawkins took office, and Wynter proved to be a worthy foe for Hawkins both by virtue of his talent for intrigue and his positions as Master of Naval Ordnance and also Surveyor of the Ships. The struggles between these two men, which incidentally produced another major expedient at the Admiralty with the conclusion of Hawkins' first "bargain" with the Crown, made the dockyards and offices an administrative battleground.[13] Eventually, Wynter made things so uncomfortable for Hawkins that he had to call upon Cecil for help, which led to Wynter's assignment to the command of a small squadron patrolling the Irish coast.[14]

Thus a *reductio ad absurdum* occurred at the Navy Board because of the adoption of expedients. First, Cecil disposed of the Lord Admiral and his Lieutenant in order to elevate and control the Treasurer, then to keep the Treasurer predominant he was compelled to exile the naval administrator who held two offices and had the most seniority to an Irish patrolling command. The Crown may well have gained financially by adopting Hawkins' reforms, but the Navy Board lost by being deprived of its Master of Ordnance and Surveyor at a critical juncture. It should perhaps also be pointed out that Wynter's criticisms of Hawkins were not without substance, for Hawkins' second short-lived "bargain" resulted directly from Wynter's assessment of the Admiralty in 1583 after his return from Ireland.

There are, of course, numerous other examples of expedients and their effect on Elizabethan naval administration, but there are two in particular that merit some discussion because they demonstrate the range of expedients as well as their positive and negative effects. These examples are:

the introduction of contingency planning outside the Navy Board by Lord Burghley; and the conflicting ambitions and career perceptions of the Principal Officers.

Contingency planning was one of the more consequential but largely ignored of Cecil's contributions to the art of government. His famous memoranda are filled with instances utilizing contingency plans or remarking on the need for them, and the navy seemed of special interest to him in this area because of its key defensive role. Of the many instances where Cecil's contingency planning affected the Admiralty, perhaps the best example occurred in 1582. With the Spanish threat apparent and the Navy Board shaken by the Hawkins-Wynter disputes, Cecil determined to collect strategic naval data without the knowledge of the Principal Officers. He charged Lord Admiral the Earl of Lincoln to undertake a survey of the entire maritime strength of the island ranging from names and tonnage of merchant ships to names and locations of masters and mariners in selected counties.[15] Using his own servants, the Lord Admiral accomplished the task quickly and efficiently, and the result was a document of some 123 pages that became an important part of the data base for the government's strategic planning for the Armada campaign. Although Admiralty officials were not involved in the process, they ultimately benefited from the expedient, for when the time came for them to mobilize the maritime resources of England the information that they needed to do so was readily available from the Lord Treasurer.

The second of these expedients was quite different in its effect. It consisted of the inability of the government, as well as the Principal Officers themselves, to view posts on the Navy Board as full-time service positions, and it proved most harmful in the use of deputies to supervise departments in times of national crisis. Navy Board officers were, with few exceptions, active individuals with a wide range of interests, and neither the time nor their own self perceptions enabled them to accept the responsibilities of bureaucratic work on a daily basis with ease. They were, in short, constantly trying to get away from their offices, meetings, surveys and reports and onto the decks of ships where they could achieve what the Elizabethan adventurer considered something worthwhile. Thus Wynter's exile to the Irish coast was not quite so great a punishment as it might seem. Or William Borough's scurrying off to participate in Drake's raid allowed the erstwhile Willoughby and Chancellor voyager to do what he really wanted to do, leaving the important work of the Clerk of the Ships in the hands of some deputy. But the best case in point of how this expedient shaped the Navy Board undoubtedly occurred with the activities of John Hawkins.

For the first decade of his tenure as Treasurer, Hawkins showed little inclination to absent himself from the Admiralty offices. He did, however, quietly prepare the way for taking extended leaves from the office by creating an unofficial deputy. This man was Roger Langford, who first appeared in the Audit Office accounts in 1584 as a clerk earning 8d. a day and ended his career as Navy Treasurer in 1599.[16] Hawkins seems to have promoted Langford as a kind of paymaster who could hold the Treasurer's office, if not the whole Navy Board, together for lengthy periods, and when the Armada came Hawkins did not hesitate to use Langford. Sailing as Rear Admiral in Howard's fleet in the summer of 1588, Hawkins left the critical administrative tasks in the deputy's care, and he did likewise on other occasions until his death in 1595. Eventually, Langford was rewarded with the office for which he had stood deputy for many times under trying circumstances, but the administration as a unit only suffered from this practice. Langford was not, after all, a person of Hawkin's prestige, contacts, experience and will, and there seems to be a direct correlation between his caretaking activities and the decline in performance and reputation of the Navy Board in the waning years of Queen Elizabeth.[17]

It seems evident then that with the emergence of recognizable bureaucracies in England during the Tudor period, essentially two forces played key roles in the shaping of these administrative organs. The first of these was the way in which they were structured by the Crown, which by the reign of Elizabeth tended to be along rational and carefully defined lines. It seems equally clear that at almost the same time that some thought was devoted to constructing bureaucracies, expedients born of pride, power lust, economic aggrandizement and ego gratification were adopted and shaped those administrative units to suit the purposes of either an individual or in some cases a small clique. So it was the Navy Board of Elizabethan England. Recognized as a legitimate department of state, regulated by ordinance and staffed with some concern for competence, it was molded over the years by external controls and internal ambitions that as often as not ran utterly contrary to the planning that had created the unit. Because of the planning that forged it and the stresses that shaped it over the years, it does not seem absurd to suggest that the Elizabethan Admiralty, like other bureaucracies, developed a life outside that of its personnel, and that life was best expressed by the traditions, practices and procedures that were the ultimate products of rationality and expedience.

FOOTNOTES

[1] Robert Bolt, *A Man for All Seasons* (New York: Vintage, 1962), p. 42.

[2] Michael Oppenheim, *A History of the Administration of the Royal Navy* (London: Bodley, 1896), p. 3.

[3] The expansion of naval administrative staff during the period 1510 to 1540 was discussed in some detail by the author in a paper entitled "Henry VIII and the Founding of the Admiralty" delivered at the Ohio Academy of History in April 1971. Most of the documentary evidence supporting the generalization can be found in Great Britain, Public Record Office, *Letters and Papers, Foreign and Domestic of the Reign of Henry VIII* (London: H.M.S.O., 1864-), Vols. II through V.

[4] For the various grants see *Ibid.*, Vol. XXI, pt. 1, Nos. 650(79) and 718.

[5] R. K. Merton *et al.*, eds., *Reader in Bureaucracy* (Glencoe, Ill.: Free Press, 1952), pp. 21-2.

[6] Bodleian Library, *Rawlinson Mss.*, C. 840, No. 4, ff. 46-61. An excellent analysis of these documents is available in Tom Glasgow Jr., "The Maturing of Elizabethan Naval Administration," *Mariner's Mirror*, LVI (1972), 12-14.

[7] Great Britain, Public Record Office, *State Papers Domestic, Elizabeth*, Vol. XV, No. 4 (SP12/15/4). All PRO documents hereinafter will be cited by PRO call number.

[8] See the listing of Navy Tresurer's accounts in Great Britain, Public Record Office, *Lists and Indexes*, (London: H.M.S.O., 1892), Vol. II, p. 240.

[9] PRO, *AO1/1682/5*.

[10] For an example of their closeness see the Lord Admiral's will, PRO, *Prob 11/68, Brudenell 26*. The author is completing a biography of Lord Admiral Clinton (Lincoln).

[11] See Michael Lewis, *England's Sea Officers* (London: Allen and Unwin, 1939), pp. 153-4.

[12] For Hawkins' reversion see James Williamson, *Sir John Hawkins* (Oxford: Clarendon Press, 1927), p. 302.

[13] For the best analysis of Hawkins' two bargains see *Ibid.*, Book III, Chs. I and II.

[14] Thomas Woodroofe, *Vantage at Sea* (New York: St. Martin's, 1958), p. 147.

[15] PRO, *SP12/156/45*.

[16] See PRO, *AO1/1685/19*.

[17] See the critical remarks about the ability of the Navy Board in the post Hawkins-Wynter era under the heading "Government" in PRO, *SP14/41/f.5*.

CHAPTER 8

The Machinery for the Planning and Execution of English Grand Strategy in the War of the Spanish Succession, 1702-1713

John B. Hattendorf

U.S. Naval War College

In his biography of the Duke of Marlborough, Sir Winston Churchill attributed English grand strategy entirely to his famous ancestor. "Until the advent of Napoleon," Churchill wrote:

> no commander wielded such widespread power in Europe. . . . His comprehension of the war extended to all theatres and his authority alone secured design and concerted action. He animated the war at sea no less than on land, and established till the present time the British naval supremacy in the Mediterranean. His eye ranged far across the oceans, and the foundations of British dominion in the New World and in Asia were laid or strengthened as the result of his Continental policy. He was for six years not only the Commander-in-Chief of the Allies, but, though a subject, virtually master of England.

Believing that fame had shone unwillingly on Marlborough, Churchill sought "a more just and a more generous judgment from his fellow-countrymen."[1] In this, he was largely successful. Today, every general text acknowledges Marlborough's role and gives him the credit for English war strategy and policy. There is no reason to tarnish the deserved reputation of a great commander and a successful diplomat. However, overemphasizing Marlborough's role tends to ignore the fact that England fought the war as part of an alliance, and it tends to obscure two important developments in the late 17th century: (1) The dramatic growth in the size of armies and navies, and (2) the development of central bureaucracies.[2]

80

The conduct of grand strategy is the higher direction of warfare. It is the purposeful use of all the resources of a nation to achieve broad objectives in international relations. For the purpose of this conference and this paper, however, I shall limit my discussion to those elements which relate to the Navy.

The conduct of war and international relations are functions which were traditionally exercised by the Crown. In the 17th and 18th centuries, parliament had gradually asserted its right to be consulted in these affairs. During Queen Anne's reign, parliamentary influence was clearly present, but grand strategy was still formulated within the executive sphere of government. Although Parliament did not formulate policy, it could and did decide whether the nation would or would not enter into a war. Among other influential men, Marlborough thought that if the King should enter into war on his own authority in 1701, 'We shall never see a quiet day more in England.'[3] A dispute between Crown and Parliament would so divide the nation that English power in Europe would be entirely ineffective. Once the decision for war had been taken, the appropriate funds voted, and the supplies maintained, the government often paid little regard in its conduct of the war for the 'many murmurings and hollow noises of distant winds' which were heard in Parliament.[4] The obstruction or the actual failure by Parliament to supply the necessary money could alter grand strategy. In this regard, the attitude of parliament was a critical concern for those who directed the war as well as the allies who observed the situation in England.[5] In this manner, parliament could exercise a degree of control on the government, although it could not plan and execute a grand strategy for the conduct of war. This was left to officials at many levels within the government.

The growth in the size of the central government in London, accompanied by the reduction in both the size and influence of the court,[6] produced a complex system to control the armed forces. During the Nine Years War, the Royal Navy had expanded from 173 ships in 1688, with a tonnage of 101,892 tons and carrying 6930 guns to 323 ships in 1697 totaling 160,000 tons and 9912 guns.[7] The navy in Queen Anne's reign remained at substantially the same level, but by 1714 more workers were employed in industry supporting the navy than any other work in the country. The army, on the English establishment alone, grew from 18,568 to 69,095 men between 1701 and 1709.[8] At the same time, the number of diplomatic representatives abroad expanded by 70 per cent.[9] The increased involvement in continental affairs, the management of trade and colonies overseas as well as the operations of the army and navy in widely separated areas dictated that these affairs would be controlled by the cooperation of a variety of men in a variety of capacities rather than by a small group or by a single individual.

THE MACHINERY FOR GRAND STRATEGY IN LONDON

The growth of the administrative side of the central government had created many officials concerned with military and naval affairs. The Navy Board, the Transport Board, the Victualling Board, the Commissioners of Sick and Wounded, and the Board of Ordnance made essential contributions. However, these offices were rarely involved in directly making strategic decisions. Direction of this sort was left, in varying degrees, to the Admiralty, the Board of Trade, the secretaries of state, the cabinet, and the Queen. Of course, in theory, it was the sovereign who held the ultimate authority in the formulation of strategy and policy. The contrast between William III's active role and keen interest in foreign affairs with the more subdued role of Queen Anne has overshadowed Anne's contribution in this process. It is becoming increasingly apparent to historians that Anne "was not a negligible force in the politics of her reign,"[10] but her precise role is difficult to define. The Queen was closely concerned with foreign affairs and was kept informed of routine dispatches privately[11] and in cabinet. It is clear that the Queen's personal influence and interest in foreign affairs had an impact on English policy. In a private memorandum written in 1711, Robert Harley gave the "Queen's opinion and health" as the first item in his list of domestic reasons for obtaining peace with France.[12] The nature of the documents make it exceedingly difficult to find any policy which can be traced to the Queen herself. Unlike her predecessor, she had no Portland or Heinsius to whom she penned her thoughts on foreign policy. The business of formulating decisions within the central government took place within the cabinet.

The Queen was present at every cabinet meeting. Only in a brief period in 1708 following the death of her husband, Prince George of Denmark, were the "Lords of the Committee of Council" alone allowed full control of national affairs. Normally, the Queen meeting with the Lords of the Committee formed the cabinet, and the subcommittees which were formed from this group reported their recommendations and opinions to the full cabinet for approval.[13]

There appears to have been a variety of committees which dealt with various problems and which prepared matters for cabinet discussions, discussed detailed arrangements, and supervised the execution of plans approved in cabinet. For example, preparations for the expedition to Canada were being considered in committee as early as January 1711, although the plans were not presented for cabinet approval until March.[14] The existence of these committees does not by any means presuppose that they controlled all matters. They performed a significant and valuable service which was clearly accepted by those who participated.

The day-to-day management of foreign affairs was left to the secretaries of state and the Lord Treasurer. These men, as well as Marlborough when he was in London, were privy to nearly all the information relating to foreign affairs and the conduct of the war. But precautions were taken in restricting the availability of this information beyond a very small circle. Some envoys were directed to report their secret information in a separate encyphered letter that would not need to be read in a full cabinet meeting.[15] In addition to this practice there is clear evidence of management by small groups within the cabinet. In a fragmentary note passed between Godolphin and Nottingham during a cabinet meeting, the secretary of state penned in his tiny, characteristic script 'I intended to speak of this when the Prince's Council go out.' To which Godolphin replied in his flamboyant hand, 'I think you had better not speak of this but to the Duke of Marlborough and me, at first, and when it has been a little digested, it will not require so much time here, as it will do now.'[16] Indeed, there is a limitation to what any one committee can accomplish in managing the diverse affairs of government. A committee, such as the cabinet itself, required issues to be considered in depth before a sound decision could be taken by the group as a whole. At the same time, it was not necessary for those who had considered matters in detail to discuss them with other members of the cabinet, both privately and in cabinet meetings.[17] Information received by one member of the cabinet was very often shared by other cabinet members. For example, Marlborough and Godolphin's private correspondence was routinely shared with the secretaries of state.[18]

While it is true that certain members of the cabinet were closely concerned with a detailed consideration of foreign and military affairs, it does not necessarily follow that these individuals or factions within the cabinet were in complete control of policy. The evidence of cabinet meetings, when compared to the directives which were issued, reveals that decisions regarding grand strategy and the general conduct of the war were not made by any single individual. They appear to have been reached by the concensus of cabinet members acting on a consideration of facts, opinions, and reports obtained from many sources.[19]

The secretaries of state were the key administrative coordinators in relation to the various segments of the government. They provided the official certification of cabinet decisions. Nearly evrything which appeared in a secretary's official letter had been previously discussed and approved in a meeting of the cabinet or lords of the committee. Over the years, a division of responsibility was developed to handle this business as a matter of convenience among the two or three men who served as principal secretaries of state. However, the secretaries were well informed of each others activities and their daily work routinely complemented one another. When one secretary was ill or indisposed, the other secretary would handle his affairs and inform him or his staff of the action taken.

The secretaries of state were responsible for maintaining close contact with a variety of groups outside the cabinet which provided essential information and advice for the conduct of the war. The Board of Trade[20] served as an important source of information and advice on colonial defense, convoys, arms supplies, manning ships, and plans for colonial expeditions. In addition, it provided important intelligence of enemy operations overseas through correspondence with colonial officials. The London Post Office provided an administrative center for gathering secret intelligence from abroad and for deciphering intercepted diplomatic and military dispatches.[21] Foreign envoys in London played an extremely important part within the process by which the government made decisions in grand strategy. These representatives of allied governments provided information on specific points as well as recommendations for broad policy which they obtained through instructions from their own countries.

Foreign intelligence, colonial affairs, and the opinions of the allies were all matters of direct concern to the government in the formulation of its policy and strategy. In addition to providing a link between the cabinet and the various sources of such information, the secretaries of state also provided the link between the cabinet and the Armed Forces.

The business of the Admiralty, in whatever form it was managed,[22] involved a wide variety of considerations. The most important of these for strategy were the issuing of orders to commanders at sea and the gathering intelligence from reports made by the fleet. In both these areas, the Admiralty worked closely with the cabinet, through the secretary of state for the Southern department.[23] General guidance was received from the secretary of state, and the Admiralty, in turn, shared its intelligence information. The Admiralty considered the specific matters of ship assignments and the officers who manned them. In the course of planning, the Admiralty provided the secretary of state an assessment of the equipment and the capacity of the fleet to perform a particular task. But such technical matters were not allowed to remain the exclusive province of the Admiralty. In many cases, judgments on these matters were carefully reviewed at the cabinet level.[24]

The Admiralty was required to regularly report to the cabinet the state of the fleet[25] and in addition all orders to any admiral or commander-in-chief were submitted to the Queen in cabinet or to a committee of the lords of the cabinet council before they were dispatched.[26] Representatives of the Admiralty met frequently with cabinet officers in managing the fleet. Through this procedure, the Admiralty's direction of affairs was controlled and often modified. At the same time, the Admiralty's function in framing the drafts of instructions was an important contribution to the process by which a decision was reached in the cabinet. Although the Admiralty was not in a position to have the final authority in affairs at sea, its perceptions were an important influence in defining the available options which could be chosen.

The relationship of the cabinet to the Admiralty in reviewing instructions was not its only connection to the fleet at sea. There was a direct link between the secretary of state and a commander in chief, by-passing the Admiralty through a routine administrative process. First, the secretary of state directed the Admiralty to instruct an admiral that he was to receive orders from her Majesty by the hand of a secretary of state.[27] The Admiralty then issued a warrant authorizing the officer to receive such instructions. Then, the secretary of state would send instructions from the Queen under her signet and sign manual. The orders would invariably require the admiral to report his progress to a secretary of state, who in turn would provide additional instructions. These orders were not necessarily reported to the Admiralty. In some cases, commanders were ordered to make no mention of their instructions to anyone other than a secretary of state.[28]

In normal usage this arrangement created neither a conflict in direction nor an overlap in authority between the professional and political direction of fleet movements. It was clearly a complementary system by which the two sources of direction worked together, and in which the cabinet and crown maintained the ultimate authority and the responsibility for the strategic direction of affairs at sea. The Admiralty served as the administrative coordinators of the navy and the technical advisors to the cabinet. However, by regularly reporting the state of the navy, collecting and reporting intelligences, and framing instructions, the Admiralty played an active part in the planning and execution of grand strategy.

THE MACHINERY FOR ENGLISH STRATEGY ABROAD

Time and distance were as much a factor in controlling forces in Europe as they were in more distant areas. It was a matter of prudence and necessity that instructions from London be considered at the scene of action in the light of practicality and recent events. Commanders-in-chief were directed to govern themselves

> . . . by the advice and opinion of a Council of War, which Council shall consist of Flag Officers when such matters are to be therein proposed and debated as related only to the Service at Sea, and of the said officers, and the Commanders-in-Chief, and other General Officers of Our Land Forces, when such things are to be considered of as related to the Service both at Sea and Land.[29]

The war council was an important aspect in the execution of orders for it was only on the reasoning and authority of a council that an order could be modified. It was a standard practice to submit the minutes of war councils to higher authority in support of actions taken. This practice was brought into question early in the war by the court martial of Rear Admiral Sir John Munden for failure to follow his orders in attacking the French Squadron at Coruna in May 1702.[30] Although Munden never again flew his flag at sea, his acquittal was based on the validity of a war council's judgment in such circumstances.[31]

When the navy was operating jointly with a Dutch squadron, the procedure to be followed in war council was specified by treaty. Decisions were to be reached by a strict majority of votes. However, the treaty stipulation that three Dutch ships were to be supplied for every five English ships[32] insured English predominance in war council. A Dutch refusal to participate on the basis of conflicting orders or an absence of orders from the Hague, however, could reduce the possibility of success for English forces acting alone.[33]

Frequently, it was impossible to know in London what forces would be adequate in a specific situation. In those circumstances only a broad indication could be given and the specific operation had to be worked out at the scene. In 1704, for example a council of war decided that it was impractical for the fleet to attempt to carry out its instructions for an attack on Cadiz without an adequate supporting army. Instead the council decided to take advantage of the weak defenses of Gibraltar.[34] When news of the success of this operation reached London, the Lord High Treasurer remarked in a letter to the English envoy in Savoy, "Our last news from Sir George Rooke gave an account that he had possessed himself of Gibraltar, which I suppose you hear sooner than we; I know not how far it is tenable, or can be of use to us, those at Lisbon will be the best judges and directors of that matter."[35]

Such judgment and direction had to be soundly based on authoritative information as well as on a firm understanding of national policy and objectives. In affairs of this nature, commanders-in-chief necessarily joined with diplomats. The government in London expected that envoys and senior officers working together would have the necessary information and judgment to make the appropriate decisions. For example in the summer of 1711, there was some suspicion that Portugal might make a separate peace with France. When the commander-in-chief of the army in Portugal wrote home for directions what he should do if such a situation arose, he was told by the secretary of state,

> . . . you are to consult with the Ministers of the Queen and the States residing at Lisbon, and the Admirals in the Mediterranean what measures are proper to be taken, your Lordship is on the spot where these things are transacted you have a perfect knowledge of the situation of the public affairs, and I am therefore to desire you will propose what you conceive must advisable to be done at such a conjuncture, upon which at present I can not send you any further instructions.[36]

The Queen's envoys provided important information which directly facilitated the conduct of naval and military operations. Envoys served as verifying authorities for the particular needs of their respective courts, and in that process, they judged the appropriateness of the requests which those courts made to English commanders. At times, envoys were specifically instructed to provide intelligence to the fleet,[37] but their ability to serve in this function was dependent on their access to reliable information. Of course, diplomats received their own royal instructions from London as well as further instructions, gazettes, newsletters, and advice from the secretary of state. Equally important information was obtained through specially employed secret agents and through regular correspondence with English ministers at other courts. English diplomats abroad were not merely sources of information for admirals and generals, they were highly influential and active participants in war councils.[38] In one case, Richard Hill, a member of the Lord High Admiral's Council as well as the envoy at Turin retained direct control of two frigates in the Mediterranean throughout the winter of 1704-05.[39] Others, such as Marlborough and Stanhope, served in the dual capacity of envoy and commander-in-chief.[40]

The cooperation of the allies in the conduct of operations was a critical matter to the success of many plans. Without a centralized, allied command with the authority to direct operations, matters had to be settled through a continual process of war councils and negotiations. It was a method which often irritated the Duke of Marlborough who believed that it destroyed secrecy in planning and dispatch in execution.[41] Despite Marlborough's impatience with the process and its implicit denial of complete authority, the necessary consultation, negotiation, and conflicting viewpoints among the allies remained modifying influences on the course of operations throughout the war. Time and distance, the situation of affairs on distant stations, the initiative of commanders and envoys, joined with the pressures and needs of the allies in creating a situation in which plans envisaged and orders issued in London could easily be modified.

In the area of planning future operations, ministers abroad and commanders-in-chief played similarly important roles. On one occasion, London was left in some doubt as to what course actually had been taken. In 1707, the commander-in-chief of the Mediterranean Squadron was killed when his flagship wrecked in the Isles of Scilly as he was returning to England. Secretary of State Robert Harley wrote the English resident minister in Holland, that ". . . the unfortunate loss of Sir Cloudesly Shovell has left us for some time in the dark for what he had concerted with the States Flag concerning the continuance of ships at Lisbon, and the operations in those seas."[42]

On occasion, even the plan for the negotiation of treaties was left to those who were abroad. Being provided with the broad lines of policy, Lord Galway would be instructed in relation to a new military treaty with Portugal, "Queen leaves the Schemes of the new Treaty entirely to your lordship and Mr. Methuen."[43] Similarly, Marlborough was given authority to negotiate the details of troop treaties at the Hague.[44]

The Dutch had a special importance as a key location for the conduct of negotiations with the allies. In many ways it was "the Centre of Business and Intelligence." Marlborough's long service at the Hague, between 1701 and 1711, gave him a special position in addition to his duties as commander-in chief envoy, captain-general, and member of the cabinet in London. Shortly after William III's death, Marlborough was sent to the Hague on a mission to give assurances to the allies that England would carry on the planned alliance. He sailed on this mission with "a full Gale of favour" and had in effect the position of an "Ambassador General" who could give instructions to other ministers abroad.[46] It was clearly a temporary authority given in a difficult situation to ensure that all appropriate action was taken in carrying out the details of a basic decision that was made in London.[47] Ordinarily, however, Marlborough was authorized only to give instructions to others in regard to the details of troop treaties. Throughout the war, he took extraordinary care in obtaining authority and approval for his actions.[48] In general, he confined his work to relations with Holland and Germany, but the central position of the Hague and the negotiations conducted there relating to Spain, the Mediterranean, and Italy, involved him also in a wider sphere.[49] As a distinguished personality, and a victorious commander, Marlborough carried a special prestige abroad. The government at home rarely lost an opportunity to employ his remarkable talents in support of difficult negotiations.

Marlborough served, like his colleagues in other areas, as a proponent of English policy as well as being a recipient of suggestions from the allies. Much of the work of envoys abroad was part of a persistent effort to persuade the allies to conduct the war along the lines which England believed were best. Like other responsible officers abroad, envoys had to proceed on their own initiative, on occasion, in the light of what they believed would be an acceptable course of action. In a private letter to Harley, John Methuen lamented the problems he had faced in bringing Portugal into the Grand Alliance. "I was to struggle with a strong French party here," he wrote, "who were supported by all the arts and other methods of France which I could no way deal with but by giving the King of Portugal hopes of everything from the Allies."[50] However necessary this type of initiative was to the progress of diplomatic negotiations, it could easily cause a storm when the government came to review the situation. There were some influential members of the government at home who apparently opposed this license, on principle. Robert Harley admitted to Lord Raby that one of the reasons for his dismissal as a secretary of state in 1708 was his belief that ministers abroad were not independent enough. Two years later, Lord Raby could note that "they have been much less so since."[51] The relations among the various officials abroad were not always happy. Personalities might clash, perceptions could differ, responsibilities would occasionally overlap, but on the whole, envoys, generals, and admirals complemented one another in making practical and necessary modifications to strategic plans which had been outlined by instructions from London. In the colonies and on distant stations, the situation was similar. Colonial governors, assemblies, local commanders, and trading companies molded and modified their instruction from London as local conditions required.

Despite limitations, it was essentially a decentralised system in both Europe and on distant stations by which those in the field could significantly influence the conduct of the war. Most importantly, it was largely on the insight, recommendations and understanding of those who served abroad that the government in London based its decisions. The reports from abroad were the eyes and ears of the government in London. In many cases, they provided England's understanding of events abroad as well as the logic behind grand strategy.

One may summarise the process by which decisions were reached by briefly outlining one example. Let us select for this purpose the capture of Port Mahon which was so important for the naval war in the Mediterranean.[52]

The strategic value of the island of Minorca with its large harbour at Port Mahon had been understood in London for some time. As early as 1701, the Prince of Hasse-Darmstadt had proposed taking the island as part of his plan to encourage the revolt of the Catalans.[53] In 1704, Jean Philippe Hoffman, the envoy of King Charles III in London, proposed it in a memorial to the Queen,[54] and in 1706, the fleet under Sir John Leake had not been able to devote the forces which had been planned for taking it during that campaign.[55] In December 1707, the cabinet debated the issue "whether it would not be right to make ourselves masters at Port Mahon and to instruct Sir J. Leake to the purpose,"[56] but no instructions were issued at that time. During that same winter, the envoy in Spain, James Stanhope, had returned to England on personal business. In March 1708, he was ordered to return and he went with a commission as commander-in-chief as well as envoy. En route back to his port, Stanhope accompanied the Duke of Marlborough to the Hague, planning to reach Spain overland and consulting the allies en route. At the Hague he joined Marlborough and Prince Eugene and the Dutch deputies in their planning conference for the 1708 campaign. Both Marlborough and Stanhope reported the results of the conference to London where it was dealt with, at first, by the two secretaries of state, the Lord Chancellor and the Lord Treasurer.[57] One of the major points of discussion at the Hague conference was the urgent need for the fleet to operate in the Mediterranean during the winter when it could support the army in Spain. The Dutch, in particular, were strongly in favour of the idea and thought it a very practical proposal. While the Army in northern Europe went into winter quarters, the mild winter weather in the South afforded the best time for military operations in the Peninsula. While the Army was active, the fleet was needed for support. This point was discussed at a meeting of the cabinet, and referred to the Prince's Council for advice.[58] In addition, further information and advice was sought from Stanhope and from the Dutch.[59] Stanhope pressed for using Porto Spezia in Italy as a fleet base, and on this point he wrote Marlborough and Godolphin to secure their support for his views. Marlborough passed his letter on to the secretary of state, commenting that he approved of the plan in general, but did "not enter into the particulars of what he writes . . . you will be the best judges at home how far that can be complyed with."[60] However, little progress was made in London. The Admiralty delayed making its report and the Dutch offered little concrete information for carrying out the proposal they had supported so strongly.[61] Godolphin saw the great values of the plan, but wondered "how can it be done with safety?" Cadiz was surely a better location, away from the major French base at Toulon which could so easily sever the links between Spain and Italy.[62]

In Spain the military situation had not improved. The lack of supplies and ready money threatened the ability of the army to take the field. Portugal was becoming an increasingly unreliable source of supply, and the navy was urgently needed to bring relief and establish safe and dependable communications from other areas. As one officer with the army put it, "if the Fleet should not come Time enough . . . we shall be obliged to knock all our horses in the head for want of forage and defend Tarragona and Barcelona with the foot as long as we can."[63] In this situation, King Charles III wrote London urging that the stationing of the fleet in the Mediterranean was absolutely essential to maintaining himself in Spain. On receipt of this letter, Godolphin and the Lords of the Committee prodded the Admiralty to produce its recommendations on the subject, but Godolphin himself remained quite pessimistic on the matter.[64] The Prince's Council responded immediately that there was no port readily available in allied hands which could safely be used to winter the Anglo-Dutch fleet. The Italian and Spanish ports were not suitable; however, if Port Mahon could be taken, then the squadron could safely winter there.[65] Godolphin immediately recommended to Stanhope that he and the forces in Spain should dispose yourselves without loss of time to be masters of Port Mahon."[66] When this was accomplished then London could arrange for a fleet to be sustained there. Meanwhile, James Craggs was sent from Spain to solicit the support of the government for wintering the fleet in Italy, and the Admiralty unsympathetically reviewed further information on the Italian ports.[67] When Marlborough received a copy of the report from the Prince's Council in mid-July he, too, wrote Stanhope urging him to take the port.[68]

By late August, Godolphin's letter arrived in Spain reporting the opinion of the Prince's Council and including his own encouragement to take Port

Mahon. Upon its receipt, Stanhope took action. He went immediately to King Charles III and consulted him on the plan. The fleet under Sir John Leake was just in the process of subduing Sardinia and it was immediately recalled for the assault on Minorca.[69] These letters were received by Leake near Cagliari and were considered at a council of war. The council agreed to set aside other plans and proceed immediately to Minorca.[70] It was obvious to those on the scene that the value of the capture of Sardinia would be ruined if a fleet was not available to maintain the security of regular supplies of grain from that island to the army in Spain.[71]

In October the news arrived in London by express that Port Mahon had fallen to the allies on 30 September.[72] The dispatch which brought the news from Stanhope also included an unexpected development. "It is my humble opinion," Stanhope wrote, "that England ought never to part with this island, which will give the Law to the Mediterranean both in Time of War and Peace." For this reason, Stanhope allowed only English troops to man the garrison, but he made no other move which would disturb the allies.[73] Immediately upon receipt of the news, naval stores and victuàls were ordered sent from Portugal, and Stanhope was ordered "to keep secret any thought of keeping Port Mahon in our hands after Peace."[74] In December the cabinet considered the matter further and Stanhope was ordered to initiate appropriate negotiations with King Charles III to obtain Minorca "as some sort of security for the charges and expences" which England had been at for the war in Spain.[75] Negotiations on this point continued for some time and were included in the peace negotiations at Utrecht. It was not until November 1712 that the island was publically taken in the name of Queen Anne.[76]

In this example, one can see the numerous factors at work in the process by which decisions were made in grand strategy. One may see the influence of the allies in promoting the project initially, the importance and relation of the existing military and naval situation, the initiative of a commander-in-chief, the importance of the advice of an agency such as the Admiralty, the impact of key members of the cabinet such as Marlborough and Godolphin, the coordination of the secretaries of state, the strategic relationship between army and navy, the manner in which the cabinet considered proposals that were made to it and the way in which it built practically upon them in the light of actions taken in the field. The lines of command and control for the armed forces coincided with those of strategic decision making. The elements which impelled the machinery for the planning and execution of grand strategy created an effect which was distinct from what any one acting by itself might produce, and at the same time, partook of each and was formed out of all.

FOOTNOTES

[1] W. S. Churchill, *Marlborough: His Life and Times* (New York, 1933), i. pp. 3-4.

[2] For general studies of these problems see J. H. Plumb, *The Growth of Political Stability in England 1675-1715* (London 1967); Clayton Roberts, *The Growth of Responsible Government in Stuart England* (Cambridge, 1966); G. Perjes, "Army Provisioning, Logistics and Strategy in the Second Half of the 17th Century"; *Acta Historica Academiae Scientiarum Hungaricae*, xvi (1970), pp. 1-54.

[3] Brit. Lib. Addit. MSS. 40, 775 fos. 232-3, Marlborough to Vernon, 3/14 October 1701.

[4] Brit. Lib. Addit. MS. 7059 fo. 39v., Harley to Stepney, 31 October 1704.

[5] See M. A. Thomson, 'Parliament and Foreign Policy 1689-1714' in R. Hatton and J. S. bromley (eds.), *William III and Louis XIV* (Liverpool 1968), pp. 130-39; D. H. Wollman 'Parliament and Foreign 1697-1714', unpublished Ph.D. Thesis, University of Wisconsin, 1970.

[6] J. H. Plumb, *The Growth of Political Stability in England 1675-1725* (London, 1967), p. 119 and ch. 4 in general.

[7] J. Ehrman, *The Navy in the War of William III* (Cambridge, 1953), p. xx.

[8] R. E. Scouller, *The Armies of Queen Anne* (Oxford, 1966), Appendix C.

[9] D. B. Horn, *The British Diplomatic Service 1689-1789* (Oxford, 1961), p. 44.

[10] Paul Langford, *Modern British Foreign Policy: The Eighteenth Century 1688-1815* (London, 1976), p. 5.

[11] A typical example of a report used by a secretary of state to the Queen outside a cabinet meeting may be seen in the Bodlian Library, MSS Eng. His. d. 147, Boyle to Townshend, 27 May 1709.

[12] British Library, Loan 29/10, "Minutes, Windsor", 19 October 1711.

[13] For a detailed description of this process see J. H. Plumb, "The Organization of the Cabinet in the Region of Queen Anne", *Trans. Royal Hist. Soc.*, 5th Series, vol. 7, 1957, pp. 137-57.

[14] Staffordshire R. O. MSS. D(W) 1778/188, fo. 99, Lord's Minutes, 18 January 1711; fo. 134, Cabinet Minutes, 25 March 1711.

[15] P.R.O., SP. 80/18 fo. 79, Stepney to Vernon, 5 February 1702; Brit. Lib. Addit. MSS. 37,529, fo. 41, Nottingham to Hill, 3 March 1704.

[16] Brit. Lib. Addit. MSS. 29,589 fo. 395, Nottingham to Godolphin with reply, undated.

[17] For example of this see H. L. Snyder, "Communication: The Formulation of Foreign and Domestic Policy in the Reign of Queen Anne: Memoranda by Lord Chancellor Cowper of Conversation with Lord Treasurer Godolphin," *The Historical Journal* xi (1968), 144-160.

[18] Longleat House, Portland MSS. iv, fo. 31, Marlborough to Harley, 8 July 1706; P.R.O. SP. 87/2 fo. 19, Marlborough to Nottingham, 20 August 1702; Brit. Lib. Addit. MSS. 28,891, Tucker to Ellis, 2 October 1703.

[19] This statement is based on a comparison of Blenheim Palace, MSS. C1-16; Brit. Lib. MSS. Loan 29/9 and 10; Staffordshire R.O. MSS. D(W) 1778/188 with secretarial entry books, P.R.O., SP. 104 series; Blenheim MSS, Sunderland Letterbooks. This shows that these documents for the most part are not 'minutes' in the usual sense, but notes for the secretary to use in writing his required correspondence. See the rather full example printed in E. N. Williams, *The Eighteenth Century Constitution 1688-1815* (Cambridge, 1970), pp. 113-16.

[20] For a detailed study of the Board in this period see Ian K. Steele, *Politics of Colonial Policy: The Board of Trade in Colonial Administration 1696-1720* (Oxford, 1968), pp. 85-148.

[21] See K. L. Ellis, *The Post Office in the Eighteenth Century: A Study in Administrative History* (Oxford, 1958), pp. 62-3, 65-6, 127-131; K. L. Ellis 'British Communication and

Diplomacy in the Eighteenth Century', *Bulletin of the Institute of Historical Research,* xxxi (1958) pp. 158-67; J. C. Sainty, *Secretaries of State* (London, 1973), pp. 51-2.

[22] The powers of the Admiralty were vested in the office of the Lord High Admiral. These powers were exercised in the name of this office alternatively by a single individual, by an individual with the advice of a specially appointed council, or by a board of commissioners. In the event that all these methods failed, the office reverted to the crown. During the War of the Spanish Succession, all four of these methods were used to conduct Admiralty affairs. The Office had reverted to the Crown from 28 October tó 29 November 1708. P.R.O. ADM. 2/1744; Brit. Lib. Addit. MSS. 37,356 fo. 310, Tilson to Stepney, 2 November 1708. For a list of the various office holders see J. C. Sainty, *Admiralty Officials 1660-1870* (London, 1975) pp. 21-22, 32-33.

[23] This was part of an arbitrary and informal division of labour among the secretaries. In other reigns, it was not exclusively within the Southern department, *e.g.,* John Ehrman, *The Navy in the War of William III,* pp. 306, 512-3, 606.

[24] These generalisations are based on a detailed examination and comparison between P.R.O. ADM. 2/27-45. Admiralty Instructions; ADM. 1/4087-96, Secretaries of State to the Admiralty; ADM. 2/264-66, Admiralty to Secretaries of State; ADM. 3/16-27, Admiralty Minutes.

[25] P.R.O., ADM. 1/4087 fo. 39. Secretary Vernon's directions for the Admiralty to report to the King twice a week on the manning and operation of the fleet; SP. 44/104 fo. 33, Nottingham to Burchett, 30 June 1702 required a weekly report; ADM. 8, The monthly lists of ships and vessels in sea pay were also provided to the secretary of state.

[26] P.R.O., SP. 44/210 fo. 11, Sunderland to the Prince's Council, 8 March 1707; Blenheim MSS. C1-16, Cabinet Minutes, 7 March 1707.

[27] *E.g.,* Brit. Lib. Addit. MSS., 28,888 fo. 301, Hedges to Prince George, 8 June 1702.

[28] Staffordshire R.O. MSS. D(W) 1778/188 fo. 11, Ov. Minutes, 14 February 1711; P.R.O., SP. 104/79 fo. 21. St. John to Wishart, 16 February 1711.

[29] B. Tunstall (ed.), *The Byng Papers* (Naval Records Soc., LXVIII, 1931) p. 203. Instructions to Byng, 8 July 1708.

[30] Gloucestershire R.O., MSS. D1833/X4, p. 45. Rooke to Clarke, 29 June 1702.

[31] P.R.O. ADM 1/5264. Courts Martial Reports, 1702.

[32] The Treaty of Westminster, 3 March 1678; supplementary agreements of 26 July 1678 and March 1689.

[33] An example of such a consideration can be seen in Blenheim MSS. C2-33, Whitaker to Sunderland, 16 October 1708.

[34] Brit. Lib. Addit. MSS. 5440 fo. 197, Council of War of Flag Officers on Board HMS *Royal Katherine,* 17 July 1704.

[35] Brit. Lib. Addit. MSS, 37,529 fo. 57, Godolphin to Hill, 15 August 1704.

[36] P.R.O., SP. 104/111 fo. 137, Dartmouth to Portmore, 26 June 1711.

[37] Brit. Lib. Addit. MSS. 37529 fo. 76, Hedges to Hill, 4 May 1705.

[38] For example, Blenheim MSS. C2-17, War Council held with land and sea officers and Portuguese representatives at Methuen's home in Lisbon, 20 December 1706.

[39] Brit. Lib. Addit. MSS. 37,529, Hedges to Hill, 3 November 1704.

[40] *E.g.,* Lord Galway in Portugal; Stanhope, Peterborough and Argyll in Spain; Marlborough in Holland. Other envoys were officers closely connected to a commander in chief: Rear Admiral Sir George Byng in Algiers, Lord Cutts in Holland, Cadogan in Flanders and Holland.

[41] B. van't Hoff (ed.), *The Correspondence 1701-1711 of John Churchill First Duke of Marlborough and Anthonie Heinsius Grand Pensionary of Holland* (Utrecht, 1951), pp. 198-99, Letter 318.

[42] Brit. Lib. Addit. MSS. 15,866 fo. 66, Harley to Dayrolle, 6 December 1707.

[43] Blenheim MSS., Sunderland Letterbook, i, pp. 164-65, Sunderland to Galway, 20 April 1708.

[44] P.R.O., FO. 90/37 fo. 4, Darmouth to Chetwynd, 11 July 1710; Brit. Lib., MSS Loan 29/45M, Instructions to Pultney, 1706; Blenheim MSS., Sunderland Letterbook, i, p. 160, Sunderland to Marlborough, 13 April 1708.

[45] Brit. Lib. Stowe MSS. 248 fo. 1, 'Mr. Harley's Plan for Conducting the Business of the Public', 30 October 1710.

[46] Brit. Lib. Addit. MSS. 7074, Ellis to Stepney, 13 March 1702.

[47] P.R.O., SP. 104/89 fo. 230, Manchester to Blackwell, 13 March 1702.

[48] H. L. Snyder (ed.), *The Marlborough-Godolphin Correspondence* (Oxford, 1975), i, pp. xxiii-iv.

[49] Brit. Lib. Addit. MSS. 7074, Ellis to Stepney, 23 December 1701; *Marlborough-Godolphin Correspondence*, p. xxxii.

[50] Brit. Lib. MSS. Loan 29/45Y, John Methuen to Harley, 1 July 1704. Another example of Methuen's initiative may be seen in his use of unauthorized funds to support the defense of Gibralter during the 1704-05 siege. Spencer Research Library, University of Kansas, MS.E82, f. LI, Methuen to Simpson, 6 February 1705.

[51] Brit. Lib. MSS. Loan 29/45M, Raby to Harley, 30 September 1710.

[52] The most recent detailed accounts of this action are H. T. Dickinson, 'The Capture of Minorca 1708', *Mariner's Mirror*, LI (1965), pp. 195-204 and David Francis, *The First Peninsular War, 1702-13* (London, 1975), pp. 267-72, both of which are based on printed sources.

[53] Brit. Lib. Addit. MSS. 9720. fo. 84, Stepney to Blathwayt, 3 August 1701.

[54] P.R.O., SP. 100/10 Memorial of 4/15, August 1704.

[55] Kent R.O., Stanhope MSS. 63/19, Leake to Stanhope, 24 September 1706.

[56] Blenheim MSS. C1-16, Cabinet Council Minutes, Kensington, 28 December 1707.

[57] *Marlborough-Godolphin Correspondence*, p. 953.

[58] Blenheim MSS. C1-16, Minutes Cabinet Council, Kensington, 11 April 1708; P.R.O., Adm. 1/4091 fo. 622, Sunderland to Prince's Council, 13 April 1708.

[59] Brit. Lib. Addit. MSS. 15,866 fo. 106v, Sunderland to Dayrolles, 13 April 1708; Blenheim MSS. Sunderland Letterbook, i. p. 162, Sunderland to Stanhope, 13 April 1708.

[60] Blenheim MSS., Marlborough Letterbook, xxi, pp. 203-4, Marlborough to Sunderland, 17 May 1708.

[61] Blenheim MSS., Sunderland Letterbook, i, pp. 171-2, Sunderland to Stanhope, 14 May 1708.

[62] Kent R.O., Stanhope MSS. 66/7, Godolphin to Stanhope, 11 May 1708.

[63] Blenheim MSS. C2-15C, ? to Sunderland, 18 June 1708.

[64] Blenheim MSS. A2-38, Godolphin to Marlborough, 22 June 1708.

[65] Blenheim MSS. C1-6, Burchett to Sunderland, 23 June 1708.

[66] Kent R.O., Stanhope MSS 66/7, Godolphin to Stanhope, 22 June 1708.

[67] Kent R.O., Stanhope MSS 67, J. Craggs to Stanhope, 14 September 1708 and Memorials to Lord Sunderland; Blenheim MSS. C1-6, Burchett to Boyle, 19 August 1708.

[68] Blenheim MSS., Marlborough Letter Book, xxi, pp. 406-7, Marlborough to Stanhope, 15 July 1708; p. 418, Marlborough to Sunderland, 16 July 1708.

[69] Blenheim MSS. C2-32, Charles III to Leake, 23 August 1708; C2-15C, Stanhope to Sunderland, 28 August 1708; Stanhope to Leake, 24 August 1708.

[70] Brit. Lib. Addit. MSS. 5443 fo. 284, Council of War Minutes, 18 August 1708 (o.s.) on board H.M.S. *Elizabeth.*

[71] Kent R.O., Stanhope MSS. 66/2, Stanhope to Marlborough, 24 August 1708.

[72] Blenheim MSS., Sunderland Letterbooks, ii, pt. i, p. 182, Sunderland to Lord Mayor of London, 18/29 October 1708.

[73] Blenheim MSS. C2-15c, Stanhope to Sunderland, 30 September 1708 (n.s.).

[74] Blenheim MSS. C1-16, Cabinet Minutes, Kensington, 19 October 1708; Sunderland Letterbook, i., p. 227, Sunderland to Galway, 19 October 1708; p. 229, Sunderland to Stanhope, 20 October 1708.

[75] Blenheim MSS., Sunderland Letterbook, i., p. 256, Instructions to Stanhope, 9 December 1708, MSS. C1-16, Minutes Cabinet Council, Cockpit, 7 December 1708.

[76] Bedfordshire R.O., MSS. WY. 899, p. 6, Argyll to the Jurate and Vicar-General, 12 November 1712.

CHAPTER 9

Licensed to Steal: Toward a Sociology of English Piracy, 1550-1750

Joel Best

California State University at Fresno

Pirates are most often seen as romantic figures: men who led lives of freedom and violence in an age of adventure. The exploits of the best-known pirates have been the subjects of dozens of narrative histories. Although these stories have been retold many times, there have been surprisingly few attempts to analyze piracy as an activity, to identify the patterns in the pirates' lives.[1] This paper attempts to interpret piracy, particularly as it was practiced by Englishmen in the New World between 1550 and 1750, from the perspective of the sociology of deviance.

Sociologists define deviance as rule violation: acts or conditions which are subject to official sanctions from authorized agents of social control. The concept provides an analytic framework for comparing activities which might otherwise be seen as dissimilar, such as crime, mental illness, witchcraft, and piracy. Studies of deviance focus not only upon its causes, but also on its social organization and the social processes it involves.[2]

Typically, studies of deviance describe a conflict between the deviants and the agents of social control who usually represent the state. These control agents enforce the state's rules in order to protect its members, but their activities also have a symbolic function: by sanctioning deviants, the agents mark the moral limits of the social order. The definition of what is orderly and what is disorderly reflects the interests of those groups and institutions which influence the processes of rule creation and social control policy. Thus the social control agents' activities are normally consistent with the interests of the politically powerful; they are in conflict with deviants who threaten those interests.[3]

Piracy is interesting to sociologists because it is an exception to this general rule. Rather than threatening the interests of the powerful, English pirates frequently had and generally required the support of the politically powerful. The patterns piracy took changed over time, but the activity flourished only when it served the interests of the elite.

Before examining the types of support piracy received from the elite, it will be necessary to define piracy and related forms of activity, and to identify the circumstances under which piracy develops.

During the period being studied, an occasion when one ship was captured by another was subject to several interpretations depending upon certain circumstances. Such an incident could, for example, be viewed as an act of war, so long as the captors fit several criteria: they were part of a national navy, financed by the government, manned by sailors paid by that government, and sailing under the control of official orders during a period when a state of war existed between their government and that of their captives. Acts of warfare are legitimate exercises, and they can be contrasted with acts of piracy. Pirates may be defined as manning privately financed vessels with no legitimate right to capture their prizes.

While it seems easy to distinguish between acts of war and piracy, there were at least two other circumstances under which ships could be captured, and they were particularly important since they are similar to both warfare and piracy in important ways. Privateers were privately financed and controlled, but they had official permission to attack specified targets. Privateers might be commissioned during wartime with licenses to attack enemy shipping, or they might be commissioned during times of peace to attack pirates or to redress some private affairs in which the privateers had been victimized.[4] On other occasions, when governments required more control over a voyage than privateering allowed, semi-official expeditions were organized. Here the government provided some of the financing— although the largest share remained in private hands—and the basic policy for the expedition. In 1585, when Drake raided the West Indies, Elizabeth had provided nearly one third of his financing, and Drake acted as her admiral under official instructions.[5] Thus, attacks at sea could involve acts of war, piracy, privateering, or semi-official aggression, depending upon the financing of the captors and the authorization under which they operated.

It is important to qualify this set of categories in two ways. First, the line between piracy and the various legitimate forms of attack was not always clear. Privateers, for example, might choose to seize a prize when the opportunity presented itself, even when their target did not fall into the category of ships they were authorized to attack. Merchantmen, armed against piracy, could find themselves strong enough to take prizes of their own, albeit illegally. Sometimes privateering expeditions were mounted with the intention of using the license as a cover for piracy. When James I attempted to eliminate piracy by licensing privateers to capture pirate vessels, Sir Thomas Rowe noted that the licenses were "a Common Pretence of beeing Piratts."[6] Thus the categories established above are adequate only so long as they are used to judge individual encounters at sea; at various times the same ship and crew might fall into any of the categories and in particular, they might drift from privateering to piracy and back again during the course of a voyage. As a second qualification, it is important to appreciate that the various legitimate designations for aggressive activity were not always ratified by the victims of the attack. Victims were particularly likely to view privateering as piracy. In the New World, Spain defined all foreign intrusions, including smuggling, as acts of piracy.[7]

Piracy, then, can not be neatly separated from other forms of aggression. Whether a specific naval encounter should be labelled an act of piracy was often a matter of debate—both for contemporaries and for later historians. The label selected depended upon the distribution of political power at the time of the act; as the location of power shifted, so did the ways in which aggressive acts were defined. Between 1550 and 1750, it is possible to identify three forms of piracy practiced by Englishmen: the long-range missions of the late sixteenth century; the buccaneering expeditions of the seventeenth century; and the outlaw piracy of the early eighteenth century. An examination of each of these forms reveals that the definition of piracy reflected the degree to which pirates had the support of politically powerful groups.

Any form of piracy requires manpower, targets, and a reasonably safe area for operations.[8] From 1550 to 1750, manpower was easy to come by; sailors discontented with the harsh life on naval and merchant ships were attracted to the more democratically run pirate vessels. Moreover, many men who were trained as sailors or privateers during the wartime found themselves unemployed during times of peace; their skills prepared them well for piracy. Targets were also easily available in any of the well-traveled shipping lanes, and until the late seventeenth century, European navies were unable to patrol the New World effectively enough to endanger most pirates.[9] A fourth factor was more important than the first three in dictating the shape of piracy—pirates needed a base. Ideally the base was a port, where supplies could be purchased, repairs undertaken, and prizes sold. At a minimum, a safe landfall was required for supplying the vessel with fresh water, cleaning the hull, and making repairs. Obviously, pirates operating out of ports needed better connections with people on shore than those who occasionally landed at isolated islands. These connections are what gave piracy in a given period its character.

In Elizabethan England, piracy was well-connected with the most powerful elements in English society. The Crown, government agencies, and the gentry and merchants all supported illegal activities at sea, particularly those directed at Spanish shipping. During the tense years before war broke out, both privateers and unauthorized raiders sailed from English ports. Much of their raiding took place in European waters,[10] but the most famous expeditions were attempts to break the Spanish monopoly in the New World through trade—or theft. Although many of the attacks on these long-range missions were technically illegal acts of piracy, they were tolerated and even encouraged because they were in the national interest.

Drake's 1572-73 raid on the West Indies is probably the best-known long-range mission. ". . . Drake was allowed to sail without direct governmental help but certainly with the friendly connivance of the authorities" in two ships obviously equipped for warfare. Although he did not hold a privateer's commission, Drake assumed that the poor relations between England and Spain justified his attacks. After a series of minor raids, the climax of the voyage came when Drake and the French corsairs with whom he had joined forces robbed three mule trains carrying Spanish treasure. His return to England was triumphant; Drake became a popular hero in spite of the raid's illegality.

The English rivalry with Spain was based in part on religious differences and conflicting interests in Europe and the New World. Since Spain was the more powerful state, able to draw on greater resources, Elizabeth was forced to adopt those tools that were available to her. In particular, she encouraged unlicensed attacks such as Drake's as well as privateering and semi-official naval expeditions against Spanish shipping in both Europe and the New World. This policy had several advantages. First, it maximized the return on the limited funds available to the Crown. Unable to fund a large national navy, Elizabeth used privateers to provide a protective network around England and to carry out offensive measures against Spain.[12] Since privateering commissions frequently gave the Crown a share in the profits of the enterprise, the attacks also generated revenue for the state. Second, these missions demanded the attention and resources of Spain. English attacks drained away Spanish resources by forcing Spain to replace lost ships and goods. Further, they affected Spanish policy; Gerhard suggests that Spain neglected the development of the west coast of New Spain because it would have been too costly to build adequate defenses against piracy. Third, the English activities served as a symbolic source of unity. Although the Spanish defined all excursions by other nations in the New World as piracy, and although some voyages were undertaken without official commissions and were technically illegal, and the attacks mounted by some of the privateers and semi-official expeditions exceeded their commissions (and can therefore be seen as piratical), Hawkins, Drake, and other leaders of long-range missions became national heroes, honored by both the people and the state. The Crown, then, used long-range missions of dubious legality as a tool of national policy.[13]

The government agencies charged with the conduct of maritime affairs also supported piracy. These agencies collected the duties on prize-goods as well as that share of the prizes used to fund the navy, and therefore had an interest in promoting the operations of privateers. While charged with the regulation of privateering through their control over the distribution of licenses and their authorization to demand restitution for prizes taken under illegitimate circumstances, the agencies' powers were actually limited. Privateers sometimes refused to pay the restitution charges levied against them, and licenses were acquired through the use of fronts, so that there was no effective control over their distribution. Moreover, since many of the individuals involved in privateering were powerful, the agencies found it necessary to compromise their dealings in order to avoid the anger of the Crown and its favorites. Privateers who exceeded their commissions as well as outright pirates could afford to bribe officials when their voyages were financed by wealthy investors. This was certainly the case when the officials themselves backed pirate enterprises, as in the case of Sir John Killigrew, the Commissioner for Piracy in 1577.[14] The government agencies then, often found it easier to support piracy than to bring it under control.

The gentry and merchants also supported piracy by providing financial backing for most expeditions. These men combined political power and influence, prestige, and great wealth. They were motivated by individual combinations of three motives: patriotism, puritanism, and profit. The long-range missions were clearly tied to English interests; a privateer who exceeded his commission could be seen as a patriot rather than a criminal so long as he selected Spanish targets. The Protestant gentry, who saw the struggle with Spain in religious terms, were particularly likely to support the attacks.[15] And raiding was profitable; expeditions might be mounted purely for the purpose of capturing prizes, or ordinary merchant voyages might combine trade with fortuitous opportunities for plunder. The returns on investing in piracy gave merchants the capital to finance other, more legitimate enterprises, and their new wealth gave the promoters access to other honors, including peerages. As Raleigh noted, piracy was a label used for small, rather than great thefts.[16] Because piracy offered so much satisfaction, and because the men who backed it were effectively invulnerable from government sanctions, the practice of investing in and even leading expeditions flourished among the wealthy and powerful gentry and merchants.

In the late sixteenth century, the rivalry between England and Spain led the government, the investors, and the sailors to ignore the nice distinctions between piracy and privateering or semi-official voyages. While there were ordinary pirates operating during this period without support from the Crown, the government agencies, and the gentry and merchants, the best-known and most profitable long-range missions had this support in spite of their illegality.

By the middle of the seventeenth century, piracy in the New World had been broken as the other European powers established their own colonies. Since the European governments could not afford to provide adequate naval patrols to protect their colonies, and since government policies, such as restrictions on trade, were often contrary to the colonists' interests, the colonies tended to develop their own foreign policies. Frequently these policies emphasized raiding the shipping and towns of rival colonies, even at times when their European governments were at peace. The limited naval patrols, the increased amount of commerce, and the presence of the buccaneers, "masterless men-marooned or ship-wrecked sailors, deserters, escaped felons, runaway intended servants, and all such as disliked organised society," provided ideal conditions for piracy. Piracy became a major tool of colonial policy, supported by the colonial governments, colonial merchants, and, with less enthusiasm, the European governments. Piracy was an important colonial industry, based at such colonial outposts as Tortuga, Port Royal, and later Nassau.[17]

Henry Morgan, the most famous buccaneer, provides an excellent example of official support. In 1668-69, he attacked Puerto Principe, Puerto Bello, and Maracaibo. In each of these raids, he had the support of Jamaica's Governor, Sir Thomas Modyford, who commissioned Morgan, provided him with at least one major ship, and defended his exploits to England. Ordered to gather intelligence in Cuba, Morgan used his commission to justify seizing Puerto Principe. Claiming that he had learned of a pending Spanish attack, he convinced Modyford to sanction the infamous assault on Puerto Bello as a means of disrupting the enemy. Upon his return to Port Royal, Morgan prepared for the Maracaibo attack and "the Governor threw no obstacles in his way, for he fully realized that his acceptance of what had been nothing less than an open act of war against Spain must be followed up at once before he could be disavowed from England." Although Morgan was a known pirate of great cruelty who frequently ignored his instructions, Modyford used him as an agent to carry out illegitimate raids.[18]

Modyford was not alone; supporting piracy was expedient for many colonial governors. In most cases, they lacked the power to eliminate piracy; at best, pirates could be driven from the colony's ports. But there was always the risk that these exiles would choose to join a rival colony's forces; there were instances of English pirates responding to abolition campaigns by switching allegiance to the French or Portuguese.[19] A safer policy was to accept the buccaneers as mercenaries, commissioning them as privateers, using them to mount expeditions against other colonies, and not asking too many questions about their methods or the legitimacy of the prizes they brought into port. Colonial governors, such as Modyford and Colonel Benjamin Fletcher of New York, recognized that piracy brought both profits and protection to their colonies. Given the circumstances, it was better to be for the pirates than against them.[20]

101

Colonial merchants also understood the advantages of supporting piracy. While they recognized that the elimination of piracy might bring about increased trade and profits in the long-run, it was difficult to ignore the short-term advantages of cooperating with the pirates. The pirates' prizes carried goods which were otherwise difficult to obtain, and they could be purchased from the captors on favorable terms. Pirates back from a successful raid were desirable customers; Esquemeling describes the behavior of L'Ollonais' men after a raid in which each earned more than one hundred pieces of eight:

> For as to the common Pirates, in three weeks they had scarce any money left them; having spent it all in things of little value, or at play either at cards or dice . . . Thus they made shift to lose and spend the riches they had got in much less time than they were purchased by robbing. The taverns, according to the custom of Pirates, got the greatest part thereof . . .[21]

The greatest profits to merchants did not come from either buying stolen goods or catering to pirate customers but lay in sponsoring pirate voyages. As in sixteenth century England, major colonial merchants in the seventeenth century invested in the expeditions of pirates. The "Red Sea trade"—pirate voyages to the Indian Ocean—provided investment opportunities for New York merchants in the late seventeenth century. Given the profits piracy offered, the merchants' support is not surprising.[22]

The English government adopted a more ambivalent view of piracy during this period. On the one hand, it recognized piracy's uses as a tool. Pirate raids on a rival colony could be useful, particularly since the raids could be disavowed even as their fruits were being enjoyed. The government's approval is reflected in decisions to grant colonial governors the power to commission known pirates, or to pardon pirates for past crimes. On the other hand, the pirates' raids could embarrass the government, particularly during those periods when it was attempting to establish better relations with Spain. The decisions of distant governors, or even sailors, to attack a rival colony could frustrate the government's foreign policy. This ambivalence is nicely expressed in Morgan's life; the notorious buccaneer was knighted and ended his career as Lieutenant Governor of Jamaica under instructions to stamp out piracy.[23]

The buccaneers' greatest impact was felt during the second half of the century, when their raids were most frequent:

> At no other time in Western history can a few thousand desperados have created a reign of terror over so vast an area, or have exercised so great and so continuous an influence upon the policy of civilised states. During the six years of Morgan's ascendancy, from [1665 to 1671], they had sacked eighteen cities, four towns, and nearly forty villages . . . and this fearful tale of outrage does not include the English expeditions

made after 1670, nor the still more wholesale depredations of the French. The development of the Greater Antilles as productive settlements was impossible while the buccaneers continued to receive support.[24]

Increasingly, the European governments recognized the buccaneers as embarrassments, endangering both their foreign policies and the development of their colonies. In response, the ineffectual attempts to abolish piracy developed into serious campaigns, supported by adequate naval patrols. After 1685, the pirates' traditional supports in Jamaica had been removed, and, with Governor Rogers' arrival at Nassau in 1718, the last of the pirate bastions in the West Indies disappeared. Instances of support continued in the North American colonies, particularly the Carolinas, but New York's "Red Sea trade" had been suppressed in 1697 when Governor Fletcher was replaced. Piracy had lost most of its powerful supporters; the European governments could no longer afford it, the colonial governors were now required to suppress it, and the merchants now found that it interferred with their more profitable legitimate trade.[25]

By the early eighteenth century, the circumstances under which pirates operated had changed. Increased naval patrols in Europe and the New World made the risk of capture greater. Warfare was increasingly conducted by the regular navy, or by privateers who were carefully supervised so that the services of the buccaneers were no longer needed. More and more ports were closed to pirates. The effect of these changes was to make piracy a riskier enterprise.[26]

In response to the loss of their powerful supporters, the pirates were forced to adopt a new form of piracy. With the notable exception of Madagascar, there were no longer stable pirate bases. Pirates were less likely to sail to ports; privateering commissions for known pirates were difficult to obtain, and the people were more likely to refuse to deal with pirates. Without ties to any nation or colony, the pirates became indiscriminant in their choices of targets; shipping under all flags was raided. Without the support of powerful agents, the pirates became in fact what they had always been in theory—outlaws.

A portion of the voyages of Captain Bartholomew Roberts (who was described by Defoe as typical of pirates in this period) illustrates the problems with this form of piracy. At one point Roberts and a few men found themselves on a small vessel in the West Indies. They took two sloops for "Provisions and other Necessaries," and shortly after robbed a ship of clothing, food, powder, cable, and a hawser as well as goods and money. They sailed to Barbadous, but the Governor sent out a galley to attack them. They escaped from the battle by outrunning the galley—but only after throwing some guns and goods overboard to lighten their vessel. At Dominico, they watered and traded goods for provisions. Sailing to

Carriaco, they cleaned their ship and then left just ahead of two French sloops sent to attack them from Martinico. A voyage to Newfoundland followed, where they acquired a new ship, several prizes, and more supplies. Back in the West Indies, they laid in wait of ships to rob for supplies, but failing to sight anyone, they sailed to St. Christophers where they were refused entry. However, they were welcomed at St. Bartholemew and acquired more provisions. Changing ships again, they attempted to sail for the coast of Africa.[28]

This brief summary describes some of the constraints facing outlaw pirates. Without a base in a port, supplies had to be taken from prizes. Without the protection of a colonial administration, the pirates had to be prepared to fight the increased patrols from several colonies. The danger of being found by a patrol encouraged the pirates to roam the sea from continent to continent. The outcome of the voyage was also likely to be unhappy; Roberts was eventually killed in battle, his crew captured and hanged—a fate shared by many of the outlaw pirates described by Defoe.[29]

Eighteenth century pirates were not completely without support from powerful agents. Roberts was welcomed at some of the ports where he called, and other pirates were able to find occasional governors who were willing to permit trade with them and who might supply a privateering commission. Merchants sometimes traded with pirates by sending supplies on ships, purportedly on trading voyages, which were "taken" by the pirates. Pirates required and were presumably able to find receivers for the goods they stole. Pirates continued to operate, but their operations were more difficult and probably less profitable without the support of powerful groups and institutions.[30]

In summary, piracy took on different forms depending upon the degree of support it received from powerful groups and institutions. Some supporters could be found throughout the period from 1550 to 1750; merchants were willing to profit from illicit trade with pirates, and governments were careless enough in granting commissions to keep the line between piracy and privateering hazy. In 1585, Sir George Carey lobbied to have Flud, a known pirate, commissioned as a privateer, and nearly 135 years later some of the privateers, "who behaved so bravely against *Blackbeard*, went afterwards a Pyrating themselves."[31] But the trend was toward reduced support. The long-range missions of the sixteenth century pirates were supported in English ports, until the government's desire to improve relationships with other European powers led to tighter supervision. During the seventeenth century, the buccaneers flourished in the New World until the European governments found it necessary to devote resources to policing their colonies. By the eighteenth century, support was sporadic and the outlaw pirates found it more and more difficult to operate.

Piracy required the protection and support of the powerful. The elite promoted piracy by offering safe harbors, a market for stolen goods, and privateering licenses because the pirates provided useful services. Pirates attacked the shipping and settlements of rival nations, and brought financial profit to their supporters. It was a symbiotic relationship: the pirates needed support to flourish, and the powerful found the pirates useful. For the elite, piracy was a policy, albeit one which could not be openly acknowledged; the government more often found it necessary to excuse piracy than to justify it. The Crown was more likely to respond to complaints by denying direct responsibility for expeditions or by accusing its rivals of supporting pirates of their own, than to justify the illegal actions of English pirates.[33] The pirates were most useful when their links to the powerful were least obvious.

Although this paper has focused on English piracy in the New World, the relationship of piracy to powerful interests may be found in other settings. Mediterranean piracy shows a similar pattern of government support, frequently exceeded privateering commissions, and ports dependent on the trade of pirates.[34]

This relationship with powerful supporters separates piracy from other forms of deviance. In most cases of theft, there are three actors: the thief, the victim, and the social control agent. Normally, the victim and the social control agent have compatable interests which bind them together in the common cause of sanctioning the thief. Piracy, however, finds a different alliance, one between the thief and the social control agent. The government permits the pirate to operate in return for the services the pirate provides by serving as an informal navy and by providing income in the form of taxes, bribes, and returns on the investments of the regime's most powerful supporters.

Piracy is not the only example of deviance as a political tool of the elite. Although political deviance is most often defined as radicalism, corruption, or the abuse of official power,[35] it is possible to find other examples of career deviants being used to further the ends of the powerful. Blok argues that bandits in agrarian societies often have the support of landlords because, as retainers:

> they serve to prevent and suppress peasant mobilization in at least two ways: first, by putting down collective peasant action through terror; second, by carving out avenues of upward mobility which, like many other vertical bonds in peasant societies, tend to weaken class tensions.[36]

Pearce suggests that labor racketeering by organized crime was sponsored by industries which found the gangsters less threatening than social movements within the unions.[37] The recent revelations that intelligence agencies have chosen to support the Asian heroin traffic and consulted with mobsters about assassination plans continue the theme in current politics.[38] In each of these cases, deviance is fostered by the powerful because it serves their interests.

These cases of deviance being sponsored by an elite seem to have some underlying similarities. For such sponsorship to occur, three necessary conditions must be met: there must be an external threat to the elite; the consequences of the deviance must be consistent with the elite's interests; and there must be sufficient unity within the elite.[39] Each of these conditions merits further examination.

First, before deviance will be sponsored, members of an elite must perceive themselves to be threatened from the outside. This threat must be potentially serious, and the threatening agency cannot be subject to routine social control efforts. International conflict is an example of such a threat: in the case of Elizabethan piracy, the threat was posed by Spain; later, Spanish colonies threatened English colonies in the New World. The need to respond to the threat provides the elite with a motive for supporting deviance.

Second, deviance will not be sponsored unless its effects are consistent with the interests of the elite in responding to the threat. Obviously, elites have no reason to support deviants unless their deviance provides some service. Powerful groups and institutions supported piracy because it injured their enemies, protected their communities, and provided them with handsome profits. Although the deviance must be consistent with the elite's interests, this may be publicly denied by the elite, particularly if acknowledgement would exacerbate the conflict with the threatening force. In these cases, deviance may be denounced, even as it is being promoted, for the value of supporting deviance lies partly in its convenience—the threat can be met without openly acknowledging the conflict.

Third, there must be enough internal unity among the elite to provide adequate support for the deviance to flourish while at the same time maintaining secrecy regarding the support. Discretion is necessary or open conflict may develop. Normally the elite can not afford the embarrassment of being publicly linked to the deviants. Thus the Crown found it most convenient to be able to deny supporting the buccaneers, secure in the knowledge that its claims would not be contradicted by other members of the elite who also profited from piracy. Recent history offers an obvious example of the consequences of failing to maintain this discipline.

It has been argued that piracy requires manpower, targets, and safe areas of operation if it is to exist. However, if piracy is to flourish, there is a fourth requirement: it must have the support of the elite. This sponsorship will develop under conditions of outside threat, consistent with interests, and internal unity within the elite.

106

To conclude, unlike most deviance, piracy depends upon the support of powerful groups and institutions. Although isolated raiders can operate without this support, large-scale piracy requires it. The history of English piracy from 1550 to 1750 reflects the changing pattern of support. In the late sixteenth century, the illegitimate acts of the long-range missions gave England an advantage in its struggle with Spain. While European waters were under effective naval control a century later, the buccaneers were an important force in the New World. The extension of naval control to the Western Hemisphere at the start of the eighteenth century eliminated piracy's most prominent supporters, and, as outlaws, pirates found it increasingly difficult to operate. The decline of piracy was a consequence of the elimination of piracy as a form of elite policy.

Piracy, then, deserves to be seen in a sociological context. The relationships of pirates with governments and merchants shape their actions. Further, the support of these elite members is predictable: it will develop under conditions of external threat, consistent interests, and internal unity. Thus the apparent freedom of the swashbuckling pirate existed only within several constraints of the larger social web.

FOOTNOTES

[1] Some exceptions are Kenneth R. Andrews, *Elizabethan Privateering: English Privateering during the Spanish War, 1585-1603* (Cambridge, 1964); James G. Lydon, *Pirates, Privateers, and Profits* (Upper Saddle River, N.J., 1970); and B. R. Burg, "Legitimacy and Authority: A Case Study of Pirate Commanders in the Seventeenth and Eighteenth Centuries," *American Neptune,* 37 (1977): 40-49, and "Pirate Communities in the Seventeenth Century: A Case Study of Homosexual Society," unpublished paper.

[2] For basic works on deviance, see: Howard S. Becker, *Outsiders: Studies in the Sociology of Deviance* (rev. ed.; New York, 1973); John Lofland, *Deviance and Identity* (Englewood Cliffs, N.J., 1969); and Earl Rubington and Martin S. Weinberg, eds., *Deviance: The Interactionist Perspective* (2nd ed.; New York, 1973).

[3] On the relationship between deviance, social control, and elite interests, see: Joel Best, "Moral Change: A Study of the Invention and Vindication of Deviance," (unpublished Ph.D. dissertation, University of California, Berkeley, 1971); Kai T. Erikson, *Mayward Puritans: A Study in the Sociology of Deviance* (New York, 1966); Joseph R. Gusfield, *Symbolic Crusade: Status Politics and the American Temperance Movement* (Urbana, Ill., 1966); Douglas Hay, "Property, Authority, and the Criminal Law," in Hay, *et al.,* *Albion's Fatal Tree: Crime and Society in Eighteenth-Century England* (New York, 1975), pp. 17-63; Martin Loney, "Social Control in Cuba," in Ian Taylor and Laurie Taylor, eds., *Politics and Deviance* (Harmondsworth, 1973), pp. 33-60; Frank Pearce, *Crimes of the Powerful: Marxism, Crime and Deviance* (London, 1976); Stephen J. Pfohl, "The 'Discovery' of Child Abuse," *Social Problems,* 24 (1977): 310-23; and David J. Rothman, *The Discovery of the Asylum: Social Order and Disorder in the New Republic* (Boston, 1971).

[4] For example, in 1585, Spain confiscated some English vessels. Those English merchants who could give proof of their losses were eligible for licenses from the Lord Admiral to attack Spanish shipping. Andrews, *Elizabethan Privateering,* 3.

[5] Ibid., 5.

[6] M. Frank Craven, "The Earl of Warwick: A Speculator in Piracy," *Hispanic American Historical Review,* 10 (1930), 458.

[7] Peter Gerhard, *Pirates on the West Coast of New Spain, 1575-1742* (Glendale, Calif., 1960), 13. Since victims are typically allowed to define deviance, and since social control agents usually ratify their definitions, the Spanish perspective needs to be taken seriously.

[8] Jay Barrett Botsford, "Piracy," *Encyclopedia of the Social Sciences* (1934) XII, 137.

[9] Geoffrey W. Symcox, "The Battle of the Atlantic, 1500-1700," *First Images of America: The Impact of the New World on the Old,* I, ed. Fredi Chiappeli (Berkeley, 1976), 266-267.

[10] Alberto Tenenti, *Piracy and the Decline of Venice, 1580-1615,* trans. Janet and Brian Pullan (Berkeley, 1967); David Mathew, "The Cornish and Welsh Pirates in the Reign of Elizabeth," *English Historical Review,* 39 (1924): 337-348.

[11] Arthur Percival Newton, *The European Nations in the West Indies, 1493-1688* (London, 1933), 88; Mendel Peterson, *The Funnel of Gold* (Boston, 1975): 135-153; Godfrey Fisher, *Barbary Legend: War, Trade and Piracy in North Africa, 1415-1830* (Oxford, 1957): 140.

[12] The use of privateers had limitations: they were not subject to overall, coordinated direction, and, since it was in their interest to enter only those engagements they could expect to win, their overall effect was likely to be harrassment, rather than open conflict.

[13] Andrews, *Elizabethan Privateering;* Gerhard, *Pirates.*

[14] Cyrus H. Karraker, *Piracy Was a Business* (Rindge, N. H., 1953), 37; Andrews, *ibid.,* 22-31; Mathew, "Cornish."

108

[15] Craven argues the gentry later deliberately violated the injunctions by James I against piracy in order to display their dissatisfaction with the King's efforts to come to terms with Spain. Craven, "Earl of Warwick," 478; Mathew, *ibid.*

[16] Craven, *ibid.*; Andrews, *Elizabethan Privateering*; Karraker, *Piracy.*

[17] J. H. Perry and P. M. Sherlock, *A Short History of the West Indies* (3rd ed.: London, 1971), 82; Symcox, "Battle," 266-267.

[18] Newton, *European Nations*, 265; Peterson, *Funnel*, 316-335; John Esquemeling, *The Buccaneers of America* (1893; rpt. New York, 1967), 130-131.

[19] C. H. Haring, *The Buccaneers in the West Indies in the XVII Century* (New York, 1910), 216; Newton, *European Nations*, 231.

[20] Newton, *ibid.*; Perry and Sherlock, *Short History*; Lydon, *Pirates.*

[21] Esquemeling, *Buccaneers*, 100.

[22] Lydon, *Pirates*, 37-45; Newton, *European Nations*, 230-239.

[23] Newton, *ibid.*; Symcox, "Battle," 266-267; Philip Lindsay, *The Great Buccaneer* (New York, 1951).

[24] Perry and Sherlock, *Short History*, 93-94.

[25] Symcox, "Battle," 266-268; Lydon, *Pirates*, 36-59; Newton, *European Nations*, 320-333; Peterson, *Funnel*, 387-396.

[26] Symcox, *ibid.*

[27] Daniel Defoe, *A General History of the Pyrates*, ed. Manuel Schonhorn (London, 1972).

[28] *Ibid.*, 215-218.

[29] *Ibid.*, 244.

[30] *Ibid.*, 218.

[31] *Ibid.*, 83; Andrews, *Elizabethan Privateering*, 3.

[32] For a somewhat different discussion of symbiosis in deviance, see George J. McCall, "Symbiosis: The Case of Hoodoo and the Numbers Racket," *The Other Side*, ed. Howard S. Becker (New York, 1964), 51-54.

[33] On the importance of the distinction between excuses and justifications, see Marvin B. Scott and Stanford M. Lyman, "Accounts," *American Sociological Review*, 33 (1968): 46-62.

[34] Fernand Braudel, *The Mediterranean and the Mediterranean World in the Age of Philip II*, II (New York, 1973), 865-891; Fisher, *Barbary Legend*; Tenenti, *Piracy.*

[35] Jack D. Douglas and John M. Johnson, eds., *Official Deviance* (New York, 1977).

[36] Anton Blok, "The Peasant and the Brigand: Social Banditry Reconsidered," *Comprehensive Studies in Society and History*, 14 (1972), 499-500.

[37] Pearce, *Crimes*, 131-146.

[38] Alfred W. McCoy, *The Politics of Heroin in Southeast Asia* (New York, 1972).

[39] For an analogous explanation of productivity in witchhunting agencies, see Elliott P. Currie, "Crimes without Criminals: Witchcraft and Its Control in Renaissance Europe," *Law and Society Review*, 3 (1968): 7-32.

109

Crime as Disorder: Criminality and the Symbolic Universe of the 18th Century British Naval Officer

Arthur N. Gilbert

University of Denver

British army and navy justice in the eighteenth century focused on the overwhelming desertion problem in both services.[1] During the American Revolution, for example, over 50 percent of all crimes tried at the Army General Courts Martial level and close to 61 percent of all capital sentences imposed were for desertion and related offenses.[2] In the navy, the percentage of desertion and related offenses was somewhat less—39 percent—as was the comparable death sentence figure of 28 percent.[3] Therefore, in both forces desertion was the major preoccupation of the judicial systems.

In spite of this shared concern, there were important differences between army and navy justice. These differences illuminate and highlight the nature of both branches of the armed forces, although in this essay the emphasis will be on the naval justice system. The peculiar qualities of naval life, in large measure dictated by the isolation and the dangers of going to sea in the age of sailing ships, shaped a legal system which differed sharply from *any* land-based counterpart.[4] While there are many facets of naval justice worth exploring, perhaps none is as interesting as what might be termed "crime as disorder." This term can be understood by examining some significant differences between the legal concerns of the two services. This paper will deal with that concept as revealed in the treatment of the crimes of drunkenness, buggery, disrespect and disobedience, and mutiny. From this examination, it should be possible to consider the symbolic universe of the 18th century British naval officer.

Drinking, often to excess, was a problem in both the army and the navy. General Courts Martial trials in the army were filled with references to drinking. Soldiers frequently found the courage to desert at the bottom of a bottle of gin or innocently wandered off or fell asleep in a drunken stupor only to find themselves legally guilty of desertion when sobriety returned. The army would not allow a plea of drunkenness as an excuse for the breach of any law but, at the same time, it rarely included intoxification as part of the formal charge. During the Seven Years War, for example, the army indicted only one soldier for drunkenness and court-martialled only one officer.[5] In the navy, by contrast, the General Courts Martial records are filled with reports of sailors, particularly from midshipmen on up, who stood trial for drunkenness or, more commonly, drunkenness and another crime. For example, in one year, 1760, one lieutenant, four masters, a boatswain, a purser, and a carpenter were charged with excessive drinking.[6] During the American Revolution, the army held no trials for drunkenness, while in the navy, drunkenness was mentioned in General Courts Martial records ninety-seven times.[7].

To understand this discrepancy, it is essential to understand the "total" nature of naval life. As Erving Goffman and others have noted, total institutions impinge upon privacy because the dynamics of these organizations cannot allow for the individual to maintain a sphere of autonomy outside of the all-consuming institutional structure.[8] In the navy, in particular, it was not easy to draw lines between legitimate private matters and the larger interests of the shipboard community. Certain acts, which on land were relatively harmless, on shipboard could have been disastrous. On land, an occasional drunken spree did not threaten the community as a whole, but aboard ship a sailor who could not perform his duties because of an overdose of rum or gin jeopardized the whole community of mariners. The line between public and private deeds was blurred: an essentially private act on land assumed enormous social consequences on board a ship. The square-rigged vessel was a giant sea-going machine and, in battle and foul weather, the operations of the machine depended on skilled and alert personnel. Indeed, superior seamanship is often mentioned as the vital ingredient which gave the English navy its edge in combat with the French and Spanish navies in the eighteenth century.[9] Thus, drunkenness could mean disaster. Drunkenness meant a man—and, potentially, an entire ship—out of control.

Likewise, the navy showed little tolerance for another kind of disorder and loss of control—sexual deviance. Clearly, such behavior represented an assault on the order and discipline of the naval community. In comparison with the navy, Army General Courts Martial records show fewer cases of sexual deviance. This is understandable. The practicing homosexual was less likely to get caught on land because space was on his side. Between 1756 and 1763, for example, the army tried only four soldiers for crimes related to sodomy. In 1757, John Turnbull was convicted of "behaving in a sodomitical manner to John Frog" and given 1,000 lashes.[10] Two years later, Thomas Coterell stood convicted of attempted sodomy on a number of soldiers, for which he was drummed out of the service after receiving 500 lashes.[11] In 1762, Edward Minton and Simon Hoyle, stationed at Gibraltar, suffered 1,500 lashes after conviction of separate trials for bestiality with a cow.[12]

These sentences take on meaning only in comparison with the treatment of other criminals at the General Courts Martial level. It is significant that Minton and Hoyle were severely lashed, but *not hanged*, for bestiality. In fact, from 1700 to 1783, there are no records of soldiers sentenced to die for sodomy, and the Minton and Hoyle convictions took place in 1762, a year during which at least fifteen soldiers were condemned to death in the marching regiments for such crimes as murder, desertion, and robbery.[13]

Aside from the bestiality convictions, soldiers received sentences of 1,000 and 500 lashes. The lower figure comports with sentences imposed for sodomy and attempted sodomy by Army Courts Martial throughout the 18th century. A soldier named Hewett, for example, received only 300 lashes for an attempted sodomy conviction in 1747.[14] The army sentenced Edward Hammerton to 500 lashes for the same crime in 1782 and Job Lewes got the same number for his sodomy conviction in 1790.[15] These lashings were not excessive by 18th century standards. The average penalty for all crimes in the army from September 1761 through July 1762 was 778 lashes.[16] Later periods show averages well in excess of the penalties imposed for sodomy-related offenses. In 1779, for example, sentences averaged 827 lashes and in 1781, 823. In 1782, the year of Hammerton's conviction, the figure was 766.[17] From mid-century on, it was always above 600 per sentence.[18] By contrast with penalties for sodomy, the army was not at all reticent to assign the death sentence in rape cases. At least four soldiers were executed for this offense during the American Revolution.[19]

In the navy, detection of sexual deviance was certainly easier, but this hardly explains the severity of treatment for this offense at the General Courts Martial. During the Seven Years War, at least four men were condemned to death for sodomy.[20] In 1758, James Blake was hanged for sodomy and, in the following year, R. Chilton was executed after conviction of sodomizing one of the ship's boys.[21] Two years later, two seamen, Newton and Finney, were executed for consensual sodomy.

In 1761, the year of the Newton/Finney executions, navy boards handed down eleven death sentences: executions for sodomy represented 18 percent of that total.[22] In other years, no one was executed for sodomy, but the number of capital sentences for this offense must be examined in the light of the rarity of naval executions for *any* crime. Perennially short of men, the 18th century English navy used the lash liberally, but proved neither willing nor able to kill large numbers of seamen because each capital sentence

112

created a recruiting problem for the ship involved.[23] The very fact that the navy was willing to execute *anyone* for sexual deviance indicates its seriousness in the naval environment.

As in the army, lashing sentences show a great deal about the importance to the institution of particular crimes. During the Seven Years War, the navy's lash average for attempted sodomy and "uncleanliness" was 585.[24] The lash average for all other offenses was much lower. In 1760, an average of 270 lashes per sentence were given, and in 1761, the figure is 264—much lower than the figure for sexual deviance.[25] The most common naval crime, desertion, showed an average of 300 lashes per sentence in 1760-61.[26] The same pattern of extremely heavy lashing for attempted sodomy continued until the closing years of the Napoleonic Wars. During that conflict, the severest lash sentence delivered by a General Courts Martial occured in 1807, when George Shandoff and James Johnson of the *HMS Bellona* each received sentences of 1,000 lashes for attempted sodomy.[27]

A third set of crimes which had "disorder" as a major component were those offenses dealing with disrespect, disobedience, and the like. Once again, the army records show that crimes of this nature remained only marginally important; they seem to have been handled informally or at the level of a regimental courts martial. Almost all offenses of this sort handled in General Courts Martial during the American Revolution were confined to the officers' corps. The contrast with the navy is striking for, in addition to cases involving officers, there were 183 General Courts Martial in the 1776-1783 period which wholly or in part involved disrespect and disobedience.[28] Crimes of this nature took on meaning only in a rigid and hierarchical institution where knowing one's place and not questioning the chain of command were values of supreme importance.

In the navy, a sailor who, in a fit of anger, struck, or even attempted to strike, an officer was more likely than not to be sentenced to death. It was for this crime—not murder—that Billy Budd was sentenced to die in Melville's famous short story.[29] In the army, it was rare for a soldier to be tried by a General Court Martial for this offense. Once again, such crimes were probably handled informally by the officers involved or, at the very most, a soldier would have been tried by a regimental court and therefore protected from a death sentence. There were exceptions, of course. In 1761-62, three soldiers were convicted of striking an officer and two were sentenced to death.[30] In the same period in the navy, however, sixteen sailors were tried for this crime and fourteen were convicted, with six death sentences imposed.[31] From 1756 to 1806, there were 103 naval convictions for striking an officer and 72 capital sentences.[32] The conviction rate was 99 percent and of those convicted, 70 percent received capital sentences.[33] There was no crime in the navy which had a higher conviction rate. Striking an officer can be viewed as an extension of disrespect and disobedience—a violation of the hierarchical nature of the seagoing community and a violation of the order on which virtually everything depended.

The navy's concern with mutiny is too well-known to require elaboration. Suffice it to say that mutiny can be seen as another and very extreme form of loss of control. Once again, it was rare in the army for a man to be tried and executed for mutiny, whereas the navy treated mutineers very harshly and very often sentenced offenders to death. For example, during the American Revolution, only 16 soldiers were tried for mutiny, as against 198 mariners.[34] Only one soldier was capitally convicted of this crime in the entire 1776-1783 period. By contrast, the navy General Courts Martial boards handed down 100 death sentences for mutiny during the same years.[35]

A number of factors explain the difference between army and navy justice. Each branch of the service had its own code and the legal traditions of the army and navy also differed. Yet, military legal codes were loosely drawn documents, with a minimum of detail and without legal precedents to guide and influence decisions. If legal precedent was of minor importance, though, each service had an *oral tradition* that probably played a far greater role in determining which crimes were deemed most heinous. Equally significant was the fact that each legal system had functional value in its own environment. Of course, the problem of functionalism as applied to legal systems is that particular practices may be vestigal remains of another era with no apparent functional value in the community. In other words, law in theory and practice may be either disfunctional or irrelevant. Still, the imprecision, the sketchiness, and the lack of precedent in 18th century British military law suggest that officers enjoyed great leeway in applying the law and that they applied it according to the nature and extent of seriousness of the offense *to the organization*. Furthermore, since they viewed punishment as a deterrent and as an example to the military community, it seems reasonable to assume that crime and punishment statistics provide more accurate indicators of the fears and concerns of the officers than would be the case were punishment for its own sake of primary importance.

THE SYMBOLIC UNIVERSE OF THE NAVAL OFFICER

The *officers* in each service controlled the military justice systems of 18th century England. While some countries on the continent allowed enlisted men to serve on navy Courts Martial boards, this was not the case in Britain. Thus the question arises as to why naval officers were so particularly concerned with five specific crimes: drunkenness, sodomy, disobedience, striking an officer, and mutiny. The fears of these men can be best understood by an examination of the symbolic universe of the naval officer as it was formed and shaped by the environment at sea and by the common experience of all those men who attained positions of authority in the Royal Navy.

The naval ship symbolized the triumph of order, control, and will power over chaos and disorder. Officers who commanded the vessels were well aware of the thinness of the line that separated control from loss of control. Perhaps Herman Melville best summed up fear of disorder in the navy in *White Jacket:* "Were it not for regulations, a man o' war's crew would be nothing but a mob, more ungovernable stripping the canvas in a gale than Lord Gordon's tearing down the lofty House of Lord Mansfield."[36] Melville refers to two sources of disorder which, he claimed, taken together could lead to disaster. First, there was the disorder of nature, exacerbated at sea by storms; second there was the disorder of men who were no longer working together to counteract and defeat the worst chaos of nature. While concepts of discipline and good order were valued in the army as well as the navy, the army did not operate in the fickle and unstable environment of the world's oceans. A sudden storm simply lacked the same meaning on land as it did at sea where chaos might mean complete and utter destruction.

To the chaotic qualities of the oceans, tamed by a disciplined ship's crew, most particularly as it affected the naval officer. An examination of the career of a hypothetical midshipman who joined the Royal Navy in the eighteenth century illustrates this reality.

The midshipman usually began his career at a young and impressionable age, just at the beginning of adolescence. Horatio Nelson and Cuthbert Collingwood, for example, both became midshipmen at twelve years of age.[37] Although some were even younger when they joined the navy—William Bligh, for instance, was only seven years old—this was unusual.[38] An admiral, the Earl of Dundonald, wrote that he went to sea as a midshipman "at the mature age of seventeen and a half," but as his remark suggests, that was also unusual.[39] The average age of entry stood between twelve and fourteen years of age.[40]

Adolescence is a crucial time for value formation and the term "identity crisis" associated with these years has become a commonplace in sociology, psychology, and in psychohistory. Erik Erikson described it as a time of "role confusion," when problems of sexual identity can be acute.[41] In this psychological state, the adolescent develops what Erikson labels an "ideological mind," where "rituals, creeds, and programs" define both what is good and evil.[42] It is what he calls a kind of "second birth," when

> . . . each youth must define for himself some central perspective, some working unity, out of the effective remnants of his childhood and the hopes of his anticipated adulthood: he must detect some meaningful resemblance between what he has come to see in himself and what his sharpened awareness tells him others judge and expect him to be.[43]

Other studies have shown that the identity crisis of adolescence can lead to religious conversion and religious asceticism.[44]

While there may have been differences in the experiences of adolescent midshipmen, whether they served under lenient or harsh captains, the size of the ships and the areas of the world to which they sailed and the kinds of crews they encountered, the similarities are significant. Unfortunately, autobiographical accounts of shipboard life rarely mention the early years at sea. Comments in the surviving reminiscences are usually limited to anecdotes, some cursory remarks about family backgrounds, and statements as to how the young man entered the navy. Still, from accounts of 18th century naval life emerges a fairly good picture of the conditions which a young midshipman encountered aboard a warship. In his life of Viscount Exmouth, C. Northcote Parkinson wrote that all descriptions of sea life for the novice "agree in showing those days to have been of such sort as to form a period of hopeless slavery."[45] The new volunteer was lodged, by and large, on the orlop deck: a dark, dank, crowded hole which surely shocked a young man accustomed to the freedom and open spaces of land. He soon became very familiar with the lower deck conditions of which one observer, employing images of the underworld, wrote, "he can choose to live contentedly [below deck], need never trouble his head what lodgings are chalked out for him in the other world."[46]

The midshipman learned about filth, disease, and the pervasive stench of the lower deck. Of these, Donald MacIntyre wrote,

> The space is lit by candle lanterns which give but a dim, gloomy light; no special arrangements are made for ventilation, and the air is thick with the foul smells which linger everywhere between decks, compounded of stale bilge water, the sickly odor of dry rot in the timbers, of nearly 700 rarely washed bodies, with an overtone of stale cheese and rancid butter from the storerooms below.[47]

In addition to the "hellish" physical conditions which the young volunteer encountered upon boarding a ship for the first time, he was likely to be plunged into scenes of open and uncontrolled sexuality. "His shocked eyes," MacIntyre claimed, were "likely to take in scenes of unveiled debauchery, while his ears shirk from jokes and curses foul even by the standards of such a licentious age."[48]

The adolescent encounter with sexuality is often problematic in the best of circumstances. For the male, it is a time of great sexual desire, often combined with enforced continence. During this period, the midshipman found himself in an all male environment. True, there were occasional contacts with women, who sometimes accompanied mariners to sea. In port, prostitutes were welcomed aboard to satisfy the accumulated lusts of the seamen. Furthermore, there was always shore leave, which allowed the mariners some relief from their sexual repression as well as from shipboard order and discipline. There is no gauge as to how often midshipmen participated in shipboard orgies or sexual adventures ashore, but clearly contact with women was sporadic at best and during his formative period, the aspiring young officer found himself in an all male world. Moreover, the women he did encounter were women of "easy virtue," enforcing and reinforcing a perception of females neither flattering nor uplifting. Male companionship may well have seemed of a higher value in comparison, adding fuel to the sexual confusion of adolescence.

The all-male naval environment was also rigidly hierarchical. Up above were the living quarters of the ship's officers, with the captain aloof in his cabin on the quarter deck, which enjoyed access to sky and sun and from which he imposed discipline on the unruly masses below. The midshipman lived in a dichotomized world: order and discipline, imposed from above, and potential chaos and disorder dreaded from below. Above, the officers enjoyed comparatively luxurious quarters but below was the bilge, a stinking, disease-ridden bottom where the accumulated wastes of years at sea served as ballast. All of this was symbolic of the sharp lines between officers and men, order and chaos, heaven and hell. The midshipman lived in a purgatory between the two worlds—breathing the air of the lower and orlop decks and striving to escape to the "respectable" realm where lieutenants and captains walked with dignity and honor. Promotion in the navy was not merely a change in status and financial position; in a larger sense, it was movement from the bestial to the noble, from the worst to the best in man. There was probably no other environment where the lines between man as animal and man as aspiring toward God were drawn with such distinction and sharpness.

The midshipman suffered from further ambiguity which was a product of what might be termed "status anomaly": the gap between skill level and status. These upwardly mobile young men came into the navy without the skills of the older seamen whom they commanded. This situation probably produced anxiety in the young midshipmen who had only the power granted to them by their place in the naval hierarchy by which to measure their self-esteem. Understandably, this tension produced in these young men sometimes found expression in unusually cruel treatment of ordinary sailors. Midshipmen often flogged seamen—a brutalizing factor in itself—and were generally resented, even hated, by the ship's crew. One account, that of Jack Nastyface, illustrated how poor relations could be between the midshipmen and their crew:

> We had a Midshipman on board our ship of a wickedly mischievous disposition, whose sole delight was to insult the feelings of the seamen and furnish pretexts to get them punished. His conduct made every man's life miserable that happened to be under his orders. He was a

youth of not more than twelve or thirteen years of age: I have often seen him get on the carriage of a gun, call a man to him and kick him about the thighs and body, and with his feet would beat him about the head; and these, although prime seamen, at the same time dared not murmur. It was ordained, however, by Providence, that his reign of terror and severity would not last; for during the engagement he was killed on the quarter deck by a grape-shot, his body greatly mutilated, his entrails being driven and scattered against the larboard side; nor were there any lamentations for his fate! No! for when it was known that he was killed, the general exclamation was "Thank God we are rid of the young tyrant!" His death was hailed as the triumph over an enemy.[49]

Needless to say, not all crews so thoroughly detested all midshipmen, but in general, their reputations were not good. Perhaps these young men metamorphosed their own instinctual desires onto the ordinary seamen, who symbolized chaos, loss of control, and disorder—qualities that had to be stamped out in the self and in the community of mariners. In the language of psychology, the behavior of midshipmen toward the crew may have been an example of reaction formation: an attempt to deny and repress instinctual impulses, resulting in a compulsive desire for order and cleanliness which expressed itself in the need to control others.

When a midshipman became a lieutenant or captain, to a greater or lesser extent, he was marked by his earlier experiences. These experiences would make him aware of the thin line between the bestial and the noble in man in ways which would be virtually impossible to duplicate on land, where space softened the edges of this symbolic universe. Space meant flexibility and ambivalence which contrasted with the manichean vision likely to emerge from life on a sailing ship.

By contrast, the army had no equivalent to the world of the midshipman. The young army officer began his career as part of the officer's corps. He might enter the army as a cornet, but he was just as likely to enter as a lieutenant. In either case, from the start he was an officer and therefore free from the demands made on midshipmen to escape from the symbolic halfway house of the orlop deck. In addition, the young army officer could move freely in the larger civilian world. Leave was comparatively easy to obtain and, even while on duty, there would be constant interaction with non-military personnel—including respectable women. Indeed, throughout most of the eighteenth century, army units in England were quartered in local inns—a far cry from the decks of a man o' war.

Finally, isolation characterized the world of the naval officer. On land was the comfort of knowing that the larger society could be called upon to restrain chaos served as an antidote to disorder. Mutiny on land, for example, could be halted as the state brought its resources to bear on the violators: other military units could be readily brought to the scene to stamp out a revolt. At sea, there was no place to turn for help. As a result,

118

the naval justice system tried to nip disorder in the bud and to punish its manifestations with rigor.

Given the ship's symbolic qualities and its impact on the would-be officer in transit from amidships to the upper deck, there was an understandable equation of crime with disorder. Drunkenness, disrespect and disobedience, striking an officer, and mutiny were clearly attacks on good order which threatened the hierarchical order of the seagoing community which was required to preserve that community. For naval officers, these crimes served as particularly vivid reminders of the disorderly world of the lower deck which they had viewed from close quarters. However, their concern with sodomy requires further examination.

In the West, sodomy has always symbolized rebellion. It had been associated with witchcraft, heresy, and violation of what those in power viewed as the natural order of things. It was the cause of the destruction of Sodom and Gommorah, and it was common practice to accuse heretics and rebels of sodomitic practices of all kinds.[51] The sodomy accusations leveled against the Albigensians and the Knights Templar are two clear and well-known examples of this habit. The vessels of the Royal Navy, with their sharp cleavages between officers and common sailors, and with a physical environment which exaggerated the dichotomy between man as beast and man as aspirant to a higher world, together with the chaotic qualities of the ocean itself, made sodomy—the most "bestial" of all sexual acts by western standards—peculiarly abhorrent. It was a profound example of loss of control; and in that sense analogous to drunkenness, striking an officer, or mutiny. In the final analysis, it was closest of all to mutiny, for the distance between "moral mutiny" and the "real thing" was small. For the naval officer, the sodomite and the mutineer were in league with the devil in attempting to overthrow legitimacy and order.[52]

It may also have been true that the naval hierarchy sensed that homoerotic relationships, if allowed to flourish, could offer a competing set of values and loyalties to sailors whose absolute allegiance had to be to the ship and its captain. It is in the nature of total institutions to attempt to destroy competing groups and relationships which challenge the absolute power and value system of the primary organization. In this sense, sodomy perhaps was viewed as an indicator of potential homosexual bands which might subvert, much as would a band of mutineers, the power of the ship's captain.

Other evidence suggests that, in the minds of naval officers, disorder and criminality were one. There was the well-known preoccupation of officers with dirt, for example. Keeping the decks clean—"holystoning" them in the 18th century—and a thousand and one other housekeeping tasks were essential for reasons of health to keep the ship in good repair, but alone this does not explain their preoccupation with dirt. Indeed, some of the house-

119

keeping tasks actually harmed the sailors. Washing down the decks frequently caused moisture and dampness to seep into the quarters of the men, thus worsening living conditions and contributing to a variety of ailments. What, then, is the real rationale for the obsession with "cleanliness"?

Dirt, according to Mary Douglas, "is essentially disorder." She argues,

> There is no such thing as absolute dirt: it exists in the eye of the beholder. If we shun dirt, it is not because of craven fear, still less dread or holy terror. Nor do our ideas about disease account for the range of our behaviours in cleaning or avoiding dirt. Dirt *offends against order.* Eliminating it is not a negative movement, but a positive effort to *organize the environment.*[53]

In addition to waging war against dirt and, therein, disorder, it was common practice for naval officers to informally punish seamen for a crime called "uncleanliness."[54] Since uncleanliness was not ordinarily a General Court Martial offense, no formal charges or court minutes explain precisely what it comprised. It may have covered a failure to perform housekeeping tasks or undertake personal hygiene. It apparently included minor sexual lapses, such as masturbation and non-sodomitic sexual acts. Those few cases of uncleanliness tried at the General Courts Martial level almost always concerned such illicit sexual practices. In 1799, for example, George Read and Thomas Tattesell were acquitted of buggery but convicted of "an abominable uncleanness" and sentenced to 500 lashes apiece.[55] This was further evidence of the relationship between aberrant sexuality, dirt, and disorder. "Uncleanliness," Mary Douglas noted, "is matter out of place, we must approach it through order. Uncleanliness or dirt is that which must not be included if a pattern is to be maintained."[56] It is significant that there was no analogous crime in the British army.

Thus, naval officers developed and adopted at an early age rigidly defined conceptions of order, purity, cleanliness, and licit sexuality. Formed by the environment and experiences encountered at sea, they accounted in large part for the manner in which the Royal Navy defined criminality. The navy was not only at war with England's enemies, but also with dirt and disorder of all kinds. And only by understanding this symbolic university of the British naval officer can the nature of naval justice in theory and practice in the 18th century be grasped.

FOOTNOTES

[1] See Leon Radsinowitz, *The History of English Criminal Law*, 4 volumes: *The Movement for Reform*, Vol. I (London: Stevens and Sons, 1948); Douglas Hay, Peter Linebaugh, *et al.*, *Albion's Fatal Tree: Crime and Society in Eighteenth Century England* (New York: Random House, 1975); E. P. Thompson, *Whigs and Hunters: The Origins of the Black Act* (New York: Random House, 1975); and J. M. Beattie, "The Pattern of Crime in England, 1660-1800," *Past and Present* (February 1974).

[2] War Office Records, 71/84-71/97, Public Records Office, London. See Arthur N. Gilbert, "Military and Civilian Justice in Eighteenth Century England: An Assessment," *The Journal of British Studies* (forthcoming).

[3] Admiralty Papers 1/5307 1/5323, PRO.

[4] Michael Lewis, *A Social History of the Navy, 1793-1815* (London, 1960), p. 391.

[5] W.O. 71/69, Henry Butt Court Martial, 22 July 1761, and W.O. 71/47, Lt. Pomeroy Court Martial, 7 November 1761.

[6] Adm. 1/5299.

[7] Adm. 1/5307—Adm. 1/5323.

[8] Erving Goffman, *Asylums: Essays on the Social Situation of Mental Patients and Other Inmates* (Chicago: Aldine Pub. Co., 1962).

[9] See, for example, Arthur Bryant, *The Years of Endurance, 1793-1802* (London, 1942).

[10] W.O. 71/44.

[11] W.O. 71/45.

[12] W.O. 71/72.

[13] *Ibid.*

[14] W.O. 71/38.

[15] W.O. 71/66 and W.O. 71/95.

[16] W.O. 71/69 and W.O. 71/70.

[17] W.O. 71/88 and W.O. 71/91.

[18] See W.O. 71 Series.

[19] See Courts Martial of John Dunn and John Lusty, W.O. 71/82; Barth McDunough, W.O. 71/86, and John Fischer, W.O. 71/85.

[20] Adm. 12/26 *Courts Martial Digest.*

[21] Adm. 1/5300 and Adm. 1.5301.

[22] Adm. 1/5300.

[23] During the American Revolution, for example, there were 71 capital sentences in the Royal Navy out of 908 General Courts Martial for sailors below the rank of lieutenant. The capital conviction rate was 7.1 percent. In the army, by way of contrast, there were 142 death sentences out of 629 trials for a capital conviction rate of 22.5 percent. These naval figures omit one case in 1791 where 64 men were sentenced to death for mutiny. This was unusual—an aberration—and it is doubtful if the sentence was carried out.

[24] Adm. 1/5296 to Adm. 1/5302.

[25] Adm. 1/5299 and Adm. 1/5300.

[26] *Ibid.*

[27] Adm. 1/5383.

[28] Adm. 1/5307 to Adm. 1/5323.

[29] For a discussion of Billy Budd and Naval Law, see L.B. Ives, "Billy Budd and the Articles of War," in William T. Stafford, *Billy Budd and the Critics* (Belmont, California: Wadsworth Press, 1968).

[30] W.O. 71/69 and W.O. 71/70.

[31] Adm. 1/5299 and Adm. 1/5300.

[32] Adm. 12/22 to Adm. 12/28.

[33] *Ibid.*

[34] W.O. 71/82 to W.O. 71/96 and Adm. 1/5307 to Adm. 1/5323.

[35] Adm. 1/5307 to Adm. 1/5323.

[36] Herman Melville, *White Jacket or the World in a Man of War* (Boston: Dana Estes, 1892), p. 11. While Melville described the American navy, the British navy of the 18th century was quite similar and the observation is relevant.

[37] Oliver Warner, *The Life and Letters of Vice Admiral Collingwood* (London: Oxford University Press, 1968), p. 2; Carola Oman, *Nelson* (New York: Doubleday, 1946), p. 11.

[38] George MacKaness, *The Life of Vice Admiral William Bligh* (London: Angus and Robertson, 1951), p. 4.

[39] *Thomas, Tenth Earl of Dundonald, GCB, The Autobiography of a Seaman* (London: Richard Bentley, 1860), pp. 42-43.

[40] For example, Edward Pellew was thirteen, Edward Coddrington was thirteen, George Anson was fourteen, Richard Howe was fourteen, John Byng was thirteen, and his father, George, fourteen, on entering the navy. See also Michael Lewis, *The History of the British Navy* (London: Penguin Books, 1957), p. 155.

[41] Erik Erikson, *Childhood and Society* (New York: W. W. Norton, 1963), p. 262.

[42] *Ibid.*, p. 263.

[43] Erik Erikson, *Young Man Luther* (New York: W. W. Norton, 1962), p. 14.

[44] For example, see Michael Goodish, "Childhood and Adolescence among the Thirteenth Century Saints," in George M. Kren and Leon Rappaport, *Varieties of Psychohistory* (New York: Springer Publishing Company, 1976).

[45] C. Northcote Parkinson, *Edward Pellew, Viscount Exmouth, Admiral of the Red* (London: Metheum & Co., Ltd., 1934), p. 8.

[46] David Spinney, *Rodney* (London: George Allen and Unwin, 1969), p. 29.

[47] Donald MacIntyre, RN, *Admiral Rodney* (New York: W. W. Norton, 1962), p. 10.

[48] *Ibid.*

[49] See Henry Baynham, *From the Lower Deck: The Royal Navy, 1780-1840* (Barre, Massachusetts, 1970). pp. 59-60.

[50] On reaction formation, see Otto Fenichel, *The Psychoanalytic Theory of Neurosis* (New York: W. W. Norton, 1945), p. 151.

[51] Vern Bullough, "Heresy, Witchcraft and Sexuality," *Journal of Homosexuality*, Vol. 1, No. 2 (Winter 1974); Arno Karlen, "The Homosexual Heresy," *Chaucer Review*, Vol. 6, No. 1 (Summer 1971); and E. William Monter, *Witchcraft in France and Switzerland: The Borderlands during the Reformation* (Ithaca, New York: Cornell University Press, 1976), p. 197.

[52] See Arthur N. Gilbert, "Buggery and the British Navy, 1700-1861," *Journal of Social History* (Fall 1976), p. 89.

[53] Mary Douglas, *Purity and Danger: An Analysis of Concepts of Pollution and Taboo* (New York: Praeger, 1966), p. 2.

[54] Adm. 51/1561, Logbook of the *Surveillance*, 1806, for example.

[55] Adm. 12/26, *Courts Martial Digest.*

[56] Douglas, *op. cit.*, p. 40.

CHAPTER 11

Current Research on the Navy of Louis XIV: Problems and Perspective

Geoffrey Symcox

University of California at Los Angeles

Louis XIV's reign marks a critical epoch in French naval history.[1] This was the period in which France finally acquired a navy in the true sense of the term: a permanent fleet under centralized state control, endowed with the administrative and logistical underpinnings required to sustain it. For a time, in fact, Louis XIV's navy was the strongest in Europe, and in 1690 it defeated the combined English and Dutch fleets at Beachy Head, but after that it fell into increasingly precipitate decline. After 1694 during the Nine Years War, and again after 1704 in the War of the Spanish Succession, the French fleet no longer put to sea as an organized force; its administration and port facilities began to decay. By 1715 the whole edifice of naval might was close to total collapse. The naval history of Louis XIV's reign thus offers a picture of rise and decline that has always fascinated historians: how did France become a great naval power in the years between 1661 and 1690; why did this power subsequently wither and die?

To some degree the concept of this traditional architectonic structure which rose and fell needs to be re-shaped: it is a little too simple, too lacking in nuances. Recent historiography has begun to suggest that the navy's growth in the years before 1690 was marred by internal flaws and con-tradictions, whose impact was deferred until the Nine Years War and the War of the Spanish Succession revealed them with brutal clarity. It is in-creasingly evident, too, that the difficulties confronting the French navy in the later years of the reign were of a quite different order of magnitude from those that it had faced earlier on. From 1688 to 1713, with only a brief respite, the French navy was pitted against the combined forces of the two leading maritime states in Europe, whereas before it had only had to deal with them singly. Moreover, from the later 1680s the economic strength of the French state, which had provided the basic condition for the growth of naval power, was undermined by commercial recession, agricultural disasters and war taxation. Money could no longer be found to maintain the navy and rapid decline ensued.

The problem of naval finances—part of the wider problem of the crisis of state finance in the latter part of Louis XIV's reign—is thus a key element in any explanation of the decline and fall of French sea power after 1690. This much is clear, although as yet we possess only a generalized picture of how the navy's finances worked, and of the ills that afflicted them. The other key element for understanding how and why Louis XIV's navy declined is to be sought in the problem of manpower. Here again we are only at the beginning: we know that there was a desperate shortage of trained seamen from the 1690s onwards, but the reasons for this remain obscure. The two critical issues of money and manpower will therefore form the underlying theme of this essay. We shall deal with them first, and then move on to examine the naval administration, tactical and technical questions, concluding with the shift to privateering and the *guerre de course* that occurred from the 1690s onward.

FINANCES AND RECRUITMENT

Colbert's achievement as the virtual founder of the modern French navy has always preoccupied historians. This is deservedly so. Although the main lines of his work had been anticipated by some of his predecessors—notably Richelieu—Colbert rescued the navy from oblivion, made it a redoubtable fighting force, and established its administrative structure for a century and more. He created a new hierarchy of officials, dependent on himself as Secretary of State for the Navy. He overhauled the financial mechanisms, dockyards and warships, and he improved the procurement system.[2] Also, he instituted a new system of recruitment. But even though we can follow the main lines of these improvements, we are still a long way from appreciating the full extent of Colbert's achievement. Much remains obscure.

The most significant body of research on Colbert and his administration has been devoted to the system of recruitment that he instituted from 1668-9 onwards, the famous *Maritime Classes*. Modern research on the question really starts with the fine work of René Mémain in the 1930s, which provides a model for future investigations, although it focuses on the Department of Rochefort alone.[3] Since then Eugene Asher has examined the social impact of the system of *Classes* as one aspect of the reaction of French society to the demands of absolute monarchy in its widest sense.[4] Marc Perrichet's survey of the *Classes* in Britanny offers a quick key to understanding the system as a whole and to the kind of archival materials that it offers for study.[5] The system of *Classes* did not spring fully grown from Colbert's

124

mind. As Mémain has shown, the new Secretary worked through a number of experiments before settling on the final form. But it never really lived up to what was expected of it. Colbert's primary intention was to ensure that the fleet did not absorb all the available seamen, and that some men would always be left over to man fishing vessels and merchantmen. From about 1669, therefore, he issued orders to register all sailors on rolls (a formality which, Asher shows, they effectively evaded), and then to divide them into groups or *Classes*, to serve in rotation aboard the King's ships. The *Classes* not required by the fleet would be free—in theory at least—to serve in trade. This system functioned rather well in peacetime when the navy armed only small squadrons of warships, but in wartime when large numbers of sailors were needed the *Classes* broke down; there were never enough men for the fleet. At the outbreak of the Dutch War in 1672-3 Colbert had to revert to pressing men for the navy, irrespective of their designation in the system of *Classes*, while trade sank to a low level for want of merchant crews. The same scenario repeated itself in each succeeding war. Moreover the number of available sailors shrank at the moment when they were most desperately needed. From a peak of about 60,000 in the mid-1680s the numbers of men carried on the rolls dropped to just over 50,000 by 1696 and continued to fall thereafter—and these were paper figures.[6]

This crippling decline in manpower is attributable, in part at least, to the decrease in seaborne trade and fishing caused by almost constant warfare after 1688. The French navy did not train its sailors but drew from the pool of skilled manpower provided by the merchant marine. In wartime fewer merchantmen sailed, and fishing was much reduced—especially oceanic fishing off Newfoundland, that great nursery of seamen—so that the supply of trained men was not replenished in the normal way. The problem then became a vicious circle: the weakened fleet could not dominate the seas, so that trade and fishing declined still further; as a result fewer seamen were trained to replace those who died on active service or grew too old; as the supply of skilled seamen dwindled, the fleet was weakened still further, and so on. The system of *Classes* did not deal with this problem; it merely registered men and did not train them. The problem of actually creating a pool of trained seamen—as opposed to drafting those who learned their trade at sea—was not to be resolved until the nineteenth century.

Another vital factor causing the shortage of seamen would be the financial crisis that affected the navy after 1693-4. As the sailors' pay became more and more irregular—by the later years of the War of the Spanish Succession most sailors, dockyard workers and even officers had not been paid regularly for years—desertion and evasion of duty became more and more common. The two fundamental problems afflicting Louis XIV's navy—money and manpower—were thus intimately linked. Colbert's system of *Classes*, although a bold and innovative experiment, was at best a palliative for the insuperable problem of manning the fleet in wartime.

Colbert's other great achievement, again only a qualified success, was his attempt to place the navy's finances on a sound footing. The whole subject of naval finance has received less scholarly attention than its importance warrants, although it is not hard to see why: the fiscal records of the Old Regime are of such daunting complexity. The financing of Louis XIV's navy consequently remains an arcane and unexplored topic, and the only modern study devoted to it seems to be Henri Légoherel's work on the *Trésoriers-Généraux de la Marine*.[7] Légoherel points out that Colbert, as Controller-General of Finances, was admirably placed to restore the navy's financial base. He could ensure that the navy received the funds it needed, and he attempted to reduce fraud through a system of rigorous accounting. But he failed to translate personal control into permanent institutions, and when he passed from the scene in 1683, the old inefficiencies and frauds reappeared, becoming rampant under the stress of war. Colbert's son Seignelay, who was Secretary of the Navy from 1683 to 1690, no longer controlled the state finances, and so could not find the money to meet the navy's needs and maintain the momentum of development. Donald Pilgrim has recently shown that the resulting financial stringency was one of the causes of the navy's decline after about 1690; essential services were skimped on, and the logistical underpinning vital to long-term efficiency had to be neglected.[8] When the great wars broke out in 1688, the French navy, though outwardly impressive, was actually beset by serious internal weaknesses which soon impaired its fighting efficiency. The financial squeeze on the navy was to grow tighter through the 1690s, and would finally toll the knell of Louis XIV's navy during the War of the Spanish Succession.

ADMINISTRATION AND THE ROLE OF THE SECRETARIES

The lack of work on naval finances is paralleled by a similar shortage of studies devoted to other aspects of the administrative system established by Colbert to run his new fleet. But it is no longer possible to assert, as historians of Lavisse's generation did, that Colbert came to power with a clear, Cartesian plan of action, which he then implemented logically and systematically; current research, such as it is, shows him to have been far more of a pragmatist.

It is a revealing commentary on the state of scholarship in this area that we still possess no study of how Colbert actually took over the naval administration—a tortuous process that exemplifies his methods. He was in *de facto* charge of naval affairs from 1661, although titular control remained with Lionne and Le Tellier, the Secretaries of State who shared the two departments into which the naval bureau was divided. Operational command was separate and was exercised by the Admiral of France, the intractable duc de Beaufort. Until 1669 Colbert shared control of the navy in uneasy partnership with the other Secretaries; in March of that year he bought Lionne's share of the office and assumed undivided control. Shortly afterwards Beaufort's providential death allowed him to take over the Admiral's functions as well.[9] He cemented his achievement by obtaining the right of succession to the Secretaryship of the Navy for his son, Seignelay; only then was he in undisputed control and free to institute reforms.

The rather piecemeal character of Colbert's approach may be gauged from the fact that he did not abolish the old system of naval administration based on the local Admiralties.[10] All he could do was to bring them under his personal sway. To combat their inertia he set up a new series of officials and institutions directly dependent upon himself. These were the intendants and commissioners of the ports, and the *commissaires aux classes* who saw to recruitment. These maneuvers were in the best administrative traditions of the Old Regime—old institutions never died, but merely faded away. They were supplemented, and eventually (it was hoped) supplanted by new institutions more closely tied to the central authority. Behind the orderly facade of the new institutions, the old remained largely intact, with more than merely a residue of their original powers in this case. Thus, despite Colbert's rigorous personal control, the old office of *Trésorier-Général* retained its key role in naval finances, and after his death in 1683, reasserted itself.[11] Likewise, the Admiral remained the titular head of the navy, and in 1695 the office was reactivated for the comte de Toulouse when he came of age. This man resumed the direction of the coastal Admiralties, chaired the revived *Counseil des Prises,* commanded the fleet in action, feuded with the Secretary of the Navy (Jérôme de Pontchartrain), and finally headed the Council of the Navy which replaced that unfortunate Secretary in 1715.[12] In a certain sense, therefore, the naval history of the latter part of Louis XIV's reign can be written in terms of the reemergence of the old administrative system from the limbo to which Colbert had consigned it. The tension between the old and the new administrative systems forms a theme running through the entire reign; it is a theme which still awaits elucidation.

A cognate theme which would bear close attention is the pervasive influence of administrative dynasticism. It started at the top: as we have seen Colbert had tried to turn the navy into a family appanage, and the Pontchartrains who assumed direction of the navy in 1690 were far more successful. They retained control of the naval administration, with interruptions, for much of the next century. From these great ministerial dynasties a network of clients and relatives spread throughout the official hierarchy. The Bégons, who began as associates of Colbert, themselves formed a long-lived dynasty of naval administrators.[13] Many noble families, particularly Bretons, provided officers for the navy generation after generation.[14] Examination of this underworld of patronage and family ties is a formidable task, but it would give a profound insight into the way

127

in which the service *really* functioned, and led to an understanding of the obstacles to administrative and operational efficiency that were built into the very fabric of the navy.

Some comment should also be made on the role of Louis XIV's successive Secretaries of the Navy, and the place accorded to them in the historical literature. Colbert's achievement as the real founder of French seapower is undoubtedly impressive, but we can no longer afford to view it in the uncritical manner of earlier scholarship. The time has come to move beyond the cult of personality that gives Colbert, and to a lesser extent his son Seignelay, all the credit for the glories of Louis XIV's navy, while laying the blame for all its failures at the door of their successors, the two Pontchartrains, father and son. Recent work, with its emphasis on financial and institutional factors, and its attempt to place the navy in a social economic context, has begun to move away from the tradition of scholarship in which individual personalities bulked so large. My own research has made me realize how negative the historical verdict has been on the two Pontchartrains.[15] Louis de Pontchartrain (Secretary from 1690 to 1699) seems in fact to have been a conscientious and highly intelligent Secretary, whose failures stemmed mainly from the fact that the problems facing him were far graver than those that Colbert had had to confront.[16] A similar revisionist view of the Secretaryship of his son Jérôme, who held office during the navy's darkest days (1699-1715), is probably justified. At the latter's dismissal in 1715 he argued that financial penury had been the real reason for the navy's lamentable decline during his term of office. The evidence that I have seen suggests that he was right. Posterity, however, has always preferred to believe the accusations of malice and incompetence levelled against him by his former friend and subsequent nemesis, the virulent duc de Saint-Simon, who devoted perhaps the most vicious pen-portrait in his long gallery of obloquy to the unfortunate Jérôme.[17] Saint-Simon's lip-smacking indictment of Jérôme's deformities and enormities is echoed by every subsequent writer, and is often quoted *in extenso, con amore.* This is the legacy that any serious attempt to understand the naval history of Louis XIV's last years will have to demolish. Any reassessment of Jérôme de Pontchartrain might well start from the scholarly studies of Louis Delavaud, too long neglected, which dispel some of the clouds of myth.[18] But the real solution lies in dispassionate analysis of the vast wealth of untapped archival material covering this period, once we have discarded our persistent view of the Colberts as heroes and the Pontchartrains as villains.

TACTICS, TRAINING AND TECHNOLOGY

From the little that has so far been written it is evident that significant developments were taking place in all these fields, very often as a result of deliberate encouragement from Colbert and his successors. The teaching and practice of navigation, for instance, developed very rapidly after about 1670, with a new emphasis on theoretical questions.[19] Colbert strove to improve navigational methods and to provide the navy with better charts; he also tried to harness the intellectual resources of the Academy of Sciences to solving the problem of longitude.[20] Here the impact of the scientific revolution of the seventeenth century is evident, although the exact relationship between "pure" research and its practical application still awaits analysis. Colbert also established naval academies to train officers in gunnery, mathematics, seamanship and navigation, and the companies of naval cadets that he founded reflect a similar desire to raise the professional expertise of the officer corps. His concern did not extend to the rank and file, however, save for a few specialist gunners trained at artillery schools in the ports. But we can begin to speak of "training" in the modern sense of the term: the start of a military revolution that was to replace instinct and tradition with rational analysis and formal percept, turning the art of war into a science.

The same kind of care was lavished on the design and construction of warships. Colbert set up advisory boards at the main arsenals to supervise construction and investigate the principles of design, while treatises like those of Père Hoste and Renau d'Eliçagaray attest to a general quickening of interest in these questions.[21] As one commentator has recently pointed out, a revolution in naval architecture was beginning; mathematical analysis began to be applied to ship design, and the use of working drawings became more common, until by the middle of the next century it had been accepted as normal practice.[22] The design principles thus elaborated differed in some crucial respects from those of the Maritime Powers, with important tactical consequences. Between about 1660 and 1690 the French rating system was revised, so that French warships were effectively upgunned. The result was that a French warship tended to be more powerful than a Dutch or English vessel of the same nominal rate; conversely, a French warship with the same number of guns as its opponent would be larger, with a bigger crew and a heavier weight of metal, gun for gun.[23] That French ships generally carried larger crews than their enemies probably accounts in part for the greater favor that the French showed for boarding as a mode of attack. This tendency to opt for a numerical superiority in men was especially evident with privateer captains like Bart or du Guay-Trouin, most of whose victories were won by boarding rather than by gunfire.[24]

The question of naval tactics in this period remains largely unexplored, at least since Admiral Castex's work early in this century.[25] One comes away from a study of naval engagements in this period with a sense of tactical inflexibility and growing inconclusiveness. This impression of stasis is probably correct, yet the reasons for it need to be investigated. One possible line of approach might be through the analysis of contemporary

129

tactical handbooks, of which the most influential, Père Hoste's *L'art des armées navales,* is certainly worth careful consideration.[26] Did it express actual practice, or was it purely theoretical? Who actually read it, and was it ever used at the naval academies? Did it help to enforce a stifling tactical orthodoxy, or was it a liberating influence?

The general vitality of French ship design and technological expertise is attested by the invention of perhaps the only totally new type of warship in the age of sail: the bomb-ketch. The pre-history of this intriguing innovation is obscure; Jal has described how in 1680 Renau d'Eliçagaray proposed the new type to Colbert, who authorized construction. Renau's new warships were armed with two heavy-calibre mortars and soon proved their value in bombarding coastwise targets.[27] But just why this new weapon appeared at this particular time and place is a question that has never really been asked. My own theory is that the bomb-ketch must be seen as the naval counterpart to the development of heavy mortars for siege warfare, in which the French led the way.[28] The explosive shell was known from the 1580s onwards, at least, but for long played a very restricted part in actual operations. Much time was required before reliable shells could be produced in sufficient quantity to affect tactics. In the 1660s and 1670s the French took the lead in the development of mortars as practical weapons. Vauban was experimenting with them about this time, and in 1669 François Blondel composed his *Art de jeter les bombes,* which was published in 1683 and soon gained acceptance as the definitive handbook on mortar fire. By the 1680s French siege-trains always included a high proportion of heavy mortars, and the bombardment of cities and fortified places—as distinct from a regular siege "dans les formes"—had become a normal part of tactics on land.[30] The heavy shell-firing mortar was now an effective weapon, mainly because of the progress made by French artillerists and engineers. It seems only natural, therefore, that the application of mortar technology to sea warfare should have come first in France, and that it would have been pioneered by a man whose training had been in military engineering and siege warfare.

Let me conclude this section of my paper with some remarks on what is generally regarded as the antithesis of technical and tactical progress: the galley fleet. This received idea will have to be reexamined in the light of J. F. Guilmartin's recent analysis of galley warfare in the sixteenth century.[31] Paul Bamford has given us a good general survey of the French galleys, concerned not so much with tactics, however, as with problems of organization, especially the procurement of oarsmen.[32] Bamford's book posed a problem: given the apparent ineffectuality of galleys in the age of sail, why did Louis XIV continue to use them? In an earlier article Bamford ingeniously suggested that since the galley officers of France and her enemies had nearly all been trained in the Order of St. John; they were unwilling to fight each other.[33] This argument can now be supplemented by Guilmartin's demonstration that galley warfare was a strategic and tactical system with objectives and imperatives radically different from those of the sailing fleet. What Guilmartin has to say about the sixteenth century is still perfectly applicable to the age of Louis XIV. Galley warfare was a sophisticated system of amphibious warfare, in which the prime objective was the capture of fortified bases from which the galleys, with their restricted radius of action, could operate close to enemy coasts and sea-lanes. Battle was an option to be exercised only as a last resort, and "control of the sea" in Mahan's sense could never be won, let alone maintained. To judge galley warfare by the criteria of sailing operations is thus misleading, and historically invalid. In operations for which they were designed—sieges and coastal warfare—the galleys served well. Perhaps we should stop regarding Louis XIV's galleys as museum-pieces, and reassess their importance in the light of Guilmartin's book.

THE GUERRE DE COURSE

Operational history in the grand manner—big fleets and big battles—does not seem to be a popular genre today, at least for the period we are discussing. Scholarly interest has moved away from traditional political and military types of investigation, towards the social and economic matrix in which naval power functioned; hence, I think, a quickening interest in the *guerre de course*, which is only to be understood in the context of the social and economic forces that lay behind it. In any case, the privateering war waged in Louis XIV's reign is a topic of central importance in its own right: for most of the latter part of the reign it overshadowed the operations of the main battle fleet. The great wars of Louis XIV's later years seem to have been the historical climax of French privateering. Though prosecuted with vigor throughout the eighteenth century and into the Napoleonic Wars, the *course* never again attained the scale and intensity that it displayed between 1688 and 1715.[34] This phenomenon, of capital significance not merely for naval history but for the whole development of French society under absolutism, is now being scrutinized in a growing corpus of historical literature, which is currently the most important contribution to the naval history of the period.[35]

A profound fascination has always attached to privateering and piracy (the latter very rare in European waters by this time, and requiring careful conceptual separation from the regulated enomic warfare of the *course*) so that the earlier literature on the subject is replete with tales of derring-do and doubloons, but contains little of historical value. Modern investigations probably start with the work of Henri Malo on Dunkirk, or the various articles on Saint-Malo written by Léon Vignols.[36] The emphasis in the recent literature has been determinedly anti-romantic; as one writer roundly observes, "il faut donc, une fois pour toutes, débarasser la course de son panache."[37] So in place of cutlasses between the teeth and broadsides of grape we are now regaled with graphs of investment, prizes and profits. A good critical orientation in the literature is to be found in a stimulating article published recently by Jean Meyer.[38] Any survey of current work should start with the meticulous studies of John Bromley, who is largely responsible for giving the study of the *course* its present direction.[39] Then one must mention the work of Jean Delumeau and his students, who are patiently disinterring and analyzing the records of trade and privateering at Saint-Malo.[40] Their studies give us our first clear, systematic understanding of the city's commercial and privateering interests, completing E. W. Dahlgren's brilliant pioneering investigations, and Anne Morel's survey of Malouin privateering between 1681 and 1715 which was based on the Admiralty records.[41]

A point of vital importance which recurs throughout the current literature is the financing of the *course*. As yet we know comparatively little: records are scattered, and there is always the problem of investigating a group of financiers who for one reason or another liked to cover their tracks. My own impression—and it is no more than an impression—is that the financing of privateering was largely local, drawing investment from the ports concerned and their immediate orbits. Some of the more substantial ventures seem to have attracted capital from further afield, but only in the really big ventures, for instance Saint-Pol's armament at Dunkirk in 1704, did the preponderance of capital come from Paris and the court.[42] The power of local capital should not be underestimated, especially when we are dealing with a place like Saint-Malo, possibly the greatest center of commerce and privateering during Louis XIV's later years.

Here the work of Delumeau and his students raises the question of the relationship between privateering and normal trade: was the *course* just a substitute for commercial activity dislocated by war? Let me cite one example to reveal the complexity of the problem. Dahlgren's lists of merchants involved in the risky but enormously profitable trade around Cape Horn to the "South Seas" (actually Chile and Peru) reveal many who were also leading privateer owners, and it is very hard to draw a clear line between their different investments. In many ways the South Sea trade functioned as an extension of the *course*, managed by the same merchants, using the same ships, and operating at the very edge of legality—or beyond. Geographical extension is another point of contact between the South Seas traffic and the *course*. As each war progressed privateering began to shift increasingly to the colonies, as pickings became slimmer in home waters: hence Pointis's sack of Cartagena in 1697, or du Guay-Trouin's capture of Rio de Janeiro in 1711.[43] This trend was to become more and more pronounced through the eighteenth century, until the center of gravity of the *course* shifted from European waters to the West Indies.[44] The South Seas trade—a virtual Malouin monopoly[45]—was thus inextricably interwoven with privateering and was in many ways indistinguishable from it.

For the interaction of trade and privateering at Dunkirk we are far less well informed than we are for Saint-Malo, although the recent reopening of the archives at Dunkirk—which I wrongly believed to have been destroyed—should soon change this. It may well turn out to be true, as Bromley has recently argued, that Dunkirk's reputation as *the* corsair port, which rests largely on some inflated figures quoted by Henry Malo, will have to be revised: Saint-Malo may finally emerge as the great center of the *course*. But if we are to understand the full significance of privateering under Louis XIV, these two great ports are an obvious point of departure for research. From the merchants of the corsair ports the investigation leads into the tangled underworld of French state finance in one of its most chaotic periods, when the government mortgaged itself to the financiers who kept it afloat, and to the ubiquitous purveyors, suppliers and contractors who kept the war-machine going, for a handsome price.[46]

From here one moves naturally to the question of the profitability of the course, and to the issue of its strategic value. Enough people were doing well out of privateering to make it an attractive proposition, but the returns fluctuated so wildly that any answer to the question of profitability must be qualified according to the year, or even perhaps the month that one is discussing. In general it seems that privateering became more marginal as a war progressed: prey became rarer and counter-measures more effective.[47] Nevertheless many contemporaries, not least of them Vauban, believed that the *course* was the surest way to win the war at sea. Vauban's *M'emoire sur la caprerie* (1695) is the definitive statement of the economic and strategic aims of French privateering at this time, and argues strongly in favor of a *guerre de course à l'outrance* as the quickest way to ruin the Allies and so win the war, while simultaneously bringing untold wealth into France.[48]

If Louis XIV had lifted all restrictions from his privateers, as Vauban wished, would they have won the war for him? Did the *guerre de course* help to shorten the wars and bring France better terms at the peace treaties? Or was it, as Admiral Mahan argued, and most subsequent writers have assumed, a strategic blind alley? Here, as I have argued elsewhere, we must think ourselves free from the intellectual legacy bequeathed by Mahan's powerful mind.[49] He had nothing but contempt for the *course*, but I feel that the recent research outlined above must lead us to modify the preconceptions that we all bring to this question after reading Mahan. His theory of sea power is vowedly historical: grounded in historical evidence, it assumed for Mahan the force of historical law. Yet his knowledge of French maritime history was thin—even judged by what was known when he wrote—and his conclusions are open to question.[50] Mahan did not under-stand the wider historical forces that determined the shift to the *guerre de course* in Louis XIV's later wars—the crippling shortage of men and money, and the administrative paralysis that made it impossible for France to equip a battle fleet and send it to sea. Mahan was also unwilling to recognize that the French battle fleet, in the years that it had put to sea, had signally failed to win anything more than ephemeral tactical successes. He implied that the adoption of the *course* was a free—and strategically wrong-headed—choice, when in fact it was brought about by dire necessity and the manifest futility of waging war with a great fleet. In practical terms, and Mahan to the contrary, I would argue that Louis XIV could not have won a naval war against both Maritime Powers no matter what strategy he adopted. For France, the land war always held top priority, and Mahan's belief that a French victory would have resulted from a vigorous oceanic and colonial war is mere propaganda for his own time. Burdened by the simultaneous need to maintain a huge army, France could not afford a battle fleet capable of equalling, let alone defeating, the combined navies of England and Holland. France lacked the necessary reserves of money, ships and men. To challenge England and Holland to a contest of battle fleets was thus a losing proposition. In this naval poker game the Maritime Powers could always meet the ante and raise the stakes beyond what Louis XIV could afford, since their existence depended upon it, whereas France's in fact did not. Perhaps the question to ask is not why France mothballed its battle fleet and went over to privateering after 1694 and 1704, but why Louis XIV persisted so long in fighting a war of battle fleets when it obviously was leading nowhere.

In the end, therefore, I believe that Louis XIV stood no chance of winning a conventional naval war against England and Holland, with their greater reserves of ships and sailors and their more advanced commercial economies. Colbert's intensification of privateering in the later stages of the Dutch War, and the complete abandonment of the *guerre d'escadre* in the later stages of the Nine Years War and the War of the Spanish Succession, are clear recognitions of this. The *course*, on the other hand, was far better adapted to France's position as the weaker naval power, and in fact offered a number of advantages, as Vauban argued so cogently in his *Mémoire sur la caprerie*. Vauban was perhaps too optimistic when he claimed that the *course* could win the sea war for France, but he was right to argue that it would inflict serious damage on the Maritime Powers and make them eager for peace. In a war of commerce-destruction France had little to lose, whereas the Maritime Powers stood to suffer heavily, and did so, as the continual complaints from their merchants bear witness.[51] Moreover the *course* offered the only way by which the overburdened French state could continue to fight the war at sea, by shifting the costs onto the private sector.

Given France's financial prostration, and given the sterility of the *guerre d'escadre* as a strategy, there was a logic and force to Vauban's arguments which many of his contemporaries readily accepted. What he prescribed was a maritime strategy that would inflict far more damage on the Maritime Powers than the battle fleet had ever done, and at far less cost. Given that France could not win a naval war outright but only shorten it by inflicting heavy losses on the commerce of the Maritime Powers, the *course* was a far more logical strategy to follow than the chimera of victory through a great fleet.

CONCLUSION

The recent literature on the *guerre de course* indicates the new direction away from a narrowly military conception of the problem, and towards a wider understanding of the social, economic and institutional framework in which the navy operated that I feel subsequent work on Louis XIV's navy will follow. This approach has proven to be of great value in analyzing how privateering functioned, how it was financed, what motives lay behind it. A similar approach will, I am sure, prove equally fruitful when applied to other aspects of the naval history of the period. The last generation or so has seen enormous progress in the historical investigation of the institutional and social fabric of the Old Regime, largely thanks to the work of a brilliant school of French historians. Their new conception of French society under absolutism has begun to have its effect on the study of naval history as well. The new line of approach was suggested as long ago as the 1930's, in the René Mémain's brilliant study of Rochefort. His lead has been followed, to some extent, by recent historians of Saint-Malo, but the other great ports still await investigation.[52] Another instance of the application of a wider mode of historical inquiry to the problems of naval history is the series of articles in which Marcel Giraud illuminated the decline of the French navy during the War of the Spanish Succession. This is pioneer work which should be followed up.[53]

We need to know much more about the social and institutional base of Louis XIV's navy. Its administrative hierarchy has received little attention; the vital topic of naval finances is still almost completely unexplored. We also know surprisingly little about administrative personnel, the kinds of careers that were typical, and the factors that made for advancement.[54] The composition of the officer corps and the tensions within it need to be re-examined very carefully, as the recent work of Jacques Aman shows.[55] Questions of training, tactical expertise, and intellectual formation remain to be explored. These factors are of central concern if we are to understand how the officer corps functioned. Of the ordinary sailors we know hardly anything. Such studies of the common seamen as we posess do not measure up to André Corvisier's comparable work on the rank and file of the army

135

at this time.[56] The materials for a study parallel to Corvisier's exist in the records of the system of *Classes* and in the *rôles d'équipages* and related documents that are still available in considerable numbers. A related topic, which I have always found fascinating, would be an investigation of mutinies and their causes. Recent work on sixteenth- and seventeenth-century armies shows the kind of results to be expected from this kind of research, which would integrate the concerns of military history with the conclusions of current research into peasant insurrection and civil disorder under the Old Regime.[57] We must always bear in mind that Louis XIV's sailors were not professionals but peasants and fishermen drafted unwillingly from their peacetime occupations. This fact determined their capabilities and limitations as fighting men. What feelings of solidarity or antagonism bound them to the gentlemen-officers who commanded them? Above all, what motivated them to fight and die, to accept discipline or resist it?

In the long run, we must learn much more about the structural weaknesses and contradictions that prevented Louis XIV's navy from realizing the great promise that it seemed to offer in the first half of the reign. I have touched here on what I regard as the two basic structural defects that affected the French navy: shortage of money and shortage of manpower. Any explanation of these inherent flaws will not be found within the realm of naval history, narrowly construed in the traditional sense. It is to be sought in a wider understanding of French society, and in the workings of absolute monarchy and its complex institutions. The future direction for the study of the naval history of this period, in my opinion, if it is to be fruitful, lies in the approach already being mapped out: the closer intergration of social and economic history with the study of naval and maritime affairs.

FOOTNOTES

[1] The basic history of the French navy during this period remains that of Charles G. M. Bourel de la Roncière. *Histoire de la marine française.* 6 vols. (Paris, 1899-1932); vols. 5 and 6 cover Louis XIV's reign. See also Didier Neuville. *Etat sommaire des archives de la marine antérieures à la Révolution* (Paris, 1898), which has an excellent introduction; and Auguste Jal, *Abraham du Quesne et la marine de son temps* (2 vols: Paris, 1872).

[2] Paul W. Bamford, *Forests and French Sea Power 1660-1789* (Toronto: University of Toronto Press, 1956).

[3] The most important earlier work is J. Captier, *Etude historique et économique sur l'in-scription maritime* (Paris, 1907). Mémain's work is far more complete: René Mémain, *Matelots et soldats des vaisseaux du Roi. Levées d'hommes au département de Rochefort 1661-1690* (Paris, 1937), and *idem., La marine de guerre sous Louis XIV. Le matériel. Rochefort, arsenal modèle de Colbert* (Paris, 1937).

[4] Eugene L. Asher, *The Resistance to the Maritime Classes. The Survival of Feudalism in the France of Colbert* (Berkeley and Los Angeles: University of California Press, 1960).

[5] Marc Perrichet, "L'administration des classes de la marine et ses archives dans les ports bretons," in *Revue d'histoire économique et sociale,* 37 (1959). I have not yet seen John S. Bromley's article. "Comment a fonctionné le système des classes maritimes 1689-1713." in a forthcoming volume of essays edited by Jean Boisset in honor of Louis Dermigny. For this and many other items of recent bibliography I am endebted to Madame Ulane Bonnel.

[6] Discussion of this problem in Geoffrey W. Symcox, *The Crisis of French Sea Power 1688-1697: from the Guerre d'Escadre to the Guerre de Course* (The Hague: Martinus Nijhoff, 1974), pp. 14-20. The English and Dutch navies had their manpower problems too, but could draw on larger reserves of sailors. In England the defects of the system of impressment led to periodic suggestions for a recruitment plan modelled on the French: see John S. Bromley (ed), *The Manning of the Royal Navy. Selected Public Pamphlets 1693-1873* (London: Navy Records Society Publications, vol. 119, 1974) pp. 16-41, and Appendix I.

[7] Henry Legohérel, *Les trésoriers-généraux de la marine (1517-1788)* (Paris, 1965). Some further information can be obtained from Léon Vignols. "La caisse des invalides et les dilapidations gouvernementales du XVIIe au XXe siècle," in *Revue d'histoire économique et sociale,* 23 (1936-1937).

[8] Donald Pilgrim, "The Colbert-Siegnelay Naval Reforms and the Beginnings of the War of the League of Augsburg," in *French Historical Studies,* 9 (1975), summarizing his doctoral thesis, "The Uses and Limitations of French Naval Power in the Reign of Louis XIV: the Administration of the Marquis de Seignelay, 1683-1690" (Brown University, 1969).

[9] Colbert's moves can be followed in part through the documents printed by Pierre Clément (ed), *Lettres, instructions et mémoires de Colbert* (7 vols. in 8: Paris, 1861-73) 3, part I, pp. 28, 80-82, 89-93, 104-105, 137-143. Further information in Neuville, *op. cit.,* p. xii ff.

[10] A recent study of the local Admiralties is the series of articles by J. Darsel, "L'Amirauté en Normandie," in *Annales de Normandie,* from vol. 19 (1969) onwards.

[11] Legohérel, *op. cit.,* 171 ff.

[12] On the *Conseil des Prises* (or supreme prize-court), see A. Dumas, "Le Conseil des Prises sous l'ancien régime," ion *Nouvelle revue historique de droit français et étranger,* 29 (1905). On the Council of the Navy, see Georges Lacour-Gayet, *La marine militarire de la France sous le règne de Louis XV* (Paris, 1902), p. 29.

[13] Yvonne Bézard, *Fonctionnaires maritimes et coloniaux sous Louis XIV, les Bégon* (Paris, 1932.)

[14] Comte C. de Calan, "Les Bretons dans la marine française," in *Mémoires de la société d'histoire et d'archéologie de Bretagne*, 8 (1927).

[15] Symcox, *op. cit.*, pp. 103-108. A representative sample of the anti-Pontchartrain literature is Simone Goubet, "Deux ministres de la marine, Seignelay et Pontchartrain," in *Revue des questions historiques*, 59e année (1931), a remarkable exercise in the selection and misinterpretation of evidence.

[16] Patrice M. Berger of the University of Nebraska is currently engaged on a study of Louis de Pontchartrain; so far he has written "Pontchartrain and the Grain Trade during the Famine of 1693," in *Journal of Modern History*, 48:4 (Dec. 1976).

[17] Arthur de Boislisle (ed), *Mémoires du duc de Saint-Simon* (43 vols: Paris, 1879-1930): see especially vo. 21, pp. 376-381.

[18] Louis Delavaud, *Un ministre de la marine, Jérôme Phélypeaux de Pontchartrain. Son éducation et ses premiers emplois. Sa visite des ports de France en 1694, 1695 et 1696* (Rochefort, 1911: reprinted from *Bulletin de la société de géographie de Rochefort*, années 1910-1911); *idem. Documents inédits sur le duc de Saint-Simon* (La Rochelle, 1910). One may note also Pierre Clément, "Les successeurs de Colbert. I. Pontchartrain," in *Revue des deux mondes*, 33e année (Aug. 1863), although it too is marked by bias against Pontchartrain.

[19] F. Russo, "L'enseignement des sciences de la navigation dans les écoles d'hydrographie aux XVIIe et XVIIIe siècles," in Michel Mollat (ed.), *Le navire et l'économie maritime du moyen âge au XVIIIe siècle, principalement en Méditerranée, Travaux du deuxième Colloque International d'histoire maritime* (Paris, 1958).

[20] Colbert's efforts helped make French charts the best in Europe, but they were still far from perfect: see the complaints in *Mémoires de Robert Challes, écrivain du Roi* (ed. A. Augustin-Thierry: Paris, 1931), 9-10.

[21] Père Paul Hoste, *Théorie de la construction des vaisseaux* (Lyons, 1697); Bernard Renau d'Eliçagaray. *Théorie de la manoeuvre des vaisseaux* (Paris, 1689). Renau designed and built a frigate (in 1692) which proved extremely fast and manoeuverable.

[22] P. Gille, "Les écoles de constructeurs," in Mollat (ed.), *Le navire* . . . . (cited note 19 above).

[23] This point is developed by John H. Owen, *War at Sea under Queen Anne 1702-1708* (Cambridge, England: Cambridge University Press, 1938), pp. 29-30. French prizes were sometimes copied by the English and Dutch; likewise a number of captured English warships were admired by French captains. Du Guay-Trouin made the "Jersey" his flagship, and Saint-Pol led the Dunkirk squadron in the "Salisbury." Forbin, who captured H.M.S. "Grafton" and "Hampton Court," called them "deux vaisseaux de la nouvelle construction d'Angleterre et admirables, au dire de tout ce qui les a vus." (Quoted in de la Roncière, *op. cit.*, 6, p. 443).

[24] Another factor making for large crews aboard privateers was of course the need for extra men to serve as prize crews.

[25] Raoul V. P. Castex, *Les idées militaires de la marine du XVIIIe siècle, de Ruyter à Suffren* (Paris, 1911).

[26] Père Paul Hoste, *L'art des armées navales, ou traité des évolutions navales* (Lyons, 1697). The work's importance is indicated by the fact that it was translated into English at least twice, in 1762 and 1834.

[27] Jal, *op. cit.*, 2, 412-421. Fontenelle's *Eloge* of Renau summarizes his career. Further details in Charles G. M. Bourel de la Roncière, "Au siècle de Louis XIV: tanks, aéroplanes, sous-marins, torpilles et obus monstrueux," in *Revue hébdomadaire*, 25e année (Dec. 1916), pp. 455-458.

[28] Contemporary artillery treatises do not mention hollow explosive shells to be fired from mortars until about the mid-seventeenth century; prior to that mortars fired solid shot.

138

For the development of French mortar technology, see Francois Blondel, *L'art de jeter les bombes* (The Hague, 1683), pp. 4-7, 67; Pierre Surirey de Saint-Rémy, *Mémoires d'artillerie* (2 vols: Paris, 1697), preface to vol. 1; Guillaume Leblond, *Elémens de la guerre des sièges, ou traité de l'artillerie, de l'attaque, et de la défense des places* (Paris, 1743), especially p. 62.

[29] On Blondel, see Prosper Charbonnier, *Essais sur l'histoire de la balistique* (Paris, 1928); Alfred R. Hall. *Ballistics in the Seventeenth Century* (Cambridge, England: Cambridge University Press, 1952), pp. 125-127. For Vauban's experiments, see Eugéne A. de Rochas d'Aiglun (ed.), *Vauban, sa famille et ses écrits* (2 vols: Paris, 1910), especially his letter to Louvois, 17 Oct. 1671, in vol. 2, p. 56.

[30] List of the French siege-train at Luxembourg in 1684, in Alfred Lefort, *Les Français à Luxembourg. Vauban et la forteresse d'après des documents inédits* (Reims, 1900), p. 24.

[31] John F. Guilmartin, Jr., *Gunpowder and Galleys. Changing Technology and Mediterranean Warfare at Sea in the Sixteenth Century* (Cambridge, England: Cambridge University Press, 1974).

[32] Paul W. Bamford, *Fighting Ships and Prisons: the Mediterranean Galleys of France in the Age of Louis XIV* (Minneapolis: University of Minnesota Press, 1973).

[33] *Idem*. "The Knights of Malta and the King of France, 1665-1700," in *French Historical Studies*, 3 (1964).

[34] Jean Delumeau, "La guerre de course française sous l'ancien régime," in Michel Mollat (ed.), *Course et piraterie. Etudes présentées à la Commission Internationale d'Histoire Maritime, XVe Colloque, San Francisco 1975* (published in mimeo, Paris, 1975), pp. 294-295.

[35] The wider implications of naval policy in Louis XIV's later years are discussed by Lionel Rothkrug, *Opposition to Louis XIV. The Political and Social Origins of the French Enlightenment* (Princeton: Princeton University Press, 1965), notably in chapter 7.

[36] Henri Malo, *Les corsaires dunkerquois et Jean Bart* (2 vols: Paris 1913-14); *idem*, *La grande guerre des corsaires. Dunkerque 1702-1715* (Paris, 1925); Léon Vignols, "La course maritime, ses conséquences économiques, sociales et internationales," in *Revue d'histoire économique et sociale*, 15 (1927), and "Le commerce maritime et les aspects du capitalisme commercial à Saint-Malo de 1680 à 1789," in *ibid.*, 19 (1931).

[37] Jean Delumeau, *Le mouvement du port de Saint-Malo 1681-1720, bilan statistique* (Paris, 1966), p. xii.

[38] Jean Meyer, "La course: romantisme, exutoire social, réalité économique. Essai de méthodologie," in *Annales de Bretagne*, 78 (1971).

[39] John S. Bromley, "The Channel Islands Privateers in the War of the Spanish Succession," in *Transactions de la société guernésiaise*, 14 (1950); *idem*, "The Trade and Privateering of Saint-Malo during the War of the Spanish Succession," in *ibid.*, 17 (1964); *idem*, "Le commerce de la France de l'ouest et la guerre maritime, 1702-1712," in *Annales du Midi*, 65 (1953); *idem*, "The French Privateering War 1702-1713," in Henry E. Bell and Richard L. Ollard (eds.), *Historical Essays 1600-1750 presented to David Ogg* (London, 1963); *idem*, "Some Zeeland Privateering Instructions: Jacob Sautijn to Captain Salomon Reynders 1707," in John S. Bromley and Ragnhild M. Hatton (eds.), *William III and Louis XIV. Essays by and for Mark A. Thomson* (Liverpool: University of Liverpool Press, 1968(; *idem*, "Projets et contrats d'armement en course marseillais 1705-1712," in *Revue d'histoire économique et sociale*, 50 (1972); *idem*, "The Jacobite Privateers in the Nine Years War," in Anne Whiteman (ed.), *Statesmen, Scholars and Merchants. Essays presented to Dame Lucy Sutherland* (Oxford: Oxford University Press, 1973); "The Importance of Dunkirk (1688-1713) Reconsidered," in Mollat (ed.), *Course et piraterie*.

[40] Besides the works cited in notes 34 and 37 above, see also Jean Delumeau, "Le commerce malouin à la fin du XVIIe siècle," in *Annales de Bretagne*, 66 (1959); *idem*, "Les terre-

neuviers malouins a la fin du XVIIe siècle," in *Annales ESC,* 16 (1961); *idem,* "Les constructions navales a Saint-Malo à la fin du XVIIe siècle et au début du XVIIIe siècle," in *Revue d'histoire économique et sociale,* 42 (1964); *idem,* "Le commerce extérieur français au XVIIe siècle," in *XVIIe Siècle,* 70-71 (1966); *idem,* "La démographie d'un port français sous l'ancien régime: Saint-Malo (1651-1750)," in *ibid.,* 86-87 (1970). Two of Delumeau's students are at present preparing doctorates, Andre Lespagnol on the merchant community of Saint-Malo, and Mme. Martin-Deidier on the *course.* I should also note the Mémoire de Maîtrise by M. H. Tarrie and J. C. Larran, "La guerre de course en France de 1695 à 1713," (Paris I), and J. Ottenhof, "La course à Nantes pendant la guerre de la Ligue d'Augsbourg," (DES, Rennes, 1960).

[41] Erik W. Dahlgren, *De Franska Sjöfarderna till Söderhafvet i början af Adertonde Seklet. En Studie i Historisk Geografi* (Stockholm, 1900), later translated and expanded as *Les relations commerciales et maritimes entre la France et les côtes de l'Océan Pacifique. Tome premier: le commerce de la mer du Sud jusqu'à la paix d'Utrecht* (Paris, 1909); *idem, Abbe Noël Jouin, en Hubert-Historia fran Ludwig XIV's Tid* (Stockholm, 1904); *idem,* "Voyages françaises à destination de la mer du Sud avant Bougainville (1695-1749)," in *Nouvelles archives des missions scientifiques et littéraires,* 14, fasc. 4 (1907); *idem,* "Le comte Jérôme de Pontchartrain et les armateurs de Saint-Malo, 1712-1715," in *Revue historique,* 88 (1905), also published separately, Paris, 1905; *idem,* "L'expédition de Martinet et la fin du commerce français dans la mer du Sud," in *Revue de l'histoire des colonies,* 1 (1913); Anne Morel, "La guerre de course à Saint-Malo de 1681 à 1713," in *Mémoires de la société d'histoire et d'archéologie de Bretagne,* 37-38 (1957-58).

[42] List of Saint-Pol's backers in Malo, *La grande guerre des corsaires,* p. 31; *cf.* the lists of investors in Symcox, *op. cit.,* pp. 199-200, and Appendix 3. Further discussion of this point in Bromley, "Projets . . . marseillais 1705-1712," and in H. Bourde de la Rogerie, "La guerre de course sur les côtes de Cornouaille de 1690 à 1697," in *Mémoires de la société d'histoire et d'archéologie de Bretagne,* 17 (1936).

[43] Madame Bonnel informs me that Frédéric Mauro is currently engaged on a study of du Guay-Trouin's capture of Rio de Janeiro. Comte le Nepvou de Carfort, *Histoire de du Guay Trouin, le corsaire* (Paris, 1922), breaks off just before this episode. The best account is that in du Guay-Trouin's *Mémoires,* ed. Alexandre Petitot and Louis J. N. Monmerqué. *Collection des mémoires relatifs à l'histoire de la France,* vol. 75, (Paris, 1829). Du Guay-Trouin claimed that his investors made a 92% profit: a list of his backers is in Jean Meyer, *La noblesse bretonne au XVIIIe siècle* (2 vols: Paris, 1966), vol. 1, p. 337. Part of this profit came from the South Seas trade, however; Dahlgren "Voyages français . . . avant Bougainville," pp. 496-498, notes that du Guay-Trouin sent two ships on from Rio to the South Seas.

[44] Delumeau, "La guerre de course française sous l'ancien régime," p. 288.

[45] H.-F. Buffet, "La traite des noirs et le commerce de l'argent au Port-Louis et à Lorient sous Louis XIV," in *Revue des études historiques,* 102e année (1935), shows how these ports functioned as outports for Saint-Malo's South Sea trade. Dahlgren, "Voyages français . . . avant Bougainville," estimates that this traffic brought in as much as 400 million livres from 1703 to 1720—a figure curiously close to the estimate for the value of French wartime trade and privateering given by Swift in *The Conduct of the Allies.*

[46] Daniel Dessert is beginning to investigate this problem. See his articles, "Finances et société au XVIIe siècle: à propos de la Chambre de Justice de 1661," in *Annales ESC,* 29 (July-Aug. 1974), and "Le lobby Colbert: un royaume, ou une affaire de famillè?" *ibid.,* 30 (Nov.-Dec. 1975).

[47] A recent illustration of this point may be found in the figures for privateering at Dunkirk given by R. Baetens, 'The Organization and Effects of Flemish Privateering in the Seventeenth Century," in *Acta Historiae Neerlandicae,* 9 (1976), p. 67, p. 72.

[48] Discussion of Vauban's *Mémoire* in Symcox, *op. cit.*, pp. 177-187; *cf.* Armel de Wismes, *Jean Bart et la guerre de course* (Paris, 1965), p. 139 ff. A complete assessment of Vauban's concept of the *course* must wait until his papers—at present in private hands and inaccessible to scholars—are made available for research.

[49] Symcox, *op. cit.*, pp. 227-230; *cf. idem*, "Admiral Mahan, the *Jeune Ecole* and the *Guerre de Course*," in Mollat (ed.). *Course et piraterie*.

[50] In Mahan's autobiography, *From Sail to Steam* (London and New York, 1907), pp. 278-284, there is a list of the sources he used for his account of the French navy in *The Influence of Sea Power on History 1660-1783* (Boston, 1890); his discussion of Louis XIV's naval strategy is in chapters 4 and 5, *passim*.

[51] Patrick Crowhurst, *The Defence of British Trade 1689-1815* (Folkestone: William Dawson & Sons, 1977), p. 1: "The principal threat to British trade in the wars between 1689 and 1815 came from a large number of French privateers that put to sea from St Malo, Dunkirk and other ports along the French coast." For a contemporary view, see the debates on the losses to French privateers, in Parliament during February 1708, in William Cobbett (ed.), *Parliamentary History of England* (36 vols: London, 1806-19), vol. 6, pp. 618-662.

[52] H.-F. Buffet, "Lorient sous Louis XIV," in *Annales de Bretagne*, 44 (1937), is an exception. On Brest there is little of value; Yves le Gallo (ed.), *Histoire de Brest* (Toulouse: Privat, 1976) adds little to our knowledge for this period. Claude K. Bell of U.C.L.A. is at present engaged on a PhD thesis dealing with the operation of the port of Brest during the 1690's.

[53] Marcel Giraud, "Crise de conscience et d'autorité à la fin du règne de Louis XIV," in *Annales ESC*, 7 (1952); *idem*. "Tendances humanitaires à la fin du règne de Louis XIV," in *Revue historique*, 209 (1953); *idem*, "Marins et ouvriers des ports devant la crise de la fin du règne de Louis XIV," in *Eventail de l'histoire vivante: hommage à Lucien Febvre* (3 vols: Paris, 1953).

[54] I understand from Madame Bonnel that O. J. Sturcy is currently working on a study of the naval administration under Pontchartrain.

[55] Jacques Aman, *Les officiers bleus dans la marine française au XVIIIe siècle* (Geneva, 1976).

[56] André Corvisier, *L'armée français de la fin du XVIIe siècle au ministère de Choiseul. Le soldat* (2 vols: Paris, 1964). For the navy there is Jean Merrien, *La vie quotidienne des marins au temps du Roi Soleil* (Paris: Hachette, 1964), and Armel de Wismes, *La vie quotidienne dans les ports bretons aux XVIIe et XVIIIe siècles* (Paris: Hachette, 1973).

[57] J. S. Morrill, "Mutiny and Discontent in English Provincial Armies 1645-1647," in *Past and Present*, 56 (Aug. 1972); G. Parker, "Mutiny and Discontent in the Spanish Army of Flanders 1572-1607," in *ibid.,* 58 (Feb. 1973); René Pillorget, "Une émeute des gens de mer: Martigues, 16 aôut 1670," in *Actes du 93e congrès national des sociétés savantes 1968* (2 vols: Paris, 1971); G. Lemarchand "Crises économiques et atmosphère sociale en milieu urbain sous Louis XIV," in *Revue d'histoire moderne et contemporaine*, 14 (1967).

CHAPTER 12

The French Navy, 1748-1762; Problems and Perspectives_____

James Pritchard

Queen's University

The destruction of the French navy during the two mid-eighteenth century maritime and colonial wars with Great Britain remains a dismal period of French naval history and probably accounts for the relatively few studies of the navy of Louis XV. Those that do exist were written prior to the Great War and reflect the tumultuous debates over naval policy that spanned the half century between 1870 and 1920.[1] The emphasis in French naval historiography has been on battles, strategy and tactics. Biography when it appeared all too frequently became hagiography. Interesting studies of institutions within the navy appeared but they were usually written by men interested in reform of the naval ministry or by professionals with an antiquarian or juridical outlook who wished to call attention to organizations to which they had devoted their careers.[2] Eighteenth-century naval history was filled with villains and heroes existing independently of the society in which they lived. When studied for more than technique, wars and battles were often viewed as won or lost owing to external circumstances over which the navy had little control. The navy and the officer corps were portrayed in monolithic fashion and even the well-known tension between administrative and executive officers received superficial treatment. Moreover, the intellectual currents of the late nineteenth and early twentieth centuries led to great emphasis upon ideas and scorn for the limitations that materiel and institutions imposed upon past actions. The remarks of Raoul Castex (later Admiral) that "The ideas professed by the members of a military society . . . have always seemed more interesting to consider than its organization or its material resources", or, "The intellectual factor . . .affirms its preeminence over the concrete nature of things" reveals some of the limitations of these earlier studies to the historian.[3]

Generally foreign to these early studies was the idea that the navy was a complex, multi-faceted organization possessing a system of internal hierarchies of competing interests where tensions and existing reality limited the development of strategic thinking and operational planning. Equally foreign was the concept that this organization existed within a social, economic and political environment containing other systems whose dynamic relations were constantly at work. The low state of the navy during the mid-eighteenth century is often attributed to poor ideas about the use of naval power, to what might be called the "bad mistress" theory of history, to accompanying ministerial incompetence and neglect, and to a want of money. By way of compensation naval officers themselves are often portrayed as collectively inept, but personally brave, intelligent, and strongly oriented towards scientific curiosity.[4] It is also surprising how much has been written that was based on so little original reseach.[5]

The fourteen years between 1748 and 1762 form a critical period in the colonial and maritime history of France. During the first seven years, against a background of domestic political turmoil French colonial trade grew to an unprecedented volume and value, and the rearmament of a once devastated navy accompanied this phenomenal commercial growth.[6] During the next seven years French maritime commerce disappeared from the seas and the royal navy was destroyed. Despite their general inadequacy as an explanation for this disaster, the elements cited in the older histories as contributory to the navy's miserable performance do begin to identify the problems that arise out of a study of the navy during the Seven Years' War.

In the first place the view that the navy had no idea of the use of naval power must be challenged. This view ignores the navy's armament policy and ignores further the truism that this armament policy—like operational policy—reflects strategic intentions that in turn interact with naval policy. For a full picture there remain vast unknown areas requiring research into the implementation and execution of naval policy. Questions concerning the acquisition of materiel, ship construction, the organization and administration of the dockyards, manning, provisioning, recruitment and training the civilian and naval officer corps, and finances all require investigation. Within each of these general areas there are a host of subsidiary questions to be answered, and a need to correlate a multitude of apparently disconnected events. What significance lies in the number of warships decided upon? Why did the building program concentrate on 64- and 74-gun ships? Larger warships were begun only after hostilities began.[7] Why was France able to build the best warships in the world, yet unable to arm them with sufficient cannons to go to sea?

The persistence of the "bad mistress" theory of history in studies of the maritime and colonial wars is demonstration enough of the inadequacy of current French naval studies of the eighteenth century. Heavy and uncritical reliance upon published court memoirs is the main cause of this interpretation, and it is astonishing that the memoirs have not been used with greater caution, for Mme. de Pompadour was a convenient scapegoat for those administrators who sought exculpation for their own actions.[8]

In dealing with the related question of ministerial competency in the naval department between 1748 and 1762 one must first draw some conclusions about Louis XV and his relations with his ministers during the domestic turmoil that destroyed the political equilibrium in France after May 1749 when the *Controleur-général des Finances* persuaded the king to impose permanently the *vingtième* on the revenues of the privileged classes.

Only the salient characteristics that affected Louis XV's relations with his secretaries of state and ministers need recall, for the enigma of Louis XV's personality has been explored by both contemporaries and biographers.[9] Shyness which approached neurasthenia in its domination of the king's behaviour stands above all other features of Louis XV's personality. His excessive respect for his pious wife left to the royal mistresses the challenge of providing the warm, comfortable and intimate environment that he craved; yet the success achieved by Madame de Pompadour had its detrimental effect by leaving Louis XV with a profound sense of sin, tormented by religious remorse for the pain that his life caused his children whom he adored. Louis XV's natural indecisiveness was too long encouraged by this teacher, Cardinal Fleury, whose death in January 1743 left him ill-equipped to rule alone. Long reliance on the old cardinal had increased the king's shyness, further weakened his little self-regard, and left him fearful either of expressing his will or of rejecting advice that he could not accept.[10] Although intelligent, and prescient and moderate in judgment, Louis XV was reluctant to assert himself. Always able to see an alternate point of view, he too often believed his own to be wrong. Shyness, remorse, modesty and self-doubt combined to create a near paralysis of will.

Yet Louis XV was not afraid of work. His well-known, and often criticized, self-indulgence has been overemphasized for it was not a characteristic of lethargy but of boundless physical energy.[11] It is also incorrect to claim that the king rarely saw his senior advisors.[12] Michel Antoine has convincingly demonstrated that throughout his adult life Louis XV regularly presided over his four main councils.[13] Each council met for at least two hours once or twice a week; and each day of the week also contained set hours to receive the Chancellor or his deputy, the Keeper of the Seals, the four secretaries of state, the Comptroller-General of Finances, the holder of the portfolio of benefices as well as impromptu audiences at other times. But although the king reigned and worked he did not rule.

Louis XV's lack of leadership in his councils meant that his government lacked cohesion. His ministers received no sense of the collective identity that comes of working as equals below the monarch. Members of the councils failed to use their time to the best advantage. They often became caught up on detail and left important matters of state to junior officials.[14]

Put another way, minor details of administration often required their attention to the detriment of more important matters of policy.[15] Each minister had his own relationship to the king and sought to develop it as best he could. Under Louis XV the secretaries of state reached the apogee of their administrative power, and, as Antoine points out, with this came the progressive devolution of central power and the development of the bureaucratic mind.[16] Each secretary of state and minister sought allies, and during the disturbed times after May, 1749, government increasingly came to be by faction and intrigue.

Cultivation of faction may have been an essential component of absolute government for as a political mechanism it was in some cases the only feasible alternative to having the king take sides, and it permitted several points of view concerning policies to be followed and decisions to be made to be presented to the king.[17] But success required a forceful and decisive monarch to control the dynamics of such a process. Under Louis XV changes in the personnel of his councils rarely came about by force of the king's will, but more frequently by death, ill-health or unforeseen circumstances. Thus, the factional struggles among the king's senior officials were an important aspect of government.

In theory France was administered by the royal councils, but in practice the government's conciliar structure was slow and confused owing to overlapping jurisdictions. The principle that all decisions were made by the king-in-council was largely fictitious.[18] The councils were often by-passed by the various secretaries of state and the *Controleur-général des finances*, the head of the financial administration, and by their departments; indeed, the Secretary of State for the Navy had not been a member of the *Conseil d'état* during the long period stretching from 1699 to 1738, nor was he from April 1749 to August 1751 or between June and November 1758.[19]

During the twenty years between Cardinal Fleury's death and the Duc de Choiseul's consolidation of power the Secretaries of State were usually undistinguished. None were strong men, yet most were conscientious. Tramond is unduly harsh when he writes that, "The desire to maintain themselves in power while flattering national conceit is all that inspired them"[20] During the 1750's the tenure in office of some was often so brief as to leave them in ignorance of what the department was doing. These may have been the years of "ephemeral ministries" but the ministers themselves have had a very mixed press.[21] But however important an assessment of the competence or incompetence of each Secretary of State for the navy might be, it would be premature to give one. Here we should note only that rapid political and social changes occurred in the *Counseil d'état* between 1749 and 1761 when five men held the portfolio for 63, 30, 16, 5, and 36 months respectively. The naval secretaries of state attempted to carry out the extremely difficult task of fighting a war for which the navy remained

145

unprepared, and which was made more difficult by the continuing devolution of power during the decade owing to their brevity in office, the lack of strong support from the king, and the system of government itself. Regardless of the strength of character and influence of individual ministers, the French system of government had reached a state where the execution of the central will was severely limited by existing institutions and interest groups. Nowhere was this more prevalent than in the navy.

The navy department had once been geographically organized, but in 1750 its many sub-sections were divided into about nine branches or *bureaux*: funds, colonial funds, ports, manpower, consulates, colonies, archives, maps and charts, and a secretariat.[22] It was these *bureaux*, directed by head clerks or *premiers comis*, which outweighed the councils and even sometimes the Secretary of State in the decision-making process. For it was in the *bureaux* that matters were thoroughly investigated and dealt with before the Secretary of State placed them before the king either in council or in private audience. Louis XV was in no position to alter the recommendations brought before him. Here too reports to the Secretary of State from naval intendants and *commissaires-ordinnateurs* were received, read and appreciated, and outgoing replies were composed for his signature. Altogether, the *premiers, secondes* and *troisièmes commis,* copyists, and messengers numbered about 65 or 70 persons.[23]

An obviously crucial factor in executing royal policy was the Secretary of State's degree of control over his *bureaux*. In contrast to the secretaries' relatively brief periods in office, some *premiers commis* occupied their posts for twenty years and came to wield enormous influence and power; thus Arnauld La Porte almost closed the *bureau des colonies* to the secretaries of state and Joseph Pellerin *père et fils* at the *bureau de police des ports* became indispensable.[24] The Secretary of State's knowledge of procedures or *formes*, how conscientiously he read the incoming correspondence, or whether he read it at all or only the summaries provided by the *bureaux*, and if he supervised and read the replies are significant questions to consider concerning the devolution of power in the navy department.

But of this seems to suggest that a highly centralized bureaucracy staffed by professional, experienced civil officers, who, although reducing the effectiveness of the royal councils, still employed machinery to impose a self-defined but nonetheless central will on the navy two very serious qualifications are yet in order. The execution of policy was not in the hands of the men who staffed the *bureaux*. The arsenals and colonies had civilian staffs arranged in a hierarchy of *écrivains, commissaires* and *intendants*, but ultimately the object of their endeavours was to get warships in condition to proceed to sea, and these ships were in other hands, those of the military aristocracy, or, as one of their number saw it, "la bonne et ancienne noblesse".[25] This is not the place to go into the often murderous re-

146

lations between *la plume* and *l'épée;* rather it is to point to the major weakness of central authority in the navy. The department had to rely on various corps of *officiers* both within and without its jurisdiction. Within the navy loyalty, group-interest and self-image led to division and dispute. In an age of slow communication the effectiveness of authority varied inversely as to distance; Brest is more than 700 and Toulon more than 900 kilometers from Paris. The distance to Rochefort is 500 kilometers. *La grande corps* was only the most important group that had to be dealt with. A multitude of non-naval corps of *officiers* also had to be employed to work the naval will.

Naval funds, for example, were provided by the *Trésoriers-généraux de la marine,* who as *officiers comptables* were virtually independent not only of naval control, but any administrative control; they were accountable only to sovereign financial courts, in this case the *chambres des comptes.* Although the *trésoriers,* the agents of the *treasurers-général* in the arsenals and colonies, often cooperated closely with *intendants* and *ordonnateurs,* these naval officials had very little control over them, for the *trésoriers* were the private agents of men who may be regarded virtually as private bankers.[26]

Timber, too take another example, was under the jealously guarded jurisdiction of the *Grand-maître des eaux et forêts* under the direction of the *Controleur-général.* Naval commissioners searching for ship timber in the royal forests usually encountered obstacles placed at every turn by the *officiers* of the local *maîtrises.*[27] The situation was so bad in Provence where the *maîtrise* was actually one of the chambers of the *parlement* of Aix that the navy virtually abandoned efforts to draw timber from the region, even though it was the closest area to Toulon.[28]

Royal provincial intendants themselves agents of the central government were frequently unable and unwilling to assist naval commissioners to obtain timber, cannons or men. Appeals for aid to entrepreneurs with large ordnance contracts made by the Secretary of State himself were met with outright hostility or passive obstruction. Between 1748 and 1762 the French navy was unable to obtain sufficient cannon to arm the ships then in existence let alone new ones.[29] When in 1756 the navy sought to increase its potential manpower by extending compulsory registration of seamen and workers in ancillary occupations into the French interior, provincial intendants as well as local populaces objected to and obstructed the naval *commissaires des classes.*[30] Local authorities also were angered, as in 1760, when the *maire* and *jurats* of Libourne refused to call out the cavalry of the *maréchaussée* to enforce a levy of seamen.[31] Good bourgeois everywhere feared for peace and order if troops were removed to escort unwilling levies to the seaports.

The intendants were not exercising mere personal pique, but like naval commissioners they too relied on corps of venal officers to execute the central government's will at local levels and were daily engaged in delicate, complex relations with a host of these persons whose own independence from the king and his councils was being vividly demonstrated by the *parlement* of Paris.[32] Intendants frequently viewed the navy's presence in their *généralitiés* as hamfisted intrusions that disturbed local interests, and sought to remove them as rapidly as possible in order to preserve social, political and even economic order and well-being. The intendant of Montauban was particularly aggrieved. In 1756 he refused to send any of 500 house carpenters to Toulon to learn shipbuilding without express orders from the king to use force; none could be obtained any other way and he warned that the local building industry would be destroyed.[33] Four years later, efforts to levy seamen threw the whole region into an uproar. The angry intendant reported that so many boatmen and ferrymen had deserted the rivers that transportation of sufficient grain for local markets was threatened.[34]

The officer corps remains to be further investigated. Previous histories emphasize the animosity between the administrative and executive officer corps and frequently allude to the development of a strong scientific orientation among naval officers almost as compensation for a lack of military aggressiveness. But little research has been done on the recruitment and training of naval officers in the middle of the eighteenth century.[35] Preliminary investigation of the social composition of both civil and naval officer corps reveals many close family ties. Gilles Hocquart and Charles Ruis Embito, intendants of Brest and Rochefort, both had brothers who were *capitaines de vaisseau*. The uncle of the *Intendant-général de la marine et des colonies* had held similar rank while the Marquis de Massiac, *Lieutenant-général des armées navales,* married the widow of a one-time *premier commis.* A cousin of Lieutenant-général, Michel Barrin de la Galissonière, was *premier commis* of the *bureau des fonds* and intendant of Dunkerque, and *Captaine de vaisseau* (later Admiral) Sébastien Bigot de Morogues was the son of a former intendant of Brest. Whether the common background of many *officiers d'épée et de plume* led to development of identical interests or whether service or function came to shape the interest of the *officiers* of both corps requires careful study.

If senior naval administrators were members of the *noblesse de robe* they were not actually in it. By the middle of the eighteenth century their recruitment and training had become so specialized that they were more isolated from the milieu of the *robe* than other elements of France's governing elites. The lack of venality in the navy only emphasized this. By mid-century senior naval administrators no less than members of *la grande corps* were being recruited from "les enfants du corps". It was nearly impossible for anyone to obtain the crucial rank of *commissaire de la marine* unless a father or grandfather had been in the corps.[36] Moreover young men destined for senior administrative rank were trained entirely within the naval and colonial service unlike the majority of the government's administrative elite, who during their youth had a common experience in Paris and in law.[37] Sébastien Lenormant de Mézy left France for the colonies at age 16 and only returned 31 years later as Intendant of Rochefort: Gilles Hocquart was 22 years as Intendant of New France before assuming similar duties at Brest. Ranche and Hurson were both Intendants of Martinique before becoming Intendants of Havre and Toulon respectively. But if separate from other members of the *noblesse d'état* and the *robe*, how different were these officers from their counterparts in *la grande corps?*

Access to membership in both corps during the 1750's was increasingly limited. The son of Jean Bart held the highest rank in the navy, *vice-admiral*, from 1752 to 1755, but Jean Bart himself would probably not have gained entry into the officer corps.[38] In 1761, the commandant of the company of *gardes de la marine* at Toulon was anxious that future candidates for the navy offer original proof of 100 years of nobility to qualify for entry. He asked that certificates of nobility signed by provincial intendants, syndics of local nobility, or the mayor and aldermen of towns no longer be accepted as evidence because it was well-known that these authorities were too often influenced by recently acquired wealth.[39] The same attitude persisted among *la plume.* In 1756, while pleading for extra staff needed to replace men put into La Galissonière's ships, the intendant of Toulon assured the minister that the replacements would be dismissed at the end of the temporary crisis; he agreed that they were unsuitable for the *corps de la plume,* "where it is customary to admit only the children of the corps of young persons of family."[40]

The royal galley corps was reunited to the sailing navy in 1748, but its influence by no means ended. The few Knights of Malta wielded influence far beyond their number in the officer corps because many officers in the Mediterranean felt that the union brought a personal and national loss of prestige. Officers felt humiliated when galleys from Genoa, Spain, and the Papal States visited Toulon. The majority of the Knights of Malta were French and when the famous "galères de la religion" visited Toulon, French naval officers felt acutely the lack of a separate galley corps. The divisive effect of the galleys on the sailing navy remains to be investigated. For example as late as 1760 the intendant of Brest was tearing his hair because officers who had received permission to arm a galley to exercise convicts in the roadstead now proposed that two galleys be used to keep English frigates out of the entrance to Brest Roads.[41] With 256 convicts per galley an angry intendant foresaw the disappearance of a considerable portion of the strongest members of his labour force and warned the minister of the consequences.

In the middle of the eighteenth century one may argue that a French naval officer corps existed in name only. So little control was exercised over personnel that when in April, 1758, Louis XV ordered all officers who were absent from their departments to return immediately, no list of these officers could be found in Paris and the minister had to delegate the task of recall to the naval commandants in the ports.[42] Naval officers identified themselves with the ports where they were registered for payment of their appointments, not with the service. Permission to return to their home department was continually given, being almost never refused, and the zeal of the few who sought transfers in order to find active service was remarked upon. The tremendous distances between the arsenals and between each of them and Paris, the lack of central authority over the corps, and the sharp cultural and professional differences between the Mediterranean and Atlantic maritime traditions obstructed formation of any common identity among naval officers. No "band of brothers" was in the making; indeed the multiple divisions between the officer corps are probably more important to any consideration of French naval weakness than the better known feuding between these officers and the *officiers de plume*. A shocked and horrified Berryer once wrote, "In the navy, they all hate each other."[43]

One cannot leave off the discussion without a mention of naval finances. Two recent studies unfortunately shed little light on the years prior to and during the Seven Years' War.[44] Do the navy's debts lie at the heart of any account of the navy's defeat? Certainly lack of financial resources is a convenient explanation, for to accept it requires little investigation of the navy itself. Besides, to say that the navy lacked financial resources is a little like saying Hamlet was moody. The questions when? how much? where? and why? remain unanswered.

I am not in a position to answer these questions, but two factors need to be considered. First, the French absolute monarchy was never able adequately to finance its navy. In wartime extraordinary expenses were urgently demanded and in peacetime economy became the order of the day. Nevertheless, the French navy played a critical role in the American War of Independence even though it encountered the same financial problems as it had earlier at mid-century. Second, the navy lacked not money so much as credit. Why this occurred is the key question. By 1758, men like Abraham Gradis of Bordeaux had placed their whole fortunes at the service of the navy.[45] Marseille's Chamber of Commerce had loaned at least 4,000,000 *livres* to the navy at Toulon.[46] A commission agent helped the *ordonnateur* of Brest raise a rapid naval loan for 132,000 *livres* on his personal signature.[47] Then suddenly this crucial assistance ceased. The cause of the navy's financial misfortunes may well lay in the pernicious action of Abbé de Bernis at Foreign Affairs during the summer of 1758 whose investigations into the navy led to the establishment in October of a committee of investigation to liquidate the navy's debts.[48] Instead of liquidating its debts the establishment of the committee and subsequent suspension of royal payments appears to have liquidated naval credit. Naval provisioners feared for their accounts and demanded cash payments which were not available. The insanity of Bernis' behaviour during a summer when the English made three descents on the French coast and when the fortress of Louisbourg in North America and the island of Gorée off Africa were captured is to be wondered at.

The navy's financial difficulties improved late in 1761 after the Duc de Choiseul arranged to pay five percent interest on bills of exchange of the colonies and staged the marvelous "Affaire du Canada" which saw the governor and intendant of Canada and several lesser persons clapped in the Bastille.[49] Financial confidence repidly returned and with it an outburst of patriotic fervor that saw various corporate bodies donate to the navy the costs of the largest ships ever built in the old regime, nearly a year before hostilities were concluded.[50]

One could continue listing areas where research needs to be carried out, but they did not correlate disconnected events and explain their bearing on the development of war and the French absolute monarchy. The normative approach of earlier historians was to abstract the war-making institution or part of it from its environment, but it is necessary to study the navy as one of the major institutions of the absolute monarchy. First, however, one must describe the organization.

Organizational research was practically non-existent when the foundations of modern naval historiography were laid, but during the last half-century it has become a field of study in its own right; it is also inter-disciplinary in scope. Under the impulse of research into economics, political science, psychology and other behavioural sciences, organizational research has developed modes of explanation. Whether the models need to be accepted by historians is a matter of personal temperament as much as rational argument, but the insights they contain are frequently very useful.[51]

Chief among them is the idea that organizations and their activities are not exclusively the products of rational thinking and planning. Drawing up organizational charts of the French navy for the middle of the eighteenth century, or describing the navy's "formal" organization is only superficially useful. It is silly, for example, to suggest that the French navy enjoyed little influence at court because it lacked an instrument like the English parliament to transmit political pressure. One must proceed to the informal organization, or to the network of personal relationships that existed alongside and within the "formal" structure. Such "informal" organizations existed and are important because individuals had different interests and aims from the "formal" organization. These often conflicted with the interests and aims of the latter, or the means of achieving the latter did not exactly exist. Naval officers were interested in promotion, appointments and bounties, and while these were obtained through the navy, the latter did not exist to advance its members. On the other hand, the navy did exist to carry out the government's maritime policy, but the means to build, provision and man the instruments of this policy were not at all clearly defined. By considering the distinction between "formal" and "informal" organization the historian can hack his way through much that is anecdotal and see beyond personalities to the origin of many clashes.

Continuity versus innovation within both types of organization is another useful concept derived from organization research. Tensions arise in organizations which well may be insurmountable; in the case of the French navy, the strength of individuals and the weakness of structures, or the imbalance of power between "informal" and "formal" organizations, were crucial to naval weakness. Here organization theory has another contribution to make to the historian because of debates among theorists concerning the role of conflict in organiation. Many view conflict as "dysfunctional", or disturbing, upsetting and unnatural to efficient organizations. But this is challenged by conflict theorists who, rather than seek deficiencies in persons or organizations (e.g. lack of integration of its parts or inequitable distribution of power) to account for conflict or instability, view the latter as normal healthy features of an organization that functions in a dynamic, social and economic environment. In this view, conflict is central to all social relations, and moreover, contributes to the reintegration and renewed stability of organizations in a world of change.

Finally, organization theory has a third contribution to make in systems theory. Derived from biology, but far removed from the rigorous explanations demanded by the scientist, systems theory emphasizes the strong links that exist between all forms of life, and by analogy all human organizations. It insists, moreover, that these links are essential to the existence of life. Not only the organization, then, but also the environment in which it exists and of which it forms a part is crucial to achieving understanding. There is no intention here to apply evidence from the past in order to demonstrate the validity of one or another theory of organization. Concepts and insights from organization theory need be employed only to the extent that it is useful to do so. In brief, organization theory offers the historian a group of concepts that can be applied to study French naval organization and administration in the eighteenth century by treating the navy as a system in itself with sub-parts interacting with one another, and interacting in whole or in part within a large system containing other organizations like itself. What is intended is a dynamic rather than functional study of a war-making organization interacting within the framework of political, social, economic and cultural history. For above all war is a part of the totality of human experience.

FOOTNOTES

[1] See G. Lacour-Gayet, *La marine militaire de la France sous le règne de Louis XV* (Paris, 1902) and E. Chevalier, *Histoire de la marine française depuis le début de la monarchie jusqu'au traité de paix de 1763* (Paris, 1902) whose aim was to reveal the dangers of ministerial meddling in naval matters.

[2] The number of these studies is quite large. Some examples are: Alfred Doneaud de Plan, *La Marine francaise au XVIIIe siècle au point de vue de l'administration et des progrès scientifiques* (Paris, 1867) was written by a professor of literature at the Imperial Naval School: Andre Dupont, *Les Arsenaux de Marine de 1869 à 1910, leur organization administrative* (Paris, 1913) written by the "ancien ingénieur en chef de la marine". This honorable tradition continues in such works as P-M-Jean Conturie, *Histoire de la fonderie nationale de Ruelle, 1750-1940* (Paris, 1951) written by the "ingénieur général de l'artillerie naval", and in Florian Cordon, *Les Invalides de la marine; une institution sociale de Louis XIV, son histoire de Colbert à nos jours* (Paris, 1950) written by the "trésorier-général des invalides de la marine".

[3] Raoul Castes, *Les Idées militaires de la marine de XVIIIe siècle de Ruyter à Suffren* (Paris, 1911), p. 30.

[4] See Joannes Tramond, *Manuel d'histoire maritime de la France des origines à 1815* (Paris, 1947), pp. 370-71.

[5] Aside from Lacour-Gayet, *La marine militaire*, the general naval histories of Tramond, *Manuel d'histoire maritime*, and René Jouan, *Histoire de la marine française* (Paris 1950), are very useful. Both devote more space to analysis and interpretation than the larger work by Lacour-Gayet. The most influential book of naval history ever written, Alfred T. Mahan's *The Influence of Sea Power Upon History, 1660-1782* (Boston, 1890) was not based on any original research and his account of the French during the Seven Years' War is taken unacknowledged from Moufle d'Angerville, *Vie Privée de Louis XV, ou principaux événements, particularités et anecdotes de son règne*, 4 vols. (Londres, 1781). Mahan may not be at fault for his sources may have lifted the account. More to the point, Moufle d'Angerville was a naval *écrivain* at Brest who was sacked.

[6] Pierre Léon in F. Braudel et E. Labrousse, *Histoire économique et sociale de la France*, Tome II, *Des derniers temps de l'age seigneurial aux preludes de l'age industriel (1660-1789)* (Paris, 1970), pp. 501-503.

[7] *Le Royal Louis*, 116-guns, and *le Mediateur*, 90-guns. The first ships of such size to be laid down in the eighteenth century were ordered in May 1757, see Marine, Brest, 1L, 45 "ordre du roi", 25 May 1757; *L'Ocean*, built at Toulon, was the only 80-gun ship laid down after 1748.

[8] G. Fregault, *Francois Bigot, administrateur français*, 2 vols. (Montreal, 1948) provides a good example of such uncritical use. See also Leon Achen, "Les mémoires du Cardinal de Bernis et les débuts de la guerre de sept ans", *Revue d'Histoire moderne et contemporaine*, XII (1909); The famous *Mémoires de Mme. Du Hausset femme de Chambre de Madame de Pompadour* (Paris, 1846) are apocryphal and attributed to Senac de Meilhan.

[9] Although superficial, the best attempt remains Pierre Gaxotte, *Le Siècle de Louis XV* (Paris, 1933), translated by J. L. May, *Louis The Fifteenth and His Times* (London, 1934), pp. 74-102 and 144-191; see also G. P. Gooch, *Louis XV: The Monarchy in Decline* (London, 1956).

[10] M. Antoine, *Le Conseil du roi sous le règne de Louis XV* (Paris, Geneve: 1970), p. 601; also Alfred Cobban, *A History of Modern France*, Vol. I, *1715-1799* (Harmondsworth, Middlesex: Penguin Books, 1961), pp. 49-53.

[11] See e.g. L. Kennett, *The French Armies in The Seven Years' War: A Study of Organization and Administration* (Durham, N.C.: Duke University Press, 1967), p. 3. who sees the king's slaughter of several hundred deer during The Seven Years' War as an example of indolence and search for diversion. On Louis XV's physical need for vigorous activity see Gaxotte, *Le siècle de Louis XV*, pp. 145-47.

[12] E. G. R. La Roque de Roquebrune, "La direction de la Nouvelle-France par le ministère de la marine", *Revue d'histoire de l'Amerique française,* VII (1952-53), 472 for this traditional view.

[13] Antoine, *Le Conseil du roi,* p. 120; see *ibid.,* pp. 118-75 for organization of the councils.

[14] J. F. Bosher, "French Administration and Public Finance in Their European Setting", *The New Cambridge Modern History,* Vol. VIII, *The American and French Revolutions, 1763-1793* (Cambridge, The University Press, 1965), p. 568.

[15] In the navy this often took the form of correspondence with the Comptroller-General of Finances and provincial intendants concerning continual administrative obstruction between the navy's contractors and some wretched *comptable* who refused to budge without direct orders from the top, or concerning disputes between junior naval administrators and local *officiers.*

[16] Antoine, *Le Conseil du roi,* p. 210.

[17] J. A. W. Gunn, ed., *"Introduction", Factions No More, Attitudes to Party in Government and Opposition in the Eighteenth Century England, Extracts from Contemporary Sources* (London, 1972), p. 7.

[18] Wolfram Fischer and Peter Lundgreen, "The Recruitment and Training of Administrative and Technical Personnel" in *The Formation of National States in Western Europe,* Chas. Tilley, ed. (Princeton, N.J.: Princeton University Press, 1975), pp. 430-509.

[19] Jerome de Phélypeaux, Comte de Pontchartrain, was never minister of the navy. See J. C. Rule, "Le roi bureaucrate" in *Louis XIV and Kingship,* ed., J. C. Rule (Ohio State University Press, 1969), p. 27. Maurepas only became minister in 1738, see M. Antoine, *Le Counseil du roi,* p. 198.

[20] Tramond, *Manuel d'histoire maritime,* p. 361.

[21] Lacour-Gayet, *La marine militarie,* p. 210 for the phase.

[22] G. Dagnaud, "L'Administration centrale de la marine sous l'ancien régime", Extrait de *la Revue Maritime* (Paris, n.d.) pp. 29-33; and H. Fontaine de Resbecq, "L'Administration centrale de la marine et des colonies", *Revue maritime et coloniale,* LXXXVIII (1886), 414.

[23] Ibid., 414, 418 gives 65 employees in 1753 and 7 *premiers commis,* 62 *commis* and an unknown number of lesser employees ten years later.

[24] The *premiers commis* of the navy have not been the subject of special study but see C.-V. Piccioni, *Les Premiers commis des affairs étrangères au XVII*^e *et au XVIII siècle* (Paris, 1928); and J. F. Bosher, "The 'Premiers Commis des Finances' in the Reign of Louis XVI", *French Historical Studies,* III (1964), 475-94.

[25] Marine, B³, 551. ff. 137-8. Comte de Carne-Marcein to Choiseul, 7 November 1761.

[26] J. F. Bosher, *French Finances, 1770-1795: From Business to Bureaucracy.* (Cambridge, The University Press, 1970), pp. 3 ff., 67 ff., 92 ff.

[27] E. g. Marine, D³, 1, f. 340 Circular letter from Berryer to intendants and *commissaires* in the provinces, 28 November 1758.

[28] Marine, D³, 2, ff. 168-178v "Exploitation et fournitures des bois de construction", [anonymous], 13 December 1758.

[29] J. S. Pritchard, "Ordnance Problems in the French Navy, 1748-1758" (Unpublished paper presented to the Third Annual Meeting of the French Colonial Historical Society, Montreal, May 5-7, 1977).

[30] E. g. Marine, B³, 532, ff. 299-300, La Galazière, intendant at Montauban, to Machault, 6 October 1756 objecting to the enthusiasm of naval commissioner Rostan of Bordeaux.

[31] Marine, B³, 549, ff. 287-7, Tourny, intendant of Bordeaux, to Berryer, 7 April 1760 who excuses them.

[32] The contentious question of the limited effectiveness of the provincial intendants is most convincingly dealt with by Maurice Bordes, "Les Intendants de Louis XV", *Revue Historique,* CCXXIII (1960), 45-62.

[33] Marine, B³, 532, f. 319. St. Priest to Machault, February 1756.

[34] Marine, B³, 549, ff. 283-4 St. Priest to Berryer, 31 May 1760.

[35] See, however, Marc Perrichet, "Plume ou épée: problèmes de carrière dans quelques familles d'officiers d'administration de la marine au XVIIIᵉ siècle," *91ᵉCongrès nationale des sociétés savantes* (Rennes, 1969), II, 145-83.

[36] Marine, B³, 530, ff. 71v-z Villeblanche, intendant of Toulon, to Machault, 12 February 1756.

[37] V. Gruder, *The Royal Provincial Intendants: A Governing Elite in Eighteenth Century France* (Ithaca: Cornell University Press, 1968), pp. 97 ff.

[38] Francois-Cornil de Bart (1677-1755) entered the navy in 1692. His son, Philippe Francois de Bart, became governor-general of St. Dominique in 1756.

[39] Marine, B³, 551. ff. 137-9 Comte de Carné-Marcein to Choiseul, 7 November 1761.

[40] See note 36.

[41] Marine, B³, 547, ff. 169-72, Chevalier de Grasse du Bar, Capⁿᵉ de Vᵃⁱᵘ to Berryer, 17 March 1760.

[42] Marine, Brest, 1A, 751, f. 106. Copy Moras to Du Guay, 10 April 1755.

[43] Cited in Brun, *Guerres maritimes*, I, 446, Berryer to Hurson, 6 May 1761.

[44] Henri Légohérel, *Les Tresoriers-généraux de la Marine, 1517-1788* (Paris, 1965) is both too general in treatment and too juridical in its focus. He follows Lacour-Gayet for his opinions of the 1750's, but the data provided is very valuable; Denise Ozanam, *Claude Baudard de Sainte-James: Trésories général de la marine et Brasseau d'affaires (1738-1787)* (Genève: Droz, 1969) is an important contribution to business history that covers a later period.

[45] On Gradis see *Jean de Maupassant, Un grande armateur de Bordeaux: Abraham Gradis 1699?-1780)* (Bordeaux, 1917); Marine, E. 204, piece no. 76, dated June 1759 shows that Gradis shipped 1,555,247 *livres* worth of supplies and freight to Canada in 1758.

[46] Brun, *Guerres maritimes*, I.

[47] Marine, Brest, 1E, 511, ff. 30, 38, Robert to Moras, 21, 1 & 26 April 1758: see also Marine, Brest, lE, 511, f. 364, Hocquart to Berryer, 1 December 1758 for the case of the Sieurs Arnoux, *père et fils*, who are owed 5,000 *livres* and begged 16 to 20,000 *livres* on account in order to survive.

[48] The records of this commission are in Bibliothèque nationale, Fonds Français, nos. 11, 334 to 11,339. "Registre des deliberations de M.M. les commissaires nommes par arrêt du Conseil du 18 Octobre 1758, . . ."

[49] For one account of the "Canada Affair" see Frégault, *François Bigot*, II, 341-88.

[50] In all, 16 ships were donated by the *Etats* of Languedoc, Burgundy and Brittany, the Marseilles Chamber of Commerce, the City of Paris, the six merchant guilds of Paris, the Postal administration, the *payeurs des rentes*, the companies of The Receivers-General, and seven court bankers, *trésoriers* and army provisioners; see Maufle d'Angeville, *La Vie privée de Louis* XV, IV, 14-15. It is ironic that the last group made up of war profiteers had their 74 gun gift (?) renamed *le Citoyen* in their honour. Marine, Brest, 1E, 512, f. 112, Hocquart to Choiseul, 25 January 1762.

[51] This and the following paragraphs are heavily indebted to and largely inspired by Carl Axell-Gemzell, *Organization Conflict and Innovation: A Study of German Naval Strategic Planning 1888-1940*, Lund Studies in International History 4 (Lund, 1973), pp. 1-31.

CHAPTER 13

French Maritime Historical Studies: An Overview

Ulane Bonnel

*Delegate in France of
the Library of Congress*

At the outset a few definitions are in order.[1] What is meant in French by "maritime" and "naval" history and why have I chosen to speak of "French maritime historical studies" when our subject is "French naval policy"? The broad span of the sea-related past constitutes "maritime" history of which only those aspects directly related to operational combat forces can properly be termed "naval" history. If the word "naval" is more restrictive in French than in English, it is possibly due to the nature of French archival sources. From the time of Colbert to the end of the "ancien régime" and to a certain degree even to the creation of an independent ministry of Colonies in 1894, naval and colonial matters as well as overseas trade were administered by the same ministry whose purpose was to provide the French State with territorial, economic and military oceanic power commensurate with national goals and commitments. The records of that "ministère de la Marine et des Colonies" necessarily reflect these manifold activities—often more economic than naval—and their study understandably leads to an appreciation of the overall maritime picture of which the "fighting navy", however prestigious, was only a part.

In addition to these connotations which varied somewhat from one period to another, reflections on the theme proposed to us led me to situate it within the wide scope of maritime history. Defining naval policy is no mean task in any period and naturally enough attracted brilliant political minds. Achieving the means of attaining that policy is even more arduous, and mobilized the material and human resources of the nation. The study of such vital questions as logistics and manning may be thought of, and rightly so in my opinion, as naval history, but they certainly fall as well within the realm of maritime history. So does the civilian function of supplying nuts and bolts, which, if it draws less limelight than combat with enemy forces, is no less essential to the final outcome of war.

Finally, the kinds of studies based on French naval records undertaken since 1970 are to be classified in their great majority as maritime rather than more strictly speaking naval history.

When the invitation to participate in this Symposium reached me, I decided to make a survey of work going on in French naval records. I quickly found that the state of readers' records was not conducive to the production of neat columns of foolproof statistics. After consulting the French Navy's Historical Service, the reader's service of the Archives Nationales, the Central Registry of Doctoral Dissertations (Fichier central des Theses), various university specialists, particularly those who have made significant contributions to the work of the International Commission for Maritime History, and a great number of friends, a general view of the French scene emerges. The figures given here, however, must be considerd to be indications rather than true statistics. On the whole they tend to under-estimate reality, for the lacunae almost certainly outweigh the number of projects undertaken but abandoned before completion.

The overall view is provided by the files of research requests granted by the French Navy's Historical Service from 1970 to 1 July 1977. Having adopted the time span of 1600-1850, and having eliminated all university work below the doctorate, genealogical research, requests from mass media, publishing houses searching for illustrative material and other such quests of iconography or for details, as well as regional or local studies of limited scope, I found a total of 462 researchers authorized to work on French naval records. Of this number, 161 are not French: 50 are from the United States, 22 from Canada, 20 from Great Britain, five each from Australia and the Federal Republic of Germany, three from Belgium, Ivory Coast and the Netherlands, two from each of 13 countries ranging from France's neighbors, Italy and Spain, to South Korea, and one from each of 17 other countries.

The subjects are so wide-ranging as to defy classification. For 11 studies of the French Navy at war, 24 other projects concerning wars, campaigns and battles, and 36 administrative, institutional, supply and personal subjects, there are 66 topics related to the history of French overseas territories, 36 with diplomatic and consular overtones, 35 economic studies, mainly of maritime commerce with other nations, and 34 concerning French presence and influence outside of the French zone. Somewhat to my surprise, I found 49 biographical subjects listed, 30 studies of port cities and port installations, 20 ship histories and 12 regional or local seacoast topics. It was also a surprise to find only two demographic subjects listed. I wonder if that means that the subject has been exhausted, or that people are tired of demographic studies, or that no one has had the courage to tackle naval personnel records? However, the study of the French Navy's recruiting system ("inscription maritime", or the "système des classes") is beginning: 8

157

studies have been undertaken and another is underway on a related topic, the French "marines". Among titles concerning voyages of discovery and of exploration, several pertain to accounts of travelers in remote parts of the world, particulary in Latin America. Nine titles concern shipwrecks. Is underwater archeology responsible for this sudden interest, or is a new rash of treasure hunting about to break out? All of us old Paris hand recall the frantic search for treasure maps some twenty years ago. Privateering (10), fishing (4), and the merchant marine (3) are still represented, and the study of navy chaplains (2) and of the medical corps along with related topics such as hospitals, naval medicine and hygiene (10), call attention to a trend that is only beginning. Histories of art, science, communications, and of course naval techniques are represented, as are black (4), cultural (4), social (8) and lexicographic (3) studies.

Although the foregoing is based on declarations of intention, as requests for authorization to consult naval records may be called, most of them are pursued to fruition, particularly those presented to universities for doctoral degrees.

The various sources I consulted gave the following results as to doctoral dissertations in progress or completed during the period 1970-1977:

French university doctorates:	
doctorate d'Etat (Lettres)	19
doctorate de 3ᵉ cycle "	41
doctorate d'Université "	1
Ecole des Chartes	12
doctorate in law	6
doctorate in medicine	4
doctorate in architecture	1
doctorate in ethnology	1
doctorates (type not indicated; presumably French)	39
Total French degrees	124
Foreign university doctorates	58
Grand Total	182

Obviously, scholarly research in French naval and other related records is flourishing. Not all subjects are naval or even maritime, but there is widespread appreciation of the rather fabulous store of historical raw materials to be found in naval records. Foreign students were among the first to recognize that along with the diplomatic service, the navy constitutes an excellent point of contact with other countries. Indeed, in the case of former colonies, and for the period under consideration here, the navy was often the only point of contact. The number of requests to consult hydrographic service or consular records, not to mention campaign reports or ministerial letters, attests the awareness of scholars of that fact. Various aspects of maritime trade also constitute popular subjects, as do foreign relations as seen through a naval spyglass, if I may be allowed such an expression. Purely "French" subjects are often chosen by foreign scholars, as are "European" topics. This is so true that French scholars can no longer work on French maritime history without consulting the historiography in other languages, particularly in English. This trend, visible for many years, has become even more pronounced in this decade. By adding to the 58 candidates for foreign doctorates mentioned above, African and Middle Eastern doctoral candidates, of whom some may be preparing French degrees although I found no evidence to this effect, the total rises to 74. Of that number, 42 may be classified as maritime, 24 as colonial and only 4 as naval history, making a total of 70. Only 4 topics out of 74 fall outside the above classification.

Among foreign doctoral candidates, Africans tend to study their own continent, generally their own region, and scholars from the Middle East seem to have a preference for the study of trade and of consular and diplomatic relations in their area. It is an Egyptian, however, who is studying the crucial question of French trade with Cadiz in the 18th century. A Spaniard has chosen to write on d'Aubenton de Villebois, a study which should throw light on many aspects of the 18th century. The West Indies continue to furnish topics for scholarly research as do various other island groups: the Comores and the Seychelles in particular. Various aspects of Franco-Irish and Franco-British relations are being studied, as are many areas of maritime trade and of fishing. British, Canadian and United States scholars are also working on administrators and administrations: Maurepas, Choiseul, Castries, Pontchartrain, Colbert, Rouillé, Le Normand de Mézy, Beauharnais, Vaudreuil, Bigot, Desclouzeaux are names that appear in readers' files. Several studies concern Delisle and Malouet. One is on Vauban. Institutional histories are in progress on the "Counseil d'Etat", the "Conseil de Commerce", the "Conseil d'Amirauté", the "Inscription maritime" and on naval training schools. A particularly interesting subject concerns French naturalists and botanists in French colonies in the 18th century. A Panamanian is studying the history of the Panama Canal, beginning in 1840, and a Belgian is working on the Chappe telegraph. Two studies on Albania are being pursued, as are two others on Georgia (USSR). Greece and Turkey are also well represented. To turn to the New World, an excellent study of the Rotch family of whalers is now completed and the author will, I understand, soon be convoked for his oral examinations. A great many Canadian subjects were noted in addition to some of the administrative studies listed above; several topics concern French Louisiana, and many others, as would be expected, are related to the American Revolution.

Two recently completed United States dissertations are to be cited in respect to the latter: Howard Killion's fine, perceptive study of Suffren's campaign in the Indian Ocean and Jonathan Dull's excellent work on arms and diplomacy, or the French Navy's role in American independence.

Scholarly publications other than dissertations are also numerous. The first to be cited is of course the Navy Department's monumental series of *Naval Documents of the American Revolution* which has made fine use of French archival sources to document the role of France in the winning of American independence. Brian Morton pursues his edition of Beaumarchais' correspondence. The important contributions of Donald Pilgrim on the navy of Louis XIV, of Geoffrey Smycox on the same period, of James Pritchard on the middle years of the 18th century, of Stephen Roberts on the introduction of steam technology in the French Navy are well known, as is Patrick Crowhurst's on trade, commerce raiding and convoys. Finally, the outstanding works of P. W. Bamford (galleys, ship timber, industrial enterprises under contract to the Navy) and of John Bromley (French privateering) must be cited although they are certainly familiar to all present here.

In France too maritime history has come into its own within the past twenty years, gaining considerable momentum in the 1970's. One of the most productive centers has grown up around Michel Mollat, Sorbonne professor, president of the International Commission for Maritime History and director of the inter-institutional, multi-disciplinary laboratory of maritime history. One of the most interesting long-term projects, now one of the major undertakings of the laboratory, is the revised edition of Jal's famous *Glossaire Nautique*. The main burden of the lexicographic research and of the drawing up of definitions is borne by Christiane Villain-Gandossi, but many other experts are consulted. Definitions are in French and equivalencies are given in up to 18 other languages. Letters A and B have been published in the form of soft-cover brochures, C is soon to be off the presses and D, followed by bibliographic references, is ready to be printed. At the end of the alphabet, a bibliographic supplement, an index and equivalents in Arabic will complete this project. It is difficult to overemphasize the importance of this basic reference tool.

In the vast realm of underwater archeology, actively pursued in France, the laboratory of maritime history has been asked to collaborate with the "Direction des Recherches Archéologiques Sous-Marines" (DRASM) at Marseilles. It is hoped that this collaboration will produce good results. Be that as it may, underwater exploration attracts amateurs as well as properly mandated official explorers, hence the urgent necessity of protecting sites and artifacts. The work done in the Mediterranean is quite widely known, but I wonder how many people are aware of the recuperation of cannons and other objects from the *Juste* which sank at the entrance of the Loire river after the battle of the Cardinals in 1759?

A new collection of Sorbonne publications devoted to documents and accounts of voyages, also a laboratory activity, is to be launched with Etienne Taillemite's annotated edition of journals and logs of the Bougainville expedition, due to appear in late 1977 or early 1978. This important work, which the author has allowed to become the first title of the new collection, will set a high standard of excellence for the future.

The laboratory of maritime history also sponsors a survey of maritime ex-votos. Coastal regions from the Belgian to the Spanish borders have already been covered and a descriptive card file established, supplemented by photographs. For the Mediterranean coast, work is nearing completion from Spain to the Rhone river and for Corsica. For the area east of the Rhône, liaison has been established with the University of Provence and with local naval and maritime museums, and the joint survey is progressing. An exhibit of Atlantic, or Western facade, ex-votos drew some 24,000 visitors at Nantes, Caen and Dunkerque in 1975-1976, and another exhibit is planned for the Mediterranean coast in 1978. Jean LePage, who has done a great deal of the work on ex-votos, is also preparing his doctor's dissertation on religious practices of seamen.

Professor Mollat's university courses are often connected with laboratory activities, as would be expected, but do not fall within the scope of this paper.

To a certain degree, the preparation of symposia sponsored by the International Commission of Maritime History (ICMH) and the publication of their proceedings are inseparable from other phases of M. Mollat's undertakings, in the sense that the same people produce the major part of the work, often on their personal time. From 1957 to 1969, 12 such symposia were organized in Paris (4), Lourenço Marquès, Lisbon, Venice, Vienna, Beirut, Seville, Brussels and Bari and the proceedings of 10 of them have been published.[2] In this decade, 6 symposia have been held, the proceedings of the Greenwich meeting (1974) have been published[3] thanks to the National Maritime Museum, and the reports and papers of the San Francisco symposium (1975) were pre-printed by off-set.[4] Proceedings for the Moscow (1970) and the Exeter (1976) meetings are being printed and it is hoped that those of the Varna symposium (1977) can be made available in the not-too-distant future.

The ICMH has another long-term publication underway: the *Bibliography of the History of Great Maritime Routes*, edited by Charles Verlinden. Four sections have appeared to date and the fifth is ready for the printer. This too is a major accomplishment and a basic reference tool for all maritime history specialists.(5)

Among other university professors who have left, or are leaving, their mark on maritime history, Jean Delumeau, for the quality of his own work and for that of students formed by him, deserves a special mention. Since his election to the Collège de France, he has apparently put maritime history aside in order to devote his time to occidental religious mentalities in modern times. However, in addition to Professor Mollat, Professors Mauro, Goubert, Crouzet, Perrot, Pedelaborde (all of Paris), Février (Aix) and Béranger (Rennes) are presently advisors to doctoral candidates whose dissertations concern maritime history. Furthermore, maritime history specialists would of course not fail to give their attention to anything published by Professors Pierre Chaunu (Spanish America), Jean Meyer (Nantes, Bretagne), Jean Bérenger (Colonial America), Bertrand Gille (maritime economy).

Recent economic histories of the trade of various French ports, the work of confirmed historians, are of great interest to the maritime historian. Among them, Charles Garrière, Marcel Courdurie and Ferréol Rebuffat on Marseilles, Paul Butel and Jean Cavignac on Bordeaux, Jean Meyer on Nantes, Levot on Brest and Pierre Dardel on Rouen and Le Havre may be cited. Jean Tarrade's doctoral dissertation on colonial commerce at the end of the "ancien régime" is not to be overlooked. A great number of excellent studies of more limited scope exist but even so the surface of this promising field of investigation has hardly been scratched.

The same can be said for histories of finance directed at least in part towards naval and maritime affairs. The trend is going in that direction, however. Claude-Frédéric Lévy's study of capitalism during the reign of Louis XIV clearly shows that maritime and colonial matters, particularly the slave trade, were at the heart of the kingdom's finances. Daniel Dessert, who has already published articles that have received widespread attention, has undertaken what promises to be the definitive study of financiers during Louis XIVth's reign. It is in fact the subject of his "doctorat d'Etat". Professor Goubert, his advisor, has another outstanding candidate for the "doctorat d'Etat" in Jean-Louis Journet, whose dissertation concerns naval supplies and civilian contractors of the Royal Navy, 1611-1715. These greatly needed works are awaited in many different circles with impatience, all the more that the two young men recently co-authored a provocative article on the Colbert lobby that has whetted many an appetite. Other young university teachers are numerous, active and highly qualified. Among them we shall cite only those who have already appeared on the international scene in ICMH symposia: Philippe Bonnichon and Michel Fontenay at the Sorbonne, André Lespagnol at Rennes, Charles Frostin at Tunis, Michel Morineau at Clermont-Ferrand, and of course Marc Perrichet at Caen. Denys Lombard at the "Ecole des Hautes Etudes en Sciences Sociales," Paris, is one of the prime moving forces behind *Archipel: études interdisciplinaires sur le monde insulindien*, now in its twelfth volume (Bureau 732, 54 boulevard Raspail, 75006 Paris). Lombard is already an accomplished historian and writer, and much is expected of him. These names will certainly continue to appear in bibliographies and their work can hardly fail to be significant. An even younger maritime historian, still teaching in a lycée but coming up fast, is Patrick Villiers. He too has a real contribution to make, as does Anne Pérotin, archivist, and specialist of Spanish colonization in America, one of the best trained and most gifted of the younger historians I have had the privilege of meeting. Two other ladies must be mentioned here: Mme Jeanne Santraud, Professor of English at Paris IV, for her outstanding book on the sea and the American novel, and Nicole Charbonnel, doctor of law, for her work on trade and privateering at La Rochelle, 1775-1815.

Paris, as is well known, is not all of France and important centers of maritime history exist in the provinces. As to university centers, Nantes, Rennes, Brest, Bordeaux and Aix-Marseilles are perhaps the most important, although the publications of all universities should be checked for significant contributions. At present Nantes is in the forefront, thanks to its Medical School and its former Dean (and also President of the University), Professor Jean Pierre Kerneis, who has created, inspired and directed a remakable center for the history of medicine. Dr. Kerneïs' students have produced 125 dissertations for the degree of doctor of medicine, all of which concern seagoing doctors—whether of the Royal Navy, of privateersmen or of merchant vessels—and in general the history of naval medicine and hygiene as well as of epidimiology. This is certainly one of the most significant developments of this decade for the study of maritime history in France. Being married to a microbiologist deeply concerned with epidimiology, I have long been aware of the sobering fact that until our day (shall we say the Second World War?), "generals" who most often decided the outcome of battles, campaigns and even wars were "general epidemics". The same can be said for colonization in the tropical zone and also, obviously, for the slave trade. It is a great satisfaction to see health and medical matters receive the attention they deserve. As his own Bicentennial effort, Dr. Kerneïs undertook the study of medical doctors from la Vendée, from their training through their terms of sea duty during the War for American Independence and on through their subsequent careers, whether naval or civilian.

Nantes counts another specialist of the history of naval medicine and hygiene, Admiral (MC, ret) Adrien Carré. It was he who pioneered the subject in France in our times, particularly the system of medical care and of social and dependents' benefits developed in France in the 17th century and still in existence. He has collaborated wholeheartedly with Professor Kerneïs and with all others interested in naval history in general and in that of naval medicine in particular. It is entirely fitting that the section on individual scholars begin with him. There are many such experts in France, working more or less alone, often members of the "Comités de

163

Documentation historique de la Marine" of Paris, Nantes and Brest and of local learned societies. Many French ports, particularly those where naval shore establishments and naval/maritime museums are located, have active and competent local historians.

In Paris there are too many such individual scholars for me to be able to cite them all. Attention should be called to the work of Marcel Destombes, specialist of the history of cartography, of Jacques Aman, doctor of law whose dissertation in Letters on the "officer bleu", or the "ancien régime" reserve officer, is most enlightening, of Jacques Michel on Vice-Admiral Count d'Estaing, and of Jean Boudriot, architect, whose superb four volume work on the 74-gun ship of the line is without doubt one of the major events in France in the field of maritime history within this decade.

A fine contribution to the celebration of the bicentennial of American independence has been and is being made by the "Comité de Documentation historique de la Marine" of Paris which is producing a two-year cycle of lectures on naval and maritime aspects of the American Revolution. The texts will be published in book form and, judging by the quality of the papers already presented, they will interest a broad span of the scholarly and cultivated public.

A few guidelines as to French bibliography may be helpful. The most complete, and also official, source is the *Bibliographie de France* put out by the Bibliotheque Nationale, based on copyright deposits ("dépôt légal"), and distributed by the "Cercle de la Librairie". This *Bibliographie* is now virtually current and is of course the basis for all bibliographic research on French publications. Also bearing the general title of *Bibliographie de France* but with the sub-title of *Biblio*, the "Cercle de la Librairie" publishes a commercial trade journal carrying publishers' paid announcements of books as they appear.[6] For many years, the publisher "France Expansion"[7] specialized in bibliographic works covering all forms of edition in the French language throughout the world, the two most widely known titles having been *Francophonie* and *Repertoire des Livres de Langue française disponibles*. As of now—that is, October and November 1977—"France Expansion", the "Cercle de la Librairie" and the "Catalogue de l'Edition française" are pooling their resources in order to publish one general bibliography of books in print in the French language. It will be entitled *Livres disponibles*.

At the same time, "France Expansion" is launching a new bi-monthly journal called *A Paraître,* half of which will be devoted to a round-up of books, periodicals, collections, proceedings, etc. to be published. *A Paraître* will cover everything in French except fiction. The other half of this new journal will contain analyses of the recent and probably future evolution of publication in a given area (the first to be dealt with will be the social sciences) and of tendencies in publishing. Frequent articles will highlight liaison between universities and the publishing business, and a regular feature called "Bloc-Notes" will announce schedules of meetings (congresses, symposia, etc.), of prepublication subscriptions and of all significant events of interest to people concerned with books and other supports of the written word. Other features will present profiles of editors, authors and scholars, surveys of the various disciplines or fields, and technical studies, one of the first of which will be on micro-editions.

To conclude this general bibliographic survey, the *Bulletin critique du Livre français*[8] and the *Bibliographic annuelle de l'Histoire de France*[9] are to be mentioned.

In our own realm of maritime history, Jean Polak, well-known dealer specialized in naval, maritime, colonial and travel books, published his *Bibliographie Maritime Française depuis les temps les plus reculés jusqu'à 1914* in 1976.[10] Catherine Méhaud is putting the finishing touches to her *Bibliographie Française d'Histoire Maritime 1962-1975,* which, when printed, will be indispensable to libraries and specialists alike.

Among periodicals, *La Revue Maritime* and *Neptunia*[11] carry a few book reviews, as does *Cols Bleus.* The *Petit Perroquet,* put out by the Editions des 4 Seigneurs at Grenoble, is entirely devoted to maritime history, naval archeology and architecture and other sea subjects, including book reviews. This same publisher has brought out several fine reeditions of famous treatises, has edited numerous memoirs, many of which are related to the War for American Independence, and printed and distributed Boudriot's *Vaisseau de 74.*[12]

The special maritime history issues of the *Revue d'Histoire économique et sociale*[13] are certainly well-known and should always be checked for good articles and new books.

Two other great periodicals are indispensable to all who want to know what is going on in France in history: the *Revue Historique*[14] and the *Annales Economies Sociétés Civilisations.*[15] Widely read in France—and surely in North America—is the excellent Canadian *Revue d'Histoire de l'Amérique française.*[16] Speaking of Canada, I would like to point out the unique importance of the *Dictionary of Canadian Biography,*[17] a multivolume work in progress, not only for Canada and for France, but also for the United States and the West Indies. It is extraordinarily complete and well done.

Other printed sources, perhaps not very well-known outside of France, are the proceedings of the historical sections of the national congresses of Learned Societies and the publications of the "Ecole Pratique des Hautes Etudes" (*Bibliotheque générale de l'EPHE* and *Collection Ports—Routes—Trafics).*[18]

What better way could be found to introduce the subject of archives than to cite the *Guide to the Archival Sources of American History in France,*[19] even though I did have a great deal to do with it! Conceived to be a lasting contribution to the celebration of the bicentennial of United States independence, the guide was prepared by 10 archivists and myself who also shared with Etienne Taillemite the responsibility for producing the book. It *is* a guide, not an inventory, but as such will undoubtedly render great service to scholars. It points the way to sources that can hardly be said to be new, but that are little known and virtually unused. "New" to public use are various collections of private papers now available in the "Section des Archives privees" at the Archives Nationales. An outstanding example is the correspondence of Count Hector, director of the port and arsenal of Brest during the War for American Independence.

A bilateral Franco-Canadian guide has been in gestation for several years. Canada has long since finished its section on archives related to France, and France's contribution on archival sources related to Canada was recently completed. The manuscript will soon be sent to the printer. When available, this guide will also be a boon to the researcher.

Another bit of good news from France may be announced here: the famous old *Etat sommaire des Archives de la Marine* by Didier Neuville is being reproduced by offset and will soon be on the market. It is far from being adequate by present standards but is the best general finding aid for naval records in existence. Neuville's introductions to series and sub-series can hardly be improved upon and should be read and re-read by everyone working in the field. While Etienne Taillemite was curator of naval and colonial records at the Archives Nationales, many excellent inventories and tables were published. None is more useful than the volume of *Tables des noms de lieux, de personnes, de matières et de navires* mentioned in Didier Neuville's seven volume and in Taillemite's eighth volume inventory of the Marine B series. These tables are the work of Etienne Taillemite and of Mesdames Jacqueline Giroux and Thérèse Tour. Complete names are given with their correct spelling and their various incorrect but frequently used versions—a real boon to all who have to struggle with the fantasies of 17th and 18th century spelling. Philippe Henrat, Taillemite's successor in naval and colonial records, is carrying on this welcome and necessary policy of publication. Sales of Archives Nationales publications are handled by the "Documentation Française" (29-31 quai Voltaire, 75340 Paris cedex 7).

"New"—perhaps to North Americans, or at least more readily available—are the archival materials on microfilms made under my direction for the Library of Congress[20] and under that of Raymonde Litalien for the Public Archives of Canada. These microfilms are America-related but even so they document a very large segment of French history—a good indication, by the way, of the place occupied by the New World in French policies and endeavors during the period being considered here. Canada has worked primarily in Colonial and Army records whereas the Library of Congress has placed considerable emphasis on Naval records for the very good reason that the Navy was the best point of contact between France and North America during the colonial period and the next best, after the Ministry of Foreign Affairs (Diplomatic records have already been microfilmed to the mid-19th century), since the United States became independent. In our work, Mlle Litalien and I occasionally find important things in unexpected places. The latest discovery was made a few weeks ago by Mlle Litalien in Bordeaux: a certain Monsieur Le Moyne turned out to be a direct descendant of Le Moyne de Sérigny and the proud possessor of family records concerning Iberville, Sérigny, Bienville and Châteauguay, names that sing to Louisianan and Canadian ears.

Now the question is: what remains to be done? We need more institutional and administrative studies, not only from the standpoint of central government but from that of the grass roots, the wharf, the dockyards, the local offices and law courts. Versailles ordained, but local people, conditions and circumstances determined what was actually done. More studies of finances are also badly needed. Bosher's excellent work[21] indicated the direction to take in that vital area of investigation. Good studies are underway concerning personnel but it will surely be a long time before the picture is complete. The same can be said for the whole logistics system and for the people who made it run—or not run. There is still much to be done as regards the study of living conditions, including climate, the history of science and of techniques, of ideas and of mentalities. The economic and social impact of oceanic pursuits—whether naval, privateering or maritime commerce—on port cities and coastal regions should prove to be a stimulating and rewarding subject. Finally, let me suggest that new histories of naval operations, strategy and tactics, with less derring-do and better knowledge of what the actors were up against (including their orders, which are at times superbly ignored by historians whereas the man making the decisions on the spot could hardly afford to forget about them) would also be timely and enlightening for us all.

These remarks almost preclude the necessity of mentioning changing interpretations, for in a large measure the sources available—and consulted—obviously determine interpretations. Chronological narrations are such a thing of the past that they surely will soon return to favor. Interpretations of economic, social and cultural history naturally change as systems of value and schools of philosophical and historical thought change. Historical fashions also play their part in changing interpretations. From births, deaths, marriages, baptisms and other such demographic questions, many historians have turned to the effects of weather or of epidimilogy on the course of human events. The earnest quest to know how things really were, now producing good, provocative studies, will probably give rise one of these years to a brilliant outburst of historical syntheses.

Wishful thinking? No, a wish; almost a prediction.

167

FOOTNOTES

[1] It is my pleasure to thank the Service Historique de la Marine, the Archives Nationales, the Fichier central des Thèses, Madame Christiane Villain-Gandossi and Mademoiselle Catherine Méhaud for providing a part of the information on which these remarks are based.

[2] These publications may be ordered from the Service d'Edition et de Vente des Publications de l'Education Nationale (S E V P E N), 13 rue du Four, 75006 Paris.

[3] and may be purchased from the National Maritime Museum, London SE10 9NF.

[4] Copies may be ordered from Professeur Michel Mollat du Jourdin, 1 rue Bausset, 75015 Paris.

[5] They have been published in a variety of places. Inquiries may be sent to Prof. Mollat (see note 4).

[6] Cercle de la Librairie, 117 boulevard Saint-Germain, 75006 Paris.

[7] France Expansion, 336 rue Saint-Honoré, 75001 Paris.

[8] Association pour la Diffusion de la Pensée française (A D P F), 21 bis rue La Pérouse, 75116 Paris.

[9] Editions du Centre national de la Recherche scientifique (C N R S), 15 quai Anatole France, 75700 Paris; Canada: Presses de l'Université de Montréal, Case postale 6128, Montréal 101; U.S.A.: SMPF, 14 East 60th Street, New York, N. Y. 10022.

[10] Editions des 4 Seigneurs, 39 rue Marceau, 3800 Grenoble.

[11] Both are domiciled at the Musée de la Marine, Palais de Chaillot, 75016 Paris.

[12] *Cols Bleus*, 3 avenue Octave-Gérard, 75007 Paris. For others, see note no. 10.

[13] Editions Marcel Rivière et Cie, 22 rue Soufflot, 75005 Paris.

[14] Presses Universitaires Françaises, 108 boulevard Saint-Germain, 75006 Paris.

[15] Librairie Armand Colin, 103 boulevard Saint-Michel, 75240 Paris Cedex 5.

[16] Institut d'histoire de l'Amérique française, 261 avenue Bloomfield, Outremont, Montréal H2V 3R6, Québec.

[17] University of Toronto Press, 5201 Dusserin Street, Downsview, Ontario M3H 9Z9. The French edition is put out by the Laval University Press.

[18] Ecole Pratique des Hautes Etudes, 45-47 rue des Ecoles, 75005 Paris.

[19] France Expansion, see note 7.

[20] Available for consultation in the Manuscript Division of the Library of Congress.

[21] Bosher, J. R. *French Finances, 1770-1795.*

CHAPTER 14

Diplomacy from the Quarterdeck: the U.S. Navy in the Caribbean, 1815-1830 ___

Raymond L. Shoemaker

Indiana Historical Society

This article concerns the activities of the early United States Navy in the Caribbean just after the close of the War of 1812. Although the activities of the navy in the Mediterranean in this period have been covered extensively, and to a lesser extent those in the Pacific, there has been no adequate study made of the navy in the Caribbean during the Latin American wars of independence, that is, from 1815 to 1830. This is surprising, because naval action in that area was more important to American commerce and to foreign relations than was its activity in the Mediterranean. Next to Great Britain, the nations of Latin America, especially the Caribbean countries, were America's best customers, and, next to Great Britain, the United States was the region's most valuable supplier. In addition, the proximity of the area to the United States encouraged diplomatic connections. By 1815, long before president James Monroe announced his famous doctrine, the influence of the United States in the Caribbean was pronounced and in some localities dominant.

While the Latin Americans carried on their revolutions after 1815, Europe and the United States, once more at peace, could resume their commercial expansion into the promising markets to the south. With the Spanish monopoly broken and both belligerents needing supplies, the opportunities seemed limitless. But American merchants were reluctant to move into the Caribbean without the aid of some stabilizing influence. Since the rapidly changing conditions of an area in revolution prevented regular diplomatic representation, naval officers became the principal agents through which this stabilizing influence was established in the Caribbean after 1815. Protectors of American commerce as well as impromptu diplomatic agents, the American naval officers were, for a time, the most important representatives of the United States in the area.

The reasons for using the navy were logical. At the end of the War of 1812 the navy had reached a considerable strength, and it no longer was needed in the Mediterranean against the Barbary pirates, which the British defeated decisively in 1816. Thus it was available for use nearby home, in the Caribbean. At that time the State Department, understaffed even in Europe, was almost unrepresented in the Caribbean, since it sent recognized consuls only to Cuba, Puerto Rico, and Haiti. On several Swedish and Danish islands American resident consuls were unrecognized by the local governors. On the Spanish Main only La Guaira had an American consul before 1823, for those at Puerto Cabello, Maracaibo, Santa Marta, Cartagena, and Panama were added after that date.[1]

In contrast, Great Britain had many diplomatic and commercial representatives in the area and supplemented them with naval commanders. All these agents worked hard and with some success to shut American competitors out of the Caribbean markets.[2] If the United States wanted entrance into these markets, it would have to find a method of extending and then protecting its trade. In the chaotic Latin American scene, surrounded by British rivals and understaffed with diplomatic agents, this would not be easy. Necessity caused the State Department to turn to the many experienced naval officers for assistance.

Although American naval officers received no formal training in diplomacy, it cannot be said that they had no exposure to international affairs. All except the young lieutenants had followed the vicissitudes of American policy during the Napoleonic Wars. They were aware of their nation's commercial interest and the necessity of protecting that interest if the United States was to grow. Most of them came from merchant or naval families and, as men whose lives were tied to the sea, realized that commerce would probably expand by water.

Since the more senior officers had begun their careers fighting the French in the Quasi War of 1798-1801, they were well acquainted with the geography of the Caribbean. They knew the currents, winds, climate, and diseases of the region. The naval officers appreciated the dangers and hardships the merchants faced when doing business in the Caribbean. For several years during the Quasi War they had plied the treacherous waters in search of French warships and privateers. Here the Navy had carried out its most glorious exploits—the victories of the *Constellation* over the French frigates *Insurgente* and *Vengeance*.

A glance at a map of the Caribbean will show that four narrow passages commanded its approaches from the United States. To the east of Puerto Rico is the Sombrero Passage, which merchants generally did not use because it lay off the main trade routes. They used the second route, the Mona Passage, between Puerto Rico and Santo Domingo, primarily for the return voyage to the United States from the Spanish Main. The two most frequented passages were the Windward, between Haiti and Cuba, and the Florida Channel north of Cuba—the former for trade with southern Cuba and the Spanish Main, the latter for trade with New Orleans, Havana, and Mexico. Winds and currents encouraged the route, as the northeast trade winds prevailed in the Caribbean.

Unfortunately the difficult and narrow accesses into the Caribbean made interdiction of trade easy. Merchants trading with the rebellious Spanish colonies became painfully aware of this as Spanish privateers, who carried royal commissions but acted more like pirates, swooped down on merchantmen attempting to negotiate the passages. American commanders had the duty of protecting their countrymen from such plundering. It became increasingly clear that this protection would involve diplomatic as well as naval means, since the United States maintained that stopping non-contraband neutral trade was illegal and Spain defended the practice. This difference of opinion would cause problems, with the American naval commanders caught in the middle.

Besides their necessary involvement with commercial problems, the chaotic situation in the Caribbean and the military character of the local rulers gave a decided advantage to naval commanders performing diplomatic tasks. A demonstration of force and an atmosphere of camaraderie between naval officers and military governors sometimes produced startling results in the wake of failure by State Department agents.

Merchants in the United States were not unfamiliar with difficulties of a neutral nation trading with belligerents. America had just fought a war over this issue. The merchants also knew something about the uncertain Latin American trade. They had sent their ships and goods to that region since colonial times, as Spain enforced or ignored its navigation laws as needs at home and overseas required. During the wars and internal upheavals between 1776 and 1815, Spain allowed trade to develop between the United States and Spanish America because Madrid could not maintain communications with her colonies. By 1815 the trade of the United States with the Caribbean was second only to Britain's. Many American merchants had become heavily dependent on this trade.[3]

After the Latin American revolutions began it became increasingly difficult for the United States to deal with the erstwhile Spanish colonies and avoid a confrontation with Spain. Naturally that nation objected vigorously to American trade with the rebels as an aid to the rebellion and therefore an unfriendly act. Earlier Britain had so regarded all such trade with the rebellious American colonies, and the United States would later do the same during its Civil War. Yet over Spain's protests, the United States became one of Latin America's largest suppliers.

Another activity which did nothing to endear Americans to Spain or her loyalists in the Caribbean was the system of privateering practiced by the

171

rebels. The privateering vessels, which attacked Spanish trade, were mostly manned, commanded, and frequently owned by Americans. This arrangement was natural, since the Latin Americans had little experience with the sea, and many able-bodied American seamen were out of work with the termination of the war with Britain. The patriot (rebel) governments in Colombia, Mexico, Chile, and other places offered great rewards to American seamen for their services. Even more tempting was the opportunity to sail on a former American privateer that had merely changed its prey from British to Spanish.[4] It was not uncommon to find a patriot privateer on which English was the only language. The Monroe administration, especially Secretary of State John Quincy Adams, attempted to halt this practice, but even when United States' port officials apprehended Americans engaged in this illegal activity when their vessels put into an American port, convictions by local juries were rare. Generally the American people supported the revolutions and were loath to assist the Spanish in any way.[5]

Spanish officials in the Caribbean were furious at this practice, and if *they* captured an American serving on a patriot privateer, they threw him into prison without hope of release. The loyal Spanish population reflected the views of the officials. Cuban and Puerto Rican merchants saw the American-manned privateers plundering their ships and in some cases plunging them into financial ruin. As the people of the Spanish islands were dependent on trade, a blow to the merchants affected them all. Loyalists began to strike back, since the United States proved unable to halt unneutral acts of its citizens. Some even fitted out their own privateers to prey upon vessels going to and from rebel ports, often demonstrating even less concern with legality than their patriot counterparts. The Spanish captured American merchant ships, taking their prizes into remote ports, rather than the more legal admiralty courts at Havana, San Juan, or Santiago, where local judges and inhabitants shared in the profits gained from condemning the captured vessels.[6]

The existing American consuls in the Caribbean were powerless to protect the American merchantmen from seizure and condemnation, although they protested loudly. Spanish officials claimed that as mere colonial administrators they could not intervene; any action would have to come from Madrid. Yet Secretary Adams' efforts to solve the problem at Madrid met with delay, confusion, and defeat.[7] Adams could find no acceptable diplomatic solution. Looking for less traditonal alternatives, he found an ally in the secretary of the navy.

Unlike the understaffed secretary of state, Secretary of the Navy Benjamin Crowninshield was plagued with an overabundance of naval personnel and a dearth of constructive assignments for them. Most of the ships built during the War of 1812 were no longer needed and because of budget stringencies were placed in ordinary. With fewer ships the navy needed fewer men. There was little problem disposing of the ordinary seamen; most were happy to be done with the life of the navy and could turn to service on a merchant vessel or even a privateer. But the department also had to force out many of the officers who had entered the navy with the intent of remaining there. Crowninshield managed to persuade Congress to retain more officers than he really needed, but this meant that he had to find useful employment for them.[8] The secretary encouraged nonessential officers to take furloughs and find employment on merchant vessels until naval assignments opened.[9]

This was a stopgap measure, and Crowninshield and his successor, Smith Thompson, needed some arrangement that would give their officers employment in naval rather than commercial positions. One such plan appeared in Thompson's letters to Adams concerning Oliver Hazard Perry's successful and important diplomatic mission to Venezuela in 1819. Thompson supported such employment of officers, as there were "so many naval officers on duty and so little for them to do." He was sure that such employment would benefit both departments, as the officers could perform naval missions in hazardous areas while the State Department used them as diplomats.[10]

Thompson felt that officers made good diplomats. Adams evidently agreed, for in his communication to Thompson about Perry he mentioned two advantages of using a naval officer rather than a State Department agent—the unsettled state of affairs in Latin America, and the ability of a military man such as Venezuela's Simón Bolívar to understand another military man, such as Oliver Hazard Perry, who was backed by force.[11] Adams also knew that naval vessels visited many Latin American ports, especially in the Caribbean, which lacked an American diplomatic agent. Naval officers were in a position to establish relations with areas otherwise inaccessible to the State Department.[12]

Adams was a nationalist from a maritime state, and he showed no hesitation in expressing his esteem for the navy and its officers, professionally and personally. These men were imbued with an intense nationalism and confidence as a result of the recent wars with Britain and the Barbary powers. If Adams had not understood and respected these traits it is unlikely that he would have entrusted them with delicate diplomatic assignments, no matter how pressed he was for personnel. On several occasions Adams publicly stated his belief that only a strong navy could protect the United States. He counted several prominent officers among his friends and confidants, including Commodores Charles Stewart, William Bainbridge, John Rodgers, and James Biddle. Biddle, while on a mission to the Pacific in 1819, protected American interests so vigorously that the Chilean government officially protested to the United States. Adams, however, defended Biddle's actions. In his memoirs he wrote, "Biddle's conduct was perhaps indiscreet, and not entirely disinterested. But he turned it at least to the account of his countrymen, for whom he saved and rescued property to a very large amount. He obtained also the release of many citizens of the United States who were prisoners."[13] Adams held many agents of his own department in much lower esteem.[14]

Nor was the value of the warship in diplomatic matters lost on Adams. In a letter to one of the first naval officers thus employed, Crowninshield enjoined Captain John Downes to make "such a display of the ship . . . as may be best calculated to produce impressions favorable to the interests of the United States."[15] In the future naval officers were encouraged to use this tool for diplomacy.

As naval forces in the Caribbean increased through 1820, the United States government grew impatient at Spanish interference with American commerce. Adams made it clear to the Spanish minister in Washington that the United States would not recognize the "paper" blockade that Madrid had decreed and therefore would allow American warships to protect merchantmen from capture by Spanish privateers.[16] Through such devices as harassing privateers and convoying American vessels past blockades, the navy made it difficult for privateers to operate effectively. Spanish ministers protested this treatment in vain. The administration's tough policy vis-à-vis Spanish privateers remained the same. In fact, Adams applied continuous pressure upon the Spanish government to revoke the blockade and the privateering commissions issued under its auspices. Failing action by the Spanish government, he practically declared war on the Spanish privateers, and by the end of 1820, the navy had greatly reduced the threat to American commerce from these raiders.[17] Unfortunately, the Elizabethan expression, "if you scratch a privateer, you will find a pirate," was never more apt than in the early nineteenth-century Caribbean.

As the navy drove the Spanish privateers from the seas, more and more undisguised pirates appeared. In many cases, these pirates were actually former privateers who had shed the last vestige of legitimacy. Congress acted quickly against the growing menace to American shipping. If some members had been reluctant to interfere with the Spanish privateers, none was hesitant about how to treat pirates. In March 1819, Congress passed, "An Act to Protect the Commerce of the United States and Punish the Crime of Piracy." Over the next three years, Congress renewed the bill and increased its scope. Naval officers were authorized to seize any ship they believed to have committed or attempted piratical acts. Armed with these powers, the navy soon destroyed the large, cruising pirate vessels.[18]

This destruction, however, resulted in a change in the pirates' *modus operandi*. They became land-based and operated in small, usually oar-propelled vessels that could navigate the coves and streams lacing the

Cuban coast. These pirates would lurk in their hiding places along the shore or among the many keys on the trade routes and await the arrival of an unfortunate merchantman, suddenly betrayed by the often unreliable winds and left becalmed within striking distance of the pirate craft. To combat this odious system, the navy needed the assistance of local inhabitants and officials who could destroy the pirates' land bases. Unfortunately, the Spanish of Cuba and Puerto Rico were reluctant to provide this assistance because of profits in dealing with the pirates and Spanish hostility toward Americans.

State Department officials could not persuade the Spanish governors to move against the pirate bases. Adams discerned that naval commanders, while enforcing the piracy act of 1819, had more success impressing Caribbean leaders with the possibility of American intervention if the piracy threat continued. He also noted that a timely, if unauthorized, diplomatic effort by several lieutenants had gained the release of American prisoners in Cuba.[19]

Finally, Adams and his colleagues realized that it took too long for an officer to return to Washington for instructions. In the unstable situation in the Caribbean immediate decisions had to be made. Therefore, in 1822, the navy created the West India Squadron and appointed a commander armed with instructions from both the Navy and State Departments.[20] Over the next half decade the commanders of the West India Squadron and their lieutenants fought pirates and negotiated with most of the rulers of the Caribbean to promote and protect growing American commerce. Gradually, through a combination of subtle threats, constant pressure, and dramatic naval actions these commanders convinced Spanish officials first to permit, then to join with them in clearing out the pirate bases on the islands. Examples of their successes are numerous, but perhaps the most significant negotiation was between the first commander of the Squadron, James Biddle, and the Spanish governor of Cuba, Don Nicholas Mahy. Through coercion, persuasion, flattery, and a timely incident pointing out the necessity for cooperation, Biddle wrenched from Mahy an informal agreement not to protest the landing of American troops on the uninhabited Cuban keys. From this slight opening grew the privilege of landing troops on Cuban soil whenever American commanders felt it necessary.[21]

The list of officers who served in the West India Squadron during the Latin American revolts is impressive. The first commander was Biddle, already well known to Adams and Thompson for his adroit handling of the delicate matter of neutral rights of the United States in the midst of the struggle between the patriots and royalists in Chile and Peru in 1819.[22] In 1846, twenty years after his service in the Caribbean, Biddle negotiated the first commercial treaty between China and the United States.[23] On his return trip from China, he attempted to repeat his success by negotiating a treaty with Japan but failed.[24] Serving under Biddle was a group of junior officers later famous for their diplomatic and naval exploits. Lawrence Kearny, also operating in the Far East during the 1840s, helped to secure from China the same trade concessions as did the British following the First Opium War in 1842 and lay the foundations for the Open Door Policy.[25] Matthew C. Perry, who in 1856 convinced the Japanese to end their isolation, is perhaps the best known of the group. David Porter, the second to command the squadron, was a renowned warrior before his assignment to the Caribbean in 1823.[26] Unfortunately, his naval career was destroyed during this assignment, but he finished his life as a minister to the Ottoman Empire under Andrew Jackson and Martin Van Buren.[27] Others included David G. Farragut, Porter's adopted son, Francis Gregory, who along with Farragut and Porter's biological son, David Dixon Porter, were among the nation's first admirals, and the enigmatic Jesse Elliott, who commanded the West India Squadron in the last years of the pirate threat. Elliott summed up the dilemma that the naval officers faced in the Caribbean during these years. In a letter to the Cuban governor in 1830 Elliott complained:

> The consular agents appointed by our government for the Island of Cuba, not having been accredited by that of His Catholic Majesty, it devolves upon us to take cognizance of matters, more properly appertaining to such agents, . . . and let me trust that such a remedy may be ere long applied, as will supersede the necessity of the officers of this squadron having to content otherwise than on their peculiar element.[28]

It can be argued that this early form of gunboat diplomacy led to later American interventions and Latin American bitterness. Certainly navy commanders used stronger pressure and assumed a more threatening stance than the State Department agents. Yet the alternative was to sacrifice American commerce and prestige in the area to mollify a government that most Americans despised for its toleration of commerce raiders. Without the combination of naval and diplomatic pressure commerce would have ceased to grow, as British merchants would have gladly replaced their Yankee rivals.

In the early nineteenth century the United States was not yet guilt-ridden over use of its power, and the choice of policy was obvious—commercial expansion aided by diplomacy. The Monroe and Adams administrations used naval officers to develop and carry out this policy in the Caribbean.

FOOTNOTES

[1] John P. Harrison (ed.), *Guide to Materials on Latin America in the National Archives* (Washington, D.C., 1961), end paper map; Arthur P. Whitaker, *The United States and the Independence of Latin America, 1800-1830* (Baltimore, 1941), 152.

[2] Charles K. Webster (ed.), *Britain and the Independence of Latin America, 1812-1830: Selected Documents from the Foreign Office Archives*, 2 vols. (London 1938), I, 40-44, 50-52.

[3] Timothy Pitkin, *A Statistical View of the Commerce of the United States of America* (New Haven, 1839), 285; see also Whitaker, *Independence of Latin America*, 116-17.

[4] John Quincy Adams to John M. Forbes, special agent to Buenos Aires, July 5, 1820 and Adams to James Monroe, Jan. 28, 1819, in William R. Manning (ed.), *Diplomatic Correspondence of the United States Concerning the Independence of the Latin American Nations,* 3 vols. (New York, 1925), I, 131-32, 94; H. G. Warren, *The Sword Was Their Passport: A History of American Filibustering in the Mexican Revolution* (Port Washington, 1972), 152-53. For an excellent account of the Baltimore privateers, see C. C. Griffin, "Privateering from Baltimore during the Spanish-American Wars of Independence," *Maryland Historical Magazine*, XXV (1940), 1-25; Stanley Faye, "Privateersmen of the Gulf," *Louisiana Historical Quarterly*, XXII (July 1939). The Congress of Aix-la-Chapelle, at the urging of the Portuguese representative, singled out Baltimore for special condemnation regarding unneutral activities. Only a mild rebuke came out of the Congress in its final form, mostly because Britain would not agree to anything stronger. Charles Francis Adams, (ed.), *The Memoirs of John Quincy Adams, Comprising Portions of His Diary from 1795 to 1848*, 12 vols. (Philadelphia, 1874-1877), IV, 316-19.

[5] William Wirt to James Monroe, Sept. 10, 1818, Miscellaneous Letters of the Department of State, 1789-1906, General Records of the Department of State, Record Group 59, National Archives, n.p., reel 42; James D. Weitcott to Joseph Anderson, U.S. Comptroller, June 8, 1819, Miscellaneous Letters, reel 44; Manning, *Diplomatic Correspondence*, I, 75-76.

[6] Richard K. Wheeler, *In Pirate Waters* (New York, 1969), 80-82; Master Commandant John Elton to Secretary of the Navy Smith Thompson, Dec. 29, 1821, Letters Received by the Secretary from Commanders, Office of Naval Records and Library, Record Group 45, National Archives, 21, pt. 2, reel 9; Judah Lord, U.S. Consul in Puerto Rico, to Adams, May 18, 1822, Despatches from United States Consular Representatives in Puerto Rico, 1821-1899, M 79, General Records of the Department of State, RG 59, reel 2.

[7] Lord to Adams, Jan. 13, 1821, Consular Letters, Puerto Rico, reel 39; George Erving, U.S. minister to Spain, to Pablo Cevallos, foreign secretary, Oct. 15, 1816, Cevallos to Erving, Oct. 17, 1816, Erving to Cevallos, Oct. 25, 1816, in Manning, *Diplomatic Correspondence*, III, 1907-09.

[8] Letters from the Secretary of the Navy to Officers, Records of the Secretary of the Navy, Office of Naval Records and Library, Record Group 45, National Archives, 1816-1817, reel 12, *passim.*

[9] Matthew C. Perry to Secretary of the Navy Benjamin Crowninshield, July 31, 1817, Letters Received by the Secretary of the Navy from Officers Below the Rank of Commander, Office of Naval Records and Library, Record Group 45, 77, pt. 1, reel 17; John Gallagher to Crowninshield, April 6, 1817, *ibid.*, 5, pt. 2, reel 16.

[10] Smith Thompson to Adams, March 15, April 26, 1819, Miscellaneous Letters, reel 44.

[11] Adams to Thompson, June 5, 1818, Domestic Letters of the Department of State, 1784-1906, General Records of the Department of State, Record Group 59, 326-28, reel

15; Adams to Thompson, May 20, 1819, Confidential Letters, 1813-1822, Naval Records Collection of the Office of Naval Records and Library, Record Group 45, pp. 266-67.

[12] Natalia Summers, *Documents Relating to Special Agents of the Department of State* (Washington, 1951), viii.

[13] Adams Diary, John Quincy Adams Papers, Library of Congress, Manuscript Division, 98, reel 34 and reels 35-38, *passim; Niles Register,* XIV (March 14, 1818), 33; Adams, *Memoirs,* V,164.

[14] Adams had nothing but contempt for a trio of observers sent to Buenos Aires in 1818. Baptis Irvine, who preceded Oliver Hazard Perry to Venezuela in 1819 thoroughly antagonized Simón Bolívar and received Adams' scorn. John Prevost, an agent who accompanied James Biddle to the northwest, was so cautious he was ineffective. Adams had little use for him. Adams, *Memoirs,* IV, 159, V, 164; Diary of Adams, Adams Papers, 64, reel 34.

[15] Crowninshield to John Downes, Sept. 2, 1818, Confidential Letters, 254-56.

[16] Luis de Onis to Monroe, Sept. 5, 1815, *Annals of Congress,* 15 Cong., 1 Sess., Vol. II, 1841; Manning, *Diplomatic Correspondence,* III, 1891; Adams to Hugh Nelson, U.S. minister to Spain, April 28, 1823, in Manning, *Diplomatic Corespondence,* I, 166; Erving to Cervallos, Oct. 15, 25, 1816, in Manning, *Diplomatic Correspondence,* III, 1907-09.

[17] *Niles Register,* 1819-1820, *passim.* See especially XVII (Sept. 11, 1819), 31; XVII (Oct. 30, 1819), 143; XVII (Dec. 25, 1819), 287; XVIII (June 24, 1820), 298; and XVIII (Aug. 5, 1820), 416; Daniel T. Patterson to Thompson, Sept. 10, 1821, Letters of the Secretary of the Navy from Captains, Office of Naval Records and Library, Record Group 45, 77, reel 73, 42, reel 74.

[18] *Annals of Congress,* March 3, 1819, 15 Cong., 2 Sess., 2523, May 15, 1820, 16 Cong., 1 Sess., 2623, March 2, 1822, 17 Cong., 1 Sess., 1175; Adams Diary, Adams Papers, 65-66, reel 34; *Niles Register,* XIX-XXII (Sept. 1820-Sept. 1822), *passim;* Thompson to Lawrence Kearney, Nov. 21, 1821, Letters from the Secretary of the Navy to Officers, Office of Naval Records and Library, 240, reel 14; Kearney to Patterson, March 7, 1822, Captains Letters, 58, reel 78.

[19] Matthew C. Perry to Thompson, March 28, 1822, Letterbook of Matthew C. Perry, *Journals Kept by Naval Personnel Attached to Vessels at Sea, 1776-1908,* Office of Naval Records and Library, 20-21; Lieutenant John R. Madison to Kearney, April 20, 1820, Captains Letters, 49, reel 67; Madison to Patterson, May 15, 1820, Captains Letters, 49, reel 67.

[20] James Biddle to Thompson, Feb. 12, 1822, Captains Letters, 18, reel 78; Thompson to Lowdnes, Jan. 13, 1822, and Thompson to Samuel Smith, Jan 25, 1822, Letters to Congress, Naval Records Collection of the Office of Naval Records and Library; Thompson to Biddle, March 26, 1822, Confidential Letters, 334-35; Adams to Biddle, Domestic Letters, March 22, 1822, 296-97, reel 17.

[21] Biddle to Governor Don Nicholas Mahy, April 30, 1822, Captains Letters, 77, reel 78; Mahy to Biddle, May 2, 1822, Captains Letters, 78, reel 78; Biddle to Thompson, May 6, 1822, Captains Letters, 79, reel 78; Biddle to Adams, May 29, 1822, Miscellaneous Letters, 42-43, reel 54; Biddle to Thompson, May 18, 1822, Captains Letters, 91, reel 78; *Niles Register,* XXII (June 22, 1822), 264.

[22] Biddle to Crowninshield, 1818-1819, Captains Letters; Biddle to Monroe, *American State Papers—Naval Affairs,* 3 vols. (Washington, 1832-1861), I, 668-69; Biddle to Adams, Dec. 7, 1819, Miscellaneous Letters, reel 46; Edward Billingsley, *In Defense of Neutral Rights: The United States Navy and Wars of Independence in Chile and Peru* (Chapel Hill, 1967), 16-74.

[23] Nicholas B. Wainwright, "Commodore James Biddle and His Sketch Book," *Pennsylvania Magazine of History and Biography,* XC (Jan. 1966), 3-10.

[24] *Ibid.*

[25] J. K. Fairbank, *Trade and Diplomacy on the China Coast: The Opening of the Treaty Ports, 1842-1854* (Cambridge, 1953); Robert Hanks, "Commodore Lawrence Kearny, the Diplomatic Seaman," *Naval Institute Proceedings,* CVI (March 1970), 70-72.

[26] David F. Long, *Nothing Too Daring: A Biography of Commodore David Porter* (Annapolis, 1970), 6-108, 142-55; David D. Porter, *Memoir of Commodore David Porter of the United States Navy* (Albany, 1875), 14-85, 220-39; David Porter, *Journal of a Cruise Made to the Pacific Ocean by Captain David Porter, in the Frigate Essex, in the Years 1812, 1813, and 1814,* 2 vols. (Philadelphia, 1815).

[27] Long, *Nothing Too Daring,* 156-396.

[28] Jesse Elliott to Governor Francisco Dionisio Vives, Dec. 12, 1830, Captains Letters, 121, reel 154.

CHAPTER 15

The U.S. Navy's Pacific Squadron, 1824-1827

Linda M. Maloney

University of South Carolina

The naval squadron under Commodore Isaac Hull which assembled on the Pacific coast of South America in 1824 was a kind of pivot in the history of United States-Latin American relations. The sailing of the flagship in January 1824 was preceded by the proclamation of the "Monroe Doctrine," and it was during the cruise of the Hull squadron, 1824-27, that the independence of Latin America was finally secured by the patriot victory at Ayacucho in December 1824, the fall of Callao in January 1826, and the conquest of Chiloé in the same month. The task of the squadron accordingly shifted, during the three years, from maintenance of the rights of American neutral commerce against warring powers, the assignment of the earlier forces, to the upholding of commercial law and the fostering of an expanding American commerce throughout the Pacific in time of peace, the charge of future squadrons. The fact that the period was transitional, added to the difficulty of communicating with a government months distant, made the assignment a particularly difficult one. Hull accomplished his mission with some success, but not without a great deal of personal anguish and occasional trepidation.

Considering the magnitude of the tasks to be performed, the force assigned seems ludicrously small: frigate *United States*, 44, as flagship, and sloop of war *Peacock*, 18. Hull's predecessor, Commodore Charles Stewart, had *Franklin*, 74, and *Dolphin*, 12; he had found it necessary to add some auxiliaries, and had purchased two small schooners, *Peruvian* and *Waterwitch*, for use as dispatch vessels. Hull's instructions were to retain these two schooners with his own squadron, but when he reached Valparaiso he found that Stewart, who quite correctly regarded *Peruvian* and *Waterwitch* as his own property, had sold them preparatory to his return to the United

States. Hull therefore stretched his own authority slightly by keeping the *Dolphin* with him.[1] The three vessels were a minimum force for the objects in view. Secretary of the Navy Samuel L. Southard displayed a curiously foreshortened idea of Pacific geography in his instructions to Hull, which included injunctions to protect American commerce on the coast of South America (an extent of some 2500 miles), to cooperate closely with the Minister to Chile (based at Valparaiso, 1700 miles from Hull's main seat of operations at Callao), and incidentally, when he could spare the time, to visit the Sandwich Islands, the mouth of the Columbia river, and the coast of California. Hull did his best. Although the political situation in Peru and Chile forced him to keep his flagship on that coast he sent the *Dolphin* on a cruise among the Pacific islands in 1825, and the *Peacock* on a similar round in 1826. Both vessels visited Oahu, and the *Peacock* touched at California and Mexico, but the Columbia had to remain unvisited. The scope of these cruising instructions is indicative of the rapid expansion of American commerce and whaling in the Pacific in the 1820s, which was, however, not accompanied by an equivalent expansion in naval force.

The *United States* left Hampton Roads on January 4, 1824, after no more than the usual delays caused by recruitment problems, procurement difficulties, and a last-minute outbreak of smallpox. She made a short and easy passage to Rio and around Cape Horn, arriving at Valparaiso on March 27. *Peacock*, however, needed repairs and did not sail from Norfolk until the day *United States* anchored at Valparaiso. After that she had a difficult passage, losing a dozen men to storms and smallpox, and joined the *United States* at Callao on August 16. The flagship carried out the first United States Minister to Chile, Heman Allen. Commodore Hull was instructed to keep cordial relations with Minister Allen, but this was hardly a problem since the two were brothers-in-law.

The political situation in Chile was found to be relatively quiet, although uneasy because of the recent failure of an expedition against Chiloé. Minister Allen was cordially received at Valparaiso and Santiago, and Hull proceeded almost immediately to Callao, where he met Stewart in the *Franklin*. Peru was in a terrible state. Simón Bolívar's armies had occupied Lima with its port, Callao, and the greater part of lower Peru in 1823, but the Liberator's illness in January 1824 had weakened his position. A counterrevolutionary surge led to the fall of Lima and Callao to the Spanish royalists in February. When Hull reached Callao on April 11, he learned that Bolívar had established his government at Trujillo and was himself high in the cordillera at Huamachuco, assembling an army for a counterstroke against the viceregal forces.

It was clear by this time to all concerned that the neutrality of the United States in the South American struggle was merely formal. The United States government hoped to keep its merchant fleet from engaging in unneutral acts, such as carrying contraband, which might cause it to fall forefeit to belligerents, but the sentiments of Americans generally, as well as their economic hopes, lay with the patriots. This attitude was embodied in Hull's instructions, as well as in Allen's, which were also furnished to Hull. The Minister's instructions, in fact, were used as a model by Southard in drawing up his letter to Hull[3] so that the spirit of John Quincy Adams, and thus of the "Monroe Doctrine," of which he was the principal author, presided over the whole. It was in this spirit that Southard advised Hull, "Our relations with the government of Chile and Peru are of the most friendly character, and the desire of our government that they should continue so is undiminished. Your conduct must, on all occasions, be such as those relations require; at the same time full protection must be afforded to our citizens and their interest."[4]

This demanded that the naval commander walk a tightrope between friendship for the revolutionary governments and protection for American citizens. Southard added a caveat that "complaints have . . . been made, both by individuals, and by the government existing there, that our vessels have afforded improper protection to unlawful trade, and aided our own citizens, and those of other nations, in violations of the laws." As a matter of fact, the government of the United Provinces of Rio de la Plata, at Buenos Aires, had registered a formal protest against Stewart's alleged protection of American gun-runners who were selling arms to the royalists. John Quincy Adams had vigorously denied the fact, and Stewart was later acquitted of all such charges. He had, however, earned some unpopularity with the patriots by his vigorous and successful protests against paper blockades. Hull was to have a brief wrangle with Peruvian Admiral Martin George Guise on the same subject, but in general it may be said that, in the spirit of his instructions, he was "neutral on the side of the patriots." He maintained a constant admiration for Bolívar, although by the end of his cruise he had serious doubts about the future of Peru—doubts entirely shared by the Liberator himself.

The first problem Hull had to contend with was a blockade of the Peruvian coast from 11°3' to 14° S., or from Chancay to Pisco, proclaimed on March 16, and an anterior decree of February 21 ordering the blockade as far south as Cobija (22°30'S.). Since Peruvian Admiral Guise had but one frigate and three smaller vessels at his disposal, the blockade could only be a paper one, and in fact was being used merely as an excuse for levying tribute on merchant vessels: if a ship were caught entering a prohibited harbour, she could be permitted to enter anyway, provided her master paid the Peruvian naval commander a fee of from six to twenty-five percent of the value of his cargo. All of this was patently illegal. The United States in particular had been sensitive for years to the problem of illegal blockades, and Stewart had protested such blockades during his cruise. But Stewart's instructions, which were also given to Hull, had been very particular on the manner of dealing with illegal blockades proclaimed by the Patriots. With reference to such a blockade by the Chilean squadron in 1821, Secretary of the Navy Smith Thompson had written:

> although . . . its legality is expressly denied, yet the nature of the controversy that is carrying on in South America, being a struggle, on one side, for liberty and independence, renders it peculiarly fit and proper for the United States to avoid any collision with them, or to do any act that may, in any manner, have the appearance, or admit of the construction of favoring the cause of Spain against such a struggle. . . . Act, at present, on the defensive only; and for all violations of our neutral rights, if any occur under your observation, let strong and spirited appeals be made, through our public Agent. . . .[5]

Hull's indicated course, then, was to remonstrate to Guise's superiors in the Peruvian government. He did this on his own initiative because John B. Prevost, United States Special Agent to Peru, Buenos Aires and Chile, was at Trujillo with the government. The only quasi-diplomatic agent on the scene at Callao was the newly-arrived consul, William Tudor, but Tudor was not likely to be very helpful in this situation. Although Hull and Tudor maintained friendly relations they had very different political views. Tudor had an extravagant admiration for the Spanish Viceroy, José de la Serna, and his generals; his opinion of Bolívar and the Colombians was correspondingly low. He had established himself at Lima and presented his credentials to the royalist government, making no ackowledgment of the patriot government at Trujillo. Tudor was delighted when Guise, who was an Englishman, seized a British trader, and H.M.S. *Aurora*, Captain Prescott, was sent to remonstrate: "I offer you my congratulations," he wrote Hull,

> that chance has brought Admiral Guise on his own countrymen first, . . . that Captain P. who is such a great admirer of what are here called Patriots, who thought St. Martin a Washington in his day, and takes up his successors in the same way; and alas! there are Americans too, who from a sort of infatuation are thus willing to lower the character of the immortal patriots of America to the level of what we see here— . . . it is curious that Capt. P. . . . should have to discuss the matter with the floating customhouse. . . . I am glad that the case is likely to be made so very clear for you.[6]

Prevost took a dim view of Tudor, and Hull was worried that the consul's behavior would cause him to be expelled when the Patriots came to power again; but for the moment it was clear that he would have to negotiate with the government at Trujillo himself. He wrote to Bolívar at the end of May, protesting the illegality of the blockade, assuring him that no protection would be given to vessels carrying contraband, and that a legal blockade would be respected. Lieutenant Hiram Paulding was sent with the letters in the *Dolphin*, to land at Huacho or Trujillo and to seek Bolívar in the mountains, the Liberator's cordial response reached Hull on July 8. Bolívar, who had before him both Hull's protest and that of Prevost, said that he would himself be answerable for any legal pillage by Guise's fleet. He also made at least a gesture of good will by instructing Guise to maintain a legal blockade by keeping a ship before every interdicted port—which was, of course, impossible. He had, after all, very little control over his admiral, and could not afford to alienate him at that critical moment, as Hull realized. He laid the situation before Heman Allen, commenting:

> when I am instructed to conduct in a way to insure a continuance of the friendly feelings that now exist between the two Governments and at the same time to protect commerce, I am much at a loss how far I should be justified in using force when remonstrance is found to be unavailing, and I am the more at a loss from the peculiar situation in which the protector is placed at this time with Admiral Guise, for there cannot be doubt that he disapproves of the conduct of the Admiral towards neutrals, yet he cannot well at this time dispense with his services, and if he could, it would be difficult to get him out of the Ship he commands, nor dare he attempt to remove him for fear of the consequences. Under these circumstances were I to use force and disable his Ship and General Bolivar should fail in establishing the Independence of Peru, it would be said that America was the first to acknowledge their Independence and the first to injure their cause when endeavouring to regain it.[7]

Allen in reply insisted that Hull should maintain American rights against both warring parties, for should the independence of Peru depend on acquiescence by the United States in outrages upon its citizens, "as much as I should lament its failure yet I should say that, our country is not prepared for so great a sacrifice."[8] No further serious trouble, however, came from the Patriots. The Spanish forces began in May to be the chief thorn in Hull's side and remained so for more than a year. *Dolphin* was scarcely out of Callao Bay on her mission to Bolívar when the American brig *Nancy* came in as prize to a Spanish privateer, *Constante*, commissioned by General José Ramon Rodil, governor of Callao. She was the first of several victims of the privateer to be sent in during the winter. The usual excuse was that the vessel had Patriot property on board—which her captain always denied—or that she had stopped in a Chilean port. It was questionable, in any case, whether the privateer could legally operate under a commission from a provincial commander. The case of the *Nancy*, and of the *General Carrington*, a Rhode Island ship which soon followed her, began a long, fruitless, and increasingly heated correspondence between Hull and Rodil.

The European nations had much larger naval forces in the Pacific than did the United States. At the time of Hull's arrival the British squadron at Callao consisted of *Cambridge*, 84, frigates *Aurora* and *Tartar*, and sloops of war *Fly* and *Mersey*, under the overall command of Captain Thomas

Maling. Hull and Maling acted in close concert throughout the cruise; old hatchets were buried in a mutual celebration of July 4 on board the *United States,* where a banquet was served under an awning composed of the flags of both nations. But the British were not of much help in arguing the blockade question since, being chronic violators of international law in that respect, they were not willing to protest its violations by others. There were reports, near the end of June, of a strong French force of two ships of the line, a frigate and brig *en route* to the Pacific. It was rumored, as well, that a Spanish squadron was coming out from Cadiz: would these forces cooperate in attacking Chile and/or Peru?

Hull had a hand in putting one Spanish privateersman out of business. Late in July he left Callao for Haunchaco to water, and on July 22 ran down the privateer *Moyana.* He stopped and searched her and kept her captain on board the *United States* at night, but could find no evidence of her having preyed on Americans, so he reluctantly let her go the next day. *Moyana,* however, had so badly damaged her top-hamper and strained her hull in trying to escape from the *United States* that she fell victim to one of Guise's ships and was burned.[9]

During the remainder of the winter Admiral Guise was able to keep one or two vessels in Gallao Roads, and to make the port a hot spot with night attacks on Spanish shipping. Americans were not always able to get out of the way: on September 5 one man was killed and another wounded on board the merchant ship *General Clinton* when Rodil's gunboats attempted to seize one of Guise's brigs.[10] As the patriot armies gathered strength in the countryside, American and British residents in Lima became more and more fearful for their lives and property, since the Lima authorities were helpless to protect the city even against raids by partisan bands of *montaneros.* About the middle of August General Rodil proposed to the British and American commanders that they send their own marines into the city to guard the houses of their countrymen. Captain Maling immediately sent up a large force, which was quartered and fed by the Spanish government. To Hull this seemed an un-neutral proceeding. He offered to send some sailors and officers, to be distributed among the houses of the Americans, but not to be in any way associated with the government. The Americans, however, were more afraid of the sailors than of the *montaneros;* they declined the offer.[11]

The war at sea reached its climax—or anticlimax—in September and October of 1824. On September 12 the expected Spanish squadron arrived: *Asia,* 64, and brig of war *Aquiles,* 22. Admiral Guise, who had only the frigate *Protector,* 44, and a ten-gun brig, nevertheless offered a fight; the Spaniards ignored him and, taking advantage of a favoring wind and current, sailed into the harbor where they joined the privateers *Ica,* 28 (formerly the American *Esther*), *Pezuela,* 16 and *Constante,* 16. At the time

185

the Spanish ships approached the harbor, the *United States* was anchored in the fairway, where she would have been directly in line of the contending ships if a running fight had taken place. Hull sent his men to quarters and got under way, as did Captain Maling of the *Cambridge*. He was much surprised to see the Spaniards, as he said, "skulk into port," and expressed his contempt so openly that Midshipman Andrew Hull Foote thought "it would have taken little provocation . . . to have been complimented with a broadside from Uncle Issac."[12] Hull was astonished, and even more disgusted, to learn a few days later that the Spanish commodore had said he avoided engaging Guise because he thought the *United States* was a Peruvian frigate. Hull had a diagram drawn of the positions of the vessels in the bay and got Maling to certify that it was correct and that no un-neutral implications should be drawn from the fact of their vessels being under way. The Spaniards, having saved face, settled down to repair their ships. Guise went off to collect more force, but the squadron with which he returned on October 6 was still vastly inferior to the Spanish force. The latter sailed out to engage him, and again the neutral warships got under way to witness the action. They did not see much; a confused melee followed in a fog in which Guise managed to escape with his ships intact and unpursued.[13] As the Spanish ships continued preparing for sea Maling in the *Cambridge* decided to shadow them; Hull also called in *Peacock* and *Dolphin* from Quilca and Valparaiso. Should the Spanish squadron attack American ships he planned to pursue it with his whole force. At the same time he pointed out to the Secretary of the Navy the futility of trying to guard so long a coast with his tiny squadron, and the difficulty of acting at such a long remove from Washington,

> having the Spaniards on one side and the Patriots on the other, the former inveterate and extremely hostile towards us, and the Patriots jealous but friendly, every movement of mine is closely watched and seized upon to make difficulty where it can be done, so that barely a day passes that I do not have trouble with one party or the other, and as neither are governed by the laws or usage of nations or by common justice, and having no one to advise with or aid me in these difficulties, I feel a weight of responsibility which I most earnestly hope to be relieved from soon, by receiving instructions to meet the great changes that have taken place in this sea, and the present state of affairs.[14]

On October 20 the entire Spanish squadron left Callao, bound southward. Guise was powerless to stop them. He was expecting aid from the Chilean navy, but Admiral Manuel Blanco Encalada did not leave Valparaiso until November 15. Even then, his four ships were not equal to the voyage. He had to stop at Coquimbo to repair the frigate *O'Higgins* and brig *Moctezuma*. Luckily he found there the schooner *Dolphin*; Lieutenant John Percival had brought her to Coquimbo to heave out and clean her bottom, and he cheerfully loaned his carpenters to Admiral Blanco.[15]

The Chilean, Peruvian and Colombian squadrons, had they combined, would have made a rather formidable force, but they were too late. On December 9, 1824, came the crowning patriot victory at Ayacucho. Lima had already fallen. The *Asia* and *Aquiles* had so many impressed Peruvians in their crews that news of the patriot victories led to mutinies on board. The *Asia* was surrendered to Mexican authorities at Acapulco, and *Aquiles* sailed to Valparaiso and joined the Chilean service.[16]

After the departure of the Spanish ships Hull's most critical problem was his rapidly deteriorating relations with General Rodil: Consul Tudor reported that "Com.̣ Hull and General Rodil are on the worst terms; the former has certainly some reason on his side, and the latter accuses the Com.̣ of insulting him with perpetual threats and other irritations."[17] The condemnations of the *Nancy* and *General Carrington* had embittered these relations, but the real crisis occurred in November with the Spanish seizure of the ship *China* in Callao harbor.

On the night of November 2 the captain of the *China*, James Goodrich, attempted to transship some goods to the American brig *Rimac*. Both traders were in the outer harbor of Callao, near the island of San Lorenzo, and *Rimac*, which had arrived only the day previous and was in need of repairs, was lying under the guns of the *United States*, with Navy carpenters on board. When the transshipment to the *Rimac* was discovered, the *China* was seized by officers of the customs and carried into the inner harbor, where she was moored under the guns of the castles. Next morning an officer from Callao demanded to search the *Rimac* for the goods which were supposed to have been received illegally from the *China*. *Rimac's* captain appealed to Hull, and Hull sent the customs officer away, with a letter to General Rodil saying that, while he would not countenance smuggling, he believed the outer harbor to be outside the limits of customs jurisdiction, and that such transshipments were usual. In fact, *China* had already landed part of her cargo for Rodil's own use, although she had not entered at the custom house. She had also sold provisions to the *Asia* and *Cambridge*.[18] Nevertheless, Rodil gave orders to proceed against the *China*, and even had her cargo unloaded before the judicial process began. The ship and cargo were valued at over $150,000, but Hull was the more disturbed at the seizure because *China* was a well-built ship which could easily be turned into a privateer.[19]

The next day the officers and crew of one of *United State's* boats were roughly handled and pelted with stones at the wharf. When Hull sent a remonstrance by Lieutenant Paulding, that officer was detained and insulted. Rodil then cut all normal communication by ordering that no boats from the *United States* be allowed to land, and threatened to seize all the American property in Callao if the *Rimac* were not handed over.[20] Hull demanded as a right, under America's treaty with Spain, that he be allowed to communicate with the Americans on shore, and threatened, if he were refused, to take his own ship and all the other American vessels away from Callao. On November 10 he summoned the trading ships, ten in number, to anchor near the *United States*. He was even angrier when he learned that Captain Goodrich and his crew had been imprisoned, and the crew forced to do manual labor on shore. The next day he sailed, with all the American traders, for Ancon, intending to wait there until the Patriots entered Lima, which was expected to happen any day. The merchants could then land their cargoes at Ancon and send them up to Lima, avoiding Callao altogether.[21]

Hull was determined, should Rodil attempt to seize any more American property at Callao or Lima, to sail against Spanish cruisers and merchant shipping. Unfortunately these, and especially the latter, were few. His frustration was evident: he was faced with an enemy who, though weak, had plenty of prey ready to hand, while he, though relatively strong, could scarcely hope to find any vulnerable point for retaliation. He had left the *Peacock* at Callao; on November 29 he returned there with the *United States*, sending the *Peacock* to Huacho for water. An interview with Captain Goodrich, who, on Hull's advice, had secretly gone on board the *Cambridge*, made him angrier than ever: the crew of the *China* had been beaten to make them work, and the mate threatened with hanging if he did not testify against his captain. Hull warned William Tudor to prepare the Americans on shore for possible violence, remarking grimly:

> I think there is not an American in this country, knowing all things which have taken place, who would not be willing to sacrifice every feeling of interest, to have their rights respected, and that would not view resistance to the violations of them here upon more liberal principles than individual interest. Capt. Goodrich will tell you what are my intentions. I have no time, if it was prudent.[22]

He wrote the Secretary of the Navy that "I know of no other alternative but to make reprisals and to retain Spanish subjects until the Americans are released."[23]

But before he could carry out his threat he had to fill his empty water casks at Huacho. *United States* returned to Callao on December 11 and Hull sent in an immediate demand for the release of Goodrich, his crew, and the *China*. His officers were not allowed to land, although his letters were received. Goodrich and his men were not permitted to come near the wharf. Hull sent a second demand, and a third, then told Rodil that he would not write again, but would proceed as he had threatened. At this critical moment, however, news was received of the battle of Ayachucho, and that Bolívar was securely in possession of Lima. Rodil was cut off by land, and would soon be blockaded again by sea. Hull, believing this might cause the General to have second thoughts, waited.[24] Within a short time Rodil relented to the extent of releasing Goodrich and his crew, though he retained the *China* and still refused to allow boats from the *United States* to land.

Everyone expected the Callao castles to be surrendered after the fall of Lima, but Rodil held out for a full fourteen months, until January 1826. During that time Callao was a dangerous harbor, for there were almost nightly engagements, particularly in the early months, between Rodil's gunboats and forts and the blockading squadrons of Guise, Blanco and the Colombian admiral John Illingworth. During this time the foreign traders based at Chorillos and *United States* was kept in that port to protect them, except for a few months' cruise to Valparaiso in the early months of 1825. With the end of the war came an end to serious difficulty over American commercial rights. One more ship was lost: the *General Brown* was seized by Blanco for blockade violations and eventually condemned after a whole series of trials and appeals. Hull took an interest in the case at first, but in August the Peruvian government refused to correspond further with him on the subject since he was not recognized as a diplomat. He then turned the matter over to Tudor, who had, despite Hull's and Prevost's fears, been recognized as United States Consul by the new government. Unhappily for American interests, Judge Prevost had died near Arequipa in March. Tudor, who spent a lot of time at Mira Flores in the mountains, looking after his health and his mining interests, was not always an effective representative. Hull, at any rate, was glad to be rid of the *General Brown* issue, since he thought her captain had, as he put it, "behaved badly," while on the other hand he said of Blanco that "I do not know of any situation that he would be at home in, other than that of keeping a dancing school, for I do not believe he is either a Sailor or Soldier, not do I believe that he is a man of honour or honesty."[25] His relations with the English admirals in Latin American service, Guise and Illingworth, were by contrast extremely cordial.

The end of the war in Peru allowed Hull at last to divide his squadron in order to carry out his orders to visit the Pacific islands. In addition to the general need to protect American commerce, he had been particularly enjoined early in 1825 to send a vessel in search of the mutineers of the whaleship *Globe* of Nantucket, who had taken refuge in the Mulgrave Islands (Mili Atoll). Lieutenant Percival in the *Dolphin* sailed from Chorillos on that mission in August. He found the survivors of the mutiny and proceeded to Oahu where he was received cordially by the merchant community, less so by the American missionaries. The latter accused Percival of undermining their work by encouraging a revival of prostitution. But an American warship was a welcome sight to the Americans with rapidly increasing property interests at the islands: during the four months of *Dolphin's* stay at Oahu, American whalers valued at $1,829,580 touched there, in addition to trading vessels worth $366,263.26.

Hull had expected *Dolphin* to return in six months. She was actually absent from the coast for more than a year, so before her return, in May 1826, he sent the *Peacock* on a similar round by way of Tahiti. The appearance of the latter at Oahu, so soon after the *Dolphin's* departure, had a profound psychological effect: it made the American force seem much larger than it was.

By the time *Peacock* was dispatched, Commodore Hull was more than anxious for word of the relief squadron. His crew's enlistments had all expired, and it was only by the most diplomatic management of the men — something which, luckily, Hull was very good at — that he succeeded in getting them home in a reasonably contented frame of mind. Commodore Jacob Jones in the *Brandywine* finally met him at Valparaiso in December 1826, and the *United States* anchored at New York on April 23, 1827, leaving *Dolphin* for the new squadron, and *Peacock* to return in the fall.

A great deal more could be said about the cruise of the Hull squadron, particularly its internal affairs, if time permitted. Two conclusions may, however, be added. First, the regard to the squadron's mission to protect American neutral rights: Hull's experience confirms the supposition that the rights of neutrals are never secure in wartime, no matter how strong the neutral or how weak the warring powers. Hull could have done more with a greater force, to be sure, but even the British with a much larger squadron were unable to prevent their traders being seized. It seems sad but true that a neutral has as many rights as the belligerents wish him to have, and no more.

Second, in the postwar period the Hull squadron looked to the future by fostering the rapid growth of American Pacific commerce. The totals of shipping at Oahu in early 1826 have already been mentioned. During the first two years of his cruise Hull kept a boarding book for the *United States* to record the vessels he spoke. Although American masters suspiciously refused to answer many of his questions about the content and value of their cargoes, he did compile a valuable list of vessels with the names of their masters and owners, home port and destination, lading, tonnage, numbers of crew and guns. Altogether in 1824 he spoke 66 different vessels, some of them twice. At least half of these were from the United States, the other half mostly British. In 1825 he boarded about 140 ships, of which again about half were North Americans, the rest British, French and Peruvian, with a scattering of other Europeans and Latin Americans. There is no book for 1826, but clearly American Pacific trade was increasing very rapidly, and Americans were already taking the lead.[27]

This information must have been of the greatest interest to John Quincy Adams, now President, to his Secretary of State, Henry Clay, and to others with their kind of hemispheric vision. But by the time Hull returned to the United States the Adams administration was declining to its close. His successor had a different world view. The Pacific squadron remained small, but American trade flourished, in a Pacific ocean which happily, for generations to come, lived up to its name.

FOOTNOTES

[1] Samuel L. Southard to Isaac Hull, Dec. 24, 1823, Letters to Officers of Ships of War (OSW), Record Group 45, National Archives; Heman Allen to Quincy Adams, April 29, 1824, Records of the Department of State, Dispatches from Ministers, Chile, Record Group 59, National Archives.

[2] Ann M. Hull to Sarah Hart Jarvis [Nov. 11] 1823, copy in possession of Eleanor Taft Tilton.

[3] Charles Francis Adams, ed., *Memoirs of John Quincy Adams* (Phila., 1875), VI, 210.

[4] Southard to Hull, Dec. 24, 1823, OSW.

[5] Smith Thompson to Charles Stewart, Sept. 8, 1821, copy, Isaac Hull Papers, Boston Atheneum.

[6] William Tudor to Isaac Hull, Friday morning [May 28, 1824], Isaac Hull Papers, Boston Atheneum.

[7] Hull to Allen, July 9, 1824, Isaac Hull Letterbook, 1823-27, New-York Historical Society.

[8] Allen to Hull, Aug. 4, 1824, copy, Dept. of State, Letters Rec. from Ministers, Chile, NA:RG 59.

[9] Entry, July 23, 1824, Log of the *United States*, 1823-27, New-York Historical Society; Wm. Tudor to J. Q. Adams, Aug. 24, 1824, in William R. Manning, ed., *Diplomatic Correspondence of the United States Concerning the Independence of the Latin-American Nations* (New York, 1925), III, 1760; Hull to Southard, Oct. 2, 1824, Captain's Letters (CL), RG 45, NA.

[10] Tudor to Rodil, Sept. 6, 1824, Manning, III, 1764.

[11] Tudor to John Quincy Adams, Aug. 24, 1824, Manning, III, 1759; Tudor to Hull, Aug. 19, Aug. 20, 1824, Hull Papers, Boston Atheneum; Hull to Rodil, Aug. 21, 1824, Hull LB, NYHS.

[12] A. H. Foote to[?], Sept. 15, 1824, Area 9 File, NA. Since Foote was Hull's cousin, not his nephew, it seems likely that "Uncle Isaac" was the Commodore's sobriquet among the young officers of his squadron.

[13] Tudor to J. Q. Adams, Oct. 17, 1824, Manning, II, 1796; Donald Worcester, *Sea Power and Chilean Independence* (Gainesville, Fla., 1962), p. 81.

[14] Hull to Southard, Oct. 19, 1824, Hull LB, NYHS.

[15] Worcester, *Sea Power*, p. 80.

[16] Worcester, *Sea Power*, p. 81.

[17] Tudor to J. Q. Adams, Oct. 17, 1824, Manning, III, 1770.

[18] Hull to Rodil, Nov. 3, 1824, Hull LB, NYHS; Hull to J. Q. Adams, Nov. 13, 1824.

[19] Hull to Southard, Nov. 4, 1824, NA:CL.

[20] Hull to Rodil, Nov. 5, Nov. 9, 1824, Hull LB, NYHS.

[21] Hull to Southard, Nov. 12, 1824, Hull LB, NYHS.

[22] Hull to Tudor, Nov. 30, 1824, Hull LB, NYHS.

[23] Hull to Southard, Dec. 5, 1824, Hull LB, NYHS.

[24] Hull to Southard, Dec. 16, 1824, Hull LB, NYHS; Hull to Heman Allen, Dec. 17, 1824.

[25] Hull to Heman Allen, Sept. 25, 1826, Hull LB, NYHS. Manuel Blanco Encalada was, by that time, President of Chile.

[26] Hull to Southard, Sept. 11, 1826, Memoranda enclosed, CL.

[27] Hull to Southard, Dec. 31, 1825, enclosed in: A List of Merchant Vessels boarded by U.S. Frigate United States, Isaac Hull Commander, during the period of 30th March [1824 to] December 1825, NA:CL.

CHAPTER 16

Russian Naval Reformers and Modernization: Naval Affairs and the Historiography of the Great Reforms

Jacob W. Kipp

Kansas State University

Several years ago the editors of the *Journal of Modern History* floated a "trial balloon" that suggested war (not peace) is the mother of all things.[1] While perhaps too ambitious in their claims for war "as the engine of social change," the editors raised an issue worthy of serious consideration. Many historians of modern Russia (since the reign of Peter the Great) have noted the relationship between military necessity and social modernization.[2] With regard to the Great Reforms of Alexander II's reign (1855-1881), this interpretation has been a popular one, either alone or as part of more sophisticated multi-causal analyses.[3]

Taken collectively, the Great Reforms marked a profound transformation in Russian society and have been viewed by many historians as "a fundamental break with the past," especially with regard to the emancipation of the Russian gentry's serfs in 1861.[4] Such change had many roots in the near and distant past, but military defeat in the Crimean War by the Anglo-French maritime coalition served as a catalyst. Historians have pointed to a crisis of the servile economy, mass popular discontent, and a conscious national interest in economic development as motives for the emancipation and the other Great Reforms.[5] In all cases, however, the war and military defeat set the stage for each of these. Indeed, Alfred J. Rieber in a provocative essay has suggested that military necessity itself served as the primary motive for the Great Reforms. Rieber's thesis, as Daniel Field has noted, has an Achilles' heel: there are few documents that link the emancipation of the serfs with military necessity.[6] Indeed, contradicting the assumptions of the *Journal of Modern History,* Field concludes that the war and its consequences inhibited the process of reform.[7] Regarding the emancipation of 1861, Field's *caveat* seems well taken. Few important military figures took an active hand in writing the Statute of Emancipation and relations between the government and the serf-holding gentry had far more importance in the actual drafting of the legislation than any abstract concerns about military modernization.[8]

While this concern for the emancipation as the very foundation of Russia's fundamental break with the past is quite legitimate, it has had one unfortunate consequence. The Great Reforms were much more than supplementary legislation, flowing inevitably from the Statute of February 19, 1861. Many of these reforms were articulated and some enacted prior to that statute.[9] The Great Reforms should be seen in *Gestalt*—as something more than the sum of their parts and as a web of social, economic and political changes. At the center of that web stood the Crimean War.[10]

The reforms enacted by the Naval Ministry during and following the Crimean War did not cause the Great Reforms but were, it can be argued, an important part of that web. In his treatment of the Crimean War Field has argued that Russian defeat was not a national disaster such as Prussia suffered after Jena but a governmental embarrassment. The war demonstrated the incompetency of the bureaucracy and military while never seriously challenging the nation's existence.[11] This point is fundamentally correct, but ignores the peculiar nature of the war. First, unlike every other major European war in which Russia had engaged down to that time, the Crimean War was a maritime war, in which superior naval power allowed one side both to choose the theaters of operation and to define the strategic objectives of its campaigns. Second, the war involved the intensive use of modern industrial technology on an unprecedented scale. Steam propulsion, the screw propellor, exploding shell and armor plate marked naval operations, and technological inferiority condemned the weaker power to disaster or prolonged inaction.[12] Technology did not have so evident or profound an effect upon the immediate conduct of land operations. The absence of a modern system of rapid transportation for troops and supplies did frustrate the Russian plans for a counter-offensive in the Crimean War, while the Anglo-French logistic use of steamships and railroads aided their efforts. Still, it was in naval affairs that the technological aspects of modern war were most visible and where Russia's backwardness was most immediately felt. Third, the Crimean War was in the geopolitical sense a maritime war: Anglo-French activities during the hostilities were concentrated upon the destruction of Russian naval power in the Black Sea as a threat to the Turkish Empire and their own interests in the Near East. The consequences of the Crimean War finally were a disaster to the Naval Ministry and Russian naval officers. The Paris peace settlement imposed upon Russia the demilitarization of the Black Sea and the destruction of all forts and naval yards on that sea, robbing the Russian Navy of its second command and destroying a center for naval reform that had grown there during the tenures of Admirals Lazarev and Kornilov.[13]

In contrast to the demoralization that marked the Russian state and bureaucracy following the Crimean War, the Naval Ministry emerged from that war with considerable *élan* and an unheard of popularity with educated Russian society. While this situation has been treated in some detail in another work, its causes should be noted here.[14] The Russian Navy achieved what few successes that tsarist arms could claim during the war: the splendid victory of Admiral Nakhimov against the Turks at Sinope, the heroic defense of Sevastopol, the successful defense of Petropavlovsk on the Pacific, and the denial of a naval victory in the Baltic to Admiral Napier's fleet. In addition, in the course of the war the Naval Ministry came under the personal direction of the Nicholas I's second son, the talented and forceful Grand Duke Konstantin Nikolaevich. Under his leadership the worst abuses of bureaucratic centralization, formalism, and obscurantism were attacked. The Naval Ministry became a haven for young, reform-minded bureaucrats and active junior naval officers. Indeed, to many contemporaries the Grand Duke's circle of reformers, the *Konstantinovtsy*, became the spokesmen for the younger generation against the incompetency and resistance to change found among the statesmen and advisors from the reign of Nicholas I. The Grand Duke himself was only twenty-six when he took over direction of the Naval Ministry.[15]

The *Konstantinovtsy* began a fundamental transformation of the navy during the Crimean War. In this task they rejected the institutional foundations upon which the tsarist navy had stood before the war, correctly asserting that such an order could not successfully prosecute or hope to win a modern maritime conflict. The old navy, like every other agency of the Russian state, had rested upon the institution of serfdom. Its officers were drawn exclusively from gentry ranks, its enlisted men largely from the enserfed population. Relations between officers and ratings were colored by the pervasive spirit of serfdom; officers considered sailors their "souls." Some progressive officers had come to recognize the incompatibility of such attitudes and values even prior to the Crimean War and rejected the knout as the best teacher and foundation for order. Such had been the views of M. P. Lazarev and so were they the views of his leading students: Nakhimov, Istomin, and Kornilov. Nakhimov observed, "It's time that we stopped considering ourselves *pomeshchiks* and them (the sailors) as serfs. The sailor is the prime mover on a warship and we only springs, who act upon him. Here are they whom we must ennoble, teach, and stimulate in their bravery, heroism—if we are not egotists but real servants of the fatherland."[16] Such sentiments were shared by the younger officers who

194

served under Nakhimov, Istomin, and Kornilov until their untimely deaths during the war. Their subordinates—Butakov, Likhachev, Metlin, Shestakov, Popov and Krabbe—became leaders in the cause of naval reform following the war. They assumed important responsibilities with the Naval Ministry; Metlin, and later Krabbe, became the Grand Duke's immediate subordinates in administering the Navy. Shestakov directed the acquisition of modern warships in the United States, while Popov and Likhachev commanded naval forces dispatched to the Pacific. Butakov supervised the liquidation of the Black Sea Fleet and wrote the first Russian treatise on naval tactics under steam before becoming commander of the first squadron of Russian ironclads in the Baltic.[17]

These professional naval officers were linked with a circle of young bureaucrats, whom the Grand Duke had recruited to the Naval Ministry prior to and during the war. A. V. Golovnin, the son of an admiral himself, served as the Grand Duke's personal secretary. M. Kh. Reutern undertook the inspection of naval facilities and became the leading expert within the Naval Ministry on economic affairs. He spent a number of years following the Crimean War abroad in Europe and the United States, studying naval administration and budgetary policy. D. A. Tolstoi directed the Ministry's chancellery and reduced the volume of its correspondence while increasing its efficiency. D. A. Obolenskii managed the Commissary Department. All became important statesmen during the reign of Alexander II.[18]

In the person of the Grand Duke Konstantin Nikolaevich the two circles—naval and civilian—found their common link. It was the Grand Duke in his capacity as general-admiral who had the task of rebuilding Russian naval power after the Crimean War, and it was through his patronage and support that both circles prospered and gained influence. The common program of reform shared by both the civilian and naval reformers can be summed up briefly: technological modernization, administrative rationalization, professionalization, and increased efficiency. This program carried over into nearly all aspects of naval affairs in the post-Crimean period and was an intregal part of radical changes in the nature of the service, the deployment of its warships, the development of its technological foundations, and the evolution of its mission.[19]

For the purpose of this paper the discussion of naval reforms will be limited to three areas: terms of service for the lower ratings, the education of naval officers, and naval justice.

In 1853 recruitment for the navy followed the basic pattern set by the army. While early in the century there had been special levees in coastal *gubernias* for the navy, it had not established any claim for recruiting among the maritime professions, and this right was one for which the Grand Duke fought.[20] Term of enlistment was twenty five years, and the sailors were drawn from the peasantry and other tax paying estates.[21] Their conditions of service were harsh by any standard with corporal punishment as the most common method for education and discipline. Technology had, however, begun to force innovations in recruiting that contradicted the estate nature of naval recruitment even prior to the Crimean War. During the reign of Nicholas I and largely on the initiative of Black Sea officers, "free sailors" for service on steam warships were recruited. Their term of service was ten years and they were freed from all taxes and obligations. In 1850 there were approximately 100 free sailors with the Baltic Fleet and 1600 with the Black Sea Fleet.[22] In terms of the total complement of the navy this was a small number. On the eve of the Crimean War the navy numbered 90,885 men and at its end 100,085.

By the Naval Ministry's own estimates the results of this system of recruiting and training were hardly better than disastrous. Of 108,737 men taken into the navy during the period 1829-1855 more than 34,000 were unfit for combat.[23] A disproportionately high percentage of those recruited never went to sea; in 1856, 47,400 men were in various shore commands providing what amounted to uncompensated labor services.[24] Naval reformers found the ill health and bad morale among the lower ratings serving ashore intolerable. They proposed to replace such labor with hired civilian workers and reduced the number of shore personnel to 5,832 by 1865.[25]

Naval reformers also found the recruitment system based on serfdom inefficient and counter-productive. Such sentiments were not unique to the Naval Ministry, and the tsarist government did suspend recruiting for both the army and navy from 1856 to 1863. However, the Naval Ministry under reform-minded leadership pressed more forcefully for the reduction of the term of service—first to 10 years and after 1874 to 5-7 years.[26] Strenuous efforts were made to increase literacy among the ratings through the organization of classes: by 1865 over 10,000 sailors out of 40,000 could read.[27] Naval reformers also placed a heavy emphasis upon long-range cruises as the best training device, and they considered the summertime exercises of the old Baltic Fleet as poor foundations for a professional navy. As Admiral Krabbe observed: "Sailing in the course of a short summer in our northern waters on poorly built ships, officers and men do not feel either love of or calling to naval affairs . . . ."[28] Long-range cruises became a priority item in the Naval Ministry's budget. During the most difficult financial crisis, when funds were being cut from the program to construct new screw-propelled warships after the Crimean War, the Grand Duke would tolerate no reduction of this item:

> If money is not appropriated for prolonged cruises it would be better not to have a fleet for in that case all the other sacrifices for it amount to an absolutely useless expenditure.[29]

The Grand Duke won his funds, and the long-range cruises to the Mediterranean, Atlantic and Siberia were expanded with more than twenty warships on such voyages in each year during the late 1850's and early 1860's.[30]

The *Kontstantinovtsy*'s plans for the transformation of the term of service for naval ratings culminated in two proposals. The first, made by the General-Admiral in a report to the Senate in 1859, proposed the termination of conscription as the basis for naval recruitment and the establishment of a volunteer system. Alexander II affirmed the criticisms of a number of senior admirals and officials on the proposal and rejected it as impractical. Yet, the proposal was the first measure that both systematically criticized the former system of conscription and offered an alternative. The Grand Duke noted the former system was infused with the spirit of serfdom, cut the armed forces off from the nation's life, and was the root-cause of low morale among enlisted personnel. He wished to reform not only the recruiting system but also the conditions of service. "It is quite worthwhile to reach the point where in all Russia the holy obligation to serve the Tsar and Fatherland would be fulfilled by the nation with joy and this depends completely upon the means of its recruitment to service and the conditions of that service itself."[31]

Konstantin Nikolaevich's plans included making the naval service competitively attractive so that the navy might enlist better educated and more qualified cadres. The transformation of the system of naval recruitment did not occur until a general statute establishing a universal conscription system was proclaimed in 1874 at the initiative of the Minister of War D. A. Miliutin. This statute did not, however, resolve the problems of the Naval Ministry, arising from the need for literate recruits with technical skills. This problem was to plague the tsarist navy for the rest of its existence. While this matter was stillborn, the Naval Ministry did manage to achieve a second and basic transformation of the terms of naval service in the early 1860's: the abolition of corporal punishment.

The origin of the decree abolishing corporal punishment in the army, navy, and civil affairs has often been attributed to the initiative of Prince N. A. Orlov in his essay of March 1861. Historians have noted that the Naval Ministry and the Grand Duke Konstantin Nikolaevich were supporters of this matter, but have viewed such support as a general manifestation of humanitarian sentiment.[32] While such feelings did contribute to the *Konstantinovtsy*'s views, these also contained a rather rational and technical element. Experience proved to the *Konstantinovtsy* that corporal punishment and long-range cruises on modern warships were incompatible.

Returning from one such long-range cruise, the clipper *Plastun* sank with great loss of life in the Baltic. The commission that investigated the disaster discovered that one seaman, Savel'ev, who throughout the voyage had been subject to frequent punishment, had been sent to work in the powder magazine stacking shells immediately prior to the disaster. On the testimony of survivors the investigating commission not only established that the explosion which sank the *Plastun* originated in this area, but it also learned that Savel'ev had been sent to work in the magazine only shortly before the explosion, knowing that he was to undergo a flogging on the completion of that task.[33] The investigating commission's observations on this disaster were published in the Naval Ministry's journal, *Morskoi sbornik*, in late 1860.

The Grand Duke Konstantin Nikolaevich took to heart these conclusions. His support for the abolition of corporal punishment was founded upon this institution's incompatibility with the new conditions of service: "Neither the severity nor the frequent use of the knout lends support to discipline but on the contrary, its severity and frequent use can weaken the force of military discipline."[34] Unlike other navies where the abolition of corporal punishment followed its termination in both the army and civilian affairs, the Russian Navy led the struggle for its abolition.

The need to improve the education of Russian naval officers had been apparent to many progressive figures even prior to the Crimean War. As part of this process libraries and clubs for naval officers had been organized on a voluntary basis in the 1840's, and at the end of that decade Admiral F. P. Litke, the tutor of the Grand Duke Konstantin and a naval officer-explorer of worldwide recognition, had secured the founding of a permanent professional journal within the Naval Ministry for naval officers, *Morskoi sbornik*.[35]

During the Crimean War the need for a thorough overhaul of the system of instruction for naval cadets became increasingly evident. As a first step in this process the Naval Ministry sponsored a series of articles on problems of education in general, prior to turning its attention to the specifics of the reform of the navy's officer training institutions. This series, which marked the first public discussion of educational reform during Alexander II's reign, achieved great popularity.

In the first half of the nineteenth century education had been treated by the state as a matter of preparing the young for service. Behind the entire system stood the notion of ascription: those who were to be educated already had an hereditary calling for such service, whether military, naval, or civilian. Young men, really still boys, were sent to institutions, cadet corps, lyceums, and schools, on this basis. Typical of this mentality is the request of the future admiral A. V. Kornilov for admittance to the Naval Cadet Corps in the 1820's. Kornilov, then twelve years of age and having finished his elementary schooling presented himself in this fashion:

> I am in no way equipped for the service of (his) Imperial Highness and have the desire to embark upon the path of a cadet in the Naval Cadet

Corps and therefore I, your lowliest subject, request that Your Imperial
Highness issue an order for my enrollment in the Naval Cadet Corps.[36]

While in Kornilov's case the young nobleman did prove a dedicated sailor
and fine naval officer, the early enrollment of youngsters in the Naval
Cadet Corps forced them to come under the sway of "the tyranny of the
rod." I. A. Shestakov left a depressing picture of the abuses that the young
cadets endured there during the reign of Nicholas I. As an eleven-year-old
Shestakov himself had received two hundred blows from a birch rod for
"rudeness" and considered his sentence light, for some of the senior teachers
thought nothing of giving six hundred strokes as a standard punishment.
While Admiral I. F. Kruzenstern attempted during his tenure as director of
the corps to limit the use of corporal punishment, most of the staff ignored
his efforts and continued to rely upon the public imposition of corporal
punishment as the single most expedient means of insuring discipline.
Neither the physical or psychological consequences of such punishment
upon their charges seems to have concerned the staff.[37] For many of the very
young among the cadets this system must have undermined any affection
that they felt towards the sea or naval service.

In 1860 a commission investigating naval education under the chairman-
ship of Admiral Putiatin concluded that: "Children enter naval training
institutions at too early an age when their calling to the sea is unclear and
when it is impossible to determine. . . . Many youths who complete the entire course of instruction find that they have prepared themselves in a
specialty altogether unsuited to them."[38] How naval education and education in general might be reformed to reduce or remove this problem was the
topic of an entire series of articles from 1856 until the publication of the
commission's report in 1860.[39] Reform-minded authors, like the surgeon
N. I. Pirogov, stressed the role of education as preparation for life and not
the terms of service within the civil or military bureaucracies. Basic education would best be carried out in public institutions devoted to general and
unspecialized education.[40]

With regard to the education of naval officers this meant a transformation of not only the Naval Cadet Corps but also the technical schools that
trained navigators, engineers and artillerists. Admiral Putiatin's project included the following basic features: entrance into all naval schools was to be
limited to young men between the ages of fourteen and sixteen; admission
to the Naval Corps was still to be restricted on an estate basis to some
noblemen, officers, and civil servants; a competitive examination and
physical were to be initiated to replace seniority on the rolls of those seeking
entrance; the program of instruction within each institution was to be
changed to stress practical preparation of officer cadres and their special instruction in the naval arts, foreign languages, and sciences; and the assignment of graduates on the basis of special examination to determine their
suitability for various types of duty.[41]

Putiatin's proposals were the subject of lively discussion by naval officers in *Morskoi sbornik* and some important changes were suggested. Rimskii-Korsakov, the Director of the Naval Cadet Corps, took the opportunity to stress the need for practical naval experience in the education of officer cadres. While Putiatin's proposals had confined training cruises exclusively to the two middle years of a cadet's tenure, Rimskii-Korsakov favored their inclusion from the very start on the grounds that such experience was absolutely necessary for the cultivation of a love of the sea in a nation where such a feeling was quite weak. Rimskii-Korsakov also stressed the advantages of practical experience in learning the naval arts.[42] Rimskii-Korsakov's suggestions were incorporated into the project and the Naval Corps opened in 1867 with a four-year program of instruction.[43]

The reform of naval education for the officer cadre had emerged as an issue out of the Crimean War when it had become apparent that the older system built upon the foundations of the Naval Cadet Corps did not function. The discussion of educational reform in the Naval Ministry had far wider ramifications. Since the issue was raised publicly in *Morskoi sbornik*, the Navy's discussions stimulated a general interest in the problem of educational reform throughout the Russian state and society. In 1861 when Alexander II turned his attention to the reform of public education he appointed Admiral Putiatin as Minister of Education. When the admiral's tenure was cut short by embarrassing student riots at the universities in the fall of that year, the Emperor again turned to an official of the Naval Ministry, the Grand Duke Konstantin Nikolaevich's personal secretary, A. V. Golovnin. During Golovnin's tenure, 1861-1866, major reforms in the empire educational system were carried out at the university, middle, and elementary levels.[44]

In the case of judicial reform, as in the area of education, the Naval Ministry played a leading role in the process of reform. Naval justice, like the civil judiciary system, suffered from serious flaws, reflecting the influence of serfdom throughout the national life. Russian statesmen in the first half of the century had tried to transform the empire into a state under law through systematic codification, but had not altered the complex court system which was ponderously slow and offered many opportunities for corruption and bribery. Usually historians date the beginning of judicial reform in Russia from Alexander II's commission to State Secretary D. N. Bludov to prepare a report on judicial reform in 1861.[45] The Naval Ministry had, however, been concerned with the reform of its own system of justice for at least five years prior to Bludov's assignment, and the proposals of Naval Ministry personnel in the area of judicial reform had an important impact upon the general plans for the reform of the courts. In contrast to the Naval Ministry, the Ministry of War did not seriously begin the task of judicial reform until 1862 with the appointment of a special committee under General N. A. Kryzhanovskii.[46] The Naval Ministry's views on judicial reform took on a "radical" cast from the first consideration of the matter, and it was the Naval Ministry that championed those features of judicial change which in the statute of 1864 did give Russia a judicial system on a par with that in Western Europe of the same period.

The task of studying the reform of naval justice the Grand Duke Konstantin Nikolaevich entrusted to two civilian jurists, P. N. Glebov and K. S. Varrand. Glebov had the task of drafting a project for regulation of the naval judicial system and its judicial process.[47] This assignment had three components: an examination of the existing system, a consideration of foreign systems as possible models, and the drafting of a preliminary project. On the first point, the office of Naval Auditor reported in 1859 that one of the basic causes for desertion from the fleet was dissatisfaction among the lower ranks with both the naval courts and the system of punishments.[48] The fundamental problem with the old system lay in the fact that a commander could and often did dispense justice to his subordinates in a manner resembling that of a landlord with his peasants. He instigated charges, directed the investigation, and confirmed the sentences of the court-martial. He was judge, jury, and prosecutor rolled into one, and his actions transpired behind closed doors without any oral testimony, public discussion, or even counsel for the accused. Glebov described the outcome of this system candidly:

> The very basis of the present system of naval justice and the dysfunction of the judicial part of the naval department lead inevitably to the predominance of individual action over the spirit of legality . . . , the consequences of which are apparent and harmful for public morality.[49]

Glebov and other reform-minded officials in the navy proposed fundamental changes in both the organization of the courts and in its proceedings. First, they universally championed the idea of public trial. Second, they supported oral testimony. Third, they defended the right of each accused to have his own counsel, and fourth, promoted trial by jury.[50] In all of these proposals the navy was far in advance of other agencies of the Imperial Government. Neither Count D. N. Bludov, the Director of the Second Section of His Imperial Highness Personal Chancellery, nor Count V. N. Panin, the Minister of Justice, greeted this project enthusiastically. Bludov observed that the project was based upon a system quite alien to the existing order and could cause confusion. He judged trial by jury as "premature."[51] While the Naval Ministry had intended that the Second Section, the Ministry of Justice, and the Ministry of War were to review Glebov's project of April 1860, it did not halt the matter there. The project was at the same time sent to "different persons known for their erudition in legal matters" and after that, when the project was improved according to their comments, the ministry proposed "to forward it for the consideration of the State Council."[52]

The collection of comments on Glebov's project stimulated a wide interest in judicial reform. Many figures noted the sweeping nature of the proposals, but concluded that the project contained those features necessary for a new court system. Professor A. I. Chebyshev-Dmitriev wrote that "the transformation of the naval judiciary has great significance. . . . The good features of the reform of the Navy's judicial process could advance the matter of reforming the entire criminal process."[53] Professor V. D. Spasovich applauded the project's radical break with the existing court system as the only sound approach to reform in this area.[54] B. P. Mansurov, a close associate of the Grand Duke Konstantin Nikolaevich and a former official of the Naval Ministry, gloated over the fact that: "the first example [of court reform] will be given, although not by that department which most of all is obliged to concern itself about the organization of the judiciary."[55]

Some commentators noted the danger of reforming the naval judicial system without transforming other military courts or the general judicial system. Konstantin Pobedonostsev recognized this problem.[56] B. G. Glinka worried about the deterioration of army morale and "the disastrous consequences for our army."[57] While these fears about the immediate reform of the naval judiciary did postpone the implementation of Glebov's proposals, they could not stem the tide of popular support within educated society for its principles. These became the foundations upon which State Secretary V. P. Butkov and S. I. Zarudnyi worked out the Court Statute of 1864.[58]

The enthusiasm of Russian liberals for Glebov's proposals should not prevent a clear assessment of the practical nature of his suggestions for the navy. The navy had made technical modernization and the creation of a "Blue water" fleet the keystone of all its actions after the Crimean War. The Grand Duke Konstantin Nikolaevich considered long-range cruises in foreign waters as an important part of his transformation.[59] Russian sailors were to be in frequent contact with other navies and to learn from them. Such contacts both Glebov and Varrand reported would not bring the intended result if Russian officers and seamen found their own position grossly inferior to that of sailors in other fleets. If Russia was to have an oceanic force, manned by competent cadres with a high morale, the courts had to be reformed:

> Our naval officers and lower ranks who take part in foreign cruises are constantly in uninterrupted contact with different lands; they hear and see how courts function in such countries—how dearly appreciated and protected by law are the person of the officer and even the lower ranks—and can not but suffer a loss of self respect through a contemptuous glance at the picture of the performance of the courts that we have, can not but feel in themselves some regret that we are subordinated to a different order. . . . The strength and fiber of military forces are always undermined when the ranks' self respect begins to suffer— when they are insulted and do not value their own system.[60]

A modern navy needed long-range cruises and that had made judicial reform an imperative to the Naval Ministry, when other branches of the imperial government were unwilling to consider either immediate or profound changes in this area.

In conclusion, the decision to create a modern navy following the Crimean War pressed the Naval Ministry into fundamental reforms in the areas under discussion—terms of service for the lower ranks, naval education, and justice. None of these areas related directly to the emancipation of the serfs. Yet, they are important elements in the web of transformations that historians identify with the Great Reforms. It seems possible to conclude that the Crimean War stimulated these reforms. Naval affairs, a peripheral topic for most scholarship on this period, then assumes a new significance.

FOOTNOTES

[1] "Trial Balloons," *Journal of Modern History*, XLVI (December 1974), 686-687.

[2] Thomas Esper, "Military Self-Sufficiency and Weapons Technology in Moscovite Russia," *Slavic Review*, XXVIII (June 1969), 185-208; Richard Hellie, "The Petrine Army Continuity, Change, and Impact," *Canadian-American Slavic Studies*, VIII (1974), 237-53; Richard Pipes, "The Russian Military Colonies, 1810-1831," *Journal of Modern History*, XXII (September 1950), 205-219; John Sheldon Curtiss, *The Russian Army Under Nicholas I, 1825-1855* (Durham, North Carolina: Duke University Press, 1965); L. G. Beskrovnyi, *Russkaia armiia i flot v XIX veke* (Moscow: Nauka, 1973); W. Bruce Lincoln, "General Dmitrii Milyutin and the Russian Army," *History Today*, XXVI (January 1976), 40-47; and Jacob W. Kipp, "Consequences of Defeat: Modernizing the Russian Navy, 1856-1863," *Jahrbucher für Geschichte Osteuropas*, XX (June 1972), 210-225.

[3] A. Kornilov, *Kurs istorii Rossii XIX veka*, 2nd edition (Moscow: M. & S. Sabashnikov, 1918), 125-132; M. N. Pokrovskii, "Krymskaia voina," in: *Istoriia Rossiiv XIX veke* (St. Petersburg: Granat, 1910) IV, 1-68; E. V. Tarle, "Krimskaia voina," in: *Sochineniia* (Moscow: Akademiia Nauk SSSR, 1959), IX, 554-555; P. A. Zaionchkovskii, *Otmena krepostnogo prava v Rossii*, 1st edition (Moscow: Gosudarstvennoe izdatel'stvo politicheskoi literatur, 1954), 73-77; Terence Emmons, *The Russian Landed Gentry and the Peasant Emancipation of 1861* (Cambridge: Cambridge University Press, 1968), 47-50; and Alfred J. Rieber, *The Politics of Autocracy: Letters of Alexander II to Prince A. I. Bariatinskii 1857-1864* (Paris: Mouton & Co., 1966), 15-58.

[3] C. E. Black, *The Dynamics of Modernization: A Study in Comparative History* (New York: Harper & Row, 1966), 122. For interesting essays on the various aspects of this fundamental break with the past see: C. E. Black, ed., *The Transformation of Russian Society: Aspects of Social Change since 1861* (Cambridge: Harvard University Press, 1960).

[4] Essays on the historiography of the Great Reforms are contained in the following works: P. A. Zaionchkovskii, "Sovetskaia istoriografiia reformy 1861 goda," *Voprosy istorii*, (February 1961), no. 2, 197-208; Alfred Rieber, *The Politics of Autocracy . . .* , 15-20; M. V. Nechkina, "Revoliutsionnaia situatsiia v Rossii v iskhode 1850-kh—nachale 1860-kh godov (Issledovatel'skaia problematika i osnovnye zadachi izucheniia, in: *Revoliutsionnaia situatsiia v Rossii v 1859-1861 gg.* (Moscow: Akademiia Nauk SSR, 1960),

3-14; Charles C. Adler, Jr., "The Revolutionary Situation, 1859-1861: The Uses of an Historical Conception," *Canadian Slavic Studies,* III (1969), 383-399; L. G. Zakharova, "Otechestvennaia istoriografiia o podgotovke krest'ianskoi reformy 1861 goda," *Istoriia SSR* (1975), 54-76. I. D. Koval'chenko, *Russkoe krepostnoe krest'ianstvo v pervoi polovine XIX veka* (Moscow: Izdatel'stvo Moskovskogo Universiteta, 1967), 3-20; and Daniel Field, *The End of Serfdom: Nobility and Bureaucracy in Russia, 1855-1861* (Cambridge: Harvard University Press, 1976), 51-56.

[5] Rieber, *The Politics of Autocracy . . .* , 17-28.

[6] Field, *The End of Serfdom . . .* , 54-55, 386.

[7] *Ibid.,* 55.

[8] *Ibid.,* 56. This path has been pursued by other scholars. See: L. G. Zakharova, "Pravitel'stvennaia programma otmeny krepostnogo prava v. Rossii," *Istoriia SSR* (1975), no. 2, 22-47.

[9] It is quite true that traditionally historians have dated the process of reform in many areas as beginning after the promulgation of the Emancipation Statute in 1861. See: G. A. Dzhanshiev, *Epokha velikikh reform,* 5th edition (Moscow: A. I. Mamontov, 1894), *passim.* Yet, the process of reform articulation and passage clearly predates 1861. In the important area of economic reorganization this was the case. The reform of the national banking system which was undertaken with the clear objective of creating a free market for capital in the hope of encouraging private investment was considered the economic twin of the emancipation by many reform-minded officials, since free markets in both labor and capital were seen as the essential foundations for Russia's economic development. On this topic see: I. Gindin, *Gosudarstvennyi bank i ekonomicheskaia politika tsarskogo pravitel'stva* (Moscow: Gosfinizdat, 1960), 26-30; L. E. Shepelev, *Aktsionernye kompanii v. Rossii* (Leningrad: Nauka, 1973), 66-80; and Jacob W. Kipp, "M. Kh. Reutern on the Russian State and Economy: A Liberal Bureaucrat during the Crimean Era, 1854-1860," *Journal of Modern History,* XLVII (September 1975), 437-459.

[10] Alexander Gerschenkron, "Russia: Agarian Policies and Industrialization, 1861-1917," in: *Continuity in History and Other Essays* (Cambridge: Harvard University Press, 1968), 140-147. The war has been presented not only as a watershed in state policy but also as a turning point in the mentality of the intelligentsia. See: Sh. M. Levin, in: *Ocherki po istorii russkoi obshchestvennoi mysli: Vtoraia polovina XIX—nachalo XX veka,* (Leningrad: Nauka, 1974), 293-404.

[11] Field, *The End of Serfdom . . .* , 54-55.

[12] Wilhelm Treue, *Der Krimkrieg und die Entstehung der modernen Flotten* (Gottingen: Musterschmidt, 1954).

[13] Jacob W. Kipp, "Consequences of Defeat: Modernizing the Russian Navy, 1856-1863," *Jahrbucher für Geschichte Osteuropas,* XX (June 1972), 210-225; and "Imperial Russia: The Archaic Bureaucratic Framework, 1850-1863," in: Ken J. Hagan *et al., Naval Technology and Social Modernization in the Nineteenth Century* (Manhattan, Kansas: Military Affairs, 1976), 32-67.

[14] Jacob W. Kipp, "Charisma, Crisis, and the Genesis of Reform: The *Konstantinovtsy* and Russian Naval Modernization, 1853-1858," in: *Acta No. 2 (Washington, D.C., 13-19 VIII 1975) Commission Internationale d'Histoire Militaire,* edited by Robin Higham and Jacob W. Kipp (Manhattan, Kansas: United States Commission on Military History, 1977), 85-96.

[15] Gosudarstvennaia Publichnaia Biblioteka im. Saltykova-Shchedrina: Otdel Rukopisei, (hereafter cited as GPB), fond 208 (A. V. Golovnin), delo 10/124-141.

[16] A. A. Samarov, ed., *P. S. Nakhimov: Dokumenty i materialy* (Moscow: Ministerstvo Oborony Soiuza SSR, 1954), 613.

[17] On the careers of these officers see: K. G. Zhitkov, "Svetloi pamiati Grigoriia Ivanovicha Butakova," *Morskoi sbornik*, no. 4, (April 1912), *neof.*, 1-47; I. A. Shestakov, "Polveka obyknovennoi zhizni: Vospominaniia Admirala Shestakova," *Russkii arkhiv*, (1873) *kn.* 2, 163-193; and Jacob W. Kipp, "Russian Naval Reformers and Imperial Expansion, 1856-1863," *Soviet Armed Forces Review Annual*, I (1977), 119-139.

[18] Russia, Morskoe Ministerstvo, *Istoricheskii obzor razvitiia i deiatel'nosti morskogo ministerstva za sto let ego sushchestvovaniia (1802-1902 gg.)*, edited by S. F. Ogorodnikov, (St. Petersburg: Morskoe Izdatel'stvo, 1902), 138-140.

[19] This program was delineated by the Grand Duke Konstantin Nikolaevich in a memorandum on the goal and significance of the fleet in 1856. See: GPB, fond 208 (A. V. Golovnin), delo 10/ 259-262.

[20] *Ibid.*, 237-238.

[21] Beskrovnyi, *Russkaia armiia i flot XIX veke*, 539-546.

[22] *Ibid.*, 539-540.

[23] Russia, Morskoe Ministerstvo, *Obzor deiatel'nosti morskago upravleniia v Rossii v pervoe dvadtsatipiatiletie tsarstvovaniia G. Imp. Aleksandra Nikolaevicha, 1855-1880 gg.*, edited by K. A. Mann, (St. Petersburg, 1880), I, 2.

[24] *Ibid.*, 2-16.

[25] *Ibid.*, 22. It should be pointed out that the overall size of the navy declined also during this period from 125,169 in 1855 to 20,986 in 1870. A large portion of the decline that took place in the 1860's was a conscious choice by the Naval Ministry to seek funds for ship construction by reducing personnel costs. The Navy did, however, accept the notion of "fewer but better" during the post Crimean period.

[26] "O sokrashchennykh srokakh sluzhby dlia nizhnikh chinov flota, oznamenovavshikh den' (8 Sentiabia 1859 g.) sovershennoletiia Gosudaria naslednika tsarevicha!" *Morskoi sbornik*, XLIII (Sept. 1859) *of.*, lxviii.

[27] Russia, Morskoe Ministerstvo, *Obzor deiatel'nosti morskago upravleniia . . .*, I, 372-377.

[28] Gosudarstvennaia Biblioteka im. Lenina: Otdel Rukopisei, (hereafter cited as GBL), fond 169 (D. A. Miliutin), karton 42, delo 30/2.

[29] GPB, fond 208 (A. V. Golovnin), delo 12/100.

[30] Russia, Morskoe Ministerstvo, *Obzor deiatel'nosti morskago upravleniia . . .*, I, 193.

[31] GPB, fond 208 (A. V. Golovnin), delo 23/68-69.

[32] Dzhanshiev, *Epokha velikikh reform*, 178.

[33] "Gibel' klippera *Plastun* (izvlechenie iz sledstvennago proizvodstva)," *Morskoi sbornik*, L (Dec. 1860), no. 13, *of.* 154-183.

[34] Dzhanshiev, *Epokha velikikh reform*, 182.

[35] S. F. Ogorodnikov, "50-letie zhurnala *Morskoi sbornik*," (St. Petersburg, 1898), 1-9. On *Morskoi sbornik* see also: E. D. Dneprov, "*Morskoi sbornik* v obshchestvennom dvizhenii period pervoi revoliutsionnoi situatsii," in: *Revoliutsionnaia situatsiia v Rossii v 1859-1861 gg.*, (Moscow: Nauka, 1965), 229-258.

[36] N. V. Novikov & P. G. Sofinov, eds., *Vitse-Admiral Kornilov*, (Moscow: Voennoe Izdetel'stov Ministerstva vooruzhennykh sil Soiuza SSR, 1947), 25.

[37] I. A. Shestakov, "Polveka obyknovennoi zhizni: Vospominaniia Ivana Alekseevicha Shestakova," *Russkii arkhiv*, (1873) kn. 2, cc. 192-195.

[38] Russia, Morskoe Ministerstvo, *Obzor deniatel'nosti morskago upravleniia . . .*, II, 603.

[39] *Ibid.*, 601-602. The articles are quite numerous and can be found in *Morskoi sbornik*.

[40] N. I. Pirogov, "Voprosi zhizni," *Morskoi sbornik*, XXIII (1856), no. 9, *neof.*, 559-597, and "Shkola i zhizn'," *Morskoi sbornik*, XLV (Jan. 1860), no. i, *neof.*, 278-294.

[41] E. V. Putiatin, 'Proekt preobrazovaniia morskikh uchebnykh zavedenii s uchrezhdeniem novoi gimnazii, (St. Petersburg: Tipografiia Morskago Ministerstva, 1860), 112-113. For

criticisms of Putiatin's proposal see: Russia, Morskoe Ministerstvo, *Zamechaniia raznykh lits na proekty preobrazovaniia morskikh uchebnykh zavedenii Admiral Grafa Putiatina, 1860-1861* (St. Petersburg, 1861).

[42] V. A. Rimskii-Korsakov, "O morskom vospitanii," *Morskoi sbornik* (July 1860), no. 7, *neof.*, 209-250. Rimskii-Korsakov's views were similar to but more systematic than those expressed by I. A. Shestakov two years earlier. See: Shestakov, "Staryia mysli na novoe delo," *Morskoi sbornik*, XXXIII (Jan. 1858), no. 1, *neof.*, 1-33.

[43] T. Maksimov, "Morskoi korpus i Nikolaevskaia akademiiav S. Peterburge," in: *Sbornik kratkikh svedenii po morskomu vedomstvu, vypusk 14* , (St. Petersburg: Tipografiia Morskago Ministerstva, 1867).

[44] V. Z. Smirnov, *Reforma nachal'noi i srednoi shkoly v 60-kh godakh XIX v.* (Moscow: Izdatel'stvo Akademii pedagogicheskikh Nauk RSFSR, 1954), *passim*. Not only were Naval Ministry personnel leaders in the Ministry of Education, but N. I. Pirogov's progressive ideas on education served as the basis for the Ministry's most important reform projects during the early 1860's.

[45] Dzhanshiev, *Epokha velikikh reform*, 365-374. For an excellent treatment of the Naval Ministry's role in judicial reform see: E. D. Dneprov, "Proekt ustava morskogo suda i ego rol' v podgotovke sudebnoi reformy (Aprel' 1860 g.)," in: *Revoliutsionnaia situatsiia v Rossii v 1859-1861 gg.* (Moscow: Nauka, 1970), 57-70.

[46] A. V. Fedorov, *Russkaia armiia v 50-70-kh godakh XIX v.* (Leningrad, 1959), 111-112.

[47] GBP, fond 208 (A. V. Golovnin), delo 22/103. The first article on the reform of justice, which established the ideological line of the Konstantinovtsy, circulates among them under the title: "O ustnosti i glasnosti."

[48] "Ob issledovanii prichin chastykh pobegov, sdelannykh nizhnimi chinami Morskogo vedomestva v 1854-1859 gg.," GPB, fond 208 (A. V. Golovnin), delo 23/27. While the number of desertions had declined from 647 in 1856 to 230 in 1859, the General-Auditor of the Navy felt that further reductions in the rate of desertion were not possible without a reform of the court system.

[49] P. N. Glebov, "Vvedenie ili ob'iasnitel'naia zapiska k proektu ustava morskogo sudoustroistva i sudoproizvodstva," *Morskoi sbornik*, XLVI (May 1860), no. 5, *neof.*, 22.

[50] *Ibid.*, 34. Glebov outlined the principles of his project in these terms: "Independence of the courts. . . , publicity of the judicial process and press coverage of the activities of the court, oral or verbal proceedings in court, the finality and immutability of court verdicts, the guarantee of the right of defense for the accused, the guarantee by an appeals court of the observance of the lawful rules and rites of the judicial process."

[51] *Obshchaia ob'iasnitel'naia zapiska k proektu novogo ustava po prestypleniiam i prostupkam: Materialy po preobrazovaniiu sudebnoi chasti v Rossii*, Tsentral'naia spravochnaia biblioteka, Tsentral'nyi Gosudarstvennyi Istoricheskii Arkhiv v Leningrade, VII, 72. cited in: Dneprov, "Proekt ustava morskogo suda i ego rol; v podgotovke reformy (Aprel' 1860 g.)," in: *Revoliutsionnaia situatsiia v Rossii v 1859-1861 gg.* (1970), 64.

[52] GPB, fond 208 (A. V. Golovnin), delo 23/40.

[53] Russia, Morskoe Ministerstvo, *Svod zamechanni na proekt ustava o voenno-morskom sude* (St. Petersburg, 1861), ch. 1, 951.

[54] *Ibid.*, 837.

[55] *Ibid.*, 612.

[56] *Ibid.*, ch. II, 31-32.

[57] *Ibid.*, ch. I, 218.

[58] Dzhanshiev, *Epokha velikikh reform*, 379-388.

[59] GPB, fond 208 (A. V. Golovnin), delo 22/105. Konstantin Nikolaevich expressed himself quite plainly on the place of long-range cruises in the reformed navy: "In order to have a good fleet most of all it is necessary to send it to sea as often as possible and to keep it at sea for as long as possible, endeavoring to secure for the officers diverse naval exercises in a good climate, where our vessels can meet with foreign fleets. The consequences of such exercises will be better ordered and this will inevitably lead to various improvements in the navy. Officers and sailors will become partial to the service and get the necessary knowledge and experience, . . . which the fleet could never get from short-range cruises or shore training."

[60] Glebov, "Vvedenie ili ob'iasnitel'naia zapiska k proektu ustava morskogo sudoustroistva i sudoproizvodstva," *Morskoi sbornik*, XLVI (May 1860), no. 5, *neof.*, 22-23. Glebov recognized that his proposal was founded upon foreign models and that it broke with the past. He also noted that the foreign systems of naval justice which he took as his guides, especially that of France, were an integral part of a national system of justice based upon the same general principles. This he accepted as necessary. As early as 1859 in his comments on the French system of naval justice Glebov stated his opinion that such principles were gradually infecting the judicial systems of all western Europe—Holland, Belgium, Sardinia, Prussia, and a large part of Germany. See: "Morskoe sudoproizvodstvo vo Frantsii," *Morskoi sbornik*, SLVI (Nov. 1859), no. 11, *neof.*, 101-104. K. Varrand provided the readers of *Morskoi sbornik* with extended commentaries on the British system of naval justice and its foundations in the general system of English law. See: "Morskoe sudoproizvodstvo v Anglii," *Morskoi sbornik* (Dec. 1860), no. 13, *neof.*, 323-351, and "Zamechatel'nyia ugolovno-sudebnyia dela angliiskago flota," *Morskoi sbornik*, LIII (May 1861), no. 5, *neof.*, 88-118.

CHAPTER 17

The Manning Question in the Royal Navy in the Early Ironclad Era

Eugene L. Rasor

Emory and Henry College

During the entire nineteenth century the Royal Navy enjoyed extraordinary preeminence as the "Senior Service" and the "first line of defense"of the most powerful empire in the world.[1] This was also the formative period of the ironclad era when technological shifts were being made from sail to steam propulsion, from wood to iron and steel construction, and from muzzle-loading, smooth-bore to breech-loading, rifled guns. Change was cumulative. Alterations in one sphere or at a particular level inevitably caused changed circumstances elsewhere. It is a truism among navalists that the seamen of the Elizabethan era, the men serving under Sir Francis Drake, could have, with relative ease, fought under Lord Nelson at Trafalgar. One doubts seriously whether such a thing would have been possible under Admiral Sir John Jellicoe at the Battle of Jutland.[2]

A dramatic transformation was taking place throughout the navy. It is the thesis of this paper that the Admiralty perceived this, and, for the first time, became sensitive to and considerate of the personal and human needs and feelings of the bluejacket, the man of the lower deck. A crisis in manning occurred at mid-century and the response was quite different from anything that had occurred previously. Historians have tended to concentrate on the technological, engineering, and strategic spheres and have neglected the social and environmental aspects of the Royal Navy in the nineteenth century.[3]

The "manning the navy" question was not ignored at the time. The problems of recruitment and retention of enlisted men were the subject of debate in newspapers, in periodicals, on the floor of Parliament, and in two formal governmental investigations.[4] All commentators recognized the seriousness of the problem. Without men the fleet was worthless and it was the navy, as the preamble of the Naval Discipline Act of 1860 stated, "whereupon the good Providence of God, the Wealth, Safety and Strength of the Kingdom" depended. The solutions of the past no longer provided a reliable and politically acceptable method of recruitment and retention which would guarantee sufficient numbers of men in peacetime and fulfill the expanded requirements of wartime.

In 1850 a senior Admiralty official informed the Prime Minister that the most serious problem facing the Royal Navy was manning in an emergency. A decade later, in an unusually perceptive series of articles in *Blackwood's Magazine,* an anonymous author[5] stressed that Great Britain was not endangered by technological competition—at that time with France—over ships and guns. The future existence of the empire was dependent upon "this man-difficulty. . . . We decline to compel them, we fail to lure them."[6]

Although the inability of the Royal Navy to recruit and retain enlisted men was not a new problem,[7] during the 1850s the situation became critical. Mobilization for the Russian War of 1854-56 required more men than the navy could secure and operations in the Crimea, Pacific, and Baltic were adversely affected. At one point the Admiralty ordered the commander of the campaign in the Baltic to get under way and enlist Scandinavian sailors en route. When the war ended, the navy rapidly discharged hundreds of men and in the process released many skilled and experienced bluejackets and retained some of the worst of the wartime recruits. Later in the decade, incidents involving China, India, France, and Italy again created increased demand for men. In these crises the response was so poor that for the first time ever during peacetime the navy offered a bounty to encourage enlistment. The bounty failed to attract the required numbers of men, but the offer so alienated bluejackets already in the service that the navy paid a half bounty to appease them. At the end of the decade, the beginning of the Volunteer Movement in 1859, served to further reduce the manpower pool from which the service drew.[8]

Not only did the navy in the 1850s have trouble attracting the men it needed, it faced dissatisfaction among those who did enlist. In 1859-60 a series of disturbances which the Admiralty insisted upon calling "mutinies" occurred aboard individual warships. These incidents were widely publicized and members of Parliament raised anxious questions about the state of the navy.

Under similar circumstances in the past the government had immediately resorted to some form of compulsory service, and that alternative was theoretically available in the 1850s. Such variations as impressment, the ballot, a lottery, and calling up all merchant seamen were discussed and considered, and never adopted. Obviously, compulsion was excluded as a practical alternative due to political expediency. The Russian War was the first to be fought without resort to some form of compulsory service.[9]

Up to this time the standard method of recruitment in the Royal Navy was hire-and-discharge, a short-term service. An entire crew would be assembled, serve for a "commission"—three to five years—and then let go en masse. This was now dropped. In his budget speech of 1852 Chancellor of the Exchequer Benjamin Disraeli denounced it as "unsatisfactory and irrational. . . . It dismisses the seasoned seaman when he is most qualified [loud cries of 'hear, hear']." The system was described as "hand-to-mouth."[10]

Vocal lamentations were expressed about the demise of another tradition: the close and supportive relationship between the Royal Navy and the merchant service. At one time the merchant marine had acted as "the nursery for naval seamen," virtually all training and initial experience at sea having been acquired there. Whether life was actually better, safer, and more lucrative outside the Royal Navy is now open to conjecture, but the merchant seaman of the mid-nineteenth century certainly believed that it was. He was attracted elsewhere, often to America. He saw the Royal Navy as "a black nightmare in which he would be scrubbed till clean and then flogged to death." Seamen unions and benefit societies discouraged service in the navy.[11]

Technological developments exacerbated the problem of recruiting. There now existed an increasing demand for skilled professionals: engineers, gunners, engine room artificers, divers. They were reluctant to join for many of the same reasons as the merchant seamen, plus they were abused and antagonized by the naval seamen who saw them as a threat. The sailors called them "chimney sweeps" and resented the higher pay and additional privileges offered by the Admiralty to attract them.[12]

Finally, much discussion was heard about the merits and superiority of the process of recruitment utilized in France, the *Inscription Maritime*. Again, there are those who doubt its actual potential, but critics of the Admiralty at the time never tired in praising its dependability, effectiveness, and predictability. It incorporated a combination of quotas and the ballot. For rapid expansion in an emergency it was a system that worked. Fifty thousand trained seamen could be raised whereas the maximum available in Great Britain was about ten thousand, it was claimed.[13]

We have seen that under the circumstances and during the crises of the 1850s previously acceptable methods of recruitment were rejected: compulsory service was deemed inappropriate even during wartime and short-term service, hire-and-discharge, was abandoned. The bounty had created disruption and had failed. A need was also felt to renew the attachments between the navy and merchant service.

Manning the navy was the subject of two formal investigations of the 1850s, both instituted during separate governments of the Tory, Lord Derby, in 1852 and 1858-59.[14] A departmental committee of naval officers chaired by Admiral Sir William Parker, with Sir Charles Henry Pennell, Chief Clerk of the Admiralty as secretary, studied the problem in 1852-53. Admiral Collingwood had suggested the basic idea in 1805 but Pennell was credited with formulating the most important of the recommendations: the Continuous Service system or long-term service. It incorporated fundamental changes.

Young men were recruited between the ages of fifteen and sixteen. To be eligible they must have parental permission, must read and write, and attain certain weight and height standards. These "boys," as they were called, were trained aboard specialized training ships for two years. Now the Royal Navy nurtured its own seamen. At age eighteen each signed an "engagement" for ten years. Upon expiration the seaman renewed the contract for another ten years and was then eligible for a pension. Continuous Service was to be the primary recruiting practice after 1853. Subsequently, there was much praise for its success. Continuous Service established the career-oriented, permanent, professional naval ratings for the more technologically complex and sophisticated ships of the late nineteenth century.[15]

Continuous Service was implemented by an Order-in-Council of 1 April 1853, unfortunately not a propitious time. Mobilization, demobilization, and frantic recruitment for responding to international crises caused chaos, as has been noted. With the return of the Lord Derby government in 1858-59, a Royal Commission, a higher level investigative body, studied the manning question. The Earl of Hardwicke was chairman and the other members were consciously selected for their association with the merchant service. Two prominent ship-owners and a former President of the Board of Trade were members. It endorsed Continuous Service. However, its important recommendations concerned the source for large numbers of seamen in an emergency and improvement of conditions within the navy. These related to the question of merchant seamen.[16]

Implementing the primary recommendation of the Royal Commission, the Royal Naval Reserve was formed in 1859. Experienced merchant seamen were recruited to serve twenty-eight days a year for training drill and to be subject to call in an emergency. Annual pay depended upon experience and competence. The system was endorsed by the seamen unions. As with Continuous Service, the Royal Naval Reserve was hampered by delays. Ultimately it would attain its projected strength and provide sufficient numbers of trained seamen in an emergency.[17]

The departmental committee of 1853 had warned the Admiralty to improve the environment on the lower deck; the Royal Commission of 1859 stressed that as one of its major recomendations. Life on the lower deck had to be made more attractive and humane. Basically the reforms were in the nature of incentives and inducements for recruiting and retention. Long-term service must be made popular and the merchant seamen must be

211

enticed into affiliating with the Royal Naval Reserve. Between 1849 and 1866 the following reforms were implemented: wages were increased; uniforms were introduced and provided free, along with mess kits and bedding; discipline and punishment practices were drastically humanized and ameliorated—flogging was renounced; improvements were made in medical and sanitary arrangements; good conduct incentives, educational opportunities, and ships' libraries were provided; paid leave and monthly pay in advance were instituted; the food ration was increased, the rum ration decreased; and gratuities, pensions and arrangements for allotments were improved.[18]

The process of change was slow and haphazard. Some inducements to recruiting disappeared, e.g., prize money, once so prominently advertised; and some poor conditions and policies continued, e.g., the notorious hulks, the home of seamen when not aboard ship, were replaced by barracks only in the 1890s; no opportunities developed for opening commissioned status to the lower deck.[19]

A number of officials at Whitehall, the location of the Admiralty, contributed to the social transformation just described. Sir Charles Henry Pennell's contribution has been mentioned. More importantly, Admiral Sir Maurice Berkeley, who served on eighteen Boards of the Admiralty during this period, has been most linked to the reforms in recruitment and manning.[20] Admiral Sir William Fanshawe Martin was given most credit for instituting the humanitarian reforms, especially concerning discipline and punishment.[21] Finally, it was during the administration of the Duke of Somerset, First Lord of the Admiralty between 1859-66, that the consolidation of the various personnel reforms and dramatic improvements took place.[22]

Why had the Admiralty changed its policies? Perhaps unconsciously, and certainly slowly, these leaders perceived that the requirements of technological progress could not be fulfilled by traditional recruiting and personnel practices. Oftentimes it was outside pressures, primarily parliamentary and journalistic, which forced the Admiralty to institute reforms affecting the conditions and welfare of the seamen. Admiralty action during this exceedingly disruptive period was uncharacteristically kind and generous. Altered circumstances, outside pressures, and serious crises made for unprecedented responses.

Meanwhile the Admiralty resorted to more elaborate and sophisticated recruiting measures such as colorful advertisements and highly-publicized recruiting teams, the latter projecting quite different images from those of the old press gangs. They even went after Irish recruits.[23] The deterioration of the British economy which began in the 1870s assisted the recruiting drive. More recruits responded, and the efforts were successful.[24]

Continuous Service and the Royal Naval Reserve provided the solution to the manning question, though admittedly in a delayed and unspectacular manner. The primary source for the former shifted from the merchant service to young boys who could be induced to make the navy a career. This was much more expensive, but also more reliable. And for the emergency the navy resumed its reliance upon the merchant service, again at added expense. Together these measures created the modern regular navy of Great Britain, the "Standing Navy" of professionals.

FOOTNOTES*

[1] Sir William Laird Clowes, *The Royal Navy, A History*, 7 vols. (London: Low and Marston, 1897-1903), volumes V, VI, and VII; C. J. Bartlett, *Great Britain and Sea Power* (New York: Oxford University Press, 1963); Michael A. Lewis, *The Navy in Transition, 1814-64* (London: Hodder and Stoughton, 1965); Arthur J. Marder, *The Anatomy of British Sea Power* (New York: Knopf, 1940); Peter K. Kemp, *The British Sailor* (London: Dent, 1970).

[2] Charles Johnstone "Manning the Fleet; A Re-arrangement of Existing Corps and Their Training," *Journal of the Royal United Service Institution* 35 (April 1891): 367-94.

[3] A perusal of the historiography of the Royal Navy of the nineteenth century will provide proof for this contention. For example, a recent survey is entitled, "The Condition of the Fleets," and, as usual, "fleets" is stressed. The writer, Ruddock F. Mackay, calls for "more studies of technical development," yet only two lines in eight pages are devoted to social history, and nothing is included about personnel or "conditions" on the lower deck. Essay in Robin Higham, ed., *A Guide to the Sources of British Military History* (London: Routledge and Kegan Paul, 1971), pp. 238-45.

[4] Hans Busk, *The Navies of the World* (London: Richmond, 1859), pp. 198-203; "By a Captain, R.N.," "Hints on Educating and Manning the Navy," a pamphlet (Bath: Hayward and Payne, [1855]); [G. A. Elliot], "Reform in the Navy," *Cornhill Magazine* 3 (January 1861): 90-94; W. S. Lindsay, *Manning the Royal Navy and the Mercantile Marine* (London: Pewtress, 1877). There was frequent debate in Parliament. For example, Great Britain, Parliament, *Hansard's Parliamentary Debates*, 3rd series, 111: 279-82; 3rd series, 150: 886-911.

[5] Charles Hamley.

[6] [Charles Hamley], "Fleets and Navies," 4 parts, *Blackwoods Magazine* 85-87 (June 1859 to February 1860): 641-60; 324-39; 758-75; 226-43.

[7] Leslie Gardiner, *The British Admiralty* (London: Blackwood, 1968), pp. 163-64; Sir Herbert W. Richmond, *Naval Policy and Naval Strength* (London: Longmans, Green, 1928), p. 247; [William H. Ragan], *Admiralty Administration*, 2nd ed., revised (London: Longmans, Green, 1861), pp. 85-86; Bartlett, *Great Britain*, pp. 138-40, 168-69.

[8] Roy Taylor, "Manning the Royal Navy: the Reform of the Recruiting System, 1852-62," *Mariner's Mirror*, Part I, Vol. 44 (November 1958): 302-13; C. I. Hamilton, "Sir James Graham, the Baltic Campaign and War-Planning at the Admiralty in 1854," *Historical Journal* 19 (March 1976): 89-112; Michael J. Salevouris, "Rifleman Form: the War Scare of 1959-60," Ph.D. dissertation, University of Minnesota, 1971, pp. 111-26; Christopher Lloyd, *The British Seaman* (Cranbury, N.J.: Fairleigh Dickinson University Press, 1970), p. 280; Michael A. Lewis "An Eye-Witness at Petropaulovski, 1854," *Mariner's Mirror*

44 (November 1963): 265-72; Barry M. Gough, "The Crimean War in the Pacific:British Strategy and Naval Operations," *Military Affairs* 37 (December 1973): 130-36; [Hamley], "Fleets," pp. 641-60; *The Times*, 24 January 1854 and 3 December 1860; *Hansard's*, 3rd series, 155: 278-79; 3rd series, 155: 363-65; Francis W. Hirst, *The Six Panics* (London: Methuen, 1913).

[9] Olive Anderson, "Early Experiences of Manpower Problems in an Industrial Society at War: Great Britain, 1854-56," *Political Science Quarterly* 82 (December 1967): 526-45; James Stewart, "The Press-Gangs of the Royal Navy," *U.S. Naval Institute Proceedings* 86 (October 1960): 81-87; M. R. D. Foot, ed., *War and Society* (New York: Barnes and Noble, 1973), pp. 193-94.

[10] [John Murray], "The Financial Statements of the Right Honourable Benjamin Disraeli," *The Quarterly Review* 183 (December 1852): 236-74; Taylor, "Manning," pp. 302-13.

[11] Stephen Jones, "Blood Red Roses: The Supply of Merchant Seamen in the Nineteenth Century," *Mariner's Mirror* 58 (November 1972): 429-42; Henry Baynham, *Before the Mast* (London: Hutchinson, 1971); David Roberts, *Victorian Origins of the British Welfare State* (New Haven: Yale University Press, 1961), pp. 85-87.

[12] Sidney Knock, *"Clear Lower Deck,"* (London: Alan, [1932]), pp. 16-19; Bartlett, *Great Britain*, pp. 203-10; Lewis, *Navy*, pp. 14-15.

[13] Roy Taylor, "Manning the Royal Navy: The Reform of the Recruiting System, 1847-61," M. A. thesis, University of London, 1954, p. 27; James Reddie, "On Manning the Navy," *Journal of the Royal United Service Institution* 11 (June 1867): 279-362; Lindesay Brine, "The Best Method of Providing an Efficient Force of Officers and Men for the Navy," *Journal of the United Service Institution* 26 (June 1882): 183-338; [Hamley], "Fleets," pp. 641-60; [Ragan], *Admiralty*, pp. 29-34.

[14] Great Britain, Parliament, *Parliamentary Papers* (Commons), 1852-53: LX [1628]; (Commons), 1859, 1st session: VI [2469]; *Hansard's*, 3rd series, 150: 1061.

[15] H. I. V. Neale, "Manning the Navy—Seamen," *Naval Library Pamphlets* 3 (#712): 253-56; J. M. Moody, "Recruiting for Her Majesty's Service," *Journal of the Royal United Service Institution* 29 (1885): 565-629; Sir J. C. D. Hay, "On the Necessity for Training Seamen for the Sea Service," *Journal of the Royal United Service Institution* 28 (June 1904): 652-76; Sam Noble, *'Tween Decks in the Seventies* (New York: Stokes, 1925); Henry D. Capper, *Aft-From the Hawsehole* (London: Faber and Gwyer, 1927); Taylor, "Manning," pp. 302-13; Lewis, *Navy*, pp. 185-91; Reddie, "Manning," pp. 279-362; *The Times*, 24 February 1859.

[16] Lindsay, *Manning*, pp. 19-38; Baynham, *Mast*, p. 120; *The Times*, 24 May 1859.

[17] James L. Kerr and Wilfred Granville, *The R.N.V.R.* (London: Harrap, 1957); W. F. Caborne, "The Royal Naval Reserve," *Journal of the Royal United Service Institution* 33 (January 1889): 41-47; G. H. Gardner, "On the Formation of Reserves of Officers and Seamen for the Royal Navy, and the Evils and Inadequacy of Impressment to Provide the Same," *Journal of the Royal United Service Institution* 15 (1871): 601-42; Lord Thomas Brassey, *British Seamen* (London: Longmans, Green, 1877); Jones, "Blood Red Roses," pp. 429-42; Lloyd, *Seamen*, pp. 280-82; Lewis, *Navy*, pp. 185-91; Sir Frederick W. Grey, "Suggestions for Improving the Character of our Merchant Seamen and for Providing an Efficient Naval Reserve," a pamphlet (London: 1860); J. C. Wilson, "Is Our Merchant Service Any Longer a Feeder to the Royal Navy?," *Journal of the Royal United Service Institution* 20 (1876): 61-84.

[18] Eugene L. Rasor, *Reform in the Royal Navy* (Hamden, Conn.: Archon, 1976), pp. 21-111; Sir Frederick W. Grey, *On the Organization of the Navy* (London: 1860) pp. 3-14; [Elliot], "Reform," pp. 90-94; Taylor, "Manning," pp. 302-13; Lewis, *Navy*, p. 223.

[19] Rasor, *Reform*, pp. 21-111; [Harry Pursey], "Lower Deck to Quarter Deck, 1818 to 1937," *Brassey's Naval Annual* (1938): 87-105; Peter K. Kemp, *Prize Money* (Aldershot: Gale and Polden, 1946), pp. 1-33; Henry Baynham, *Men from the Dreadnoughts* (London: Hutchinson, 1976), pp. 195-96; Baynham, *Mast*, pp. 134-36; "E.R.F.,"

"Discipline and Seamanship in the Navy, Past and Present," *Fraser's Magazine* 15 (March 1877): 269-84; Elliot, "Reform," pp. 90-94.

[20] Taylor, "Manning," pp. 302-13; Foot, *War*, pp. 185-89.

[21] Moody, "Recruiting," pp. 565-629; Rasor, *Reform*, pp. 120-21.

[22] Colin F. Baxter, "Admiralty Problems during the Second Palmerston Administration, 1859-65," Ph.D. dissertation, University of Georgia, 1965, pp. 115-16; Grey, *Suggestions*; Rasor, *Reform*, pp. 118-20.

[23] Great Britain, Public Record Office, *Admiralty Digests*, IND 18091; IND 18146; IND 18222.

[24] Baynham, *Mast*, pp. 157-60.

* Much of the research for this paper was conducted among the Admiralty records and documents located at the Public Record Office and the Naval Library at Earl's Court, and among the collected papers at the National Maritime Museum, Greenwich. This fact could have been more easily demonstrated in a bibliography. Also, I was unable to gain access to the collection of pamphlets on naval manning compiled by John Bromley and published by the Naval Records Society.

215

CHAPTER 18

Manning and Training the Japanese Navy in the 19th Century

Peter G. Cornwall

University of Alaska

The system of manning and training evolved by the Imperial Japanese Navy in the closing decades of the nineteenth century provides an interesting example of how a relative latecomer to the naval scene, with a minimal naval tradition, was able to create a viable personnel policy while emerging as a major naval power. In this period, established and emerging navies alike were obliged by rapid technological and social change to reconsider existing methods of manning and training, or to evolve new, and thus the experience of Japan should prove of interest when compared to that of Western navies, with due allowance for the peculiarities of individual situations.

Although Japan did not have an extensive naval tradition,[1] the Imperial Navy, which came into existence as an independent force in 1872, was able to draw upon the experience of its predecessors, the navies of the central feudal government (the bakufu) and the various feudal domains. Before the opening of Japan in 1853, exclusion edicts had prevented the development of a merchant marine engaged in overseas trade, and the building of vessels suitable for such a trade. Thus, a source of supply of trained seamen, utilized freely in the west, was not available. During the period of isolation this was not a serious handicap, of course, and the bakufu was able to meet its slight naval needs by recruiting seamen from the Shiaku Islands, in the Inland Sea, whose inhabitants, in return for a trade monopoly, were obliged to furnish seamen on request.[2] Although with experience these men proved to be competent to handle western-style vessels, this was at best a limited source. In 1861, therefore, after the opening of Japan had made the need for naval development apparent, a bakufu committee on military affairs recommended the enlistment of fishermen, a practice already followed in the navies being created by some of the feudal domains.[3]

This suggestion was not adopted by the bakufu, however, nor initially by the Imperial government which came to power after 1868. The first ships of what was to become the Imperial Navy were those taken from the bakufu and feudal domains, and their existing crews became the nucleus of the navy's enlisted force. When additional seamen or stokers were required, they were supplied by the former domains or government request, a procedure which worked well as long as the navy was small, and its ships few.

In 1868, however, even before the Imperial forces were in complete control of the country, the decision had been taken to create a strong navy, with initial emphasis to be placed on the education and training of personnel. This was to take precedence over the production of iron and the building of ships in what seems to be a wise allocation of limited resources.[4] This policy and the naval growth of the 1870's made an increase in personnel necessary. Late in 1870 interim regulations were issued for a system of national conscription, but significantly the navy preferred to seek its men through voluntary enlistment. In 1871 volunteers were sought from among the sons of fishermen, of strong physique, and between the ages of 18 and 25. Although the Conscription Law promulgated in 1873 made all male subjects betwen 17 and 40 liable for service in the navy, the latter did not avail itself of this opportunity, but continued to meet its needs through voluntary enlistment. At this time, the term of service for conscripts was 3 years in either the army or the navy, and this period was considered by naval authorities to be too short to allow the necessary training, and some return in terms of service for this investment. Together with the lesser manpower needs of the navy, this was a prime reason for the preference for voluntary enlistment until 1889.[5] In that year, the Conscription Law was amended to extend the period of naval service to 4 years, and from this time the navy recruited its enlisted personnel by a combination of conscription and volunteer service. The increased length of service in the navy was compensated for, in some degree, by higher pay, better food, and generally better conditions than those prevailing in the army.[6]

Utilizing the existing army conscription facilities, in German fashion, naval recruiting officers classified men who had reached the age of 20 and who lived in coastal districts or on islands into seamen, stokers, artificers, and miscellaneous trades, in accordance with their physique and civilian trades or skills. After this initial selection process, the men required for that particular year were chosen by lot, and commenced their training. The remainder of those eligible were placed for one year in a conscript reserve, from which men could be drawn as replacements for casualties, and which could be mobilized in time of war. Those who were the sole support of their families were exempt from service, while students at certain specified schools, usually of the normal or middle school level, were deferred until age 28, and those staying abroad were deferred until they reached 32, at which time, if still abroad, they passed into the militia.[7] Conscripts served for 4 years, and at the end of this time inducements such as advanced training with the possibility of qualifying for a higher rate, a modest family allowance, and the chance of promotion to petty officer were offered, in the hope that the most able would choose to remain in the service.

Volunteers for the Imperial Navy were accepted in the trades of seaman, signalman, carpenter, stoker, artificer, musician, and cook after 1889. After 1896, sick-berth attendants were recruited. Seamen and stokers were taken between the ages of 17 and 21, while to permit the enlistment of skilled or semiskilled men, carpenters, artificers, cooks and sick-berth attendants could enter between 17 and 26. Signalmen were selected on the basis of aptitude from the seaman branch, and music pupils were enrolled between the ages of 16 and 19, and discharged within 3 months if found to be without musical talent. With this single exception, volunteers signed on for a period of 8 years. Ineligible for volunteer service in the navy were members of the army reserves, those with a record of imprisonment or who were known gamblers, the insolvent and bankrupts who had not discharged their obligation, and those awaiting trial for a criminal offence. Volunteer service offered certain advantages, and the benefits conscripts enjoyed upon re-enlistment were the result of their being henceforth considered volunteers.[8]

The number of volunteers to be raised each year was decided by the Navy Minister on the basis of estimated need, and quotas were assigned to the various naval stations charged with inducting and training recruits. The proportion of volunteers to conscripts was also decided by the Navy Minister and recruiting figures for Kure Naval Station show the pattern of voluntary enlistment after 1889. During that year 139 conscripts entered the naval barracks, as opposed to 129 volunteers. In the following year, 1890, the figures were 427 and 309, but in 1891 only 104 conscripts were taken to 124 volunteers, while in 1892 146 volunteers were raised, with conscription limited to 16. Figures for 1894 were 616 volunteers and 346 conscripts, for 1895, 504 and 156, and ten years later, in 1904, 1,822 and 419, and in 1905, 2,245 and 1,059.[9] The increase in volunteers in 1894-95 and 1904-05 was due largely to patriotic enthusiasm accompanying the Sino-Japanese and Russo-Japanese Wars, but for the service generally voluntary enlistment continued to equal or be in advance of conscript service. In 1910, for example, 3,487 volunteers were raised to 3,235 conscripts.[10] With a higher retention rate, and the reclassification of re-enlisting conscripts, volunteers made up an even higher proportion of the enlisted force than recruiting figures indicate, and estimates range from 50 to as high as 70 percent.[11]

Advancement within the service was the result of success in examinations, and a minimum time in grade, with sea service counting for 1/3 more than shore time.[12] During hostilities, this time in grade was reduced by one half, and, in outstanding cases, a man could be promoted by selection, rather than by examination. Volunteers and re-enlisted conscripts who showed trade proficiency and some leadership skill were eligible for promotion to petty officer, and progress through the three classes of this rank was again by examination and service. A man promoted to petty officer was obliged to serve for six years from the date of promotion, unless retirement age—45 for petty officers and 40 for men, was reached first. A very few highly qualified petty officers were promoted to warrant officer, a rank carrying status and prestige akin to that of the commissioned officer.[13] Re-enlistment in the Imperial Navy was for successive periods of 3 years, and was conditional on physique, trade progression, and the recommendation of the man's commanding officer. Following active service, petty officers and men were transferred to the first and second reserves until total service time, active and reserve, had reached 14 and 12 years, respectively.

The training of enlisted men in the early navies of Japan developed in a somewhat erratic manner, although this should not be surprising, considering the magnitude of the task. New skills had to be learned in the handling of Western-style ships, and an attempt was made, in the early 1860's, to sound enlisted men abroad for practical experience. Eight ratings were in fact sent to Holland, where a ship was building for the bakufu navy.[14] This pattern, however, was not subsequently followed up as extensively as with officers, some of whom received training in foreign warships, or in naval schools in Great Britain, France, Germany, and the United States.[15] For enlisted personnel, most early training was a matter of practical work aboard recently acquired ships, often under the guidance of men who had themselves only recently learned the management of these new vessels. Foreign instructors were an invaluable, if expensive, source of knowledge, and the Dutch, French, and British who assisted the bakufu navy before 1868 all provided instruction for enlisted personnel as well as for officers. In 1870 the decision had been taken to follow the British pattern in naval development and, in 1873, following the creation of the Imperial Navy as an independent service, a request was made to the British government for a training mission from the Royal Navy, the choice of personnel to be left to the Admiralty. An earlier British mission of 1866, had included, at Japanese request, senior enlisted men as well as officers, and in a similar fashion 16 of the 34 members of the mission of 1873 were leading or able seamen.[16] Their task was to teach their Japanese counterparts by example, and the training vessel attached to the Naval School was used to train seamen as well as cadets. British non-commissioned officers and men also served on board other training vessels as advisors.[17] This pattern of practical training on board ship, in Royal Navy style, continued after the termination of the British mission in 1879, although from the mid-seventies a tendency to identify training with the naval stations at which these ships were based was evident.

By the 1880's basic instruction was being provided for seamen, stokers, carpenters, and artificers and the beginning of specialization could be seen in the use of torpedo and gunnery training ships, established in 1878 and 1881 respectively, and in attempts to create a shore training facility for the engine room force.[18] Between 1889 and 1901, as part of a series of organizational changes, Japan was divided into four naval districts, and barracks were constructed in each of the four major naval stations: Yokosuka, Kure, Sasebo, and Maizuru. With this innovation came some semblance of pattern in the field of training. The barracks were responsible for the enlistment and basic training of all recruits, volunteer or conscript. Military drill and preliminary trade training lasted 6 months, with the emphasis on practical work, both ashore with the use of training aids and mock-ups and on board the training vessels attached to the barracks. For seamen, the course of instruction consisted of general seamanship, boat pulling, and introductory gun and torpedo drill. Facilities included models for instruction in ship types and nomenclature, examples of knots and splices, and practice guns and torpedo tubes. Drills for stokers involved shovelling pebbles, to represent coal, into dummy fireboxes, while artificer recruits were provided with the facilities and tools necessary for basic bench and shopwork. Similar introductory trade training was available for signalmen, after they had mastered the elements of seamanship, for carpenters and, from 1889, for cooks.[19] At the end of the 6 months, the recruits, now 4th class men, were posted to the fleet or to shore establishments for a period of practical experience which varied according to individual ability.

For those likely to benefit from it, specialist training was offered, on the condition that the man so trained remain in the service for a period of time after completion of the course. Usually, this advance training was given at two levels. An ordinary course, for first and second class men, brought with it an obligation to serve not less than four years after completion, while a higher course, for petty officers and first class men entailed three years active service after finishing the course. In this fashion the Imperial Navy sought to overcome a difficulty facing other navies: that of providing technical training for men who then left to seek more lucrative employment in the merchant service or ashore. Following the general pattern of basing training ashore, rather than afloat, the torpedo and gunnery training ships were abolished in 1893, and specialist schools established in their place. Electrical specialists, drawn from the ranks of serving torpedomen, were trained at the Naval Torpedo School and, from 1901 instruction was given there in wireless telegraphy.[20] Interestingly, these schools, while providing training for both officers and enlisted men, were also charged with research and development in their respective fields. For the enlisted men of the engineering force a series of schools evolved, including, for a time, the facilities of the former Naval Engineering College, when the Imperial Navy experimented with line-engineer amalgamation between 1887 and 1893. This development culminated in the Naval Mechanical and Engineering School, where, as in the Torpedo and Gunnery Schools, both officers and enlisted men were trained, and where instructors were expected to conduct investigations into engineering and related problems, in addition to their teaching duties. For enlisted men, courses were available in the trades of stoker, blacksmith, armorer, machinist, carpenter, and engine room artificer, with electrical artificer added after 1907.[21] Students for the Mechanical and Engineering School were chosen in the same manner as those for the Torpedo and Gunnery Schools, and in this instance the re-quirement of a period of active service after graduation was particularly meaningful.[22]

Advanced training was also provided for clerical personnel, a small special group who were recruited in an irregular fashion as the need arose, and trained in the barracks and in the Naval Paymasters College, which also gave advanced training to cooks and stewards.[23] Sick-berth attendants, a specialty then rare in the world's navies, were trained after 1896 in the naval hospitals attached to the naval stations, and bandsmen at Yokosuka Naval Barracks, and through civilian musical facilities.[24]

In the area of advanced training in practical seamanship, the approach taken was, of necessity, somewhat different. Faced with an initial shortage of non-commissioned officers, the Imperial Navy began the specific training of seamen chosen for promotion to this rank as early as 1873. With the passage of time, however, it was discovered that actual service, particularly under sail, provided a sound education in seamanship. Consequently, in 1891, the program was abandoned and the seamanship training vessel abolished. Henceforth, petty officers were to be chosen from among seamen who displayed practical ability, and who were capable of passing a promo-tion examination.[25] By the early years of the twentieth century, however, it was apparent that the use of steam for both propulsion and auxiliary power had resulted in a decline in the skills which traditionally had been identified as seamanship, a condition noted, with varying degrees of intensity, by the navies of the day.[26]

The Japanese solution, decided upon in 1907, was to commission a vessel for advanced training in seamanship, in which petty officers and senior men could be trained to act as instructors in this subject throughout the fleet. Chosen for this duty was the *Chin'en*, a former Chinese battleship captured in 1895. The course of instruction lasted for six months, and was intended to provide the students with a knowledge of the work necessary for the operation, safety, and maintenance of the ship, the management of its boats, and the use and care of its basic equipment. Special courses for warrant officers provided training in basic navigation and an introduction to engineering, electricity and wireless telegraphy to fit them for command in the event of emergency.

In this fashion, warrant officers, petty officers, and first class men were given at least an introduction to the entire range of practical seamanship. The training attempted to simulate conditions which in service would occur only by chance and which most of the students might never experience in a normal career yet for which they must be prepared. The knowledge thus gained would then be passed on to the lower ranks, when the training ship graduates returned to their own ships and assumed instructional duties. The problem of the retention of the skills of the seaman in an age of steam was one which plagued the navies of the world in the late nineteenth and early twentieth centuries, and it is typical of Japan that a solution should be sought in the establishment of a formal training institution.

Specialist training and progressively advanced courses were thus available to enlisted men of all trades, yet, while valuable for theoretical instruction and directed practice, they needed the reinforcement of constant in-service drill for the greatest effect. It is significant that the most advanced courses were intended primarily for future instructors who would teach, not in schools, but on board ship and in active formations ashore. Prior to 1897, practical training in service was the responsibility of the individual commanding officer, and efficiency depended to a large extent on his initiative and zeal. In that year, however, regulations to ensure a uniform standard of training throughout the service were issued, and these were updated in 1901 and 1905. The aim was to provide a systematic program of practical training, where such did not interfere with the regular duties of the men. In addition to general and division drill, training companies were organized by trade and branch to improve the technical capabilities of individual petty officers and men, and instructors were found from among the specialists on board. Thus, for example, the gunnery officer and his staff were responsible for gunnery training, the senior division officer for seamanship, and the navigating officer for helmsmanship and signalling. This instruction was to be accomplished in formal five month courses to be held twice a year, and men so trained were awarded an "assistant" certificate which, after two years satisfactory performance of actual duties, would be upgraded to the level attained in the specialist school ordinary course; assistant gunners would become gunners, for example.

All areas of training emphasized physical and moral development as well as technical skill, and in these areas Japan possessed something of an advantage when compared to other naval powers. The Imperial Navy was essentially a "short-legged" force, and did not engage in protracted cruises. Thus, opportunities for physical training ashore existed in the naval stations and ports, and physical exercise was constantly encouraged. Moral or spiritual training, not unfamiliar in Japanese tradition, was intended to foster a spirit of patriotism and loyalty in the men, while emphasizing the military virtues of courage and obedience. Officers, by their conduct and through formal lectures, were to set a pattern of military behaviour, and to enforce discipline while correcting such faults as the men might develop. Specifically, officers were to read and explain Imperial proclamations, and to instruct their men in the necessity of obeying the Imperial will. Lectures were to illustrate the duty of a warrior to his country and, by illustrations from noted battles and ship actions, and the deeds of famous warriors, to stimulate in the men a spirit of heroism.[27] In this fashion, esprit de corps was to be created and the initial lack of an indigenous naval tradition overcome.

This lack of tradition was not entirely negative, however, as can be seen when we compare the Japanese system of manning and training with those of the west. The absence of a significant Japanese naval past and the consequent absence of a body of senior officers committed thereto, meant that the Imperial Navy was less hampered by the "inertia of tradition" than were the older, established navies in the west. Thus, the spirits of a bygone age were less likely be be invoked in defence of sail training, and rearguard arguments based on courage and physical conditioning had little applicability in the face of spiritual training and the skills of the warrior. The absence of a fleet of sailing vessels which had been rendered obsolete by technological advance was also a benefit to Japan, for thus there were no old hulks to be used as training vessels, and as receiving ships for newly enlisted men. Recruits could therefore be given their basic training in barracks, and be spared the difficulties of accommodating themselves to life on board a western-style vessel while learning new skills and naval discipline. The Imperial Navy was able to resolve the question of initial training afloat or ashore, in favor of the latter, some sixteen years before its former mentor, Great Britain, took a similar step.[28] Of relatively recent origin, and with a comparatively young body of senior officers, the Japanese Navy was able to innovate, and to adjust its training methods to rapidly changing conditions.[29]

Japan enjoyed other advantages, also. Its enlisted personnel were an homogenous body, and the problems of linguistic and ethnic division, apparent in the Austro-Hungarian Navy, and even in that of the United States for a time, were not present.[30] Also, with the early development in Japan of an effective system of public education, the navy was not faced with the necessity of training a great number of illiterates. In this, the Imperial Navy stands in great contrast to that of Russia. In theory, seamen of the Russian Navy were to be taken from the sea-going, technically competent sector of the population. These men, however, were too valuable to the merchant service to be spared, and thus the navy recruited its seamen from among the often illiterate peasants of the interior.

Similarly, France and Italy found that coast-dwellers taken into the navy by the *inscription* system were often lacking in education and technical aptitude, a situation not apparent among the better-educated Japanese.[31] Internal developments in Japan also influenced the composition of the engine room force. In the earlier industrial powers, and in particular in France and England, skilled men recruited as mechanics or artificers often proved to be a divisive element, with trade union membership and political connections. Such were the difficulties encountered that, in time, those countries were obliged to adopt a program of enlisting boy artificers or apprentices, and training them wholly within the service.[32] With no significant union movement, Japan was able to take advantage of whatever skills the civilian sector could provide.

The system of training adopted, with its balance of volunteer and conscript, also conferred certain advantages upon Japan. Eight year volunteers gave a degree of continuity, a significant return for the time and money invested in them and, like their English continuous service counterparts, provided a source of non-commissioned officers, who then were regarded by many as the backbone of the fleet.[33] In this latter regard, both Japan and England enjoyed an advantage over those continental navies relying on a short-service conscript system, such as those of Germany, Italy, and Austria-Hungary, who were obliged to utilize boy-entrant apprentice schemes to provide a source of future petty officers.

One of the major advantages of the Japanese system was the relatively low turnover of personnel. Although the continental navies permitted voluntary enlistment, the bulk of their personnel were conscripts, and even volunteers were reluctant to serve for longer than the period of compulsory service. In the German Navy, for example, 90 percent of the recruits in the early twentieth century served only the stipulated 3 years, and only the petty officers could be considered long-service personnel, retiring after 12 years. It has been estimated that, in the first decade of this century, some 28.5 percent of the personnel of the German Navy were changed each year, compared to 10 percent of Great Britain, and 14.5 percent for Japan.[34] Rapid turnover was not limited to navies employing conscription, however, and the same estimates show a 38 percent annual turnover in the United States Navy for this same period.[35] This high rate of changeover meant that fleets so affected were virtually useless as fighting units for 3-6 months each year, as new men were taken on board and familiarized, to some extent, with their duties. A tremendous strain was placed upon the petty officers and officers who had to train the recruits as rapidly as possible. In effect, the battle fleet was the training fleet. Japan's balance of long service and 4 year conscript enlistment spared her this difficulty, to a great extent.

In defence of the European system, it must be mentioned that the object of short-term conscript service was to provide a reserve to permit rapid mobilization in time of emergency. Britain, unable for political reasons to adopt conscription, provided for this eventuality by the creation of nucleus crews and the Royal Naval Reserve. Japan did have a reserve system, as we have seen, but interestingly did not intend it to man a rapidly growing fleet in time of war. In the Imperial Navy the emphasis was on the active fleet itself, and it is significant that in 1904, during the Russo-Japanese War, only half of the available men in the first and second reserves were called to the colors, 4,647 of 8,084, and these served largely in auxiliary facilities and in shore stations.[36]

Japan, therefore, by selective borrowing and learning from the experience of others, was able to evolve a pattern of manning and training suited to her own needs, and which capitalized on such advantages as she possessed. Naturally, this was not a smooth, even development, and many mistakes were made along the way, and weaknesses were apparent in some areas, as was seen in signals and wireless telegraphy in the early 20th century. This was, however, a system devised within the Navy itself for manning and training was seen as serious professional business, best left to professionals. There was no such public debate as accompanied the introduction of new methods of recruiting and training in the navies of the west, for example. Japan had found a way to obtain, train, motivate and retain enlisted men for her navy. That the system worked can be seen in the reports of foreign observers, and in the results of two victorious wars, in 1895 and 1905.

FOOTNOTES

[1] For a discussion of the early use of sea power in Japan see Arthur J. Marder, "From Jimmu Tenno to Perry: Sea Power in Early Japanese History," *The American Historical Review*, 51 (October 1945): 1-34.

[2] Ikeda Kiyoshi, *Nihon no Kaigun* (The Japanese Navy),(Tokyo: Shiseidō, 1966) I, pp. 6, 77. Zaidan Hōjin Kaigun Yūshū Kai, *Kinsei Teikoku Kaigun Shiyō* (Society for the Perfection of the Navy, comp., A Short History of the Imperial Navy in Modern Times) (Tokyo, 1940) p. 197.

[3] Kaigun Kyōiku Hombu, *Teikoku Kaigun Kyōiku Shi* (Naval Education Department, A History of Education in the Imperial Navy) (Tokyo: Kaigun Kyōiku Hombu, 1911) I, pp. 35-36.

[4] *Teikoku Kaigun Kyōiku Shi*, I, pp. 61-62.

[5] Ikeda, *Nihon no Kaigun*, I, pp. 77-78. *Kinsei Teikoku Kaigun Shiyō*, p. 198. To indicate the differing manpower needs of the two services, the army in 1895 took 21,662 conscripts into active service, while the navy enrolled only 780. The figures for 1898 were 52,040 and 1,412 respectively. Gotaro Ogawa, *Conscription System in Japan* (New York: Oxford University Press, 1921) p. 46.

[6] Ogawa, *Conscription System in Japan*, pp. 33, 188-189.

[7] A translation of the Conscription Law of 1889, as amended in 1895, appears in U.S. National Archives, Record Group 38, Records of the Office of the Chief of Naval Operations, Office of Naval Intelligence, Register E - 7 - d 15271, "Entry of Enlisted Personnel, Japanese Navy."

[8] Volunteer regulations are to be found in O. N. I., E - 7 - d 15271.

[9] Kure Shi Shi Hensan Shitsu, *Kure Shi Shi* (Kure City History Compilation Office, comp., A History of Kure City), III (Tokyo, 1964) p. 120. It is interesting to note that, for the service as a whole, of the 18,470 volunteers examined in 1904, 13,506 were rejected on the grounds of physical disability, and 1,967 for other reasons. O. N. I., O - 12 - a 06-295, "Translation of Report on Japanese Navy for 1904-05."

[10] O. N. I., E - 8 - a 1716, "Annual Report of Japanese Navy Dept. for Fiscal Year Ended March 31, 1911."

[11] O. N. I., E - 7 - d 08-90, "The Japanese Navy," in a report dated January 27, 1908, states that "about one half" of the enlisted force is made up of conscripts (p. 19) while Ikeda suggests that, by the time of the Russo-Japanese War, the ratio of volunteers to conscripts was 6 : 4 or 7 : 3.

[12] For example, promotion from third class to second class man required a minimum of 6 months sea time, or 8 months ashore. Similarly, from first class man to third class petty officer required 12 months at sea or 16 months on a shore station. J. C. Balet, *Military Japan: The Japanese Army and Navy in 1910* (Yokohama: Kelly and Walsh, 1910) pp. 174-175.

[13] The rank of warrant officer was introduced in 1872, when 29 were appointed. Of the 27,557 men of all ranks on active service in 1900, 1,562 were commissioned officers (including 40 of flag rank), 291 were midshipmen, 579 warrant officers, 4,530 petty officers, and 20,495 men. Kaigun Daijin Kambō, comp., *Yamamoto Gombei to Kaigun* (Secretariat of the Navy Ministry. Yamamoto Gombei and the Navy) (Tokyo: Kaigun Daijin Kambō, 1927). Reissued by Hara Shobō, (Tokyo, 1966) p. 401.

[14] *Teikoku Kaigun Kyōiku Shi*, I, p. 50.

[15] Between 1868 and 1906 seventeen Japanese students attended the United States Naval Academy at Annapolis. U. S. National Archives, Record Group 24. U.S. Naval Academy, Annapolis, *Registers*.

[16] *Teikoku Kaigun Kyōiku Shi*, I, pp. 51-52, 182-184.

[17] Instructions from then Lieutenant Commander A. C. Douglas, commanding the British mission, to boatswain second class Willoughby for such duties are to be found in Archibald C. Douglas, *Life of Admiral Sir Archibald Lucius Douglas* (Totnes, Devon: Mortimer Brothers, 1938) pp. 70-71. Willoughby was to be accompanied by a chief petty officer and two leading seamen or AB's and Douglas was careful to spell out their duties during the various drills (one seaman was to be stationed aloft in each top during general sail drill, for example), and to ensure that the position and authority of the Japanese officers aboard was respected.

[18] From 1879 to 1883 torpedo training was also carried out ashore, in a former Christian church built by the French at Yokosuka. *Teikoku Kaigun Kyōiku Shi*, I, pp. 75, 77.

[19] For a western observer's impression of these facilities, and the training conducted therein, see George Kennan, "War by Prearrangement," *The Outlook*, Vol. 77 (Saturday, August 13, 1904) p. 894. See also Erin, "The Japanese Navy," *The Naval Annual*, ed. T. A. Brassey, (1904) p. 199.

[20] *Teikoku Kaigun Kyōiku Shi*, VII, Supplement, pp. 45-46. Unfortunately, the quality of instruction given in these early wireless courses was not particularly good, and the navy suffered inconvenience and embarrassment in its attempts to communicate with shore stations and foreign men-of-war. Subsequently, instructors from the Torpedo School were sent to the wireless school operated by the Ministry of Communications for intensive training, and the course at the Torpedo School was lengthened and patterned after that of the civilian agency, indicating the navy's willingness to learn from other government departments, as well as from abroad. O.N.I., E - 8 - a 1078, "Annual Report of the Japanese Navy Dept. for Year Ending March 31, 1910."

[21] *Teikoku Kaigun Kyōiku Shi*, VII, Supplement, pp. 53-59.

[22] Regulations governing these schools will be found in O. N. I., E - 7 - d 397, "Regulations Governing Education of Officers and Enlisted Men, Japanese Navy."

[23] Opportunities for advancement in the clerical branch of the service were few, and numbers were kept small by the Navy's practice of appointing civil servants to clerical positions in shore establishments.

[24] For example, bandsmen were sent to Tokyo in 1908 to study string music, as the prelude to the formation of an orchestra. *Teikoku Kaigun Kyōiku Shi*, I, p. 83.

[25] *Teikoku Kaigun Kyōiku Shi*, I, pp. 72, 80.

[26] For an example of this point of view see Rear-Admiral S. B. Luce, "Naval Training," United States Naval Institute *Proceedings* 16 (March 1890): 372. The same author repeats his argument for the "school of the topman" as late as 1910 in his "Naval Training II," United States Naval Institute *Proceedings* 36 (March 1910): 118-119.

[27] Kaigun Daijin Kambō, *Kaigun Seido Enkaku*, (Secretariat of the Navy Ministry, comp., History of Naval Organization) (Tokyo: Kaigun Daijin Kambō, n. d., [c. 1941]) XII, p. 42. Spiritual education, in a formal sense, remained of considerable significance throughout the history of the Imperial Navy. For later examples see Kaigun Heigakkō, *Seishin Kyōiku Shiryō, Shōchoku Kinkai, Shōchoku Shū* (Naval Academy, Materials for Spiritual Education, Reverent Explanation of Imperial Proclamations, Collection of Imperial Proclamations) (Etajima: Kaigun Heigakkō, 1943).

[28] "Barracks in Place of Training Ships," United States Naval Institute *Proceedings* 31 (September 1905): 738.

[29] In 1905 the age span of admirals in the Japanese service was from 53 to 62, while that for Great Britain was 61-65, for Germany 57-61, and for Russia 67-85. For rear admirals the figures were Japan 44-56, Great Britain 48-60, USA 60 average, Germany 51-55, France 54-62, and Russia 49-59. O. N. I., E - 7 - c 99,"Appointment, Education, and Promotion of Japanese and Russian Naval Officers," and O. N. I., E - 7 - c 06-69, "The Japanese Naval Personnel."

[30] The composition of the enlisted force of the Austro-Hungarian Navy in 1914 was 31.3% Croatians, 20.4% Magyars, 16.3% German Austrians, 14.4% Italians, 10.6% Czechs, 2.8% Slovenes, 18% Poles, 1.2% Romanians, 0.8% Ruthenians, and 0.4% Slovaks. Anthony E. Sokol, *The Imperial and Royal Austro-Hungarian Navy* (Annapolis: United States Naval Institute, 1968) p. 79. For the American situation, see Lieutenant W. F. Fullam, "The System of Naval Training and Discipline Required to Promote Efficiency and Attract Americans," United States Naval Institute *Proceedings* 16 (1890): 479 and Lieutenant E. B. Barry, discussion of a paper by Rear-Admiral S. B. Luce on "Naval Training," United States Naval Institute *Proceedings* 16 (1890): 413.

[31] O. N. I., E - 1 -d 1396, "Recruiting and Training of Enlisted Men in Foreign Navies."

[32] Theodore Ropp, "The Development of a Modern Navy: French Naval Policy, 1871-1904." Unpublished doctoral dissertation (Harvard University, 1937) pp. 370-371. See also O. N. I., E - 1 - d 1396, "Recruiting and Training of Enlisted Men in Foreign Navies."

[33] For a statement of the value of senior petty officers to the Imperial Navy, see Ikeda, *Nihon no Kaigun*, I, pp. 79-80. For an early, favorable account of the English system in which boys were recruited between 15 and 16, and served for 10 years after reaching the age of 18, see Lieutenant Commander F. E. Chadwick, "The Training of Seamen," United States Naval Institute *Proceedings* 6 (1880): 17-27.

[34] O. N. I., E - 1 - d 1396, "Recruiting and Training of Enlisted Men in Foreign Navies." The figure for Japan is calculated from the Annual Report of the Japanese Navy for 1904-05. O. N. I., O - 12 - a 06 - 295. It must be recognized that these percentages are, at best, generalizations.

[35] O. N. I., E - 1 d 1396. In 1908, 77% of the men of the U.S. Navy were serving under their first enlistment. In this same year, the desertion rate stood at 13.1%. Luce, "Naval Training II," pp. 104-105. In 1910, the desertion rate for the Imperial Navy was 0.45%, although any direct comparison is rendered difficult by differing social and economic conditions. O. N. I., E - 8 - a 1716, "Annual Report of the Japanese Navy Dept. for the Fiscal Year Ending March 31, 1911."

[36] O. N. I., O - 12 - a 06-295, "Translation of Report on Japanese Navy for 1904-05."

CHAPTER 19

The Recruitment of Japanese Navy Officers in the Meiji Period

David C. Evans

University of Richmond

The main concern of the men who brought about the Meiji Emperor's "Restoration" of 1868 and set Japan on its path to modernity was to meet the "external alarm" of Western power. To this end they wished to construct a navy which could "illumine the military might of the Imperial Country abroad" and "display the Imperial effulgence to the eight kinds of barbarians outside the country in the four quarters."[1] For all their addiction to ornate Chinese phrasing, the Meiji leadership understood that an effective navy would require the nurturing of a professional officer corps trained in the latest Western technology. "The heart of a warship is its officers," stated an early memorial, ". . . and mastery of the difficult arts and sciences necessary to the naval officer is not easily acquired."[2]

A modern navy required not only training institutions, the establishment of which was a fairly straightforward matter, but also wholly new methods of selecting officers. The class- and rank-bound military system of the old regime, the Tokugawa shogunate, had to be overturned. Hereditary status was not sufficient qualification to command a Western warship, as several high retainers of the Tokugawa had been disconcerted to learn. In the face of the Western challenge, ability and training could be the only criteria for selecting naval commanders.

In the first Meiji years, however, vestiges of the social and political interests of the old order remained which worked against such a system of naval officer procurement. Middle- and low-level members of the samurai class—Japan's old warrior-administrator aristocracy—had brought about the Meiji Restoration and actually governed the country. Many of them believed initially that the samurai should continue to rule society and retain their monopoly of arms. In 1869 the government reaffirmed the special status of the samurai class, designating it anew as *shizoku* (samurai families). A small group of former court nobles and territorial lords, the *kazoku* (peerage), was also created above the *shizoku* at this time. Below these were the *heimin* or commoners. Thus, a legally privileged and influential aristocracy persisted at the opening of the modern era.

Another vestige of the previous regime was the narrow geographical interest represented by the new government. The Restoration leaders stemmed from several semi-independent domains (*han*) of southwestern Japan—Satsuma, Chōshū, Tosa and Hizen, the so-called "Satchōdohi" group. Acting together as "imperial" or "loyalist" forces, these domains had overthrown the Tokugawa shogun and taken the lead in the government of the early Meiji years. In most cases Satchōdohi men had transferred their loyalties from domain to nation. But strong particularist and localist sentiments inevitably persisted, particularly in the armed forces. Units from the southwestern domains had won the Restoration War of 1868 and formed the backbone of the new military. Satchōdohi men saw the military as their own preserve.

The early navy probably reflected more than any other branch of government the continued strength of the old class system and the regional character of its foundations. To begin with, the navy had a strong samurai cast. While some army units of imperial forces in the Restoration War had incorporated commoners thus breaking the samurai monopoly of arms, samurai had held all positions of leadership in navy forces. In the anti-Tokugawa domains as indeed in all of Japan only men of samurai status had been selected for the difficult and expensive course of naval training. Many of the loyalist navy men remained in the sea service after the War, where they were eventually joined by a number of retainers of the old Tokugawa House navy. No officer lists survive from the early 1870s, the period of the navy's founding, but the 200-odd officers of that time were almost certainly samurai to a man.[3]

The geographical origins of these officers were scarcely less exclusive than the social. The few former Tokugawa vassals held specialist positions ashore, but officers of the southwestern anti-Tokugawa domains held all of the sea billets.[4] Satsuma and Hizen men were most prominent because their domains had built up the largest forces of Western steamships before the Restoration.

Satsuma men constituted a plurality of the early navy officers.[5] They exercised strong influence in the corridors of the Navy Ministry as well as in the fleet. A Royal Navy officer who had instructed Japanese cadets reported in 1881 that the navy was little more than "an instrument of patronage in the hands of the Satsuma clan."[6] This "clan" was not a family but a clique, the former retainers of the Satsuma domain who used their position of strength in the navy to further their own interests. Satsuma men crowded

230

into the best ministry and fleet positions in the 1870s and after that could not be dislodged. Of fifteen officers who made the rank of admiral during the Meiji period—the era of the Meiji Emperor's reign, 1868-1912—thirteen were from Satsuma.[7]

In the first years of Meiji, however, the navy established rather enlightened recruiting practices which sought to ignore social and geographical origins in favor of merit. In time these practices produced a new generation of professionally trained officers less exclusive than the early officer corps, as figures on the composition of the corps show. When these professionals came of age and entered leadership positions, the Satsuma stranglehold on the navy was broken. The monopoly of leadership that the samurai class exercised in the early years also began to weaken then. These are the basic contentions of the following study, which will further suggest a few of the wider implications these matters had for the navy and nation of Japan. The full story of Japan's modern naval leadership will require studies of many other aspects of its development, principally technological adaptation and elite formation. The broadening of recruitment and officer composition recounted here, however, constitutes a fundamental transformation which helped make the naval service an efficient and modern force.

RECRUITMENT

Japan's leaders showed insight into the requirements for building a modern navy. They were convinced that the human side of the naval enterprise, the development of capable naval officers, should have priority over the acquisition of hardware. This conviction was doubtless aided by the lack of money to buy ships in early Meiji. Still, the Japanese attitude contrasts strongly with that of contemporary Chinese "Self-Strengtheners," who concentrated on getting "solid ships and effective guns."[8] The central figure on the Japanese government's early military planning staff, Ōmura Masujirō, wrote in the first year of the new regime, "Nothing is more urgent than the establishment of a naval school when it comes to priorities for promoting the navy."[9]

Given this emphasis on education, it is not surprising that the government set up a naval officer school well before the navy acquired a separate institutional identity under its own ministry. The Kaigun Sōrenjo (Navy Training Facility) was estabished in October 1869. This school was erected on grounds adjacent to the former Tokugawa naval center, at Tsukiji in Tokyo. It was later renamed the Kaigun Heigakuryō (Naval Studies Dormitory) and Kaigun Heigakkō (School of Naval Studies). For convenience' sake we shall call it simply the Naval Academy. In 1888 it was moved to Etajima, a small island in the Inland Sea to the west of Kure. From the early 1870s it was almost the only path of entry into the executive branch of the officer corps. Our investigation of recruitment thus can focus on the

231

requirements for admission to it. "Non-combatant" officers such as engineers, paymasters, and physicians could not aspire to the positions of leadership of "officers of the line" and therefore will not be included in this study.

The Naval Academy opened on February 11, 1870, with a ceremony and a lecture, appropriately enough, on the life of James Watt.[10] In attendance were some fifty pupils. Most of them were "tribute students," young samurai who had been ordered to the school at the government's behest by seventeen domains of the Restoration's anti-Tokugawa coalition. There were also "day students" who lived in the city, commuted to school, and paid fees.[11] Although this category was meant to include entirely private volunteers, academy fees were so high that most of the day students also were the samurai nominees of domains, receiving support from their native provinces. Satsuma, for example, had sent its full quota of five tribute students but increased its contingent with nineteen day students, so that it had more young men at the academy than any other domain.[12] Such practices tended to provoke antagonisms between groups of students from different domains. For this and other reasons, the tribute system was abolished at the end of 1870.[13]

In January 1871 the Naval Academy announced that applications for admission would be accepted from the public and that entry would be based on competitive examinations. Its recruiting notice read:

> On the second day of the eighth month of this year, the year of the sheep, a total of fifty persons will be chosen to be students at the Naval Academy. Therefore, those wishing a career in the navy, whatever their social and geographical origins, are to fill out an application as shown below and present it in person, accompanied by their guarantors, to the Naval Academy by the twenty-ninth day of the sixth month.[14]

The notice also stated that except for some minor expenses the student would be completely provided for throughout his schooling.

Thus almost from its inception the Japanese Navy provided a free course of professional training officially open to all who could demonstrate the necessary qualifications. This policy went into effect before the arrival of the British training mission under Commander Archibald Douglas that did so much to shape educational methods during the years of its activity, 1873–79. Japanese recruitment policy is not attributable to this British contingent, though other foreigners may have suggested such a course to the Japanese. The Royal Navy itself followed more socially exclusive policies in its officer procurement at the time.[15]

Throughout its history the Imperial Navy upheld the principle of universal recruitment based on merit, but this policy was hard to translate into practice. Traditional attitudes concerning class roles kept commoners from applying to the navy in any numbers. The Academy's entrance examinations were initially based to a certain extent on subjects a samurai was likely to have studied but not a commoner.[16] English and mathematics were featured on the examinations, but only those with means—usually samurai—could attend the "institutes of Western learning" which offered preparation in such subjects.[17] The Naval Academy for a time (1870-86) offered a preparatory course of its own, entry to which was on the basis of competitive examination, but few of its students proved capable of progressing to the regular course.[18]

Despite these early difficulties, the academy began to attract large numbers of applicants, generally above 500 per year for 30 to 50 openings in the 1890s and nearly 2,000 per year for 200 openings after 1900.[19] This upswing in numbers arose in part from the public's growing awareness of the navy after the victories of the Sino- and Russo-Japanese Wars. Another cause was the rapid development of a sound public school system.[20] The academy announced in 1897 that thenceforth entrance examinations would be based on the curriculum of the common middle school. The announced rationale for the new policy was that middle schools were finally able to provide an adequate preparation for naval studies, in fact a broader and more useful education than academy entrance examinations had earlier prescribed.[21] From then on the navy relied largely on the public school system for its officer candidates, taking a significantly different path from the army, which set up its own system of specialized military high schools (Yōnen Gakkō).

Recruitment was also made easier by more widespread application facilities. Before 1889 prospective cadets could take examinations for entry only in Tokyo. After that date other locations were gradually added to the list, so that by 1901 applicants could report to navy recruiting centers in eighteen major cities from Aomori in the far north to Kagoshima in the far south.[22]

In late Meiji times an applicant had to be between sixteen and twenty years of age. He presented himself for testing with a certificate of residence from local government authorities and recommendations from two guarantors, usually close family members. After passing the physical examination—a hurdle that often eliminated half of the applicants—he took a battery of written tests. The major subjects were native language arts (Japanese and *Kambun,* or Chinese texts), English, and mathematics. Minor subjects included chemistry, history, geography and others derived from the national middle school curriculum.

Married men were ineligible to apply. Those with criminal records and those whose families were undergoing bankruptcy proceedings were also excluded. Finally, those "considered incapable of upholding the honor of the naval officer . . . because of poor family background or poor moral character" were not considered.[23] It is difficult to determine exactly what

233

"poor family background" meant, because there are no official pronouncements on the subject. The army excluded applicants from the *mizu shōbai* (the entertainment demimonde) and from families in disreputable petty trades.[24] In the absence of information we can only speculate that the navy may have had a similar policy.

SOCIAL ORIGINS

This provision concerning "family background," announced first in 1904, by which time applications were coming in a flood, casts some doubt on the navy's announced policy of open recruitment. Further, it appears that places were reserved for imperial princes (*kōzoku*) and a few sons of the peerage. Yet actual figures on the class backgrounds of academy graduates show a noticeable broadening by this time. Commoners (*heimin*) accounted for only 11 percent of graduates in the first eight academy classes (1873-81), but by the last decade for which we have record, 1892-1901, they accounted for 34 percent (see table 1).

TABLE 1

SOCIAL BACKGROUND OF NAVAL ACADEMY GRADUATES
1873-81, 1882-91, 1892-1901

	1873-81 Academy Classes 1-8		1882-91 Academy Classes 9-18		1892-1901 Academy Classes 19-21	
	Grads.	Percent	Grads.	Percent	Grads	Percent
Kōzoku/Kazoku (royalty & peerage)	2	1.2	5	1.2	10	1.6
Shizoku (samurai)	144	85.7	331	77.5	387	63.7
Heimin (commoners)	19	11.3	90	21.1	209	34.4
Unknown	3	1.8	1	0.2	2	0.3
Totals	168	100.0	427	100.0	608	100.0

SOURCES: *Kyūgokai kaiin meibo* [Membership list of the (navy officers') relief society] (n.p., 1902) provides class designations for all Academy graduates through 1901. Information from this source was collated with lists of graduates in Kaigunshō, Kaigun Heigakkō, *Kaigun Heigakkō enkaku* [History of the Naval Academy], 2 vols., Meiji Hyakunenshi Sōsho, no. 74 (Tokyo: Kaigunshō, 1919; reprint ed., 2 vols. in 1, Tokyo: Hara Shobō, 1968), Koseisho Engokyoku, *Moto kaigun shikan meibo* [Register of former navy officers] (Tokyo: Kōseishō Engokyoku, 1952) and standard biographical reference works.

Cadets of samurai background (*shizoku*) nevertheless predominated. They comprised over 70 percent of all graduates up to 1900. While it is tempting to explain their preponderance by a biased admissions policy at the academy, other factors may account for it.

In his pursuit of a naval career the aspirant of samurai background inherited definite advantages from the past. Samurai families placed great emphasis on education. Their sons were powerfully motivated to seek public leadership roles. The military profession of course enjoyed a special position of honor among them. Samurai traditions of this kind, still very much alive in late Meiji, kept the *shizoku* a majority of academy graduates until after the turn of the century.

The superior initiative of the samurai is indicated by their general prominence in public life. In 1890 about 72 percent of the 31,324 government officials stemmed from samurai backgrounds.[25] Because persons of samurai family made up only 5 percent of the population, their representation was strong indeed, assuming that the government did not favor them in recruiting. This is a generous assumption, perhaps, but the government had no announced policies of favoring samurai over commoners. Samurai prominence did not end in Meiji. A study of several hundred leaders of Japanese society conducted in 1959 found that over one-third came from such backgrounds and concluded, ". . . the indication that two out of five persons in top-most positions in Japan were of noble or *samurai* origins— nearly one hundred years and three or four generations removed from feudal society—points to a high level of status inheritance and leadership continuity."[26]

A more fundamental question than why samurai strength in the navy persisted, however, is why the service was opened up to commoners at all. The fact is that the samurai leaders of the Meiji regime did not insist on a samurai monopoly of leadership in any government department in early Meiji; there was no concerted opposition to the rise of commoners by the samurai as a class. The gradual abrogation of samurai privileges helped spark major uprisings like the Satsuma Rebellion of 1877, but even then foreign policy issues, Westernization and local autonomy were the crucial issues, not the loss of samurai status per se.

The willingness of the Meiji leaders, themselves samurai, to sweep away their class is to be explained by several factors. As military men they were acutely attuned to the imperatives posed by the Western threat; their patriotism, nourished by Restoration struggles, made them ready to take extreme measures. Their class, though a privileged stratum with roots in a feudal past that resembled Europe's, was with almost two million members too large to be cohesive. It had little of the European aristocracy's conservatism because centuries earlier it had been removed from the land and dispossessed. Samurai lived in castle towns as salaried retainers of their domain lords, the daimyo. By the end of the Tokugawa age financial troubles of the daimyo plunged many samurai into genuine penury which made the much vaunted austerity of the warrior class a grim necessity. What made their position intolerable for most samurai was the hereditary system of office holding within domain governments. The Neo-Confucian values of the samurai prescribed that political leadership—which alone could give a gentleman fulfillment— should go to men of ability, training, and moral quality. Yet no matter what their personal merit, most ended up as clerks, gate-guards, or other near-menials while a handful of favored families held the important posts. Large numbers of middle and lower samurai were left with little more than their pride and frustration. These emotions contributed powerfully to the Restoration and the changes which came after it.[27]

The preponderant view in early Meiji was that thenceforth, in mastering the new knowledge and new skills necessary to meet the challenge of the West, a man's ability would have to count for more than his social pedigree. It is little wonder that the navy, being a highly technical service resting on Western science and nautical practice, attempted to recruit its future officers on the basis of demonstrated aptitude for learning.

GEOGRAPHICAL ORIGINS

Admiral Suzuki Kantarō related that when he was considering a naval career in 1883,

> There were classmates of mine and others who were against my entering the navy. They said that the army was a Chōshū affair, and the navy Satsuma; in the services there was no chance of raising oneself and making one's way into the world; and anyway, there was no chance of getting in.[28]

This is how the recruiting policy of the military appeared to many. But Suzuki persisted in his ambition. Suzuki reasoned that Satsuma could hardly control entry to the navy if candidates were admitted through competitive examination. Suzuki attended a preparatory school and soon after gained admission to the Academy. In 1918, as a vice admiral, Suzuki became superintendent of the academy. Suzuki checked school records for evidence of favoritism toward applicants from Satsuma (after 1871 Kagoshima Prefecture) during the Meiji era. Suzuki found none and concluded that the authorities had been admirably fair out of concern for the fortunes of the navy.[29]

Questions of Satsuma influence and Satchōdohi favoritism are best answered by tabulating the geographical origins of naval officers. Early officer lists show that Satsuma had a plurality in the corps and that the Satchōdohi group provided over half the officers. About a third of the nation's prefectures were entirely unrepresented.[30] But academy graduates began to replace the tight group of Satchōdohi veterans during the 1880s. These new officers came from all over Japan. Graduates by 1890 came from all but three of the forty-five prefectures (excluding Hokkaido and Okinawa); Satchōdohi representation by then had fallen to a third of the total.[31] Also, statistical tests show evidence of the broadening of academy recruitment. The prefectural origins of academy graduates slowly begin to reflect prefectural population distribution in the Meiji period.[32]

Satsuma men were numerous in the earliest academy classes, but their representation fell off rapidly as the years went by. They accounted for 25 percent of the graduates of the first through the seventh classes (1873-1881). In the decade of the 1880s their portion dropped to 10 percent, in the 1890s 8 percent. For the entire Meiji period up to 1912 they accounted for a little over 6 percent of all graduates, a good representation certainly, but much lower than one would expect from a policy of favoritism.

Actually Tokyo and Hizen (Saga Prefecture) ranked ahead of Satsuma as suppliers of Naval Academy graduates in the Meiji period. Tokyo had over 11 percent of the total, Hizen 8. In fourth and fifth places were other areas of Restoration prominence, Chōshū (Yamaguchi Prefecture) and Tosa (Kōchi Prefecture), with 5 and 4 percent, respectively.

Tokyo's leading position is to be expected. Tokyo was the only site of examinations for admission to the academy until the 1890s. Also, it was the metropolis. It had private wealth and educational opportunities unmatched elsewhere. The Tokyo press kept the navy in the public eye. The government's vigorous reforming efforts fostered an atmosphere of enterprise in the city that encouraged aspirants to something as novel as the naval service.

If we are to continue to argue that recruitment did not involve favoritism, however, we must explain the presence at the top of the list after Tokyo of the Satchōdohi regions and particularly the strong if not overwhelming representation of Satsuma. The first point to be made is that Hizen, Chōshū, and Tosa, like Satsuma, got progressively smaller shares of academy graduates while maintaining their leadership positions; their margin of leadership depended to a degree on their strength in the early years and had shrunk considerably by late Meiji.

Second, there is evidence that a couple of the leading areas stayed on top because they consistently put up more candidates for the academy than others. In the mid-1880s applicants from Satsuma and Hizen (along with those of Tokyo) numbered over twice those from other areas.[33] The early power of Satsuma and Hizen in the national government stimulated the enthusiasm of many native sons of these areas, and in this sense early success bred later success. Yet it is a mistake to assume that Satsuma and Hizen men came in such numbers because they got special treatment. Their rate of success in passing entrance examinations was lower than those of applicants from some other areas in the years for which we have record.[34]

Third, Satsuma and Hizen made special efforts to put up superior candidates for the navy. They set up their own preparatory schools for the service academies and formed societies to aid their prospective cadets. In the late 1870s the Shimazu, formerly the ruling house of Satsuma, established the Zōshikai, a military academy in Kagoshima, and the Azabu Chūgaku, a middle school in Tokyo.[35] High ranking Satsuma navy officers

237

founded the Kagoshima Education Association in late Meiji to support Naval Academy candidates from that prefecture.[36] In 1879 Hizen navy men formed the Chishinkai (New Knowledge Society), which extended monetary aid to Hizen candidates for the academy and later ran a small institute of naval science to train naval aspirants.[37]

Thus an element of local boosterism helps explain the continued strong showing of Satsuma and Hizen in the naval officer corps of Meiji. Satsuma and Hizen elders in the navy saw that the old style of feudal patronage could not perpetuate their control given the large scale of the navy's new institutions and the imperative of technical competence. They relied instead on schools and aid associations which gave their young men an advantage under the new system. Their organizations, it should be noted, constitute just a few examples in the naval sphere of a phenomenon that was widespread in the Meiji period and exists even today. Regionally-based organizations for the support of promising native sons seem to be a permanent feature of modern Japanese society.

We would expect that after Meiji, in the Taishō (1912-26) and Shōwa (1926-) eras, the numbers of academy graduates from regions of Restoration prominence like Satsuma and Hizen would have ceased to be worthy of special notice. Public education by then provided nationwide an adequate preparation for naval officer training. Yet the Satchōdohi regions continued in the later periods to account for a far larger proportion of academy graduates than, say, their size and populations would lead one to expect.

It may be suggested that strong traditions of military life in these areas is one underlying cause of their flourishing in the naval officer corps. Southwestern Japan has of course been famous since ancient times for its hardy and high-spirited warriors. In the Meiji era the peripheral location and economic backwardness of the Satchōdohi areas, especially Satsuma, helped keep traditional values alive while much of the rest of the country moved on to more cosmopolitan views with the progress of modernization. A resurgence in numbers of officers from these areas in the generally anti-military decade of the 1920s—a fact in the army officer corps as well as the navy—points to the survival there of powerful military sentiment.[38]

Economic necessity played its part too. A military career was an attractive means of gaining a livelihood in districts of chronic poverty like Satsuma. At the same time it must be recognized that other regions of scarcity, the Tōhoku for example, provided few naval cadets.[39]

A final reason for Satchōdohi prominence is very simply the concentration of samurai in the population of these areas. Kagoshima Prefecture (roughly the equivalent of the old Satsuma domain) had by far the largest shizoku population in Japan. In 1898 it had 256,000, more than double that of any other prefecture. The ratio of shizoku to commoners was also highest there. Almost a quarter of the population was of samurai family. Over 13 percent of the Satchōdohi populations taken together was of samurai background; the rate for the rest of the nation was 4 percent.[40]

Statistical tests in fact show a significant correlation between *shizoku* populations and the number of Academy graduates of the prefectures, not only for the Meiji era but more recent years as well. That is, statistics support the contention that over the entire nation prefectures with large numbers of *shizoku* fairly consistently produced large numbers of executive navy officers.[41]

THE NEW GENERATION COMES TO THE FORE

Beneath the leadership circle of the navy, solidly Satsuma in the first decades, the new group of academy-trained officers grew steadily from the 1870s. Satsuma elders and other holdovers from domain navies resented them and were successful for a time in holding them back. But in 1893 a series of reforms began to bring proper recognition and responsibility to the younger generation of officers. The author of these reforms was the prodigious Yamamoto Gonnohyōe, then Chief of the Navy Minister's Secretariat. He was himself a Satsuma man, but also an academy graduate and veteran of training abroad who was deeply concerned with promoting the efficiency of the navy. He proclaimed that his goal was to develop "a vigorous navy through the process of replacement," by which he meant the advancement of able junior officers from the academy.[42] When he initiated the reforms which would bring this about he also acted decisively to remove dead wood from the officers' ranks. He retired about ten percent of the officers in the executive corps, including some Satsuma admirals, in 1893-95. Senior Satsuma men bitterly complained, regarding him as a traitor to the Satsuma cause. His nickname was "the tyrant captain."[43]

The effect of Yamamoto's reforms (which continued during his tenure as Navy Minister, 1898-1906) is apparent in the geographical origins of officers who attained admiral's rank in the Taishō and Shōwa periods. They came from all over Japan. In Taishō twenty-five admirals came from fourteen prefectures; in Shōwa, thirty-six from twenty-one. Only two Taishō and two Shōwa admirals came from Satsuma.[44] Further testimony to Yamamoto's policy is the fact that after his term in office very few holders of key navy posts (Navy Minister, Vice Minister, Head of the Military Affairs Bureau, Chief of the Navy General Staff, Commander in Chief of the Combined Fleet) were from Satsuma.[45]

Because of Yamamoto's reforms in late Meiji, the impartial and achievement oriented recruiting practices long in force at the academy began to have their effect on navy leadership. Domain-based patronage gave way to professional qualifications as criteria for advancement.

Yamamoto's reforms and the rise of academy graduates unfortunately did not put an end to factional politics in the navy. The basis of clique align-

239

ments changed, however, from regional loyalties to professional ones. Sea commanders of the "Fleet Faction" at the time of the Russo-Japanese War resisted the brilliant, young, and politically gifted officers that Yamamoto had brought into the Navy Ministry. In the naval arms limitation controversies of 1922 and 1930 strong animosities developed between the "command group" in the Navy General Staff and the "administrative group" in the Ministry.

Yamamoto's reforms nevertheless contributed to the high morale of navy officers in late Meiji. The direction of his policies was already evident before the Sino-Japanese War. He was bringing the academy trained generation into its own. Naval officers could go into action with the assurance that professional performance would be prized above all and that Satsuma connections were no longer a major consideration. They had increasing evidence that they were part of a truly national force unimpeded by regional interests.

The Chinese navy of 1894 provides an instructive contrast. Admiral Ting Ju-ch'ang, a former cavalry officer, boasted that he had no detailed knowledge of ships or navigation. He was clearly selected for his post because of his personal loyalty to Li Hung-chang. He commanded a regional force, the Peiyang Fleet, whose officers had no place and no honor in Chinese society. When Japanese attack was imminent, the Court ordered Ting to be most vigilant under threat of "dreadful punishment."[46] Many other elements went into Japanese naval victories and Chinese defeats in that war. But the personnel policies the Japanese followed in fostering their executive officer corps were of great importance to the Japanese success.

CONCLUSION

Measured against a sociological model of modern recruitment so far implicit in this study, one featuring universal enlistment based on achievement without barriers of social class or other inherited characteristics, the Japanese Navy in the Meiji period was remarkably rational and by extension modern. From the early 1870s on there was no formal preference given to applicants of samurai status or Satchōdohi background in selecting future executive officers. Tabulations of the class and geographical backgrounds of Naval Academy graduates show the beginnings of a universal system of recruitment. They reveal a slowly broadening social base and a wide geographical base in the officer corps. At the same time they show a strong presence of men from Satsuma and southwestern Japan that persisted in the Taishō and Shōwa periods. This presence is probably to be attributed to powerful traditions of military service in a large population of *shizoku* there, not biased entrance procedures at the Naval Academy.

The Japanese Navy's officer recruitment policy appears enlightened not only in reference to the sociological model but in comparison to the historical reality of contemporary European navies. A few examples may be offered. The Royal Navy was clearly moving toward universal recruitment in the mid-nineteenth century, but "special recommendations" from captains and flag officers were required to take entrance examinations until after 1900. Open competition was not officially instituted until 1914.[47] In Germany the naval officer corps was open to upper middle class youths, and the navy attempted to raise educational prerequisites for the Marineschule. With the rise of the navy's prestige in the 1890s, however, the service adopted aristocratic pretensions of an old Prussian stamp. Those of middle and lower middle class backgrounds were largely excluded.[48] In Russia only the sons of nobles and of navy officers could gain admittance to the Naval Cadet Corps.[49]

Yet the implication of these comparisons, that the Japanese navy as a whole was more modern or more rational than the European, may not be correct. For one thing, Japan did not possess the rich capital of scientific culture that allowed Germany, for example, to neglect technological considerations somewhat in favor of class. When Japan was opened to foreign contact in the 1850s and 1860s, its leaders were profoundly shocked to discover their inferiority to the West in science, technology, and organization. It was with a terrible sense of urgency that Japanese leaders set about organizing their armed forces. Their pursuit of Western technology, and the lack of a foundation for it in Japan, allowed for no priority in the recruitment of officers other than ability.

241

FOOTNOTES

[1] Kaigunshō, Kaigun Daijin Kambō, *Kaigun seido enkaku* [History of navy organization], 18 *kan* [books] (Tokyo: Kaigunshō, 1937-41; reprint ed., 26 vols., Meiji Hyakunenshi Series, nos. 152-77, Tokyo: Ha*r*a Shobō, 1971-72), *kan* 2, vol. 2:33.

All Japanese names in the notes and the body of the paper are given in the Japanese order, that is, surname first.

[2] Ikeda Kiyoshi, *Nihon no kaigun* [The Japanese navy], 2 vols. (Tokyo: Shiseidō, 1969), 1:58.

[3] In 1872 the navy had 217 officers, 234 in all if warrant officers are included. Kaigun Daijin Kambō, "Kaigun kansen kakuchō enkaku" [History of warship and ship expansion] (1904), in Kaigunshō, Kaigun Daijin Kambō, *Yamamoto Gonnohyōe to kaigun* [Yamamoto Gonnohyōe and the navy] (Tokyo: Kaigunshō, 1904-27?; reprint ed., Meiji Hyakunenshi Series, no. 4, Tokyo: Hara Shobō, 1966), p. 401.

This book consists of several separate works issued by the Kaigun Daijin Kambo (Navy Minister's Secretariat) in pamphlet and mimeographed form for internal use only; they were produced at various times before World War II. The postwar publishing house of Hara Shobō put them into one volume and gave it the title of *Yamamoto Gonnohyōe to kaigun*.

[4] Takahashi Shigeo, "Sokenki no kyu-Teikoku Kaigun" [The old Imperial Navy in the period of its establishment], *Gunji shigaku* [Historical studies of military affairs] 7 (June 1971):45.

Regarding former Tokugawa vassals ashore, it can be noted first that in 1872 the Navy Minister himself, Katsu Awa (Katsu Kaishū), was a former Tokugawa retainer. Division Chief Akamatsu Noriyoshi and hydrographic officer Yanagi Naoyoshi were other prominent men who had come over to the new service from the old regime; Matsushita Yoshio, *Nihon gumbatsu no kōbō* [The rise and fall of Japan's military cliques], 3 vols. (Tokyo: Jimbutsu Or*a*isha, 1967) 1:53-56. Many of the instructors at the Naval Academy came from the Tokugawa's Nomazu School or the shogunate's naval center; they stemmed from pro-Tokugawa domains and Tokugawa territories such as Kikuma, Toba, Nirayama, Zeze, Owari, and Shizuoka; as instructors they received naval commissions. See the list of teachers in Kaigunshō, Kaigun Heigakkō, *Kaigun Heigakkō enkaku* [History of the Naval Academy], 2 vols. (Tokyo: Kaigunshō, 1919; reprint ed., 2 vols. in 1, Meiji Hyakunenshi Series, no. 74, Tokyo: Hara Shōbō, 1968), 1:13-15.

[5] The earliest list of executive officers that can be pieced together, from the year 1883, shows more men from Satsuma (Kagoshima) than any other area, accounting for 28 percent of the total. My compilation, from Kōseishō, Engokyoku, *Moto kaigun shikan meibo* [Register of former navy officers] (Tokyo: Kōseishō, 1952), no pagination.

[6] John Curtis Perry, "Great Britain and the Imperial Japanese Navy, 1858-1905" (Ph.D. dissertation, Harvard University, 1962), p. 130.

[7] Matsushita, *Nihon gumbatsu no kōbō* 3:306-11.

[8] Ssu-yu Teng, John K. Fairbank et al., eds., *China's Response to the West. A Documentary Survey 1839-1923* (New York: Atheneum, 1963), p. 53.

[9] Ikeda, *Nihon no kaigun* 1:58.

[10] Kaigunshō, Kaigun Heigakkō, *Kaigun Heigakkō enkaku* 1:3.

[11] Ibid. 1:1.

[12] Ibid. 1:7-12; Matsushita Yoshio, *Meiji gunseishi ron* [A treatise on the history of the Meiji military establishment], 2 vols. (Tokyo: Yūhikaku, 1956), 1:135, 140, n. 9.

[13] Matsushita, *Meiji gunseishi ron* 1:140, n. 8, 9.

[14] Kaigunshō, Kyōiku Hombu, *Teikoku Kaigun kyōiku shi* [History of education in the Imperial Navy], 7 vols. (Tokyo: Kaigunshō, 1911), 1:154.

[15] In Britain candidates for officer training competed for entry by taking examinations, but to enter this competititon they had to be nominated by a captain or flag rank officer of the Royal Navy. "Special recommendations" of this kind were practically speaking not needed after 1903, but open competition was not officially instituted until 1914. Michael Lewis, *England's Sea Officers. The Story of the Naval Profession* (London: George Allen & Unwin, Ltd., 1948), pp. 100-103.

[16] Examinations in the first years required a knowledge of historical works like Rai San'yo's *Nihon gaishi,* the same author's *Nihon seiki,* and Iwagaki Matsunae's *Kokushiryaku;* Kaigunsho, Kaigun Heigakko, *Kaigun Heigakko enkaku* 1:22. The *Kokushiryaku* was a standard text in domain schools *(hanko)* for samurai; *Nihon rekishi daijiten* [Encyclopedia of Japanese history], 1964 ed., s.v. "Kokushiryaku."

[17] A number of these rapidly sprang up in Tokyo to meet the demand for Western studies brought about by the government's Westernizing reforms. In 1872 there were sixteen such institutions enrolling over a thousand students. Fukichi Shigetaka, *Shizoku to samurai inshiki* [The *shizoku* and samurai mentality] (Tokyo: Shunjusha, 1956), pp. 175-76.

The Kōgyokusha, located across the canal from the Naval Academy in Tsukiji, was most popular with naval aspirants. It provided preparatory training to many future naval officers in the 1870s and 1880s. *Nihon rekishi daijiten* s.v. "Kōgyokusha."

[18] Kaigunshō, Kaigun Heigakkō, *Kaigun Heigakkō enkaku* 1:19-32, 89-91, 128-31, 235-39, 316-17, 356-57, 387.

[19] Kaigunshō, Kyōiku Hombu, *Teikoku Kaigun kyōiku shi* 7: Appendix, pp. 4-5 and graph no. 4.

[20] In 1890 there were 55 middle schools, almost all of them public, with 11,000 pupils. Seven years later, in 1897, 157 such schools accommodated 52,000 pupils. Mombusho, *Zu de miru waga kuni no ayumi. Kyōiku tōkei hachijūnenshi* [The progress of our country's education as seen in graphs: eighty years' history in educational statistics] (Tokyo: Mombushō, 1957), p. 139.

[21] Kaigunshō, Kaigun Heigakkō, *Kaigun Heigakkō enkaku* 2:53-54.

[22] Ibid. 2:160.

[23] This and other stipulations for applicants taken from Ibid. 2:59, 217, 219.

[24] From the forthcoming Princeton University Ph.D. dissertation of Theodore Failor Cook, Jr., "The Japanese Officer Corps: Origins, Education, and Career Patterns in a Military Elite, 1872-1945."

[25] Ōshima Tarō and Fukushima Shingo, "Kanryōsei to guntai" [The bureaucracy and the military] in *Iwanami Kōza Nihon rekishi: kindai 4* [Iwanami Studies in Japanese history: the modern period, no. 4], Iwanami Kōza series, no. 17 (Tokyo: Iwanami Shoten, 1972), p. 17.

[26] James Abegglen and Hiroshi Mannari, "Leaders of Modern Japan: Social Origins and Mobility," *Economic Development and Cultural Change* 9 (October 1960): part 2, 126.

[27] Thomas C. Smith, "Japan's Aristocratic Revolution," *Yale Review* 50 (1960-61): 370-83 and idem, " 'Merit' as Ideology in the Tokugawa Period," in R. P. Dore, ed., *Aspects of Social Change in Modern Japan* (Princeton, N.J.: Princeton University Press, 1967), pp. 71-90.

[28] Suzuki Kantarō, *Suzuki Kantarō jiden* [Autobiography of Suzuki Kantarō] (Tokyo: Ōgikukai Shuppanbu, 1949), p. 25.

[29] Ibid., p. 26.

[30] Executive officer list of 1883, Kōseishō, Engokyoku, *Moto kaigun shikan meibo;* see n. 5 above.

[31] Information on geographical backgrounds comes from my collation of officer lists in Kōseishō, Engokyoku, *Moto kaigun shikan meibo;* Kaigunshō, Kaigun Heigakkō, *Kaigun Heigakkō enkaku;* Sawa Kannojō, *Kaigun Heigakuryō* [The Naval Studies

Dormitory] (Tokyo: Kōa Nipponsha, 1942); and Suikōkai, *Kaigun Heigakkō, Kaigun Kikan Gakkō, Kaigun Keiri Gakkō* (The Naval Academy, Naval Engineering College and Navy Paymasters' School] (Tokyo: Akimoto Shobō, 1971).

[32] The Statistical Package for the Social Sciences was used to compute Pearson correlation coefficients of the relation betwen populations of the prefectures (excluding Hokkaido and Okinawa) and the Academy graduates from the prefectures for various periods. The Pearson coefficient (R) for two variables will of course be zero if they are unrelated and will have a value of $+1$ if they are positively and perfectly related. When R is less than .7, little can be claimed for the relationship, since less than half of the variation (.7^2 or .49, the coefficient of determination) can be attributed to the influence of the relationship and more than half can be the result of other factors.

   Using prefectural population figures of 1885 from Naikaku Tokei Kyoku, *Nippon Teikoku dai go tōkei nenkan* [Statistical yearbook of the Japanese Empire, no. 5] (1886), pp. 38-40, the coefficients are as follows for the Academy graduates of these periods: 1873-90, .05; 1891-1910, .20; 1911-20, .35. Taking population figures of 1898 from Naikaku Tokei Kyoku, *Nippon Teikoku dai nijū tōkei nenkan* [Statistical yearbook of the Japanese Empire, no. 20] (1901), pp. 54-57, the coefficients are, for the graduates of these periods: 1873-90, .22; 1891-1910, .30; 1910-30, .39. Using population figures of 1913 from Irene B. Taeuber, *The Population of Japan* (Princeton, N.J.: Princeton University Press, 1958), p. 48, the coefficients are: 1891-1900, .25; 1901-10, .48; 1911-20, .58; 1921-30, .37; and 1931-41, .61.

   Although no strong causal relationship is indicated for any period, the important fact is that the correlations are larger in successive periods, showing that officers' geographical origins were moving toward the pattern of national population distribution.

[33] Based on figures in Kaigunshō, Kaigun Heigakkō, *Kaigun Heigakkō enkaku* 1:364-65, 372-73. 375-76, 419-20 for entrance examinations of 1884, 1885, and 1887 that involved 1,195 applicants.

[34] Ibid. The success rate of applicants from Aichi Prefecture was 25 percent, Tosa (Kōchi) 24 percent, and Yamagata and Ishikawa, 19 percent; Saga's rate was 18 percent, Satsuma's 10.

[35] Ikeda Kiyoshi and Etō Jun, "Kaigun no Meiji" [The Meiji era of the navy], *Bungei shunjū* [Literary arts, spring and autumn] 50 (November 1971, special enlarged ed.): 111.

[36] Uzaki Rojō (Uzaki Kumakichi), *Satsu no kaigun, Chō no rikugun* [The Satsuma navy and the Chōshū army] (Tokyo: Seikyosha, 1911), p. 89.

[37] Chishinkai, *Saga han kaigun shi* [History of the Saga *han* navy] (Tokyo: Chishinkai, 1917), pp. 419, 479.

[38] In the Meiji period about 24 percent of all Naval Academy graduates stemmed from the Satchōdohi areas, which had about 7 percent of the population. In 1911 their representation fell to a still-respectable 18 percent. It rose again to 23 percent in 1921-30.

   In the army Satchōdohi men accounted for about 17 percent of entrants to the Military Academy for the decade after the turn of the century; their representation rose to over 21 percent in the period 1921-32. Theodore Failor Cook, Jr., "The Japanese Officer Corps." I am indebted to Theodore Cook for pointing this out and for making valuable methodological suggestions bearing on my analysis of the navy officer corps.

[39] Aomori Prefecture ranked thirty-ninth and Akita forty-third out of forty-five prefectures (excluding Hokkaido and Okinawa) in the number of Naval Academy graduates produced during the Meiji period. These two prefectures and Morioka, another Tōhoku prefecture, were in the bottom ten for the period 1873-1941 (academy classes 1-70).

   Kyūshū, the region containing the old Satsuma and Hizen areas, supplied 26 percent of the academy graduates of 1911-30 while accounting for 15 percent of the national population (1920 population figures from Taeuber, *Population of Japan*, p. 48; again taking Hokaido and Okinawa out of the reckoning). The Tōhoku produced 8 percent of the graduates in this period and had 11 percent of the population.

244

[40] All figures in this paragraph are reckoned on the basis of population statistics for 1898 found in Naikaku Tōkei Kyoku, *Nippon Teikoku dai nijū tōkei nenkan,* pp. 54-57.

[41] Using the same computation procedures and sources of population figures as outlined in note 32, I computed coefficients of the relation between the *shizoku* prefectural populations in 1898 and Academy graduates of the prefectures for various periods. The periods and their coefficients are: 1873-90, .76; 1891-1910, .60; and 1911-30, .74.

Two other tests are of interest. I computed R for the relation between prefectural *shizoku* populations of 1898 and Academy graduates of *shizoku* backgrounds from the prefectures over the years 1873-1901; the result was .76, evidence of a strong relation. To determine if prefectures with many commoners (*heimin*) produced many *heimin* officers, I computed R for prefectural *heimin* populations of 1898 and *heimin* Academy graduates of 1873-1901; the figure was a weak .35.

[42] Ko Hakushaku Yamamoto Kaigun Taishō Denki Hensankai, *Hakushaku Yamamoto Gonnohyōe den* [Biography of Count Yamamoto Gonnohyōe], 2 vols. (Tokyo: Ko Hakushaku Yamamoto Kaigun Taishō Denki Hensankai, 1938), 1: 345-46.

[43] Ikeda, *Nihon no kaigun* 1: 116,17.

[44] Matsushita, *Nihon gumbatsu no kōbō* 3: 306-11.

[45] Ikeda, *Nihon no kaigun* 1: 116.

[46] Observations on the Chinese naval forces are drawn from John L. Rawlinson, *China's Struggle for Naval Development, 1839-1895* (Cambridge, Mass.: Harvard University Press, 1967), esp. pp. 161, 166-67.

[47] See n. 15 above.

[48] Holger H. Herwig, *The German Naval Officer Corps. A Social and Political History 1890-1918* (Oxford University Press, 1973), pp. 37-60.

[49] Review of A. Krotkov's *Morskoi Kadetskii Korpus* (St. Petersburg, 1901) in *Marine Rundschau* 14 (April 1903): 525-26.

245

From Tirpitz to Hitler: Continuity and Discontinuity in German Naval History_____

Keith W. Bird

University of Bridgeport

Until recent years, historians of German history virtually ignored the navy in their studies of the Weimar Republic and the Third Reich. Apart from operational histories, the navy's relationship to society and state had been largely overshadowed by the role of the army in modern German history. The history of the Tirpitz era and the Imperial navy had, however, beginning in the early sixties, attracted the attention of scholars who saw a close link between the development of a navy and the political, social, and economic problems of Wilhelmian Germany.[1] The parallel between the development of Germany as a maritime power before the first World War and the apparent intention of its Führer to make a second bid for *Weltmacht* aroused the interest of historians seeking to establish the continuity or discontinuity of German history. The current interest in the German navy in all three of its phases—Imperial, Republican, and National Socialist—is closely related to trends in German historiography as well as the research opportunities created by the extensive archival resources in the field of German naval history.

The tradition of naval history in Germany is as recent as the creation of the German fleet itself and is directly tied to its development and fate in the years 1888-1945. Constantly forced to justify its existence and lacking the proud heritage of the army, the supporters of the navy found history itself to be a valuable tool. At the same time, however, as the aftermath of World War I was to prove, the manipulation of Hitler own versions of history blinded the leaders of the navy and prevented them from critically evaluating their past.[2] Even after the Second World War, German naval writers, with few exceptions, were closely tied intellectually, if not official-ly, to the navy. The official bias which marked the majority of naval studies began with the creation of the *Reichsmarineamts Nachrichtenbüro* in 1897 and the alliance forged by Tirpitz with a prominent group of university professors, primarily economists and historians. The large naval rearmament program that had begun in 1898 was accompanied by an intensive propaganda campaign utilizing the combined efforts of active and retired naval officers, civilian employees, industrial interests and members of the many national associations and federations, such as the *Kolonialgesellschaft* and the *Alldeutscher Verband*. The contacts and traditions established during this time period were to persist through the history of the German navy, including the creation in 1956 of the West German *Bundesmarine* — a continuity which exists today.[3]

Although historians have long considered the building of the navy as the visible sign of Imperial Germany's *Griff nach der Weltmacht*, the economic, social, and political implications of the fleet in both foreign and domestic politics were largely neglected. Yet, the government's naval policy served as a focal point for the conflicts between agrarian and industrial interests and the debate over whether *Weltpolitik* or the traditional continental foreign policy should be pursued by Imperial Germany. The first scholar to analyze the interrelationship between the domestic, constitutional struggles and the naval planning of the Wilhelmine era was the Berlin historian Eckart Kehr. Contrary to those historians who emphasized the "primacy of foreign politics" in their studies of the German navy, Kehr's thesis, based upon the documentary evidence available in the twenties, indicated that Germany's naval program was the result of a coalition of agrarian and industrial interests directed against the emerging working class.[4] Kehr's publications, however, never seriously challenged the main stream of historical scholarship in post World War I Germany which rejected his view of German diplomacy as being exclusively defined by internal political and economic considerations ("primacy of domestic politics").[5] Nor did the defenders of the navy regard Kehr, a Marxist, as a particular threat to the officially-sanctioned interpretations of the Tirpitz era.[6]

After the Second World War, Kehr's work received careful attention from "revisionist" historians such as Fritz Fischer and his students and the question of "continuity" in German politics from Bismarck to Hitler became the issue of a heated historical debate in West Germany.[7] At the same time, the return of the captured naval documents to the Federal Republic and the centralization of the military archives in Freiburg allowed scholars to study in detail the course of a "traditional, conservative *Führungsgruppe*" under three regimes.

Unlike the army and the Luftwaffe records, the German naval archives survived the war virtually intact. It is, therefore, not surprising that the some hundred and fifty thousand volumes, dating from 1850 and the frail beginnings of a Prussian navy, would become a rich mine for historians seeking a better understanding of the course of German history. In 1971, Volker R. Berghahn published the first major work dealing with the navy and its relationship to the state and society of Imperial Germany. Berghahn's massively documented *Der Tirpitz-Plan. Genesis und Verfall einer innenpolitischen Krisenstrategie* supported Kehr's findings by indicating the interdependence of internal and external factors in the development of German naval policy. The navy, Berghahn argues, was built against "Reichstag and England." The "crisis strategy" which led to the decision to create the fleet had two aims: first, the maintenance of the quasi-constitutional Imperial government and the status quo of the ruling elite against the Reichstag and the growing threat of Socialism; second, the building of a fleet which would give Germany a chance of victory over the world's most powerful navy.

Berghahn, thus, challenged a number of interpretations of the Tirpitz program defended by historians such as Walther Hubatsch who emphasized the basically defensive character of the fleet building or Gerhard Ritter who stressed the importance of international developments for German naval planning before World War I.[8] Tracing the dozens of alternative building plans considered and approved within the *Reichsmarineamt* between 1900 and 1907, Berghahn demonstrates that Tirpitz did not simply respond to internal crises by formulating new navy laws but took advantage of the appropriate situation to introduce bills already carefully conceived by the navy. Berghahn also characterizes Tirpitz's technique as one of proceeding by steps *(stufenweise)*. Berghahn's contention that the building of the Kaiser's fleet could be understood not with the tools of traditional military history but only by applying the "categories of modern social history" created a new dimension in the writing of German naval history if not German history in general.[9] Berghahn also discredited the popular view of the Imperial Navy as an "un-thought-out technical exercise or meaninglessly by constructed military monstrosity."[10]

In 1972, the *Militärgeschichtliches Forschungsamt* in Freiburg sponsored a conference on the theme "Navy and Naval Politics in Imperial Germany 1871-1914." This conference demonstrated the breadth and direction of new research and the nature of the issues involved in the debate over Berghahn's interpretations. The papers, later published by the *Forschungsamt*, convincingly document the bankruptcy of German naval planning in the period before World War I. Peter-Christian Witt's study of Reich finances and armaments, for example, reveals the government's failure to replace the anticipated costs in shipbuilding after the *Dreadnought* "break-through."[11] The financial needs of the military, especially the navy, threatened the government's system-stabilizing *Sammlungspolitik* and, in the end, caused the government to lose the support of those very political, social, and economic groups whose interests it was trying to preserve.

248

With the Moroccan crisis, the dilemma of German *Weltpolitik* became obvious and the armament needs of the army received priority. The return to Germany's more traditional continental policy in 1911 and the stronger position of the Army's General Staff clearly showed the navy's failure to fulfill either its domestic or foreign policy goals. Hopelessly caught in a trap of their own making, Germany's leaders embraced war as the only means of maintaining their power and status.[12] Given these circumstances, which the officers of the navy and their supporters refused to acknowledge, it is not surprising to discover in other essays that the Imperial officer corps became "Prussianized" or that Tirpitz's strategic plans were built upon sand.[13]

Although critics, especially the older German naval officers and historians, found Berghahn's "working model" of Wilhelmine *Weltpolitik* too ordered and exact, it succeeded in establishing the interrelation between naval policy and state policy and stimulated research into the navy's role in Weimar and the Third Reich.[14] Moreover, Berghahn's investigations lent support to Fritz Fischer's analysis of the continuity of Germany's war aims. Although Fischer had acknowledged the deep differences between Bethmann-Hollweg and Hitler,

> the similarity in the directions, even if not in the essence, of German aims in the two World Wars is striking. This similarity can be traced to the geographical position of Germany as well as to the continuity of ideas about the position of Germany and the world.[15]

If German politics could be viewed as a continuum, so the argument would go, then the Weimar period, for both the navy and society, could be viewed as the bridge between the Empire and the Third Reich when Germany's leaders assessed their mistakes and made plans for a fresh, but more systematical attempt "to upset the international status quo and to put the clock back at home."[16] From this standpoint, the rise of National Socialism and the origins of the Second World War became intertwined with the goals of Germany's ruling elite. The issue of whether 1933 represented a "break" for the navy's planning or goals therefore became closely tied with an investigation of the navy's political inclinations during the National Socialist period.

The question of Adolf Hitler's understanding of sea power or his conception of the role of a navy in achieving his objectives of pursuing Germany's "traditional" goal of *Weltmacht* has historically been a topic of much debate.[17] In 1965 Andreas Hillgruber produced the framework for studying Hitler's naval programs by establishing the existence of the Führer's *Stufenplan*. According to Hillgruber, German power would be expanded in carefully calculated stages: first, restoring Germany's great power status after the defeat of 1918 and the Versailles Treaty; second, establishing preeminence in Central Europe; then, from this position securing continental hegemony and *Lebensraum* in the East (at the expense of the Soviet Union);

249

and finally, transforming the greater German Reich into a *Weltmacht* through overseas expansion.[18]

Hillgruber's work inspired a number of monographs illuminating different aspects of Hitler's "Program" such as Klaus Hildebrand's *Vom Reich zum Weltreich*, a study of the colonial policy of the Third Reich.[19] Then, in 1973, one of Hillgruber's students, Jost Dülffer, published a massively documented study of German naval policy after 1918 which has stimulated a controversy in Germany similar to that created by Berghahn. Dülffer's *Weimar, Hitler und die Marine: Reichspolitik und Flottenbau 1920-1939* (Düsseldorf, 1973), represents a continuation of the "Kehr-Berghahn" thesis of the duality of foreign and domestic policy in German naval planning. Analyzing the navy's construction programs for Weimar and the Third Reich, Dülffer traces the continuity in German naval history from Tirpitz to Adolf Hitler. Even in the defeat of 1912, the navy kept alive the idea of a battle fleet as a means of re-establishing Germany's great power status and as an alliance factor (particularly with England). The navy's leaders regarded the Weimar Republic as only a transitional phase and the Versailles Treaty as a temporary delay in achieving German *Weltmacht*. Although Tirpitz had (according to Kehr-Berghahn) stressed the "system-stabilizing" role of naval construction, the navy's post-war leaders believed that an expansion of the fleet could proceed only after a national "social consolidation" had occurred. Because the officers also believed that the nation's desire for a fleet would be the signal for its recovery from the "sabotage" of the Republic's supporters, they welcomed both the "national" and "social" aims of Adolf Hitler's party and the seizure of power in 1933.[20]

Tracing the origins of Hitler's attitudes toward the navy in the years before 1933 to the Führer's direct intervention in the construction of a new fleet, Dülffer convincingly supports his thesis that the navy played a central role in both Hitler's short- and long-range "Program." Outlined by Dülffer, it appears that Hitler hoped to use the issue of naval rearmament as a means of persuading the British to accept Germany's bid for continental hegemony. Voluntarily limiting German naval strength to 35% of the Royal Navy in June 1935 did not imply, as others have argued, Hitler's rejection of a fleet or even a temporary delay in the Führer's timetable for German expansion. A "35% fleet was militarily sufficient for Hitler's continental phase and, at the same time, provided a base for Germany's expansion overseas by providing Hitler with a means of compelling England to accept an alliance or, if needed, the basis for a much larger naval expansion that could challenge and defeat English naval power."

In the "turn against England," evident in the 1937 naval planning as well as Hitler's drawings for 100,000-ton super battleships, Dülffer argues that Hitler was already thinking beyond this continental stage. Hitler, therefore, not only gave naval construction priority in labor and raw materials but, as Dülffer reveals, the Führer threatened to replace Raeder if he could not increase the pace of construction.

The navy's skepticism over Hitler's foreign and domestic policies expressed itself during 1938-1939. Hitler, however, refused to allow the navy to reverse his priorities of completing battleships first in favor of more U-boats which Raeder and his junior officers wanted as an immediate deterrent (another Risk-fleet!). Moreover, the pace and scale of the navy's construction program threatened to create an economic and social crisis. Thus, for the second time in German history, the building of a large fleet proved to be a decisive factor in domestic politics, but as Dülffer indicates, its importance had acquired a different meaning. Instead of serving as a means of achieving social integration (a la Tirpitz), Hitler's naval program proved to be a considerable step in the direction of social disruption. Since the dynamics of National Socialism did not permit any compromise in either domestic or foreign affairs, war appeared as the only alternative *(Flucht nach vorn)*. In this sense Dülffer argues that the social and economic dislocations caused by the massive *Flottenbau* contributed more directly and immediately to Hitler's long-range social objective of destroying the existing order and creating a new order than the Führer had originally envisioned.

Dülffer's reconstruction of Hitler's short- and long-range naval plans has, much like Berghahn's analysis of the Tirpitz fleet, been criticized for being too precise and too rigid for such a complex historical problem. It seems curious, for example, that although the navy was to be incorporated into Hitler's *Stufenplan*, the naval leaders themselves never developed a "clear naval strategy" which would dictate not only operations planning but ship construction and armaments priorities as well. As a number of reviews have pointed out, the navy seemed to ignore the problems of diesel fuel which, in the final analysis, would curtail naval movements more than the enemy. Dülffer's analysis of the social and economic impact of the "Hitler fleet" is, as the author acknowledges, incomplete and must await more specialized studies in such areas as the role of the naval shipyards in the armaments industry and Hitler's influence on naval planning and operations.[21]

The navy's vision of World Power is also the topic of Michael Salewski's three-volume study *Die deutsche Seekriegsleitung 1935-1945*. Unlike Dülffer, Salewski, in his first volume, does not vigorously pursue the reasons for the fleet building after 1935 nor does he challenge the traditional interpretation of Hitler's foreign policy as "continental." In fact, he sidesteps the important questions of German-English relations by arguing that this requires a special study. Thus, although he traces the development of the fleet and its role in war, he does not raise the fundamental economic, political, and social issues tied to naval construction and planning in the

Third Reich. Salewski, for example, refers to a 1940 study of the *Seekriegsleitung* which called for a fleet of 60-80 super battleships, a worldwide system of naval stations and a *"Tschechische Losung"* for all conquered peoples as "understandable" in the *Zeitgeist* of 1940.[23]

What Salewski documents so impressively is the parallel to the First World War—the emphasis on the "big ships" over U-boats and the pressure on the naval leaders to risk the navy's few heavy units to avoid the shameful inactivity of the First World War. What is perhaps most significant about Salewski's contribution to our understanding concerning the role of the navy in Hitler's wartime operational plans is his description of Raeder's Mediterranean strategy in late summer, 1940. Raeder's fruitless attempts to convince Hitler against attacking Russia (which Hitler had already decided on at the end of July, 1940) in favor of attacking England in the Mediterranean revealed the failure of the navy to "educate" the continental-minded strategists of Hitler's OKW and the navy could only watch as their struggle against England was relegated to a secondary priority. As Salewski indicates, the navy became more and more after June 22, 1941, an auxiliary to army operations—a situation which the naval leaders never really challenged. With the entry of the USA into the war, the position of the navy became hopeless and the major concern of the naval command was to maintain discipline and prevent a repeat of 1917-1918.

In his second volume, Salewski provides an excellent insight into the attitudes of the navy to Hitler and National Socialism as reflected in the July 20 attempt on Hitler's life.[24] Although the memoirs of Raeder and Dönitz stress the "apolitical" character of the navy and their duty as soldiers, the documents reveal the close identification of traditional navy goals with those of Hitler's in the pre-war period and, as a result of the demands of total war, a growing "politicalization" of the navy. Raeder for a long time mistakenly believed that Hitler was *"steuerbar"* and the navy's vaunted "independence" was a result of its emphasis on obedience and loyalty. While Raeder learned how wrong he was about the former, Dönitz carried the latter to such extremes that he and the navy became the model for the other branches of the armed forces and their officers. As Salewski and others have argued, the key to understanding the political attitude of the navy, as in the case of the navy's role and development in Weimar and the Third Reich, can be traced back to the trauma of war and revolution and the lessons gleamed from the experiences of the navy's brief existence in German history.[25]

The studies of Berghahn, Dülffer, and Salewski represent the primary emphasis of naval research in West Germany today—the naval armaments programs under Tirpitz, Raeder, and Hitler and German naval leadership during the Second World War. Correspondingly, it is because the above authors have outlined the broad political and social ramifications of German naval construction and its relationship to foreign policy, that

Werner Rahn argues for a consideration of the original military objective of the navy in an overall national defense program. Rahn's *Reichsmarine und Landesverteidigung 1919-1928. Konzeption und Führung der Marine in der Weimarer Republik* (Munich, 1976) thus provides a necessary perspective to the larger plans and ambitions of the navy as presented by Dülffer. According to Rahn, the Weimar navy never received any clear military assignment from the political leadership—a fact that encouraged the independence of the navy. The development of naval planning and construction plans reflected not only the navy's conception of its immediate role in national defense but its long-range goal as a "political instrument" to make Germany a maritime power—which usually received priority over the former.

Rahn's topic is perhaps an indication that future research in German naval history will concentrate more on specific issues suggested by the "working models" created by Berghahn and Dülffer.[26] Wilhelm Deist's recent *Flottenpolitik und Flottenpropaganda. Das Nachrichtenbureau des Reichsmarineamtes 1899-1914* (Stuttgart, 1976) represents another example of this development. Deist indicates the close relationship between the Tirpitz "plans" and naval construction stages with the propaganda campaign. The evidence not ony reveals the navy's manipulation and ultimate goals but the very nature of the Imperial *Weltanschauung.*

In addition to the writings of the West German historians, there exist a number of other studies which treat different phases and problems of German naval history. Among the numerous English-language monographs and dissertations focusing on German naval issues, several have received particular attention from German scholars. Daniel Horn's study of *The German Naval Mutinies of World War I*, a damning indictment of the German naval officer corps, agrees with the leftist view popular during the Weimar period that an "Admirals' rebellion" had triggered the November, 1918 Revolution, although Horn indicates that the naval mutinies were in fact the outcome of a twenty-year-old social conflict in the navy.[27] Horn's view of a "feudalized" naval officer corps has been more extensively investigated by Holger Herwig who described the "Prussianization" of the predominantly middle-class officer corps in his *The German Naval Officer Corps: A Social and Political History 1890-1918.*[28]

It is interesting to note that both Horn and Herwig have been severely scored for their critical portrayal of the Imperial officer corps by the official and military naval historians. Herwig's recent *Politics .of Frustration: The United States in German Naval Planning, 1889-1941* (Boston, 1976) demonstrates not only the "continuity" of Germany's naval ambitions but also the importance of an external factor in the strategic deliberations of the German navy in two world wars—the United States. From the Wilhelmine era to the Third Reich, argues Herwig, the German naval leaders regarded war with the United States, an "inseparable ally" of England, as inevitable and necessary if Germany was to survive and share in the redistribution of territories (World War I) or create a *Weltflotte* (World War II). Herwig's comparative history suggests another useful approach in evaluating the development of German naval planning.[29]

Wallace L. Lewis' dissertation, "The Survival of the German Navy 1917-1920. Officers, Sailors, and Politics," bridges the period from the Imperial period to the Republic and reveals the existence of a "civil war" between radical and national elements of the navy in the first years of Weimar.[30] The author's dissertation, "Officers and Republic: The German Navy and Politics," investigates the period of 1918-1928 and is primarily concerned with probing the "inner structure of the navy and its position in the state." As compared to Carsten's analysis of the navy as "reactionary," my findings indicate the growing "politicalization" of the naval officer corps—a result of the officers' inability to adjust to the new conditions as well as the leftists' failure (or refusal) to reach any accommodation with the military. The navy, with its dreams of a *Weltflotte* and its hatred of communism, proved particularly ripe for National Socialist ideology and promises.[31] The extent of the navy's attempts to circumvent the Versailles Treaty in the period 1919-1935 can be seen in A. W. Saville's "The Development of the German U-Boat Arm," although, as critics have pointed out, Saville is less concerned about the military and political aspects of these violations than the legal and moral issues.[32]

East German historians have until recently been restricted in their access to the naval archives and have based their research on contemporary naval literature from the period 1918-1945 and postwar secondary sources. At the same time, the East German naval historians demonstrate "little understanding for the military necessity of naval operations" and adhere dogmatically to the thesis that "German fascist imperialism rearmed for the struggle for World Mastery" aided by the "reactionary, chauvinistic, imperialistic elements of finance capital."[33] Gerhard Zimmer's "Die Marinerüstung und die Rolle der Kriegsmarine innerhalb der aggressiven Aussenpolitik des faschistischen deutschen Imperialismus" is an example of a competent summary of the navy's rearmament plans in the period of 1933-1939.[34] Zimmer, however, fails to prove the obligatory thesis that the armaments industries had any influence on the number of naval contracts or the pace of construction. In fact, as Dülffer demonstrates, many of the armaments industries supplying the navy had objections to the schedules demanded by the 1939 Z-Plan and only accepted contracts under pressure from Berlin.

The value of the naval archives as a resource for social scientists is demonstrated by Carl-Axel Gemzell's *Organization, Conflict, and Innovation: A Study of German Naval Strategic Planning, 1886-1940.*[35] In this book, Gemzell develops a sociological framework to examine a bureaucratic institution such as the navy and then tests his model by studying the navy's interest in expansion northward in four periods of German naval history (1888-1914, 1914-1918, 1918-1939, and 1939-1940). In each period the navy's strategic interest in Scandinavia centers around a combination of personal ambitions and rivalries, internal as well as external. Although Gemzell's study of innovation in naval planning does not take into account all the factors such as the ties between industry and the navy, he does reveal a continuity in naval planning during the period 1888-1940.

The issues and questions raised by the works discussed above will continue to occupy the attention of scholars for some time. The relationship of the navy and its leaders to industry and labor during all phases of its development is a major topic, as are the official and unofficial ties that existed between the retired officers and their active duty comrades serving in the *Reichsmarine und Kriegsmarine*. Current research in military history today, as evidenced by the papers presented at the 1974 spring conference in Freiburg, "Rüstung und Wirtschaft am Vorabend des Zweiten Welkrieges," emphasizes the close ties between armament and economics and between military technology and industry, the cooperation of scientific research and economics with the military, and the other less examined topics of military history such as material and personnel reserves and transportation problems.[36]

A lecture delivered in June, 1975, at the *Militärgeschichtliches Forschungsamt* in Freiburg signaled what may be the beginning of revisions in the history of German naval operations in the Second World War. In a discussion of F. W. Winterbotham's book, *The Ultra Secret*, Jürgen Rohwer sketched a preliminary assessment of the effect of the British ability to read the German code on operations such as the *Bismarck's* May, 1941, sortie and the U-boat campaign.[37] While Rohwer was hesitant to call the British cryptanalysis coup "decisive," the role of cryptography can no longer be ignored.

Biography should also become a subject for historians of German naval history. A new biography of Tirpitz is badly needed as well as serious studies of Raeder and Dönitz. In the case of the last two commanders of the German navy, the memoirs—written close on the heels of Nuremberg and without the benefit of the naval archives—are simply too self-serving and apologetic to serve as useful guides to reconstructing the past.[38] Helmuth Schubert's two-volume treatment of Admiral von Trotha as an example of "psycho-history" may prove useful as a model for further investigations.[39]

With the availability of guides now being prepared by the National Archives, access to the mass of microfilmed German naval documents should be easier and one can expect a deluge of dissertations and monographs over the course of the next several years. Those who wish to consult bibliographies should refer to the works of Dülffer, Salewski, and Bird. Jost Dülffer's critical bigliography, *Zur deutschen Marinegeschichte der Zwischenkriegszeit (1920-1929)* (Frankfurt, 1972), is also quite useful. The absence of any general work on the history of the navy in the period 1919-1945 that reflects the level of scholarship of Dülffer or Salweski remains a problem.[40]

Ironically, as Theodore Ropp points out, in spite of the persistent Marxist influence on German naval historiography and "the fact that a naval industrial complex was, even at the time, seen as a prime factor in German navalism, very little formal economic or econometric analysis has been done of it, in spite of the Witt and Berghahn works."[41] Ropp's questions as to the relationship of the arms industry to the naval program or the crisis of heavy industry in the 1890's are still unanswered and the "new" combination of sociology and politics in German history writing (with Marxist or non-Marxist flavor) has not yet produced what he labels as a "kind of Mardern model of navalism." The research of scholars such as Klaus Saul (*Staat, Industrie, Arbeiterbewegung im Kaiserreich* [Düsseldorf, 1974]) and Timothy Mason (*Arbeiterklasse und Volksgemeinschaft. Dokumente und Materialien zur deutschen Arbeiterpolitik 1936-1939* [Opladen, 1975]) represent major reinterpretations of the Imperial and National Socialist period which can also be expected to affect the writing of naval history in the late 70's as Fischer's did in the late 60's.

FOOTNOTES

[1] Jonathan Steinberg was one of the first scholars to explore the extensive archives of the German navy in his *Yesterday's Deterrent: Tirpitz and the Birth of the German Battle Fleet* (New York, 1965).

[2] See Philip K. Lundeberg, "The German Naval Critique of the U-Boat Campaign, 1915-1918," *Military Affairs* 27 (Fall, 1963), pp. 105-118. The East German government and historians regard the leaders of the rebel sailors of 1917-1920 as the forerunners of their regime. In the Weimar Republic, the German retired officers also acted as the watchdogs for the "official" accounts of World War I. See Admiral von Trotha's complaints to Admiral von Levetzow about one of the officers in the *Marine-Archiv*, Berlin, 4 May 1933, *Nachlass* Levetzow N239/103. Cf. Walther Hubatsch's letter to Widenmann on how to discourage an American professor by the name of Gatzke from pursuing a study of Tirpitz. Hubatsch was concerned that the pendulum was swinging towards a critical reassessment of Tirpitz and the pre-war fleet-building program. Gottingen, 24 March, 1952, *Nachlass* Wilhelm Widenmann N158/29. Raeder's manipulation of documents and control over the naval archives follows the "Tirpitz mold" which he learned as one of Tirpitz's *Nachrichtenbüro* officers.

[3] This statement is based on research made possible by a grant from the *Deutscher Akademischer Austauschdienst* conducted during the summer of 1975 in Freiburg in preparation for an article on the development and position of the *Bundeswehr* in the state and the society of the Federal Republic.

[4] *Schlachtflottenbau und Parteipolitik 1894-1901* (Berlin, 1966) and *Der Primat der Innen-politik,* edited by Hans-Ulrich Wehler (Berlin, 1966).

[5] See Widenmann's critical but appreciative assessment of Kehr in his letter to Schuster, 11, April, 1944, *Nachlass* Widenmann, N158/19. Widenmann felt that the book was interesting but there was a danger that the domestic aspects of naval development might be over-emphasized at the cost of the more important issues of foreign policy.

[6] For example, such contemporary works as Ulrich von Hassell, *Tirpitz* (Stuttgart, 1920) or Hans Hallmann, *Der Weg zum deutschen Schlachtflottenbau* (Stuttgart, 1933), or more recent publications such as Walther Hubatsch, *Die Ära Tirpitz* (Göttingen, 1955) and Gerhard Ritter, *Staatkunst und Kriegshandwerk,* II (Munich, 1960).

[7] See John A. Moses, *The Politics of Illusion. The Fischer Revolution in German Historiography* (New York, 1975).

[8] In a review of *Der Tirpitz Plan,* Jonathan Steinberg indicated that Berghahn makes obsolete much earlier work on the subject including "several efforts" by Steinberg. *The Historical Journal,* XVI (1, 1973), pp. 196-204.

[9] "Der Tirpitz-Plan und die Krisis des preussisch-deutschen Herrschaftssystems," in Herbert Schottelius and Wilhelm Deist, eds., *Marine und Marinepolitik im Kaiserlichen Deutschland 1871-1914* (Düsseldorf, 1972), p. 89. See also the introduction to *Modern deutsche Sozialgeschichte* (Koln, 1973), by Hans-Ulrich Wehler.

[10] "Der Tirpitz-Plan und die Krisis", p. 89.

[11] Published in *Marine und Marinepolitik* as "Reichsfinanzen und Rustungspolitik 1898-1914," pp. 146-177.

[12] Berghahn, "Der Tirpitz-Plan und die Krisis", pp. 109-115.

[13] Holger Herwig, "Zur Soziologie des kaiserlichen Seeoffizer-korps vor 1914," pp. 73-78, and Paul Kennedy, "Maritime Strategie-probleme der deutsch-englischen Flottenrivalitat," pp. 178-210. Both contributions appear in *Marine und Marinepolitik.*

[14] See Steinberg's review (footnote 8 above); Hans Herzfeld's review of Berghahn's *Der Tirpitz-Plan, Militärgeschichtliche Mitteilungen,* 11 (1972), pp. 196-198. Cf. Friedrich Forstmeier's "Der Tirpitzsche Flottenbau im Urteil der Historiker," *Marine und Marinepolitik,* pp. 34-53.

[15] Fritz Fischer, "A Comparison of German Aims in the Two World Wars" in J.C.G. Rohl, *From Bismarck to Hitler. The Problem of Continuity in German History* (London, 1970), p. 146, as quoted in Klaus Hildebrand, "Hitlers Ort in der Geschichte des Preussisch-Deutschen Nationalstaates," *Historische Zeitschrift,* 217 (1973), p. 601. See also Fritz Stern's *The Failure of Illiberalism* (New York, 1972), pp. 147-158, and Fritz Fischer's *World Power of Decline* (New York, 1974).

[16] Berghahn, *Germany and the Approach of War in 1914* (New York, 1973), p. 214.

[17] See, for example, Kurt Assmann's *Deutsche Seestrategie in Zwei Weltkriegen* (Tubingen, 1957). F. H. Hinsley, however, argued in his 1951 study, *Hitler's Strategy* (Cambridge), that Hitler did understand seapower and recognized its importance well enough to initiate military and political campaigns that would guarantee Germany's continental hegemony before he offered a direct challenge to the maritime powers.

[18] *Hitlers Strategie, Politik und Kriegfuhrung 1940-1941* (Frankfurt, 1965).

[19] *Vom Reich zum Weltreich Hitler, NSDAP und koloniale Frage 1919-1945* (Munich, 1969).

[20] Cf. Keith W. Bird, "Officers and Republic: The German Navy and Politics." Unpublished dissertation, Durham, North Carolina, 1972. B. R. Gruner B. V. will publish an expanded version as *Weimar, the German Naval Officer Corps and the Rise of National Socialism* (Amsterdam, 1978).

[21] Reviews of Dülffer can be found in the *American Historical Review,* LXXIX (February, 1974), pp. 176-178 (Keith W. Bird); *Central European History,* VII (September, 1974),

pp. 275-278 (Harold Gordon); and *Militärgeschichtliche Mitteilungen* 14 (1973), pp. 247-253 (Bernard-Jürgen Wendt). For a selection from the Dülffer "debate" see *MOV-Nachrichten*, 11/12, 1973, pp. 252-253 (Rolf Guth) and *Marineforum*, 6 (1975), pp. 160-162 (Edward Wegener). Cf. Dülffer's "Der Beginn des Krieges 1939: Hitler, die innere Krise and das Machtsystem," *Das nationalsozialistische Herrschaftssystem, Geschichte und Gesellschaft* (Heft 4, 1976), pp. 443-470.

[22] Volume one "1935-1941" was published in 1970 (Munich) and the second volume "1942-1945" in 1975. Volume three, a collection of documents, was published in 1974.

[23] See Friedrich Forstmeier's review of Salewski in the *Militärgeschichtliche Mitteilungen*, 11 (1972), pp. 211-217.

[24] I am indebted to Dr. Salewski for providing me with proofs from volume II in preparation for an earlier version of this article.

[25] Salewski's "Der 20 Juli 1944: Marine und Nationalsozialismus" (see note 24) supersedes the only previously existing published account of the German navy and National Socialism—Walter Braum's *"Marine, Nationalsozialismus und Widerstand"*, *Vierteljahreshefte für Zeitgeschichte*, XI (January, 1963), pp. 16-48.

[26] Rahn's dissertation title (Hamburg) was *Verteidigungskonzeption und Reichsmarine in der Weimarer Republik. Planning und Fuhrung in der Ara Behncke und Zenker 1920-1928*. Rahn's study is complimented by Gaines Post, Jr.'s excellent analysis of the relationship between foreign policy and military planning, *The Civil-Military Fabric of Weimar Foreign Policy* (Princeton, 1973). Post describes German naval planning as presumptuous and displaying "romantic" tendencies.

[27] New Brunswick, New Jersey, 1969. Cf. Admiral Ruge's review of Herwig's book in the *United States Naval Proceedings*, 102 (July, 1975) p. 84.

[28] Oxford, 1973.

[29] Cf. Jost Dülffers "Der Einfluss des Auslandes auf die national-sozialistische Politik", in *Innen-und Aussenpolitik unter nationalsozialistischer Bedrohung, Determinanten internationaler Beziehungen in historischen Fallstudien*, edited by Erhard Forndran, Frank Golszewski, Dieter Riesenberger (Oplanden, 1977).

[30] Unpublished dissertation, Iowa, 1969.

[31] Cf. F.L. Carsten, *Reichswehr and Politics 1918-1963* (Oxford, 1966).

[32] Unpublished dissertation, University of Washington, 1963. Eva H. Haraszti, *Treaty-Breakers or "Real-Politiker"? The Anglo-German Naval Agreement of June, 1935* (Boppard am Rhein and Budapest, 1974), does not provide any new evidence or significant research.

[33] See Manfred Krüger, "Die Grundzüge der imperialistischen deutschen Marineideologie," Phil. Habil., Rostock, 1963, and W. Wunderlich, "Das seestrategische Denken im imperialistischen Deutschland in Vorbereitung des Zweiten Weltkrieges," unpublished dissertation, (2 volumes) Leipzig, 1966.

[34] Unpublished dissertation, Humboldt-Universität zu Berlin, 1970.

[35] (Lund, 1973). Cf. Gemzell's *Raeder, Hitler, und Skandinavien. Der Kampf für einen maritimen Operationsplan* (Lund, 1965).

[36] The papers from this conference were published by the *Militärgeschichtliches Forschungsamt*.

[37] *The Ultra Secret* (New York, 1974). See the new material provided by the "Joint Session on Code-breaking and Intelligence in the European Theatre, World War II" (Washington, 29 December 1976), American Committee on the History of the Second World War *Newsletter*, 17 (May, 1977), pp. 3-8.

[38] Raeder's two-volume memoirs *Mein Leben* (Tübingen, 1956 and 1957) was written primarily by Admiral Erich Förste who organized—in the absence of documents—the reports and accounts of commanders and department heads. These were presented to

Raeder for his reaction and approval before the final version was written. The story of the manuscript can be found in the *Nachlass* Förste, N328. Dönitz had published three autobiographical accounts: *Zehn Yahre und Zwanzig Tage* (Frankfurt, 1963); *Mein wechselvolles Leben* (Frankfurt, 1968); and *Deutsche Strategie zur See im Zweiten Weltkrieg. Die Antworten des Gross admirals auf 40 Fragen* (Frankfurt, 1970). Walter Görlitz's uncritical *Karl Dönitz. Der Grossadmiral* (Göttingen, 1972) is not satisfactory.

[39] Major Schubert recently completed his research at the *Militärgeschichtliches Forschungstamt* in Freiburg.

[40] Rolf Guth's *Die Marine des Deutschen Reiches 1919-1939* (Frankfurt, 1972) provides an overview of the period but is arranged in handbook fashion without any new research or insights. The *Handbuch zur deutsche Militärgeschichte* published by the *Militärgeschichtliches Forschungsamt* is more useful but only *Reichswehr und Republik 1918-1933* (Frankfurt, 1970) has been published (the section covering 1933-1945 has not yet been completed). The naval documents available on microfilm should be supplemented by a reading of the extensive (and continually growing) collection of *Nachlasse* available in the holding of the *Militärarchiv* in Freiburg. These private papers (such as the Widenmann papers) should stimulate the writing of biographies. The expansion and development of the German archives after 1960 is also a subject worthy of closer study. Tobias R. Philbin III's study of Admiral Franz Hipper (Ph.D. dissertation, Kings College, University of London) is also an encouraging sign in this area. Holger Herwig's article on Admiral Levetzow demonstrates the usefulness of these studies for an understanding of this period of German history. See "From Kaiser to Führer: The Political Road of a German Admiral, 1923-33," *Journal of Contemporary History*, IX (April, 1974), pp. 107-120.

[41] Letter to author, January 28, 1976.

CHAPTER 21

Naval Attachés, Intelligence Officers, and the Rise of the "New American Navy," 1882-1914

Jeffrey M. Dorwart

Rutgers University at Camden

The only major new interpretation of U.S. naval history to appear during the past decade of tumultuous revisionist historical writing has been Peter Karsten's *The Naval Aristocracy.*[1] This sociological and psychological analysis of Academy graduates during the late 19th and early 20th centuries presented one of the most comprehensive and heavily documented attempts yet made to explain the development of a modern U.S. Navy. Professor Kenneth J. Hagan called it "the most provocative book on American naval history ever to appear."[2] Indeed, there is much in Karsten's volume to provoke discussion and stimulate debate. Were American naval officers as militaristic, racist, intellectually conformist, and socially inbred as Karsten suggests? Did a divisive generation gap, conflicting elitist cliques, and career anxieties really explain the officers' interest in updating and expanding the Navy? One might, for example, challenge Karsten's argument that the diverse ideas employed by this group of officers to promote a modern navy were mere rhetoric masking economic motives.

It is not the purpose of this paper to take issue with Karsen's sweeping interpretations. Instead I wish to examine one group of naval officers which he used to buttress his primary thesis in the hope that this will induce other historians to test additional aspects of Karsten's controversial study.

Karsten contended that most naval attachés and intelligence officers were youthful insurgents, tormented by career anxieties and visions of a New Empire. Moreover, he claimed that these officers used the Office of Naval Intelligence to promote naval expansion and imperial expansion, thus providing more jobs for officers and accelerating their own promotion up the ranks. The intelligence office, Karsten insisted, was the "Bastion of the Young Turks."[3]

This view may be examined by surveying some of the early naval intelligence officers and attachés whom Karsten referred to as Young Turks. Lieutenant Theodorus Bailey Myers Mason became the head of the newly created Office of Naval Intelligence in June 1882. During his three-year tenure, which coincided with the first stirrings of the new Navy, Mason never made O.N.I. a bastion for young reformist officers. From the beginning his intelligence bureau held a precarious position within the Navy Department. It enjoyed no legal existence, was attached informally to the Bureau of Navigation, and relied entirely upon that body for funds and support. Other bureaus and most officers ignored it. It was not uncommon in those first years for intelligence officers aboard ship to casually report that their Chinese servants had thrown intelligence forms overboard with the ship's garbage.[4]

Bright young officers avoided duty with Mason. If O.N.I. was created to provide jobs for Young Turks, these same officers appeared reluctant to grasp this new opportunity for advancement. Eventually Mason found fifteen men to serve in the intelligence office between 1882-85, although some had to be detached from other branches to assist him.[5] Karsten claimed that these staff intelligence officers and the Navy's first attachés were the Young Turks who dominated O.N.I. However, of the fifteen only 4, Mason, Charles C. Rogers, Sidney A. Staunton and French E. Chadwick, became activists in the new Navy. William H. Beehler and William Driggs sympathized with the insurgents and periodically sided with them. The other nine could not be termed Young Turks. What about career anxieties? All officers in the 1880's expressed a certain amount of disillusionment with the slowness of promotions. Several lieutenants on Mason's staff had in fact each been in the service for nearly twenty years. Mason himself was a veteran of fourteen years in the Navy. But only one, J. P. S. Lawrance, recorded strong career frustrations, and only one, Robert H. McLean, resigned because of slow advancement. Three others, John S. Abbott, Lovell K. Reynolds and M. Fisher Wright, had little time to ponder career anxiety since all died within a few years after their tour in O.N.I.[6]

Karsten singled out Mason, the chief intelligence officer, as a typical Young Turk, who was torn by career anxiety because he had lost hope for promotion and who resigned in disgust. Mason, in fact, accepted the Navy's promotion system. "Promotion, except in rare cases during war, is by seniority," Mason wrote a few months before entering O.N.I., "and it is probably best that it should be so."[7] Moreover, Mason did not resign. A recurrence of a tropical fever contracted years before in Panama so incapacitated him that he sought medical retirement. And even as he lay dying, Mason believed a miraculous recovery would allow him to return to the Navy.[8]

If Mason was no anxious careerist, one must look elsewhere for the roots of his desire to modernize the Navy. His many professional essays and articles abound with concern for American security in the face of rapidly changing naval technology. As early as 1875, Mason presented a paper to the Naval Institute at Annapolis; in it he described a fanciful version of a future naval battle in which foreign steel warships armed with rifled ordnance brushed aside the American fleet and devastated the Atlantic coast. Several years later, while on station in Chilean waters during the War of the Pacific, he personally observed the results of a naval battle between Chilean and Peruvian ironclad warships. Even these nearly obsolete Latin American men-of-war were far more destructive than any ship in the U.S. Navy. They worried Mason.[9]

In historical hindsight concern for these tiny ships appears absurd. Even Mason knew that it would be difficult to convince anyone that Chilean cruisers posed a direct threat to American ports. But these warships merely represented the larger question of the dangers posed to American security by rapidly improving foreign naval weapons. Early intelligence reports reinforced this concern, and Mason hoped to use O.N.I. to convince the Navy, Congress, and American public opinion of future threats. "Our people must be made to understand that a navy is for war," he warned in 1885, because "once that fact is well understood there will be no necessity of making excuses for its existence in time of peace."[10]

Mason's close friend and classmate, Raymond Perry Rodgers, became second chief intelligence officer in April 1885. He served until 1889, and during his tenure O.N.I. fit Karsten's image as a breeding ground for insurgent Young Turks. Rodgers assembled the most brilliant and activist staff in the Office's history. Articulate and irreverent, they lashed out at poor attitudes, inadequate training, obsolete equipment and inefficient organization in the Navy. The Navy Department was full of the biggest wranglers in history, naval attaché in Paris, Berlin and St. Petersburg Benjamin H. Buckingham wrote in 1888. He wished the German Kaiser could control the American Navy for awhile to set things straight. Nathan Sargent, the first O.N.I. representative in Rome and Vienna, deplored the Navy's treatment of maneuvers as nothing more than dress parade reviews. Staff intelligence officer John C. Colwell concluded simply: "Radical changes are what the navy needs, and radical changes will be made for us before many years, unless we indicate those needs and so have a voice in the making."[11]

It was not all iconoclastic criticism. Rodgers' dynamic group wrote thoughtful essays on weapons technology, naval reserve systems, mobilization of national resources, general staff organization, and acquisition of coaling stations. These essays described the use of seapower in terms of economic rivalries, defense of the national honor, and survival of the fittest. But once again, as with Mason, the O.N.I. under Rodgers considered security issues of prime importance. Rodgers' childhood companion and senior staff intelligence officer, Seaton Schroeder, best expressed the atmosphere in O.N.I. "Eternal vigilance is the price of preparedness."[12]

The naval intelligence office between 1885 and 1889 reached an ever-widening audience. Congressmen consulted it when preparing naval legislation. Secretary of the Navy William C. Whitney turned to Rodgers' staff for information, and the State Department cooperated fully in exchanging views.[13] It was within the naval establishment itself, however, that Rodgers' office had its greatest impact. Bureaus and boards relied on O.N.I. for the latest overseas blueprints of ship designs, the most recent armor and ordnance specifications, advances in electricity, boilers, engines and torpedoes. This vital information aided construction of the new Navy's first steel warships. Rodgers' people sent key information to the Naval Institute, the Torpedo Station at Newport, and the new Naval War College. Captain Alfred T. Mahan expressed the college's indebtedness to O.N.I. in a November 1888 letter to Rodgers. "I take this opportunity to thank you not only for the particular favor, but also for the kindness and readiness shown by you, throughout my connection with the College, in forwarding all matters in which I have asked you to help."[14]

Commander Charles H. Davis, Jr. replaced Rodgers in September 1889. According to Karsten, O.N.I. became a bastion of the Young Turks under Davis. Such a view is understandable. The office's activism had grown during the previous four years, and more could be expected from the new chief intelligence officer, son of the brilliant Rear Admiral Charles Henry Davis. The younger Davis appeared equally capable, already identified prominently with progressive officers working on scientific and coastal survey duties. Moreover Davis had married into the family of Henry Cabot Lodge of Massachusetts, and numbered other expansionists among his inner circle of friends.[15]

There were other factors pointing to increased O.N.I. contributions to naval expansion. The new Secretary of the Navy Benjamin F. Tracy expressed interest in departmental reforms, promotion of the Naval War College and construction of bigger warships. Walter R. Herrick, Jr., one of Tracy's biographers, claimed the secretary inspired the most revolutionary changes in doctrine ever experienced by the Navy Department. Whether or not Tracy's influence was that immense, in 1889 intelligence officers and naval attachés voiced enthusiasm for the new secretary. Tracy encouraged this feeling by moving the intelligence office from the Bureau of Navigation to the office of the Assistant Secretary of the Navy James R. Soley. Davis and his staff now had immediate access to the secretary and hoped to operate as an informal general staff.[16]

Late nineteenth-century naval and imperial rivalries also promised increased responsibilities for intelligence officers and attachés. Big munitions firms turned out more sophisticated and destructive hardware. Naval powers experimented with submarines, new torpedoes, fleet tactics, and range finders. International tensions forecast confrontations, and the United States faced complications with Spain, Britain, and Germany. The world was alive with excitement and danger, providing fertile ground for naval intelligence. American intelligence officers and attachés adopted this spirit and flooded O.N.I. with detailed reports.[17]

However, despite this atmosphere, O.N.I. stagnated under Davis and his immediate successors, French E. Chadwick and Frederic Singer. During much of the 1890's the Office slipped into near obscurity. The staff sat at their desks serving time. Dynamic junior officers such as John Baptiste-Bernadou and Washington I. Chambers left, and no new Young Turks took their places. Intelligence officers and naval attachés in the field wondered why their reports were ignored by the Navy Department. Enthusiasm for intelligence work waned, and many officers wrote simply: "Nothing of note was observed."[18] Young intelligence officer and insurgent William S. Sims wrote from the Asiatic Station in 1895, "I don't know why the Department puts up with it but many ships entirely neglect it."[19]

O.N.I. publications during the 'nineties, cited by Karsten as examples of insurgent propaganda, became nothing more than pedestrian accumulations of facts, comparing the merits of one boiler over another. Rather than promoting commercial empire, O.N.I. essays slipped into racist rhetoric and explained how savages did not suffer from gunshot wounds like "civilized" people because "like the horse" they can't go into shock.[20]

Frustrated and neglected, naval attachés turned to other enterprises in the 1890's. Francis M. Barber and Raymond Rodgers, now naval attaché in Paris, promoted U.S. business overseas. Rodgers introduced one American businessman to Nathan Sargent in Rome. "Any assistance that you can give him will I am sure promote our American interests."[21] Other attachés during the late 19th century, including Sims in Paris, John C. Colwell in London and William Beehler in Berlin, though, refused to participate in this game. Moreover until the William Howard Taft administration, O.N.I. did not actively promote big business.

Several reasons can be found for O.N.I.'s failure to become a bastion of the Young Turks under Davis. He never gave it firm leadership. He was moody and erratic, given to flights of depression and sarcasm. He would discuss the need for reform, then extol the virtues of his father's old sailing navy. Trying to live up to Rear Admiral Davis' reputation, the younger man found himself overshadowed in the O.N.I. by his immediate superior Soley. The assistant secretary even took over responsibility for ordering blueprints and other routine work. Davis' staff observed how completely Soley dominated their chief. At the same time, Secretary Tracy presented O.N.I. with a paradoxical situation. He demanded more information, especially during the war scare with Chile in 1891, but hoarded this intelligence for his inner strategy group of Soley, Mahan and several other officers. Davis was squeezed out.[22]

Appointment of Chadwick as new chief intelligence officer in late 1892 failed to reverse the office's decline. As first naval attaché between 1882-89, Chadwick had done more than anyone to lay the foundations for O.N.I. as a potential bastion of the Young Turks. But in 1892-93 he failed to revive the intelligence agency. Shortly after transfer to head the Bureau of Equipment, Chadwick expressed concern for the office's future. "Elsewhere it is regarded as an essential part of a general staff, and it would at once drop into its proper place in the event of war, necessity bringing a result in our case which is arrived at elsewhere by the foresight bred of the eminency of war."[23]

Four years later, in 1897 Richard Wainwright, a dynamic young officer with sweeping views of naval and imperial expansion, assumed charge of O.N.I. Soon he established intimate relations with Assistant Secretary of the Navy Theodore Roosevelt. If the intelligence office was ever to become a bastion for Young Turks it should have occurred under the tutelage of these aggressive navalists. Instead O.N.I. focused narrowly on compiling plans for possible military operations against Spain. These plans remained incomplete when Wainwright left naval intelligence for a tour of duty aboard the *Maine*. When the Spanish-American War broke out in April 1898, retired officers, reservists, and civilian clerks manned O.N.I., concentrating desperately on providing information on enemy preparations for a Naval War Board composed of Mahan, Arent S. Crowninshield, and Montgomery Sicard. The harried intelligence office had only limited success. "What we appear to suffer from most," Sicard wrote Secretary of the Navy John Long in May, "seems to be an absence of correct information from abroad."[24]

Fortunately O.N.I.'s inadequate service during the Spanish-American War did not matter because Spain's naval capabilities had long been declining. But knowledge of such shortcomings plagued the office for the next fifteen years, particularly the chief intelligence officers Charles D. Sigsbee, Seaton Schroeder, and the second tenure of Raymond Rodgers. They became obsessed with the menace to the United States posed by growing German and Japanese naval power. Their fear of national humilitation was much more than the rhetoric masking economic motives interpreted by Karsten. These intelligence officers worried consistently about foreign threats. Obstacles confronting U.S. naval attachés added to their concern. Major powers viewed the United States now as a potential ally, or enemy. "The possibility of national alliances has deprived our attachés of the independence they once had and made them objects of suspicion and espionage like the attachés of other nations," one American naval agent observed.[25]

The Navy Department responded to these new complexities in naval intelligence by strengthening O.N.I.'s position in the organization. In February 1899, legislation formally established the office with its own appropriations and provisions for civilian clerks. In 1900 Henry Clay Taylor, Chadwick and other O.N.I. veterans helped attach the intelligence office to the newly-formed Navy General Board, an advisory body which many hoped would become a formal naval general staff. Along with the Naval War College, these two organizations planned the Navy's long-range policies and war portfolios. Such activity forced intelligence officers and naval attachés to redefine their work. Comprehensive new intelligence instructions replaced the earlier casual observations and reports. "The General Board submits that information of detached, isolated facts produces but little of value," Board president George Dewey wrote the Secretary of the Navy in December 1901, "and that the salient idea governing such investigations should be to define a route and a method of attack or defense, and to learn every point of interest connected with that proposed operation."[26]

Following such orders, O.N.I. agents roved through Latin America, the Pacific Ocean and East Asia. The Office prepared memoranda for President Roosevelt on the Russo-Japanese War of 1904-1905, preparation for a world cruise of the battleship fleet and on Latin American revolutions which might affect isthmian policies. Many former O.N.I. operatives predicted that their long struggle for creation of a central policy board and general staff to plan for national security was becoming a reality. From Mason's days down through 1900 this had been a dominant theme in O.N.I. thinking, around which technological, economic and political questions revolved. But with full integration into the naval establishment, intelligence officers lost their earlier creativity. They reflected General Board views and offered little new information or ideas. Many accepted the General Board as the most that could be expected in terms of a body to plan overall operations. Others failed to recognize the significance of developments in diesel engines, submarines, and aircraft. Most reinforced assumptions that the big-gun battleship marked the zenith of naval development.

Although O.N.I. had long ceased to attract Young Turks, it still harbored a few progressive intelligence officers and naval attachés in the decade preceding World War I. For one, Albert Parker Neblack observed that his fellows seemed more interested in promotion than improvement of the service, and failed to introduce new theories on naval tactics to update primitive practices.[27] At the same time John H. Gibbons noted that while the new Navy had been launched twenty years ago, it still lacked coherent building policies or homogeneous fighting units.[28] Raymond Rodgers, back for another tour, continued his earlier insurgency and attempted to modernize O.N.I. When he reentered the office in 1906, he discovered numerous rumors of war with Japan and other supposed enemies. One report claimed that Japanese Admiral Togo was in Berlin disguised as a German, carrying huge sums of Chinese money with which to buy weapons from the Kaiser to fight the United States. Other intelligence alluded to Japanese attempts to buy the Italian Navy and sinister plots to blow up the American Great White Fleet on its world cruise. Rodgers warned his young intelligence officers and attachés to learn the difference between rumor and hard information. He stressed the importance of precise reports and realistic analyses of foreign conditions. The times and generation had changed for Rodgers, but the requirements for good information continued unchanged.[29]

Despite Rodgers' warnings, naval intelligence personnel continued to struggle in their information-gathering assignments. During the William Howard Taft administration they spent more time as salesmen for American arms merchants than as collectors of fresh intelligence.[30] Nor did the end of dollar diplomacy and the emergence of Wilsonian idealism improve the situation. The quality of data diminished each year. On the eve of the Great European War of 1914, former naval attaché Reginald Rowan Belknap believed that O.N.I. had become anything but a bastion for Young Turks. "Regarding the Office of Naval Intelligence as the body responsible for giving us a correct estimate of possible enemies' forces," Belknap informed the General Board, "I think we need some radical changes in equipping our naval attachés as field agents of the Office."[31]

A sketch of naval attachés and intelligence officers between 1882 and 1914 has suggested some general observations. First, it is difficult to accept Karsten's stereotype of these officers as a unified band of Young Turks or agents of New Empire. Some were, others were not. Between 1885-89 the majority were insurgents, manning O.N.I. as a bastion of the Young Turks. During this interval the intelligence bureau helped lay the foundation for the new Navy. At other times, however, most intelligence people simply served their time or actually resisted rapid changes. While a few suffered career anxiety, others evidently were motivated by different concerns. Naval attachés and intelligence officers presented a rich variety of arguments for naval reform and expansion including commercialism, imperial rivalry, security fears, national honor, natural law, and technological modernization. They were most concerned with national defense, not promotion of economic empire or insurgency. Indeed the monotonous nature of gathering and collating information over the years often discouraged Young Turks from seeking duty as intelligence officers or naval attachés. In the final analysis, Karsten's treatment of O.N.I. personnel between 1882 and 1914 seems an over-generalized and simplified approach to a complex subject.

FOOTNOTES

[1] Peter Karsten, *The Naval Aristocracy: The Golden Age of Annapolis and the Emergence of Modern American Navalism* (New York, 1972); "No Room for Young Turks?" *United States Naval Institute Proceedings*, 99 (1973): 37-50. (Hereafter *USNIP*.)

[2] Kenneth J. Hagan, "The Navy in the Nineteenth Century, 1789-1889," in Robin Higham, ed., *A Guide to the Sources of United States Military History* (Hamden, Conn., 1975), 164.

[3] Karsten, *Naval Aristocracy*, 296.

[4] William S. Hogg to N. Mayo Dyer, 3 Sept. 1888; Dyer to Bureau of Navigation, 4 Sept. 1888; Dyer to Bureau of Navigation 22 Nov. 1888, all in Office of Naval Intelligence, General Correspondence, Letters Received, 1886-1899, Record Group 38, National Archives. (Hereafter, RG 38, NA.)

[5] A. G. Berry, "The Beginning of the Office of Naval Intelligence," *USNIP*, LXIII (1937): 102-3.

[6] Register of Personnel of the Office of Naval Intelligence, 1882-1918, RG 38, NA; U.S. Navy, *Register of the United States Navy* (Washington, 1871-1900).

[7] T. B. M. Mason, "A Medal of Honor for Officers," *The United Service*, IV (1881): 10.

[8] T. B. M. Mason Papers, Division of Naval History, Smithsonian Institution.

[9] T. B. M. Mason, "The Lessons from the Future," *The Record of the United States Naval Institute*, II (1875): 1-22; "The War Between Chile, Peru, and Bolivia: Shakings from the Log-Book of a Lieutenant," *The United Service*, II (1880): 553-574; *The War on the Pacific Coast of South America between Chile and the Allied Republics of Peru and Bolivia, 1879-'81*, Office of Naval Intelligence, War Series, No. II (Washington, 1885).

[10] Mason, "Discussion," *USNIP*, XI (1885): 71.

[11] Colwell, "Discussion," *USNIP*, XVI (1890): 509; Buckingham to Royal B. Bradford, 17 Sept. 1888, Letters from U.S. Naval Attachés, RG 38, NA; Sargent, "Suggestions in Favor of More Practical and Efficient Service Exercises," *USNIP*, X (1884): 233-40.

[12] Schroeder, "Gleanings from the Sea of Japan," *USNIP*, XXXII (1906): 79; *Naval Mobilization and Improvement in Matériel, June 1889*, O.N.I., General Information Series, No. VII (Washington, 1888).

[13] Hon. Hilary A. Herbert to Rodgers, 8 Feb., 13 June, 18 July 1886; 23 Jan. 1887; 22 Aug. 1888, all in O.N.I. General Correspondence; Walker to Whitney, 8 and 15 Sept. 1887, The Papers of John Grimes Walker, Naval Historical Foundation Collection, Library of Congress; Thomas F. Bayard to Whitney, 14 Jan. 1887, O.N.I., General Correspondence.

[14] Mahan to Rodgers, 1 Nov. 1888, *ibid.*

[15] See Charles H. Davis, *Life of Charles Henry Davis, Rear Admiral, 1807-1877* (Boston, 1899); Lewis Randolph Hamersly, *The Records of Living Officers of the U.S. Navy and Marine Corps* (New York, 1902), 106; *Dictionary of American Biography*, 5, pp. 107-8.

[16] See Walter R. Herrick, Jr., *The American Naval Revolution* (Baton Rouge, 1966); B. Franklin Cooling, *Benjamin Franklin Tracy, Father of the Modern American Fighting Navy* (Hamden, 1973).

[17] Letters from U.S. Naval Attachés, RG 38, NA.

[18] Pickering to Secretary of the Navy, 14 March 1892, O.N.I., General Correspondence.

[19] William [Sims] to his family, 9 March 1895, The Papers of William S. Sims, Naval Historical Foundation Collection, Library of Congress.

[20] Karmany in *Notes on Naval Progress, July 1894*, O.N.I., General Information Series, No. XIII (Washington, 1894): 163-64.

[21] Rodgers to Sargent, 8 June 1893, Letters from Attachés, RG 38, NA.

[22] Singer to Sargent, 23 Oct. 1892; 9 Dec. 1889, Nathan Sargent Letterbooks, RG 45, NA.

[23] Chadwick, "Naval Department Organization," *USNIP*, XX (1894): 499.

[24] Sicard to the Secretary of the Navy, 19 May 1898, Naval War Board Records, Record Group 80, National Archives.

[25] Barber to Bureau of Navigation, 23 Jan. 1899, Letters from Attaches. See O.N.I., General Correspondence, "Cases," 1900-1906 for Sigsbee and Schroeder.

[26] Dewey to the Secretary of the Navy, 3 Dec. 1901, General Board File 409, General Board of the Navy Papers, Operational Archives, Washington Navy Yard.

[27] Niblack, "An Answer to Criticisms of 'The Elements of Fleet Tactics,' " *USNIP*, XXXII (1906): 1065-67.

[28] Gibbons, "The Need of a Building Program for Our Navy," *USNIP*, XXIX (1903): 323.

[29] Howard to Rodgers, 1 July 1907, O.N.I., General Correspondence, case 8444. Also, see Rodgers to Bernadou, 13 Apr. 1907, case 8038; Rodgers to Gibbons and Howard, 16 May 1907, in case 8139.

[30] See William R. Braisted, "China, the United States Navy, and Bethlehem Steel Co., 1909-1929," *Business History Review*, 42 (1968): 50-66.

[31] Belknap, "Naval Attachés," typescript dated 18 Dec. 1913, in General Board File 429, General Board Papers.

CHAPTER 22

The U. S. Navy and the Near Eastern Crisis, 1893-1897

William Still, Jr.

East Carolina University

The purpose of this paper is to suggest that historians should recognize the importance of Turkish-American relations in the mid 1890's and the role played by the United States Navy in these relations. Traditional scholarship has emphasized the crisis with Great Britain over Venezuela and the growing problem with Spain over Cuba. Yet, during this same period the United States became involved in a controversy with the Ottoman Empire which threatened to catapult this country into intervening by force in Turkey. The so-called Armenian massacres were the basic cause for this crisis, although relations were complicated by a long history of unresolved difficulties between the two countries, along with the international tension surrounding the gradual decay and collapse of the "sick man of Europe."

The traditional policy of the United States was non-involvement so far as the Near Eastern question was concerned. In reality, however, this country was frequently involved, partly because of American interests in the Ottoman Empire and partly for humanitarian reasons. American commercial interests were negligible, but missionary interests were widespread and important. By the last decade of the 19th century there were several hundred missionaries operating mission stations, schools, and hospitals. They had generally been left alone by Ottoman officials because they made little effort to convert Moslems; instead they concentrated on the Christian minorities, particularly the Armenians. This policy of non-interference began to change in the late 1880's because of the growing nationalism among the Armenians and the suspicion on the part of Turkish officials that the missionaries were encouraging the Armenians in their increasing militancy. By 1890 clashes between the Armenians and the Turks were frequent. These clashes reached a peak during the decade when thousands of

Armenians were slaughtered. Some missionary property was destroyed, and the missionaries themselves were fearful for their lives. The United States Navy was requested to provide protection, a mission in keeping with its peacetime responsibilities.

Throughout most of the 19th century the navy had maintained a squadron in the Mediterranean Sea and northern European waters. The growing obsolescence of the wooden vessels of the old Navy and the importance of other stations, such as those in Latin America and the Pacific, resulted in the gradual reduction and temporary demise of the European Squadron in 1889. The station was reactivated in 1893 under the command of Rear Admiral Henry Erban. The squadron, however, consisted of only one steel warship—the protected cruiser *Chicago.* Although there were a number of factors that persuaded the Navy Department to re-establish the European Station, the most important one was the trouble in the Ottoman Empire.[1]

In 1893 Admiral Erban made a brief cruise in Turkish waters, but reported the missionaries in no immediate danger. This assessment exasperated the missionaries and also Alexander Terrell, the American minister to Turkey, who demanded the stationing of a permanent naval force in the Levant. As a result of pressure brought on President Grover Cleveland's administration by missionary interests, especially the powerful American Board of Commissioners for Foreign Missions in Boston, the missionary arm of the Congregationalist Church, the Navy Department ordered a second cruiser, the *Marblehead,* to the Mediterranean.[2]

In 1894 Erban was relieved by Real Admiral William A. Kirkland, a colorful figure in the old navy where he was known as "Red Bill" because of his sandy hair, florid complexion, and fiery nature. Alfred Thayer Mahan, who admired Kirkland and hated Erban, wrote of Kirkland, "He is irascible, profane and gouty—a warm heart, but that is of little account when the temper is violent and uncontrolable." As Admiral Yates Sterling wrote, "he was in no sense the drawing room type." Considering Kirkland's personality it is not surprising that his thirteen-month tour as commander of the European Squadron was stormy and controversial. He publicly criticized the missionaries in Turkey, and the New York *Times* quoted him as calling them a "bad lot"; Kirkland as much as admitted it to Mahan when he wrote, "I met several liars and sons of bitches in the east, not all of them outside the limits of the Church," and added, "I left them a first class reputation to malign and guess they'll . . . make a riffle at it." He was right. They did in letters to the press, their home churches, and to Washington officials. What angered the missionaries the most, however, were not his personal remarks about them, but his opposition to maintaining a naval force in Turkish waters. Kirkland made two cruises to the Near East and in both cases reported that the missionaries were in no immediate danger, reports that were published in the newspapers. There is little doubt that the controversy generated by his reports and the reaction to them resulted in his relief, apparently ordered by the president himself. As the *Army and Navy Journal* concluded, "to shock the religious sentiment [in] . . . the United States is to commit the unpardonable sin."[3]

In November, 1895, Acting Rear Admiral Thomas O. Selfridge, Jr., arrived in France to assume command of the European Squadron. Selfridge had the reputation of being a "by the book" or no-nonsense commander. His flag was hoisted on the cruiser *San Francisco* which sailed immediately to join the *Marblehead* in Turkish waters. His orders were virtually the same as those given to his predecessor, "to personally investigate and report fully on the danger to American missionaries." Selfridge's arrival coincided with a new outbreak of terror against the Armenians in the interior of Turkey. A number of American mission stations, schools, and private residences were looted and burned. Missionaries flooded their native country with appeals and petitions, personal letters to the mission boards, to newspapers, church congregations, influential individuals and government officials. Religious and business leaders organized rallies in New York, Boston, Baltimore, Chicago and other cities. Religious journals like the *Independent,* the *Congregationalist,* the *Baptist Philadelphers Commonwealth,* and the *Methodist Western Christian Advocate* began to demand intervention by force.[4]

Terrell, the American minister in Constantinople, also urged the use of force. On November 27, he telegraphed the State Department that a "fleet" was necessary to induce the Turkish government to pay ("under the muzzle of its guns") for the damage to missionary property. He even mentioned an ultimatum. Expressing similar sentiments a few days later, he wrote, "If an American Squadron with [England's] . . . consent, unexpectedly rush[ed] the Dardanelles and held the Porte under its guns, it would be the surest way of obtaining indemnity for the past and security for the future." Like most proponents of gunboat diplomacy, he believed that such action would not bring on war with the Ottoman Empire.[5]

The Cleveland administration's response to the increasing demand for involvement in the Turkish crisis was cautious. A third cruiser was sent out to join Admiral Selfridge's squadron in Turkish waters, and the Sultan was petitioned to allow one of the American warships to pass through the Dardanelles to Constantinople.[6] When the request was refused, the State Department dropped the idea. On December 2, Cleveland sent his annual message to Congress. It devoted as much space to the Turkish crisis as to the Venezuelan situation, but the tone remained cautious. He emphasized that no American lives had been lost, although property had been destroyed, and that the naval vessels were there to gather information and act as a place of refuge for American citizens.

However, in the following weeks his position changed. He began seriously to consider sending strong naval reinforcements into Turkish waters, and landing a force from these ships if necessary. This change in policy resulted from Terrell's recommendations, the appeals from religious groups, and perhaps more importantly, the increasing political pressure on him to take a stronger stand.[7]

Inevitably the Turkish problem became embroiled in American politics. Republicans criticized Cleveland for his failure to respond to missionary appeals. Members of Congress began to recognize the political sensitivity of the issue. Senator Orville Platt of Connecticut and Representative George A. Boutelle of Maine requested that additional naval vessels be sent to the eastern Mediterranean. On December 10, Senators Wilkinson Call of Florida and George F. Hoar of Massachusetts introduced resolutions calling on the administration to prevent by peaceful negotiations or by force of arms if necessary, the cruelties inflicted on the Armenians.[8]

On December 19, Admiral Selfridge was ordered to concentrate his squadron at Alexandretta, to take on board all Americans, and if necessary to "land a force." Alexandretta was selected because the city of Marash, some ninety miles inland, was considered the point of greatest danger. Selfridge's reply made it clear that he considered the whole idea ludicrous. He only had approximately 3,000 men (including a few dozen marines) to man his vessels, and Marash was a distant ten days' journey, "there being for a large part of the way nothing but bridle paths." The plan to land a force was dropped temporarily.[9]

Early in January, 1896, newspapers carried stories that a powerful fleet of American warships would be concentrated in Turkish waters. The Sunday, January 5, edition of the New York *Herald* included an entire page on this "naval demonstration." The article suggested that the North Atlantic Squadron, at that time anchored in Hampton Roads, was under orders to sail for the Mediterranean, and that other squadrons, including the Asiatic, would assemble there. Other newspapers carried similar stories. The New York *Times* headlined its account, "May coerce the Sultan." In the following days the press seethed with rumors. The usually authoritative *Army and Navy Journal* reported on January 11, "We have absolutely reliable authority . . . that the administration has prepared a plan of campaign against Turkey." Both the New York *Herald* and *Times* were critical of a naval demonstration. The *Herald* asked in one editorial, "Is jingoism again rampant?" And the *Times* said, "We can see no immediate need for sending even a single ship to say nothing of a fleet to reinforce Admiral Selfridge's command."[10]

There is evidence that the Cleveland administration seriously considered some sort of naval demonstration. Shortly before Christmas, 1895, Rear Admiral Francis M. Bunce, in command of the North Atlantic Squadron, made a hurried trip to Washington. The squadron's scheduled cruise to the West Indies was cancelled, and most newspapers blamed the change on the Turkish crisis. On January 2, Bunce ordered his ship commanders to make a detailed list of "fittings and articles" that would "unnecessarily endanger the officers and crew when under fire. . . ." Three days later orders were issued for instructions in "arranging the knapsacks, etc. of the landing force. . . ." The *Army and Navy Journal* outlined in detail the military preparations contemplated.[11]

It is, of course, possible that the squadron was being readied in case of trouble with Great Britain over the Venezuela boundary dispute. The dispute did coincide with the Turkish crisis. On December 17, Cleveland sent his message to Congress recommending strong action if Britain refused arbitration over the boundary. However, neither Cleveland nor Richard Olney, his secretary of state, wanted or expected war with Great Britain.

Secretary of State Olney was responsible for the strong position taken on the Venezuelan matter, and was equally responsible for the aggressive policy adopted towards Turkey. Assistant Secretary of State Alvey Adee wrote, "Mr. Olney came very near directing a demonstration against Alexandretta to collect our demands, but he was distrustful of the way the European powers would take it." On January 23, 1896, a medical missionary recently returned from the Ottoman Empire had an interview with the secretary of state. During conversation the secretary asked, "Suppose this country should send a fleet there to demand an indemnity from Turkey for the losses of property that have suffered in these riots?" The missionary replied: "It would be hazardous." Olney later said, "The Government means to insist upon the indemnity, but in doing this it might be necessary to bombard a Turkish port which would jeopardize the lives of the missionaries in the interior."[12]

Olney did not contemplate war; he simply looked on a solution to the Turkish situation the same way he approached the Venezuelan boundary controversy. A vigorous policy of direct action was the type of diplomacy he preferred. If, as a number of historians have suggested, Olney was convinced that vigorous diplomacy in the Venezuelan controversy would aid his political party in the coming election, certainly the same was true of the Turkish problem.[13]

Congress was also making warlike gestures. The New York *Herald* reported on January 9 that the Senate Foreign Relations Committee devoted its first meeting of the new year to "Armenian affairs." On January 2, Senator Shelby Collum, Chairman of the Foreign Relations Committee, introduced a resolution to support Cleveland in any appropriate measure that he might adopt. After two days of debate in which one senator, William P. Fyre of Maine, urged that American warships "sail up the Dardanelles and plant themselves before Constantinople," the resolution was adopted. The House followed suit.[14]

274

The *Nation* reported that there was more debate over the Armenian resolution than over the Venezuelan correspondence. It went on to chastise Congress for abandoning the Monroe Doctrine, and chided that august body for standing behind the President even if "vigorous action were required."[15]

Whatever action the Cleveland administration had contemplated was abandoned in late January or early February. This was done because Admiral Selfridge's reports continued to stress that the missionaries were in no immediate danger, but that the use of force would clearly endanger them. More than likely the other diplomatic and domestic problems that faced the administration at the time as well as the possibility of complications with European powers were also factors in the decision. By the middle of February, 1896, Postmaster General William L. Wilson could write in his diary that the Cuban situation was the only diplomatic problem that "causes anxiety."[16]

Although the possibility of armed intervention disappeared, the United States maintained a small naval force in Turkish waters until shortly before the outbreak of the Spanish American War. Violence continued to occur periodically in various parts of the Ottoman Empire. Also the State Department and its representative in Constantinople insisted that Americn claims could be brought to a successful conclusion only through judicious application of naval pressure.

This pressure included the stationing of a warship at Constantinople. In January, 1896, the State Department instructed minister Terrell to obtain permission for the 800-ton gunboat *Bancroft* to pass through the Straits. The Turkish government simply ignored the request. National pride precluded acquiescence, but a direct refusal might further antagonize the United States and possibly bring on armed intervention. At the same time the United States was not one of the treaty powers with the right to keep a stationnaire at Constantinople, nor was it likely that the signatory powers would agree to allow an American warship to pass through the Straits. For months the matter dragged on as American officials tried to obtain support from the powers. The *Bancroft* never did reach the Sultan's capital although she did get as far as Smyrna. The gunboat remained in the eastern Mediterranean until she was withdrawn along with the other units of the European Squadron in January, 1898.[17]

United States naval policy toward Turkey during the Armenian crisis of the 1890's was a failure. The United States along with other great powers accepted gunboat diplomacy as an acceptable means of solving international disputes, particularly with non-developed areas. Lord Palmerston as British Prime Minister had once stated, "Diplomats and protocols are very good things but there are no better peace-keepers than well-appointed three deckers." Yet, the pressure of naval forces and even the threat of a naval demonstration failed to persuade the Ottoman government to settle various differences with the United States. Several years would pass before the Sultan would agree to pay an indemnity for the destruction of American property during the massacres.

Although missionary property was destroyed, no American missionaries were injured or lost their lives. Was the presence of warships or the threat of coercion responsible for this? Certainly the missionaries thought so. Yet, naval vessels could provide little protection for the missions in the interior far beyond the range of their guns. In fact, some contemporaries including missionaries actually feared that a naval demonstration might result in a massacre of foreigners. When the British Prime Minister urged such a demonstration, the German minister to Russia pointed out that the ships would "always come too late to rescue foreigners from a massacre in Constantinople."[18]

The Ottoman Empire would continue crumbling; the Armenians would continue declining in numbers; and the American missionaries would continue calling upon the Navy for protection.

FOOTNOTES

[1] New York *Times*, August 5, 1893; Hillary Herbert to Erban, May 20, 1893, Henry Erban Papers, New York Historical Society, New York City.

[2] Walter Gresham to Terrell, December 15, 1894, Diplomatic Instructions of the Department of State, 1801-1906, General Records of the Department of State, R.G. 59, National Archives Microfilm Publication M77, roll 167; *The Army and Navy Journal*, December 29, 1894, 296. See also Erban to Terrell, March 10, 1894, Official Correspondence of the U.S. European Squadron, Records of the Naval Operating Forces, National Archives Record Group 313.

[3] On Kirkland's personality see Alfred Mahan to his wife, August 29, 1894, Alfred Mahan Papers, Library of Congress; Yates Sterling, Jr., *Sea Duty: the Memoirs of a Fighting Admiral* (New York, 1939), 35-36. On Kirkland, the missionaries, and Turkey see Bartlett to Judson Smith, June 10, 1895, American Board of Commissioners for Foreign Missions Archives, Houghton Library, Harvard University; Kirkland to Herbert, April 17, 1895, Area File of the Naval Records Collection, 1775-1910, Naval Records Collection of the Office of Naval Records and Library, R.G. 45, National Archives Microfilm Publication M625, roll 28; New York *Times*, August 18, 21, 1895. See several letters in the Boston *Transcript*, May 20, 1895 and the New York *Daily Tribune*, October 13, 1895. For correspondence between Kirkland and Herbert concerning the controversy over his relief see the William A. Kirkland Papers, East Carolina University Manuscript Collection, Greenville, North Carolina; *Army and Navy Journal*, October 26, 1895, 115.

[4] Herbert to Selfridge, October 30, 1895, M625, roll 229. For the religionists' pressure, see the documents in roll 92 of the Grover Cleveland Papers, Library of Congress. See also Kennedy to Cleveland, November 18, 1895, and Washburn to Kennedy, December 10, 1895, Cleveland papers, roll 91.

[5] Terrell to Olney, November 24, 27, 30, 1895, to Adee, December 1, 1895, Despatches from United States Ministers to Turkey, 1818-1906, General Records of the Department of State, R.G. 59, National Archives Microfilm Publication M46, roll 59.

[6] *Army and Navy Journal*, November 2, 1895; New York *Times*, November 15, 1895, Terrell to Olney, November 7, 1895, M46, roll 59.

[7] In roll 92 of the Cleveland papers are a large number of documents urging the President to take a stronger stand.

[8] Boutelle to Olney, November 21, 1895, Richard Olney Papers, Library of Congress; Olney to Boutelle, November 23, 1895, Domestic Letters of the Department of State, 1784-1906, General Records of the Department of State, R. G. 59, National Archives Microfilm Publication M40, roll 128; Robert L. Beisner, *Twelve Against Empire: The Anti-Imperalist, 1890-1900* (New York, 1971), 146; Frederick E. Gillett, *George Frisbie Hoar* (Boston, 1934), 270; Olney to the President of the Stanford Manufacturing Company, December 26, 1895, M40, roll 128; Merle Curti, *American Philanthropy Abroad: A History* (New Brunswick, 1963), 131-132.

[9] Herbert to Selfridge, December 19, 1895, Ciphers Sent, Confidential Correspondence of the Navy Department, National Archives Record Group 45; Selfridge to Secretary of the Navy, December 21, 1895, M625, roll 29; New York *Herald*, December 20, 23, 1895.

[10] *Army and Navy Journal*, January 11, 1896, 331; New York *Herald*, January 7, 12,·1896; New York *Times*, January 13, 1896; New York *Sun*, January 13, 1896.

[11] Secretary of the Navy to Bunce, December 21, 1895, Bunce to commanding officers of vessels, January 2, 1896, Bunce to Lieutenant Fuller, January 5, 1896, in Records of the North Atlantic Squadron, Records of Naval Operating Forces, National Archives Record Group 313; *Army and Navy Journal*, February 8, 1896, 410.

[12] Memo dated December 18, 1897, attached to a letter from Angel to Sherman, M46, roll 64; Minutes of conversation, January 23, 1896, Olney papers.

[13] Gerald G. Eggert, *Richard Olney: Evolution of a Statesman* (University Park, Pennsylvania, 1974), 242, Ernest R. May, *Imperial Democracy: The Emergence of America as a Great Power* (New York, 1961), 60-61.

[14] Congressional *Record*, 54th Cong., 1st sess., 1895-1896, XXVIII, pt. 1, 144-145, 854-855, 959, 962-963, 1000-1002, 1007; pt. 2, 1011, 1014-1016.

[15] *The Nation*, February 22, 1896, 140.

[16] *The Cabinet Diary of William L. Wilson, 1896-1897*, Festus P. Summers (ed.) (Chapel Hill, 1957), 25.

[17] There is considerable correspondence on the efforts to persuade the Turkish officials to accept the *Bancroft* as a stationnaire in the Olney papers, and in M46, rolls 61, 62. See also *Foreign Relations, 1896*, 926-929; Mavroyeni Bey to Secretary of State, June 16, 1896, Notes from the Turkish Legation in the United States to the Department of State, 1867-1906, General Records of the Department of State, R.G. 59, National Archives Publication T815, roll 8.

[18] Hugo van Radolm to Holstein, November 19, 1895, Norman Rich and M. H. Fisher (eds.), *The Holstein Papers* 4 vols. (Cambridge, 1963), III, 501-502.

CHAPTER 23

A Biography of a Biographer: Alfred Thayer Mahan

Robert Seager II

University of Kentucky

The act of writing a biography of Alfred Thayer Mahan is one fraught with interpretive dangers. Especially when the task has been undertaken by a historian whose previous experience in the art form is confined to a joint study of President John Tyler and his second wife.[1] And more especially since Mahan, a veritable saint in the hagiolatry of the U.S. Navy, was himself the biographer of two of the greatest naval folk-heroes produced by the English-speaking world—Horatio Nelson and David Glasgow Farragut.[2]

Further, when one biographer is foolhardy enough to undertake the study of another, the reader should understand that he will learn much more about the author than his subject. Thus, a reader of *Alfred Thayer Mahan: The Man and His Letters* (Naval Institute Press, 1977) will discover that its author is a student in the traditional "warts and all" school of biography, if indeed there is such a school, and that his matriculation therein is without benefit of the Creator, Karl Marx, Sigmund Freud, the New Leftists, or the Cliometricians. In sum, his is a rather non-faddish approach to biography in which the subject ultimately emerges as neither saint nor sinner, genius nor dunce, exploiter nor exploited.

The author's biography of Mahan reveals, too, in its transparent inadequacies, that the biographical enterprise is a difficult and inexact business. At best, biography is history writ small and crooked. The biography of a biographer, however, is even more narrowly circumscribed, since it is history seen by one observer through the eyes of another, the latter usually far removed in time and space from his own subject's original line of vision. It is, therefore, the delayed image of a confused image, a blurred reflection cloudier than the shadows on the walls of Plato's cave—shadows further distended by egos, attitudes, biases, and mores of both observers. This writer's view of Mahan's view of Nelson's view of himself thus has built into it certain obvious technical problems and limitations.

At the same time, however, the biographical act should attempt to illuminate both the subject and the age in which he lived. For this reason, if for no other, it is helpful if the subject contributed to his age in a manner significant enough to warrant illumination. Certainly, Farragut and Nelson met the test of historical significance, as biographer Mahan demonstrated. And so too does Captain Mahan himself. His famous book, *The Influence of Sea Power Upon History, 1660-1783,* published in 1890, not only revolutionized the manner in which thinking men regarded navies and naval warfare, it had a powerful impact on the way Americans looked at, and acted within, the competitive state system in which they found themselves living at the turn of the twentieth century.[3]

Mahan did not make these contributions to the world naval community and to his country with his biographies of Nelson and Farragut. Instead, he made America and the world conscious of naval power with his three great narrative studies of the influence of sea power on history, his so-called "sea power series."[4] Biography was not Mahan's strong suit. It was, as he conceived it, a device by which the nineteenth century moral and ethical principles in which he strongly believed might best be handed down to successive generations. At another level, he regarded biography as a microcosm of the larger historical stage upon which various God-given principles and cosmic laws moved, awaiting human discovery and understanding. He used biography to illustrate the workings of these principles at the heroic human level, pausing only to pass personal judgments on the character of his chosen subjects—that is, on their moral turpitude, ethical constancy, and professional behavior as they made their ways through their naval careers and through their personal lives.

He seems also to have believed in the adage that if one cannot speak well of the dead one should say little or nothing about them. Certainly, his biography of Farragut was wholly uncritical and non-analytical; it was a paean of praise to the saintly Hero of Mobile Bay. His biography of the Hero of Trafalgar was similar in tone and thrust, save in Mahan's rather naive treatment of the unsightly wart that was Nelson's adulterous relationship with the provocative Lady Hamilton.

The last was an interpretive reaction deeply rooted in Mahan's upbringing, in his own family life, and in his Victorian sense of manners. It was also related to his notions of sexual propriety and to his opinion of the acceptable social role of nineteenth-century middle-class women. His personal relations with his own wife and his two daughters thus seem to have had much to do with his horrified attitude toward the Nelson-Hamilton liaison at Naples in 1798-1799, and with his controversial interpretation of Nelson's responsibility for the dubious political judgments that flowed, in part, from that illicit romance. His unbending hostility toward adultery, coupled with his propensity to sustain Nelson in all other matters, almost wrecked an

279

otherwise excellent biography. Specifically, it involved him in a bitter literary struggle with British critic Francis Pritchett Badham which adversely affected the sale and professional impact of the study and forced him into a "Second Edition, Revised" in a vain attempt to support more convincingly his initial defense of Nelson's erratic political behavior at Naples in June 1799. In fine, Mahan judged his biographical subjects in the light of his own belief in an omnipotent personal God (giver of universal principles and laws), against the yardstick of a rigid sexual morality, and with reference to his own sense of acceptable professional behavior.[5]

Mahan came to his study of Farragut in 1891 fresh from the widely-heralded triumph that was the publication of his *The Influence of Sea Power Upon History*, and from his less well-known victory over his daughter Helen's developing interest in young men. His conflict with Helen occurred in July 1890 when he bluntly told the 17-year-old girl to avoid the company of those around her whose "aims and principles [are] entirely worldly—living, that is, for this world and not for the next." Nor should the young lady allow herself to "attach undue importance to, and care too much for, the comforts and pleasures of this world." As for her possible marriage:

> Since marriage and relations with men must needs be in your thoughts, let all your thoughts be under His care. . . . Ask Him that if He wishes you to marry He may guide you to the man to whose care He will entrust you. . . . To be dwelling on and looking for marriage continually is morbid. . . .

If you thus commend your future to God, He will surely direct it. Unlike the Emperor Constantine at Milvian Bridge, the prayerful Helen received no convenient sign from Heaven in the matter. She died in 1963, at age 89, unpursued, unimpaired, and unmarried. Her sister Ellen died in 1947 at age 70 in a similar state of grace.[6]

Indeed, Mahan successfully crushed the desire of both of his daughters for personal independence, for lives of their own, by reducing them to little more than servants in his house. Not only did he seal them off from possible suitors, he forbade their reading of the literature of the day that in any way touched explicitly upon sexual relationships. To the novels of Emile Zola, for example, he reacted with "utter loathing—a moral feeling resembling physical nausea." This attitude toward sexual realism he conveyed to his daughters, both of whom paid obeisance to the wishes of their imperious father in this and all matters. Unhappily, their unquestioning and selfless obedience to him over the years was occasionally punctuated with severe bouts of mental depression.[7]

Mahan approached Farragut with his mind already made up on just what immutable "principles" were demonstrably operating in God's Universe. Developed in his first *Influence of Sea Power* volume, these principles were essentially two in number: the strategic principle that naval command of the sea had powerfully influenced, if not mainly determined, the course of history; and the tactical principle that the achievement of firepower concentration in combat invariably won the great fleet battles that ensured command of the sea. Underlying both of these views was his belief that the study and understanding of what he termed the "Art of War," its axioms, principles, and laws, as these were revealed in history by the Creator, was the proper business of naval officers, especially those intellectuals among them who were attached to the nascent Naval War College, founded in 1884. Such officers, on the other hand, should not overly concern themselves with what Mahan deprecatingly called the "Materials of War," that is, the navy's ships, ordnance, and propulsion systems. Technological changes in naval architecture and weapons, he maintained, in no way influenced the workings of the universal principles that had governed warfare through the ages.

To a large extent, therefore, his biography of Farragut was a display case for many of the intellectual and professional biases he had come to embrace since his first assignment to the War College faculty in 1886. In it, he argued, as he had not in *The Gulf and Inland Waters*, his 1883 book on the naval history of the Civil War, that the Confederacy had been defeated by the ability of the U.S. Navy to seize and exercise command of the sea. This it had accomplished with its blockade and with its stirring victories on the Mississippi and at Mobile Bay.[8] Throughout the book he called attention to the "leading principles of warfare," urged upon his readers the study of "tactical science," and affirmed the existence of a "science of strategy." In Mahan's telling of it, the self-educated Farragut was a brilliant strategist and tactician because his heart was morally pure and because "the custom of reading had made him familiar with the biography and history of his profession." And in a final crescendo of patriotic fervor, Mahan concluded the volume with the observation that the heroic Farragut was the equal of Lord Nelson in all naval matters logistical, strategical, and tactical, a comparison that amused British reviewers of the book no end.[9]

Similarly, Farragut the man emerged from Mahan's pages as a cardboard figure absolutely perfect in his personal qualities, particularly in his marital and religious life. Just as Mahan later claimed that God had personally brought him to the discovery of the concept of the influence of sea power on history,[10] so too was Farragut depicted as being on intimate speaking terms with the Creator. Specifically, in his description of the Battle of Mobile Bay, Episcopalian Mahan assured his reading audience that God had spoken directly and personally to the Episcopal Commodore, urging him to push on through the Confederate mine field that had claimed the *Tecumseh*. As Farragut asked at that critical moment: "Oh, God, who created man and gave him reason, direct me what to do. Shall I go on?" And God responded: "Go on."

With such excellent command connections as these, Farragut could scarcely be viewed as less than an exemplary husband as well. Predictably, Mahan pronounced him wholly ideal in this regard, noting that "infidelity or neglect of a wife was, in truth, in the estimation of the Admiral, one of the most serious blots upon a man's character, drawing out always his bitterest condemnation." He especially lauded Farragut's tender care of his invalid first wife, a woman "so helpless" that her husband "was obliged to lift her and carry her about like a child." Such attitudes toward God and marriage, apparently shared by Farragut and Mahan alike, made the latter's *Life of Nelson* a difficult book to write.[11]

Nevertheless, it was a far better book than his *Farragut* which was slapped together in five months in late 1891 and early 1892 while Mahan was simultaneously finishing his brilliant *The Influence of Sea Power Upon the French Revolution and Empire, 1793-1812,* (1892), and while he was serving briefly and uselessly in Washington as an advisor to Secretary of the Navy Benjamin P. Tracy during the American-Chilean war scare. Indeed, Mahan dashed off *Farragut* mainly to ingratiate himself further with Tracy, whose protégé he had become. The book was also part of his strategy to avoid hated sea duty, to draw the Secretary's favorable attention to the historical, analytical, and theoretical work being done at the Naval War College, and to arrange with Tracy his reassignment to Newport as head of the struggling institution. The Secretary ultimately obliged him on all counts.

Historiographically considered, however, the *Farragut* volume was little more than an unimaginative rewrite of Loyall Farragut's eulogistic biography of his father (1879). To this ready-made base Mahan added some warmed-over operational data he had included in his *The Gulf and Inland Waters.* He then applied to the derivative product a thin coating of sea-power hypothesis and the gratuitous comparison of Farragut with Lord Nelson noted above. In so doing, he knew that he had produced a distinctly second-rate piece of work. "The great defect in my *Farragut*," he later lamented, "was that I had no data with which to depict the *man.*" Conversely, his complaint about his study of Nelson was that there was far too much intimate personal material about the British admiral to be mastered by a biographer. The timing of *Farragut* was also poor in that it was published at precisely the same time as was his second *Influence* book. In the wake of Nelson at Trafalgar, Farragut at Mobile Bay sank out of sight. From the standpoint of royalties earned, *Farragut* was Mahan's greatest disaster, as commercially disappointing as it was interpretively superficial.[12]

The departure of the able Tracy from office in March 1893 marked the beginning of Mahan's two-volume *Life of Nelson,* by far his most deeply researched and most readable book. Banished to sea as captain of the U.S.S.

Chicago by an unsympathetic Francis H. Ramsay, Chief of the Bureau of Navigation, who muttered something to the effect that it was not the business of naval officers to write books, Mahan found himself in England on three occasions in 1893-1894. There he did considerable research in Nelson primary source materials, especially personal letters; and there he began to set his *Life of Nelson* to paper. His punishment for this activity was two unfavorable fitness reports from Rear Admiral Henry Erben, commander of the European Station, a rough, ready, and eczematous sailor of the old school who flew his broad pennant in the *Chicago*. Erben, who was certainly no intellectual, correctly charged Mahan with paying more attention to the Nelson manuscript than to his duties as skipper of the vessel.[13]

But out of his unhappy two-year cruise in the *Chicago* came Mahan's scheme for his *Life of Nelson*. The book, he decided, would "contribute something further towards disengaging the figure of the hero from the glory that cloaks it." Eulogy that it turned out to be, the study did nothing of the sort. The Hero remained fully cloaked, except perhaps in the boudoir of Lady Hamilton. Nevertheless, biographer Mahan did work out a definite methodological approach to Nelson, as he had done five years earlier in his *Admiral Farragut:*

> The author's method has been to make a careful study of Nelson's voluminous correspondence, analyzing it, in order to detect the leading features of temperament, traits of thought, and motives of action . . . and partly by such grouping of incidents and utterances . . . to emphasize particular traits, or particular opinions, more forcibly than when such testimonies are scattered far apart, as they would be if recounted in a strict order of time.

This, he held, could not be done satisfactorily "without concentrating the evidence from time to time."[14]

So it was that in his *Nelson* book Mahan began to work toward the notion of what he would come to call "subordination," or the methodological device of grouping ("concentrating") selected facts around various transcendent historical themes thought to exist in the Universe—such as the influence of sea power on history. The act of "concentration, the watchword of military action, and the final end of all combination" came most naturally and easily to the military historian, said Mahan, because such historians best understood that "facts must be massed as well as troops if they are to prevail against the passive resistance of indolent mentality." The purpose of this particular manipulation of data was therefore to "prove" the philosophical existence of various historical themes lurking in the Universe, awaiting discovery. Once individually discovered and proven, they would at a future date be brought collectively together by some historian chosen by God—a devout person who would then properly synthesize them into the harmonious Oneness that would at last reveal to mankind the larger cosmic meaning of History and God's dominant role therein. Mahan developed his ideas on subordination at length in his presidential address to the American Historical Association in 1902.[15]

But describing the methodology that he called "subordination" was easier than applying it to the writing of biography. Because of this, Mahan complained to his publisher, and to others, that a biography of Nelson, about whom there was such a wealth of primary factual material, involved for him a much more difficult job of organization, concentration, and synthesis than he had experienced in philosophizing about history in his first two *Influence* books, both of which were broadbrush treatments based largely on secondary sources. As he described the different and more complex historiographical problems he encountered in writing his *Life of Nelson:*

> I find biography, according to my aims and aspirations, far harder work than philosophizing over history. . . . I find that difficulty greater than I had thought—writing biography. I mean . . . the handling of an immense amount of material . . . its proper sorting and adjustment . . . greatly taxes me, for my strength has been, as far as I can judge, rather in singling out the great outlines of events and concentrating attention upon them, than in the management of details. . . . The expenditure of labor has been much greater than on the same amount of product in other books; from which I reason that biography is not an economical use of brain power for me. . . . I have to confess . . . the extreme difficulty of the mosaic work, which most accurately defines my attempt; mosaic, because built up of innumerable minute fragments; difficult, because necessary so to blend them as not to show the joints nor make the differences of shading conspicuous.[16]

Equally difficult was how to explain the rust on Nelson's moral armor in a book, written by a confirmed Anglophile, that was laudatory throughout—not only of Nelson himself, but of the strategic, tactical, and historical sagacity of the entire Royal Navy in the years 1775-1805. How, then, was it that a man of Nelson's outward religious devotion, undoubted courage in combat, professional integrity, and strategic brilliance, could commit open adultery with a common, vulgar strumpet like Lady Hamilton? Or so Mahan regarded her. How could Horatio Nelson, the very "Embodiment of the Sea Power of Great Britain," the tactical genius who had literally saved the magnificent British Empire at the Nile, and again at Trafalgar, abandon a nice, sexless, homely women like Lady Nelson and flee to the arms of a beautiful, clever, amoral, sexually aggressive tart like Emma, there to father by her a bastard daughter?

For Mahan, this was not a rhetorical question, as some historians today might assume it to be. It was for him a tragic Jekyll and Hyde contradiction in Nelson's personality that demanded theoretical resolution. But in attempting to explain the interpretive dilemma inherent in the Lord Nelson-Lady Hamilton liaison, biographer Mahan brought down on his head the polite laughter of British reviewers of the book.

The somewhat circuitous solution to the problem worked out by the author was to extol and defend Lady Nelson as an estimable woman who was kind, gentle, good, and long-suffering—a fine wife whom Nelson truly and deeply loved in his heart of hearts, even though there was a seven-year period at the end of his life during which he seemed not to persist in his fundamental connubial commitment to her. "My sympathies are greatly enlisted on behalf of Lady Nelson," he told his publisher as the manuscript took final shape; "I have been careful to bring out Lady Nelson's side." In adamantly defending Lady Nelson, he was also, in a manner of speaking, lauding the virtues of his own wife of 25 years, Ellen Evans Mahan, an unexciting lady who in thought, word, deed, personality, and plainness was very much like Frances Nelson. She was certainly very much unlike the beautiful, scheming, and sensuous Emma Hamilton, the evil serpent in the Hero's garden on whom Mahan placed the blame for Lord Nelson's marital and political lapses in Naples in 1798-1799. But how did Nelson fall under the influence of such a terrible woman in the first place? The biographer's explanation was disingenuous at best. Nelson's "unhappy passion" for Lady Hamilton, he argued, was caused by his battle wounds, "especially that on the head received at the Nile" in August 1798. If so, the passionate sequela of a scalp crease lasted for seven long years.[17]

Armed with the convenient, if not persuasive, medical rationalization that it was "That Hamilton Woman" who had seduced the war-weary Nelson to the Neapolitan-Royalist cause in 1798-1799 and made of him such a violent and irrational anti-Jacobin, Mahan nonetheless chose to defend on narrow political grounds the admiral's subsequent judgments in support of Britain's leading Italian allies against France. These dubious comrades-in-arms were King Ferdinand I and Queen Maria Carolina, ruling monarchs of the opéra bouffe Kingdom of Naples (Kingdom of the Two Sicilies). It was to the morally relaxed and relaxing court of these improbable rulers that Emma's husband, the aging and senile Sir William Hamilton, was accredited as British minister; it was also the place to which Nelson repaired for rest and recuperation immediately after his great victory at the Nile. While Mahan agreed that Nelson's political actions in Naples in June 1799 might be viewed as erratic, harsh, and impulsive, he undertook to explain these failings, as well as the Hero's sexual improprieties, in larger and less personal philosophical terms. Nelson, he maintained, was simply a dichotomous individual. In his essential personality, character, and genius, he was the miraculous, creative, brilliant synthesis of a dialectical contradiction.

Sheer nonsense, snorted British historian Spenser Wilkinson in his otherwise highly favorable review of Mahan's book in the *National Review* for July 1897:

285

When Captain Mahan begins a synthesis, when, having taken his hero to pieces, he puts him together again, I cannot feel quite satisfied. The question here is: How do judgment and determination come together in the same man? Captain Mahan finds the cement in the shape of "genius." This is to my mind a synonym for miracle, and amounts to giving up the problem. . . . In him [Nelson] judgment and determination are inseparable; they are two sides of the same thing. If to Captain Mahan their union seems miraculous, the reason is that his career has been a different one. . . . The passionate attachment to Lady Hamilton is just what was to be expected from a man of Nelson's temperament. It matters little to us what Lady Hamilton's character seemed to be to others; to Nelson she supplied what his character absolutely required—a person from whom his devotion could meet with an expressive response.

True, Nelson's fiery temperament expressed itself in almost identical ways on King George's quarterdecks and in Lady Hamilton's boudoir. Mahan scarcely needed to conjure up a dialectical synthesis of contradictory traits to obscure that obvious fact. As William O'Connor Morris delicately instructed the author, in another complimentary notice of the book, Lady Nelson's "somewhat cold, emotionless, and commonplace nature made her no fit helpmeet for a hero of his enthusiastic character."[18]

Other reviewers, mostly friendly, joined Wilkinson and Morris in further criticizing Mahan for being far too lenient on the Hero for two ill-advised political decisions he made in June 1799 when British and Neapolitan-Royalist forces recaptured Naples from the French and their Neapolitan-Republican allies.

The first of these was Nelson's role in arbitrarily cancelling a capitulation-amnesty agreement worked out on the scene by the Royalist commander, Cardinal Fabrizio Ruffo, with the assistance and concurrence of Captain Edward J. Foote, the senior Royal Navy officer present. This arrangement was made on June 23, the day before Nelson, his squadron, and Emma returned to Naples. In voiding the agreement, designed to prevent the senseless shedding of blood, the admiral clearly exceeded his authority from King Ferdinand I. Worse, his act triggered a local bloodbath as the victorious Royalists wreaked vengeance on their defeated Republican compatriots.

A second decision made by Lady Hamilton's lover four days after he arrived in Naples, was to order the arrest, kangaroo court-martial, and speedy hanging of Admiral Francesco Caracciolo, a Neapolitan career officer who had defected to the Republican cause in the city during the French occupation in the Spring of 1799 and had then shown the bad manners to fight against the Royal Navy. Since it was not then, nor was it to become, the historical habit of victorious British admirals to hang defeated enemy commanders, whatever their manifold political sins and wickednesses, the Caracciolo affair subsequently entered British naval annals as one of Nelson's less glorious moments.

Mahan's labored defense of the Hero in both instances was built on highly technical, legalistic, and semantic grounds. It turned on his dubious assertion that Nelson was merely acting on the orders of, or was otherwise carrying out the will of, Ferdinand I who remained in Sicily during June. Nelson's powers, said Mahan, were "unlimited powers as representative of the King." But no evidence, other than circumstantial, was adduced to support this contention. To be sure, Mahan admitted that Nelson had displayed a lamentable lack of generosity in both the amnesty and Caracciolo matters; but this he also blamed on the noxious influence of Emma Hamilton, who had long served as the reactionary Queen Maria Carolina's confidante and agent on the confused Neapolitan political scene. He further absolved Nelson of all wrong-doing with the observation that "despite his fearlessness of responsibility, he was always careful not to over-pass the legal limits of his authority, *except* when able to justify his action by what at least appeared to himself adequate reasons." Such an exception, of course, can be used to rationalize any decision.[19]

Leading the attack on Mahan's vigorous defense of Nelson was F. P. Badham, British expert in Classical and New Testament history, and amateur naval historian, who emphasized in a half-dozen polemical reviews and articles in 1897-1899 that the admiral had absolutely no authority whatever from Ferdinand I, legal, diplomatic or other, to behave as he had at Naples in June 1799. To drive home his point, Badham cited documentary evidence reposing in the British Museum and in the Public Record Office, some of it in the Italian language, that Mahan had either overlooked in his research or had minimized in his account.

Not until late 1898, following his return from active duty in Washington during the Spanish-American War, was Mahan able to launch a counter-attack. By this time it had become apparent to him, and to Little, Brown and Company, his publisher, that Badham's effective assault had cut sharply into the sales of the book and that a second edition (which was finally published in mid-1899) might stimulate sales and allow him to correct errors which, he privately admitted, had crept into the first edition. But, he assured his publisher, "nothing has turned up that affects the *Life* as a *portrait*. The errors of fact are entirely unimportant. The pages . . . require altering not because erroneous, but in order to meet an ill-founded attack."

To parry that attack he did little more than add 18 pages to the end of Volume I of the first (1897) edition. This addendum incorporated some additional English and Italian primary source material and caused him, he complained, "more trouble than any equal amount of result I have ever pro-duced." No other changes were made in the so-called "Second Edition, Revised." Nor in the revision did Mahan give an inch in his earlier defense of Nelson's erratic command at Naples. While his arguments in 1899 were more detailed, and were better researched, they were no more persuasive than they had been two years before; and the evidence on which they were based was no less circumstantial.[20]

Nevertheless, the Nelson biography and the bitter controversies it aroused convinced Mahan that biography was not his forte. He therefore turned down an offer to write a life of William B. Cushing, hero of the destruction of the Confederate ram *Albemarle* in the Roanoke River in North Carolina in 1864. He had known Cushing personally in the service and had liked him. Mrs. Cushing was eager to turn over to him the intrepid Lieutenant's personal papers, intimate material of the kind he had not had available for his *Admiral Farragut*. But Mahan said no. "There will be very little money in it judging by *Farragut*," he concluded.[21]

Not only were Mahan's biographies of Farragut and Nelson financial disappointments to him at a time when he could command up to $500 for an article in a popular magazine, biography as a form did not well lend itself to his subordinationist method of writing history. It did not adapt itself easily to the arbitrary selection, arrangement, and concentration of facts designed to illustrate and support historical truths he had already discovered and affirmed. The transcendent notion of the influence of sea power on history, for example, was far easier for Mahan to demonstrate than was the earthy influence of a scalp wound on the political and sexual life of Horatio Nelson. As Mahan defined what he meant by "subordination," and as he later extolled its methodological values and virtues in the writing of history:

> Facts won't lie if you work them right; but if you work them wrong, a little disproportion in the emphasis, a slight exaggeration of color, a little more or less limelight on this or that part of the grouping and the result is not truth, even though each individual fact be as unimpeachable as the multiplication table.[22]

But he had so much difficulty working the facts "right" in defending Nelson at Naples that he abandoned the biographical enterprise for good. From an economic standpoint, it was simply not worth his time and energy. Nor did he relish losing public debates to the likes of F. P. Badham. His enormous ego rebelled at such visible defeats.

What did survive the Nelson biography in a theoretical and methodological sense was Mahan's subsequent use of the idea of the dialectical clash of opposites, and their resultant syntheses, to explain the inevitability of war in history, and to argue that only through such bloody conflict had mankind made progress toward higher forms of civilization. He maintained in 1902, for instance, in his presidential address to the American Historical Association, that history

> may indeed be the conflict of two opposites, as in the long struggle between freedom and slavery, union and disunion, in our own land;

but the unity nevertheless exists. It is not to be found in freedom, not yet in slavery, but in their conflict it is. Around it group in subordination the many events, and the warriors of the political arena whose names are household words among us to this day. All form part of the great progress as it moved onward to its consummation [in civil war].

By June 1903 he was saying that "the two great oppositions inherent in naval administration—civil versus military, unity of action against multiplicity of activities—are but a reflection of the essential problem of warfare . . . the difficulty of the Art of War consists in concentrating in order to fight and disseminating in order to subsist. . . . The problem is one of embracing opposites." And as he told historian James Ford Rhodes on another occasion: "The line between controlling events and being controlled by them, would, I imagine, be difficult to draw; and, as in most matters, truth is best secured by holding both sides of the proposition—men both control events and are controlled by them. A mighty movement cannot be withstood, but it may be guided or deflected. Between events and man's will there is a resultant of forces."[23]

None of this came from Hegel or Marx. In fact, there is no evidence whatever that Mahan ever read the works of those prominent nineteenth-century dialecticians. The idea came instead from the curious Neo-Pythagorean works of his uncle, the Reverend Milo Mahan, amateur numerologist, Professor of Ecclesiastical History at The General Seminary in New York City, and later rector of St. Paul's Episcopal Church in Baltimore. Milo argued in two books written in the 1860's that there was symmetry, proportion, and order in the Universe. This order was revealed in the predictable mathematical relationships of various numbers found throughout the Universe and especially in the language of the Bible. These "Divine Numbers," as he called them, proved the existence of a supernatural intelligence that pervaded Scripture, History, and the Universe. In sum, they revealed the existence of the rational God who had scattered them throughout His creation, including His Word, for the purpose of giving men clues to the fact of His being. Indeed, some of the numbers found in the Bible, said Milo, "occur so often in connection with certain classes of ideas that we are naturally led to associate the one with the other." For example, he associated the number *Eight* with the *Resurrection* of Christ, arguing that *Eightness* and the *Resurrection* were expressions of the same reality. Buried in his "Divine Numbers" he discovered also the operation of what might be termed a Pythagorean Dialectic. The numbers *Eight* and *Thirteen*, he asserted, held, in their dichotomy, and in their synthesis, the key to all historical conflict and progress. As he explained this to his readers, among them his nephew:

These two, in their larger meaning, stand for two ideas which are the soul of history. The life of States, like the life of man, is a continuous manifestation of *defection, decay, apostasy, corruption, disintegration*—in short, of all that is expressed in the numeral Thirteen and in the various multiples. On the other hand, it is equally a manifestation of revival, renewal, reformation—in short, of that great idea, the cornerstone of Christian life, which finds its perfected reality in the Resurrection of Christ, and one of its most expressive symbols in the numeral Eight. History is the conflict of these two principles. Progress is the resultant of these two forces.

And how was this "progress" measured? In the material achievements of modern civilization, the goals of which, Milo affirmed, were "to replenish the earth and to subdue it, to cover every sea with ships, and every land with cities, to bind and control the wild elements of nature, to wed religion to commerce, and by their joint influence to preach the Gospel to all nations." Thirty years later his nephew Alfred was saying much the same thing in his advocacy of American imperialism.[24]

As a scriptural literalist, Milo Mahan based his analysis of Biblical numbers on his conviction that there were exactly 1,656 years between the Creation and the Flood, a belief that reduced all else in his system to mathematical and historical nonsense.

Nevertheless, he manipulated his "Divine Numbers" in much the same way that his famous nephew later worked, grouped, concentrated, and otherwise subordinated historical facts to support predetermined conclusions, chief among them the deterministic influence of sea power on the course of history. And in addition to helping Mahan later resolve his awkward Lord Nelson and Lady Hamilton problem dialectically, Milo imparted to his nephew a dialectical explanation of war as a God-given boon to mankind. War, both uncle and nephew believed, was a noble, glorious, uplifting human undertaking, an inevitable concomitant to history and to progress in history.

Still, dialectical abstraction and methodological subordination were not particularly useful to Mahan as a biographer, however helpful they were to him as sea power theorist, propagandist for U.S. imperialism, and advocate of American navalism. For this reason, the pragmatic Philosopher of Sea Power abandoned biography after two attempts at it. It was too difficult to research and write; it involved bringing together and synthesizing too many minute factual details, many of which did not "fit" his "mosaic"; it was commercially nonproductive; and it did not always lend itself to teaching clear moral lessons. Put another way, Mahan found it to arduous to "concentrate" and thus "work" his biographical facts "right." No wonder, then, that he turned back to the less demanding and far more permissive enterprise of "singling out the great outlines of events, and concentrating attention upon them," rather than undertaking again the complicated management of biographical details. Biography, he ruefully concluded, was definitely not "an economical use of brain power" for him.

290

Whether it is for any historian is largely a personal matter. But what this biographer has learned from his consideration of Alfred Thayer Mahan as a biographer is how *not* to write biography. He hastens to add, however, that he has no idea how biography *should* be written. Nevertheless, he has tentatively concluded that dialectical interpretations of history—whether Christian, Marxist, Hegelian, or Pythagorean—are exercises in religious superstition; that methodological subordination or concentration (however the term is defined) is intellectually and procedually dishonest, in that it leads invariably to a conscious manipulation of part of the available data to the end of sustaining preconceived biases; that to search for historical laws and principles in the Universe, in order thereby to demonstrate the existence of God, is about as realistic as joining an expedition to interview the Wizard of Oz; and that biography is no proper pulpit from which to preach moral, sexual, political, or ethical values to the young. Most importantly, he has learned from sad personal experience, as did Mahan, that writing biography is definitely not the royal road to financial success. Why, then, should a historian bother to write biography? This biographer answers simply: Because it is fun. Warts and all.

FOOTNOTES

[1] Robert Seager II, *And Tyler Too: A Biography of John and Julia Gardiner Tyler* (New York, 1963).

[2] A. T. Mahan, *Admiral Farragut* (New York, 1892); Mahan, *The Life of Nelson: The Embodiment of the Sea Power of Great Britain.* 2 vols. (Boston and London, 1897; Second Edition, Revised, 1899).

[3] A. T. Mahan, *The Influence of Sea Power Upon History, 1660-1783* (Boston, 1890); Robert Seager II, *Alfred Thayer Mahan: The Man and His Letters* (Annapolis, Md., 1977), 197-218, and *passim.* Cited hereafter as Seager, *Mahan.*

[4] Mahan's "sea power series" included, *The Influence of Sea Power Upon History, 1660-1783; The Influence of Sea Power Upon the French Revolution and Empire, 1793-1812.* 2 vols. (Boston, 1892); and *Sea Power in Its Relations to the War of 1812.* 2 vols. (Boston, 1905). *See also,* Mahan to James Ford Rhodes, May 20, 1906, in Robert Seager II and Doris D. Maguire, eds., *Letters and Papers of Alfred Thayer Mahan.* 3 vols. (Annapolis, Md., 1975), III, 159. Cited hereafter as *LPATM.*

[5] Parenthetically, Mahan would have been pleased to have read the biographies of himself written by Charles Carlisle Taylor and Capt. William D. Puleston, U.S.N. Both were eulogistic tributes to the Hero of Sea Power, not unlike Mahan's biography of Farragut. *See,* Charles Carlisle Taylor, *The Life of Admiral Mahan: Naval Philosopher* (London, 1920); and William D. Puleston, *Mahan: The Life and Work of Captain Alfred Thayer Mahan, U.S.N.* (New Haven, Conn., 1939).

[6] Mahan to Helen Evans Mahan, October 28, 1893; July 9, 1890; July 20, 1890, *LPATM,* II, 168-169; 13-17.

[7] Ellen Kuhn Mahan, "Recollections," *LPATM*, III, 725; Mahan to Helen Evans Mahan, December 26, 1894; June 14, *ibid.*, II, 379; 455-456; Mahan to John M. Brown, April 9, 1905, *ibid.*, III, 128; Mahan to Ellen Evans Mahan, June 15, 1894, *ibid.*, II, 288-289.

[8] Mahan, *Farragut*, 115-116, 117, 199, 207, 237, 239.

[9] *Ibid.*, 70, 218, 219, 220, 231, 239-240, 266, 288-289, 309-312, 314-315, 318.

[10] A. T. Mahan, *From Sail to Steam: Recollections of Naval Life* (New York, Reprint Edition, 1968), 276-277.

[11] Mahan, *Farragut*, 74-75, 88, 266-267, 277-278, 325.

[12] Seager, *Mahan*, 233-235, 648.

[13] *Ibid.*, 254-307.

[14] Mahan, *Life of Nelson* (1897), I, vi-vii.

[15] Seager, *Mahan*, 448-451.

[16] The quotation on the difficulty of writing biography is a composite of remarks found in Mahan to James R. Thursfield, November 21, 1895; January 10, 1896; Mahan to John M. Brown, April 11, 1896; August 31, 1896, *LPATM*, II, 436, 441, 451, 456.

[17] Mahan, *Life of Nelson* (1897), I, 36, 42-43, 142-143, 350-351, 370-372, 385-388; Seager, *Mahan*, 52-53, 81-88, 342.

[18] Spensor Wilkinson, "The New Nelson," *National Review* (July 1897); William O'Connor Morris, "Captain Mahan's Nelson," *Fortnight Review* (June 1, 1897); Seager, *Mahan*, 340-343, 665.

[19] Mahan, *Life of Nelson* (1897), I, 428-443. The concluding quotation is on p. 439. Emphasis added. *See* also, Seager, *Mahan*, 343-345.

[20] Seager, *Mahan*, 340, 345-347. For the war of words between Badham and Mahan, the so-called "Badham Contention" (1897-1900), *see*, F. P. Badham, "Nelson at Naples," *Saturday Review* (May 15, November 3, 1897), and his comments in *Athenaeum* (July 1, July 15, August 5, 1899); also, "Nelson and the Neapolitan Republicans," *English Historical Review* (April 1898), 262-282; and *Nelson at Naples: A Journal for 10-30 June, 1799.* Pamphlet. (London, 1900). Mahan responded with comments in *Athenaeum* (July 8, July 22, August 12, 1899); "The Neapolitan Republicans and Nelson's Accusers," *English Historical Review* (July 1899), 471-501; "Nelson at Naples," *ibid.* (October 1900), 699-727; and *Nelson at Naples.* Pamphlet. (London, 1900). For a comparison of Mahan's treatment of Nelson in Naples in the first and second editions of the biography, *see*, Mahan, *Life of Nelson* (First Edition, 1897), I, 428-443, and *ibid.* (Second Edition, Revised, 1899), I, 428-461.

[21] Mahan to John M. Brown, July 2, 1897; July 24, 1898; September 4, 1898; September 10, 1898, *LPATM*, II, 516, 568, 593.

[22] Mahan, *From Sail to Steam*, 168; Mahan, "Subordination in Historical Treatment," reprinted in *Naval Administration and Warfare* (Boston, 1908), *passim*; Seager, *Mahan*, 432-434.

[23] Mahan, "Subordination in Historical Treatment," *loc. cit.*, 256-257; Mahan, "The Principles of Naval Administration," *National Review* (June 1903), in *Naval Administration and Warfare*, 275-280; Mahan to Rhodes, March 26, 1899, *LPATM*, II, 629; Seager, *Mahan*, 438, 451.

[24] Milo Mahan, *Palmoni; or the Numerals of Scripture* (New York, 1862), and *Mystic Numbers* (New York, 1875, published posthumously); both are reprinted in John Henry Hopkins, ed., *The Collected Works of the Late Milo Mahan, DD.* 3 vols. (New York, 1875), II, 7-154; 155-715, together with a brief "Memoir of Milo Mahan," by Hopkins, which appears as the introduction to volume III. For a discussion of Milo Mahan, *see* Seager, *Mahan*, 445-448. Milo Mahan (1819-1870) was the half-brother of Dennis Hart Mahan (1802-1871), for many years professor of military engineering, fortifications, and tactics at the U.S. Military Academy.

CHAPTER 24

The Culebra Maneuver and the Formation of the U.S. Marine Corps' Advance Base Force, 1913-1914_____

Graham A. Cosmas and Jack Shulimson

U.S. Marine Corps Historical Center

In January 1914, a Marine brigade of 1,723 officers and men defended the tiny Caribbean island of Culebra against a simulated attack by units of the United States Atlantic Fleet. Conducted during the fleet's annual winter maneuvers, this exercise was for the Marine Corps a crucial test of its ability to perform the advance base mission which was becoming increasingly the principal rationale for the Corps' existence.[1]

The United States Navy, in the efficiency-minded Progessive Era, was trying to orient its permanent peacetime organization, training, equipment, and deployments toward its expected wartime strategy. Influenced by the doctrines of Alfred Thayer Mahan, naval leaders directed their shipbuilding programs and training activities toward creation of a battle fleet able to take command of the sea, at least in the Western Hemisphere. As part of the Navy, the Marine Corps also had to find a specific role toward which it could direct its own organization and training. The Corps' traditional missions of providing ships' policemen and sharpshooters for the fighting tops had been largely eliminated or made superfluous by modern warship technology. Fortunately for the Marines, the technological limitations of those same warships opened the way for a new mission.

This mission was occupation and defense of an advance base for the fleet. Modern battleships, in contrast to the old sailing ships of the line, required frequent refuelling, maintenance, and replenishment of stores and ammunition. Therefore, if the fleet were to operate any distance from its home ports, it had to have either permanent bases in potential overseas theaters of operations or an extensive train of supply and repair vessels.

293

Since the United States had only a few overseas possessions, the large train was the only feasible solution for the American Navy. In any naval campaign, the fleet would have to secure a temporary advance base at which to leave the train while the fighting ships sought the enemy. The fleet, then, required an accompanying land force to seize, fortify, and defend such a base. Further, in defensive operations, for example against a European power invading the Caribbean, land forces would be needed to deny such advance bases to the enemy.

Already part of the naval establishment, the Marine Corps was the logical organization to perform the advance base mission for the Navy and, indeed, any landing mission in connection with fleet operations. Traditionally, the Marines had provided ships' landing parties and guarded Navy shore installations. Moreover, during the Spanish-American War, a Marine battalion, deployed with the fleet on board its own transport, had secured Guantanamo Bay as a coaling station for the vessels blockading Santiago de Cuba, in effect establishing an advance base, although it was not called so by name. From its establishment in 1900 as a strategic planning and advisory staff for the Secretary of the Navy, the General Board assigned the advance base mission to the Marine Corps. On 22 November 1900, Brigadier General Charles Heywood, then Commandant, formally accepted the mission and pledged that the Marine Corps would cooperate gladly in carrying it out, although he warned that the effort "will necessitate very careful consideration and considerable time will be necessary for accomplishing it."[2]

In 1900, the General Board visualized the advance base force as consisting of a permanently-organized 400-man Marine battalion trained in field fortification, the landing and emplacement of heavy guns, the installation and operation of mine fields, and other coast defense activities. This battalion was to form the nucleus of a wartime expeditionary force of 1,000 men capable of seizing and holding an advance base. From 1900 through 1912, the General Board, the Navy War College, and the Marine Advance Base School refined and elaborated on the theoretical structure of the advance base force. By 1912, the Navy and Marines had adopted for planning purposes an advance base brigade divided into two 1,300-man regiments and capable of withstanding an attack by light cruisers and an accompanying landing force. One of these regiments, the fixed defense regiment, would consist of artillery, engineer, signal, searchlight, and mining companies and would have as its main armament large-caliber warship guns in temporary shore emplacements, supplemented by harbor-defense mines. The second, or mobile defense, regiment, composed of infantry reinforced by field gun and machine gun units, would repulse enemy landing forces. Both regiments, particularly the fixed defense regiment, were supposed to be kept fully organized, equipped, and trained, ready to embark on their own transports and sail with the fleet in the first days of war.

Despite the elaboration of advance base theory and doctrine during these years, practical obstacles prevented the formation of a permanent advance base force ready for deployment with the fleet. Congress never appropriated funds specifically for equipping the force, which meant that it had to compete for dollars with other programs in the rapidly-expanding Navy. The semi-independent Navy Department bureaus, especially the Bureau of Ordnance, gave the advance base force consistently low priority. As a result, in 1912 only a partial advance base outfit had been assembled, and most of the equipment composing it was obsolete.

Even if the equipment had been available, the Marine Corps would have had difficulty in providing men to use it. Although the Corps nearly doubled in size between 1900 and 1912, from 5,000 men to nearly 10,000, most of these additional Marines were required for ships' detachments and guarding Navy yards, missions which expanded as the Navy did. During most of this period, the Marines maintained a 1,000-man brigade in the Philippines, theoretically an advance base force but in fact little more than a colonial garrison. What manpower the Marines could spare from these missions was committed most of the time to the various Caribbean expeditions and interventions of the era of the "Big Stick" and "Dollar Diplomacy."

The warship detachments, which included about 2,500 Marines, were a bone of contention between the Marine Corps and a group of progressive-minded Navy officers led by Captain William F. Fullam. Fullam and his adherents, who were strong supporters of the advance base mission, argued that the Marines would have enough men to form a permanent advance base force if they would only remove what the Fullam group considered the obsolete and useless warship detachments. Marine Corps leaders, reluctant to surrender any mission, insisted that service on shipboard maintained the naval identity of the Corps as well as providing Marines with many of the skills required for advance base operations. The Marines advocated further enlargements of the Corps so that it could meet all of its responsibilities. This issue came to a head in 1908, when Fullam and his cohorts persuaded President Theodore Roosevelt to issue an executive order withdrawing the Marines from battleships and cruisers and redefining the Marine mission in terms of naval base defense and expeditionary duty. After a vigorous lobbying campaign by the Marine Corps, Congress forced Roosevelt in 1909 to put the Marines back on shipboard. The Navy Department subsequently disavowed its initial support for removing the ships' detachments out of fear that taking the Marines off warships would open the way for transfer of the entire Corps to the Army. For the next four years, the problem of Marine manpower distribution remained unresolved.

Although hampered by lack of equipment and conflicting missions, the Marine Corps gradually had begun harnessing its resources to carry out the advance base function. As early as 1901, the Corps temporarily established a small advance base school at Newport, Rhode Island. During the winter of 1902-1903, a Marine battalion of 500 men landed on Culebra island and emplaced some guns during the annual fleet maneuvers. In 1904 and again in 1907, the brigade in the Philippines conducted similar advance base drills. Prodded by the General Board, the Marines and the Navy Department in 1910 renewed and intensified the advance base effort. The Marines re-established their advance base school at Newport and moved it the following year to Philadelphia. Although interrupted periodically by deployment of its staff and students on expeditions, the school developed a systematic curriculum and increasingly focused the professional training and thought of Marine officers on the advance base problem. During 1911 and part of 1912, a Marine battalion of 300 officers and men was stationed at Philadelphia in connection with the school, constituting the nucleus of an Atlantic Coast advance base force. Furthermore, the Navy Department began collecting all the available advance base material on the East Coast, which had been scattered among a number of navy yards, at Philadelphia, and in 1912 allotted $50,000 to the Bureau of Ordnance for advance base accessories.

In this same period, the Marine Corps began consolidating its shore-based establishment for greater efficiency and expeditionary effectiveness. Taft's Secretary of the Navy, George von L. Meyer, in 1910 set forth as a major objective the concentration of most Marines at one principal station on each coast, that for the Atlantic Coast being Philadelphia. During the following year, the Marine Corps centralized recruit training at four depots and organized Marines stationed at the larger navy yards into permanent 100-man expeditionary companies. The closing of six minor navy yards and naval stations during 1911 allowed some enlargement of the Marine detachments at the remaining yards. In 1911 and 1912, the Marines began routinely forming provisional brigades of up to 2,000 men and regiments of 700 to 1,000 men, from navy yard companies and ships' detachments, for service in Cuba, Nicaragua, and the Dominican Republic. While these expeditions diverted men from advance base training, they provided Marines with invaluable experience in organizing and maneuvering what were for the Marine Corps unprecedentedly large troop formations.

By the end of 1912, all of the elements for the creation of a permanent advance base force were there to be put together. Despite the continuing diversion of Marine manpower to the Caribbean and the persistent shortages of equipment, the Marines and Navy had perfected advance base doctrine and had conducted much theoretical and some practical training, to the point where it could be put to the test.

In early 1913, the General Board decided that the time had come to conduct an actual advance base maneuver. During January, the board, after informal consultations with Marine Major General Commandant William P.

Biddle, Lieutenant Colonel Lewis C. Lucas, the Commandant of the Advance Base School, and other Marine officers, drew up a proposal to the Secretary of the Navy for an advance base exercise. On 5 February, Admiral of the Navy George Dewey, President of the board, emphasized in a letter to Secretary of the Navy Meyer that the advance base force "is an adjunct of the fleet . . . and its location, as well as its state of preparedness should be such as to enable it to go with the fleet upon short notice." It was time, he declared, to go beyond the "spasmodic efforts during the past 10 years" to organize and equip an advance base force. Dewey recommended that the assemblage of advance base equipment at Philadelphia be completed "without delay" and that an advance base brigade be organized and make an actual landing, emplace guns, and conduct target practice during the Atlantic Fleet's 1913-1914 winter maneuvers. Secretary Meyer on the same day, 5 February, approved Dewey's proposal and instructed Biddle to make the necessary arrangements for the maneuver.[3]

From February through April, the Navy and the Marine Corps worked out the size and organization of the Marine force that would participate in the maneuver. These deliberations were overshadowed by renewed violence in revolution-wracked Mexico, where General Victoriano Huerta had deposed popular President Francisco Madero. As a precautionary move during February, elements of the fleet entered Mexican waters and the Marine Corps formed a 2,000-man provisional brigade which deployed to Guantanamo for possible later commitment to Mexico. With most of his available men assigned to the Guantanamo brigade, Major General Biddle initially expressed doubts about forming a full-scale advance base brigade for the exercise and recommended instead use of only a fixed regiment of about 800 Marines. The General Board, supported by Meyer's successor in the new Wilson administration, Josephus Daniels, rejected Biddle's proposal and insisted that both fixed and mobile regiments be employed, at reduced strength if necessary. By early April, the Marine Corps had agreed to assemble a brigade of about 1,600 men for the maneuver, with two regiments, each of about 800 men. General Biddle also had submitted a detailed statement of his requirements for guns, equipment, and shipping. By this time, the likelihood of American military intervention in Mexico had diminished, and the Marine Corps had completed plans for withdrawing the brigade from Guantanamo, which would free sufficient men for formation of the projected advance base units.[4]

As serious planning for the maneuver began, the Marines' old nemesis, Captain William F. Fullam, now Aide for Inspections, challenged the Corps' ability to perform the advance base mission. Fullam used as his point of departure the report of a Navy board of officers who had inspected the Philadelphia Navy Yard during March, examining, among other functions of the yard, the advance base preparations there. In its report, issued on

19 April, the board found, to no one's surprise, that despite all of the effort since 1900, no effective advance base force yet existed and apportioned the blame for this situation about equally between the Navy Department and the Marines. The board's specific recommendations supported many longstanding Marine Corps proposals, including enlargement of the barracks and facilities at Philadelphia, provision of transports for the advance base force, and the securing of a special appropriation from Congress for completing the advance base equipment and organization. Most important, the inspection board echoed the Marine refrain that the Corps did not have enough men to meet all of its responsibilities.[5]

Beginning on 1 May, Fullam bombarded the Secretary of the Navy and the General Board with a series of memoranda on the inspection board's findings. He largely ignored those parts of the board report detailing Navy Department shortcomings and instead focused on the Marine Corps' failure to maintain permanent advance base battalions. Turning to his favorite hobbyhorse, Fullam argued that the Marines would have enough men for this purpose if they withdrew their ships' detachments. Fullam in his memoranda made several forward-looking proposals, including one for the establishment of what amounted to an amphibious task force of warships and transports with an embarked Marine battalion. Nevertheless, his principal and most controversial theme remained what he considered the maldistribution of Marine manpower, an allegation which the Marine Corps consistently challenged. For every Fullam memorandum, the Marines provided, in effect, the same answer: that the Marine Corps would form at least permanent fixed defense battalions if its manpower were increased or its expeditionary responsibilities reduced.[6]

For the most part, the General Board sided with the Marines against Fullam. On 21 July, the board in its major comments on Fullam's proposals rejected out of hand any removal of Marine ships' detachments, remarking that "this action, if persisted in, may eventually cause the loss of the Marine Corps to the Navy and its absorption by the Army." Like the Marines, the General Board pointed to the lack of equipment as the principal obstacle preventing development of an advance base force. Although rejecting Fullam's recommendation that Marines be taken off warships, the board agreed that Marine manpower was poorly distributed and that the Corps could find enough men for the advance base force without any overall increase in numbers. The board proposed that the brigade in the Philippines, which was serving no real advance base purpose, be withdrawn and that other overseas Marine garrisons be reduced to free men for advance base units. At the same time, the board expressed its confidence in the capability of the Marine Corps to conduct the advance base mission, a capability that the board believed would be "fully demonstrated by the exercises which have been laid out for the Marines . . . this coming winter." The questions raised by Fullam had little impact on the plans and preparations for the forthcoming Caribbean maneuver, but they made the success or failure of that maneuver all the more critical for the Marine Corps. By this time, the Joint Army-Navy Board had decided that the major United States Pacific naval bases would be Pearl Harbor and San Diego and that responsibility for garrisoning the Philippines belonged to the Army.[7]

With the return of the Marine brigade from Guantanamo in April and May, the organization of the units which were to take part in the winter maneuver went rapidly. On 30 June, the Commandant informed Secretary Daniels that five of the six companies of the fixed defense regiment had been formed at Philadelphia. These included artillery, mining, engineer, and signal companies, organized according to plans already drawn up by the Advance Base School. The Commandant planned to assemble the sixth company of the fixed regiment on 15 July, using men drawn from the recruit depots. Biddle also declared that the three-inch landing gun battery for the mobile regiment had been organized and was being trained at the New York Navy Yard, while the same regiment's automatic rifle company was training at the Marine Barracks in Washington, D.C. The four infantry companies for the mobile regiment, which required no specialized training, would be formed, according to Biddle, "as has heretofore been the case when the Marine Corps has been called on to furnish expeditions; that is, by an equitable reduction in the number of men at the . . . navy yards on the Atlantic coast, utilizing so far as possible the companies already organized, and adding to each organization a small proportion of those men who have nearest completed their fourteen weeks' course of training at the recruit depots."[8]

The assembly of supplies and equipment kept pace with the organization of the brigade. Guided by Commandant Biddle's requests, the bureaus issued materiel to the Advance Base School, either from their existing stocks or from new purchases. On 23 May, for example, Rear Admiral Nathan C. Twining, Chief of the Bureau of Ordnance, reported that he had already agreed to spend $50,000 for advance base equipment and now "will probably be able to supply for advance base purposes approximately $100,000" from available bureau funds.[9]

In spite of these additional purchases, the Marines had to depend heavily on what was on hand, much of which was obsolete, especially for such crucial items as five-inch and three-inch naval guns and mines. Only after much difficulty did the Marines obtain one high-powered five-inch 51-caliber naval gun for experimental purposes and prevail on the Bureau of Ordnance to borrow two 4.7-inch heavy field guns from the Army for testing as possible anti-ship weapons. The fixed regiment's five-inch battery had four five-inch 40-caliber guns, which were less effective against ships. The bureaus flatly refused to purchase draft animals for the mobile regiment's field guns, despite Marine protests that "it is . . . neither desirable nor practical to land men from the fleet to take the place of animals for this purpose."[10]

The Marines had better fortune securing transports and landing craft. At Biddle's suggestion, the Navy Department refitted the receiving ship *Hancock* at the New York Navy Yard, as a Marine transport. The Marines planned to use the *Hancock,* a 6,000-ton former ocean liner, to carry the fixed regiment and the brigade headquarters, while the existing smaller Navy transport, the *Prairie,* would embark the mobile regiment. After jurisdictional wrangling between the Bureaus of Ordnance and Construction and Repair, the Navy Department collected or built an odd assortment of landing craft. These included, in addition to the small boats of the transports, two 24-foot cutters, two motor sailing launches, two steam launches, a large steel lighter with a derrick specially constructed for landing heavy guns, and four Lundin lifeboats which could be rigged together in pairs to support rafts.[11]

By mid-summer, most of the equipment and supplies for the fixed regiment had been assembled at Philadelphia, and the troops had begun their arduous training. Captain Frederick M. Wise, commander of Company I, the three-inch naval gun company, recalled:

> . . . The easy days at Philadelphia were over. With drills and four hours a day schooling, we didn't get out of the yard until four-thirty in the afternoon. Then we had to study at night. . . .
> Hours every day in the yard we had to haul those three-inch naval guns around. We had to build a portable railroad. We had to dig pits. We had to build gun-platforms. We had to mount the guns. And then, when we had it all done, we had to tear the whole business down and do it all over again.[12]

In September, when the *Hancock* arrived at Philadelphia, the Marines added embarkation and disembarkation drills to their training schedule.

By this time, planning for the exercise was well under way. In late July, the General Board and Assistant Secretary Franklin D. Roosevelt selected Culebra, a small island 16 miles east of Puerto Rico, as the advance base site for the maneuver. During the next two months, the General Board worked out the overall schedule and objectives for the problem; Rear Admiral Charles J. Badger, Commander-in-Chief, Atlantic Fleet, prepared detailed plans for the joint activities of the fleet and the brigade; and the Advance Base School drew up the plans for the fortification and defense of Culebra.[13]

The resulting scenario and schedule of activities, approved by Secretary Daniels on 20 October, assumed that a European power, designated RED, would declare war on the United States (BLUE) on 15 December 1913. The BLUE Atlantic Fleet, with its train, would concentrate at Culebra to meet the advancing RED fleet. On 7 January 1914, the BLUE fleet would return to the U.S. east coast to counter a sudden threatened attack by a RED detachment. The BLUE train would remain at Culebra, and on 8 January the BLUE advance base force, the actual Marine brigade, would arrive on Culebra and establish its defenses. On 18 January, a presumed RED light cruiser task force, accompanied by a fast transport carrying about 1,000 troops, would appear off Culebra, its mission to destroy the BLUE advance base and capture the train. From 18 to 23 January, the U.S. Atlantic Fleet, playing the role of the RED aggressor force, would conduct a series of simulated attacks on the advance base brigade, including a landing of sailors and Marines. These joint exercises would end on the twenty-third and the Marines then would remain on the island for target practice and other training, and a possible second attack by the fleet, re-embarking for home on 9 February.[14]

Although the aggressor force in this exercise was code-named RED, the scenario was clearly derived from the Navy's BLACK plan for war with Germany. Since the turn of the century, a long series of Navy War College studies and plans had assumed that in a naval war with Germany, "Culebra is the key to the Western Atlantic and Caribbean regions," either as a concentration point for the U.S. fleet or an advance base for the attacking German fleet. In fact, as is now known, German war plans for naval operations against the United States called for the early seizure of Culebra. For the Marines, then, the forthcoming maneuver was a rehearsal for probable wartime operations as well as a test of their organization and capability to carry out the advance base mission.[15]

Marine preliminary activities for the maneuver began on 1 November when Captain Earl H. Ellis, who had recently completed a study of advance base problems at the Navy War College, left for Culebra to reconnoiter the artillery positions and camp sites designated in the Advance Base School defense plan. Upon his return, Ellis confirmed the feasibility of the planned deployments. While Ellis was still at Culebra, the Navy Department, as a result of renewed diplomatic pressure by the Wilson administration on the Huerta regime in Mexico, pushed forward by a month the formation of the mobile regiment. On 27 November, the regiment, commanded by Lieutenant Colonel John A. Lejeune, sailed from Philadelphia on the *Prairie* for Pensacola. From Pensacola, the regiment could deploy either to Mexico or to Culebra.[16]

At Philadelphia, the fixed regiment, commanded by Lieutenant Colonel Charles G. Long, began loading its equipment on board the *Hancock* on 18 December. This embarkation had many modern features, including the appointment of a single embarkation officer and a fairly sophisticated combat loading plan, which was partially disrupted by the last-minute arrival of some of the supplies. Despite difficulties in moving the heavy equipment from the warehouse to the pier, the regiment had finished embarking all of its men and materiel by noon on 3 January. Besides the six companies and

301

staff of the fixed regiment, the *Hancock* carried the brigade commander, Colonel George Barnett, and his staff and the brigade hospital. Also attached to brigade headquarters and embarked on the *Hancock* was a Marine aviation detachment of two officer-pilots and 10 enlisted mechanics with two primitive wood and fabric pusher biplanes borrowed from the Navy.[17]

At Pensacola, the mobile regiment had spent a cold, damp December, warmed for some of the younger officers by what Lieutenant Colonel Lejeune characterized as "a very gay time with the girls." On 19 December, Lejeune received orders from Headquarters Marine Corps to embark his men so as to sail on 3 January. In contrast to the fixed regiment with its heavy equipment, the more lightly armed mobile regiment had little difficulty in loading on board the *Prairie*. By 7 p.m. on 3 January, Lejeune could report his four infantry companies, automatic rifle company, and landing gun company all embarked.[18]

By 4 January, both the *Hancock* and *Prairie* were steaming toward Culebra. Conditions on both ships were crowded and uncomfortable. The appropriations for refitting the *Hancock* had run out, and the job was only partially completed. Compounding the difficulties, and despite the Marine Corps' emphasis on serving on board Navy ships, the majority of the fixed regiment had not been to sea before. Most of the men suffered from seasickness. Long remarked, "The carelessness of seasick men resulted in bad odors," but observed that the ship's food was well prepared and served "considering the circumstances." Life on the *Prairie,* if anything, was even worse. Lejeune bluntly stated that the ship "is unfitted for use as a transport." His 2d Battalion commander, Major Wendell C. Neville, compared the Marine junior officers' quarters to "a cheap Bowery lodging house."[19]

Except for the creature discomforts, the voyage was uneventful. Most of the higher-ranking officers spent much of their free time speculating on who would be chosen the new Commandant. In November, Major General Biddle had announced his intention to retire, and Colonel Barnett and Lieutenant Colonel Lejeune, both of whom had powerful political support, were active candidates for the position. Secretary Daniels had delayed naming Biddle's successor until Congress passed a law limiting the Commandant's term in office to four years. As the transports steamed toward Culebra, all Marines knew that Daniel's decision was imminent. Most informed observers, including Lejeune, who was aware of his own relatively junior rank, believed Colonel Barnett to be the front-runner. Nevertheless, for both Barnett and Lejeune, successful performance in the Culebra maneuver was all the more imperative.[20]

On 9 January, a day later than scheduled, the *Hancock* and *Prairie* dropped anchor off Culebra. Both regiments began disembarking the

302

following day. Because the *Hancock* was too large to safely enter the principal anchorages of Culebra, the Marines of the fixed regiment had to transfer themselves and their equipment onto their landing craft in the open sea. Although hampered by contrary winds and the unsuitability of some of the craft, the regiment by 18 January had managed to move its men and equipment to shore, haul its guns and materiel to the headlands where its batteries were to be located, blast out gun pits, and mount the guns, as well as setting up camp and completing mine firing stations and other installations. The fixed defense regiment was deployed along the southwestern and southern shores of the small, mountainous island, with the five-inch and three-inch naval gun batteries and the mine fields positioned to protect Great Harbor, a deep indentation in the southern shore where the hypothetical fleet train was presumed to have taken refuge.

As with the embarkation, the disembarkation of the mobile regiment went more easily. Lejeune positioned one of his infantry battalions on the southeastern tip of Culebra to protect the flank of Great Harbor, with one company located on the offshore islet of Culebrita. The other infantry battalion, supported by the automatic rifle company, deployed along the western and northwestern shores of Culebra, covering the most likely landing beaches. Lejeune placed his three-inch landing gun company on a 480-foot hill from which it could support the infantry defenses. The Marines of the mobile regiment dug trenches commanding the beaches, cleared fields of fire, and cut trails connecting their various defensive positions. They installed barbed wire entanglements, and the automatic rifle company, applying a lesson from the Russo-Japanese War, erected bomb-proof roofs over several of its gun positions. The Marines were hampered in their work by the hard rocky soil, the tough tropical vegetation, and inadequate tools. Lejeune complained:

> Machetes were of no value, the edges turning after slight use and the handles cracking. The picks were made of soft metal, and the scythes were useless for the same reason. The metal of the drills was too soft, the wire cutters did not cut. . . .[21]

While the two regiments established their positions on shore, Barnett set up brigade headquarters at the abandoned U.S. naval station near the head of Great Harbor. By the eighteenth, the Marine defenses were ready. Everyone heaped praise on the way the men had worked. Barnett later recalled:

> . . . It was a never-ending joy to be associated with men and officers who worked night and day as loyally, as incessantly under great difficulties and with as much *esprit de corps* as these men did. It was certainly a perfect joy to see them work. They dug and they blasted and pulled and dragged these guns up those mountains in a perfectly phenomenal manner.[22]

303

On the night of the 18th, ships of the Atlantic Fleet which had arrived off Culebra two days earlier, began the joint exercise. For the next two days and nights, the fleet conducted a series of simulated attacks on the Marine defenses. The destroyers made day and night reconnaissances and attempted to sweep the mine fields. Acting the part of enemy light cruisers, the battleships simulated the bombardment of the Marine shore batteries. Simultaneously, the Marine mining company tracked the enemy ships and pretended to detonate mines under them. During the day, the Marine aviators flew reconnaissance and spotting missions over the attacking ships. Marine gunners blazed away with such enthusiasm that Barnett found it necessary to order that:

> Owing to the expenditure of the very limited supply of blank ammunition for the Five-Inch Batteries, . . . those batteries will . . . simulate fire by firing one blank charge as the first round. To simulate succeeding rounds they will fire smoke pots in the afternoon and green stars from Very's pistol at night.[23]

The climax of the joint exercise occurred in the early morning hours of 21 January, when the mixed regiment of 1,200 sailors and Marines from the fleet attempted a landing. For this part of the maneuver, Rear Admiral Badger departed from his general policy for the exercise of not assigning umpires or determining victory or defeat in any particular engagement. Badger appointed Captain William S. Sims of the destroyer flotilla and eight other Navy officers umpires for the landing.

Shortly before dawn on the 21st, the assault regiment, supported by the guns of the destroyers of the 6th Division, began its landing at Firewood Bay, on the western side of Culebra. The Marines reacted rapidly. They placed heavy rifle, machine gun, and artillery fire on the approaching boatloads of sailors and Marines. Observing the action with Lejeune, Sims reported that the landing boats "were plainly visible . . . from all occupied positions, . . . due partly to the moon, which was one-quarter full, to the searchlights of the bombarding vessels playing on the hills above, to a bonfire fired by the defense, and to the fact that all bluejackets were in white uniform." As the boats reached shore, Lejeune reported, the attackers "huddled together in masses along the narrow strip of beach, . . . literally surrounded by a semi-circle of fire." The destroyers simulated a heavy bombardment that, in Sims' judgment, would have possibly silenced the Marine landing gun battery, which was firing from a dangerously exposed position; but the Chief Umpire concluded that "it is improbable that the landing force could have effected a successful landing in sufficient numbers to have made any impression on the defense. . . ." Nevertheless, as the result of a prior agreement with Barnett, Sims allowed the naval force to continue its attack from the beach. At 0700 he ordered a ceasefire and declared a victory for the defense, which had held its main line of resistance and maneuvered its reserves effectively to contain enemy breakthroughs.[24]

Although the landing and its repulse were the highlights of the maneuver, the Marines of the advance base brigade remained on Culebra for two more weeks. The joint exercise with the fleet continued through the twenty-third with additional simulated bombardments and mine sweepings. Also on the twenty-third, a 350-man fleet Marine battalion, in a second landing attempt, overran the mobile regiment company on Culebrita. After the end of the joint exercise and the departure of the fleet, the fixed regiment conducted target practice and experimental firings of the five-inch 51-caliber naval gun and the Army 4.7-inch field gun. The Marines concluded from these tests that both guns deserved further consideration as advance base weapons. The mining company attempted to fire its mines, but only succeeded in detonating one; the connecting cables to most of the mines had leaked and short-circuited the firing mechanism. During the same period, the mobile regiment conducted infantry maneuvers and field artillery target practice. Two special boards of Marine and naval officers made studies of alternate advance base sites in the Culebra area and reviewed and elaborated on the existing Culebra defense plan. Early in February, good news arrived for Barnett. At three o'clock one morning, he recalled later, his aide "came running into my room yelling like a wild Indian, telling me I had been appointed Major General Commandant of the Marine Corps." An impromptu celebration parade by pajama-clad officers and men followed in the hot and rainy darkness, concluding with champagne from the *Prairie's* mess.[25]

Even as the target practice and training continued, the Marines began dismantling their batteries and moving their heavy equipment back on board the transports. By 9 February, as originally planned, both regiments had completed re-embarkation, and the *Hancock* and *Prairie* sailed for the United States. The brigade arrived at Pensacola on 15 February. Barnett then left the brigade to assume his new duties as Commandant in Washington, turning over command to Lejeune.

The various elements of the brigade went in different directions from Pensacola, due to the continuing tension with Mexico. Part of the mobile regiment soon sailed on the *Prairie* for Vera Cruz, where, as Lejeune wryly put it, "they will wait for something to happen."[26] The fixed regiment went to Mobile and New Orleans to take part in Mardi Gras festivities. Captain Frederick H. Delano, adjutant of the mobile regiment, looked on these visits as "not good for discipline, but suppose they have to be done to keep the service in the public eye."[27]

For the Marine Corps, the Culebra maneuver was significant from many points of view. The maneuver demonstrated that the Marines could organize an advance base force on short notice and carry out all the complex steps of an advance base operation. The Marines had learned many practical lessons, including the need for expeditionary packaging of supplies and equipment, a more accurate assessment of the proper number and types of landing craft, the importance of adequate ground transportation once on shore, and the value of aircraft for reconnaissance and possibly bombing enemy ships. Many of the practices employed by the Marines in the maneuver, such as combat loading of vessels, would become mainstays of later amphibious doctrine. Participating in the Culebra maneuver, besides Commandant-designate Barnett, were two other future Commandants of the Marine Corps: Lieutenant Colonel Lejeune, commanding the mobile regiment, and Major Wendell C. Neville, commander of one of Lejeune's battalions. Captain Earl H. Ellis, the brigade intelligence officer, would become one of the Marine Corps' most influential early articulators of amphibious doctrine.

Most important, a Marine advance base force at last came into being. The two regiments of the brigade, although diverted to expeditionary duty at Vera Cruz and later in Haiti, the Dominican Republic, and Cuba, maintained a continuous existence until replaced by the East Coast Expeditionary Force following World War I. It can be said, then, that the advance base brigade at Culebra was the forerunner of the modern Fleet Marine Force.

FOOTNOTES

[1] This paper is based on the following sources: Records of the General Board of the Navy, Operational Archives Branch, Naval Historical Division, Washington, D.C., particularly Files 408 and 432 for the years 1900-1915; Records of the U.S. Marine Corps, RG 127, U.S. National Archives, especially File 1975 for the years 1900-1915; Black War Plan, Ref. No. 5y, War Portfolio No. 1, General Board Records, hereafter *Black War Plan*; General Records of the Navy Department, RG 80, U.S. National Archives; Capt. Earl H. Ellis, Report of a Reconnaissance Made of Culebra Island and Adjacent Cays, 8-23 Nov 1913, with Enclosures, USMC Records, FRC, Suitland, Md., hereafter Ellis, *Reconnaissance Report*; Biographical and Subject Files, Reference Section, History and Museums Division, Headquarters Marine Corps; George Barnett Papers in Personal Papers Collection, History and Museums Division, Headquarters Marine Corps; John A. Lejeune Papers, William F. Fullam Papers, William S. Sims Papers, and Josephus Daniels Papers, Library of Congress; Annual Published Reports of the Secretary of the Navy and the Commandant of the Marine Corps, 1900-1915; *Army and Navy Journal*, 1900-1915.

The following secondary sources have been consulted: Robert Debs Heinl, Jr., *Soldiers of the Sea* (Annapolis, 1962); Frank O. Hough, Verle E. Ludwig, and Henry I. Shaw, Jr., *Pearl Harbor to Guadalcanal*, Vol. I of *History of U.S. Marine Operations in World War II* (Washington, 1958); Jeter A. Isely and Philip A. Crowl, *The United States Marines, 1775-1975* (New York, 1976); Raymond G. O'Connor, "The U.S. Marines in the Twentieth Century: Amphibious Warfare and Doctrinal Debates," *Military Affairs*, 38:3 (Oct 1974), pp. 97-103. We are grateful to Dr. Allan R. Millett for permitting us to examine the pertinent draft chapters of his forthcoming history of the U.S. Marine Corps.

[2] President, General Board, ltr to Secretary of the Navy, dtd 6 Oct 1900, and BGen Comdt, USMC, ltr to President, General Board, dtd 22 Nov 1900, File 408, GB Records. For general development of the early advance base force, see Graham A. Cosmas and Jack Shulimson, "Continuity and Consensus: the Evolution of the Marine Advance Base Force, 1900-1924" (Paper Delivered at Citadel Conference on War and Diplomacy, 1977).

[3] Proceedings of the General Board, Vol. 5 (1913), pp. 10, 18, 22, 32; President, General Board, ltr to Secretary of the Navy, dtd 5 Feb 1913, and Secretary of the Navy, 1st Endorsement, to MGen Cmdt, dtd 5 Feb 1913, File 1975-10, RG 127.

[4] MGen Cmdt, USMC, ltr to Secretary of the Navy, dtd 24 Feb 1913, File 5503, RG 80; President, General Board, ltr to Secretary of the Navy, dtd 8 Mar 1913, File 432, GB Records; MGen Cmdt, USMC, ltr to Secretary of the Navy, dtd 10 Apr 1913, File 1975-10, RG 127.

[5] Report of Inspection of Navy Yard, Philadelphia, conducted 25-28 Mar 1913, from Board of Inspection, Navy Yard, Philadelphia, to Secretary of the Navy, dtd 19 Apr 1913, File 1975-10, RG 127, and Permanent File Binder No. 27, RG 38, Board of Inspection for Shore Stations.

[6] See Aide for Inspections, memos to Secretary of the Navy, dtd 1 May, 23 June, and 28 June 1913, File 432, GB Records; MGen Cmdt, USMC, ltr to Secretary of the Navy, dtd 17 May 1913, File 1975-10, RG 127; MGen Cmdt, ltr to Secretary of the Navy, dtd 7 June 1913, File 432, GB Records.

[7] President, General Board, memo to Secretary of the Navy, dtd 21 July 1913, File 432, GB Records.

[8] MGen Cmdt, USMC, memo to Secretary of the Navy, dtd 30 June 1913, File 408, CB Records.

[9] Chief, Bureau of Ordnance, memo to Navy Department (Materiel), dtd 23 May 1913, File 1975-10, RG 127.

[10] Chief, Bureau of Ordnance, memo to Navy Department (Materiel), dtd 26 May 1913, and HQMC, Memo to Secretary of the Navy (Personnel), dtd 11 July 1913, File 1975-10, RG 127; Senior Member, General Board, ltr to Secretary of the Navy, dtd 26 July 1913, File 408, GB Records.

[11] MGen Cmdt, USMC, memo to Secretary of the Navy, dtd 10 April 1913; Chief, Bureau of Navigation, memo to Council of Aides, dtd 24 April 1913; and Navy Department, memo to Bureau of Ordnance, dtd 21 May 1913; File 1975-10, RG 127. Senior Member Present, General Board, memo to Secretary of the Navy, dtd 26 July 1913, File 432, GB Records; Bureau of Construction and Repair, memo to Navy Department (Materiel), dtd 15 Aug 1913, File 5103, RG 80.

[12] Frederic M. Wise, A Marine Tells It to You (New York, 1929), p. 119.

[13] Acting Secretary of the Navy, ltr to President, General Board, dtd 15 July 1913, File 1975-10, RG 127; 2d Senior Member, General Board, ltr to Secretary of the Navy, dtd 26 July 1913, with Navy Department Approval, dtd 29 July 1913, File 432, GB Records; C. E. Vreeland, memo to Secretary of the Navy, dtd 13 Sept 1913, Subj: Comprehensive Plan for Work of Advance Base Expedition from date of Embarkation to Completion of Work, File 1975-80-20, RG 127; Charles G. Long, memo to MGen Cmdt, dtd 5 Oct 1913, forwarding Advance Base School plan for defense of the Island of Culebra, in Ellis Reconnaissance Report; U.S. Atlantic Fleet, memo, dtd 13 Oct 1913, re: Joint Exercise of Fleet and Advance Base Detachment, Winter 1914, in Ellis Reconnaissance Report, hereafter Atlantic Fleet Plan.

[14] Atlantic Fleet Plan.

[15] *Black War Plan*, p. 1, and "Studies and Conclusions of Naval War College, 1901-13," App. D, *Black War Plan*. For references to the German plans, see Richard W. Turk, "The United States Navy and the Taking of Panama, 1901-03," *Military Affairs* 38 (October 74); pp. 92-96, and John A. S. Grenville and George Berkeley Young, *Politics, Strategy, and American Diplomacy: Studies in Foreign Policy, 1873-1917* (New Haven, Conn., 1966), pp. 305-307.

[16] *Ellis Reconnaissance Report* and LtCol John A. Lejeune, Report to Brigade Comdr, Subj: Maneuvers and Operations, dtd 31 Jan 1914, File 1975-80-20, RG 127, hereafter Lejeune, *2d Regiment Report*.

[17] 1st Adv Base Regt, Order No. 1, dtd 17 Dec 1913, File 1975-80-20, RG 127, and LtCol Charles G. Long, Report to Brigade Comdr, Subj: Operations of 1st Regiment from Dec 18, 1913 to January 25, 1914, dtd 30 Jan 1914, File 1975-80-20, RG 127, hereafter Long, *1st Regt Report*.

[18] Lejeune, *2d Regt Report* and LtCol John A. Lejeune, ltr to Augustine Lejeune, dtd 30 Dec 1913, Lejeune Papers.

[19] Long, *1st Regt Report;* Lejeune, *2d Regiment Report;* CO 2d Battalion, 2d Advance Base Regiment, Report to CO, 2d Regiment, Subj: Maneuvers and Operations, dtd 27 Jan 1914, File 1975-80-20, RG 127.

[20] Josephus Daniels, *The Wilson Era: Years of Peace, 1910-1917* (Chapel Hill, 1944), pp. 322-324; *Army and Navy Journal* 6 (Dec 1913), p. 437; Folder, "Candidacy for Commandant, 1900-1913," Lejeune Papers.

[21] Lejeune, *2d Regiment Report*.

[22] U.S. Congress, House, Committee on Naval Affairs, *Hearings on Estimates Submitted by the Secretary of the Navy, 1915*, 63d Congress, 1st Session, 7 Dec 1914, p. 446.

[23] 1st Advance Base Brigade, Brigade Order No. 6, dtd 19 Jan 1914, File 1975-80-20, RG 127.

[24] Chief Observer, memo to CinC Atlantic Fleet, Subj: Report of Chief Observer on Landing Operations by the Fleet on 21 January 1914, dtd 23 Jan 1914, File 1975-80-30, RG 127; LtCol John A. Lejeune, Report to Brigade Commander, "Battle of Firewood Bay," dtd 24 Jan 1914, File 1975-80-20, RG 127.

[25] Col George Barnett, memo to CinC Atlantic Fleet, Subj: Report of Maneuvers and Operations from January 3 to January 24, 1914, dtd 3 Feb 1914, File 1975-80-20, RG 127; Lt Col Charles G. Long, Report to Brigade Comdr, Subj: Target and Mine Practice and Reembarkation of 1st Regiment, Jan 24 to Feb 8, 1914, File 1975-80-20, RG 127. Quote is from MGen George Barnett, "Soldier and Sailor Too" (Unpublished MS, n. d., History and Museums Division, HQMC), Chapt. 24, p. 8.

[26] LtCol John A. Lejeune, ltr to Augustine Lejeune, dtd 5 Feb 1914, Lejeune Papers.

[27] Frederick H. Delano, ltr to Mrs. Delano, dtd 14 Feb 1914, Frederick H. Delano Papers, Military History Research Collection, Carlisle Barracks, Carlisle, Pa.

CHAPTER 25

The Lengthy Shadow of H. H. Mulliner

Donald C. Gordon

University of Maryland

The name of H. H. Mulliner is not now exactly a household word, but for many years, in the eyes of those Britons who saw the arms manufacturers as the main source of war-mongering, he personified the sinister influence of this group. Mulliner was the managing director of the Coventry Ordnance Works from 1906 until 1909, when he was discharged for the political activity which brought him his notoriety. The Coventry Ordnance firm was owned jointly by three of the larger shipbuilding and engineering firms of pre-World War I Great Britain: John Brown, Fairfield Engineering, and Cammell Laird.[1] These firms could build dreadnoughts and other types of naval vessels, but were dependent upon others for gun mountings; Coventry was supposed to build the gun mountings that would make the parent firms fully capable of complete battleship construction.

In pursuit of orders, Mulliner naturally came into contact with the Director of Naval Ordnance, Captain Reginald Bacon, who formed the opinion that Mulliner was "a very sharp, clever man."[2] Admiral "Jackie" Fisher, on the other hand, apparently regarded him as a "shady company promoter," and warned J. L. Garvin, his newspaper editor confidant, to steer clear of him.[3] But despite either the cleverness or shadiness, the Admiralty did not give the Coventry firm the orders Mulliner hoped for.

Mulliner, however, had other concerns than simply awaiting Admiralty orders. Business frequently took him to Germany, and he found there, according to his testimony, that those firms from which he wished to secure machine tools and other equipment were apparently so busy filling orders they had received from the Krupp firm, that he could only conclude that that giant firm was embarked upon a huge program of expansion of its already formidable arms and shipbuilding capacity. This seemed particularly true of the Krupp capacity in the construction of gun mountings.

In May 1906, Mulliner wrote to General Hadden of the War Office about his observations of the German activities, and Hadden passed the letter along to the Admiralty. In addition to this initial letter to Hadden, Mulliner followed with others, giving further information based on later observations derived from his German trips and other contacts. He apparently saw some of the leading Admiralty figures, for he later stated that Admiral John Jellicoe had seen his original letter, and implied further that he had had interviews with Jellicoe.[4] The burden of his communication with the Admiralty was that although Germany was not actually building more naval vessels, there was substantial expansion in German shipbuilding capability, and most especially in the ability to fabricate gun mountings and turrets.

But the government of Sir Henry Campbell Bannerman, triumphant at the polls just a few months before Mulliner's German reports, was not likely to heed such warnings even if they had come to the attention of higher government echelons. The Prime Minister was among the more formidable exemplars of the Gladstonian principles of peace, retrenchment and reform, and in the pursuit of these verities the naval building program of the late Tory Government, which had called for the laying down of four dreadnoughts a year, was abandoned. Two or three each year would suffice, especially when one bore in mind the great superiority that Britain possessed over Germany in pre-dreadnought battleships.

But there were other signs and portents of German activity than those which came from Mulliner. Gradually the evidence seemed persuasive that, as he had stated, Germany was engaged in creating the facilities that would allow her to outbuild and overtake Britain in the naval race. Indeed, she had already embarked on the acceleration of her naval construction program. *The Westminister Gazette*, editorial voice of the moderate imperialist Liberals, edited by J. A. Spender, carried a story from its Berlin correspondent on May 18, 1908, on German naval expansion, predicting the need for Britain to put at least six dreadnoughts on the ways in 1909. Unless there was an increase in the British construction program over that currently planned, Germany would have thirteen and Britain only twelve dreadnoughts by 1912.

The Mulliner cries of alarm were reinforced by reports from the British military attaché at Constantinople, by the comments of Sir Trevor Dawson, another Briton engaged in the arms trade, and by tales relayed by an Admiral Garcia and a Captain Fliess of the Argentine navy whom the Germans had allowed a close inspection of the Krupp yards. Within three days of that visit the latter were telling "Jackie" Fisher that in Krupp's yards they had roughly counted some one hundred 12" and 11" guns, together with other evidence of an immense capacity for ship and gun construction.[5] Further, the annual report of the British naval attaché in Berlin, Captain Philip

Dumas, dealing with German naval developments, spoke of the increasing capacity of Krupp for gun fabrication.

Oddly, despite the ample apparent evidence of German acceleration, Prime Minister H. H. Asquith could tell Lloyd George and Reginald MacKenna, the First Lord, among others, that Mulliner's was the only information on the matter that the government had.

MacKenna, however, had been doing some arithmetic, and also found what seemed to him evidence that the rate of German construction was being accelerated by placing orders in the German shipyards before the adoption of the annual naval construction budget. Sir Edward Grey, the Foreign Secretary, when confronting the German ambassador, Metternich, with British suspicions, had found the answers of that usually honest gentleman unsatisfactory.[8]

All of these concerns, added to the underlying anxieties about German naval ambitions, led to the greatest uproar about British naval affairs and national security in decades, and culminated in the 1909 cry of "we want eight, and we won't wait," the eight being the dreadnoughts necessary to keep Britain safely ahead of Germany in the number of the new behemoths of the sea.

So it was that Mulliner suddenly found himself in the midst of events and moving among the powerful of the land. His warnings apparently remembered, he had several interviews with highly-placed officials which culminated in a meeting at Downing Street attended by many members of the Cabinet and Admirals Fisher and Jellicoe.[9] Prime Minister Asquith's notes on this meeting, dated February 19, 1909, indicate that the main topic was the capacity of the Germans to build gun mountings and turrets. The Krupp capacity was apparently estimated at fifty-four turrets a year, with the figure underlined in Asquith's notes. Since ten turrets equalled two dreadnoughts, the rate of German shipbuilding had apparently accelerated greatly.[10]

With these indications of German increase in ship and armament capacity too clear to ignore, the British officials reacted. The story of that reaction is well known. It is encapsulated in Churchill's summation of the conflict that raged in the Cabinet: economizers wanted four dreadnoughts, navalists six, so they compromised on eight. And while there was some opposition in Parliament, the "we want eight" program was carried on the contingent basis that four ships would be laid down immediately, and the remaining four if circumstances justified — as they soon seemed to do.

In the final analysis, however, it seems that there had been no German shipbuilding acceleration. Whether there ever had been, or whether the proposed acceleration had been abandoned because of the British reaction, is not clear. There is one oddity of the situation, however, and that is that while the more left-wing members of the British Liberal party were strong in their opposition to the increase in British construction, August Bebel, the leader of the German Social Democrats, their counterpart across the North Sea, was hoping that the British would carry through on the increased program and thus exert a cautioning influence on the German naval enthusiasms.[11]

Though Mulliner was shortly after the "naval scare" to move from the marginal place he actually held in history to a more central role in mythology as a war-monger, for a brief moment or two he was cast by some in an heroic role. Memories of the 1909 scare did not, of course, die out. Lord Cawdor, First Lord during the Balfour ministry, lauded Mulliner's efforts to warn the nation of its peril, and deplored the fact that these efforts had cost him his position with the Coventry firm. It was alleged by one Conservative M. P. that the Admiralty had finally granted some contracts to the Coventry firm contingent on Mulliner's dismissal. Indeed, the firm had received contracts for the construction of five large gun mountings with exactly the design that had been rejected by the Admiralty when Reginald Bacon, Mulliner's replacement at Coventry, had been Reginald Bacon, Director of Naval Ordnance.[12]

But while there were Mulliner defenders, querulous voices were heard to complain that the sources of the "scare" had not yet been identified, and others, such as John Dillon, the Irish parliamentary leader, protested that the Government promoted the naval panic on the basis of "misleading information."[13]

Such weighty authorities as Sir Llewellyn Woodward and Professor Arthur Marder dismiss the influence of Mulliner in the creating of the 1909 naval crisis as essentially marginal. But Mulliner's position among the *malefici,* those by whom evil comes to mankind, was not marginal in the minds of the pacifists and others to whom armaments-cum-capitalism were the seeds of war. In their literature and propaganda, in their prayers and incantations, poor Mr. Mulliner was to have the central role of villain until rivalled by the somewhat more sinister *persona* of Sir Basil Zaharoff.

For this strange and no doubt unwanted pre-eminence in reputed villainy, Mulliner may have had no one to blame but himself. He had dwelt in a decent obscurity during the years when he was seeking Admiralty orders, but, dismissed from his post at Coventry Ordnance for an apparent lack of success in obtaining such orders, Mulliner surfaced in a series of letters to the *Times* and other papers in which he revealed in perhaps exaggerated form the part he had played in alerting the Admiralty to the aspects of the German threat with which he claimed familiarity.

In the Commons on July 26, 1909, Prime Minister Asquith had stated that the knowledge of the expansion of German naval arms capacity had not come to the notice of the Government until the summer of 1908. In reply to the charge that if the Government had not known, the Admiralty certainly had, the Prime Minister replied that the Admiralty was not in the habit of withholding information from the Cabinet.

All this was too much for Mulliner, who like the good Englishmen he was, appealed to a higher authority by writing to *The Times*. In a series of letters from August 1909 to January 1910 he stated that when he had become aware of what was going on in Germany he had taken pains to inform the Admiralty. He had interviews in 1906, 1907 and the earlier part of 1908 with principal Admiralty officials. Further, he quoted Reginald McKenna as stating on July 17, 1908 that knowledge of the Krupp expansion had come to the Admirlty in 1906.

McKenna later indicated that his statement of July 17 simply meant that the Admiralty had indirect knowledge of some German intentions, none too clear, in 1906, as opposed to the realized facts of 1909.[14] Mulliner was not content with this, but stated that he had told the Admiralty officials only of German expansion that had actually taken place. He also asserted that Krupp alone possessed productive resources "far greater than all the ordnance firms in this country and the Woolwich Arsenal combined."

But it was in the letter of December 17, 1909 to *The Times* that Mulliner bared the story of his consultations with the Imperial Defence Committee, as he called it, and also of the meeting a week later with Admirals Fisher and Jellicoe and several members of the Cabinet. He also candidly stated that he had been concerned to secure orders for his firm. With this letter and others yet to come, Mulliner had made himself a public figure to a degree greater than before.

This was not yet enough, however, to make the Mulliner name evoke hissing in British left-wing and pacifist circles. That was to come from later circumstances: in part from the charges made in the German Reichstag in April 1913 by Karl Liebknecht against certain German armament firms. Liebknecht alleged that Krupp had bribed German army officers to disclose military documents, and he also revived an old charge that German small arms firms had planted stories in the French press likely to arouse German fears and secure more arms expenditure. These allegations were publicized in the British press, and prompted *The Economist* to write several articles on the financial structure of the major British armament firms.[15]

A present day scholar of the British arms firms and their history has spoken of the new vigor roused in critics of the British arms industry by the German scandal. The theme of the new criticism was that it "was not government policy but capitalist intrigue which was properly to blame for the persistence of the arms race."[16] This was surely the theme of a series of articles on the arms traffic that appeared in the Liberal *Daily News*, starting in their issue of May 20, 1913. While the series of eight or so articles was an effort at a general exposé of the arms trade, the author eventually got around to Mulliner and the Coventry works to a degree that made Mulliner the centerpiece of the series.

Heavier condemnation, however, was shortly to fall upon Mulliner's head. On March 18, 1914, Philip Snowden, one of the leading members of the Labour party, and later Chancellor of the Exchequer, laid into Mulliner with gusto in a speech in the Commons. He started with a quotation from Lord Welby, a recent Permanent Under-Secretary of the Treasury, and a gentleman of strong pacifist inclinations:

> We are in the hands of an organization of crooks. They are politicians, manufacturers of armaments, journalists. All of them are anxious for unlimited expenditures and go on inventing scares to terrify the public and to terrify Ministers of the Crown.[17]

So, said Snowden, "We had a scare in 1909." And of the authorship he had no doubts:

> Now we had it on the authority of Mr. Mulliner himself that for three years before 1909 he was constantly writing to the Government and appealing to them in other ways to spend more money upon armaments, and giving them information, which was afterwards found to be totally untrue, in relations to what Germany was doing. I do not suppose it is a very usual practice for Cabinet Ministers to interview commercial travellers and touts, but they made a departure on this occasion, and after three years of importunity, they enlisted the services of this gentleman, who was received by the Prime Minister and other Members of the Cabinet; and then the Prime Minister and the First Lord of the Admiralty came down to this House with that bogus story about the acceleration of the German programme, and it has since come to light that their only authority was the man whose works were standing idle at the time, and who was so anxious to get Government work.[18]

The Liberal-oriented *Economist* called the Snowden speech a "terrific attack on the armament ring" which made a "deep impression" on the House of Commons.

Snowden's statement about Mulliner and his relations with the Cabinet was a strange mixture of truth and untruth. Mulliner was certainly a good cut above the commercial traveller and "tout" class into which Snowden cast him, but it was unusual for the leading members to enlist the "knowledge" of a businessman in such a relatively formal fashion as a meeting at 10 Downing Street. At least one prominent historian has fastened on this circumstance to enhance the Mulliner role in the stirring up of the "scare."[20] On the other hand, Snowden was certainly in error when he held that Mulliner was the only authority on which the government of the day relied when it proposed the increase in the British dreadnought program.

Snowden devoted relatively little of his effort to the denunciation of the "naval scare" and Mulliner; the bulk of what he was later to call the longest and most sensational speech he ever made as a private member of the

314

Commons was a denunciation of the "international armaments ring," in which he damned British arms firms such as Vickers and Armstrong for a variety of sins.[21]

Snowden's references to an armaments ring were certainly more explicit than had been contained in any of the previous debates on the naval issue of 1909. The thrust of previous charges made against the Admiralty had generally been that it lacked accurate information, that it had allowed itself to be misled, and that in turn it had, with Milliner's aid, misled and panicked the Cabinet and the Parliament into excess naval appropriations. Snowden's charges tended to put the whole matter into a more sinister and conspiratorial light. The 1909 matter was no longer one of inadequate intelligence or of a panicky yielding to fear. It was the result of a conspiracy of armament firms, whose chief agent was Mulliner, to deceive the government, and of a governmental subservience to their machinations that amounted almost to complicity.

While Snowden had not included in his attack all the charges that were subsequently to be levelled at the arms firms, he had managed to get in two of the more frequent accusations: that of forming rings with which to mulct the British and other governments placing contracts, and that of using shady political influence in order to secure such orders. This latter argument was supported by the fact that there were a number of former naval and military officers who worked with armaments firms. Such men as Sir Cyprian Bridge, Sir Henry Brackenbury, Sir Charles Ottley, and Admiral Lord Beresford were among their ranks. In addition, critics of the arms trade were fond of elaborating on the statistics that indicated that in 1909 the stockholders of Armstrong-Whitworth, one of the two largest naval construction firms in Britain, included sixty noblemen, their wives, sons and daughters, fifteen baronets, twenty knights, eight members of Parliament, twenty military and naval officers and eight journalists.[22]

That there should have been this association amongst those who must be regarded as forming part of the pre-war British establishment can be regarded as surprising only because there were so few of them. And as a present day student of the arms trade in Britain has pointed out, ". . . mere ownership of armament shares would not guarantee—to anyone other than a convinced propagandist—that an M.P. or peer would necessarily vote or act in a way designed to bring work to the munitions factories." Such men might be influenced by a variety of other factors, including party discipline, concern for the public good, and if one has to adhere to the crassest of economic determinism, by the very variety of their own investments, for the average British investor spread his money around in a number of firms.[23]

The statistics on the number of the stockholders who were in the ranks of the nobility and upper class appeared in H. N. Brailsford's *The War of Steel and Gold*, one of the most influential books turned out by the brilliant

315

group of Radical and Marxist journalists in Britain in the decade before the 1914 war. As with Snowden, so now with Brailsford, Mulliner was once again cited: "The naval scare of 1909 was a remarkable achievement in the manipulation of public opinion, and the whole credit of it seems to belong to Mr. Mulliner." Mulliner was "the unique source of all alarmist statements current about German preparations,"[24] yet those statements passed without question. Those Ministers of the Crown who had adopted Mulliner's figures, Brailsford implied, were either simpletons or weaklings, but part of the blame rested on those who had allowed the origin of the scare to go unpublicized.

The outbreak of war in 1914 threw the criticism of the armament industry into an entirely different perspective. Many of the former advocates of disarmament swung into support of the struggle against Germany, and dissension thus broke out among those who had formerly been brothers in the ranks of the "peace mongers." Outright criticism of the war was made difficult, however, both by law and censorship and the prevailing tone of the public opinion. There were, however, liberal and labor intellectuals who were concerned to create a post-war international order in which the tragedy of the war would not be repeated. Foremost amongst them was E. D. Morel, who was the secretary and leading spirit of the Union of Democratic Control, the most significant of the groups formed in Britain by those who before the war had been among the leading critics of British foreign policy. Its principal aim was to create a new order which would banish war from international relations. The centerpiece of the UDC program was the principle of open diplomacy, with so-called democratic control of foreign policy. But Morel stated that in opposition to such a consummation there were vested interests "concerned in keeping Europe in a condition of fear and apprehension" of which "none perhaps is more insidious and more dangerous than the interests bound up with the armaments industry; and in no country are they more powerful than in our own."[27]

Morel went on to advocate the nationalization of the arms firms. It should be noted that there were echoes of the same demand in the United States. Wilson and Bryan at least toyed with the idea, and it received some support among members of the House of Representatives.[28]

The demand for the nationalization of the British arms firms put forward by the UDC was not part of the general demand for the social ownership of the commanding heights of British business. While many of its members and of the various groups such as labor unions associated with it were doubtless socialists, the UDC program was dominated by anti-war rather than anti-capitalist ideas. The "capitalist equals imperialist equals war-monger" phraseology had not made its appearance in any great strength. The UDC attacked the armaments firms more than the capitalist system as a whole.

316

In singling out the armaments industry for nationalization, the UDC was acting on the charge of men like Philip Snowden that arms manufacturers were the war-mongers, and any illustration of that thesis still centered on the alleged conduct of Mulliner. Certainly that conception and the Mulliner illustration were not to lie neglected in the next several decades.

In the covenant of the League of Nations were enshrined not only the ideals of disarmament, but also the idea of nationalization. Article VIII of the Covenant stated:

> Members of the League agree that manufacture by private enterprise of munitions and implements of war is open to grave objections.

To this, a sub-committee of the Temporary Mixed Committee of the League added in 1921 what many interpreted as an indictment of the arms industry. It seemed to accuse the arms traffickers of inciting war scares, bribing officials, exaggerating reports of arms programs of possibly hostile powers, corrupting the press and creating armaments rings. These points were less of a condemnation of the arms industry than they might seem, however, for the sub-committee took no evidence, and was apparently doing little more than setting forth a series of *pro* and *con* statements. Yet the fact that these charges were enumerated was frequently interpreted later as an endorsement of them.[29]

This set of alleged indictments against the arms firms was received with apathy in both the United States and Great Britain at the time. One student of the Nye Committee and its labors held that it came ten years too soon to arouse interest.[30] Thus, in the decade of the 1920s, the issues of nationalization of arms firms and of the alleged duplicity of such firms in the formenting of war dropped from sight. As the historian of the Vickers Company writes, "Private manufacture did not again figure very prominently in the news until the Disarmament Conference which opened in Geneva in February in 1932." This assessment is supported by the minimal attention paid to the question of the influence of private arms firms in Philip Noel-Baker's book, *Disarmament*, published in London in 1926, and one of the more scholarly discussions of the subject. Noel-Baker contented himself with repetitions of Article VIII of the League Covenant, and the allegations listed by the Temporary Mixed Commission of the League in 1921.[31]

The calm and indifference of the 1920s, however, yielded to the storms of the thirties, and the issue of the arms traffic emerged once again with more than simply renewed vigor. A new dimension was added to the controversy by the inquisitorial role of the Nye Committee in the United States and the Bankes Royal Commission in Great Britain. One of the reasons for the change lay in the antics of William Shearer at the 1932 Geneva Conference on arms limitation mentioned by the historian of the

317

Vickers Company. Of the Shearer affair, little need be said. He emerged briefly with a legal action seeking $250,000 from the American ship-building companies which had employed him for lobbying services in both Washington and Geneva. Since the Conference had been a failure, and since there was the human tendency to seek scapegoats, Shearer attracted a good deal of critical attention to himself. His conduct was roundly denounced by President Hoover as an effort to create international hatred and distrust, and he was the subject of a lack-lustre inquiry by a sub-committee of the Senate Naval Affairs Committee. As Professor John Wiltz states, Shearer's importance was not so much in what he did as what people thought he had done, surely words appropriate to the Mulliner of two decades before.

But there were deeper forces at work than the peccadilloes of a Shearer. The depression, the Manchurian incident and the consequent Sino-Japanese conflict, the Chaco war in South America, and the increasingly strident nationalist tone of politics in many parts of the globe all aroused fears of yet more wars to come.

In the United States, for those steeped in the agrarian-populist tradition, the prevailing depression only exacerbated their hostility to the business-financial community. Add to this the disillusion over American entry into the war in 1917 and the fear of involvement in yet another such conflict, and one finds most of the necessary elements for the creation of the public opinion that gave birth to and supported the labors of the Nye Committee. But the demand for such an investigation as the Nye Committee carried out came not alone from the populist and quasi-pacifist elements in American life. The movement for such an inquiry was prompted in some measure by a famous article in *Fortune*, the magazine of American big business,[33] and received indirect support also from the American Legion.

The Mulliner incident was apparently not cited as an instance of the nefarious activities of the armaments firms in any of the testimony given before the Nye Committee. But in a twisted fashion, the Nye Committee had at least some of its origins in the currents of thought in British life stemming from the Mulliner incident. A "key figure" in the creation of the Nye Com-mittee was Dorothy Detzer, the able and charming lobbyist and in-defatigable secretary of the Women's International League for Peace and Freedom. But while Miss Detzer and the WIL had long been advocates of disarmament, it had taken her contacts with Fenner Brockway, a leading member of the British Labour party and a conscientious objector during the war, to reveal to her what she came to regard as the true assessment of the relations between governments and the world of finance and arms produc-tion.[34] Brockway was the author of *The Bloody Traffic*, certainly one of the most harshly worded condemnations of the arms trade written in either Britain or the United States in the 1930s. And as he acknowledged in the work, much of the book was based on the publications of the Union for

Democratic Control. In this Brockway to Detzer to Nye combination, the Mulliner instance can scarcely have been lost to sight, since Brockway had retold the oft-told tale of how Mulliner had "scared the Cabinet"; Mulliner was once again presented as the sole source of Admiralty information of possible German naval construction acceleration.[35]

A powerful voice in American affairs, Senator William Borah of Idaho, could also have only had the Mulliner incident in mind when he regaled the Senate with an account of the pre-war naval rivalry between Britain and Germany which had been exacerbated by "the propaganda, sordid and vicious, which was constantly in those days disseminated by the munitions manufacturers. They carried on with ability and persistency a campaign of misrepresentation."[36]

And in the book which was to attach to the arms manufacturers the powerful pejorative description of *Merchants of Death*, Mulliner once again makes a rather bedraggled appearance. He first shows up anonymously as the smart little arms promoter from Leeds who scared the proud British Empire to death in 1909, and later gets a fuller treatment in a chapter almost totally dependent on the pamphlet literature of some of the leading critics of the Asquith government's foreign and naval policy. The basic error of the whole Engelbrecht and Hanighan account, however, is the implicit assumption that Mulliner was the sole source of the story of alleged German naval expansion.[37]

If one of the major theses of the authors of *Merchants of Death* was that arms makers caused war scares, then it is surely remarkable that in the 1930s they still had to fall back on the Mulliner example as their central piece of evidence, at least as far as the British arms firms were concerned.

The activities of the Nye Committee were widely noted in Britain; after all, the first testimony given to that body dealt with the activities of British armaments firms, with Vickers prominently mentioned because of its relations with the Electric Boat Company of Connecticut. British critics of the arms trade called for the creation of a comparable British investigatory body. The general tone of the demand was reflected in the words of *The Economist*:

> The state of affairs revealed by the evidence [before the Nye Committee] is so alarming, and the threads leading to this side of the Atlantic so numerous, that there is a very strong case for a parallel inquiry, with similar powers of compelling evidence, in Great Britain.[38]

And in October 1934, the government of the day yielded in part, at least, to the pressure, though it had previously rejected all such demands.[39]

This Royal Commission, when it came into being, did not have powers equal to its American counterpart. It was not empowered to subpoena witnesses, nor place them under oath; it was not equipped with counsel nor an investigative staff. Yet the personnel of the Commission commanded respect. The Chairman was Sir John Eldon Bankes, a Justice of the High Court. Other members were drawn from a variety of fields: the cooperative movement, League of Nations activity, journalism, international law and industry. Sir John as Chairman welcomed all who wished to appear as voluntary witnesses. And certainly sufficient of those witnesses spoke of the Mulliner incident to keep his name well before the members of the Commission: at least six witnesses mentioned the Mulliner affair as an example of the scandals associated with the arms traffic.

One or two of the witnesses deserve closer attention.[40] Perhaps the most notable of them was David Lloyd George, a member of the Cabinet in 1909, and foe of the naval expansion which the Government of the day ultimately embarked upon. Lloyd George's view was that Mulliner was then working up the agitation purely to get orders for his firm. He had left the Cabinet with the impression that the Germans were about to build at a much greater rate than authorized in their naval laws. This had not simply been an inference from the figures that Mulliner had advanced: ". . . he stated as a fact that the Germans were preparing and were in a position to add to their fleet so many ships that we would be in a minority by a given date. It was absolutely untrue."[41]

Another and less notable witness added a somewhat ironic note to the testimony. Walton Newbold, a one-time prominent member of the critics of the arms firms and of naval expansion, and the man who had assisted Philip Snowden in the preparation of his speech of 1914, had come full circle in his perception of the role of the arms firms. The whole incident had been blown out of proportion because it was used as a piece of political propaganda by the Radicals against the Liberals and the Liberals against the Tories.

Much of his testimony rings somewhat oddly when one knows that Newbold capped his political career as a Communist candidate for a parliamentary seat.[42] But its whole general tenor was more than substantiated by the impressive appearance before the Commission of Sir Maurice Hankey, the man who had been in the center of British war planning for decades, and of whom Balfour had said, "Without Hankey we would have lost the war." It is not too much to say that Hankey, with some twenty-four years of experience as secretary of the Committee of Imperial Defence, and twenty years as Secretary to the Cabinet, was the most formidable personage in the British civil service, and he had been anxious to present his testimony to the Commission. Hankey simply riddled the arguments of the advocates of the nationalization of the arms industry. More particularly, Hankey came to the defense of Mulliner.

In his testimony, Hankey pointed out how overworked the Mulliner case had been: six witnesses before the Commission had mentioned him and the 1909 "scare." Further, Hankey's memoranda for the Commission stated that Mulliner's evidence about the accumulation of the means of arms production in the German plants had been substantially correct and had been confirmed from other sources.[43]

And, indeed, the Mulliner case had been overworked, as Sir Maurice said. The final report of the Royal Commission stated:

> The Mulliner incident is the only evidence that has been put before us to substantiate the charge that armament firms disseminate false reports concerning the military and naval programmes of other countries.[44]

Referring to the wider number of charges against the industry which had been listed by the Temporary Sub-Committee of the League in 1921, the Commission felt that very few instances had been brought to its attention, only three in fact, of which the Mulliner and the Shearer cases were two, to support the charges which the League body had listed.[45]

With this recitation of the oft-told Mulliner tale before the Royal Commission, the gentleman in question makes his last prominent appearance on the stage. For the times were essentially not propitious for continued attacks on the arms industry; both having powder and keeping it dry became more and more an appealing course.

Andrew Undershaft, Bernard Shaw's archetypal arms manufacturer in *Major Barbara*, pronounced his creed thus:

> To give arms to all men who offer an honest price for them without respect of persons or principles: to aristocrats or republicans, to Nihilist and Czar, to Capitalist and Socialist, to Protestant and Catholic, to burglar and policeman, to black man, white man and yellow man, to all sorts and conditions, all nationalities, all faiths, all follies, all causes and all crimes.

To this Shavian creation, history added the figure of H. H. Mulliner, and while Andrew Undershaft will in all probability have a greater longevity in men's memories than Mulliner, the latter is not without his small measure of fame or notoriety. In the literature of the critics of the arms trade, Mulliner was the most widely cited instance of the evils of the trade. In their cast of evil *dramatis personae,* there were indeed other reprobates. But none, with the possible exception of Basil Zaraohff, who cast about himself an aura of mystery, attracted the attention won by Mulliner.

Yet surely, if the trade were as rich in villains as Lord Welby back in 1914, had claimed when he said, "We are in the hands of an organization of crooks," then remarkably few of them were discernible. Mulliner stands alone, and one can only entertain the idea that this is small evidence indeed on which to hang so rich a fund of invective and vituperation. As Hankey said, Mulliner had been overworked.

Further, as there is more than ample evidence today, his role as villain was exaggerated. Philip Noel-Baker writing in 1935 still called the 1909 naval scare "Mr. Mulliner's Panic." This does seem a trifle unfair. Mulliner's offense was not that he had used corrupt means to acquire arms sales by the conventional process of bribing officials or exercising some other form of undue influence on government officials, but rather that he had panicked the Admiralty, the Cabinet, the Committee of Imperial Defence, the Liberal Party and the Commons into accepting a story of German acceleration of naval construction, an acceleration that later admittedly did not occur, though it may have been planned at the time. And out of this scare Britain decided to build eight battleships rather than the previously planned four. But herein may lie Mulliner's ultimate defense, for the four additional ships that the scare with which his name was linked for decades made up the bare margin of British superiority in dreadnoughts in January 1915.[46]

The Mulliner episode triggered numerous expressions of fear then, fear of the malign influence in British society and politics of armaments firms. Of course this was but one more manifestation of fears that have come to the fore in western society since the time of the Greeks. As Professor Keith Nelson remarks, "distrust of the politician, soldier and business man as they relate to war is nothing new." And he traces expressions of these fears back to Aristotle and Polybius.[47]

Such apprehensions come in waves. The 1909 naval alarms, the Krupp scandals disclosed by Leibknecht, set off one wave, but in the decade after World War I virtually nothing of importance concerning the role of the armaments industry appeared. The 1930s offer a perfect spate of attacks on the arms maker once again, and then the flood diminishes once more, to be revived by the "farewell address" of President Eisenhower in January 1961. Since then, and with the additional stimulus of the Vietnam War, there has been an inundation of works dealing with the "warfare" state or the "garrison" state.

There is no doubt that the enormous growth in the dimensions of the arms industry, with the multiplication into the thousands of the firms with whom the Pentagon deals today, sets the problem apart from the decades before World War I. But the Mulliner story offers the cautionary lesson to critics of the so-called military-industrial complex that they should not allow advocacy to out-run intellectual probity.

Perhaps a final word from the Bankes Royal Commission. As the members of that body stated in their report, "The causes of war are remote and intractable, its instruments near and tangible." And because of that, I would add, the more available as targets.

FOOTNOTES

[1] Great Britain, *Parliamentary Papers*, Vol. 7 (1935-36), "Royal Commission on the Private Manufacture of and Trading in Arms," Cmnd. 5292, 310, 1499.

[2] Ibid., 311.

[3] Alfred M. Gollin, *The Observer and J. L. Garvin, 1908-1914* (London, 1960), 67.

[4] *The Times* (London), Dec. 17, 1909.

[5] Memo of McKenna signed by Fisher, May, Jellicoe and Onslow, ff. 21-25, McKenna MSS, 3/23, Churchill College, Cambridge.

[6] Foreign Office 371/458/6310, Feb. 12, 1908, Public Record Office, London. *See also* G. P. Gooch and H. W. V. Temperley, *British Documents on the Origin of the War, 1898-1914* (London, 1926-38), Vol. VI, 252, for statement made to the British ambassador.

[7] Asquith MSS, Vol. 21, f. 136, Bodleian Library, Oxford.

[8] Gooch and Temperley, Vol. VI, 287 et seq.

[9] Gt. Brit., *Parl. Pap.*, 1935-36, Vol. 7, Comnd, 5292, 314.

[10] Asquith MSS, Vol. 21, ff. 94-96.

[11] For Bebel comment, *see* Sir Henry Angst to Grey, May 1, 1911, F.O. 800/104/f128, PRO, London.

[12] Great Britain, *Parliamentary Debates*, Commons, 5th Series, 15, 417-427.

[13] Ibid., 22, 2535.

[14] Ibid., 8, 1840.

[15] *The Times* (London), 9, 21 April, 1913; *The Economist* (London), 26 April, 1913, 977-978 and 3 May, 1913, 1044-1045.

[16] Clive Trebilcock, "Radicalism and the Armaments Trust" in *Edwardian Radicalism*, ed. A. J. A. Morris (London, 1974), 181-82.

[17] Gt. Brit., *Parl. Debates*, Commons, 5th Series, 59, 2134-2135.

[18] Ibid., 59, 2136.

[19] *The Economist* (London), 31 March, 1914, 693.

[20] Oron Hale, *Publicity and Diplomacy* (New York, 1940), 348-349.

[21] Philip Snowden, *An Autobiography* (London, 1934), Vol. 1, 348-349.

[22] G. H. Perris, *The War Traders: an Exposure* (London, 1913), 6.

[23] Clive Trebilcock, "Legends of the British Armaments Industry, 1890-1914: a Revision," *Journal of Contemporary History* (June, 1970), 9.

[24] H. N. Brailsford, *The War of Steel and Gold*, Garland Library of War and Peace, (London, 1914; reprint edition, New York, 1971), 90-91.

[25] Ibid., 317.

[26] A. J. P. Taylor, *The Trouble Makers: Dissent over Foreign Policy, 1792-1939* (London, 1957), 178, gives an instance of this acceptability.

[27] E. D. Morel, *Truth and War*, Garland Library of War and Peace (London, 1916; reprint edition, New York, 1972), 183.

[28] William Jennings Bryan and Mary Bryan, *The Memoirs of William Jennings Bryan* (Philadelphia, 1925), 391; U.S. Congress, House, *(Congressional Record)*, 63rd Congress, 2nd Session, Vol. 51, pt. 1, 392, 400.

[29] Gt. Brit., *Parl. Debates*, Commons, 5th Series, 288, 944-45, April 18, 1934; J. D. Scott, *Vickers: A History* (London, 1962), 239-240.

[30] John E. Wiltz, *In Search of Peace: The Senate Munitions Inquiry, 1934-36* (Baton Rouge, La., 1963), 6. But even Wiltz seems to regard the allegations made against the arms firms and listed by the Temporary Mixed Commission as the judgement of that body.

[31] Philip J. Noel-Baker, *Disarmament*, Garland Library of War and Peace (New York, 1926; reprint edition New York, 1972), 302-204.

[32] Wiltz, *In Search of Peace*, 9-12.

[33] "Arms and Men," *Fortune*, March, 1934, 53-57, 113-126.

[34] Dorothy Detzer, *Appointment on the Hill* (New York, 1948), 147-149; Fenner Brockway, *Towards Tomorrow* (London, 1977), 102.

[35] Fenner Brockway, *The Bloody Traffic* (London, 1933; reprint edition, New York, 1972), 7, 148-151.

[36] U.S. Congress, *Congressional Record*, Senate, 73rd Congress, 2nd Session, 3688-3692, March 5, 1934.

[37] H. C. Englebrecht and F. C. Hanighan, *Merchants of Death* (New York, 1934; reprint edition, New York, 1972), 11 and Chapt. IX.

[38] *The Economist* (London), 8 Sept., 1934, 436.

[39] Gt. Brit., *Parl. Debates*, Commons, 5th Series, Vol. 288, 944-945.

[40] Among those who referred to the Mulliner affair were Viscount Cecil of Chelwood, Fenner Brockway, William Arnold-Foster and Philip Noel-Baker, *Minutes of Evidence*, "Royal Commission on Private Manufacture . . ." *passim*. (Not in Cmnd, 5292; consulted in State Paper Room, British Library, London.)

[41] Ibid., 537-538, 3880-3890.

[42] Ibid., 145, espec. 780-784, but much of Newbold's testimony sheds some light on differences within so-called peace circles prior to the 1914 war.

[43] *Minutes of Evidence*, "Royal Commission. . ." 695-698; also, Appendix, Second Memorandum of Evidence, 724-725, and Annex VI, 740-751.

[44] Gt. Brit., *Parl. Pap.*, 1935-36, Vol. 7, 519.

[45] Ibid., 500.

[46] Arthur Marder, *From the Dreadnought to Scapa Flow* (London, 1961), Vol. I, 179.

[47] Keith Nelson, "The 'Warfare State': History of a Concept," *Pacific Historical Review*, Vol. 40 (May, 1971), 128.

CHAPTER 26

U.S. Naval Intelligence and the Ordnance Revolution, 1900-1930

John C. Reilly

U. S. Naval Historical Center

Since the Korean War an increasing amount of attention has been given to American naval policy between 1865 and 1941. A number of older works deal with the Spanish-American War and World War I, but these tend to focus on higher policy and operations rather than on the how-it-was-done that at least some historians find interesting. In recent years we have seen such useful works as Herrick's *Naval Revolution;* Alden's *American Steel Navy;*[1] and Braisted's two volumes on *The United States Navy in the Pacific.*[2] These, with other books and articles, have given us a fresh look at the American Navy during its transition from wood to steel, from sails to propellers, and from line-of-sight muzzleloaders to remotely-controlled long-range rifles. The development of warships during most of the period considered here was outlined by Hovgaard as long ago as 1920 in his *Modern History of Warships.*[3] More recent treatments of some of the essentials of capital-ship development in the U.S. Navy to 1930 have been provided by Breyer, in *Battleships and Battle Cruisers,* and by Hough in *Dreadnought.*[4]

The naval ordnance of this period has received but little attention from historians. Besides the Bureau of Ordnance's *Naval Ordnance Activities, World War,*[5] the only sizable works which treat the development of modern ordnance and gunnery have been Peter Padfield's *Guns at Sea,*[6] a general history covering the period from the Armada through World War II, and the same author's *Aim Straight,*[7] a life of Sir Percy Scott which devotes considerable attention to Scott's efforts to improve British naval gunnery. The influence of the Scott-Sims relationship makes this helpful to the student of American naval gunnery. Sims' own work has been described by Elting Morison in *Admiral Sims and the Modern American Navy.*[8] A chapter in another of Morison's works, *Men, Machines, and Modern Times*, is a particularly interesting discussion of the technical, but also of the human, aspects of the controversy attending Sims' campaign to improve the shooting of the American fleet.[9] Dr. E. R. Lewis has recently crafted a valuable discussion of the development and adoption of American battleship ordnance after World War I.[10]

And there we are. This has hardly been a comprehensive review of the available literature on the general subject of American ship and artillery development from 1900 to 1930, but it gives a general idea of the ground. If one were to assemble a collection of books and articles on this admittedly broad area, it would not take up a great deal of library shelf space. I do not believe that it would be saying too much to suggest that a great deal of work remains to be done on the history of our naval technology. We have, for instance, nothing to compare with Schmalenbach's *Geschichte der Deutschen Schiffsartillerie;* with le Masson's *Histoire du Torpilleur en France;* with Parkes' *British Battleships* or March's *British Destroyers;* or with the series of volumes entitled *Le Navi d'Italia* issued by the Ufficio Storico della Marina Militare in Rome. We might note, here, that Schmalenbach's work is the only one of its kind: the only full-length treatment, to date, of the development of a navy's gunnery and fire control.[11]

This brings us, in a roundabout fashion, to the point of this paper: the records of the Office of Naval Intelligence for the period in question. We should neglect no possible source of historical information. This is particularly true in the area of naval technology, where a great deal of the total source record does not seem to have survived. Technical records have, apparently, not fared too well. A great deal of destruction has taken place with what has sometimes seemed to be less than an adequate degree of discrimination. One holder of records could remark that "Real historians do not care about the details of ship construction; this is the province of the 'buff types' who, in my opinion, are too much concerned with counting the 'trees' (or the nuts and bolts)." Another source could write that its policy board had "recommended disposal of most series of earlier records directly relating to the construction and design of vessels . . . These records were destroyed because such technological information was not of historical value."[12] Given the rather bleak and fragmentary state of the surviving source materials, it is particulary gratifying to find such a trove as this O.N.I. material, held by the National Archives.

Some background may be helpful. The period of gradual renaissance, following our Civil War, which saw such innovations as the introduction of the naval apprentice system and the creation of the Naval War College—both the work of Rear Admiral Stephen Luce—also saw the establishment of the Office of Naval Intelligence. Secretary of the Navy William Hunt signed General Order Number 292 on 23 March 1882, establishing this office within the Bureau of Navigation[13] "for the purpose of collecting and recording such naval information as may be useful to the department in time of war, as well as in peace." The Navy Department Library was placed under the new organization, and "commanding and other officers" were "directed to avail themselves of all opportunities which may arise to collect and forward . . . professional matter likely to serve the object in view." Lieutenant Theodorus Mason was appointed to head the new office, which he did until 1885; until his death in 1899 he continued to serve the Navy's new intelligence effort.

This was, of course, hardly the first glimmering of naval interest in overseas developments. As early as 1827, Secretary of the Navy Samuel Southard had addressed letters to our ambassadors and ministers to maritime powers, asking them to provide such information as "they may be able to procure without inconvenience" on ships, personnel, shore facilities, naval expenditures, "and, generally, anything which will enable this department completely to comprehend the extent and character of the naval means of the nation" to which each representative was accredited.[14]

In the years after the Civil War American naval officers were sent to Europe to study technical developments there. Some of the results of this work were published in 1878 under the title . . . *European Ships of War,* . . . with later editions titled the *War-Ships and Navies of the World* . . .[15] Another volume by Lieutenant Edward Very appeared as *Navies of the World in 1880.*[16] These, with the Austrian J. F. von Kronenfels' *Das Schwimmende Flottenmaterial der Seemächte,*[17] are still valuable references on naval technical development in the post-Civil War years.

The new O.N.I., whose purpose was to put this kind of information-gathering on a systematic basis, was another product of the kind of "New Navy" thinking that held naval warfare to be more than a matter of individual skill and gallantry. While "damn the torpedoes" might have been adequate in 1864, by 1882 it seems to have been clear that more than this was needed.

In July, 1882, a new Secretary of the Navy, William Chandler, took office. He evidently took naval intelligence seriously, since one of his first acts was to sign a rather detailed set of ground rules for the new activity. Its mission, as Chandler defined it, was to "collect, compile, record, and correct information" on a rather free-wheeling assortment of subjects, with heavy emphasis on the ships, war material, ports, coast defenses, and military capabilities of foreign powers. "The facilities for obtaining coals and supplies in all quarters of the globe" were of obvious interest to a Navy without Britain's network of coaling stations. Information on our own navy, merchant marine, and coast defense was also to be collected, along with "information which may be of use to our officers in their professional studies," or to the American merchant marine. Information was to be published and disseminated to the officers of the Navy. Technical bureaus having archival information of value, as well as the Department library, were directed to provide access to information of intelligence value. "The younger officers . . . ," Chandler went on, "will be encouraged in collecting and reporting intelligence and in writing original articles on naval subjects."[18] In 1883 two series of intelligence publications began to appear. The first, *Information from Abroad,* included only four titles issued between 1883 and 1893; these dealt with military and naval operations. The *General Information Series* also began publication in 1883. Twenty-one of these volumes appeared, on an annual or biannual basis, into 1902. Eight individual monographs, or *War Notes,* discussed the operations of 1898 in the Caribbean and the Philippines.

The *General Information Series* included information on naval organization, operations, and training, but from the beginning concerned itself heavily with the ships and ship systems of other powers. Its technical notes are extensive, and various volumes include articles, some quite lengthy, dealing with warship design, ordnance and gunnery, armor, and machinery. Such new developments as the torpedo also received attention. Like the single works I have mentioned, this series is a helpful first reference on many aspects of the development of ships and ordnance before and during the first years of the new American navy.

Number XXI of the *General Information Series,* issued in July, 1902, was the last of these collections to appear. This does not mean an end to the availability of this type of information, since the attaché reports which made up a great share of the source material for this publication series continued to be received and are available for research today.

The United States accredited its first naval attaché in 1882, when Lieutenant Commander French Chadwick was sent to London. Others were ordered to Paris, Saint Petersburg, and Berlin in 1885; to Rome and Vienna in 1888; to Tokyo and Peking in 1895; and to Madrid in 1897. Concerned with the distribution and readiness of the Spanish fleet after the destruction of *USS Maine* in 1898, O.N.I. sent out two ensigns—senior ensigns, be it admitted[19]—in the guise of Englishmen. Reporting in cipher by commercial cable, one of these officers tracked Cervera's squadron through the Caribbean while the second followed other Spanish forces across the Mediterranean. Ensign Henry Ward, assigned to the Caribbean, was arrested at San Juan, Puerto Rico, but succeeded in convincing the Spanish naval authorities of his British *bona fides* and continued on his way.[20] Between 1903 and 1919 fourteen more capitals in Europe and Latin America received naval attachés. The officers selected for this service first came to Washington for a period of temporary duty. Examination of O.N.I.'s files, with visits to shipyards and to the Bureaus of the Navy Department, were calculated to put the new man "in the picture" with respect to the personnel and material situation of our Navy. Arriving at his new post, a turnover period of two weeks to a month was required to enable the new attaché to take up where his predecessor had left off. The officer being relieved then returned to O.N.I. for debriefing.

The *modus operandi* of these early naval attachés seems to have been pretty aboveboard, although items in the files citing a source as "X" or "Z" would indicate that they were not averse to a hot tip if such should come along. Rear Admiral Albert Niblack, himself once an attaché, would later write that

> The method of obtaining information in foreign countries has been principally by exchanging information of equal importance, and the acquisition of information of [sic] any questionable method has been strictly frowned upon. It has been the aim of the office to use only reputable business methods and avoid anything savoring of "gum-shoe" methods. This point can not be too strongly emphasized.[21]

Niblack went on to mention that early living allowances were inadequate, and that no officer could serve as an attaché without some means of supplementing his pay. This, in turn, tended to foster a feeling that naval attachés were simply well-to-do dilettantes enjoying the foreign social whirl.[22]

Possible prejudice notwithstanding, the Navy attracted some capable people into its attaché corps. Such names as Niblack and Chadwick; William Sims; Nathan Sargent; Charles Vreeland; Reginald Belknap; Walter Gherardi; John Bernadou; Joseph Reeves; Albert L. Key; and John C. Breckinridge, of the Marine Corps, appear among others.

Results of their labor can be seen today in the voluminous records of the Office of Naval Intelligence, contained in National Archives Record Group 38, Records of the Office of the Chief of Naval Operations. These files date back to the office's earliest days and include letter books and other documents. We are, however, primarily concerned here with one large collection within this broad area, which deals in wide and frequently lavish fashion with our basic topic. The revolution—and I do not believe it hyperbolic to call it that—in naval science during the early decades of our century profoundly altered the manner in which naval warfare was carried on and, thus, also dislocated a good bit of naval thinking. Mahan, in 1890, had posited six factors affecting the development of a nation's sea power:[23] geographic position; physical conformation; extent of territory; population; national character; character of government. A seventh factor now came into play. Naval readiness was now much more than a matter of cutting and shaping wood, putting ropewalks to work, and recruiting marlinespike seamen and squint-down-the-tube gunners. It was now very much involved with the new scientific and industrial capabilities of the naval powers and would-be powers. And the rate of change was rapid, something very familiar to us today. "Conventional" warships took new forms; the heyday of the mixed-caliber predreadnought battleship was not too much longer than that of the big shell-gun frigates of the late 1850s.[24]

The new all-big-gun battleship quickly grew in speed, hitting power, and protection, making early specimens at least obsolescent before their tenth birthday. The armored cruiser and battle cruiser enjoyed brief careers. Torpedoes were delivered by growing—both in numbers and power—generations of surface and subsurface craft. "Hot-running" air-steam machinery increased the torpedo's range and payload, which in turn had its effect on tactical concepts. Steel breechloading guns grew in size and power, firing farther and faster. New means of controlling them made more accurate shooting possible at ranges that Farragut, or even Robley Evans, would have dismissed as visionary nonsense. This was very much an era of what Hayek[25] has, in another context, called the "religion of the engineers"; the men of the Navy were disciples of this oily cult. The engineers and scientists of the nineteenth century had evolved the belief that machines and formulas were the tools with which Man, the Civilizer, would ultimately set the universe in order. This applied to war just as it did to all other forms of human activity. If we are to understand what the Navy was doing and thinking at this time, I submit that it is particularly important to understand the technical framework within which it operated.

The group of records which seems most fruitful from this standpoint is officially known to the National Archives as Record Group 38, Entry 98: *Reports ("Registers") of Naval Attachés, 1886-1939.* Some 300 shelf-feet of reports deal with what might seem, at first glance, to be a rather mind-boggling array of topics. Long before the rest of the Navy adopted an alphanumerical system of subject file classification,[26] O.N.I. had established its own. This runs in roughly alphabetical fashion, beginning with *Aeronautics* and ending with *War Operations,* followed by a "catchall" heading entitled *Secret and Confidential Information, Various Subjects.* "Various," in this case, puts it mildly. The subject headings are identified by combinations of letters and numerals, such as A-1 for *Aeronautics* and F-1 for *Gun Carriages.* These general headings are further divided into subgroups; for instance, *Armor* (A-7) is subdivided into A-7-a through A-7-c. In some instances, these subheadings indicate specific subject subgroupings, while in other cases the distinction, if any, is not clear.

The subject arrangement, in places, seems a bit odd. One heading includes information on radio equipment, on "resources," and on some ships of various nations. Fuels and fueling are lumped together with "guide books." It seems as if, as time went by and new subjects came to be, they were simply fitted into whatever numerical slot might be available. The subject-heading system alone is simply not adequate for a detailed subject search, since information on, say, ordnance and gunnery is widely dispersed under a number of headings; the same holds true for material on ship development. Fortunately, a register of individual document entries exists, and a careful scanning of this with the help of an archivist is suggested. Archivists have told me that this register is not one hundred per cent complete; but it will, at least, enable a researcher to "zero in" on specific areas containing items of value. Around 1940, while these records were still in Navy hands, some reports were pruned from the collection for inclusion in what is now National Archives Record Group 45, the *Naval Records Collection of the Office of Naval Records and Library.* A cross-reference finding aid to these items exists, and can lead to these reports.

Individual attaché reports vary considerably in size and format. Some are typescript documents prepared by the attachés themselves, describing and discussing their findings. Some contain replies to official queries addressed to the government involved. Others may be rather eclectic collections of items on a general subject, often from different sources and covering an extended period of time. Published sources, such as newspapers, magazines, and military or technical journals, were evidently as carefully culled then as now.[27] *The Engineer, le Yacht, Rivista Marittima,* and *Marine-Rundschau* are typical of the numerous titles represented; foreign-language items are usually accompanied by English translations.

The subject range covered is broad. Such things as Admiralty prize questions, economic and social conditions, geography, and merchant shipping are included. Chemistry, metallurgy, and marine engineering are reported on. Of particular interest here are the lengthy series of reports dealing with ordnance, gunnery, and fire control. Torpedoes and torpedo defense receive their share of attention, as do mines and mine countermeasures. This last area, incidentally, may deserve closer examination in the light of the remarkable American mine warfare effort of World War I. Until 1915, the U.S. Navy had purchased its mines overseas; only then did we begin to manufacture small quantities of a Vickers-designed mine that the British themselves were finding unsatisfactory in services.[28] To what extent did we profit from an acquaintance with foreign developments and techniques, well represented in this collection? An experienced British ordnance officer is described as having collaborated in the design and trial of the automatic anchor for the new Mark 6 mine,[29] but did the rest of the design for the mine and its exploder mechanism, as well as the doctrinal concepts for its use, spring from native ingenuity alone?

Gunnery training and techniques were emphasized in intelligence collection, just as they were in the operations of the major fleets. Conspicuous in this context are a number of reports submitted by William S. Sims.[30] These, as might be expected, provide material of value to any student of the development of gunfire control in our fleet; something which, as I have mentioned, still remains to be done. Sims' reports, of course, do not stand alone, but form only a fraction of the material to be found here dealing with naval gunnery. Since these are intelligence records they do not, unfortunately, seem to include anything of particular significance on American developments. They do, however, give us a considerable amount of information on the state of the gunnery art overseas. We see, for instance, that as early as 1906 the British Admiralty was using simple mechanical devices to indicate range rate.[31] Some notes on Japanese fire control are also to be found.[32] Considering the general scarcity of information on the Japanese Navy, even this modest accumulation is most welcome.

The First World War produced the expected increase in reporting. Virtually every aspect of operations and material, including ship design, was included. New developments, such as the art—one could hardly call it a science—of antisubmarine warfare as well as defense against aircraft attracted attention. Besides the usual attaché corps, additional observers were ordered to duty with the Allied forces, especially the Royal Navy; their reports helped to swell the flood.

Opinions and conclusions varied. In one report dated 10 May 1915,[33] an O.N.I. officer was "more than surprised to note the extreme ranges at which hits are now being made by both the English and the German men-o-war." Looking at the Dogger Bank, Coronel, and Falklands actions, he concluded that future naval engagements would be fought at twice the average Russo-Japanese War range, or 15,000 yards and up, and at high speeds. "Here again," he goes on, "the victor must be able to make hits at very long ranges while steaming at Full Speed, and, in some cases, be able to accomplish this in a heavy sea way." Another report, dated 1916, is titled "Inaccuracy of British and German Fire at Long Ranges"[34] and concludes—from the same kind of battle experience—that long-range shooting is profitless. This sort of thing, not rarely encountered here, suggests the earlier ship-type controversy after the Russo-Japanese War, with Mahan claiming that Tsushima had demonstrated the superiority of mixed-caliber battleship batteries while Sims drew the opposite conclusion from the same data.[35] This might suggest to us that, while facts are always of importance, their evaluation and interpretation are equally so. If we are to understand what has happened during any period, not only this one, we need to avoid the extremes of, on the one hand, bogging down in the nuts and bolts or, on the other hand, assuming that decisions are made in a vacuum and that military planners and organizers have no thought for the tools or methods with which they must work. "Real historians" who think in such terms might well wonder why our own politico-military thinkers are so concerned with such mechanical matters as the range of a *Backfire* bomber or the number of MIRV's that can dance on the nose of an SS-18 ICBM.

During the war years, particular attention was paid to British gunnery and fleet operations. Observers' notes are frequently detailed and just as frequently of broad general interest, touching at various times on the entire spectrum of warfare at sea.[36] Some of them have a human interest that has little to do with technology. An American officer, aboard a British battle cruiser based in the Firth of Forth, made this note on 24 April 1916 when German battle cruisers were reported off Lowestoft; "7 P.M. Panic. Raise steam full speed at once."[37] From such items as this, we can judge these observers as being, by and large, people who believed in telling it like it was.

The details of naval operations and the development of tactical doctrine take up a good deal of space in these records. We were still fairly new at the game ourselves; early in 1913 the General Board of the Navy was discussing the desirability of working out a "system of tactics" for destroyer types,[38] and at Jutland the Royal Navy was still discovering that there were new lessons to be learned about naval warfare in the machine age.

At a time when guns and gunnery absorbed the kind of interest and concern that missilry would to a later generation, much of the product of our intelligence effort naturally dealt with guns and fire control. Information on land and naval ordnance, from small arms to major-caliber weapons, takes up a considerable amount of space. Guns, ballistics, ammunition and propellants, breech mechanisms, and methods of manufacture are generously represented. Gun mounts for surface and antiaircraft use receive attention; such titles as "Guns for Attack and Defense of Air Craft,"[39] "Krupp Naval Guns for use Against Air Aircraft,"[40] or "Ehrhardt Anti-Balloon Gun"[41] reflect early awareness of a new dimension in warfare. When our battleships of the Fiscal 1912 *Nevada* (BB-36) class were under consideration, opinion was far from unanimous concerning the structural or military advisability of placing part of their 14-inch batteries in triple turrets. Besides the Bureau of Ordnance's own calculations, we had available data on the selection of triple turrets by Italy[42] and Russia.[43] Further details came in on the study of four-gun turrets, notably by France for its abortive *Normandie*-class battleships of World War I.[44] These apparently held little interest for American ordnance designers, since quadruple or larger turrets seem to have received no more than theoretical consideration from World War I into the 1930s.

During the early years of this century, the French Navy had a great deal of difficulty with its cellulose-nitrate *Poudre B,* or Type B smokeless powder. Massive explosions in the battleships *Iéna,* in 1907, and *Liberté,* in 1911, took a large toll of lives. The most recent discussion of this can be found in Admiral Rickover's book on the loss of the battleship *Maine.*[45] The citations for this treatment include a number of books and articles, with two French parliamentary publications equivalent to our Congressional "committee

333

print." A fairly cursory search of the O.N.I. files turned up sixteen different reports on French smokeless powder, including five on accidents and others devoted to possible defects in *Poudre B*.[46] This is extensive coverage for one specific subject, possibly indicating that, only a few years after the loss of *Maine* at Havana, American naval officers may have had the same reaction to the thought of internal explosions that a discussion of surprise attacks might produce in the Pearl Harbor Survivors' Association. During the years after World War I, the question of battleship gun elevation took on considerable importance.[47] Since capital-ship construction had been suspended under the Washington Treaty, navies inevitably turned to modernization of their existing battle lines to compensate—at least to some extent—for this. Congress appropriated six and a half million dollars in 1923 for across-the-board elevation of the turret guns in thirteen battleships,[48] but rescinded this in the following year.[49] Gun elevation funding was later restored, on a class-by-class basis, as part of the general modernization packages for the *Nevada, Pennsylvania*, and *New Mexico* classes. Elevations—and, thus, ranges—of foreign guns were looked into, both by direct inquiry to governments signatory to the Washington Treaty and by such means as observation and photo interpretation. The quality of information varied; for instance, much of the available data on Japanese turret mounts was vague and contradictory. Press reports, statements by Japanese ordnance officers, and even correspondence with the Vickers Company, designers of the 14-inch mounts for the *Kongo* class, were examined. A 1924 estimate cites various sources, giving ranges of possible elevations of 20 to 30 degrees for the new *Mutsu* class and of 15 to 25 degrees for the *Kongo, Fuso,* and *Ise* classes.[50]

Estimates of British capabilities were reported as early as 1919.[51] By 1934, the Bureau of Ordnance, examining "all available data," was able to specify maximum ranges for British battleship guns which come close to those later cited by Oscar Parkes from Admiralty records.[52] The Bureau underestimated the range of *Nelson*'s 16-inch guns by 700 yards and overestimated that of the 15-inch weapons of the *Royal Sovereign* and *Queen Elizabeth* classes by 900 yards.[53] Such items as these remind the potential researcher that, in most areas, our knowledge of foreign developments seems to have run the gamut from surprising accuracy to educated guesswork. Since we, today, are working with the benefit of such aids as other declassified records, twenty-twenty hindsight, and the researches of others, we can subject much of what is found here to the kind of cross-checking that should be done with any other type of source material. After a bit of delving in these files, anyone who has followed the military-policy debates of recent years through jungles of "guesstimations" as to what the rest of the world is doing will, in all likelihood, feel that the things can't have been very different in days of yore.

In 1919, a new intelligence publication, the *Monthly Information Bulletin*, began to appear. In format and content it differed considerably from the old *General Information Series*, and included articles—sometimes quite lengthy—on social and political happenings. Russia, China, and the Near East, for instance, came in for a great deal of description and analysis. The *Bulletin* was distributed to all ships in commission, "except very minor craft," and to Naval Districts and shore stations, as well as to the State Department and to the Army. The components of the Washington headquarters establishment, as well as all flag commands afloat and ashore, received it. It was evidently more widely disseminated than the old more-or-less-annual hardcover volumes, though it is often of less minute technical interest. Ships, ordnance, aviation, and military hardware in general are described,[54] though usually in fairly general fashion. The first volumes are generously laden with material on wartime developments, with heavy emphasis on German and, to some extent, Austrian hardware and practices. German damage control, for instance, is discussed for 63 pages in one 1923 issue.[55] A German gunnery officer named Georg von Hase published a work called *Die Zwei Weissen Völker* in 1920. The author gives an interesting and rather detailed account of German naval gunnery as he had seen it, particularly as the gunnery officer of the battle cruiser *Derflinger* at Jutland. The book aroused interest on both sides of the Atlantic; a second German edition appeared in 1923, and an English translation in 1921.[56] The Naval War College reprinted von Hase's account of Jutland,[57] while the *Monthly Information Bulletin* reproduced lengthy extracts from it.[58]

Naval gunfire control had moved ahead during the First World War. By the Armistice, our Navy was equipped, or was equipping itself, with a combination of American and British fire-control instruments. Much had been learned from the Royal Navy during our wartime association, and such domestic inventors as Hannibal Ford were pursuing their own technical directions. The general quality of German wartime gunnery spurred interest in the systems which had made it possible, and descriptions of the Imperial Navy's fire control instruments and procedures. This is backed up by intelligence reports in the O.N.I. files, some of which describe and illustrate German equipment.[59] Given the relative degree of apparent technical sophistication of British and German equipment for main-battery fire control, I believe it might reasonably be asked if the reputed difference in the quality of the two navies' gunnery performance might not have had more to do with organizaton and training than with hardware. This is, on my part, nothing more than a superficial impression. I think it might, however, be a valid subject for future study. A detailed comparison of British and German gunnery tools, training, and performance during World War I could have much more than mere antiquarian value if it can tell us something about the ways in which men and machines can interact to produce results. If the Kaiser's navy could do a better job with less elaborate gear, how much of this was due to superior training? Or did it also mean that perhaps more sophistication is not necessarily better from a military standpoint? If this has not already been done—the Naval War College could probably tell us something about that—then this group of records could, in all likelihood, make a valid contribution.

Notes of humor, sometimes a bit mordant, crop up from time to time. Before World I, a German arms-brokering firm contacted our attaché to find out if the U.S. Navy was interested in purchasing some destroyers, then under construction for a third party who had apparently had second thoughts. The simple printed prospectus enclosed by the German firm made the famous Francis Bannerman Sons of New York look like a neighborhood five-and-dime store.[60] Their list of available items ran from battleships and battle cruisers through machine guns and small arms to such things as lances (in your choice of wood or steel) and field kitchens. Whether you planned to fight Hottentots or continental armies, they could fill your needs. This was less colorfully done than the kind of advertising we are used to seeing in contemporary journals, but the message was the same.

In 1931, we find a report from the attaché to the Netherlands, who had visited a Dutch licensee of the German Siemens-Halske firm, manufacturers of fire-control gear. During the years after World War I, a certain amount of commercial dickering seems to have taken place between the U.S. Navy and German or German-controlled manufacturers of optics and fire-control devices, and we maintained our wartime interest in German developments. The director of this Dutch firm, a former captain in the Imperial German Navy, showed our attaché some of his wares. In parting, the American officer inquired into the health of the fire-control business; the *Herr Direktor* responded "that their business was excellent and showed an increase after each Disarmament Conference."[61] This kind of thing raises a smile, but the undertone of tragedy makes it no more than a half-smile.

Where does all this leave us? We have said a few things about naval technology; we have picked a few nits. Does it give us any practical direction? I believe it does.

To begin with, I do not believe that we can understand the naval thinking of these earlier decades without a good grasp of the naval technology that influenced it. This may seem a truism to such an audience as this, but I think it can bear repetition. As I mentioned earlier, the availability of sources has been seriously affected, not only by records-management practices but by a belief that history and technology are two utterly separate things. This I cannot believe; nor, I would imagine, can you. We can no more begin to understand our post-Civil War naval history without some technical orientation than we can, say, interpret the life of Francis of Assisi without bringing in religion. A look at these records brings this home very clearly. The naval attachés who assembled this collection of reports already had some years of Navy experience before getting into the intelligence business. Many of them, at least, were people of above-average drive and mental capacity. Whether you choose to think of them as simon-pure national heroes or as venal accessories of Merchants of Death, Incorporated, one thing they were not: dunces. They well knew the needs of the service as higher authority saw them, and this in itself tells us something about the mind-set of the men who affected the naval directions of American policy during these decades. Like any other source, this one does not stand alone. But I believe that thoughtful incorporation of it with other bodies of available information will very likely add useful new dimensions to our understanding of where we have been, and—I hope—of where we are going.

FOOTNOTES

[1] Walter R. Herrick, *The American Naval Revolution* (Baton Rouge, 1967). John D. Alden, *The American Steel Navy* . . . (Annapolis/New York, 1972).
[2] William R. Braisted, *The United States Navy in the Pacific, 1897-1909* (Austin, 1958; reprinted 1969); *The United States Navy in the Pacific, 1909-1922* (Austin, 1971).
[3] William Hovgaard, *Modern History of Warships* (New York, 1920; reprinted 1971).
[4] Siegfried Breyer, *Battleships and Battle Cruisers* . . . (Garden City, N.Y., 1973) and Richard Hough, *Dreadnought; A History of the Modern Battleship* (New York, 1964; reprinted 1975).
[5] U.S. Navy Bureau of Ordnance, *Navy Ordnance Activities, World War, 1917-1918* (Washington, 1920).
[6] Peter Padfield, *Guns at Sea* (New York, 1974).
[7] Peter Padfield, *Aim Straight* . . . (London, 1966).
[8] Elting Morison, *Admiral Sims and the Modern American Navy* (Boston, 1942).
[9] Elting Morison, *Men, Machines, and Modern Times* (Cambridge, Mass., 1966).
[10] E. R. Lewis, "American Battleship Main Battery Armament: The Final Generation," *Warship International*, XIII (1976), 276-303.
[11] Paul Schmalenbach, *Die Geschichte der Deutschen Schiffsartillerie* (Herford, Germany, 1968; revised 1976). Henri le Masson, *Histoire du Torpilleur en France* (Paris, 1967). Oscar Parkes, *British Battleships* . . . (London, 1957; revised 1966). Edgar J. March, *British Destroyers* . . . (London, 1967). Stato Maggiore, *Le Navi D'Italia* (Series of 7 volumes; Rome, 1962-69. Most volumes revised.)
[12] I cite no source for these two quotes, though both are recent and authentic. My purpose in using them is not to criticize, but to illustrate an attitude.
[13] O.N.I. remained under the Bureau of Navigation until 1890, when it was placed directly under the Assistant Secretary of the Navy; in 1898 it returned to BuNav. In 1909 it came under the direction of the Aid for Naval Operations. In 1911 the Chief Intelligence Officer was retitled the Director of Naval Intelligence. O.N.I. became part of the new Office of the Chief of Naval Operations in 1915, and in 1922 was designated the Intelligence Division of OPNAV although the term "O.N.I." continued in general use.

[14] "Notes on the Early History of Naval Intelligence in the United States," *The O.N.I. Review,* XII (April-May 1959), 169.

[15] Chief Engineer James W. King, USN, *Report of . . . J. W. King . . . on European Ships of War and their Armament . . . etc.* (Washington, 1877; revised 1878). Three editions of an enlarged version were published as *The War-Ships and Navies of the World . . .* (Boston, 1880; 1881; 1882).

[16] Edward Very, *Navies of the World* (New York, 1880).

[17] J. F. von Kronenfels, *Das Schwimmende Flottenmaterial der Seemächte* (Vienna, 1881). A second volume, covering new developments during 1881-82, was published in 1883.

[18] Secretary of the Navy William E. Chandler letter of 25 July 1882 to Lieutenant Theodorus B. M. Mason.

[19] *Naval Operations of the War with Spain.* Appendix to the Report of the Chief of the Bureau of Navigation, 1898 (Washington, 1898), 33.

[20] "Notes on the Early History of Naval Intelligence in the United States," 176.

[21] Rear Admiral A. P. Niblack, USN, *The History and Aims of the Office of Naval Intelligence* (Washington, 1920), 6.

[22] *Ibid.*

[23] A. T. Mahan, *The Influence of Sea Power Upon History, 1660-1783* (Boston, 1890), 25-89.

[24] During 1856-59 the U.S. and Britain each completed six large wooden steam screw frigates armed with shell guns. For a few years, until the advent of the armored warship, it could be said that these were the most powerful warships of their day. The steel predreadnought battleship could be said to have come into existence in the 1890s; the all-big-gun *Dreadnought* was completed in 1906.

[25] Friedrich A. Hayek, *The Counter Evolution of Science; Studies on the Abuse of Reason* (New York, 1964), 143 ff.

[26] A Navy-wide system of alphanumerical subject classification was promulgated in 1923 with the first edition of the *Navy Filing Manual.*

[27] They may have been more carefully examined then. "In general, unclassified information is grossly neglected. . . . The remarkable achievements of technical intelligence collection systems over the past two decades have led to the excessive dependence upon such sources to the neglect of unclassified information." (W. T. Lee, "Intelligence: Some Issues of Performance," in *Arms, Men, and Military Budgets; Issues for Fiscal Year 1978,* ed. F. P. Hoeber and W. Schneider, Jr. (New York, 1977), 311.

[28] Robert C. Duncan, *America's Use of Sea Mines* (White Oak, Md., 1962), 38, 46.

[29] Ibid., 50; *Navy Ordnance Activities, World War,* 115.

[30] O.N.I. reports from this collection are cited here by subject file and "Register" (report) number, with verbal title and date where appropriate. Sims material in this file includes such items as: R-2-c, 02-323: Remarks on that Portion of the Fighting Efficiency of a Fleet which is Dependent on the Straight Shooting of the Guns (1901). R-4-a, 02-161A: Marksmanship, Gun Pointing, Telescopic Sights, Gun Mounts, etc. (1902). R-4-a, 02-261: The Morris Tube Target and its Importance . . .; The Essential Requirements of Training and Elevating Gear for Heavy Turret Guns (1902). R-4-a, 02-161B: Superiority of English Marksmanship over that of U.S. (1902). R-2-c, 05-228: Gunnery and Battle Practice, British Navy (1905). R-4-a, 06-462: Tactics and Target Practice, Japan (1906). R-4-a, 07-521A: Comparison of U.S. Army and Navy Methods of Fire Control (1907).

[31] R-2-c, 06-472: Rate of Change Instruments for Fire Control (1906).

[32] R-4-a, 402: Fire Control, Japanese Navy (1910-37).

[33] R-2-b, 5226: Battle Practice—Deductions from Naval Engagements of European War.

[34] U-1-i, 7318.

[35] A. T. Mahan, "Reflections . . . Suggested by the Battle of the Japan Sea," U.S.N.I. *Proceedings,* XXXII (June 1906), 447-471. W. S. Sims, "The Inherent Tactical Qualities of All-Big-Gun, One-Caliber Battleships . . . ," *Ibid.*, (December 1906), 1337-1366.

[36] Typical of these are: U-1-d, 5788: Notes of Naval Interest from Abroad (1915). R-2-d, 8750: Gunnery Notes, England (1917-18). U-1-i, 7039: British Battle Cruisers and Miscellaneous Notes (1916). U-1-i, 6109A: Various Notes on the British Navy (1916). U-1-i, 7288C: Confidential Notes (1917).

[37] U-1-i, 7288B: Notes from Fleet Diary, April 2, '16 to . . . July 20 (1916), p. 7.

[38] Proceedings of the General Board of the Navy (1913), p. 40. In Operational Archives Branch, Naval Historical Center.

[39] E-12-b, 669 (1909-11).

[40] E-12-c, 3338 (1912).

[41] E-12-b, 1019 (1911).

[42] F-1-a, 1105: Triple Gun Turrets, Italy (1911).

[43] F-1-b, 5638: Three-Gun Turrets, Russia (1908-15). Austria also mounted triple turrets in its VIRIBUS UNITIS class.

[44] F-1-a, 2128: Four-Gun Turrets (1912-14).

[45] "Investigation of the Explosion on Board the French Battleship Jena, March 12, 1907" (Appendix C), in H. G. Rickover, *How the Battleship Maine was Destroyed* (Washington, 1976), 141-144.

[46] For the sake of brevity; I cite only report numbers here:

A-2-d,	1855A	A-2-c,	1320
	1855B		1321
	1855C		1414
	1855D		2079B
	2790		2336B
	3110		2355
A-2-a,	736		2491
	1530	A-2-b,	295

[47] See, for example, Hector C. Bywater, "Elevation and Range of British Naval Guns," *Scientific American, CXXIX* (July 1923), 26, 71. This attracted some public, as well as naval, attention.

[48] An Act of 4 March 1923 provided $6,500,000 to elevate the guns of *Florida* (BB-30) through *Idaho* (BB-42).

[49] A Deficiency Act for Fiscal 1924, approved 2 April 1924, repealed this appropriation.

[50] E-11-a, 16145 and 16145A: Elevation of Japanese Guns.

[51] E-12-a, 08-708: Elevation of Guns (1908-24).

[52] Parkes, *op. cit., passim.*

[53] E-11-a, 18593: Elevation of Guns, British (1927-34).

[54] "H. M. Battleships 'Nelson' and 'Rodney,'" *Monthly Information Bulletin,* XI (May 1929), 18-27.

[55] "Germany: Damage Control," *Monthly Information Bulletin,* V (1 May 1923), 49-111.

[56] The Library of Congress holds the 1920 and 1923 German editions, plus the 1921 English edition titled *Kiel und Jutland.*

[57] *The Battle of Jutland, 31 May—1 June 1916* (Monograph No. 1) (Newport, R.I.: Naval War College, 1920), pp. 5-46.

[58] *Monthly Information Bulletin,* II (15 May 1920; 15 June 1920; 15 July 1920).

[59] R-3-c, 13826B and 13826C: Fire Control System, German Navy.

[60] Correspondence and sales circular from George Grottstuck, Berlin, in U-1-e, 07-800: Photographs and Particulars of Six Torpedo Boat Destroyers for Sale (1907).

[61] R-3-c, 13826D: Fire Control System, German Navy. (1921-37).

CHAPTER 27

Airpower and the British Admiralty between the World Wars

Geoffrey Till

Royal Naval College at Greenwich

The weaknesses of British naval aviation and the deficiencies in the Admiralty's attitudes about airpower at sea became apparent from the start of the Second World War. These deficiencies are often attributed to the Admiralty's having a kind of battleship complex which led it to exaggerate the power of the big gun in warfare at sea and to underestimate the revolutionary effect of new weapons such as the submarine and aircraft.

One reason for this was certainly a persistent tendency to overestimate the effectiveness of anti-aircraft gunnery. "The Navy hold the view," the First Sea Lord told the Government in 1936, "that our anti-aircraft fire will be so severe in future, [that] we hope to make the problem of attacking ships one which is an improper one to carry out."[1] In the following year, the Naval Staff argued that in the event of a large German air attack on the Fleet the presence of RAF fighters might be ". . . possibly as great an embarrassment as assistance. If they attacked the enemy when the latter were within gun range of the Fleet, they would run serious risk of being shot down by our own gunfire, as the Naval Staff do not believe that any Commander-in-Chief would withhold his anti-aircraft fire and be content to rely solely for the security of his Fleet upon the unassessable outcome of a contest between fighters and bombers."[2] For this reason, and for others too, the Admiralty generally believed that the main function of airpower at sea was to provide the conditions in which naval gunfire would win the battle. Three months before the Second World War started, the Naval Staff noted that "of our 6 Capital ships, only *Hood*, *Renown* and *Repulse* have sufficient speed to catch the German ships. Our battleships would have to cooperate with aircraft carriers in hopes that the enemy's speed could be reduced as a result of torpedo aircraft attacks and the raiders then brought to action by the battleship."[3] The persistence of the view, at least in some quarters, that airpower could only be ancillary is often held to be a prime cause for some of the naval reverses of the Second World War.

At the time, and indeed subsequently, the reason for such errors in judgment was thought to reside in the conservative nature of sailors. Don't they often, it was argued, fail to recognise the potential value of new weapons? Didn't they battle for years against the transition to steam, dismiss the submarine as "unfair, underhand and damned unEnglish" and repeatedly fail to learn the lessons of convoy? Perhaps this conservatism had something to do with the way in which sailors administer themselves—or with the nature of the society from which they sprang. More generally, perhaps, a reluctance to recognise the implications of technical change is somehow a part of the "military mind"? To Basil Liddell Hart, the Admiralty's perverse adherence to an outmoded weapons system like the battleship simply demonstrated the fact that "a scientific habit of thought is the least thing that military education and training have fostered. Perhaps this is an unalterable condition, for the services might hardly survive if they parted company with sentiment—if the bulk of their members detached themselves from the loyalties which are incompatible with the single-minded loyalty to truth that science demands."[4]

When confronted with the proposition that the Fleet Air Arm was deficient because of the conservatism of the Admiralty, however, some authorities seek to reverse the equation. The Admiralty was conservative about the possibilities of naval aviation because the Fleet Air Arm was deficient. The deficiencies are explained, instead, by reference to the malign influence of circumstances beyond the Admiralty's control. Admiral Sir Herbert Richmond was one of the Navy's severest critics about most things but even he made something of an exception where the state of the Fleet Air Arm was concerned. "The fons et origo of our deficiencies," he told a friend in the Air Ministry, "lies in the separation of the Naval Air Service from the Navy and not in a lack of appreciation on the part of the Navy of the possibilities and future of aircraft in war at sea."[5]

Richmond was here referring to the particular circumstance which some authorities claim to be the biggest single source of weakness in British naval aviation—the so-called "dual control" system. As a result of a politico-military compromise of 1923-24, responsibility for the Fleet Air Arm was divided between the Air Ministry and the Admiralty. This meant that the design, supply, maintenance and number of naval aircraft was a matter of negotiation between the two services; that general administration, planning and development was shared between two departments of state and, more obviously; that the personnel of the Fleet Air Arm were partly naval and partly RAF. The arrangement was intended to solve a demarcation dispute in which the Air Ministry claimed ultimate responsibility for all defence operations in the air while the Admiralty did the same for those at sea. It was a most cumbersome system, riddled with semantic and philosophical obscurities, which inevitably became a cause of rancorous disputes between the two services until the Admiralty resumed full control over naval aviation in the late 1930's. In view of all this, it is not surprising that naval writers tend to see this arrangement as the main author of the Fleet Air Arm's misfortunes. Obviously the needs of naval aviation were different from those of the RAF proper and, equally obviously, the Air Ministry would give the latter precedence over the former. In such a situation, naval aviation was bound to suffer—especially in those areas where Air Ministry influence—or interference—was at its height, such as aircraft design and supply and the training and provision of air personnel.

There are, therefore, two explanations for the undoubted deficiencies of British naval aviation at the outbreak of war in 1939. The first is the view that the Navy, and especially its elite, the Gunnery Branch, suffered from a battleship complex which blinded them to the possibilities of airpower at sea. The second is that such difficulties as existed must be largely attributed to circumstances beyond the Admiralty's control, such as, for example, to the general neglect of defence during the interwar period and, more particularly, to the control over naval aviation exerted by the Air Ministry.

Assessing the relative importance of these competing explanations is a most complex task and, in a limited space, it seems best to focus on one particular aspect of the case in the hope that it will shed light on the issue as a whole. Consideration of the factors that determined the actual *size* of the Fleet Air Arm seems an obvious facet to concentrate upon for one of the most common criticisms of the force was of the few aircraft it deployed at the outbreak of World War II. In September 1939, for instance, there were only about 147 torpedo/spotter/reconnaissance aircraft, 41 amphibians and 30 fighters serving at sea with the Fleet. This was a tiny force compared to the naval (air) wings of the U.S. and Japanese navies of the time.

While such low numbers may possibly have reflected low perceptions of the importance of airpower at sea, they also helped create them. Low numbers, for example, encouraged the development of multi-purpose aircraft because naval officers, having few aircraft available, naturally wanted to make each as individually versatile as possible in order to produce a force of adequate flexibility. This led to several generations of generalist aircraft which, especially in fighter categories, did not compare well with their foreign counterparts. The quality of the aircraft also had an obvious bearing on the quality of the force as a whole and there were plenty of naval officers who recognised the consequent dangers of this policy. "It seems to me," wrote Admiral Backhouse (a future First Sea Lord), "that if we continue to provide in one aircraft for every possible duty we shall merely defeat our object of getting a type which is of real utility at sea, having regard to what we want them to do and what they are likely to meet in the way of enemy aircraft."[6] Such doubts proved in the end to have been entirely justified but low numbers more or less obliged the Admiralty to proceed with the policy. Interestingly, it was the airmen themselves who came up with this particular answer to the problems of low numbers.

In a more general way, low numbers meant that naval airpower could not achieve its object and demonstrate its power by substituting quantity for quality. It could not make up for the undoubted deficiencies of individual aircraft by launching massed or sustained air attacks. The Fleet Air Arm, therefore, found it difficult to make the kind of dramatic impression probably needed to persuade the doubtful and attract major institutional support. British naval aviation therefore found it difficult to make that quantum jump from being a supportive, ancillary weapon to being a primary and even decisive one.

Most senior naval officers were convinced of the importance of airpower at sea but thought that it lay mainly in providing the best conditions for the big guns to win the battle. Reconnaissance aircraft would find the enemy, strike aircraft would slow him down and attack his carriers, spotters would direct the fire of the fleet and fighters would help defeat enemy air interference. There was an important exception to this quite cautious assessment, which concerns the prospect of launching (or dealing with) air attacks on warships in harbour. From 1914 onwards, British naval aviators had devoted considerable thought to this idea. A massed torpedo strike on the High Seas Fleet in harbour was in preparation at the end of World War I but peace came too soon for it to be tried out. Associated exercises were repeatedly practised during the interwar period, especially in the Mediterranean Fleet, and, of course, bore abundant fruit in the attack on Taranto in 1940. This apart, the notion that airpower could win battles on its own was far from the thoughts of most naval officers although nearly all were agreed that none could be won without it, at least in normal circumstances.

Since the size of the force was clearly fundamental to its anticipated role, an analysis of the reasons why the Fleet Air Arm was so small should throw light on the general issue of whether naval conservatism or external circumstances had most to do with the slow development of British naval aviation.

One of the most obvious reasons for the low numbers was the limited carrying capacity of the fleet. The Washington Naval Treaty of 1922 limited U.S. and British carrier tonnage to a common ceiling of 135,000 tons but in a way which, in the economic circumstances of the time, particularly penalised the British whose first generation carriers were ". . . in the nature of gropings, experimental and obsolete."[7] Partly by being able to capitalise on British experience, partly by wisdom and partly by accident, the U.S. Navy was able to start its naval air wing with second generation carriers able to operate far more aircraft per ton of carrier displacement than the British. Thus the four British carriers *Argus, Hermes, Eagle* and *Furious* totalled some 70,350 tons (over half the British allowances) but operated only 84 aircraft between them. This was only slightly more than the aircraft complement of the *Enterprise* whose tonnage was less than half this total at a theoretical 33,000 tons. With a common upper limit and with the maintenance of their present carrier force, the British were condemned, therefore, to a permanent numerical inferiority. The U.S. Navy also benefitted from a newly acquired and apparently fortuitous lead in certain aspects of carrier technology. The production of an efficient athwartship arrester gear, for example, meant, in conjunction with a safety barrier, that the U.S. Navy could park some aircraft on deck while landing others—and this had important implications for the size of the carrier's aircraft complement and the manner of its operation. The British, on the other hand, had temporarily abandoned arrester gear altogether—a retrograde step undertaken, curiously enough, at the insistence of the airmen themselves. Ominously, their own experience led the British (and the Air Ministry especially) habitually to under-rate the ability of U.S. and even the new, larger British ships actually to operate the aircraft they carried.

The British carrier force was not only individually deficient in such important respects as these but it was also quite diverse in age, speed, design, aircraft complement and general reliability. This meant it was extremely difficult to operate the force as a unit, however desirable such a practice was thought to be—and this too reduced the number of aircraft that could be brought to bear in fleet exercises. Finally, the carriers themselves were the product of a process of technical innovation which was disagreeably fast in that it often rendered specific design features and sometimes whole carriers obsolete even before they were completed. The pace of change slowed down during the interwar period but this earlier experience led the British to a certain agnosticism about the possibilities of technical advance which so hindered attempts to increase the number of aircraft operated by the Fleet as to be partially self-confirming. A disinclination to take technical risks, for instance, conspired with financial constraints to delay the launching of *Ark Royal* from 1929 to 1937—a delay which of course prolonged the period when aircraft numbers were restricted by the existence of the older carriers.

Another severe constraint on the numerical expansion of the Fleet Air Arm was an acute shortage in personnel volunteering for flying duties. To a certain extent, this may be attributed to a general feeling among the younger generation that their seniors disapproved of this specialisation to the extent that their careers were likely to suffer as a consequence of their choice. It is hard to find evidence actually to justify this feeling (and indeed, one of the first batch of volunteers actually ended up as First Sea Lord) but it undoubtedly existed. On the other hand, the Admiralty argued that the main reason for the continued shortfall in volunteers was the young officer's reluctance to be seconded to another service, the RAF, at a formative and sensitive part of their careers. An opinion survey of December 1926 conducted in the Mediterranean Fleet showed that young officers were indeed deterred from joining the flying service by fears about their career prospects in a force which seemed to have two masters. "It is not clear," they said, "who will be the pilot's Friend." Many also argued that "they joined the Navy to become Naval Officers and they do not intend to waste the four most valuable and receptive years of their service in a job where they have little or no opportunity of handling and dealing with men, learning command and gaining sea-sense."[8] The Admiralty was convinced that these feelings were both inevitable and would also impede progress under the present system. This conviction was a most important reason for their determination to regain control of the Fleet Air Arm.

The problem of finding enough personnel was, however, not uncommon in the flying services. The RAF solved the problem for themselves by inaugurating a scheme for short service commissions (not, at first, considered suitable for the Navy) and for the employment of non-commissioned officers as pilots. The U.S. Navy also resorted, among other things, to the use of enlisted men. The Admiralty wanted to do the same, but the Air Ministry stuck rigidly to the letter of the 1923-24 agreement (under which it was agreed that Fleet Air Arm pilots and observers should be officers of the Navy or Air Force) and refused to consider the idea of rating or petty officer pilots until forced to do so by the government in 1936.

Dual control limited the expansion of naval aviation in much more severe and direct ways than this however. In the early postwar period, the RAF was in such an organisational shambles that even the Navy agreed it was largely inevitable that the naval air wing should shrink practically to vanishing point. In April 1918, for example, the Royal Naval Air Service consisted of nearly 3000 land and sea-based aircraft: within two years this number had declined to just over 50. In the early and mid 1920's, however, the Admiralty's assessments of their future air requirement usually envisaged a force of between 300 to 400 aircraft complete with a refashioned carrier force. By the early 1930's, the Naval Staff were planning for a Fleet Air Arm in excess of 500 sea-going aircraft and such plans lay beneath the considerable expansion of naval airpower started in the late interwar period.

The operation of the Ten Years Rule stretched such programmes out but, even so, when in 1926 the Admiralty proposed a quite modest plan aimed at creating a Fleet Air Arm of 241 aircraft by 1935, the Air Staff described this proposal as being ". . . out of proportion to the present financial stringency" and recommended 144 aircraft instead. "The

[Admiralty] programme," they commented, "has evidently been drawn up with the idea of cramming aircraft into every possible space which can take them in every suitable ship in the British Navy."[9] They doubted whether such large numbers of aircraft were needed or could even be operated by the Royal Navy. They also remained unimpressed by the advances made in this area by the U.S. Navy.

The Air Staff, however, could not actually veto Admiralty air expansion schemes. The procedure had been laid down by the Balfour Committee Report of 1923 and subsequently confirmed by the Trenchard-Keyes concordat of the following year. The Air Staff could only make things awkward for the Admiralty and force them to justify their programmes before higher authority. The Cabinet and the Treasury, on the other hand, could act against the Navy's schemes and did so with considerable effect especially in the late 1920's and early 1930's. From 1929 to 1932, for example, only eighteen aircraft were added to the Fleet Air Arm's strength despite the Admiralty's efforts. What made the situation particularly galling for the Admiralty was the fact that the Treasury won its battles with ammunition openly supplied by the Air Ministry. In 1934, for example, the Naval Staff sought authorisation for a new carrier with a complement of seventy-two aircraft—*Ark Royal*—to commission in 1938. The Air Ministry objected that this involved an increase of 45 per cent in the present strength of the Fleet Air Arm (itself something of an indictment of policy to date) which, they told the Chancellor of the Exchequer, was not justified by any strategic necessity. They doubted whether the carrier could operate seventy-two aircraft efficiently and noted that "the effectiveness of aircraft carriers as an adjunct to a fleet has still to be fully demonstrated . . . (and) . . . there is surely much to be said for gaining experience if possible by the expenditure of other countries." A delay was suggested so that the Admiralty could see how the new Japanese and U.S. carriers turned out in practice. Finally, the Air Ministry denied that it was being "unduly obtrusive in interesting itself in . . . a major proposal for increased provision for the Fleet Air Arm which is an integral part of the RAF."[10] As it happened, the Admiralty won this particular battle but the fact that it had to be fought at all demonstrates the peculiar difficulties the Royal Navy had to face in expanding the strength of its airpower.

The Air Ministry's opposition to naval air expansion programmes was a general function of the rivalry between the two services for resources at a time when defence budgets were very low. It was therefore important that the claims of the airmen took a considerable hold on the public imagination on both sides of the Atlantic. One British naval officer wrote: "The deliberate propaganda of the Air Ministry directed as it is to instilling the public mind with the idea airpower is of the first importance and has become almost a substitute for sea-power is slowly creating a dangerous situation."[11] Even when in the mid 1930s defence funds began to swell as a result of the increased likelihood of war, the Admiralty's plans were constrained by the priority in the allocation of economic and industrial resources accorded to the RAF and Air Defence. In Chatfield's view, so much energy was devoted to air defence that the Navy was ". . . going through a most anxious time." He told the other Chiefs of Staff in January 1938 that, "Our battlefield was composed largely of old ships, many of which had fought at the battle of Jutland. If we had to despatch an adequate fleet to the Far East to meet that of Japan, we could leave practically no modern ships at home to deal with the German and Italian fleets which were composed of comparatively new ships. Moreover, our new ships, when completed were now going to sea without their fire control instruments owing to the heavy demands occasioned by the high priority of equipment given to the air defence of Great Britain."[12] In the same way and possibly with rather more overall justification, the Airmen saw the navy as the main threat to their well-being and even, at one stage, to their actual survival.

This general rivalry between the two services narrowed down to a number of symbolic controversies. The "bomb versus the battleship" debate was one,[13] the argument whether guns or aircraft should defend Singapore was another, and the dispute over the control of the Fleet Air Arm was a third. Beneath the dispute over control, lay the view that the Fleet Air Arm and the RAF themselves were necessarily in a state of mutual opposition. This may be deduced from a remarkable letter sent by Secretary of State for Air Lord Thomson to Prime Minister Ramsay MacDonald in early 1930: "The Fleet Air Arm is an integral part of the Royal Air Force; the machines allocated to it are included in our total strength, and each machine so allotted means one less immediately available for Home Defence against attack by the shore-based aircraft of European Powers. The Navy, of course, needs some aircraft, and an adequate number can always be made available in case of emergency; but the principal danger we have to guard against is air attack by shore-based aircraft."[14] Such a total lack of sympathy for naval needs makes the Admiralty's determination to regain total control over the Fleet Air Arm readily understandable.

For the same reason, whenever proposals were made for the limitation of aircraft by means of international arms control measures, the Air Ministry invariably suggested that naval aviation should bear the brunt of such limitations. Their reason for doing so was quite simple in that such proposals were nearly always based on the idea that each participant should accept a single ceiling to cover all aircraft in its armed forces. The Air Ministry naturally measured their air requirements against the most powerful air fleet within striking range which for many years was that of France. How, they asked, can we hope to match French air strength if a sizeable proportion of the air fleet authorised us by treaty is taken up by the

Admiralty's vainglorious desire to compete with U.S. naval aviation? When it was suggested in 1931 that air disarmament should begin with the complete abolition of all seaborne air forces, for instance, the Chief of the Air Staff, while admitting that this was too much to hope for, nevertheless urged "that negotiations should be opened as early as possible with the U.S.A. for the drastic limitation of the aircraft carrying capacity of the fleets of the two countries on the basis of parity and at as low level as can be secured."[15]

The conflict between the air demands of the two services, was also very apparent in the Admiralty's failure to have the number of shore-based aircraft available for trade protection greatly increased. The Air Staff usually maintained that the needs of the Metropolitan Air Force must come first and so were unsympathetic to the substantial reinforcement of Coastal Command, lest "The permanent subtractions from our air striking powers which will result will vitally endanger the security of the whole of Great Britain and ultimately of the whole Empire."[16] The same argument applied to the Naval Staff's desire to build up sea-going aviation for trade protection purposes. In August 1939, for example, the Admiralty requested aircraft to equip four reserve carriers to hunt down surface raiders but the Chief of the Air Staff insisted that it was "imperative to resist further inroads into a Metropolitan Air Force which would already be very hard put to it to carry out its responsibilities in war . . . it would be preferable that we should face the risk of losses on our trade routes in the Atlantic rather than accept a further reduction of our Air Forces at home, which we could not afford."[17]

The tension was not, in fact, significantly eased by the general expansion of Britain's air strength in the late 1930s. "The problem [of building up the Fleet Air Arm]," noted the First Lord, "is aggravated at every point by the strain put upon the national resources by the much larger expansion of the R.A.F. which is taking place over the same period."[18] The apparent clash between the requirements of maritime and metropolitan airpower, of course, remained throughout the Second World War.

All this seems to indicate that the air requirements of the Navy and the Air Force were indeed in conflict and that any increase in their share of the nation's air resources which one or the other side won for itself was almost bound to be at the expense of the other. Since both protagonists were biting on the same apple in this way, it was entirely natural for the Air Staff to argue that air resources absorbed by maritime aviation could not be devoted to the prosecution of strategic bombing and so the needs of the former should be tailored to suit the interests of the latter.

The Air Staff's policy was clearly hostile in that it unavoidably put obstacles in the way of those who wanted to expand the number of aircraft deployed for maritime purposes but the extent to which this hostility had practical results depended in large measure on the influence over Fleet Air

Arm actually exerted by the Air Ministry. As has already been shown, the dual control system gave the Air Ministry a fair amount of institutional authority over Fleet Air Arm policy and the effectiveness of this was reinforced by the usefulness of many of their arguments to the Treasury in their own efforts to limit naval expenditures.

Even though external circumstances such as these posed difficult problems for the Admiralty, it might still be argued that the Royal Navy displayed a want of energy in dealing with them (especially, perhaps, in comparison with the similar efforts of the U.S. and Japanese navies)—and that this want of energy largely reflected an overcautious and unimaginative approach to the possibilities of airpower at sea. The dual control system, however, not only created additional problems which impeded the development of naval aviation but also made it difficult for the Admiralty to solve them—and not least because it destroyed, weakened or diverted the officers and agencies which might otherwise have done so.

In the first place, the great majority of the Royal Navy's first generation of flyers had either left the service or had been absorbed into the Royal Air Force. For something like fifteen years the Fleet Air Arm was deprived of the kind of senior management which could have argued the air case against battleship admirals and provided the long term vision of future war at sea needed to inspire the rank and file to overcome present adversities. An exception to this was the sadly truncated career but impressive achievements of Admiral Sir Reginald Henderson who was responsible for considerable advances in the development of naval aviation—not the least of which was the Royal Navy's armoured carrier programme. By its effects on the leadership of the Fleet Air Arm, however, the dual control system made this kind of inspiration from on high the exception rather than the rule it might well otherwise have been.

Again the peculiar workings of the dual control system meant that naval aviation was inadequately represented in the Naval Staff—and not least because it obliged such naval air agencies as existed to spend a disproportionate amount of their time on humdrum administrative and technical tasks. This left them too little opportunity to reflect on their present purposes and their future directions. The first manual on the employment of airpower at sea, for example, only came out in 1936 and even that was something of a trial balloon. With a temporary absence of inspiration from on high, a lack of institutional muscle, and an imperfect vision of the way ahead, it is perhaps unsurprising that British naval aviation briefly faltered at the problems set it by unfortunate circumstances.

This brief indecision contributed to the rather moderate rate of advance made by British naval aviation during the interwar period. It resulted in an actual level of performance which did not dispel scepticism amongst the uncommitted to the degree that the potential of airpower at sea properly warranted. In short, by its effects on the leadership of British naval aviation and the quality and quantity of much of its equipment, the dual control system does much to explain the continued dominance of the view that naval airpower would develop as something which would aid the big-gun battle fleet rather than as something which might some day replace it.

There are therefore two alternative, and to some extent competing, explanations for the relatively poor state of the Fleet Air Arm at the onset of the Second World War. The first is the conventional naval case which largely attributes the blame to the way in which the Navy's air wing was jointly administered by the Admiralty and the Air Ministry. The equally familiar prosecution case attaches blame principally to the Navy's habitual conservatism about new weapons and new techniques. It is obviously very difficult to assign relative weight between these two explanations and the answer will certainly lie somewhere between the two extremes. Nonetheless, the fact that such naval conservatism that existed in this area can be shown to be at least partly the product of the dual control system suggests that a verdict biased towards the naval case is likely to be nearer the mark. In short, the British Admiralty in its development of airpower at sea during the interwar period appears to have been more sinned against than sinning.

FOOTNOTES

[1] Admiral Sir Ernle M. Chatfield at "6th Meeting of the Vulnerability of Capital Ships Enquiry", 27th May 1936. Cab 16/147, Public Record Office (PRO) London. Quotations from Crown-copyright records are by permission of the Controller of H. M. Stationary Office.

[2] Admiralty Memo to Sir Thomas Inskip, Minister for Coordination of Defence, dated 20 April 1937. Cab 64/25, PRO.

[3] Chiefs of Staff Paper 930 of 20th June 1939. Cab 53/II, PRO.

[4] Quoted in R. Hough, *The Hunting of Force Z* (New English Library, London) p. 67.

[5] Letter of 14th Oct 1942 to Air Marshal Sir Wilfred Freeman in Richmond MSS at the National Maritime Museum, Greenwich, London. Quoted by permission of the Trustees.

[6] Minute, 4th Sep 1931 in Adm 116/2792, PRO.

[7] Lord Lee of Fareham (First Lord) at the 14th Meeting of Washington Naval Conference, 30 Dec 1921. Adm 1/9271, PRO.

[8] Keyes Papers, 8/13 at Churchill College, Cambridge.

[9] Air Staff Memo of 1st July 1926. Air 8/82, PRO.

[10] Air Ministry letter of 23rd Jan 1934. Air 5/1124, PRO.

[11] Letter of 3rd Sep 1925 by Capt R. M. Bellairs to Admiral W. H. H. Henderson, Henderson MSS, National Maritime Museum, Greenwich. Quoted by permission of the Trustees.

[12] Admiral Sir Ernle M. Chatfield at 227th Meeting of the Chiefs of Staff Committee of 19th Jan 1938. Cab 53/8, PRO.

[13] This issue is explored further in my "Airpower and the Battleship in the 1920's" in *Technical Change and British Naval Policy*, ed by Bryan Ranft (Hodder & Stoughton, London 1977, Holmes & Meir, New York).

[14] Letter of 13th Jan 1930. Adm 116/3479, PRO.

[15] Memo by Air Marshal Sir John M. Salmond of 2 Oct 1931. Adm 116/2793, PRO.

[16] Air Marshal Sir Edward L. Ellington, Chief of the Air Staff, in Chiefs of Staff Paper 504 of 23 July 1936. Cab 53/28, PRO.

[17] Air Vice Marshal Sir Cyril L. M. Newall at the 310th Chiefs of Staff Meeting of 2nd Aug 1939. Cab 53/11, PRO.

[18] Air Bolton M. Eyres-Monsell, First Lord of The Admiralty, Memorandum CP 13 (39) of May 1936. Cab 16/152, PRO.

CHAPTER 28

The Stark Memorandum and the American National Security Process, 1940

Mark M. Lowenthal

Library of Congress

In the period prior to the entry of the United States into World War II American military planners tried to grapple with the nation's position in the world as it then was, the current and expected American security needs, and with probable or preferable courses of action for war itself. Many of these planning papers were drawn up in conjunction with representatives of the British military staffs, leading to a vast profusion of ideas, memoranda and plans. But in terms of overall American and Allied grand strategy for the war few of these numerous documents can be said to have been of the same seminal importance as the memorandum produced by Admiral Harold R. Stark, Chief of Naval Operations, in the autumn of 1940.

Much has already been written analyzing the final Stark Memorandum, work which has largely taken the production of the memorandum as a given.[1] Little has been done to place the Stark Memorandum firmly within the context of contemporary events in United States policy planning. Yet a deeper analysis of Stark's purposes, especially his more immediate ones, reveals a great deal more about this important paper itself and this crucial period in the evolution of United States policy and strategy in general.

The ensuing analysis of the Stark Memorandum proceeds from a view of the policy process as a longer continuum than is possible by focusing in on only the crucial decisions. Decision-making analysis of this sort implies an activity that is actually all too rare in government—the conscious selection of distinct policy options which are indeed "decisive," terminal or mutually exclusive, decisions which are easily isolated from surrounding events. The assumed frequency of these opportunities, which are in fact rare, distorts perceptions of the policy process by showing it only when working in the extreme, ignoring or accepting as a given the more usual periods of policy formulation—the continuum—during which the broad working patterns and relationships are established. Major decisions are not made on a day-to-day basis, even during true periods of crisis. Rather, some decisions are made, after which reactions and results are awaited before the next set of options is confronted. Nor are there many decisions which are unique or epochal. Most decisions represent extensions, implementations, renewals or alterations of these rarer major decisions, highlighting once again the need to comprehend the broader continuum of policy formation.

These basic premises are especially valid in an examination of the Stark Memorandum. Examining this document in relative isolation tends to obscure its relationship to the contemporaneous policy events, and, perhaps more important, the motives for which Admiral Stark drafted his memorandum in the first place.

An examination of the events surrounding the drafting and presentation of the Stark Memorandum reveals at least three different purposes behind Stark's efforts, operating at three different levels. On the personal level Stark wrote the paper in part to clear his own mind, to put his thoughts in order so as to clarify them. This, since a primarily personal purpose, requires little further explanation or examination. Stark's immediate purpose within the policy process, however, forms the crux of his reasons, an effort to coax President Roosevelt into a further definition of his own policy preferences, desires and plans. Finally, there was a long-range policy goal, the stating of Stark's own strategic preferences. The personal purpose was quickly satisfied. However, events created a competitive interplay between the immediate and long-range policy purposes which greatly affected the Stark Memorandum's ultimate effect.

The events preceding the Stark Memorandum are well known. Throughout the period of the "Phony War" in Europe United States policy remained much what it had been in the prewar period, friendly to the democracies but stand-offish as well, lacking any firm purpose or sense of direction. For President Roosevelt, as for the leaders then in power in Britain and France, the true magnitude and nature of the conflict were not totally apparent. Roosevelt's policy during this period can best be described as a search for influence without direct involvement.[2]

This shadowy period of policy ended abruptly with the German offensive in the west, which opened a Pandora's box of grave strategic problems and threats. In this period of uncertainty the President's professional military advisers began to take the lead in policy planning through memoranda which suggested lines of policy rather than the plans which responded to policy decisions.

Roosevelt, willing to help the Allies, still felt constrained by the state of public opinion.[3] The mainstay of current military planning was RAINBOW 4, which concentrated on the defense of the Western Hemisphere but also looked forward to United States task forces being sent to South America and the Eastern Atlantic if necessary. This plan stressed the importance of the eventual naval situation and the fate of the British fleet, whose future had been the subject of constant veiled warnings from the Allies during the German attack.[4] These concerns slowly converged with worries over the Western Hemispheric possessions of the Allies. Here, indeed, was a true policy crisis, i.e., an easily definable problem, representing an intensification over past conditions, and requiring a prompt decision, solution or response within a short period of time.

Virtually all of the summer of 1940 was spent in efforts to solve the immediate problem of the German threat. Roosevelt, more so than his professional advisers, had ultimate faith in Britain's ability to survive, as evidenced by the "Strategic Hypothesis" he drew up on June 13, 1940. At that date the President assumed not only Britain's continued resistance through the autumn, but that of French forces as well, although not of France itself. The Joint Planners' analysis of this hypothesis was much more pessimistic, even presuming a possible invasion of Britain, and with the United States not yet able to influence the outcome of the war, a conclusion the Joint Planners wanted kept from the President.[5]

British pressure and American needs continued to converge, brought to unity especially by Lord Lothian, the British Ambassador, and culminating in the Destroyer-Base Deal on September 2, 1940. This exchange of bases for overage destroyers represented a fundamental, basic and epochal policy decision. The United States went from neutral to non-belligerent, and rooted the nation's own security interests in Britain's survival. Whether he realized it or not, Roosevelt had selected a line of policy which carried its own momentum and logic of development unless it were to be reversed. Roosevelt, canny politician that he was, undoubtedly was aware of the nature of his decision, but he neither rushed to embrace these consequences nor chose to advertise his awareness. How far, or at what pace Roosevelt would follow through on these implications remained unclear, and thus there was a fundamental policy decision embedded within a great deal of ultimate vagueness.

This point must be stressed in order to understand the policy purposes for which Admiral Stark drafted his memorandum. Even while the decision to send the destroyers was evolving the United States had begun to send a mission to Britain for a first-hand appraisal of the military situation. The Air Corps and Army representatives on this mission, Major General Delos C. Emmons and Brigadier General George V. Strong, returned to Washington at the end of September 1940 and reported "that sooner or later the United States will be drawn into this war. . . ." They confirmed the wisdom of the decision to support Britain and at the same time promoted a further effort to give a greater definition to policy.[6] Virtually simultaneous with the Emmons-Strong report were the recommendations of the Standing Liaison Committee, the War-Navy-State coordinate body, that it was necessary to draft a more realistic estimate of the world situation and of American policy and preparedness to meet this situation.[7]

These activities underscored just how limited the decision underlying the Destroyer-Base deal was. The Joint Planners responded to the directive for a new national estimate on September 25, 1940. Their initial effort reflected the more optimistic reports coming from Britain but was quite pessimistic on American preparedness and the nation's ability to respond to various possible demands and threats. The spring of 1942 was seen as the period in which the United States would be ready to respond to the various presumed threats, Japan being viewed as the most immediately troublesome one.[8] However, the memorandum fell short of current policy needs on at least two points. First, it did not attempt to define policy any further, but rather reflected the presumed current state of policy, a proper scope of activity for the Joint Planners but not totally responsive to the Liaison Committee's needs. Second, the memorandum was reactive in tone, relying on possible enemy intentions rather than capabilities, and presuming American policy from there.

Little help could be had at this time from President Roosevelt, who had actively entered the campaign for his third term in October 1940. Thus, there was still a need to pressure Roosevelt to examine the implications of his policy and further define its limits as he saw them.

It was at this juncture that the Stark Memorandum emerged as perhaps the focal point of this pressure on the President. Admiral Stark had written a rough paper embodying his views on the strategic situation, something he did habitually to clear his own mind. He then circulated these rough notes among members of his staff, particularly those involved in war plans.[9]

The Admiral, an accomplished staff and planning officer, was under pressure from his own subordinates for clear guidelines on action and policy. Admiral James O. Richardson, Commander-in-Chief of the United States Fleet, had made known his dissatisfaction with the deployment of the fleet at Hawaii during a meeting with the President that October. Richardson had questioned the fleet's deterrent effect on Japan and felt it was unready for action. Admiral Robert Ghormley, who stayed on in London after Emmons and Strong had left, also felt that he lacked guidance on policy in his continuing talks with the British.[10]

On November 4, 1940 a near-final version of the Stark paper had emerged, now a product of the Chief of Naval Operations and his war planners. However, the reason for the memorandum was still Stark's, as he stated in the paper itself. While noting the nation's desire to remain at peace, Stark stated that the possibility of war had to be faced. Stark then said,

. . . I believe our every effort should be directed toward the prosecution of a national policy with mutually supporting diplomatic and military aspects, and having as its guiding feature a determination that any intervention we may undertake shall be such as will ultimately best promote our own national interests. We should see the best answer to the question: "Where should we fight the war, and for what objective?"[11]

With the answer to that question Stark felt he could then better carry out his own professional responsibilities and duties, and best advise the President as to the forces available for preferred policies. The Admiral then went on to state his own views on national objectives, which included preserving the United States' territorial, economic and ideological integrity, retaining its interests in the Far East and preventing "the disruption of the British Empire, with all that such a consummation implies." While this statement was not novel, having been the basis of the Destroyer-Base deal, it was significant as a full acceptance of the implications, which went to the heart of the present policy problem. Stark faced the fact that while Britain might not lose the war if alone, neither could it win alone. In so doing the Chief of Naval Operations moved past the President, who in his campaign speeches was then denying the need for American intervention.[12]

Stark then went on to present an analysis of the strategic situation around the globe, after which he detailed four possible courses of action. Underscoring his purpose once again he noted, "An early decision in this field will facilitate a naval preparation which will best promote the adopted course." The four choices were:

A) essentially Hemispheric Defense, which would keep the nation out of war as long as possible but minimize any American influence on the outcome of the war.

B) a full offensive against Japan and a defensive in the Atlantic, which would leave Britain to fend for itself against Germany and run the risk of a necessary reorientation to the Atlantic should Britain be defeated.

C) equal efforts in both Europe and the Far East, which would spread U.S. forces thin without increasing Britain's offensive power or necesarily holding Japan, would not allow offensives in either theater and could lead to disaster should either front fall.

D) an offensive in the Atlantic as an ally of Britain, coupled with a defensive stance in the Pacific, which would improve the United States' strategic position but undoubtedly involve land operations beyond the Western Hemisphere.[13]

Given his statement of national objectives and his estimate of the British position, Admiral Stark felt that Plan D (or Plan Dog) was the wisest choice, coupled with a defensive stance in the Pacific.[14]

Stark still was not ready to present his memorandum, but again referred it back to his planners. He again confirmed his purposes in letters to his major subordinates on November 12, 1940, the day he formally submitted the paper to Secretary of the Navy Frank Knox. To Admiral Richardson he wrote that he hoped Roosevelt ". . . will give some definite pronouncement on it in order that I may send you something more authoritative than I otherwise could do." To Admiral Thomas C. Hart, commander of the Asiatic Fleet, Stark noted that the President now had the memorandum. ". . . I do not expect any immediate decision, but do hope that it will serve to clarify matters so that, at least, those in authority, will be fully aware of the implications of any particular policy that may be adopted with respect to the war."[15]

An immediate decision from Roosevelt was not forthcoming. Army War Planners took objection to the memorandum's breadth, and the stating of goals which were beyond available strength. General Marshall, who generally agreed with Stark, now sent the paper to the Joint Board and Joint Planners, who were tasked with the preparation of a national estimate and appropriate plans.[16] By now Stark had also received Roosevelt's comments, but there is no record as to what they were. Stark wrote to Marshall, "I am holding the Presidential comment very tight but will tell you when I see you."[17]

Two developments are apparent here. First, Stark's hopes for a relatively quick policy decision on the options presented to Roosevelt were dashed by the President's own diffidence and the cumbersome vertical processes of the Joint Board system of planning coordination. Second, this lack of decision within Washington gave the British an opportunity to use the memorandum for their own, longer-range ends.

The contents of the memorandum had been made available to Captain A. W. Clarke, Britain's Assistant Naval Attache, on a private, unofficial and seemingly clandestine basis, probably by a friendly member of the Navy War Plans Division. From British telegrams this disclosure can be placed around October 31, 1940, twelve days before Stark submitted the memorandum to Secretary Knox.[18] Moreover, based on a letter from Stark to Ghormley on November 16, 1940 it can be assumed that the Chief did not know of this disclosure, for he advised Ghormley, ". . . I think it would probably be best for the British not to know that it [the memorandum] is in your possession. . ." and then went on to report that ". . . we are letting Captain Clarke read it here. . . ."[19]

Clarke now saw the paper for a second, official time, and the British were generally pleased with Stark's preferred option of defeating the European Axis first, Plan D, although they differed with his more limited plans for the Pacific, where Britain hoped to find relief under the American aegis.[20] However, Churchill's views, as stated in a minute to the Admiralty and to his representative on the Chiefs of Staff, General Sir Hastings Ismay, in late November 1940, were that ". . . Britain should, as far as opportunity serves, in every way contribute to strengthen the policy of Admiral Stark, and should not use arguments inconsistent with it." Churchill felt that Stark was ". . . working upon lines which would be likely to bring the United States into the war in the best possible manner for us" and that he was ". . . much encouraged by the American naval views. The paragraphs about our being incapable of winning alone are particularly helpful."[21]

It was in these two developments that Stark lost his immediate purpose but gained his longer-range one. The failure of Roosevelt to act allowed the President seemingly to keep all his options open, as he wished. Simultaneously, this lack of action or decision by the President left the British free to seize the opportunity offered by the Stark Memorandum and continue conversations with Ghormley on the favorable basis which it afforded. The British were pressing for staff talks in Washington by late November 1940, a plan to which the President agreed on November 29, 1940.[22]

Interestingly, this decision was wholly consistent with Roosevelt's failure to act on the Stark Memorandum. Stark had now accepted war as an eventuality. Roosevelt still preferred to think of it as a possibility, and agreed to the staff talks in that spirit, as a contingency, a further exploration without commitment. Roosevelt's decision for the staff talks was a tacit approval of Stark's paper at best, but far from a formal endorsement or willingness to act upon its premises and proffered options.

Work on the Stark Memorandum continued, however, within the Joint Planners, and by December 10, 1940 they had produced an agreed memorandum for presentation to the President. Basically, the new draft represented an adjustment to Army objections to even a limited war against Japan; Plan D remained the recommended course should war with Germany and Japan occur, but this now explicitly accepted the idea of losses in the Far East while the war against Germany was prosecuted.[23] This plan was tentatively approved by the Joint Board on December 21, 1940. Efforts to have Secretary of State Cordell Hull join in a presentation to the President failed on January 3, 1941, the Secretary feeling he should not be involved in presenting a military paper to the President, despite urgings from Stark and Marshall on the need to have a definite and agreed policy upon which to base planning for detailed cooperation with Britain should the United States enter the war.[24] Thus, even at that date Stark's immediate policy purpose remained manifest.

However, by mid-February 1941 Stark informed the Secretary of the Joint Board, Colonel W. P. Scobey, that although the new draft had been shown to the Secretaries of War and the Navy it was improbable that they would indicate their concurrence or submit the paper to the President for formal approval. Stark advised that, "No further action in connection with this paper is required at this time."[25] Deliberations over the Stark

Memorandum had been overtaken by preparations for the upcoming staff talks, the ABC talks. Stark's immediate purpose had been overtaken by the broader significance of his memorandum.

What, then, was the significance of the preparation of the Stark Memorandum and the Admiral's admitted purposes? What did the failure to gain those purposes signify? Three points stand out.

In the absence of clear decisions from the President as to the implied directions of American policy Stark found himself forced to temporarily usurp Roosevelt's role of defining fundamental policy in order to elicit responses upon which he could build his forces and plan their use. This effort was co-equal with similar efforts elsewhere, although it was natural that the Navy took the lead, given their relative readiness compared with the Army's and the proper assumption that the Navy would bear the brunt of any initial hostilities. In short, there was a noticeable and conscious lapse in policy definition at the top which Stark tried to fill, or rather prod into action, just as he himself was being prodded by his own subordinates.

Once the memorandum was presented it became lost for nearly a month in the time-consuming vertical processes of the Joint Board and its committees. Nearly six months after the fall of France the United States still lacked a body adequately geared to handle crisis situations. Nor, as Hull's diffidence over joining in a presentation shows, was there adequate political-military liaison, or an appreciation of the necessary unity between diplomacy and the military.

The ultimate failure of Roosevelt to act on the Stark Memorandum allowed the British to seize the initiative it offered them. By approving the request for staff conversations the President tacitly approved Stark's conclusions without formally committing himself to them as guidelines for future policy. The President still was not willing to be prodded where he would not yet go himself.

The drafting, submission and fate of the Stark Memorandum illustrate and highlight all of these shortcomings, tendencies and trends in the United States' national security policy process during the crucial winter of 1940-41. An examination of Stark's purposes, the detailed process surrounding and the effects of his memorandum affords greater insight into American policy at that juncture. It is ironic that while failing to achieve his immediate purpose, getting a firm policy definition from President Roosevelt, Admiral Stark had successfully drafted the foundation for the strategy by which the Allies eventually won the war.

FOOTNOTES

[1] See, for example, Louis Morton, "Germany First: The Basic Concept of Allied Strategy in World War II," in Kent Roberts Greenfield, ed., *Command Decisions* (Washington, 1960), 35; Mark S. Watson, *Chief of Staff: Prewar Plans and Preparations* (Washington, 1950), 118; and Maurice Matloff and Edwin M. Snell, *Strategic Planning for Coalition Warfare, 1941-1942* (Washington, 1953), 25.

[2] This analysis of Roosevelt's policy is based on the author's doctoral dissertation, "Leadership and Indecision: American War Planning and Policy Process, 1937-1942" (Harvard University, 1975), 152-225, 1065-67.

[3] On Roosevelt's diffidence see, for example, his refusal to allow the publication of his June 13, 1940 message to French Premier Paul Reynaud, summarized in Winston S. Churchill, *Their Finest Hour* (Boston, 1949), 183-87; see also Joseph P. Lash, *Roosevelt and Churchill, 1939-1941* (New York, 1976), 161-62.

[4] J. B. No. 325 (Serial 642-4): Joint Army and Navy Basic War Plan—Rainbow No. 4, May 31, 1940, RG 225, National Archives. There are numerous references to the fate of the British fleet in Churchill's telegrams to Roosevelt; see Department of State, *Foreign Relations of the United States, 1940* (Washington, 1958), III, 51, 53-55.

[5] Roosevelt's hypothesis and the Joint Planners' evaluation are in WPD 4199-1: Op-12-CTB, Memorandum, Captain Russell S. Crenshaw (Director, Navy War Plans Division) to Admiral Stark, June 29, 1940, RG 165/281, National Archives.

[6] WPD 4368: *Observations in England:* Memorandum, Emmons and Strong to General Marshall, September 25, 1940, RG 165/281, National Archives. A copy was sent to President Roosevelt on October 9, 1940.

[7] Standing Liaison Committee meeting, September 23, 1940, Minutes of the Liaison Committee, 1938-1943, RG 353, National Archives.

[8] WPD 4321-9: *The Problem of Production of Munitions in Relation to the Ability of the United States to Cope with its Defense Problems in the Present World Situation:* Memorandum, Army War Plans Division to General Marshall, September 25, 1940, RG 165/281, National Archives.

[9] Letter, Stark to Admiral James O. Richardson, November 12, 1940, in File: Ghormley Official Correspondence concerning war plans, 1940-1941, Com Nav Eu, Series II, Item 65, Operational Archives, Navy History Division.

[10] Richardson's testimony in *Pearl Harbor Attack:* Hearing before the Joint Committee on the Investigation of the Pearl Harbor Attack, 79th Congress, 2d session (Washington, 1946), I, 265-66; and James O. Richardson and George C. Dyer, *On the Treadmill to Pearl Harbor* (Washington, 1973), 424-36. Ghormley's requests can be found in various letters to Stark in October and November 1940 in File: NA London (Admiral Ghormley) Letters to GNO, 1940-1941, Navy WPD, Operational Archives, Naval History Division.

[11] Memorandum, Stark to Secretary of the Navy Frank Knox, November 4, 1940, in President's Secretary's File (PSF), Box 63, Departmental Correspondence, Navy Department, November-December 1940, Franklin D. Roosevelt Papers, Hyde Park, N.Y.

[12] *Ibid.*

[13] *Ibid.*

[14] *Ibid.*

[15] The November 12 version of the Stark Memorandum is in PSF, Box 4: Safe File, Plan Dog, Roosevelt Papers, Hyde Park. Letter, Stark to Richardson, November 12, 1940, cited in n. 9. Letter, Stark to Hart, November 12, 1940, *Pearl Harbor Attack Investigation,* XIV, 972.

[16] WPD 4175-15: *National Policy of the United States:* Memorandum, Colonel J. W. Anderson (Acting Asst. Chief of Staff, War Plans Division), to Marshall, November 13, 1940,

and Memorandum, Marshall to Secretary of War Henry L. Stimson, November 13, 1940, RG 165/281, National Archives. J. B. 325 (serial 670): *National Defense Policy for U.S.:* Memorandum, Marshall to Joint Board, November 18, 1940, RG 225, National Archives.

[17] WPD 4175-15: Memorandum, Stark to Marshall, November 22, 1940, RG 165/281, National Archives. The copy of the November 4 draft of the Stark Memorandum cited in n. 11 has some marginal comments which appear to be in Roosevelt's handwriting but are not very substantive, mostly agreeing in very broad terms. Other comments on this draft appear to be those of Knox.

[18] Telegram No. 2490, Nevile Butler (Counsellor, British Embassy in Washington) to Foreign Office, October 31, 1940, Annex III to Memorandum COS (40) 1014, December 5, 1940, CAB 80/24, Public Record Office, London.

[19] Letter, Stark to Ghormley, Serial 044212, November 16, 1940, File: Ghormley—Official Correspondence concerning war plans, 1940-1941, Com Nav Eu, Series II, Item 65, Operational Archives, Naval History Division.

[20] Telegram No. 2750, Butler to Foreign Office, November 20, 1940, Annex IV to Memorandum cited in n. 18. See also, Memorandum, Admiral Sir Sidney Bailey to Vice Chief of Naval Staff, November 14, 1940, ADM 199/1159, Public Record Office, London.

[21] Minute, Churchill to Ismay, et al., November 22, 1940, Annex I to Joint Planners Memorandum JP (40) 762 (S), December 11, 1940, CAB 84/24, Public Record Office, London.

[22] On British pressure for staff talks see Department of State, *Foreign Relations of the United States, 1940* (Washington, 1955), IV, 220-21; and Telegram No. 2802, Lord Lothian to Foreign Office, November 25, 1940, in Paper A 4909/131/45, FO 371/24243, Public Record Office, London. On Roosevelt's acceptance see Telegram No. 2851, Lord Lothian to Foreign Office, November 29, 1940, Annex I to Memorandum cited in n. 18.

[23] On Army objections see WPD 4175-15: *National Policy of the United States:* Memorandum, Brigadier General L. T. Gerow (Acting Asst. Chief of Staff, War Plans Division) to General Marshall and General William Bryden (Deputy Chief of Staff), December 12, 1940, RG 165/281, National Archives. The final agreed memorandum is in J. B. No. 325 (Serial 670): *Study of the Immediate Problems Concerning Involvement in War,* December 10, 1940, RG 225, National Archives.

[24] WPD 4175: *Conference with Secretary of State:* Memorandum, Brigadier General Gerow to Marshall, January 3, 1941, RG 165/281, National Archives. Gerow's memorandum also notes the Joint Board action on December 21, 1940.

[25] Memorandum, Stark to Colonel W. P. Scobey, February 18, 1941, in J. B. No. 325 (Serial 670), cited in n. 23.

361

The U.S. Marine Corps and an Experiment in Military Elitism: A Reassessment of the Special Warfare Impetus, 1937-1943 ___

John W. Gordon

The Citadel

By the time of American entry, World War II had already emerged as the golden age of the so-called "special forces."[1] Commencing in 1940, British commando exploits compensated for conventional military failures and argued convincingly that twentieth-century strategic, political, and technological realities had indeed produced a viable new form of warfare. Loosely described as "special warfare," this new category proved to have enormous psychological and political appeal.[2] Certainly by early 1942, the Americans—conditioned by two years of what seemed to be British commando successes—were ready to try their hand at special warfare. Not surprisingly, and befitting its sea-going light infantry heritage, the very first American service to so experiment was the U.S. Marine Corps.

This paper is an examination of that experiment. Specifically, it examines the response of the Marine Corps, an institution which patently regarded itself as elite, to what is seen as an elitist, special warfare impetus. For the product of that experiment was the formation, it was charged, of an "elite within an elite"—the famous marine raider battalions, the first such American venture of the war. Differing fundamentally from the equally-elitist parachute battalions (the so-called "paramarines" were never actually employed for special operations), it happened that the raiders contained six future marine generals, a future movie star, and a son of the President of the United States. But whereas the U.S. Army's ranger battalions and a whole gaggle of British commando outfits finished out the war, the marine raiders did not.[3] Instead, this sojourn into the world of special-purpose forces of an elitist cast lasted only two years, from early 1942 to early 1944. And the experiment, by most accounts, was far from being a happy one.

Forces of this sort have never been easy to evaluate. What with their powerful cult-appeal and the animosity which they spark in orthodox soldiers, they tend to generate more emotion than rational analysis. More of a problem than a help is terminology. What made the term "special force" so appealing was precisely its lack of precision. After 1940, the British used it as a functional descriptor for a unit created to perform the tricky, high-risk functions of raiding, harrassing, and intelligence-gathering behind enemy lines. The assumption was that these were beyond the normal operations of war; both the mission and the mystique then combined to demand special organization, special training, and special people.[4]

This idea surfaced as an adjunct to those same developments in tactics, mobility and communications which made World War II the era of the *Blitzkrieg*.[5] In contrast to the linear, static fronts of World War I, armored, mechanized and air armies could now strike deeply into enemy territory. But the corollary was that the bases which sustained them were also vulnerable—provided, of course, that there existed the means to reach and attack them. This is a crucial point; despite their cult-of-toughness aura, the advent of special forces was very much a function of twentieth-century technology. The key pre-conditional developments were 1) infiltration and access to enemy rear areas—provided by aircraft, submarines, or motor vehicles, and 2) high-level control and feedback—provided by long-distance radio apparatus. Thus, while the idea was hardly new, the capabilities of what was basically an eighteenth-century, Rogers' Rangers, light-infantry-style concept had now been drastically expanded by technology.[6]

In the first year of the war, British experimentation with such forces yielded commandos and the special raiding units employed in the Libyan desert. But their formation also reached back to a popular mythology about guerrilla-romantic Lawrence of Arabia—A.J.P. Taylor's "only old-style hero" of World War I—and to a British general staff study of irregular warfare which commenced in 1938.[7] Pushed off the Continent two years later, the British fell back on "lessons" drawn from the age of sail. An allegedly atavistic bent towards "looking for the open flank"—a happy return to the days of Pitt's conjunct operations—supposedly led military-romantic Winston Churchill to push through the formation of the commandos.[8] Raids by these tough, selected troops[9] not only bolstered civilian morale, but also, thought Churchill, overcame his generals' "dull mass" military conservatism.[10]

These forces, which contained such diverse personalities as actor David Niven and the Prime Minister's son, Randolph, sanctified the practice of using "special forces for special roles in special terrain."[11] And from the start, the Americans were indeed interested. Early in 1941, major American newspapers and magazines ran articles on commando activities.[12] Then, as the British sensed the obvious propaganda value, they themselves grew freer with information, and even more articles, including one by novelist Evelyn Waugh, appeared in *Life, Newsweek, Harper's,* and *Time.*[13] Well before Pearl Harbor, they had had their effect: they made clear to the Americans that these audacious new forces were as much a part of modern warfare as airplanes or tanks.

None of this was lost upon the U.S. Marine Corps. Well aware of what the British were doing, it was reminded that its own recent knowledge of such operations was nonexistent. Despite some practice exercises and a claim that "landing raids had been discussed extensively" in the 1935 *Tentative Landing Manual,* such guidelines were cursory and far too theoretical.[14] At any rate, the response of the Commandant, General Thomas Holcomb, was to dispatch Brigadier General Julian C. Smith to England. By July 1941, half a year before the United States entered the war, as British War Office records reveal, Smith was receiving extensive briefings from Admiral Sir Roger Keyes of Combined Operations, and enjoying at least one personal dinner chat with Prime Minister Churchill. In short, British willingness to share knowledge seems to have been summed up in the words of one officer, who reported that he had told the American "all I know."[15]

But none of this had any effect until Pearl Harbor. Thereafter, Japanese victories reproduced for the Americans the same conditions that first led the British to special warfare: in defeat, even when fortunes were lowest, a way was needed to strike back, if only with weak, token gestures. The Marine Corps in particular came under heavy pressure to be ready to mount such attacks. And the pressure was hard to avoid, especially since it came from what the Commandant described as "very high authority." Very high authority indeed: applying the pressure was Secretary of the Navy Frank Knox, and the President of the United States.[16]

Almost immediately, Holcomb found himself in an awkward position. Exposed to every futuristic scheme for commando adventures that came along, he found himself dealing with more than a few that would have been a credit to that great luminary in such matters, Hector G. Bywater.

One plan of an altogether serious nature, however, involved the future director of the future Office of Strategic Services. This of course was Colonel William (Wild Bill) Donovan, a rather dashing figure who also happened to be a Columbia Law classmate of Franklin D. Roosevelt. In World War I, he had served heroically (and here he actually does begin to look like Pat O'Brien) with the 69th "Fighting Irish." He was also an "old friend" of Rough Rider alumnus Frank Knox, now the Secretary of the Navy. Known to the press as Roosevelt's "Man of Mystery" and "America's

Secret Envoy," Donovan had met not-so-secretly with Churchill and the British intelligence chiefs. By now, he was flooding FDR with ideas about what he called "militarized raiders or 'commandos.'"[17]

For his part, General Holcomb seems always to have regarded Donovan with something less than fondness. These feelings did not diminish when Holcomb was informed that Colonel Donovan, U.S. Army Reserve, was about to become instantly Brigadier General Donovan, U.S. Marine Corps Reserve, and placed in charge of the entire marine commando project.[18] It should be added that this pleased Holcomb all the less, since, up to this point, he himself had not been aware of the existence of such a project.

Granted rights of rebuttal, he rolled out Major General Holland (Howlin' Mad) Smith, who argued rather predictably that the Corps "should not have to go outside . . . its ranks to secure leaders."[19] But while the generals were still working themselves up to full-cry over this intrusion into their inner sanctum, the OSS marched to the aid of the Marines. What had happened was that Donovan had found a better job—head of the newly-created and super-elitist, super-glamorous, "Oh, So Secret" OSS. But the drive for a marine commando effort certainly did not vanish with Donovan; by now, far too many influential people believed in the idea.

One who so believed was named Roosevelt—Captain James Roosevelt, USMCR, who enjoyed a rather obvious access to the President. It also happened that FDR's eldest son had just finished serving as Donovan's "military advisor and liaison officer." In fact, the day after *Newsweek's* article on the British commandos appeared, Captain Roosevelt had seized the moment to submit a commando project of his own.[20]

But the key proposal may have come from a man who could at least claim a personal knowledge of guerrilla warfare. This was an enigmatic figure named Evans Carlson, who had supposedly horrified his fellow marine officers by reading *The Daily Worker.* And while Carlson's heroism under fire earned him a brace of Navy Crosses, it is hard to resist feeling that his greatest feat was his success in introducing, into American military perpetuity, the Chinese Communist term "gung-ho."

Lean and tough looking, Carlson comes across as a sort of American Orde Wingate. An Old China Hand *par excellence,* in 1937 he had pulled off a feat which impressed Edgar Snow, Joseph Stilwell, and just about everybody else who knew about China: he slipped past Japanese lines to reach the Chinese Communist 8th Route Army.[21] But eventually, his own political views began to color his official reports, and he grew disenchanted to the point that he resigned his commission.[22]

By Pearl Harbor, however, he was back—helped, perhaps, by the President, to whom he had long since, at FDR's invitation, begun sending "eyes only" reports on China.[23] Carlson's commando scheme came at just the right moment. Under considerable pressure, Holcomb now, early in 1942, at last agreed to the formation of a marine special force. To be known as "raiders," rather than by the British term "commandos," which Holcomb found objectionable, they were to "spearhead amphibious landings. . .; conduct raiding expeditions requiring . . . surprise and . . . speed"; and mount "guerilla-type operations . . . behind enemy lines."[24] With this charter, the Marine Corps' foray into the realm of elite forces for special warfare was now in fact under way.

In the next months, two battalions of these raiders were raised, trained, and sent to the Pacific.[25] But from the start, Carlson and his battalion caused trouble. After a flock of organizational revisions, he also demanded a lot of exotic gear, including folding bicycles, which one regular disparaged as "Boy Scout equipment."[26] Far more objectionable, however, were what he called his "gung-ho" sessions. A Chinese expression which meant "work together," Carlson used it to symbolize his brand of "ethical indoctrination." Nor was Carlson's sense of decorum ever quite the same as everybody else's, as on the first occasion that he stood before his new battalion. While the troops in ranks carefully scrutinized their new commander, that figure, Lieutenant Colonel Carlson, was seen to walk up to the microphone, take out his harmonica, and launch into a solo rendition of *The Star Spangled Banner* [27]

But of course the main event for the raiders was the Guadalcanal landings in August 1942. These established a pattern which obtained throughout the Solomons campaign. Short one regiment, General Vandegrift used Lieutenant Colonel Merritt Edson's raiders and a parachute battalion to secure Tulagi, just across from Guadalcanal. They succeeded—but as regular infantry, not as a special force. From that point on, Edson's raiders and the paramarines, as often as not, would find themselves lumped together as provisional infantry.[28]

But Guadalcanal also brought about a dramatic and potentially useful employment of raiders: the diversionary hit-and-run raid against Makin Island. The brainchild of Admiral Nimitz's CincPac staff, this probe of the Gilberts was not exactly a Doolittle raid on Japan itself, but nevertheless amounted to the first such effort attempted by American ground forces in the war.[29]

Carlson got the assignment. Arriving by submarine on a pitch-black night, there followed a feat of American arms which General Holland Smith once described as "a piece of folly."[30] The raiders paddled ashore in rubber boats, but almost immediately got into an all-night skirmish with the Japanese. Bombed next day by enemy planes, they were left stranded on the island by a violent and insurmountably high Pacific surf.[31]

Yet their fortunes now shifted. Discovering that virtually all the Japanese on the island had actually been killed (apparently by air strikes which had conveniently hit the wrong people), they destroyed a fuel dump and bagged the ultimate trophy, the enemy commander's Samurai sword. That night the raiders managed to get back to the submarines. Unfortunately, in the confusion, they also managed to leave behind nine men whom, when they returned to the island, the Japanese lost no time in beheading.[32]

Carlson was blamed for botching the job. He was also blamed for losing his nerve. Of the raid's bleakest moment he had supposedly admitted that, "If I had heard a Japanese voice say 'Surrender,' I would have surrendered." Hard after naval defeat at Savo Island, this was not the kind of language that pleased superiors. According to one story, when the report reached Nimitz, he insisted that the objectionable part be stricken, saying that "no report from my command will have any word, or even idea, of surrender in it."[33]

Nonetheless the admiral was happy enough to accept the captured Japanese sword. It also comes as no surprise that Hollywood made sure that the Makin raid was well-represented at the box office. Shortly there appeared the first of the raider movies. Entitled *Gung-Ho!*, it starred—as New Englander Evans Carlson—of all people, Southern-drawling, Chapel Hill-educated, cowboy-hero Randolph Scott (who at least looked like Carlson, even if he didn't talk like him). Followed by *Marine Raiders* (Robert Ryan, Pat O'Brien, and Ruth Hussey), these cinematic efforts ensured that the raiders got their fair share of glory.[34]

They also continued to get their fair share of regular-infantry fighting. Along with the parachutists, Edson's battalion beat back a Japanese thrust on Guadalcanal, but this costly, orthodox infantry action once again left only Carlson's unit available for the real raiding job. In November 1942 his battalion mounted its second foray behind Japanese lines. If Carlson had botched Makin, it is apparent that under conditions of extreme hardship his raiders now did everything right. By destroying an enemy unit, blocking a key trail, and sending back intelligence, his force made an important contribution at a critical juncture of the Guadalcanal campaign.[35]

That such feats were possible greatly impressed Rear Admiral Richmond Kelly Turner, Commander, Amphibious Force, South Pacific. In fact, Turner was so impressed that he ordered the partial conversion (without bothering to consult with the Marines first) of every marine regiment to raiders. Reasoning that "night landings by small units will be useful." and that the "problem of mopping up outlying [enemy] detachments" will be a prevalent one, it seemed obvious to Turner that the marine division, in its present form, was far too large.[36]

As this early stage of the Pacific fighting, this kind of meddling might indeed have produced a major interservice rhubarb.[37] Actually, however, the plan drew as much opposstion from the Navy as from the Marines. When Admiral Nimitz agreed with Holcomb that orthodox marine units were already capable of raider-type operations, and that no alteration was presently either feasible or called for,[38] he effectively terminated Turner's plan.[39]

Nonetheless, the raiders continued to be misemployed as standard infantry.[40] But for that matter, their time was already running out. In late 1943, a Chief of Naval Operations staff subsection produced the memorandum which sealed their fate. Declaring that any operation "so far carried out . . . could have been performed equally well" by a regular unit, it urged that the raider experiment be terminated, "so as to make all . . . organizations uniform and to avoid . . . elite or selected troops."[41] By now, the final act was obvious: the conversion of the raiders into standard infantry. Early in 1944, this was accomplished. By using the raiders to reconstitute the 4th Marines, a regiment which had fallen at Corregidor, both the interest of unit pride and public relations were well served. With this pragmatic solution, the two-year-long experiment with these "elite or selected troops" had indeed come to an end.[42]

What had the experiment revealed? For one thing, it showed that there was about the raiders much which fit the established British pattern—the elite status, the publicity, the cult of personality engendered by some of the commanders, and so on. Equally clear was the fact that the experiment represented to the Americans, as earlier theirs had to the British, a way of satisfying a profound psychological need—perhaps most pronounced in these two liberal democracies—to "out-tough" a militaristic and obviously tough foe. It was also a salient departure from the professional officer corps model. The raiders and their ilk sanctioned an heroic, officer-as-warrior ethic, not the standard, manager-of-violence role fostered in the staff colleges.[43] Early in the war this may have been a psychological necessity—perhaps even an acceptably American counterfoil to what Samuel Huntington has shown to be the Japanese officer-as-warrior model.[44]

At any rate, the same criticisms made of the British special forces were also made of the raiders. One of the most telling came from Field Marshal Slim of Burma, who conluded that all such forces, "trained, equipped and mentally adjusted for one kind of operation . . . , were wasteful."[45] Few of the marine generals would have disagreed with him. There was also the collateral sin of syphoning off "the best men." This had permitted Carlson to "select anybody he wanted," and General Vandegrift recalled bitterly how Edson, "armed with appropriate orders," had arrived "to comb our units" in the middle of the preparations for Guadalcanal.[46] This, a well-nigh universal trespass of special forces, was felt all the more keenly in a smaller service like the Marine Corps, especially as it expanded from one to six divisions by the end of the war.

But the most potent criticism of all went far beyond the elitism, the jealousy, and the premise that only special units could perform special missions. Instead, it involved the very essence of amphibious doctrine—what J. F. C. Fuller called "the most far-reaching tactical innovation" of the war.[47] Signified by the creation of the Fleet Marine Force in 1933, the Marine Corps had transformed itself into a task-organized, seaborne land army able to assault a hostile shore.[48] Having at last acquired its own mission and role, relegated to the past was the old light infantry, police-force-for-the-Navy arrangement. Instead, the new paradigm called for Fort Benning tactics and standard Army-style organizations only slightly modified as battalion landing teams and the like.[49]

The careers of the key generals—Holcomb, Smith, and Vandegrift—had been deeply wedded to that process of attainment (and to their Corps' newfound status). But whereas the British had embraced special warfare as an alternative to the machine-warfare paradigm, neither the Commandant nor his senior commanders ever accepted it as a viable approach to amphibious warfare. Rather than an adjunct to their carefully-evolved doctrine, it was seen as its very antithesis. These generalist generals could only regard with suspicion, if not malice, any departure from their Corps' generalist solution to the problems of amphibious warfare. And in their eyes, the raiders represented a dangerous departure indeed. As Holland Smith put it, all that the Makin raid had succeeded in doing was to alert "the Japanese to our intentions," resulting in high casualties and near-disaster at Tarawa a year later.[50]

For as the Solomons campaign gave way to the Central Pacific drive, the character of the war altered—in ways which appeared to vindicate the generalist, not the specialist, approach. Between the advent and the termination of the raiders, American air and sea power had burgeoned, making available far more efficient ways to disrupt the enemy. Put simply, fast carrier strikes and command of the sea had rendered the raiders superfluous.[51] Contrary to what Admiral Turner had argued, outlying enemy forces did not have to be mopped up by marine raiders. Instead, their islands could be by-passed and left, in Admiral Halsey's phrase, "to die on the vine."[52]

Yet to these legitimate military criticisms must be added a rather messy ideological one. From the start, many had believed that Carlson the marine officer was also Carlson the Red.[53] Even after the war, when Carlson had retired and was working with a group called "Americans for Preservng the Peace," Vandegrift was still writing Nimitz to assure him that Carlson was "not a subversive." By doing away with officer and NCO privileges in his raider battalion, Carlson had come across as a radical out to undermine the old sureties between the ranks. Even thirty years later, the memory of his "gung-ho" talks, in which the troops could voice opinions freely, still so affronted one senior officer that he remarked that, "whenever I here . . . the infamous expression 'Gung-Ho,' I am almost nauseated. It is a Chinese communist slogan."[54]

Nor had the organizational structure been particularly conducive to success. Lacking either a British Directorate of Combined Operations or a comparable old-boy network, the independent raider battalions had been wide open to bureaucratic predators.[55] But the problem may have run deeper than these surface effects: perhaps the real trouble all along had been that Carlson was ahead of his time. Twenty years before the United States embarked upon its brief Indo-Chinese fascination with revolutionary warfare (or more precisely, its doctrinal antidote, counterinsurgency warfare), Carlson had been the first twentieth-century American soldier to grasp and apply a set of populist, revolutionary military concepts. In the not unbiased view of Carlson's friend, 1948 Progressive Party presidential candidate Henry A. Wallace, what had happened was that Carlson had tried to teach "his men what they were fighting for," but in the end, "Some high officers didn't like that . . . ," and Carlson was removed from command.[56]

At any rate, his role had been trenchant: for all the years since, his image has lurked in the Marine Corps' institutional memory, and similar special warfare adventures have been successfully resisted. The experiment had not been doomed from the start; at best, however, the reaction to it had been one of extreme skepticism. Initially, the British connection had predominated. As one general remembered it, Winston Churchill "had sold . . . [President Roosevelt] on the idea, and the Marine Corps had to suffer for it."[57] Thereafter, the Makin raid's dubious results, the perennial misemployment of raiders, and Carlson's alleged radicalism had fatally discredited the experiment in its first year. In its second year, the raiders were overtaken by the ascendancy of American naval power—in effect, their *modus operandi* became an anachronism belonging to the dark days after Pearl Harbor, and their elitism an embarrassment to the standard, workhorse infantry battalions which now began the drive across the Pacific.

And so the experiment ended. As Binkin and Record declared last year, World War II was indeed the "golden age of amphibious warfare."[58] As we have seen, in many respects it was also the golden age of special warfare. But in the Marine Corps, successfully reconciling the two golden ages proved a feat beyond the institution's grasp.

370

FOOTNOTES

[1] The author gratefully acknowledges the research assistance of The Citadel Development Foundation and the Military History Institute, U.S. Army War College.

[2] See Winston S. Churchill, *Their Finest Hour (The Second World War)* (Boston: Houghton Mifflin, 1949), pp. 166; 246-7; 466-8; Great Britain, War Office, *Reorganization of Special Service Units to form "Commandos," 1941-1942* (WO 32/9729); and Brigadier Dudley Clarke, "The Birth of the Commandos," *The Listener* 10 (November 1948): 799-800.

[3] Colonel John W. Hackett, "The Employment of Special Forces," *Journal of the Royal United Service Institution,* 98 (February 1952): 26-41.

[4] U. S. Department of the Army, *Special Warfare; An Army Speciality* (Washington: Office, Chief of Information, 1962), pp. 34-45. Roger A. Beaumont, *Military Elites* (New York: Bobbs-Merrill, 1974), pp. 1-14, emphasizes units in their qualitative, as opposed to their functional, sense.

[5] Larry H. Addington, *The Blitzkrieg Era and the German General Staff: 1865-1941* (New Brunswick: Rutgers University Press, 1971), pp. 28-46.

[6] Poet Robert Graves describes the transition from linear tactics to 1917's *Instructions for the Training of Platoons for Offensive Action.* Robert Graves, *Good-bye to All That* (New York: Cape and Harrison Smith, 1930), pp. 292-293.

[7] Great Britain, War Office, *General Staff Report on the Raising of Insurrections: Possibility of Guerrilla Activities* (WO 193/150); A. J. P. Taylor, *English History 1914-1945* (Oxford: Oxford University Press, 1965), p. 49.

[8] Hackett, "Special Forces," p. 27; Michael Howard, *The Mediterranean Strategy in the Second World War (the Lees-Knowles Lectures at Trinity College, Cambridge, 1966)* (London: Weidenfeld and Nicolson, 1968), pp. 1-2.

[9] Great Britain, War Office, *Commandos and Special Service* (WO 193/405). R. A. Bagnold, "Early Days of the Long Range Desert Group," *Geographical Journal* 105 (January 1945): 30-46; and interviews held in 1972 and 1976 with Brigadier R. A. Bagnold, Brigadier Guy Prendergast, and Major General David L. Lloyd Owen.

[10] Great Britain, War Office, *MO3 Battle File: SAS Regiment* (WO 201/747); and Vladimir Peniakoff, *Private Army* (London; Cape, 1950), pp. 192; 238.

[11] Personal interviews with General Sir John W. Hackett, June 8 and 23, 1972, at King's College, London, England; Ward Just, *Military Men* (New York: Knopf, 1960), pp. 143-150.

[12] Hanson Baldwin, "Desert Fighters," *The New York Times* (February 13, 1941).

[13] For example: Evelyn Waugh, "Commando Raid on Bardia," *Life,* November 17, 1941, pp. 63-74; "Raid on Rommel," *Newsweek,* January 12, 1942, p. 18; "British Commandos Raid Hitler's Europe," *Life,* January 26, 1942, pp. 17-21; and "Butcher and Bolt," *Time,* June 8, 1942, pp. 25-29.

[14] U. S., Department of the Navy, *Special Marine Corps Units of World War II* (Washington: Historical Division, Headquarters, U.S. Marine Corps, 1972), p. 1.

[15] General Thomas Holcomb, seventeenth Commandant of the Marine Corps (1936-1943). See Karl Schuon, *U.S. Marine Corps Biographical Dictionary* (New York: Franklin Watts, 1963), pp. 106-108.

[16] Letter, Lt. Col. T. Ely, DCO's Office, to Major A. Daniell, War Office (31 July 1941), in Great Britain, War Office, *Commandos and Special Service* (WO 193/405).

[17] *Special Marine Units,* p. 3, quoting CMC ltr to CG, PhibForLant, dtd 11 Feb 42 (Cent Files, HQMC).

[18] Corey Ford, *Donovan of OSS* (Boston: Little, Brown, 1970), pp. 98-112; 125; 162.

[19] *Special Marine Units,* p. 2.

[20] Ibid.; for Smith, see *Marine Corps Biographical Dictionary,* pp. 206-208.

[21] Ford, *Donovan*, p. 112; and Letter, Captain James Roosevelt, to Commandant of the Marine Corps, 13 January 1942, in Raider files.

[22] *Marine Corps Biographical Dictionary*, pp. 34-35. The standard biography is Michael Blankfort, *The Big Yankee: The Life of Carlson of the Raiders* (Boston: Little, Brown, 1947).

[23] U. S., Department of the Navy, *A Report of the Military Activities in the Northwest of China with Especial Regard to the Organization and Tactics of the Chinese Eighth Route Army (Ex-Communist): Pr   'd by Captain Evans F. Carlson, U. S. Marine Corps, 23 March 1938* (copy lodged in Army War College Library, October 31, 1939); Blankfort, *Big Yankee*, pp. 175-272; and F. Tillman Durdin, "Finds China Runs 'Occupied' Areas/Capt. E. F. Carlson of U. S. Marines Makes 2,000 Mile Trip . . . ," *The New York Times* (August 9, 1938).

[24] Blankfort, *Big Yankee*, pp. 170-174. Elliott Roosevelt, ed., *F. D. R.: His Personal Letters* (New York: Kraus Reprint Co., 1970), II, pp. 1497-8; 1525-6.

[25] *Special Marine Units*, pp. 3-4.

[26] For Edson, see *Marine Corps Biographical Dictionary*, pp. 65-66. His executive officer, Major Samuel Griffith, had, along with future Commandant Wallace M. Greene, just returned from observing commando training in England. *Marine Corps Biographical Dictionary*, pp. 90-91.

[27] U.S., Department of the Navy, *Oral History Transcript of Lieutenant General Alan Shapley* (Washington: History and Museums Division, Headquarters, U. S. Marine Corps), p. 74. Hereinafter cited as *Shapley Transcript*.

[28] Blankfort, *Big Yankee*, pp. 18-19.

[29] Lieutenant Colonel Frank O. Hough, Major Verle E. Ludwig, and Henry I. Shaw, *Pearl Harbor to Guadalcanal (History of U. S. Marine Corps Operations in World War II)* (Washington: USGPO, 1958), I, pp. 263-273.

[30] Ibid., pp. 285-6; and U. S., Department of the Navy, *Oral History Transcript of Major General O. T. Pfeiffer* (Washington: History and Museums Division, U. S. Marine Corps, 1974), p. 196. Hereinafter cited as *Pfeiffer Transcript*.

[31] Colonel Robert D. Heinl, *Soldiers of the Sea: The United States Marine Corps, 1775-1962* (Annapolis: United States Naval Institute, 1962), p. 357; and General Holland M. Smith and Percy Finch, *Coral and Brass* (New York: Scribner's, 1949), p. 132.

[32] See "James Roosevelt's Copies of Opns. Orders for Makin Island Raid, dtd 7 Aug 42 (PC 112)," lodged in Archives, Marine Corps Historical Center; and U.S., Department of the Navy, *Solomon Islands Campaign—Makin Island Diversion* (dtd October 20, 1942), in Raider file.

[33] "The Makin Island Raid," *Marine Corps Gazette* 27 (April 1943), No. 1, p. 31; and *Special Marine Units*, p. 14.

[34] The account given in *Pfeiffer Transcript*, pp. 197-8.

[35] For the movies, see John B. Moran, *Creating a Legend: The Complete Record of Writing About the United States Marine Corps* (Chicago: Moran/Andres, 1973), pp. 640-1.

[36] U. S., Department of the Navy, *Report on Operations—1st Parachute Bn—Lunga Ridge—Guadalcanal (13-14 Sept 1942) (a38-1)*. See *2nd Raider Bn—Misc Reports—Guadalcanal* (A39-1); Field Marshal Lord William Slim, *Defeat into Victory* (London: Cassell, 1956), especially pp. 541-460.

[37] Vice Admiral George C. Dyer, *The Amphibious Came to Conquer: The Story of Admiral Richmond Kelly Turner* (Washington: USGPO, 1969), pp. 450-2.

[38] Ibid., and *Special Marine Units*, pp. 15-16, quoting CincPac ltr to CMC, dtd 24 Sep 42, and CMC memo to CNO, dtd 2 Sep 42.

[39] Ibid., pp. 22-25.

[40] Jeter A. Isely and Philip A. Crowl, *The U. S. Marines and Amphibious War: Its Theory and Its Practice in the Pacific* (Princeton: Princeton University Press, 1951), p. 172. Hereinafter cited as Isely and Crowl, *The U. S. Marines and Amphibious War*.

[41] *Shapley Transcript*, pp. 79-80.

[42] Asst. Pac Sec, War Plans Div, CNO memo to ACS, Plans, dtd 24 Dec 43, quoted in *Special Marine Units*, p. 34.

[43] *Shapley Transcript*, p. 80.

[44] Samuel P. Huntington, *The Soldier and the State: The Theory and Politics of Civil Military Relations* (New York: Random House, 1957), pp. 125-130.

[45] Slim, *Defeat into Victory*, pp. 455-458.

[46] *Shapley Transcript*, p. 74; and General Alexander A. Vandegrift, with Robert Asprey, *Once a Marine* (New York: Norton, 1964), p. 100.

[47] Quoted in Theodore Ropp, *War in the Modern World* (Toronto: Collier Books, 1969), p. 306.

[48] Isely and Crowl, *U. S. Marines and Amphibious Warfare*, especially pp. 14-71; and Raymond G. O'Connor, "The U. S. Marines in the 20th Century: Amphibious Warfare and Doctrinal Debates," *Military Affairs* 38 (October 1974): 97-103.

[49] For views of the marine officer corps, see Peter Karsten, *The Naval Aristocracy: The Golden Age of Annapolis and the Emergence of Modern American Navalism* (New York: The Free Press, 1972), pp. 21n; 82-3; Heinl, *Soldiers of the Sea*, pp. 210; 165-6; and Brig. Gen. Dion Williams, "The Education of a Marine Officer," *Marine Corps Gazette*, November 1934, pp. 24-32.

[50] Smith, *Coral and Brass*, p. 132.

[51] Clark G. Reynolds, *Command of the Sea: The History and Strategy of Maritime Empires* (New York: William Morrow, 1974), pp. 527-543.

[52] Dyer, *Amphibians*, I, p. 596.

[53] Compare *Shapley Transcript*, pp. 71; 74, with U. S. *Department of the Navy, Oral History Transcript of Major General O. R. Peatross* (Washington: History and Museums Division, Headquarters, U. S. Marine Corps, 1975), pp. 75-6.

[54] *Pfeiffer Transcript*, p. 199; Papers of General A. A. Vandegrift lodged in Archives, History and Museums Division, Headquarters, U. S. Marine Corps: General Vandegrift to Admiral Nimitz, CNO, memo dtd 9 Oct 46; Vandegrift to Colonel E. F. Carlson, Letter dtd 11 Aug 45; and Vandegrift to General Thomas Holcomb, letter dtd 22 Apr 46; all in PC 465.

[55] Ibid., pp. 196; 199; 233.

[56] "Mrs. Carlson Tells General's Hope of Peace," *San Francisco Chronicle*, May 28, 1947.

[57] *Pfeiffer Transcript*, pp. 194-5.

[58] Martin Binkin and Jeffrey Record, *Where Does the Marine Corps Go From Here?* (Washington: The Brookings Institution, 1976), p. 88.

CHAPTER 30

The Prewar Career of Ernest J. King

Thomas B. Buell

Commander, U. S. Navy

Ernest J. King had but one aim in life during his first forty years of naval service: he wanted to become the Chief of Naval Operations. He sought that goal with zealous ambition and single-minded determination. He made no secret of it. He would tell anyone who would listen, and his goal was common knowledge throughout the Navy.

King did achieve his goal, but not as soon as he had hoped. It was not until after the war began that the President elevated him to Commander in Chief, U.S. Fleet (Cominch), and several months later made him Chief of Naval Operations (CNO) as well. Had it not been for the Second World War, King would have finished his career as a rear admiral in November, 1942, having reached the retirement age of sixty-four. And he would have been a sad and sorry man, for the Navy was the only life he knew or cared for. Retirement was incomprehensible. He would refuse even to think about it.

The Navy would not have missed him. He had some friends, but there were many more who did not like him. Naval historians would have noted that he had had an unusual career, having served in all three branches of the naval service: surface, submarines, and finally aviation. But historians would have noted nothing else extraordinary. King had risen to the temporary rank of vice admiral, had remained in that rank for a year and a half, and then had reverted to his permanent rank of rear admiral. Many other flag officers had achieved that much, and more. Superficially, then, his career would have been no different than other prewar flag officers who strove for the top, failed to make it, and then retired into anonymity. And if a historian had looked more deeply into King's prewar career, he would have found those who said that King's ambition to become CNO had been stymied because he was tactless and temperamental, he chased men's wives, and he drank too much.

King's searing ambition and his zeal to achieve were established as a boy in Lorain, Ohio, in the last two decades of the nineteenth century. A small town of between four and five thousand people, Lorain was surrounded by a rural population in the most abolitionist and radical Republican county in Ohio. King's family were literate, industrious Scottish immigrants, many of them active in labor politics, the kind of people who support libraries and value education and who were accepted by the rural natives even though they were foreigners. King's father and grandfather had shown their mettle by becoming skilled working-class foremen—they had been "born to manage things," King liked to say, and so had he.

His neighbors admired King as a bright boy from a good family. His high school class of 1897 was small—thirteen pupils—but it undoubtedly was a good school, and in Lorain it was the equivalent of college. Everyone could see that King obviously had brains and talent, for he was class valedictorian as well as a popular student leader. When King decided that he wanted to attend the Naval Academy, all were proud and delighted. Young Ernest King's fortunes became everyone's concern, for an Annapolis graduate would bring stature to their town, and King was doing what the people of Lorain admired most: he was advancing himself; he was entering a respected profession. He left for Annapolis with the encouragement and best wishes of the entire community.[1]

King was thus determined to excel at the Naval Academy, but his thinking was influenced by a drunken upperclassman who entered his room one evening while King was a plebe. The upperclassman accused King of bragging that he would stand first in his class. King denied it. King's classmate Adolphus Andrews, however, was in the room also, and Andrews boldly confirmed that *he* intended to be number one. The upperclassman berated Andrews for his presumptuousness, and King was impressed. He began to think about the implications. If he graduated first in his class, he reasoned that from then on he would be too visible for comfort throughout his naval career. As too much would probably be expected of him, King concluded that it would be best if he graduated about third or fourth, which would still confer prestige but was not nearly as conspicuous.[2]

King nevertheless strove to become the battalion commander, who wore four stripes and was the senior midshipman officer. King won the position through support from his classmates and approval from the Naval Academy administration. As the two groups were natural adversaries, King had to be many things to many men. He was popular with his classmates, who appreciated his class loyalty, his gregarious personality, and his forthrightness in representing the Battalion of Midshipmen with the administration. On the other hand, the administration recognized King's respect for law and authority and capitalized upon his ability to influence the other midshipmen to stay within the regulations.[3]

A career naval officer must decide early in life how to balance candor and independent thought against obedience and subordination to authority. One of King's first tests came during his senior year. In a letter to a Navy junior, King described his first major confrontation with a senior officer, who also was the father of the Navy junior:

> I was the "four-striper" that year and accordingly of some conse-quence in the battalion. For sail drill I was port captain of the main top. The main topsail yard (and main topsail) of the *Chesapeake* were very large, even somewhat out of proportion to the rest of the yards. When furling sail it was always a race to see who could complete the furling in the quickest time—which handicapped those who were furling the main topsail. On the day in question, while busy furling sail, someone was jiggling the topsail buntwhip which did not lighten the labors of those who were trying to stow the large and unwieldy bunt.
>
> Your father, standing on the horse-block with his trumpet, directed appropriate remarks to the main topsail yard as to our lack of speed and efficiency. When he had done this for about the third time, I turned on the foot ropes and said, "We will get the . . . blank, blank . . . topsail furled if you will stop the . . . blank, blank . . . jigging of the topsail buntwhip." I can see the people on deck now—eyes popping out of their heads—mouths wide open—waiting for the thunder and lightning to strike—me. But what happened was that your father leaped down off the horse-block, ran to the main fife-rail where he stopped the . . . blank, blank . . . jigging of the topsail buntwhip.
>
> Believe it or not, that ended the incident—no words to me—no report! We could only assume that your father heeded my cry of distress because he sensed it to be genuine—because I spoke in language that voiced an appeal which he understood as coming from one who felt he needed help.[4]

Such episodes undoubtedly confirmed in King's mind that his outraged outbursts were justified if he spoke against a wrong or an injustice. But King's outspoken bluntness went to extremes, owing to his sense of self-righteousness and an undisciplined temper. Tact and discretion too often lost out to emotional excesses, especially in his early career. Together with his intellectual arrogance and lack of humility, King simply considered that he had more brains than anyone else in the Navy and acted accordingly.

With this attitude, he entered the fleet as a junior officer in the first years of the twentieth century and got off to a shaky start.[5] Not surprisingly, he soon clashed with his senior officers. For example, as a division officer in the USS *Cincinnati* before the First World War, King cursed and yelled at his executive officer who had tried early one afternoon to get King out of bed and on deck to supervise his men. Indeed, King was indiscriminate in picking fights, for he would take on a flag officer as readily as a lieutenant commander. Older officers often felt intimidated in his presence, and they resented the way King made them feel inferior. Another of King's excesses was his drinking, which frequently caused him to miss morning musters.

His fitness reports in those early years reflected his erratic performance; one does not go about defying senior officers without getting hurt.

Fortunately for King, he had friends in the naval officers corps who recognized his ability and wanted to help him succeed. These officers gave King second and third chances, they forgave him, and they counseled him as he sat in their staterooms in the aftermaths of King-inspired uproars. King was receptive and repentant, and, after several years of commissioned service, he began to take stock of himself.

He would not give up his parties ashore, he decided, but he would never again be late for anything. His punctuality became a legend.

He was too soft and easy-going with enlisted men and subordinate officers, he decided, so he would have to become tougher—mentally and physically—if he hoped to succeed in the Navy.

He would continually develop his intellect, he decided, through reading, self-study, writing for the Naval Institute *Proceedings,* and through inventions as, for example, a fire control computer that he designed and built with his partner and classmate, William S. Pye.

He would carefully select those duty assignments, he decided, that would give him the broadest experience and which would carry the greatest weight with promotion selection boards.

The most important decision of all, however, was that he would become a flag officer entirely through professional merit. In later years his pride and sense of propriety made him unwilling to ingratiate himself with such influential cliques as the "Gun Club" or Franklin D. Roosevelt's inner circle of friends. He vowed to be so superior as a professional naval officer that he could remain aloof from the shameless intrigues of Washington and still become an admiral. Thus, except for a brief and stormy tour as Assistant Chief of the Bureau of Aeronautics in the late nineteen twenties, King avoided Washington duty until he was promoted to rear admiral some thirty-two years after graduating from the Naval Academy.

Still, he was not a stranger in Washington. King's first three tours of shore duty were at Annapolis in order to be with his wife, who had established her permanent home there. Thus he was near enough to Washington to keep in touch with the Navy Department and his detailer, yet far enough away to avoid Washington's high cost of living and political atmosphere. It was a good compromise.

Within these constraints, however, King was a "ticket puncher." He carefully appraised which jobs would benefit his career and pestered his detailers to give him the assignments that he wanted. But it was often difficult for King to decide which jobs were best. He constantly agonized, for example, between the merits of staff duty and shipboard duty in his earlier years. There were rewards for serving as a staff officer under such famous mentors as Admirals Henry T. Mayo and Hugo Osterhaus. King "learned" how to be an admiral under such men. Their influence could get King good jobs later on, and their fitness reports carried weight with selection boards. On the other hand, staff officers were often suspected of wearing their bosses' stripes, which aroused jealousy and resentment among those toiling in unglamorous shipboard jobs.

As King was a superb staff officer, he was always in demand. But King chose his flag officers carefully, and he turned down those who could not help his career. But Mayo seemed a good bet, as Mayo was to serve as Commander in Chief, Atlantic Fleet during the First World War. It was a fortunate decision. King was promoted to captain in 1918, having served as a commander for only fourteen months. His early promotion (although not unique at the time) marked the transition into King's long period of almost continuous command assignments. During the seventeen years before he made captain, King's sole command had been a destroyer. Yet after leaving Mayo in 1919, King experienced seventeen years in command during the next twenty years that he strove to become the Chief of Naval Operations.

King was so junior a captain in the years immediately following the war that he found he would have a long wait to get enough seniority for a major command at sea. Thus King's first sea command as a captain, in July, 1921, was a lowly refrigerator ship, the USS *Bridge*, rather than a cruiser or a destroyer flotilla which he would have preferred. King intended to endure his "beef boat" command no longer than necessary. After a year he confronted his detail officer at the Bureau of Navigation, Captain William D. Leahy. "Of course, I still wanted to go back to destroyers," King wrote in his memoirs, "but Leahy told me I was too senior for a division and too junior for a flotilla. I reminded him that he had 'promised' me an assignment to destroyers, but he said he was sorry but there was no job for me. Finally, he asked about my going into submarines since I could learn to be commander of a submarine division in three or four months."[6]

Thus King transferred to the submarine service in 1922 solely because, at the moment. there were no suitable sea assignments available in the surface Navy. At the submarine school he remained aloof from much of the technical training required of his junior officer classmates, and he avoided taking the written and practical examinations necessary to become a qualified submarine officer—perhaps for fear of failure. He tried new tactics and procedures once he took command of his submarine division, but his novel ideas did not achieve his expectations. When he took his division to sea, King discovered that the submarines were uncomfortable and unreliable, and he got seasick in heavy weather. Thus King's tour as a division commander was frustrating and unhappy. After a year he was ready to come ashore as commander of the U.S. Submarine Base, New London.

The New London shore command afforded King comfortable quarters for him and his family, as well as the prestige of being the senior naval officer and Navy Department representative in Connecticut. By the summer of 1925, after King had been in command of the base for almost two years, he received a disturbing letter from Admiral Charles F. Hughes, the Chief of Naval Operations. Hughes was one of the many senior naval officers over the years who was generous with advice because he believed King was a future flag officer. His letter is but one example of the counseling that King received throughout his career:

> You would be surprised to know how your record of services is looked upon. Get a job at sea where you can do some of the drudgery of the service. Do not depend upon a battleship cruise to round out your service record.
>
> I cannot explain but I am sending this in friendship.
>
> I appreciate what you have done and are doing but you are sure to be compared with others that have taken the hard knocks of the service and have come through with credit. I do not know what to advise but it should be at sea and in no fancy job—a tanker, beef ship or repair ship and not a division commander.
>
> I hope you will take this as it is intended—a helpful hint and do not say to anyone that I have written.
>
> Hope you will find the chance to have some target practices and some steaming.[7]

King's reply clearly reveals how he had planned his career thus far, together with his ambitions for the future.

> I wish to thank you very much indeed for your letter of the 12th—and deeply appreciate the motives which prompted the writing of it. It is merely the plain truth to admit that you are quite right in saying that I would be "surprised"! It has given me "furiously to think"—and I am going to ask you to continue your great kindness by listening to some of my thoughts.
>
> I have always been looking to the future—and have so far felt myself fully able and qualified to do any job that any of my contemporaries, at least, might be called upon to do—I have never, in any degree, knowingly avoided or shirked any duty of any kind—I came into submarines chiefly for my own professional benefit and had hoped to do some work with aircraft in the next few years. I might add that group command work has always seemed to me to be the best possible preparation for the future—and I like that kind of work!
>
> However, I understand that it is not my opinion and views which count, but those of the Selection Board as a whole—nor have I any idea that it is practicable or proper to attempt to "argue" the matter with the Board.
>
> I assume that one of the things "against" me is the amount of staff duty I've had—some five years in all—I can only say that never have I requested such duty nor have I ever sought it—in fact, I have declined such duty no less than three times. My last staff duty ended in April 1919 (six years ago) and rounded out a continuous "cruise" of five years and two days, and I realized *then* that I could not afford to do any more staff duty, for several years to come, at any rate.

I realized the necessity of experience in single-ship command—I went to command the *Bridge* for that very reason, even when BuNav demurred somewhat because the *Bridge* was "not a suitable command for a captain." I may say that I do not see that any particular merit is to be acquired in the command of a repair ship or tender—and—I commanded the *Bridge* for a full year, and I am doing repair ship and tender work right here.

My place on the sea-going roster calls for me to go to sea about June 1926—and when I was in Washington last month, I was told that I need not expect to go before my turn came, presumably because the Bureau is hardpressed for captains' billets at sea.

I have figured out, over a year ago, what I wanted to do at sea my next cruise—and when I say "what I wanted to do," I know you will believe that I was trying to use some judgment about my future. My last two fitness reports have stated my preference for sea duty as (1) light cruiser and (2) destroyer Squadron—what I hoped for was to get a year of each kind of duty.

Captain Leahy recently told me that I was not far enough up the list to be sure of getting a light cruiser (even in June 1926)—the other available single commands are *Rochester*, *Galveston*, *Pittsburgh*, *Huron* (?), *Chaumont* (?), *Henderson* (?), *Dobbin*, *Medusa* and *Black Hawk* (?) within the next year. It certainly seems to me that a light cruiser most fully meets all the requirements which you indicate—Gunnery and engineering, and tactics and communications—and I'd only be too glad to increase my knowledge and experience in all of those lines.

Admiral, I find that I've written quite a letter, but you have been so kindly thoughtful of my professional welfare that I wanted very much to tell you my story—my career to date seems, to *me*, not unfitting for future usefulness.

With many thanks again for your letter, whose confidence expressed in me is very encouraging, and with the assurance that I shall most carefully heed your friendly warning, I am

most sincerely yours,
/s/ E. J. King[8]

Thus in the summer of 1925 King still wanted to remain in the surface Navy, but he wanted nothing to do with Hughes' "drudgery of the service." He still wanted a warship, but the ominous warnings from Leahy turned out to be true. There was no suitable sea command available for King after he left New London, and it once again appeared that he was stymied.

In the late winter of 1925-1926 while King was in Washington, he was invited to call on Rear Admiral William A. Moffett, the Chief of the Bureau of Aeronautics. Moffett explained that Congress was about to pass legislation requiring commanding officers of aircraft carriers and naval air stations to be naval aviators or naval aviation observers. As naval aviation was such a new organization, its aviators were too junior for major aviation commands. "Moffett told me," said King in his memoirs, "that he wanted to get a few able captains who would like to take up aviation. Naturally, I was interested since I had been in submarines for almost four years and didn't see where I was going to get a proper job for myself on the list of captains. After mulling over the situation for a couple of months when I had time [King was then raising the submarine S-51], I wrote to Admiral Moffett that I'd like to go into aviation since it seemed to me that aviation was the coming thing in the Navy."[9]

Despite King's switch to naval aviation, he did not intend to forsake the surface Navy. Even after writing to Moffett, he still would have gladly accepted a cruiser command at the last moment. In a letter to a classmate at the Bureau of Navigation in May, 1926, King wrote, "I suppose that Bill Leahy has told you of my strenuous desires to get command of one of the scouts—I hope that you will keep me in mind for that duty."[10]

King was relieved at New London by another classmate, Adolphus Andrews, fresh from duty at the American Embassy in Paris, who (the reader will recall) declared as a plebe that he intended to be number one in his class. Andrews' career is worth reviewing because it contrasts with King's style of personal advancement and is the epitome of the kind of careerism that King scorned. Both wanted to be flag officers, but each in his own way. Andrews had become notorious for courting people in power while climbing over his classmates. Over the years he served as naval aide to Presidents Harding and Coolidge and was a confidant of Franklin D. Roosevelt. "How does Andrews succeed," wrote a jealous classmate to King, "in walking from one job which does not count as a cruise to another similar one and incidentally have the latter held open for him for a matter of months? It evidently pays to keep in close touch with the throne."[11]

Having qualified as a naval aviator, King sought the major command he knew he would need to make admiral: one of the new carriers, Lexington or Saratoga. But there were distractions along the way. In February, 1928, King was on temporary duty in the bitter waters off Provincetown, Massachusetts, trying to salvage the sunken submarine S-4, when he received a letter from Moffett offering him command of Langley, a small, slow converted carrier once a collier.[12]

"I hardly know how to reply at this time," wrote a harried King in response. "In the first place, I have been given this job of salvaging the S-4, which I hope to finish 'some time in April' but you never can tell. In the second place, developments regarding the Lexington and Saratoga commands may, in June or thereabouts, be of interest and importance to me. In the third place, I don't know when my present cruise [commanding seaplane tender Wright] began nor when it is supposed to end, although that doesn't really matter to me if I can get a good job!

"All in all, it looks as if I had best ask to let matters stand as they are for a time, if that can be done. I shall hope to get to Washington in time to talk with you about all of these matters before a decision has to be made."[13]

In the end King got the command he wanted, the *Lexington*.[14] Although King and Moffett later found that they could not stand each other, Moffett recognized that naval aviation needed King's talents and so had given King the one ship that guaranteed his promotion to rear admiral. King's method of command on *Lexington* was as a driver rather a leader. He was audacious and sometimes outrageous, but he got things done. *Lexington* performed brilliantly. King was selected for rear admiral in 1932, a year ahead of his classmates.

King's first flag assignment was Chief of the Bureau of Aeronautics, a billet which had suddenly become vacant with Moffett's death in early 1933. Moffett earlier had refused to sponsor King as his heir apparent despite King's many appeals for consideration. After his death it was generally understood that one of Moffett's favorites, Commander John A. Towers, a pioneer naval aviator, was in line to take over the bureau.[15] King went to Washington to get the job for himself.[16]

As King thought he was without political connections in Washington, he resorted to the direct approach by presenting himself before the CNO, Admiral William V. Pratt, and boldly asking for the job. Although Pratt regarded King as his fourth choice, he wanted to be fair. He sent King around to the Secretary of the Navy, Claude A. Swanson, who knew King casually, as well as to several key senators and congressmen, so that King could personally make his case.[17] Then King left town as he felt he had nothing more to say. Meanwhile, unknown to King, friends were working on his behalf. The most influential was Windor R. Harris, managing editor of the Norfolk *Virginian-Pilot*, whom King "had known for several years." Harris had political clout, and both he and Senator Harry F. Byrd of Virginia nominated King to the new President, Franklin D. Roosevelt.[18] It is reasonable to assume that Harris also spoke to Swanson, who had been both a senator from and the governor of Virginia. On 19 April 1933 Swanson nominated King to the President.[19]

And so King came to Washington for a three-year tour as a bureau chief, and his education began in the ways of bureaucracies. But, consistent with his independent philosophy, he remained aloof. He did almost nothing to further himself with Roosevelt, even though the President ultimately would decide whether King would achieve his dream of becoming CNO. Nor did he see much of Secretary Swanson, who was usually so sick that he was absent from the Navy Department for weeks and months at a time. Furthermore, King had no real friends in the naval hierarchy. For example, he constantly feuded with the CNO from 1933 to 1937, William H. Standley,[20] and he quarreled with the Bureau of Ordnance, the domain of the influential "Gun Club."[21]

As for Congress, King privately got along well with Carl Vinson, but he was a mediocre witness before congressional committees. Owing to his inexperience, King triggered a sensational congressional investigation of the aviation industry by naively volunteering sensitive testimony at the wrong time. It was all thoroughly distasteful to King, and it reinforced his general contempt for the Congress as a body.[22] All in all, then, King did not make good use of his three years in Washington to promote his drive to become the CNO. Nevertheless, he still had been a competent and effective bureau chief.

King returned to sea in 1936, even though Swanson, by then an invalid, had pleaded with him to remain in Washington an extra year to help him run the Navy Department. He first commanded the Navy's seaplanes (a job he had not wanted), and then the carriers. King was superb as a carrier task group commander. Many of the tactics and doctrine which he developed became standard practice during the Second World War.

In the spring of 1939 King reached the moment of truth. Leahy was about to retire as CNO, and it was then or never for King. His published memoirs record his hopes: "Although King had little conviction that it would fall to him, he thought they might do worse, and could not help hoping that lightning would strike . . . he still could not help hoping . . . he believed that his record would speak for itself."[23]

King had never had a chance of becoming the Chief of Naval Operations. Secretary Swanson, together with Admiral Leahy and the Chief of the Bureau of Navigation, Rear Admiral J. O. Richardson, had submitted their joint recommendation for flag assignments to the President on 24 January 1939.[24] King's name was not included. Roosevelt chose one of his dearest, closest friends, Harold R. Stark, to be his CNO. Later in the year King was ordered to the General Board, the traditional twilight cruise for admirals marking time until retirement.

It is fairly obvious why King was passed over, not only for CNO but for four stars, as well. Roosevelt and King were strangers. On the other hand, Stark had known Roosevelt since 1915, when Stark's destroyer had served as Roosevelt's private yacht in the waters off Campobello. Their friendship had matured over the years, and Stark was a good man whom Roosevelt could trust. "It will be grand to have you here as CNO," he wrote to Stark. "As in the case of Bill Leahy, you and I talk the same language."[25] Stark had also cultivated Secretary Swanson, whom he knew so well that Stark could send him familiar, intimate letters signed "Affectionately, Betty."[26]

King's friends told him he had been passed over because of his drinking, an assertion which King resented.[27] Richardson gratuitously asserts in his memoirs that he so admired King that he wanted him on the General Board to have him available on short notice should his services suddenly be required.[28] Richardson's claim is unconvincing, for he implies that King's later ascendancy was all part of Richardson's master plan. Although there were isolated exceptions, outstanding flag officers who still had a future simply were not sent to the General Board.

Another factor is that of seventy-four flag officers then in the Navy, only three were aviators: King, Halsey, and Charles A. Blakely. Obviously the attitudes and influence of the surface ship hierarchy would predominate in selecting the Navy's top leadership. King had chosen naval aviation, but aviation's time had not yet arrived in the Navy. In fact, King was in some ways an outcast, having turned away from the surface Navy but still resented by some naval aviators as an opportunistic latecomer who was never really one of them. King's hopes to become CNO before the Second World War had been wishful thinking.

FOOTNOTES

[1] King's family heritage is contained in his manuscript memoirs (hereafter cited as *King*) which served as the basis for King's autobiography *Fleet Admiral King: A Naval Record* (New York: Norton, 1952). These memoirs were lent to the author by Walter Muir Whitehill, who collaborated with King on his autobiography. The analysis of Lorain, Ohio, in the late nineteenth century is from the author's conversations with historian Theodore Ropp in early 1977.

[2] Memorandum of conversation, E. J. King and W. M. Whitehill, 31 July 1949, Whitehill Collection. King graduated fourth and Andrews eighteenth in the sixty-seven member class of 1901.

[3] *King*, Chapter II, pp. 32-33.

[4] E. J. King to R. S. Grant, 23 April 1946, E. J. King Collection, Manuscript Division, Library of Congress (hereafter cited as LCMD).

[5] The following paragraphs are extracted from the first six chapters of *King*.

[6] *King*, Chapter VII, p. 50.

[7] C. F. Hughes to E. J. King, 12 June 1925, Whitehill Collection.

[8] E. J. King to C. F. Hughes, 17 June 1925, Whitehill Collection.

[9] *King*, Chapter X, Part I, pp. 1-2.

[10] E. J. King to T. R. Kurtz, 13 May 1926, LCMD.

[11] J. V. Babcock to E. J. King, 24 May 1926, Whitehill Collection.

[12] W. A. Moffett to E. J. King, 8 February 1928, LCMD.

[13] E. J. King to W. A. Moffett, 13 February 1928, LCMD.

[14] King preferred *Lexington* to *Saratoga* because she did not have flag accommodations and would allow him to operate without an admiral aboard.

[15] *King*, Chapter XIII, pp. 2-35.

[16] E. J. King, memorandum for the record, 23 June 1948, Whitehill Collection.

[17] W. V. Pratt to the Secretary of the Navy, 14 April 1933, Whitehill Collection; *King*, Chapter XII, p. 26.

[18] W. R. Harris to Franklin D. Roosevelt, 15 March 1933; H. F. Byrd to Franklin D. Roosevelt, 23 March 1933. Both letters in Franklin D. Roosevelt Library.

[19] Secretary of the Navy to the President, 19 April 1933, Franklin D. Roosevelt Library.

[20] Their conflict is often cited in King's manuscript memoirs, but see also W. H. Standley to E. J. King. 10 January 1937, LCMD, which was written after Standley had received a conciliatory letter from King after Standley's retirement.

[21] *King,* Chapter XIII, pp. 8-9.

[22] For King as a witness, see *Ibid.,* pp. 10-12. The congressional investigation dealt with the charge of excess profits in late 1933 and culminated in a provision in the Vinson-Trammel Bill of 27 March 1934 that limited profits to ten percent. King's dislike for Congress is reflected in his Naval War College thesis of 1933.

[23] *Naval Record,* pp. 291-293.

[24] Secretary of the Navy to the President, 24 January 1939, Franklin D. Roosevelt Library.

[25] Franklin D. Roosevelt to H. R. Stark, 22 March 1939, Franklin D. Roosevelt Library.

[26] H. R. Stark to Claude A. Swanson, 28 September 1938, Franklin D. Roosevelt Library. "Betty" was Stark's nickname.

[27] Memorandum of conversation, E. J. King and W. M. Whitehill, 31 July 1949, Whitehill Collection.

[28] J. O. Richardson, *On the Treadmill to Pearl Harbor* (Washington: GPO, 1975), pp. 8-9.

CHAPTER 31

The Washington Years of Willis Lee: Preparing for Battle

Paul Stillwell

U. S. Naval Institute

It is ironic that the man who commanded all of the Navy's Pacific Fleet battleships as an admiral did not command a single battleship as a captain. Willis Augustus Lee, Jr., was the U.S. Navy's primary battleship commander through most of World War II. But in the years just before the war, when other members of the Naval Academy's class of 1908 were getting battleship commands, Lee was in Washington, preparing the men and ships of the U.S. Fleet for the war that was sure to come.

In the late 1930s, Lee had commanded the light cruiser *Concord* (CL-10), followed by a tour as operations officer and chief of staff for Rear Admiral Harold R. Stark, Commander Cruisers, Battle Force. In the spring of 1939, Stark was tapped as the next Chief of Naval Operations, and he took several staff members, including Lee, with him to Washington. In Lee's case, it meant a return to the Division of Fleet Training (Op-22), part of the CNO's staff. He had been there before, in the early and middle 1930s, with duty as navigator and executive officer of the USS *Pennsylvania* (BB-38) in between. It was apparently the shore duty for which the Navy considered his talents best suited. Though a bona fide member of the Gun Club, he was more interested in finding improved ways to operate ships and weapons than in designing or manufacturing them. When he reported to Main Navy on Constitution Avenue in June, 1939, the fifty-one-year-old Captain Lee was second man in the division. The director was Rear Admiral Herbert Fairfax Leary, a gunnery man who had finished fifth — two spots ahead of Chester Nimitz—in the Academy's class of 1905. Leary was brilliant, loud, and impatient. The calm, quiet Lee would serve as a good balance wheel and buffer between the admiral and the other fourteen officers who comprised Fleet Training.

Op-22 prepared directions, reports, and analyses on all phases of fleet training and exercises. These included annual competitions in gunnery, communications, engineering, and overall battle efficiency.[1] In lieu of combat itself, the competitions provided the necessary performance incentives to the peacetime Navy. On the results rode the fitness reports of officers and prize money for enlisted men. Lee's two passions were tactics and gunnery. He concentrated on those and left the details of running the individual specialties to the officers handling the appropriate desks. He was far less interested in which ships won the E's than in determining the maximum capabilities of men, ships, and weapons, then finding the best ways to employ those capabilities. There was considerable work to be done, for many new classes of ships had recently entered the fleet or were about to. Above all, the division's business was tactical training of the fleet for war.[2] Personnel training, such as boot camp or instruction within individual ratings, was handled by the Bureau of Navigation.

Although he had finished 106th out of 201 in his graduating class at Annapolis, Willis Lee had a superb mind which was particularly adept at mathematics. As a ship's captain, he had calculated mooring, now maneuvering, board solutions in his head while his deck officers struggled to do them with pencil and paper. He possessed great curiosity, seeking to know how things worked and how they could be made to work better. Yet his outward appearance and manner belied his intellectual capacity. Officers who served with Lee remember him as looking like a farmer. His necktie was seldom pulled up far enough for the knot to cover his collar button. He walked with a slouching gait, had a middle-age paunch, smoked constantly, and seldom cleaned the thick glasses he wore as the result of a boyhood mishap with gunpowder. He had something of an Oriental appearance and was known by the nicknames "Chink" and "Ching," both of which he used himself.

Captain Lee often worked ten- or twelve-hour days at the Navy Department, then took work home with him in the evening. He and his wife Mabelle — whom he had met while he was a Navy ordnance inspector in Illinois during World War I — had no children. After they had supper together, she often went to bed early because of a chronic heart condition. Lee would settle down in an easy chair with a pack of cigarettes and a pot of coffee nearby. He did his homework far into the night. Sometimes, instead of going to bed, he'd then pick up a detective novel and read some more before dozing off in the chair—perhaps as late as four o'clock in the morning. After a few hours of sleep, he put on his jacket and walked to work. Thus, if his clothes looked as if he had slept in them, he probably had.

Lee didn't own a car. Parking spaces were at a premium near the Navy Department, and autos were expensive. The Lees lived in an apartment about two miles away at 1921 Kalorama Road. It was not far from Rock

Creek Park and Connecticut Avenue in northwest Washington. Rear Admiral Nimitz was chief of the Bureau of Navigation at the time, and he wrote years later that he got to know Lee better during those years because of the long walks they took together:

> It was his custom . . . to join me in my office in the old Navy Dept Bldg on Constitution Ave—at the end of the working day and we would walk towards NW Washington—where both of us lived. This gave us much opportunity to exchange ideas and to discuss the state of the nation & the world. I was always impressed by his interest in & knowledge of world affairs—and by his sound wisdom. During the winter of 1940—on the coldest days—he would come, prepared to walk—in a thin suit & without gloves—while I—clad in an overcoat & with warm gloves—still felt the cold. I marvelled at his disregard of the weather and at his rugged physique. . . .[3]

Hot or cold, rain or shine, it was all the same to the imperturbable four-striper who had grown up in a small town in the rolling hills of north central Kentucky. He grew fond of the outdoors and developed into a crack shot. As a midshipman, he won the national pistol and rifle championships in 1907. He won five gold medals, one silver, and one bronze as a member of the U.S. Rifle Team in the 1920 Olympic Games. His shooting experience undoubtedly contributed to his knowledge of ballistics and proved helpful as he analyzed fleet gunnery exercises for Op-22.

Despite his abilities, Lee was unpretentious, even self-effacing. Officers considerably his junior felt no awkwardness over the difference in years because he paid little attention to rank. Other officers often stayed late at the office, not because they were afraid of him but because the avuncular, storytelling Lee was so interesting to be around. His philosophy was, "Don't give me a hard worker; I want an easy worker."[4] He sought not the juniors who made an effort of everything but the people who got the job done with a minimum of fuss. One such was Commander James L. "Jimmy" Holloway, Jr., (father of the current CNO) who reported to Fleet Training in 1940. He still takes pride in a fitness report evalution Lee wrote on him: "This officer does not waste time searching for a perfect solution but takes a reasonable solution and goes ahead and gets something done."[5]

Holloway was one of the "Uncle Ching's boys," and there were others working nearby. Across the hall from the Division of Fleet Training was the office of the Interior Control Board, of which Lee was chairman after June, 1940. The members came from various bureaus and from divisions within OpNav. The board's purpose was to establish specifications and requirements for the construction of new ships and weapons. The only officers whose primary duty assignment was board membership were Commander Jeffrey C. Metzel and Lieutenant Commander Milton E. "Mary" Miles. Miles kept a pot of coffee in the board office, so it was often the site of mid-morning coffee breaks during which ideas were exchanged.

Lieutenant Commander Percival E. "Pete" McDowell joined the group in 1940. The ideas Metzel, Miles, and McDowell came up with were imaginative, sometimes even bizarre. Lee had the ability to direct these men into productive channels, encouraging them to follow up on the ideas which seemed useful. Some of the suggestions—such as Miles' Chinese plan—put forth at the morning meetings were far afield from the Interior Control Board's normal business.

Like Lee, Miles had spent many years on the Navy's China Station. They had first met when serving in Asiatic Fleet destroyers in the early 1920s. On his way to duty at the Navy Department, Miles and his hardy family had made a journey of hundreds of miles along the rugged, tortuous Burma Road. The Chinese had been involved in an undeclared war with Japan since 1937. As U.S. involvement in the Far East war came inevitably nearer in 1940 and 1941, Miles sought to put a team of Navy men ashore in China to collect intelligence and coordinate U.S. efforts with those of the Chinese.[6] Lieutenant Commander Arthur H. McCollum, head of the Far East Section of the OpNav Intelligence Division, joined the coffee break discussions when the Chinese plan was hashed out, and so did Lieutenant Commander Aubrey B. "Abie" Leggett, the officer who moved in under Miles on the Interior Control Board when Metzel left to command a destroyer.

Admiral Leary went to sea himself in January, 1941, leaving Captain Lee as Director of Fleet Training. By then, the routine business of running the exercises and competitions was still taking place, but its significance paled against the urgent need to prepare for war. Of all the officers in Fleet Training then, Lee's closest soul-mate was Pete McDowell. The two were kindred spirits, and it fell to McDowell to beef up the fleet's antiaircraft capabilities in conjunction with the Bureau of Ordnance. Antiaircraft defense was a particular interest of Willis Lee, and it was a subject on which he and McDowell frequently tangled with Captain Garret L. "Mike" Schuyler, director of BuOrd's Research Division.

Captains Lee and Schuyler were close personal friends and often had lunch together, but they were frequently at odds professionally. The BuOrd research head had a tendency to pontificate on his business, and Lee sometimes had to deflate him with a well-aimed remark. Captain Lee had little tolerance for "pedigreed bunk," as he called it, and he could be quite stubborn on occasion—rearing back in his chair, putting both hands flat on his desk, and appearing "as immovable as a Missouri mule."[7] Schuyler championed 5-inch guns as the fleet's primary AA guns. His rationale was that they had greater range than .50-caliber machine guns and 1.1-inch guns and thus could knock off attacking airplanes before they got close enough for the smaller caliber weapons to hit.[8] Lee's people acknowledged the value of the 5-inch but contended the smaller guns were also useful to knock off planes that the 5-inch batteries were bound to miss. They were pushing for the acquisition of the 20-mm. Swiss Oerlikon and 40-mm. Swedish Bofors guns. Fortunately, the Chief of the Bureau of Ordnance, Rear Admiral William H. P. "Spike" Blandy, was also working actively to get the light AA guns into U.S. production.[9]

McDowell, meanwhile, was frequently off traveling. He saw the need for antiaircraft training centers as the new light guns became available. Ships that reached port would then be able to send their men ashore and let them blaze away at towed sleeves or drones so their shooting eyes would be sharper when actual planes were coming in. Lieutenant Commander Ernest M. "Judge" Eller spent a few months in the Division of Fleet Training in 1941 after returning from nearly a year observing antiaircraft guns in combat in England. One of the tasks assigned him by Captain Lee was to find a suitable location for the primary East Coast training center. He located a spot at Dam Neck, Virginia, near Virginia Beach. Eventually, there were some ten AA training centers on each coast.

McDowell and Eller were also involved in the quest for an effective gunsight for the light weapons. Once, on a train trip to the Massachusetts Institute of Technology, McDowell was tipped off by another naval officer on the existence of a "black box" in the laboratory of Dr. Stark Draper at MIT. It turned out to be a sight designed for tanks. It was composed of two airspun gyroscopes, one vertical and one horizontal. As a result, it could generate lead angles and the proper elevation for range. The gunner could keep his eye on the target rather than having to lead it as was customary with the sights then in use. An excited McDowell packed it up and went with Eller and Holloway to test it at the Naval Proving Ground, Dahlgren, Virginia.

They wired it onto a machine gun with baling wire and started testing it by firing tracer bullets. The results were amazing, for it was the best performance that had ever been demonstrated by an automatic gunsight. Even after it fell off the gun and was wired back on, it continued to shine. As soon as the test results were reported to Captain Lee, he went to Rear Admiral Blandy and recommended that the new sight, designated Mk 14, be acquired by the Navy and put into production. It was.[10]

One of the best-kept secrets of those prewar months was the development of shipboard radar. Willis Lee, who saw the device's potential, was instrumental in getting it installed aboard ships of the fleet for search and fire control. As a battleship commander in the Pacific during the war, he would sit for hours and peer at luminescent radar scopes, watching ships and airplanes moving to and fro.

As Director of the Division of Fleet Training, Captain Lee was a peripatetic figure, strolling the corridors of Main Navy to find out the latest. One of his fellow officers thought a walkie-talkie would have been in order to keep up with him. Even in the large one-room office occupied by his division, Lee was frequently up and about. He went from desk to desk, not to interfere with the work of others, but to probe and learn. He was a leader, not a pusher. Calm and soft-spoken, he was nevertheless sharp and not to be buffaloed. His manner was often folksy and laced with a dry sense of humor. Invariably, those who served with him recall the perpetual twinkle in his eye. As one of the officers in Fleet Training worked over a report or study or table of mathematical calculations, Lee would walk up and ask, "Having any problems?" A quiet question here, a suggestion there, and the officer would work it out. The officer felt the better for it, because he had come to the answer himself. Lee had been only the catalyst, not one who forced his solutions on others. After a day of such wandering, it's no wonder he had to tackle his own full briefcase at night. As with many other Navy offices, Fleet Training had to deal with a mountain of paperwork from the Fleet. Lee put his penciled initials and notes on thousands of routing slips, reports, and carbon copies of outgoing letters.

As the summer of 1941 turned to autumn, there was good news in the Lee household. At two o'clock one September morning, Lieutenant Commander Nealy A. Chapin, the Fleet Training duty officer, gave a pleased Mabelle Lee the news that her husband had been selected for promotion to rear admiral. It wasn't much of a surprise. Captain Lee had been serving in a two-star billet for months, and the Chief of Naval Operations had utmost confidence in him. Once, Admiral Stark had puckishly graded Lee's military appearance "exceptional" on a fitness report. It wasn't outstanding, but it was an exception to the norm. When news of the selection came through, the subordinates of the Fleet Training director sent him a message, "Congratulations to the first man to make flag rank without two-blocking his tie."[11]

The promotion came on November 4, and a little more than a month later, the nation was at war. Admiral and Mrs. Lee were at home when the Japanese struck Pearl Harbor. A call from the Navy Department summoned Lee to the office. Unflappable as ever, he took the news in stride while some around him were devastated. He put Jimmy Holloway, head of Fleet Training's gunnery section, in charge of allocating .50-caliber ammunition which was in short supply and dearer than gold. The half million rounds on hand weren't enough for more than a few days of fighting. The equipping of ships and training of crews, already being conducted in earnest, became even more urgent.

Admiral Ernest J. King soon moved to Washington as Commander in Chief, U.S. Fleet (Cominch), and Admiral Stark was effectively moved aside as a result of the Pearl Harbor disaster. On December 30, 1941, Admiral Lee reported to King's staff for temporary additional duty as assistant chief of staff. In another paper transaction, Fleet Training went out of business on January 20, 1942, and was reincarnated immediately as the Readiness Division (F-4) of the Cominch staff.[12] The duties and responsibilities remained much the same, although the new title was more descriptive of the division's function—to make the fleet ready for war.

Security was important in a Washington at war. On one occasion, with Lee's permission, Mary Miles dressed up in the type of apron busboys wore in the Navy Department cafeteria. So attired, he got hold of a drawer of classified files from one office, loaded the material into a pushcart and took it nearly a mile to the Federal Bureau of Investigation. He returned to his office without being detected, and the "theft" wasn't reported for two days. Lee himself also demonstrated the laxity of the building's security, coming and going at will with a picture of Adolf Hitler attached to the identification card he wore on his uniform. When no one challenged him for that, he tried a picture of Mae West and got by for another half day.[13]

Miles was also at work on more serious pursuits. The morning coffee break sessions had continued to develop plans for sending the intelligence mission to China. For a Navy at war, virtually anything that would aid the fleet in preparing for combat could be placed under the "Readiness" rubric. Admiral Lee was the patron of the affair for a couple of reasons. Even though he was just a new rear admiral, he had the necessary rank to cut across departmental lines—White House, War Department, Navy Department, State Department. And, because he was not in Naval Intelligence per se, he could not do so without attracting suspicion or attention. Thus, the Interior Control Board became the Washington cover for the mission, and Lee made the top-level decisions.[14] Lee and Miles were working with Lieutenant Colonel Hsaio Sin-ju, the assistant Chinese military attache in Washington. Their aim was to insert a naval intelligence team which could provide aerial and electronic intelligence, weather reports from the Chinese mainland, and bulletins on the movement of Japanese shipping. And, going beyond a purely intelligence-gathering role, they had in mind a rear-guard action which would strengthen the Chinese soldiers and deny the Japanese use of resources on the Chinese mainland.

In early 1942, Miles was summoned to Admiral King's office. Acting on Admiral Lee's recommendation, King was sending Miles to China "to find out what is going on out there." As Miles' memoirs recount, Admiral King told him, "You are to go to China and set up some bases as soon as you can. The main idea is to prepare the China coast in any way you can for U.S. Navy landings in three or four years. In the meantime, do whatever you can to help the Navy and heckle the Japanese."[15] On April 5, Miles left on his mission, heading first for Brazil and then to Africa, for trying to reach China by going across the Pacific was out of the question at a time when Japan was on a yet-unchecked rampage.

While Commander Miles was in China—and he stayed there the rest of the war—Jeff Metzel was his Washington contact. Metzel, who often stayed at the Navy Department for days at a time, took care of his Interior Control Board business during the day and tended the reports and requests from Miles at night. Metzel maintained a frantic pace, and he constantly threw off intellectual sparks. One of his 1919 Naval Academy classmates said that Metzel ". . . had a new idea on how to win the war about three or four times a day, and about every ten days he had an excellent idea."[16] Willis Lee had an affinity for these "brilliant screwballs." He was able to stimulate their thinking and then send them off to perform the service at which they were most valuable.

Pete McDowell continued his own gadfly missions on behalf of the boss. Lee gave him plenty of freedom and then covered for him if he had to. McDowell was the admiral's alter ego, attending conferences on his behalf. If a meeting seemed to be drifting in the wrong direction, he would make a quick call to Lee who would come in, get a quick briefing, and present his views. The tenor of these meetings often changed quickly as a result of his intervention.

In the course of his travels, McDowell talked to Lieutenant Commander Arleigh Burke, a classmate of his who was stationed at the Naval Gun Factory in Washington. Burke told him that York Safe and Lock Company was not making good breech mechanisms for the 40-mm. gun and that the Navy should get them from the Pontiac division of General Motors instead. McDowell passed the information on to Admiral Lee, who told him to make the recommendation to Commander Ernest E. Herrmann at the Bureau of Ordnance. Soon, Captain Theodore D. Ruddock, Jr., of BuOrd's Production Division called back and wanted to know where McDowell had gotten his assertions about York's breech mechanisms. Despite a lot of prodding, McDowell wouldn't tell because he didn't want to get Burke in trouble.

Before long, Admiral Lee received a letter from the Bureau of Ordnance, putting McDowell on report for "unwarranted interference" and going around collecting "misinformation" about the breech mechanism. Lee asked McDowell what he proposed to do, and he said he would lie to protect Burke. He would say that he did not really know much about the subject and didn't recall where he had heard it. Lee responded, "I don't think you're going to have to do that." He asked his secretary to bring him all the copies of the letter, and across the face of the original, he wrote a note to Admiral Blandy, "Dear Spike, In this matter, Pete performed strictly in accordance with my orders. Regards, Ching." It was typical of the way Lee operated and was the reason his subordinates held him in high esteem. He took the heat for them and showed that his loyalty went down as well as up.[17]

On May 12, 1942, the newly-formed Joint Committee on New Weapons and Equipment held its first meeting. The committee, which reported to the

Joint Chiefs of Staff, was chaired by Dr. Vannever Bush, a noted civilian scientist who was president of the Carnegie Institution of Washington. Rear Admiral Lee was the Navy member. He was already using civilian scientists in the quest for new devices which would contribute to the fleet's ability to do its job. One such was Dr. Edwin Land, then in his early thirties and later the inventor of the Polaroid camera. Lee appointed Land and McDowell as a committee of two to work on new weapons. Land was the chairman of the "committee," and McDowell was the member. Then, if someone challenged McDowell's actions or requests, he could blithely respond, "You'll have to talk to my chairman."

As before, getting antiaircraft weapons onto ships was a prime consideration. McDowell got the blueprints for all types of combatant ships in the fleet. Then he cut out circles of paper to represent the proportional sizes of various gun mounts—20-mm., 40-mm., and 5-inch. He put them down on blueprints to see how many would fit on each type of ship. Then he drafted a letter authorizing procurement of the necessary number of mounts. He showed the letter to the appropriate officer in the Bureau of Ships and asked him to sign. The man balked, saying that the mounts would disrupt the seaworthiness of the ships. McDowell pointed out that the letter authorized procurement only and not installation. Reluctantly, the officer signed, and McDowell returned to his office where he took out a period and got the letter changed from "procurement" to "procurement and installation." The letter went up the chain of command, got the requisite approval from the Secretary of the Navy, and was implemented. Thereafter, whenever a combatant went into a shipyard, light and antiaircraft guns were added everywhere there was room—and sometimes in places where there had been no room. For some of the ships, topside equipment was removed to make way for the guns.

"Uncle Ching's boys" were not alone in the production of new ideas. One cruiser skipper sent in a letter recommending that the ship's catapults be used to launch torpedoes. McDowell suggested to Admiral Lee that they send a reply which thanked the captain for his idea but told him it was totally impractical because there weren't even enough torpedoes to provide full supplies to submarines and destroyers—let alone cruisers. Lee smiled and suggested an alternate course of action. He said such a reply would only disappoint the cruiser captain and serve to dampen his morale. Instead, said the admiral, McDowell should draft a response saying that it was a good idea. He should recommend it for action and then send it on up the chain of command. But it would have to make a lot of stops, for the catapults were under the cognizance of the Bureau of Aeronatics, the ships deck under the Bureau of Ships, the catapult powder charge under the Bureau of Ordnance, the new use for the catapult under the General Board, and the possibility of a patent under the office of the Secretary of the Navy. Such a response would take months to get around, said Lee, and there would be a new endorsement perhaps once a quarter. The captain would be happy, and he would be long gone to other duty before the letter finished making the rounds. That is what McDowell did, and that is what happened to the letter.[18]

He had handled the same sort of situation somewhat differently in late 1940 when a captain in the Army Air Corps reserve submitted an idea for merchant ships to use sea sleds as a means of attacking enemy submarines. It was duly forwarded to the Navy by Secretary of the War Henry Stimson and then sent to Fleet Training for evaluation. After he had perused the suggestion, Lee wrote "Holloway tell him no possibility—the old bed-bug letter WAL" Thereupon a two-page letter was drafted for Secretary of the Navy Frank Knox to send to Stimson, explaining in logical, detailed terms why the sea sled idea was impractical.[19]

Lee had other means of getting the light touch into the flood of paper. As each new demand piled on top of the last one, priorities climbed higher and higher. Previously, action matters had been stamped "routine" or "priority." Now, everything was "urgent." Thus, Lee devised his own stamp, "frantic." There was one thing he did not have the answer for, because he was used to a Navy of men. As more and more sailors went to sea, Waves came into the Navy and took over secretarial jobs as yeomen. Admiral King ruled that the enlisted women should be addressed by their last names, just as the men were. It happened that Admiral Lee's secretary was an attractive second-class yeoman named Dorothy Angel. Lee would be embarrassed when a visitor came in and he had to call out, "Angel, please bring me the file on such-and-such."[20]

Lee detested paperwork throughout his naval career, viewing it as a necessary evil that had to be endured in order to serve as a naval officer. He was a ship operator, not a letter writer. He could sit by the hour with mathematical charts and gunnery reports, but he didn't bother with correspondence unless he could not avoid it. If a letter came in that he did not feel like answering, he might just sfuff it in a desk drawer or into one of the big side pockets of his khaki uniform. There it would stay until someone came around to track it down. Fortunately, Admiral Lee had an officer in his division who liked paperwork and did it well. Though the Readiness Division was part of the Cominch staff rather than a separate command, Lee's efficient man Friday, Commander William F. Jennings, served perfectly in the role corresponding to that of a flag secretary.[21] He and Lee had first served together in 1937 when Lee had temporary command of Cruiser Division Three and Jennings was flag secretary. Jennings had the same job as one of Admiral Stark's staff officers, and he was later Lee's chief of staff in the Pacific.

Admiral Lee had worked long hours before the war, but his schedule became even fuller as the war progressed. He was frequently at the office seven days a week. Perhaps it was just as well that he and Mabelle were not interested in the social whirl. She was a shy, retiring person and did not welcome the chore of entertaining. There was an occasional cocktail party in the Kalorama Road apartment, but mostly they stuck to themselves. When they did go out, it was often an obligatory affair or a party in the home of close friends, such as Commander Miles and his wife Wilma who had a big home in Chevy Chase. After Mary took off for China, his wife gave a small party by herself one evening. As a means of starting conversation, she devised a party game in which each guest would relate his or her most embarrassing moment or tell a whopping lie. Uncle Ching told of an experience he had supposedly had as a midshipman. He and his roommate left their ship during a cruise to Norway and proceeded to a local church. Unfamiliar with the language, they decided to watch the man in front of them and copy his actions. At one point, the man stood up, so the pair obediently followed suit. To their surprise, they were the only three on their feet. As they were leaving at the end of the service, said Admiral Lee, they spoke to the minister who happened to be bilingual and understood English. They explained their predicament, and he laughed when he told them what had happened. There was a new baby in the congregation, said the imaginary minister, and he had asked the father to stand up.[22]

But the real world of 1942 was still at work, and that meant still more requirements of the "urgent" and "frantic" variety. Submarines were cutting missions short because of a lack of pure water for refilling batteries, so Lee pushed successfully for the immediate installation of new Kleinschmidt evaporators, then being held up in the Bureau of Ships for further testing. Again, following his philosophy of moving for a workable solution rather than a perfect one, he urged production of the new proximity antiaircraft fuze, even though Commander William S. "Deke" Parsons wanted it held up until it was satisfactory. Lee and McDowell concocted a letter to BuOrd and BuShips, saying they wanted at least one radar on every combatant ship in the Navy. Admiral Lee added the prodding final sentence, "If you can't produce them in this country, buy British."[23]

As head of the Readiness Division, Lee had a hand in seeing that weapons and ammunition were procured and delivered to each ship to meet the requirements of upcoming operations. Security by then had tightened to the point that it caused problems even for Admiral Lee. He had a great deal of difficulty getting advance word on the names of ships to be involved in an operation. Sometimes, there were only a few hours to work with BuOrd and the logistics section of Cominch to meet deadlines such as the delivery of high-capacity projectiles to ships scheduled to be involved in bombardments. Truck convoys carried the new 20-mm. and 40-mm. guns to ships, and BuOrd had radio communications with the truck convoys so destinations could be changed en route to meet emergency installation needs.[24]

One such operation that called for massive preparations because of its scope was Torch, the planned invasion of North Africa in the fall of 1942. Some of the preparations came under the aegis of a new subdivision of Readiness Division called Special Weapons. Again, Commander McDowell was running with the bit in his mouth, fully aware that Captain Schuyler was not going to be pleased with the infringement on BuOrd turf. McDowell had reserve officers reading research reports and making recommendations for ideas that could be turned into hardware in one, two, or three years. They worked on landing craft, new types of amphibious ships, and getting tanks to the beach. They came up with airborne radar sets that could provide an overview of landing craft on their way to the beach and then send the picture to the bridge of the flagship by television. Still other Special Weapons projects were hedgehog rocket weapons for antisubmarine work, infrared viewing devices, and razeed destroyers for going up rivers in North Africa. Still another invention was an inflatable rubber man to draw fire in amphibious landings. It had weighted feet and could be booby-trapped. On one occasion, McDowell brought one of the "men" into Lee's office and introduced it to the admiral by saying, "Sir, I want you to meet my relief." Lee replied, in his droll way, "Pete, I can see the improvement immediately."[25]

It was time for Lee's relief. He had been on the job in Main Navy for more than three years, and the changes had been enormous. There were hundreds more ships in the fleet than when he had last been in a sea command in 1939. The biggest and most impressive of the new gunnery ships were the 35,000-ton fast battleships of the *North Carolina* (BB-55) and *South Dakota* (BB-57) classes. Willis Lee was not an ambitious man, but there was a war on, and he wanted to go to sea. He had proved his genius in gunnery and earned the approbation of Admirals Stark and King. Lee may have asked King for command of the first division of fast battleships to go to the South Pacific. In any case, King undoubtedly approved Lee for the job, for flag officer assignments during the war routinely required the initials "EJK" alongside. In August, 1942, Rear Admiral Willis Augustus Lee, Jr., fifty-four years old, went to the Kalorama Road apartment, packed a suitcase, said goodbye to Mabelle, and left for Philadelphia. There he boarded his first flagship, the *South Dakota*, for the long trip to the fleet he loved so well. Soon, he would write to his wife, "Except that I miss you, this is a welcome relief from the office in Washington."[26]

FOOTNOTES

[1] The individual sections within the Division of Fleet Training were Tactics, Gunnery, Engineering, Damage Control, and Chemical Warfare. See Admiral H. R. Stark, USN, *Organization of the Office of the Chief of Naval Operations with Duties Assigned the Divisions Thereunder* (Washington, D.C.: Navy Department, October 23, 1940), pp. 21-23.

[2] Captain Willis A. Lee, USN, confidential memorandum to Captain G. B. Wright, USN(Ret.), "Internal Organization of the Office of the Chief of Naval Operations," folder (SC)A3-1, Confidential General Correspondence of the Division of Fleet Training, 1927-41, Record Group 38 (Box 299), National Archives, Washington, D.C.

[3] Fleet Admiral Chester W. Nimitz, USN, letter to Evan E. Smith, May 8, 1962. Mr. Smith, a boyhood friend of Lee in Kentucky, was working on a biography of the admiral at the time of his death in 1963. Mrs. Smith donated her husband's papers to the author.

[4] Mrs. Wilma Miles, interview with author, Chevy Chase, Maryland, November 28, 1975.

[5] Admiral James L. Holloway, Jr., USN(Ret.), interview with author, Virginia Beach, Virginia, December 16, 1975.

[6] Miles' activities during this prewar period are covered in much greater detail in his book *A Different Kind of War* (Garden City, N.Y.: Doubleday, 1967), pp. 1-16. Unfortunately, some of the details in the early part of the book are inaccurate because it was written after Miles' death. The manuscript was produced by Hawthorne Daniel, working from Miles' notes and the memory of Mrs. Miles.

[7] Holloway, letter to author, July 13, 1977.

[8] Rear Admiral M. Eller, USN(Ret.), interview with Dr. John T. Mason, Annapolis, Maryland, August 25, 1977. The transcript of the interview is available through the U.S. Naval Institute Oral History Program, Annapolis, Md.

[9] For a detailed account of the acquisition and production of the 20-mm. and 40-mm. AA guns, see Lieutenant Commander Buford Rowland, USNR, and Lieutenant William B. Boyd, USNR, *U.S. Navy Bureau of Ordnance in World War II* (Washington, D.C.: U.S. Government Printing Office, 1953), pp. 219-231.

[10] Based on author's interviews with Admiral Holloway, Virginia Beach, July 10, 1977 and with Captain Percival E. McDowell, USN (Ret.), Winchester, Virginia, March 3, 1977, and Dr. Mason's interview with Admiral Eller. A fuller and somewhat different version is in Rowland and Boyd, *op. cit.*, pp. 379-384.

[11] McDowell interview.

[12] Rear Admiral Julius Augustus Furer, USN(Ret.), *Administration of the Navy Department in World War II* (Washington, D.C.: U.S. Government Printing Office, 1959), pp. 152-156. Included in the new Readiness Division were three major sections: F-21 (Readiness), F-22 (Training), and F-23 (Instruction). New sections added during Lee's tenure were F-25 (Antisubmarine Warfare) in April, 1942, and F-26 (Amphibious Warfare) in June, 1942. After he left for sea in August, 1942, still more sections were added during the course of the war, and the Antisubmarine Warfare Section was transferred out of the Readiness Division.

[13] Miles, *A Different Kind of War*, p. 20.

[14] Captain Raymond A. Kotrla, USN(Ret.), interview with author, Washington, D.C., May 29, 1976.

[15] Miles, *A Different Kind of War*, p. 18. Considering the posthumous nature of Miles' memoirs, there must be at least some doubt that the language in the book represents an exact transcript of the conversation between Miles and King.

[16] Vice Admiral George C. Dyer, USN (Ret.), interview with author, Annapolis, Maryland, December 12, 1974.

[17] McDowell interview.

[18] *Ibid.*

[19] Folder (SC)A13, Fleet Training Division confidential correspondence, Record Group 38 (Box 316), National Archives.

[20] Wilma Miles interview; Rear Admiral Charles H. Lyman, USN, letter to Evan E. Smith, June 16, 1962.

[21] Vice Admiral George L. Russell, USN(Ret.), interview with author, Washington, D.C., December 14, 1975.

[22] Wilma Miles interview; Mrs. Jeffrey C. Metzel, telephone interview with author, January 26, 1976.

[23] Rear Admiral John R. Waterman, USN(Ret.), letter to author, July 22, 1977; McDowell interview.

[24] Rear Admiral Nealy A. Chapin, USN(Ret.), letter to author, July 14, 1977.

[25] McDowell interview.

[26] Rear Admiral Willis A. Lee, USN, letter to Mrs. Lee, September 4, 1942. Courtesy of Miss Margaret B. Allen, Mrs. Lee's sister.

CHAPTER 32

The Navy and Investigating the Pearl Harbor Attack: A Consideration of New Source Material

William Heimdahl and Geraldine Phillips

National Archives

On March 8, 1972, President Richard Nixon signed into law Executive Order 11652 providing for the declassification and public release of millions of pages of classified documents created during World War II. Shortly thereafter, the Secretary of Defense drafted and issued on May 3, 1972, special guidelines for downgrading and declassifying records created by components or predecessor components of the Department of Defense, and declassifiers began work. One of the small but significant bodies of records reviewed by Navy Department declassifiers in 1972 under the new Department of Defense guidelines were the records of a Navy Department unit which remained in existence for less than a year during 1945-46. This unit was referred to as the Navy Liaison Office to the Joint Congressional Committee Investigating the Attack on Pearl Harbor, or the Pearl Harbor Liaison Office.

Before discussing the Pearl Harbor Liaison Office, we might briefly review the Pearl Harbor investigations conducted after December 7, 1941. Only two days after the attack, Secretary of the Navy Frank Knox undertook the first investigation of the disaster. After a brief trip to Hawaii from December 9-15, 1941, he reported to President Roosevelt that the Japanese had been successful because of Army and Navy unpreparedness for an air strike against Pearl Harbor. He avoided holding the two local commanders, Admiral Husband Kimmel and General Walter Short, specifically responsible for deficiencies by pointing out that they lacked such essential defensive equipment as sufficient fighter airplanes and anti-aircraft artillery and had not received vital information based upon intelligence intercepts available in Washington.[1]

After Secretary Knox had reported to him, President Roosevelt issued an executive order dated December 18, 1941, establishing a commission to be headed by Supreme Court Justice Owen Roberts that would conduct a more thorough investigation into the Pearl Harbor attack. After interviewing high level officials in Washington, the commission went to Pearl Harbor where it obtained further testimony and on January 23, 1942, submitted its findings to the President. Not only did it blame General Short and Admiral Kimmel for failure to prepare their commands for attack, but it stated that Washington had sufficiently alerted Pearl Harbor about the possible outbreak of hostilities.[2]

Two years after the Pearl Harbor bombing, Secretary Knox ordered an inquiry to be held to obtain information concerning the Japanese attack to prevent loss of important evidence through wartime death or absence of naval personnel having knowledge of the incident. Retired Admiral Thomas C. Hart presided over the inquiry, which lasted from February 12 to June 15, 1944. Although he was not required to submit findings or recommendations, Admiral Hart's efforts resulted in examination of a large number of witnesses who had important knowledge of facts related to the attack and events preceding it.[3]

On June 13, 1944, Congress approved legislation that extended the statute of limitations affecting the prosecution of any person connected with the Pearl Harbor catastrophe and directed the Secretary of War and the Secretary of the Navy to proceed with investigations into the circumstances surrounding the attack.[4] On July 24, 1944, the Navy opened a court of inquiry into the attack. Composed of three retired flag officers, Admiral Orin G. Murfin (chairman), Vice Admiral Edward C. Kalbfus, and Vice Admiral Adolphus Andrews, the court heard testimony from thirty-nine witnesses. In its report of October 19, 1944, the court concluded that no prosecutable offenses had been committed by any member of the naval forces in performing his duties, including Admiral Kimmel, but it did criticize Admiral Stark for failure to display sound judgement in not communicating intelligence about Japanese actions to the Pacific Fleet at Pearl Harbor.[5]

In his endorsement of the Naval Court of Inquiry findings, dated December 1, 1944, James Forrestal, who had become Secretary of the Navy after the death of Frank Knox, expressed a reservation that all possible evidence had not been exhausted, especially as it might relate to errors in judgement by Admirals Kimmel and Stark. Consequently, on May 2, 1945, he appointed Admiral H. Kent Hewitt to study the previous naval investigations and conduct any needed additional inquiries. Two junior naval reserve officers in the Secretary's office, Lieutenant Commanders John F. Sonnett and John F. Baecher, were detailed to assist with the inquiry. Although they obtained the testimony of several officers who had not been interrogated previously, Admiral Hewitt's report of July 12, 1945, differed very slightly from that of the court of inquiry.[6]

401

Three War Department investigations also occurred after the Congressional act of June 1944. The Army Pearl Harbor Board began its work on July 20 and submitted its findings on October 20, 1944. Instead of simply holding General Short accountable for deficiencies at Pearl Harbor, the Board considered that high level War Department officials, particularly Chief of Staff General Marshall, were responsible for not adequately providing vital intelligence to the Hawaiian command.[7]

Based upon reports involving the Army Pearl Harbor Board, General Marshall decided that an inquiry should be made into the War Department's pre-war handling of MAGIC, the decoded Japanese intercepts. Therefore, Colonel Carter W. Clarke looked into this aspect in September 1944 and again in July 1945. His reports concluded that Marshall and his staff had committed no transgressions in the use of the material.[8]

Because of the Army Pearl Harbor Board's criticism of General Marshall, Secretary of War Stimson decided in September 1944 that a further examination was necessary. He delegated Major Henry C. Clausen to interview those who had testified before the board in order to gather additional information. After traveling very widely to obtain his data, Clausen attempted in his report to exonerate General Marshall.[9]

Because of the contradictory nature of the previous Army and Navy investigations and the continuing public concern over the entire matter even after the Japanese surrender, Congress decided that a comprehensive examination was necessary. Senate Concurrent Resolution 27, passed on September 11, 1945, created a joint committee to investigate the Pearl Harbor attack.

Recognizing that a special office would be needed to obtain information and documentation for the joint committee and to coordinate its efforts with those of the War Department, the Navy Department decided to establish a liaison unit. As an indication of the importance of its work, the unit was set up within the Secretary's office. Rear Admiral O. S. Colclough, who became Judge Advocate General of the Navy in November 1945, and Lieutenant Commander John Ford Baecher were selected as liaison oficers, with Baecher undertaking most of the responsibility of managing the operations of the office. Baecher's experience with the Hewitt inquiry was undoubtedly one of the main reasons why he was selected to be a liaison officer. In addition, he had amassed an impressive record as a lawyer prior to his entry on active duty as a reserve lieutenant with the Navy in December 1942. A graduate of Georgetown University and Harvard Law School, he had for two years been professor of law at Santa Clara University, had served as a practicing attorney for two years with his father John A. Baecher in Norfolk, Va., had been with the San Francisco law firm of Brobeck, Phleger, and Harrison for eight years, and for one year prior to his entry on active duty had been a lawyer in the Criminal Division of the

Justice Department.[10] Before reporting to the Office of the Secretary of the Navy, he had served on the staff of the Chief of the Bureau of Yards and Docks.

Baecher's initial responsibilities were considerable. On one hand, he arranged for the painting of reception rooms, obtained executive desks and chairs to furnish them for the flag officers who were to come to the reception rooms to prepare their testimony, and ordered file cabinets, some with combination locks, to store security-classified records. More importantly, he set up a procedure whereby personnel assigned to him could promptly process requests for information and documents coming from the Committee and record the information and items furnished for the liaison office files, and with the help of some of Secretary Forrestal's aides, selected key contacts in all of the Navy Department offices to which he would have to go for assistance. In addition, he prepared the Navy's rather lengthy version of the facts of the Pearl Harbor disaster, entitled "Narrative Statement of Evidence at Navy Pearl Harbor Investigations."

The Pearl Harbor Liaison Office was only a temporary part of the Navy Department administrative structure; in fact there is very little, outside of the records that it created, that would prove it occupied rooms 1068A, 1085, and 1501 of the Main Navy Building during the latter months of 1945 and the first half of 1946. Yet, the internal records left behind by the unit provide new and interesting insights that can lead to reinterpretation of the Navy's role in the Congressional investigation launched on November 15, 1945, and document its efforts to aid or at least to meet the requests of the Congressional investigators. We will not attempt to describe all the records of the Pearl Harbor Liaison Office, but will try to provide some idea of the types of information available in them.

The charge has been made that serious obstacles were placed in the way of Admiral Husband Kimmel in his attempt to get access to MAGIC files in order to prepare his defense and that the reason that this was done was to cover up evidence of the Navy Department's failure to properly evaluate intelligence it received prior to December 7, 1941.[11] Documents found within the files of the Pearl Harbor Liaison Office provide evidence indicating that concern for protection of sources of information vital to national security and not fear of blame was Secretary of the Navy Forrestal's motive in attempting to withhold from Admirals Kimmel and Stark, the Joint Committee and other Congressional committees, and the American public certain Navy Department records relating to the Pearl Harbor disaster and its investigation. President Truman's directive of August 28, 1945, forbidding the Secretaries of State, War, and Navy, the Attorney General, the Joint Chiefs of Staff, the Director of the Budget, and the Director of the Office of Information from releasing to the public any information relating to the past or present techniques of cryptanalysis conducted under the authority of the U.S. government was in line with Forrestal's position.

403

On August 16, 1945, Chairman of the Senate Committee on Naval Affairs David I. Walsh requested that Secretary of the Navy Forrestal furnish his committee the complete file of the investigations conducted by the Navy Department into the Pearl Harbor disaster along with Forrestal's comments and recommendations as to whether these complete files should be released to the public.[12] Undoubtedly Forrestal delayed his response to this request until all pertinent issues had been discussed with the President and the President had reached a decision as to how much of the Army Pearl Harbor Board report and the Pearl Harbor Navy Court of Inquiry report should be released. The fact that the decision was made by Truman to withhold certain parts of these reports made it easier for Forrestal to insist in a letter to Walsh on September 6, 1945, that considerations of national security demanded that those parts of the investigatory records that revealed sources of enemy information had to be withheld. After making very clear his own feelings, Forrestal left it up to Walsh to decide whether the public interest outweighed national security interest in the matter.[13]

Pearl Harbor Liaison Office records also reveal that during September-October 1945, Admiral Kimmel's counsel requested and received clarification of what was meant by Truman's ban on disclosure of "specific results of any cryptanalytic unit" from Fleet Admiral E. J. King, Commander-in-Chief, United States Fleet, who stated that the proper interpretation of this phrase meant that witnesses called before the Joint Committee would be prohibited from testifying as to methods by which information relating to the enemy was acquired.[14] Any request from the Joint Committee or from Kimmel requesting to be advised of sources of information had to be approved by the President himself. It soon became apparent to the Joint Committee as well as to Kimmel, Stark, and their counsels that the Presidential ban of August 28 would seriously inhibit the investigation because it would rule out testimony of any intelligence received prior to the attack of December 7 that had been obtained through MAGIC, that is, through decryption of Japanese code messages. To remedy this situation, Chief Counsel Mitchell requested through Rear Admiral Colclough that the President's August 28th directive be modified to permit the Joint Committee to see Japanese coded messages that were intercepted and decoded by U.S. agencies prior to December 7, 1941, and that the Joint Committee be allowed to expose to the public information regarding when the messages were received, when they were deciphered, and their exact texts. Mitchell made it clear that this information could be revealed without dealing with the matter of cryptanalysis.[15] Truman granted Mitchell's request and a new presidential directive was issued on October 23, 1945, which had the effect of opening up to Admirals Kimmel and Stark and to the other Navy officer witnesses any records they wished to request in the files of the Navy Department, particularly the Office of the Chief of Naval Operations, without President Truman's prior approval.

This relatively unlimited access to Navy Department files soon ended. Later in November 1945, Admiral Kimmel requested access to certain files in the Navy Department containing copies of dispatches that originated in the White House. Similar requests were made to the Department shortly thereafter by the Joint Committee and Admiral Stark. Kimmel's request was forwarded by Forrestal to the President on November 23, 1945. It was Forrestal's opinion that only the President could grant access to White House-originated materials; Kimmel's request would prove whether he was correct.[16] On November 29, Truman gave his answer. He informed Forrestal that he had decided to deny Kimmel's request and went even further by stating: "I have found it necessary to lay down a policy that confidential files of the Department may not be available for examination by individuals."[17] Taken in its literal sense, this meant that any dispatches, letters, or other correspondence of such a nature that their disclosure would be prejudicial to the interests and prestige of the United States, even though not likely to endanger the national security, could not be reviewed or copied by Kimmel, Stark, or any other naval officer.

The November 29 Truman decision was directly contrary to the policy of furnishing information and copies of all records requested by Navy officer witnesses that had been adopted by the Navy Department under his earlier October 23 directive. After December 4, 1945, no other requests made by Admirals Kimmel and Stark or by other Navy officer witnesses for access to classified documents in Navy Department files were honored by Baecher or Colclough.

The usefulness of the Pearl Harbor Liaison Office records in determining which documents were made available to Admirals Stark and Kimmel during the period October 23–December 4, 1945, can be readily seen. It is also apparent from the foregoing that the White House, rather than the Navy Department, was chiefly responsible for restricting access to Navy Department classified documents during the Joint Committee investigation.

Another charge leveled against the Navy Department was that during the Joint Congressional investigation it deliberately withheld an ultra-secret file, designated the "White House File," which contained messages sent by President Roosevelt via naval communications channels during the last days before the Pearl Harbor attack.[18] By so doing, the White House prevented public knowledge and thus criticism of its actions immediately before December 7, 1941. This charge is not proven by the information found in the files of the Pearl Harbor Liaison Office, which shows that on November 28, 1945, Congressman Frank B. Keefe requested General Counsel William D. Mitchell to secure copies of all messages sent by President Roosevelt to Prime Minister Winston Churchill, or to an intermediary such as the British Admiralty via Navy or War Department communications systems, from November 24 to December 7, 1941. If such files were said not to exist by either department, Mitchell was to secure for the Joint Committee a certificate to that effect.[19] Copies of dispatches between the Navy Department and the British Admiralty concerning the Pacific area for the period November 1–December 7, 1941, were furnished earlier by the Navy Department to Senator Homer Ferguson, but these did not satisfy Keefe's request.

Mitchell made still another request three days later to Colclough on December 1, 1945, for all messages in the "White House File" of the Director of Naval Communications for the period October 1–December 7, 1941, sent to or received by the President or White House aides concerning Japan or military developments in the Far East.[20] The Navy Department responded in a memorandum of December 10, 1945, from Rear Admiral Colclough to Mitchell transmitting copies of two dispatches, dispatch 261854 of November 26, 1941, from Roosevelt to the High Commissioner of the Philippine Islands, and dispatch 280228 of November 28, 1941, from the Commander-in-Chief, Asiatic Fleet, to Roosevelt. Colclough commented that no other dispatches of the character described by Mitchell had been found.[21] On January 21, 1946, Baecher transmitted to General Counsel Seth Richardson a copy of a certificate signed by the Chief of Naval Communications, Rear Admiral Joseph R. Redman, stating that all pertinent files of his unit had been searched and no dispatches between Roosevelt and Churchill or any of his subordinates sent via naval communications were found.[22] The foregoing is but one instance of how the Pearl Harbor Liaison Office records provide evidence tending to refute or at least raise questions concerning the accuracy of some of the charges of Navy Department cover-up of damaging information during the Pearl Harbor investigations.

In addition to inaccessability of records to key witnesses, another criticism of the Joint Committee's investigation has been that the records furnished to the full committee were incomplete.

The Pearl Harbor Liaison Office records include documents that indicate which Navy Department records were requested by the Joint Committee and its counsel and by Navy officers called as witnesses during the hearings, the searches that were conducted by the component offices of the Navy Department for the requested records, and the results of these searches. Even more important, the Pearl Harbor Liaison Office records include copies of documents that were turned over to the Joint Committee or to witnesses called before the Committee. Comparison of these copies with the published exhibits that accompany the Joint Committee's proceedings or with other documents included in the record sometimes shows that substantial parts of the records that were turned over were not made part of the public record. The following illustrates this.

On October 12, 1945, about one month after its creation, the Joint Committee requested the Navy Department to furnish it a chronologically arranged file for the period January–December 1941 of complete copies of all intercepted code messages, including broadcasts such as the "Winds" message, that had any bearing on the Pearl Harbor hearings.[23] Lieutenant Commander Baecher transmitted this request to Rear Admiral Redman, Chief, Office of Naval Communications, asking that Redman prepare the file in duplicate and transmit it to him.[24] It took nine days for Naval Communications to assemble the "J. D. File," i.e., the file of translations of Japanese diplomatic code messages intercepted during 1941 which had been sent over more than twenty circuits including the Seattle-Tokyo circuit, the Honolulu-Tokyo circuit, the Panama-Tokyo circuit, the Tokyo-Singapore circuit, the Berlin-Tokyo circuit, and the Berlin-Rome circuit. Other messages located after October 27, 1941, were also turned over to the Joint Committee.

Comparison of the "J. D. File" retained by the Pearl Harbor Liaison Office and the Japanese diplomatic messages that were published in the exhibits to the hearings shows that none of the January–June 1941 messages that Naval Communications assembled were published and that a large part of the messages for July 1941–December 1941 were not included. For the month of November 1941 alone, the "J. D. File" now in the Pearl Harbor Liaison Office records includes 253 messages, while the published "J. D." messages for the same time period number only 83.[25] It can be properly concluded that any analysis of the Japanese diplomatic messages intercepted before December 7, 1941, by the Navy Department based solely on review of the messages printed in the Joint Committee's exhibits would have to be judged incomplete, which is the conclusion reached by at least one writer who has dealt with the topic of how the Navy made use of information derived from intercepted Japanese diplomatic code messages prior to the Pearl Harbor attack.[26]

Not all of the documents requested by the Joint Committee from Navy Department files were found. An example of this would be the war warning dispatch that was suggested to have been sent either by the Secretary of the Navy or the Chief of Naval Operations to commanders in the field, including Admiral Kimmel, on the evening of December 6 or early in the morning of December 7, 1941. Baecher made an urgent request to Rear Admiral Redman of Naval Communications on January 21, 1946, to conduct a search for this message and also look for a copy of any war warning messages that may have been phoned to Kimmel on December 6 or December 7, 1941.[27] The following day, January 22, 1946, Redman replied that no such dispatches nor any record or notation of a phone call to Kimmel were found in the records of the Office of Naval Communications.[28]

Aside from providing new answers to some of the charges made during the past thirty years in studies of the Navy's role in the investigations of Pearl Harbor, the Pearl Harbor Liaison Office records also suggest other aspects of the investigations and other issues which have been largely overlooked.

Very little attention has been given to the fact that the Joint Committee's investigation did not detract the Navy's attention from the matter of unification of the armed forces. In a memo to Chief Ship's Clerk H. L. Bryant who was assisting him in preparing the reception rooms for the Navy officer witnesses, Baecher ordered: "Be sure to see to it that each witness has an ample opportunity of reading this plan, the 'Navy Plan for Postwar Security,' which is the Navy's answer to the Army's attempt to take it over."[24]

That the Navy Department was not entirely removed from the conflict between the Committee and its general counsel, William D. Mitchell, nor from the Committee's partisanship has also been overlooked in past studies. On December 19, 1945, Baecher prepared a memorandum for the files explaining why he drafted a memorandum and delivered it to William Mitchell in the Senate Caucus Room at 2:15 p.m. on the preceding day, informing Mitchell that no search had been made in Navy Department files for documents indicating that the Japanese were suspicious or knew before December 7, 1941, that the United States had broken their codes. As Baecher explained it, Senator Brewster had asked Mitchell in a letter of November 15, 1945, whether the Japanese knew or suspected the code-breaking, and Mitchell had replied on November 17, 1945, that there was no information in the Navy or War Department files indicating that such was the case. Admiral Wilkinson's subsequent testimony that there were messages in the Navy Department files showing that the Germans had alerted the Japanese to the fact that the United States was breaking their codes resulted in an exchange between Brewster and Mitchell.[30] Baecher continues in his memo for the files: "The whole controversy was tied into the proposed questions to be put to Governor Dewey by Senator Lucas. It is the object of the Republicans to show that if the Japanese knew or suspected we were breaking their codes there was no reason why Dewey should not know it, however the net result of the exchange was to place the Navy in the light of furnishing false information to the committee's counsel."[31]

It was these latter considerations which prompted Baecher to write to Mitchell on December 18. He expected Mitchell, after reading his memorandum, to include it in the record. Mitchell did not do this immediately, nor did he put it in his own files, but at the beginning of the committee's session on the 19th Mitchell acknowledged that he had not requested nor received from the Navy Department a report on Japanese knowledge of the code breaking. At the close of the hearing on the 19th Mitchell handed Baecher's memorandum back to him with a very brief penciled notation indicating that he wanted the Navy Department's intercept files dating before December 7, 1941, searched for messages indicating that the Japanese knew that the United States had broken their codes. These messages were found and turned over later on the same day to Gerhard Gessell, counsel to the Joint Committee.[32]

The withholding of the Pearl Harbor Liaison Office records has also had another important effect on the historiography of the Pearl Harbor investigations. Very few writers in the past have shown knowledge of or have attempted to explain the role of Baecher and Colclough as Navy Department liaison officers with the Joint Congressional Committee. One of the few writers who has, Pearcy L. Greaves, chief research expert for the Republican minority members of the Joint Congressional Committee, has concluded that Baecher and other Forrestal aides were primarily concerned with shifting the blame for the attack from Roosevelt and making sure that naval officers called to testify would follow the Department's position on key points related to the attack. Greaves has described as the "highlight" of the Joint Committee hearings the testimony given by Lieutenant Commander Lester Robert Schultz.

According to Greaves, Schultz, an officer who had never testified at any of the investigations prior to the Joint Committee investigations, was brought forward to testify chiefly through the efforts of Senator Ferguson, who had received information that Schultz was on duty at the White House during the afternoon and evening of December 6, 1941. Greaves records: "This witness Schultz was flown in from somewhere in the Pacific and came directly into the committee room before the Navy liaison man, Baecher, had time to talk with him or suggest anything in the way of testimony."[33]

Documents found among the records of the Pearl Harbor Liaison Office show that Baecher did talk with Schultz before his testimony before the Committee. On November 29, 1945, a request was made by one of Baecher's assistants to the Bureau of Naval Personnel that Commander Lester Robert Schultz, Chief Engineer of the U.S.S. *Indiana*, docked at Puget Sound Navy Yard, Bremerton, Washington, be ordered for temporary duty in connection with the Congressional investigation. Because Schultz was needed at Bremerton, the decision was made to retain him on the West Coast until the Committee was ready for him to testify. According to a memorandum he prepared for the files, Baecher talked by telephone to Schultz, who was on board the *Indiana*, on the evening of December 5, 1945, about a week after the request had been made for Schultz's orders to Washington. Schultz confirmed that he was on watch at the White House on December 6, 1941, and that he received the messages which were delivered by Captain Kramer late that night at about 2230 hours.[34] Schultz told Baecher that he personally carried the messages brought by Kramer to President Roosevelt and stood by while Roosevelt read them. Schultz also said that an Ensign Carson and a Chief Yeoman Terry were also assigned to the White House during December 6 and 7, 1941. Baecher advised Schultz that he should consider himself alerted to be called upon as a witness before the Joint Committee.[35] Baecher followed up the leads that Schultz had given him concerning other naval personnel on duty at the White House during December 1941. Neither Carson nor Terry verified Schultz's story.[36]

Many of the documents referred to in this paper came from the case files of requests for information pertaining to the Pearl Harbor attack, or "Request File," dating from November 1945 to May 1946, the Office Reference Files, or "Subject Files," covering approximately the same time period, and the formerly top secret translations of 1941 intercepted Japanese Diplomatic Code Messages, or "J. D. Files." These and other office files of the Pearl Harbor Liaison Office contain much valuable information concerning which documents were requested from Navy Department records and which documents were made available to the Joint Committee, to the Committee's counsel, and to witnesses. The intra-office correspondence found in these files, some of which takes the form of hastily written notes, provides a new backdrop against which Navy Department actions during the Joint Committee's investigations can be better analyzed. Also valuable sources are the copies of formerly security-classified documents assembled by the Pearl Harbor Liaison Office for the use of witnesses, members of the Joint Committee, and the Committee's counsel and the Navy Department's official copies of the transcripts of hearings, exhibits, reports, and other records of the Roberts Commission, the Hart Inquiry, the Pearl Harbor Navy Court of Inquiry, the Hewitt investigation, the Army Pearl Harbor Board, the Clausen investigation, and the Joint Committee investigation of Pearl Harbor that were turned over to the Pearl Harbor Liaison Office. It is certainly hoped that new appraisals of the Navy's role in investigations of the greatest naval disaster in U.S. history will be enriched by the information found in these records and in other related records that are among the holdings of the National Archives of the United States.

FOOTNOTES

[1] "Report of the Secretary of the Navy to the President," Request File 91, "Knox's Report to President," Case Files of Requests for Information Pertaining to the Pearl Harbor Attack ("Request File"), Records of the Pearl Harbor Liaison Office, General Records of the Department of the Navy, 1798-1947, Record Group 80, National Archives.

[2] "Attack Upon Pearl Harbor by Japanese Armed Forces," Senate Document No. 159, 77th Cong., 2nd sess., January 23, 1942.

[3] "Proceedings of Hart Inquiry." U.S. Congress, Pearl Harbor Attack: Hearings Before the Joint Committee on the Investigation of the Pearl Harbor Attack, 79th Cong., 1st sess., 1946, pt. 26. Cited hereafter as Pearl Harbor Attack.

[4] Public Law 339, 78th Cong.

[5] Report of the Navy Court of Inquiry, Pearl Harbor Attack, pt. 39.

[6] Report of the Hewitt Inquiry, Ibid.

[7] Report of the Army Pearl Harbor Board, Ibid.

[8] "Proceedings of Clarke Investigation," Ibid., pt. 34.

[9] "Proceedings of Clausen Investigation," Ibid., pt. 35.

[10] Memorandum for William D. Mitchell, November 14, 1945, "Liaison" File, Office Reference ("Subject") Files, Records of the Pearl Harbor Liaison Office, General Records of the Department of the Navy, 1798-1947, Record Group 80, National Archives.

[11] Roberta Wohlstetter, Pearl Harbor: Warning and Decision (Stanford, Calif.: Stanford University Press, 1962), pp. 186-187.

[12] Walsh to Forrestal, August 16, 1945, "Receipts" File, Office Reference ("Subject Files"), Records of the Pearl Harbor Liaison Office, General Records of the Department of the Navy, 1798-1947, Record Group 80, National Archives.

[13] Forrestal to Walsh, September 6, 1945, Ibid.

[14] King to Secretary of the Navy, October 1, 1945, Correspondence of Secretary of the Navy James V. Forrestal, 1940-47, General Records of the Department of the Navy, 1798-1947, Record Group 80, National Archives.

[15] Mitchell to Colclough and Duncombe, October 15, 1945, "Sec Nav Files," Office Reference ("Subject Files"), Records of the Pearl Harbor Liaison Office, General Records of the Department of the Navy, 1798-1947, Record Group 80, National Archives.

[16] Forrestal to Truman, November 23, 1945, Ibid.

[17] Truman to Forrestal, November 29, 1945, Ibid.

[18] Robert A. Theobold, The Final Secret of Pearl Harbor (New York: Devin-Adair Co., 1954), p. 173.

[19] Mitchell to Colclough, November 28, 1945 (enclosure to "Statement for the Record"), Request File 22, "White House File," Case Files of Requests for Information Pertaining to the Pearl Harbor Attack ("Request File"), Records of the Pearl Harbor Liaison Office, General Records of the Department of the Navy, 1798-1947, Record Group 80, National Archives.

[20] Mitchell to Colclough, December 1, 1945, Ibid.

[21] Colclough to Mitchell, December 10, 1941, Ibid.

[22] Baecher to Richardson, January 21, 1946, Ibid.

[23] Memorandum of October 12, 1945 ("Navy Department Records Wanted by the Committee"), Request File 101, "Requests of the Committee," Case Files of Requests for Information Pertaining to the Pearl Harbor Attack ("Request File"), Records of the Pearl Harbor Liaison Office, General Records of the Department of the Navy, 1798-1947, Record Group 80, National Archives.

[24] Baecher to Redman, October 21, 1945, Formerly Top Secret Translations of Intercepted Japanese Diplomatic Code Messages ("J. D. Files"), Records of the Pearl Harbor Liaison

Office, General Records of the Department of the Navy, 1798-1947, Record Group 80, National Archives.

[25] Formerly Top Secret Translations of Intercepted Japanese Liaison Office, General Records of the Department of the Navy, 1798-1947, Record Group 80, National Archives. Pearl Harbor Attack, part 12, pp. 87-195.

[26] Wohlstetter, *Pearl Harbor: Warning and Decision,* pp. 190-211.

[27] Baecher to Redman, January 21, 1946, Request File 114, "Warning of War Message," Case Files of Requests for Information Pertaining to the Pearl Harbor Attack ("Request File"), Records of the Pearl Harbor Liaison Office, General Records of the Department of the Navy, 1798-1947, Record Group 80, National Archives.

[28] Redman to Baecher, January 22, 1946, *Ibid.*

[29] Baecher to Bryant, December 18, 1945, "Office Space Furn. & Fixt.," Office Reference ("Subject Files"), Records of the Pearl Harbor Liaison Office, General Records of the Department of the Navy, 1798-1947, Record Group 80, National Archives.

[30] Memorandum for the files, December 19, 1945, Request File 74 "Re Jap Knowledge of Code Breaking," Case Files of Requests for Information Pertaining to the Pearl Harbor Attack ("Request File"), Records of the Pearl Harbor Liaison Office, General Records of the Department of the Navy, 1798-1947, Record Group 80, National Archives.

[31] *Ibid.*

[32] Baecher to Mitchell, December 19, 1945, *Ibid.*

[33] Pearcy L. Greaves, Jr., "The Pearl Harbor Investigations," in *Perpetual War for Perpetual Peace,* ed. Harry Elmer Barnes (Caldwell, Idaho: The Caxton Printers, Ltd., 1953), p. 456.

[34] Memorandum for the files, December 5, 1945, "Schultz" file, Case Files of Individuals Connected with the Pearl Harbor Investigations ("Persons File"), Records of the Pearl Harbor Liaison Office, General Records of the Department of the Navy, 1798-1947, Record Group 80, National Archives.

[35] *Ibid.*

[36] "Lt. F. J. Terry" and "Lt. Carson" files, Case Files of Individuals Connected with the Pearl Harbor Investigations ("Persons File"), Records of the Pearl Harbor Liaison Office, General Records of the Department of the Navy, 1798-1947, Record Group 80, National Archives.

CHAPTER 33

Special Intelligence and the Battle of the Atlantic: the British View

Patrick Beesly

Former Deputy Chief,

Submarine Plotting Room, the Admiralty

First of all, a brief explanation. I shall refer throughout not to "Ultra" but to "Special Intelligence," because this was the term invariably used in the British Admiralty during the Second World War to describe information derived from decrypting enemy signals. One finds virtually no mention of "Ultra" in the secret British naval records; it was merely a security classification, akin to "Top Secret," for outgoing signals. Unfortunately due to Winterbotham's best seller, *The Ultra Secret,* the term is now almost universally used in quite the wrong sense. I only mention this because researchers into the secret British naval records, which are now slowly being released, will be misled unless the point is clearly understood.

A number of other misconceptions also stem from Winterbotham's book and from others by authors with even less knowledge than Winterbotham of maritime "Special Intelligence" and its operational uses. The impression is given in many of them that "Special Intelligence" was the only war winner, that from mid-1940 onwards we knew all of the Germans' moves and intentions, either in advance or at least currently, and that men, ships, and aircraft to do the actual fighting were hardly necessary—the cryptanalysts alone would provide.

Far be it from me to underrate the inestimable boon which the ability to decrypt enemy signals bestows on the power that possesses it. Practically no other source of information, at least up to the end of the World War II, could possibly provide such valuable raw material from which accurate and sensible appreciations of an opponent's movements and intentions might be built up. But "Special Intelligence" was only one of many sources of information upon which intelligence departments, both Allied and Axis, depended, and it had, like all of them, its own drawbacks and limitations. It

413

was not all-embracing; it was not complete; and it did not provide all the answers which the naval and air staffs required if they were to anticipate and counter every move made by their enemies. Even when "Special Intelligence" was in its most informative and current state, a very great deal still depended on the genius, and I used the word advisedly, of a few individuals to piece together, from scraps of information from all sources which were received in time to be of operational value, a clear appreciation of what was really going on, or was about to take place, at sea. The raw material needed to be carefully processed before use could be made of it.

There was a further requirement. It could serve no useful purpose, even if the intelligence department did produce an accurate appreciation, if those responsible for taking the operational decisions did not understand or failed to accept the conclusions to which intelligence had come. In World War I, the British Admiralty's Room 40 decrypted during the night after the Battle of Jutland sufficient information to show clearly the route back to Wilhelmshaven which the German Admiral, von Scheer, was taking. Room 40, however, was not a true intelligence centre and was not permitted to pass the priceless information direct to Admiral Jellicoe and the British Grand Fleet. The responsibility for doing this rested with the staff of the Operations Division, who were not trained intelligence officers, failed to understand the significance of the information laid in front of them by Room 40, and did not pass it on to Jellicoe. As a result Jutland was not the second Trafalgar which it otherwise undoubtedly would have been.

In World War II the British cryptanalysis organisation, the Government Code and Cypher School, was housed outside London at Bletchley Park. Responsibility for analysing and disseminating the results of its work in the maritime sphere rested, thanks largely to Vice Admiral Norman Denning's pre-war planning, with the Admiralty's Operational Intelligence Centre. OIC did exercise the true and full role of an intelligence centre, with enormous benefits to the Allied cause. It communicated directly, not only with the operational authorities in the Admiralty and at the RAF's Coastal Command, but also with ships and fleets at sea. On at least one occasion, however, there was a reversion to the Jutland attitude. During the ill-fated PQ.17 convoy, the First Sea Lord, Admiral Sir Dudley Pound, refused to accept Denning's accurate appreciation that *Tirpitz* and her squadron had not left Altenford to attack the convoy and gave the mistaken order to scatter which led to disaster. Such failures were, however, rare and in fact OIC's advice was very seldom ignored.

What, then, were the limitations of "Special Intelligence"? First of all, the German "Enigma" machine, when it was introduced, was an undoubted improvement on any other cipher system then in use. Nor was there only one variety of it. The German Navy developed its own model with a number of technical improvements compared to the Air Force and Army

414

types which greatly increased the difficulties for British cryptanalysts. As a result, although some of the German Air Force ciphers were cracked as early as April 1940, and the Army ones not long afterwards, it was not until the capture, in May 1941, of *U. 110*, complete with an "Enigma" machine and accompanying instructions, that any German naval cipher could be broken. For the first twenty-one months of the war at sea the intelligence scales were weighted heavily in favour of the Germans.

Another misapprehension is that "Ultra" or "Enigma" was a single cipher. The German Navy alone had thirteen different ciphers for different types of W/T traffic, not all of which were broken during the war. The capture of *U.110* did, however, enable us to read currently the main operational cipher, code-named "Hydra," then in force. Nor was the German assumption, that once the validity of the accompanying instructions had expired our cryptanalysts would once more be defeated, sound. "Hydra" continued to be decrypted, although with varying delays, throughout the war. There were, however, other ciphers: for units in the Mediterranean, for training U-boats in the Baltic, for specific operations by the heavy ships of the main fleet, and for cruiser warfare and blockade runners on the broad oceans. To my knowledge, these last two were never broken, but most of the others eventually were. The point is that the ability to decrypt one particular cipher did not necessarily or immediately lead to the penetration of all the others.

Nevertheless the cracking of "Hydra" did produce tremendous results. If it played no significant part in the sinking of *Bismarck*, it did lead, thanks to instructions broadcast to U-boats, to the mopping up of seven tankers and supply ships sent out to support the battleship on her proposed raiding cruise. "Hydra" also disclosed to us the dispositions and movements of the U-boats and enabled us to use evasive routing of convoys with some success and to gain a far greater insight into U-boat strategy and tactics. Thus, merchant shipping losses in the North Atlantic fell considerably.

Operation Paukenschlag, the U-boat campaign along the eastern seaboard of the United States after Pearl Harbor, was detected in advance by OIC, but, although this knowledge was immediately passed on to the Navy Department in Washington, the absence of any American equivalent to OIC resulted in little use being made of the information. With the creation of Op-20-G in June 1942 affairs began to take a very different course.

The German successes in the first half of 1942 were not solely due to American unpreparedness. At the end of January that year the U-boat command introduced an entirely fresh cipher, "Triton," for the Atlantic boats. Although we continued to decrypt "Hydra" and certain other ciphers, with varying delays to which I will return later, "Triton" defeated the Allied cryptanalysts until the first week in December. During these ten months we were aware, from the signals in "Hydra" to and from escort vessels, of the arrival and departure of U-boats from German, Norwegian and French ports. From "Tetis," the Baltic U-boat training cipher, we knew of the ever more rapid increase in the total number of boats. However, we no longer had any information concerning the Atlantic U-boats once they were at sea. OIC's Submarine Tracking Room, under its inspired chief, Commander Rodger Winn R.N.V.R., and Op-20-G, under the equally talented Commander Kenneth Knowles U.S.N., had to fall back on the other sources, such as high frequency-direction finding, photographic reconnaissance, sightings, and attacks for their daily forecasts of the U-boat situation. Nevertheless, thanks to the almost uncanny ability of Winn and Knowles to read Dönitz's mind, the results were considerable even during this phase.

From December 1942 until the end of the war, the British, American, and Canadian Tracking Rooms and their respective Trade Routing Departments worked in intimate and close cooperation with each other and were generally able to get a pretty close look at the cards in Dönitz's hand. Despite this, a number of serious handicaps had to be overcome. The first was the obvious one that decrypted intelligence could only be obtained from signals transmitted by W/T. We could learn nothing of messages sent by land line, or, except subsequently from prisoners of war, of instructions given to U-boat commanders before sailing, or of the deliberations of Dönitz with his staff officers, unless these were signalled to those at sea. This fact could, and often did, leave large gaps in our knowledge.

A second and even more serious limitation was the fact that the cipher settings were changed every twenty-four hours and therefore had to be broken afresh on each occasion. The time taken to achieve this varied greatly at different periods during the war. In broad terms current reading was achieved from the end of May 1941 to July or August. Thereafter time lags of from twenty-four to forty-eight hours began to occur, although there was some current reading up to the "Black Out" on 1 February 1942. When "Triton" was broken in December 1942, delays varied from nil to ten days for the first five months of 1943, when the Battle of the Atlantic was rising to its climax. The longest delay of all, apart from the "Black Out," was in July 1943—three whole weeks. From then on the time lags began to decrease and by the end of that year and throughout 1944 current reading became the rule rather than the exception; such delays as did occur rarely exceeded twenty-four hours.

To be of operational value, decrypting had to be swift. Intelligence that was more than forty-eight hours old was liable to have been overtaken by events and to be of use only as background information. In 1943 the Germans often had more than one hundred U-boats at sea in the North Atlantic alone. In order to be able to divert convoys around the large U-boat packs, spread out on three or four extensive patrol lines which were constantly shifted in the light of the latest information available to Dönitz,

416

we required continuous and up-to-date information, and this, as I have noted, was not always forthcoming in the first half of 1943. Without it we had to fall back on HF/DF, on other conventional sources, and on intelligent guesswork.

Nevertheless, the German method of controlling their wolf packs from ashore in France involved a great deal of signalling between Dönitz and his men at sea. We knew, from the escort vessels' signals, when a U-boat left port. After that it had to report having successfully passed out of the Bay of Biscay or the Iceland-Faeroes passage. It would then be given a fresh point for which to steer, followed, a day or two later, by instructions to join a particular wolf pack. Thus, delays in decrypting did not always leave us completely helpless. There were, on the other hand, many occasions when, having carefully routed a convoy clear of the waiting U-boats, our plans would be frustrated by fresh dispositions ordered by Dönitz when the new settings had not yet been cracked and we were "blind."

Here I must mention the work of the German equivalent to Bletchley Park, the B. Dienst. Just as the Germans had to signal fresh instructions to their boats at sea, so diversions and new routes had to be signalled to the Allied convoys. In 1941, and increasingly in 1942 and 1943, the B. Dienst decrypted many of these orders, until, in June 1943 the Allied code was changed. Thereafter the B. Dienst decrypted little that was of operational value, but until then the rather ridiculous situation existed that both sides were decrypting at least some of their opponent's signals without being aware that they themselves were being subjected to exactly the same form of eavesdropping.

Yet another difficulty faced OIC and Op-20-G. German naval charts were overlaid with a lettered and numbered grid, by reference to which all positions were given. Thus, 51 degrees 30 minutes North 25 degrees 40 minutes West would be described as, say, AB1234. This represented no difficulty to us once a fragment of a German gridded chart had been captured and the whole reconstructed. However, from November 1941 onwards, the Germans introduced a simple transposition code into their grid reference so that AB1234 became, for example, CD 5678, and these transpositions were changed frequently. Until each new formula had been solved we were unable, sometimes only for minutes but often for days, to say exactly which of various perfectly feasible alternatives gave the correct position.

There were other less obvious difficulties in pin-pointing the positions of U-boats and in keeping convoys clear of them. The navigation of the U-boats themselves was not always accurate, nor could we—or indeed Dönitz—always estimate their speed of advance correctly. Despite the volume of signalling, days might elapse before a U-boat on passage would report its position. Similarly our own convoys and their escorts would not break wireless silence unless they thought that their position was already known to the enemy. They might be unable to comply with diversions ordered and not report the fact, or they might, because of gales, be fifty or more miles ahead or astern of their estimated positions on our plots. Those without personal experience of it often fail to realise the meaning of the expression, the "fog of war." I can assure you that it, and just the "luck of the game," were often more decisive than many post-war historians realise.

A new situation arose in the second half of 1944. There was then a reversion to individual operations with considerable latitude left to the U-boat commanders. This called for far less signalling, and, as this phase coincided with the almost universal fitting of the Schnorkel, aircraft sightings and attacks also fell away almost to zero. Information from cryptanalysis, HF/DF, and aircraft decreased alarmingly, and had the Germans been able to bring their new types of U-boats into operational service—as Dönitz had planned—the results would have been extremely serious for the Allies. All the more so because, despite repeated assurances from his signal security experts that his ciphers were unbreakable, Dönitz began to employ "Officer Only" and "One Ship Ciphers" which could not be broken, at least quickly enough. I am only amazed that he did not introduce, even earlier, more radical changes into his ciphering arrangements.

A brief word on sources. The secret British records so far released to the Public Record Office in London, although not complete, contain many fascinating files from OIC and the Naval Section of Bletchley Park. The latter must be treated with discretion since they were usually written weeks or months after the events to which they refer. It should not be supposed that the information they contain was necessarily available absolutely contemporaneously to OIC or Op-20-G. From the point of view of the Battle of the Atlantic, the most revealing papers are the weekly reports to the First Sea Lord which Winn started to write towards the end of 1941. These are contemporary documents and show his thinking at the time. Again and again one can see his amazing ability to predict Dönitz's next moves. They also show roughly the approximate time lags prevailing week by week in decrypting. In addition, there are the reports which the Tracking Room made after every major convoy battle, based almost entirely on the relevant "Special Intelligence." They must be one of the most complete records of the German point of view still available. The only American release which I have so far seen is far less revealing of Allied contemporary thinking, but as it consists of a narrative, compiled immediately after the war and based on "Special Intelligence," it too adds greatly to our knowledge of German activities.

How much did "Special Intelligence" contribute to the Allied victory at sea over Germany? It was certainly of enormous benefit in assisting in the evasive routing of convoys, and in the concentration of naval and air forces on the critical convoys and at the decisive points. Without it the victory could only have been achieved—although I believe it would *still* have been achieved—later, and at much greater human and material cost. Who can say what would have happened if the invasion of Europe had been postponed until 1945? But what would have been the result if Dönitz had never had the benefit of the work of the B. Dienst?

"Special Intelligence" and, I must emphasize, the way in which O.I.C. and Op-20-G made use of it, was a war winner. It was not the only one. The real heroes of the Battle of the Atlantic were the men of the Allied navies, merchant navies and air forces, and, indeed also the U-boat crews. They were the ones who risked their lives and all too often had to pay a fatal price for other peoples' mistakes.

FOOTNOTE

The main British sources for this paper have been the ADM 225 series of Naval Intelligence Papers released to the Public Record Office in London in 1976. There are 67 of them but the most relevant to the North Atlantic U-boat battle are ADM 223/8, /15, /16, /18, and /19.

The American source consists of Volume II of the Op-20-G Final Report series, some 400 pages dealing with the convoy struggle with the U-boats from December 1942 until the end of the war. This was released in July 1977.

A much fuller account of the British point of view than can be given in this paper will be found in the writer's book *Very Special Intelligence: The Story of the Admiralty's Operational Intelligence Centre 1939-1945* (Hamish Hamilton Ltd., London, 1977; Doubleday & Co. Inc., New York, 1978; and Verlag Ullstein GmbH, Berlin, 1978.)

CHAPTER 34

Ultra and the Battle of the Atlantic: the German View ____

Jürgen Rohwer

Library of Contemporary History, Stuttgart

This paper presents some results of my research on the influence of radio intelligence on the Battle of the Atlantic. It has been suggested by many recent books, essays, and television shows that the use of "Ultra" gave the Allied high command continuous and complete knowledge of German strategic and tactical plans and intentions. If true, of course, this would have led to a much earlier end of the war. But it is a widespread misunderstanding to believe that only knowledge about or possession of the German cipher machine, known as "Enigma," allowed Allied cryptanalysts to decrypt and read any and all German secret messages at once.

It is largely due to Patrick Beesly's excellent book, *Very Special Intelligence*, and his essays in *Marine-Rundschau*, that some of these misunderstandings have been corrected, at least for the Battle of the Atlantic. To underline some of his points, let us review how the German navy's cipher machine, code-named "M," worked, and then examine how the radio war influenced the outcome of some typical convoy battles. (See Chart No. 1.)

"Enigma" was the code-name for a series of cipher machines developed by a private German firm. The first versions were sold to private enterprises and also to government agencies in Poland, Sweden, Great Britain, the United States, and Japan. In 1926, the German navy introduced another version of this machine, "Funkschlüssel C," but neither this type, nor "Enigma-G," used by the German army after 1928, was regarded secure because their three changeable cipher-rotors offered too few possibilities in a big wireless traffic environment. So, in 1934, the army changed to a much improved machine, "Enigma-I," which used three cipher-rotors out of a stock of five and had an additional plugboard for up to ten wire connections.

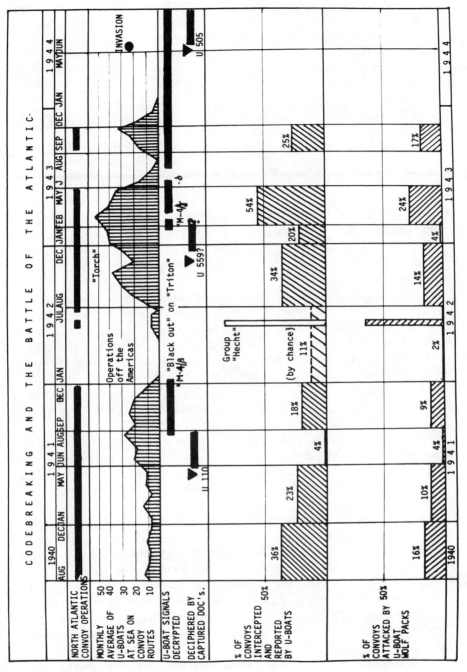

Chart No. 1

The navy used a similar machine, "Funkschlüssel M," which, by adding three more cipher-rotors to the stock, had many more possibilities to produce different cipher-alphabets without repeating a sequence of letters. The most commonly used version of this machine, "M-3," had four different settings, three of which were changed daily, and one of which was changed with each message:

> *Firstly*, you could choose three out of eight cipher-rotors. This allowed 336 different combinations of rotor-sequences. *Secondly*, each rotor had a revolving ring with 26 positions to change the inside wire connections. This gave the three inset rotors 26^3 (cubed) or 17576 ring positions. *Thirdly*, there were 1547 possible plug connections on the plugboard. And, *fourthly*, the operator could set each rotor to 26 different positions before beginning to encipher; this again gave 17576 possibilities.

By multiplying these factors you can get at the theoretically possible total of cipher combinations, which is in the area of 160 trillion. To try out so many combinations to find out the right one would take so much time, the Germans thought, that any cryptanalytic successes would come too late to be of operational value.

But the Germans greatly overrated the time needed, because they had no idea of the ingenious inventions which made the cryptanalytical machines possible. In Poland young mathematicians under Colonel Langer had solved, long before the war, the secrets of the "Enigma" machines used by the German army and air force. They had reconstructed their working mechanisms and knew the interior wire connections of the five cipher-rotors. A section of the French Deuxième Bureau under Major Bertrand assisted by delivering a large number of secret cipher documents: for instance, printed cipher procedures that they had obtained from a German traitor. British experts at Bletchley Park used, besides their own good ideas of course, this Polish intellectual achievement and the French espionage results to develop the ingenious technical means to obtain decrypts fast enough to make operational use of this intelligence possible. Their highly effective organization was also invaluable.

To explain how the commander of the U-boats (B.d.U.) directed his "wolf-packs" by radio messages and how the Allied command used "Ultra"-signals based on radio intelligence to re-route convoys, I have selected an example which may be of special interest to Americans.

In early October 1941, the American destroyer *Kearny*, deployed to guard convoys in the North Atlantic, was with her Escort Group. Map No. 1 shows the situation in the North Atlantic on 6 October 1941. Most of the German U-boats were chasing a Gibraltar-bound convoy and the North Atlantic convoy route was almost clear of U-boats. The Allied convoys east of the CHOP-line at 26° West were escorted by British Escort Groups. West of the "Mid Ocean Meeting Points" (MOMP), the fast convoys were

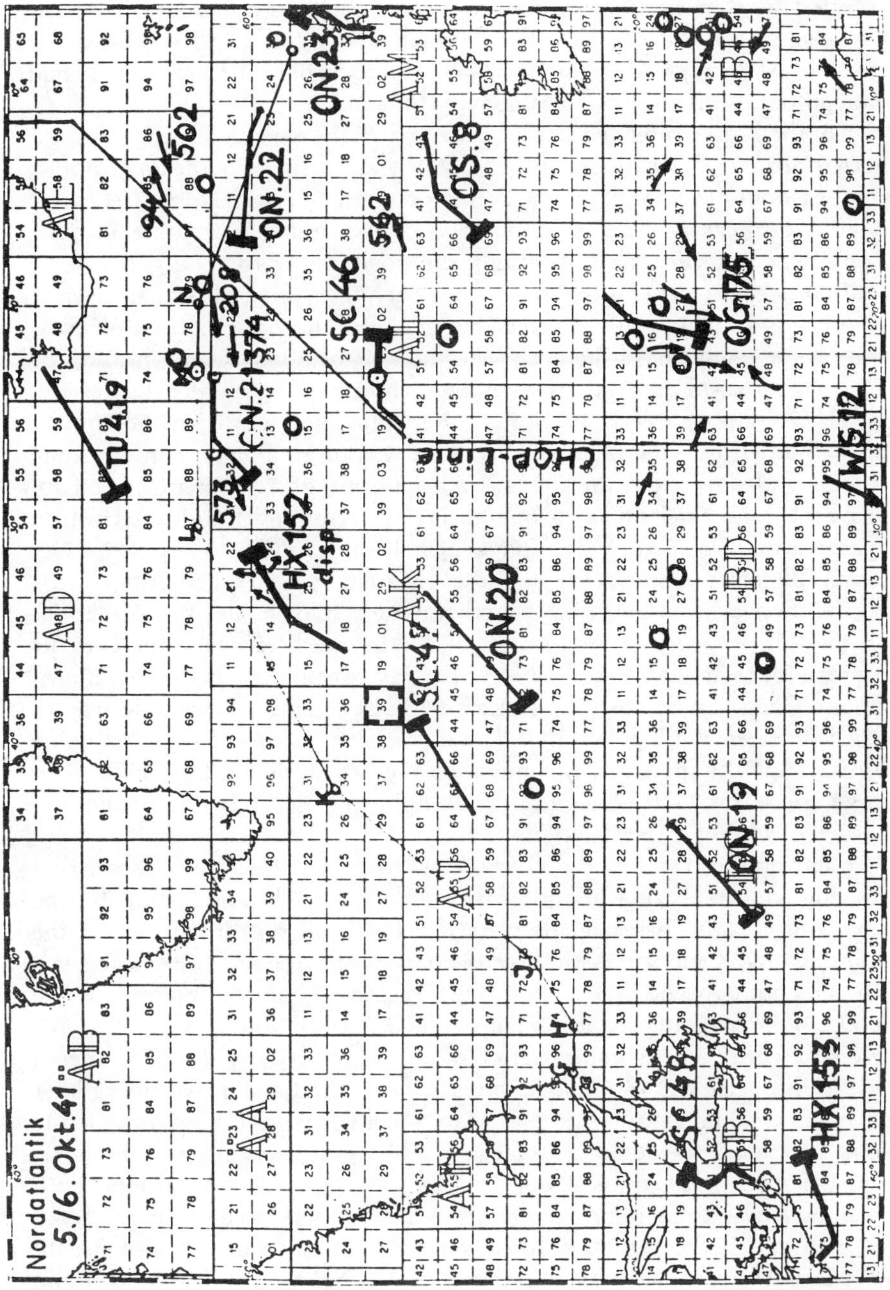
Nordatlantik
5./6. Okt. 41
TU 4.19
HX 152
disp.
ON 20
SC 47
ON 22
ON 23
SC 46
OS 8
OG 75
WS 12
ON 19
SC 48
HX 153
CHOP-Linie

Map No. 1

escorted by American task units, the slow convoys by Canadian Escort Groups. In the fall of 1941, the German decrypting service (xB-Dienst) could only decrypt Allied signals with considerable time lags. But it had enough data to reconstruct the convoy timetable.

So, the B.d.U. intended to block the way of the next pair of convoys, expected around 15 October. His first step was to signal a "heading point" southeast of Greenland for some U-boats coming out from Norway. On this day the estimate of the U-boat situation by the British Submarine Tracking Room was not very accurate. Only the positions of four outgoing boats south of Iceland were plotted fairly well after decrypting the signals of their escort vessels. They had reported the release of those submarines off Norway some eight days before. The other positions seem only to be guesswork, based on sinkings, sightings, and direction-finding (D/F) fixes.

On 8 October (see Map No. 2), the Canadian-escorted, slow convoy SC.48 had cleared the Belle Isle Strait. It was to go along a convoy route recommended by the Admiralty's Trade Division on 26 September and approved by the chief of naval operations' Convoy and Routing section in Washington (OpNav 38S) two days later. But, during the night of 8/9 October, Bletchley Park decrypted the "heading point," signalled by the B.d.U. three days earlier, lying exactly on the convoy route. The Admiralty on the 9th proposed to reroute SC.48 to the south to evade the U-boats running for their "heading point" and OpNav concurred. On the next morning the Canadian Senior Officer Escort (SOE) received the new course instruction from the OpNav 38S. The Admiralty instructed the west-going convoys ON.23 and ON.24, running on the British side of the CHOP-line, to go south also, after effecting the exchange of escort groups at the prearranged MOMP's. (See Map No. 3.)

Later on the 10th, the B.d.U. signalled to each of the three U-boats first arriving an "attack square" and ordered an adjacent "heading point" for the next four boats. These signals were decrypted by the British during the morning of 12 October. With three U-boats in position and four more nearing the southern end, the Submarine Tracking Room estimated that the B.d.U. was trying to establish a patrol line across the course of SC.48. Only two hours after the recommendation of the Admiralty, OpNav 38S ordered the SOE to turn SC.48 immediately southeast, and again two hours later gave a new route instruction. (See Map No. 4.) This re-routing order led to some problems on the 13th, because SC.48 would pass close to the west-going ON.23. Also, a fast troop convoy, TC.14, had to go around both these convoys. Some re-arrangements had to be made. (See Map No. 5.)

On the 13th the B.d.U. ordered separate "attack squares" also for the next four U-boats, and, by the next day, the Submarine Tracking Room knew exactly the area of these attack squares. The three convoys were passing close to the southern end of the patrol line, while the next westbound

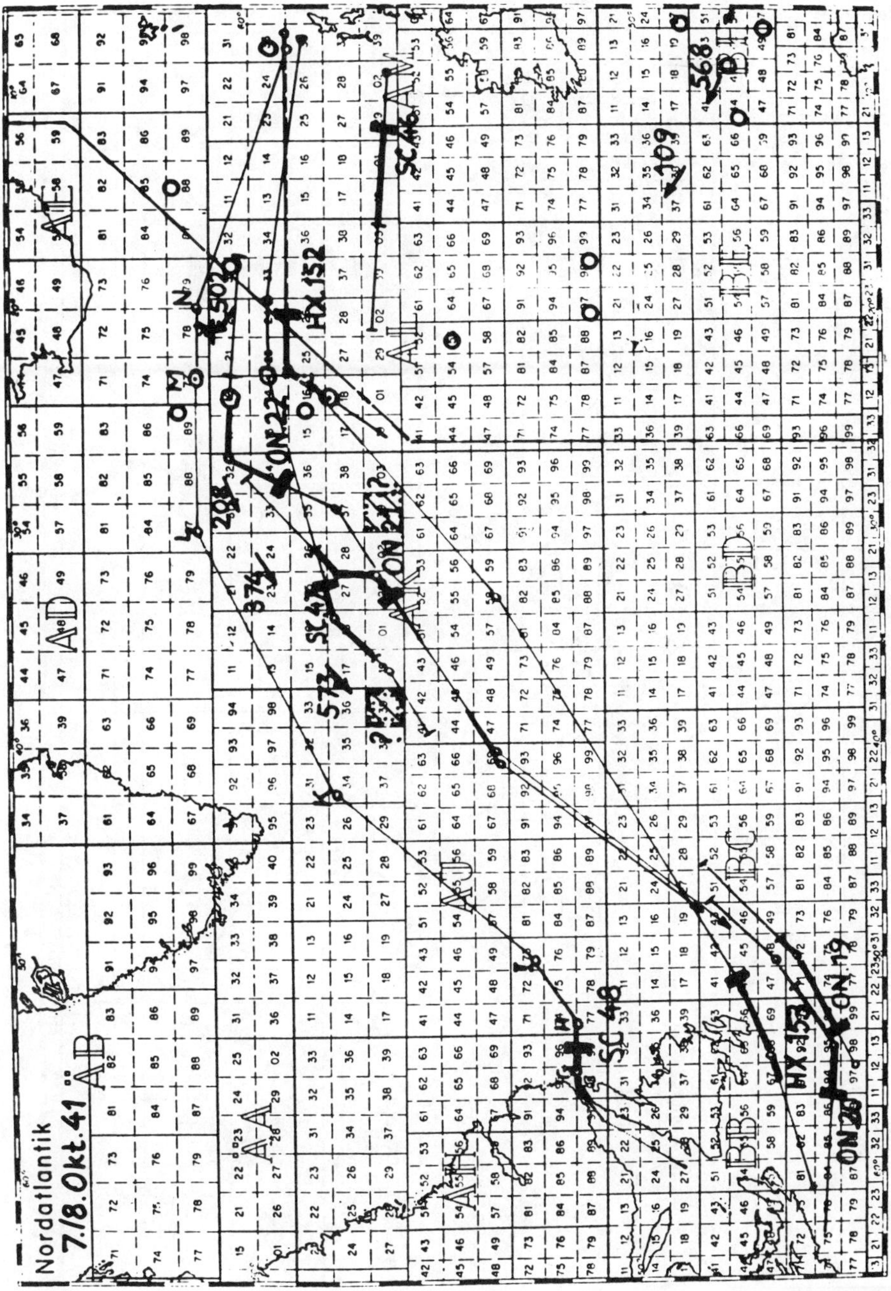

Map No. 2

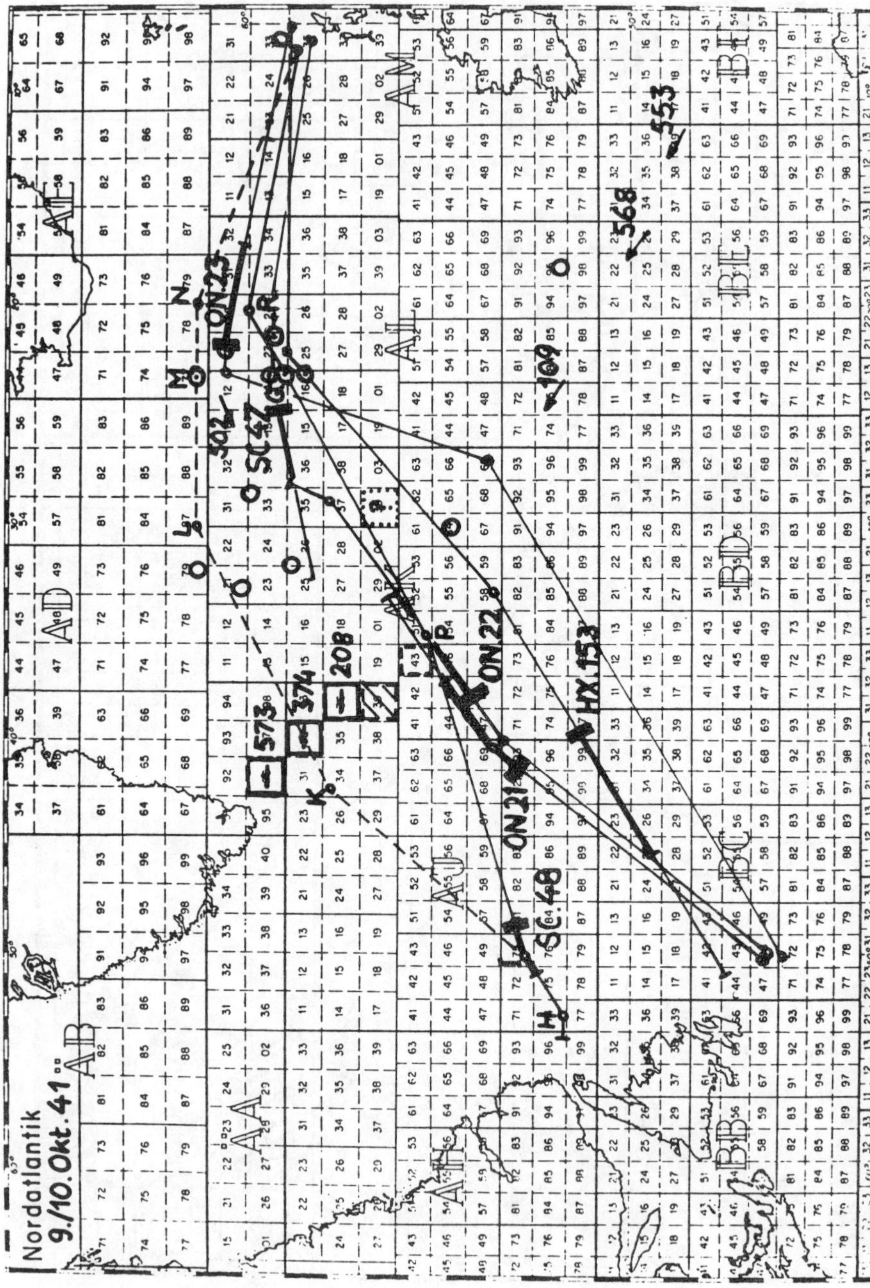
Nordatlantik
9./10.Okt.41
ON 23
SC 47
ON 22
ON 21
SC 48
HX 153
573
374
208
502
109
568
553

Map No. 3

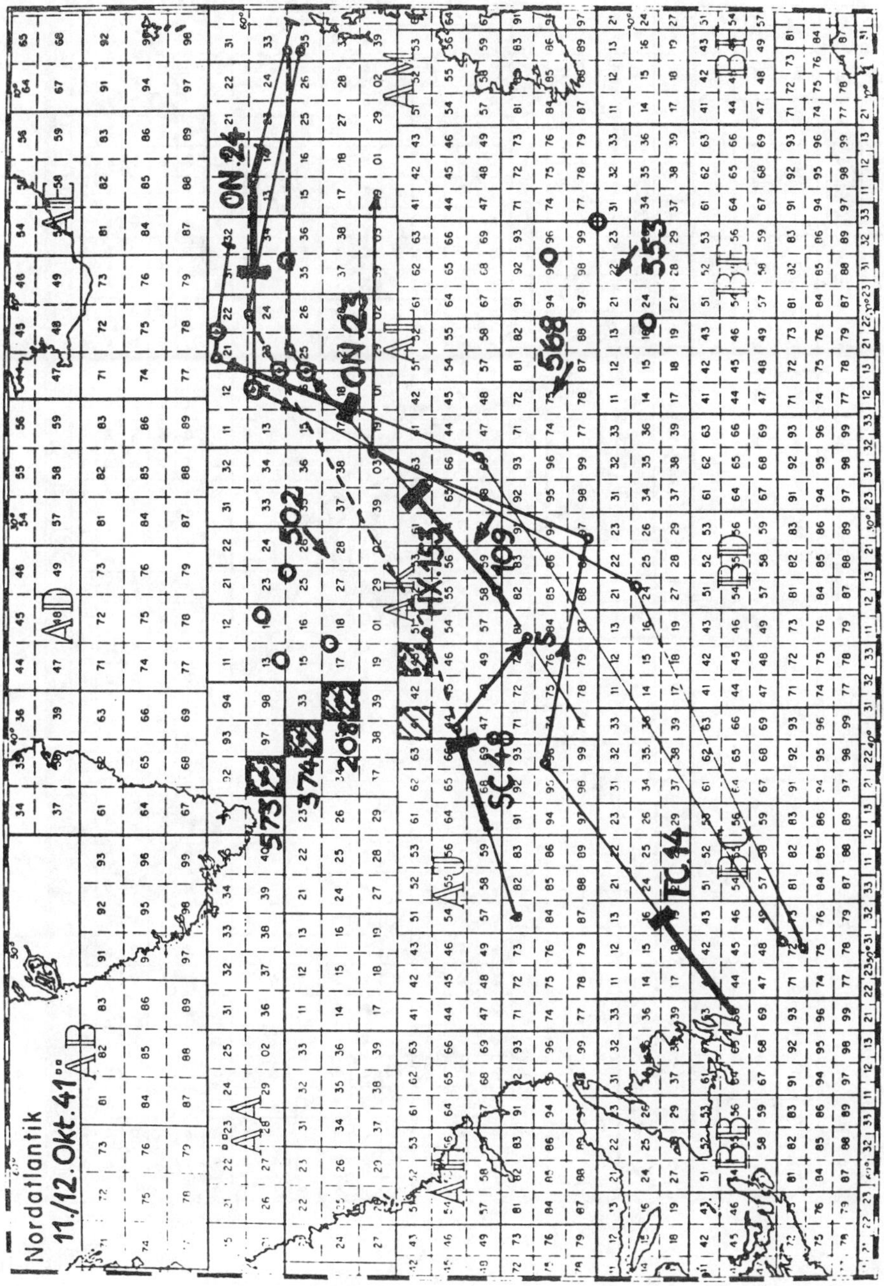
Nordatlantik
11./12. Okt. 41
AB
AD
AE
AA
AJ
AK
AL
AM
BE
BD
BF
ON 24
ON 23
HX 153
SC 48
TC 14
573
374
208
502
109
568
553

Map No. 4

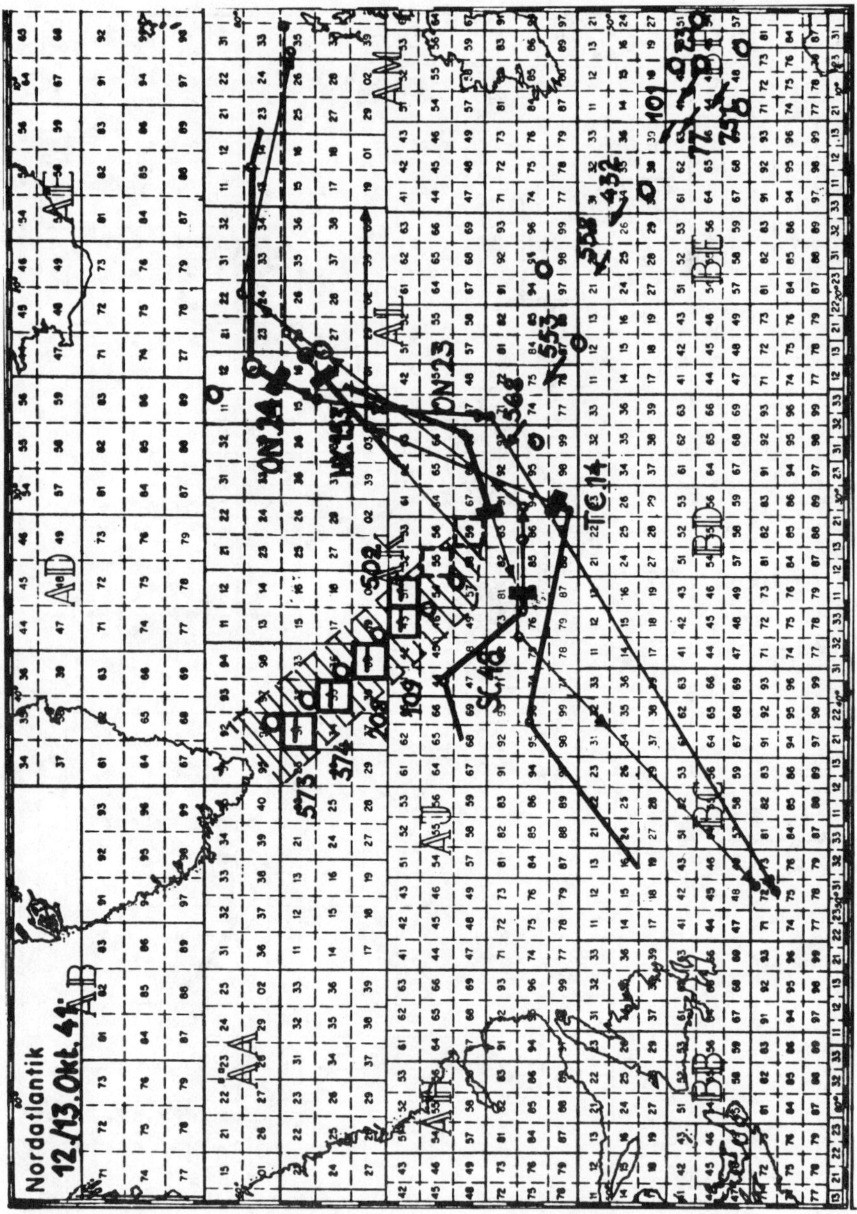

Map No. 5

convoy, ON.24, was ordered to make a short detour to the southeast, to get out of the way of TC.14 and SC.48 (see Map No. 6). All seemed to be set for a cleverly planned and well-executed evasive routing operation.

But then, in the early light of 15 October, two merchant ships were torpedoed. (See Map No. 7.) By chance, the convoy had met its attacker U-553, running up to its position in the new patrol line which the B.d.U. had ordered only a few hours earlier for the seven boats in the area and six additional boats coming up from France. Intelligence gained by decrypting could not prevent such chance contacts, even when the U-boat situation plot was, as in this case, fairly accurate. In 1941 the escorts were not equipped with high-frequency-direction-finders (Huff/Duff), which later were used so effectively to shake off the first shadower, and they had no radar which could distinguish between a U-boat and wave-echoes at distances of more than four miles.

After its success, U-553 sent hourly contact signals, homing to their target, nine U-boats which the B.d.U. had ordered to close and attack. However, the signals of U-553 were intercepted by the Allied shore listening stations. Without decryption, which cost too much time, the signals could be identified by their prefix "B-bar" and by taking bearings, as signals from boats shadowing SC.48. Therefore, the Admiralty was able, by using this other form of radio intelligence, to send in the afternoon of 15 October two corvettes escorting convoy ON.25, and two destroyers from convoy TC.14, to the assistance of the threatened convoy SC.48. Also, in the evening OpNav 38S ordered Captain L. H. Thebaud, commander of the American Task Unit 4.1.4., then escorting convoy ON.24, to disperse his merchant ships and to take his five destroyers to help SC.48. This could only be done, of course, because the allied situation map clearly showed no danger from U-boats ahead of the dispersed ships. Fifteen hours later, Thebaud reached SC.48, which had been continuously shadowed by U-boats with a loss of a third ship during the night. Once on the scene, he took command of the combined escort group of American, Canadian, British and Free French destroyers and corvettes. During the following night, U-boats sank six more ships, and U-568 torpedoed the *Kearny*.

This example, besides providing some previously unknown background about the highly publicized *Kearny* incident, serves as a model to explain the influence radio intelligence had on many of the convoy battles. It reveals not only the possibilities but also the limitations of "special intelligence" and "Ultra"-signals had in the war at sea.

In his book and articles, Patrick Beesly has explained the "blackout" in the British decrypting of German U-boat signals which lasted from January to December 1942. Graphs Nos. 1 and 2 may explain part of the British problem. The expansion of U-boat operations and the increasing number of German ships and submarines at sea led to an enormous increase in the

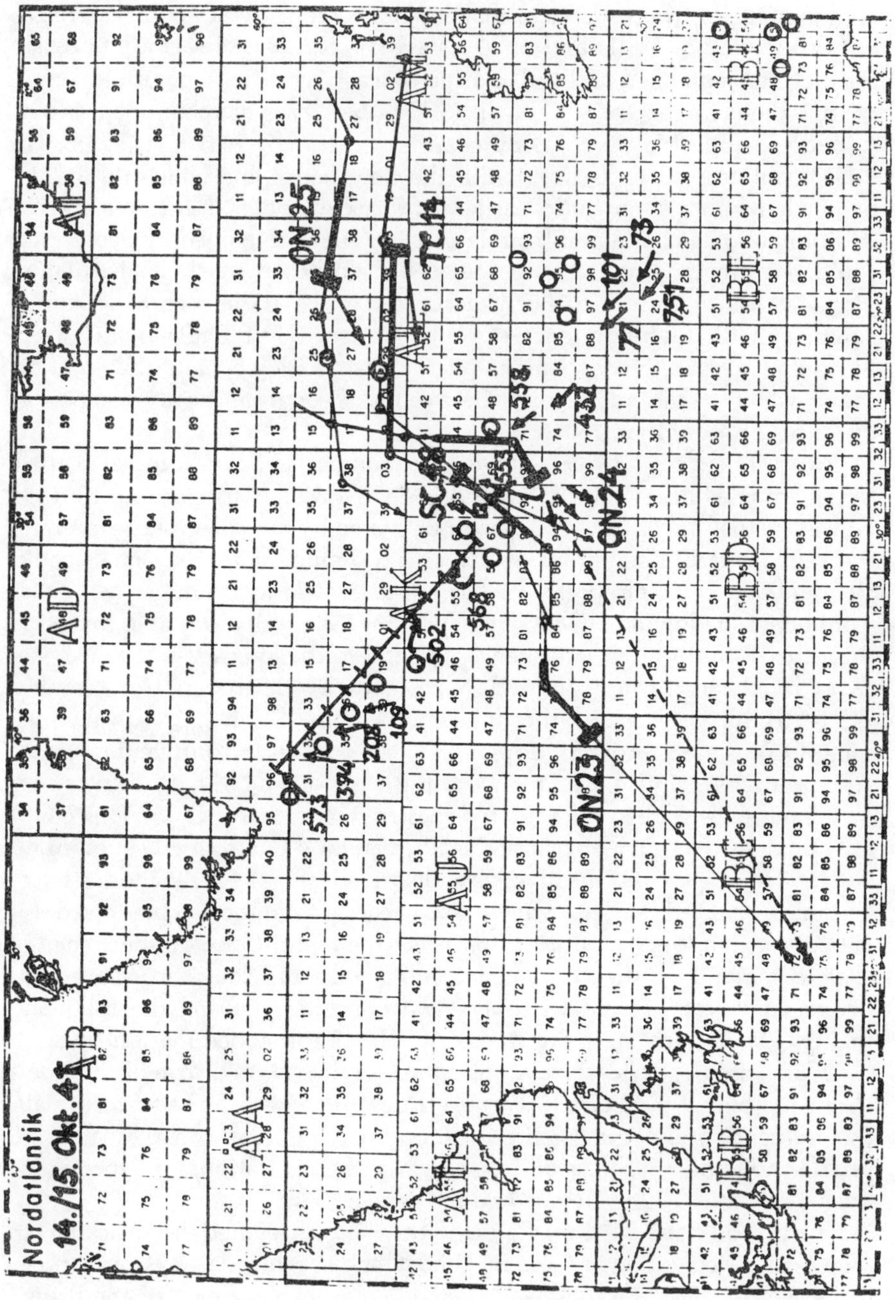
Nordatlantik
14./15. Okt. 41
ON 25
TC 14
SC 48
ON 24
ON 23

Map No. 6

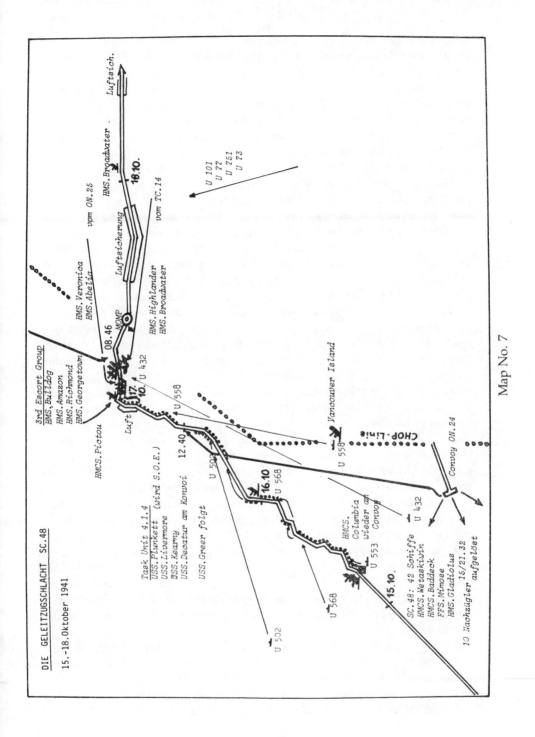

DIE GELEITZUGSCHLACHT SC.48

15.-18.Oktober 1941

3rd Escort Group
HMS.Bulldog
HMS.Amazon
HMS.Richmond
HMS.Georgetown.

HMCS.Pictou

Task Unit 4.1.4
USS.Plunkett (wird S.O.E.)
USS.Livermore
USS.Kearny
USS.Decatur am Konvoi

USS.Greer folgt

HMS.Veronica
HMS.Abelia   vom ON.25

HMS.Broadwater -   Luftsich.

HMS.Broadwater

16.10.

Luftsicherung   vom TC.14

MOMP

08.46

HMS.Highlander
HMS.Broadwater

Luft   17.
            10.

U 432
U 558

12.40.

U 502

16.10
U 568

HMCS.
Columbia
wieder am
Convoi

SC.48: 42 Schiffe
HMCS.Wetaskiwin
HMCS.Baddeck
FFS.Mimose
HMS.Gladiolus

10 Nachzügler 16/21.32 aufgelöst

15.10.

U 568

U 553

U 502

Vancouver Island

CHOP-Linie

U 558

Convoy ON.24

U 432

U 101
U 72
U 751
U 73

Map No. 7

volume of transmitted communications. From a daily average of 1000 in 1939, they rose to almost 9000 by 1943. Notwithstanding the fact that any message which could be sent by telephone or teleprinter was forbidden to be sent by radio, the share of the wireless traffic for all military communications had grown from 12 percent in 1940 to 29 percent in 1943 and, of course, only this part of the secret messages traffic was accessible to "special intelligence." In 1939 it was possible for the Germans to encipher all of the daily average of 192 wireless messages with two cipher-circuits: "home" and "foreign." However, the average daily volume of this wireless traffic rose: in 1940, 310 messages; in 1941, 473; in 1942, 1200; and in 1943, 2563. This made it necessary to establish additional traffic circuits with separate frequencies and new separate cipher-circuits, to reduce the number of signals enciphered with the same cipher-settings. To this end, in January 1942, "Triton," the new cipher-circuit for the Atlantic U-boats, was introduced. The Germans also feared that some ciphers had been compromised and this led to additional security measures: the edition of a new code-book for the U-boat short-signals and the over-encipherment of the square-grid code. In addition, some preparations were initiated to improve the cipher machine.

Nonetheless, the blackout had only limited consequences before July 1942, because the German U-boats were operating independently off the Americas in early 1942, and there was no great need for operational radio-communications. But, when they returned to attack the North Atlantic convoy routes, the blackout was of great importance. In May and June 1942, the first experimental group, "Hecht," with only six U-boats, intercepted five out of six slow westbound convoys. From July to December 1942, there were 24 U-boats on the average stationed on the North Atlantic convoy route, not many more than in the second half of 1941. From June to August 1941, the British read German signals without much time lag. During these months, U-boats intercepted only four percent of the allied convoys in the North Atlantic. From September to December the British encountered short time lags in their operational use of intercepted signals, but only eighteen percent of their convoys were attacked. However, during the second half of 1942, without decrypting, the U-boats intercepted thirty-four percent of the Allied convoys and fourteen percent of these convoys were attacked by more than two U-boats. Most of the other 20 percent could shake off the shadowers by the skillful use of the now installed Huff/Duff's, which were, I believe, of greater importance than radar in most of the convoy operations of this period.

Then, in December 1942, Bletchley Park succeeded in solving the main problems of the "Triton" cipher-circuit. It is not now clear whether this was a success of cryptanalysis alone or was arrived at by the capture of new cipher materials, perhaps from the U-559 seized in the Mediterranean. But we do know from a newly released American study written by OP-20-G at

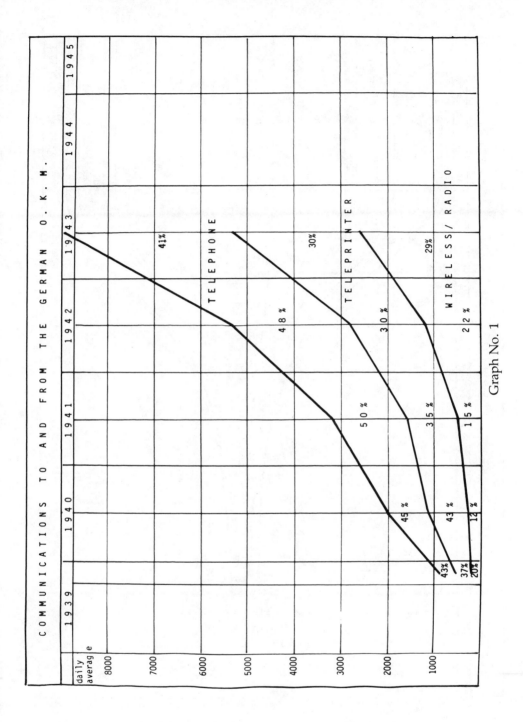

Graph No. 1

433

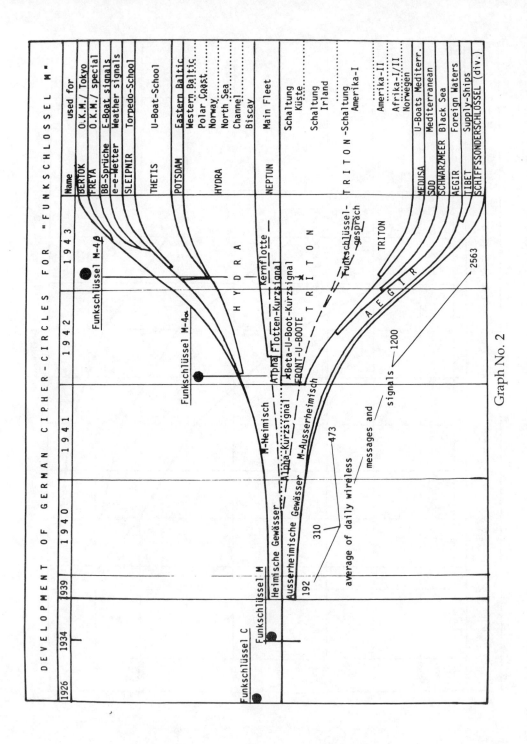

DEVELOPMENT OF GERMAN CIPHER-CIRCLES FOR "FUNKSCHLÜSSEL M"

Graph No. 2

434

the end of the war, that the average time lag in decrypting the German U-boat traffic had risen to three days at the end of December 1942. In January 1943, decrypting was often very current, but it dropped off somewhat towards the end of the month. However, from 5 to 28 February the traffic was decrypted with seldom more than a twenty-four-hour time lag.

For the U-boats, this led to a sharp drop in convoy sightings during January 1943. The number of operating submarines had increased to an average of forty but the number of convoys sighted dropped sharply to only twenty percent, and only four percent had sharp losses. All others were reported outside or at the edges of German patrol lines, so that against them no successful attack was possible. But, at this time, also, the German xB-Dienst also reached its most successful period, and could decrypt many of the routing and rerouting signals, as well as many of the U-boat situation reports sent daily by the Admiralty or Headquarters, Commander in Chief, U.S. Fleet (CominCh). Thus, even if only six to ten percent of the decrypts came in time for either side to operate, they had important consequences, as an example of operations in early 1943 may demonstrate.

On 11 February 1943 the B.d.U. ordered U-boat group "Ritter" to establish a patrol line and to move southwest, starting in three days. On 15 February, he ordered a second line, "Neptun," to begin on the 18th. Both groups were to search for convoy HX.226, which the Germans expected to cross the Atlantic according to the timetable. (See Map No. 8.) On 16 February, the xB-Dienst decrypted a position report of HX.226 proceeding northeast, so the B.d.U. ordered group "Ritter" to head north and group "Neptun" to take up its position immediately. (See Map No. 9.) But Bletchley Park decrypted this order on the 17th and the Allies rerouted HX.226 north of the German lines. Also, two westbound convoys, ON.166 and ON.167, the routes of which were planned to go through the area of the German lines, were rerouted south of group "Ritter." On 18 February, the xB-Dienst reported a position of the ON.166 and the B.d.U. now ordered "Ritter" and "Neptun" to form a long patrol line along 30° West in order to cover both possible routes on the estimated passing date, the 20th. (See Map No. 10.) On the 19th this new German order was decrypted, and the ON.166 was again rerouted south of the new combined line. In turn the xB-Dienst, the same day, decrypted a new position of the convoy, indicating the southwesterly direction of ON.166. The B.d.U. ordered four new boats to immediately form an additional short patrol line, "Knappen," southeast of "Ritter." (See Map No. 11.) This new order was also decrypted at Bletchley Park on 20 February, but now that was too late to save the convoy. While the next rerouting order was going out, U-604 already had established contact, and the B.d.U. had ordered "Knappen" and "Ritter" to close and to attack. (See Map No. 12.) In a fierce convoy battle that lasted for six

435

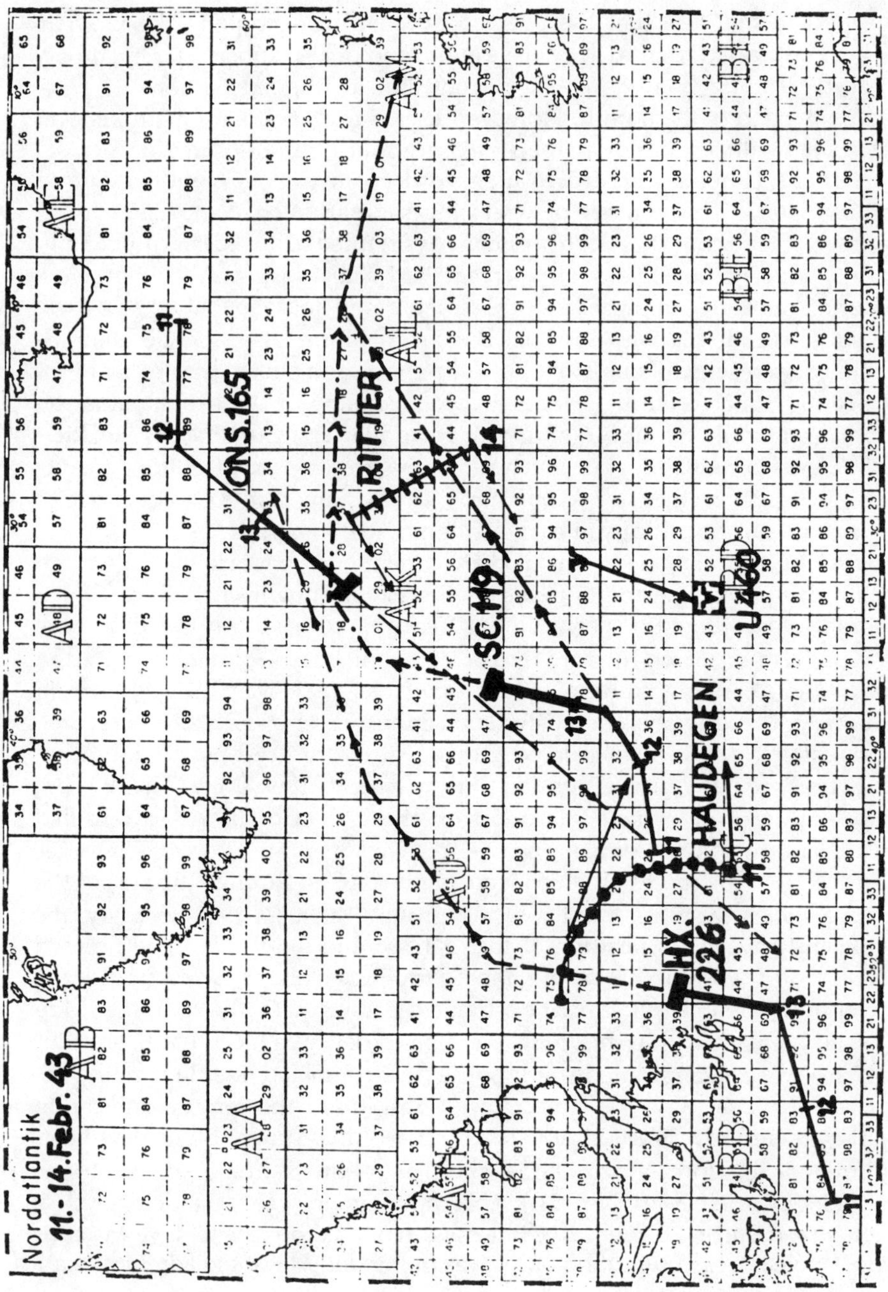
Nordatlantik
11.-14. Febr. 43
ONS.165
RITTER
SC.119
HX. 226
HAUDEGEN
U 460

Map No. 8

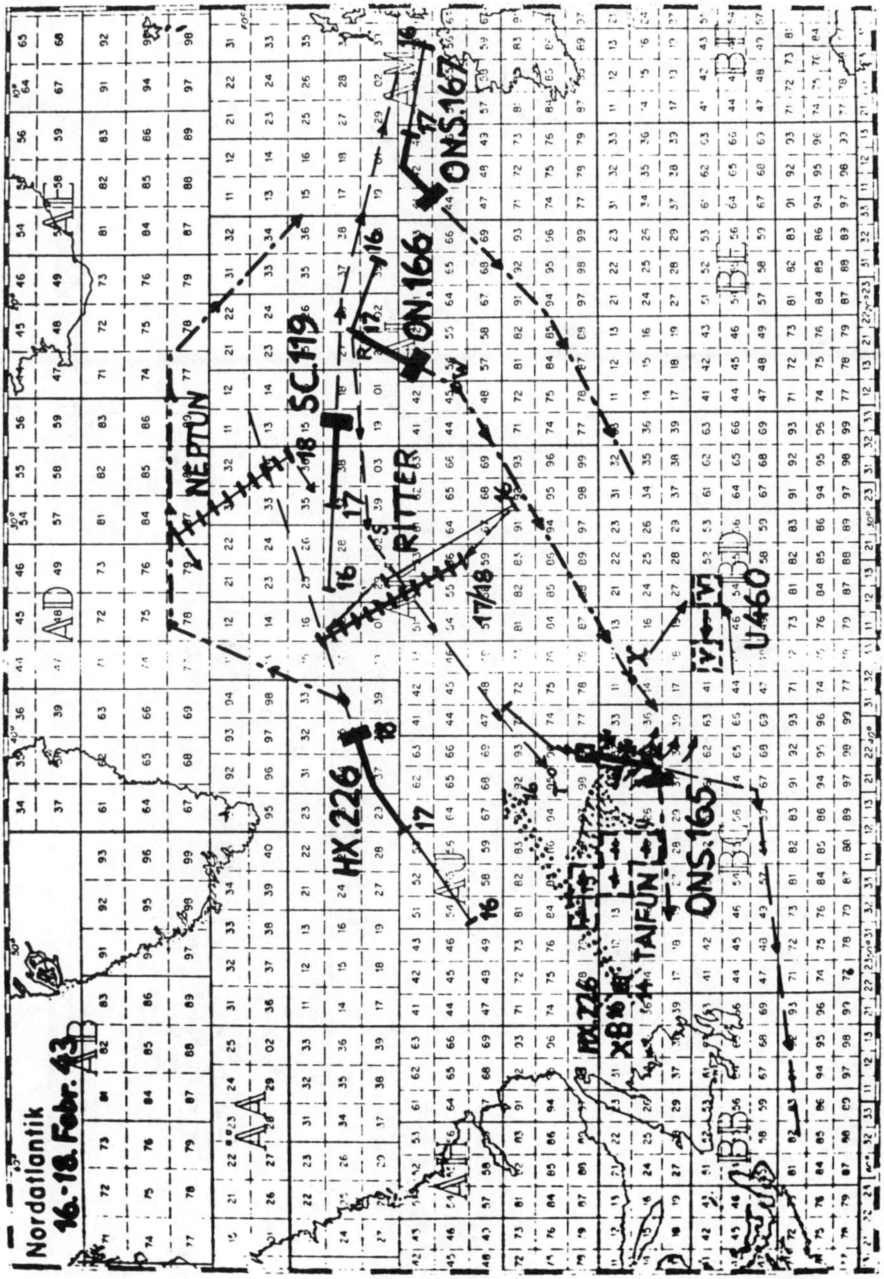

Map No. 9

437

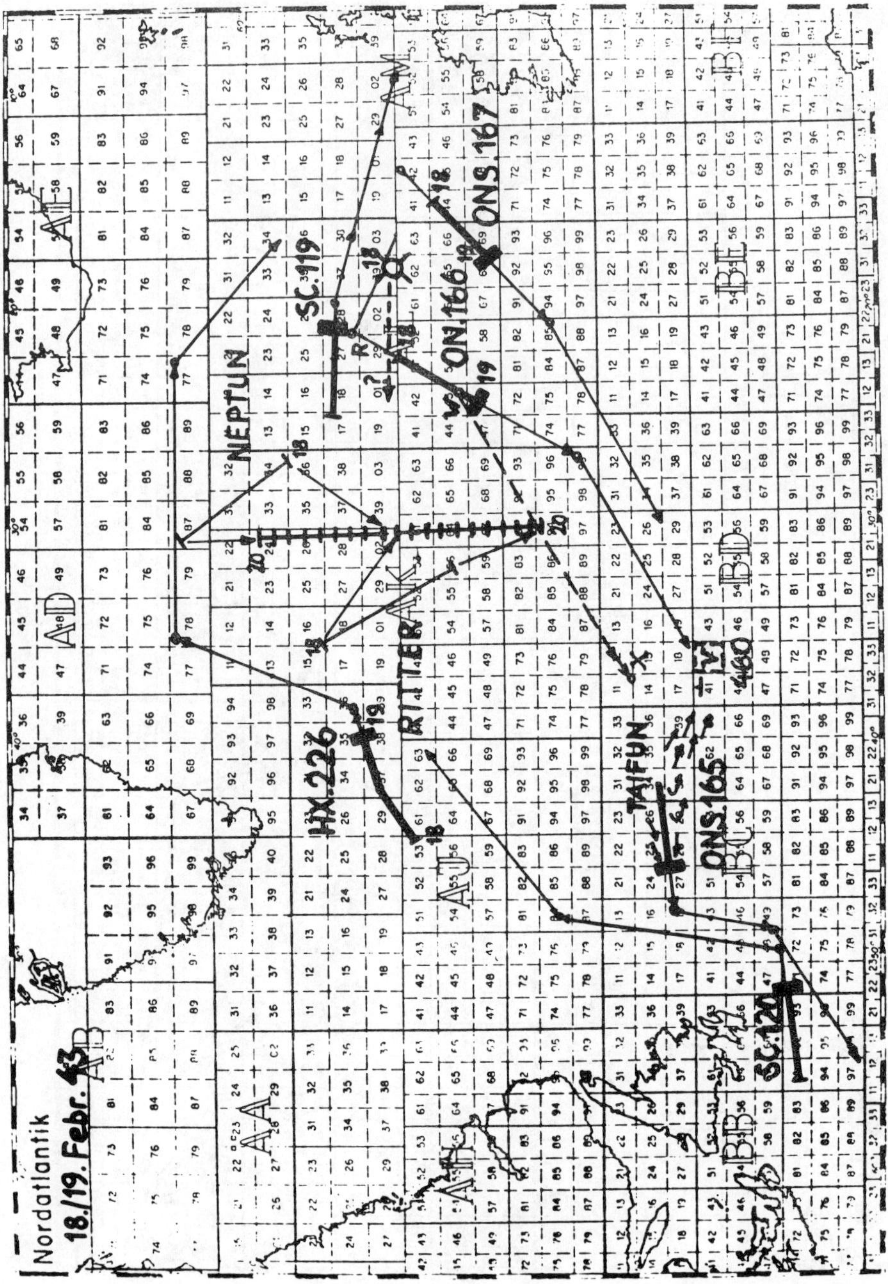
Nordatlantik
18./19. Febr. 43
NEPTUN
RITTER
TAIFUN
HX.226
SC.119
ON.166
ONS.167
ONS.165
SC.120

Map No. 10

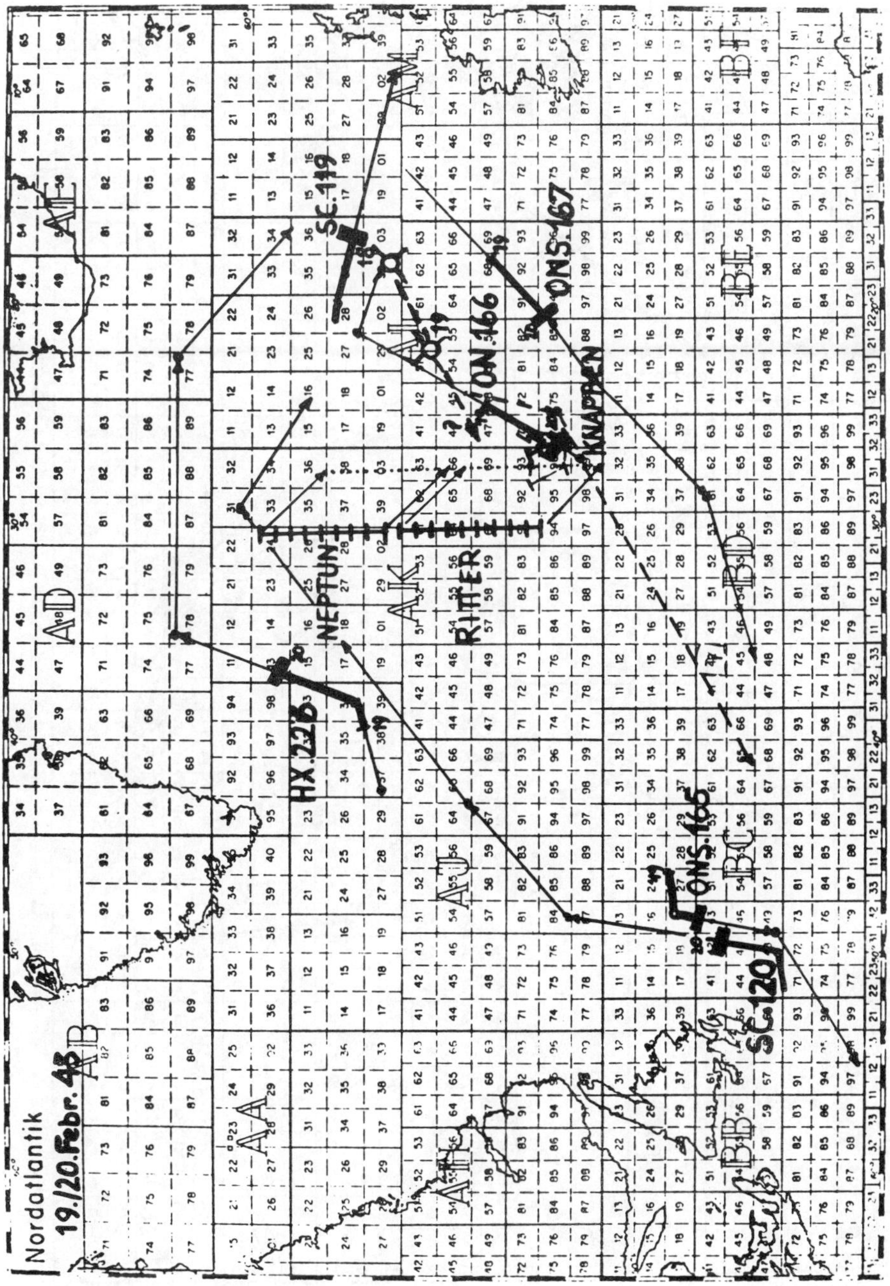

Nordatlantik
19./20.Febr. 43

SC.119

ONS.167

ON.166

KNAPPEN

HX.226

NEPTUN

AK

RITTER

ONS.165

ONS.166

SC.121

Map No. 11

439

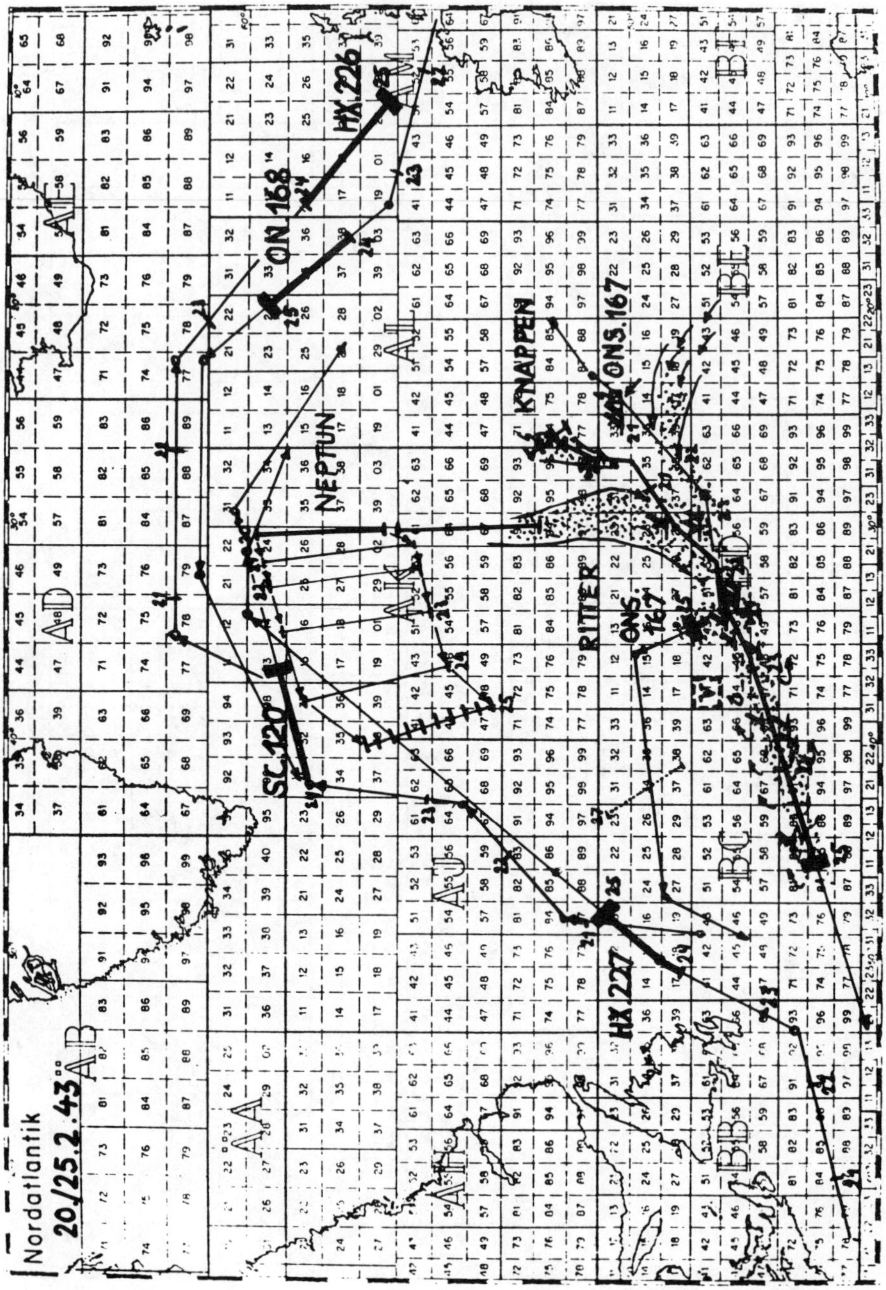

Nordatlantik
20/25.2.43
SC 120
ON 168
HX 226
HX 227
NEPTUN
RITTER
KNAPPEN
ONS 167
ONS 167

Map No. 12

days and covered 1100 miles, the U-boats sank fifteen ships and lost two of their number to counterattacks by Allied escorts.

As the number of U-boats operating in the North Atlantic increased to sixty in the first half of March, it became more and more difficult for convoys to evade the patrol lines, even with the nearly current intelligence from Bletchley Park. Moreover, in March the Germans completed preparations to set the fourth rotor to work on their new cipher machine, "M-4," and this raised the possible rotor-sequences from 336 to 1344. When Bletchley Park deciphered the key-word from this German advance in the first days of March, there was at first great fear over a new and long-lasting blackout. Without decryption on the Allied side, evasive routing might now become almost impossible. During the first twenty days of March, U-boats sank 40 ships in four eastbound convoys, which totaled 202 ships, or twenty percent of the Allied shipping in the area. Another month or two of such losses and the whole convoy system, the backbone of the Allied strategy to win the war, could collapse.

To prevent this catastrophe, at Bletchley Park all energies were concentrated to overcome the problem of the fourth rotor, and, in only about ten days, the experts arrived at the solution. This was, I believe, the greatest and most significant success the cryptanalysts at Bletchley Park enjoyed during the whole war. The achievement was due in part to some incredible mistakes made by the Germans. Eager to use the new machine, they introduced at the beginning only a small fraction of its technical possibilities. There was some overlapping in the use of the old and new machines, and of the ciphers used for weather planes of the air force and the new ones for the U-boats. Around 20 March, the British broke the new ciphers and evasive routing again could be based on decrypts. This was the beginning of the great turn of the tide. And now Commander Rodger Winn of the Admiralty could prove his suspicions that the Germans also were decrypting. Bletchley Park decrypted a German signal to U-boats which referred to their own radio-intelligence results, an unpardonable carelessness. The Allies undertook at last the big task of changing their whole signal security rules and their cipher systems. So, for the German cryptanalysts there was an almost complete blackout after 10 June 1943.

The consequences were not felt so heavily on the German side, because two weeks earlier Grand Admiral Karl Dönitz had had to admit his defeat in the convoy battles against the combined work of the Allied escorts, support groups with escort carriers, and the very long-range aircraft, all of which equipped with the new ten-centimetric radar. But he knew nothing at the time of the roles played in his defeat by Huff/Duff or by Bletchley Park and the Admiralty's Operational Intelligence Centre.

In analyzing the last two years of the Battle of the Atlantic it is not correct to assume that all and any German wireless message was decrypted by the Allies so fast as to be of operational value. At the end of 1943, the German navy alone used up to forty different ciphers, twenty-four of which were based on "Schlüssel-M." All had different daily settings, and most had two or three security grades: "general," "officers only," or "staff only." To use their own capabilities most economically and efficiently Bletchley Park had to attack each different cipher and its changing traffic volume according to established priorities. Surely the U-boat signals always had high priority. Most of them could be read, but current deciphering was often interrupted by time lags of two, three, or even seven days. Also, some short blackouts came, the longest over three weeks in July 1943.

I learned the difficulty of reaching sound conclusions about the U-boat war during my studies of the convoy operations in September 1943. When reading the summary report of the Submarine Tracking Room about convoys ON.202 and ONS.18, based on "Z-information," the code for the German decrypts, one gets the impression that the Allies had complete and up-to-date information. However, when you compare these records with German, British and American operational documents, you will find that much information which seemed to have been received in time for countermeasures nevertheless led to complete failures, because the Germans had changed their orders after two days, while the decrypts became available only after five days, and still two days off from the operation as originally planned.

What then was the role of radio intelligence for the Battle of the Atlantic? Of course, all the battles and actions during the six years had to be fought by the men in the U-boats, ships, and aircraft, with their many weapons systems, produced by the unnamed workers at home on both sides. But I am sure that without the three pillars of radio intelligence—direction-finding, traffic analysis and decryption—the commander of the U-boats could not have used his submarines as effectively as he did against the convoys, nor could the Allied commands on both sides of the Atlantic have routed their convoys so successfully around the German wolf-packs. But, from my detailed studies of all the convoy battles, I reached the conclusion, that radio intelligence had much greater influence on Allied, rather than German, operational and tactical decisions. And, if I have to place the many factors which decided the outcome of the Battle of the Atlantic in the spring of 1943 in an order of precedence, I would place "Special Intelligence" or "Ultra" at the top.

I am sure that without the work of many unknown experts at Bletchley Park, and men like Norman Denning, Patrick Beesly, Kenneth Knowles, and the late Rodger Winn, the turning point of the Battle of the Atlantic would not have come as it did in May 1943, but months, perhaps many months, later. In that case, the Allied invasion of Normandy would not have been possible in June 1944, and there would have ensued a chain of developments very different from the one which we have experienced. Of course, there would have been an Allied victory in the end, but this end might have been produced by dropping the first atomic bomb on Berlin. But this is speculation; "Ultra" was a reality, and this is what counts in history.

CHAPTER 35

Ultra and the Battle of the Atlantic: the American View

Kenneth A. Knowles

Captain, U.S. Navy (Ret.)

As events recede into history, few of them retain a significance worthy of recall.[1] The life-and-death struggle known as the Battle of the Atlantic was certainly one of these. Throughout it were woven technical achievements of the highest order, giving advantages and break-throughs first to one adversary and then to the other. But transcending all of these feats was "Ultra Intelligence," the breaking of the German U-boat cipher. It gave first to the British and then to the Americans the edge of victory at sea; and from it flowed victory in Europe. Without it the British could have been beaten to their knees. No wonder Churchill considered "Ultra Intelligence" his prime and sacred weapon—his Excalibur.

Not having experienced the harrowing years 1939-1941, we Americans viewed the U-boat conflict, at least at our entry, more as a challenge than as a struggle for survival. We recognized the seriousness of the U-boat weapon and the vital importance of the "Ultra Intelligence," but we controlled its security and use differently than the British. That is, we were far more selective in those who had a "need to know" about "Ultra," but we made use of "Ultra" more directly in anti-submarine operations.

Before proceeding further, it might be well first to look into the American naval organization developed specifically for "The Battle of the Atlantic": the Tenth Fleet, whose commander was Admiral Ernest J. King and whose chief of staff was Rear Admiral Francis (known as "Frog") Low. The Tenth Fleet was set up within Headquarters, Commander in Chief, U.S. Fleet (CominCh), using but a small segment of that staff. For example, my job was Head, Atlantic Section, Combat Intelligence, CominCh, and designated F-21. While still wearing that hat, I also wore a second hat as Chief, Intelligence Staff, Tenth Fleet. The Tenth Fleet was organized by the normal staff functions—plans, intelligence, operations, et cetera—but it also included two important additions: convoy and routing, and operations research.

A distinct advantage of the Tenth Fleet organization was the ability to use the highest command level for anti-submarine operations. This enabled us to issue orders directly to U.S. task groups in the Atlantic Theatre without incurring the delays caused by passing dispatches down through the chain of command. Of course, all related commanders were kept informed. Another advantage of the Tenth Fleet organization was the integration through the two-hat system of related tasks involving the staffs of CominCh, Tenth Fleet, and the Office of the Chief of Naval Operations. A third advantage of this organization was the security afforded "Ultra Intelligence." Within all staffs at supreme headquarters, only three persons actually dealt with "Ultra Intelligence": myself, my deputy, John Parsons, and a rating who handled files and other secretarial duties. Perhaps a half dozen senior officers within the combined staffs had knowledge that "Ultra" existed. None of the operational commands were so informed. These restrictions were deemed necessary in the American theatre because of the wide separation of commands and the difficulty of maintaining communications security among them.

On the British side, it was customary for Winn or Beesly to talk to Western Approaches, Liverpool and other shore-based commands on a daily basis when necessary, and this could be done by scrambler telephone without loss of security within the well-disciplined and relatively tight command relationships. Also, the British permitted a far more open knowledge of "Ultra Intelligence" among those assigned to operational intelligence than the Americans did. This enabled the British to operate with considerable freedom and convenience within their designated areas.

In Tenth Fleet we received "Ultra Intelligence" when available by secure teleprinter from our communications center, situated in a former girls' school on Nebraska Avenue. We also received facsimiles of high-frequency direction-finder (HF/DF) fixes, when occurring, from the center, as well as any "fingerprint signatures" of U-boat radio operators, obtained by comparison of oscillograph recordings (called TINA). The communications receiving end in Tenth Fleet was in a small, locked room adjacent to the Atlantic Theatre combat intelligence center. As previously noted, only three persons were permitted to enter and use this room. We were able to maintain a security screen around "Ultra Intelligence" largely because of tight restrictions of those requiring a "need to know," and the convenient cover of HF/DF fixes and U-boat sightings, as well as TINA "fingerprint signatures."

How did we use this sensitive yet powerful intelligence? At times more directly than did the British, yet at no time without back-up evidence, either

445

from HF/DF fixes or sightings. However, we skated on some pretty thin ice in one instance later in the war when it became imperative that we gain decisive victory as soon as possible. The occasion was a rendezvous in a remote area of the western South Atlantic involving a U-boat tanker and a group of 740-ton U-boats coming in for refueling. The tanker and two of the 740-ton U-boats were sunk. We felt the results justified the security risks, since the operation broke up very destructive U-boat attacks in that area and saved valuable shipping and cargoes. It should be remembered, too, that most of our losses were occurring in the western South Atlantic during this period. Subsequently, the commander of a surviving U-boat from this attack questioned the security of German U-boat communications, but nothing came of it as the high command was confident of their cipher system. In ordering that attack we did have a questionable aircraft sighting and a partial HF/DF fix that could be associated with it. But, in our determination to destroy this dangerous U-boat concentration, we certainly went out on a limb. I remember Commander Winn's cryptic yet appropriate signal: "Too true to be good."

In retrospect, however, I feel that Admiral King's philosophy of "the calculated risk" was sound, and it certainly paid off in rich dividends, such as the capture by Captain Dan Gallery's task group of *U-505*. She was towed with superb seamanship from the vicinity of the Cape Verde Islands to Bermuda, where Admiral Low and I inspected her. Among our finds were the first German acoustical torpedoes and their new location charts only recently put into use. Possession of these deadly acoustical torpedoes aboard *U-505*, which had wreaked such damage among our escort vessels and small carriers, was most fortuitous. After exhaustive tests of the acoustical torpedoes, we developed a counter to them called "Foxer"— towed metal bars which vibrated intensely at the proper frequency and became the sound target for those torpedoes instead of the ship's propellers.

Let me digress for the moment and refer to the German U-boat cipher. Produced in the first instance by the "Enigma" machine, it yielded a completely random cipher at any setting. In addition, U-boat positions and areas of operations were designated by coded location charts. Thus, even though the "Enigma" cipher was broken, the geographic position of a U-boat and its operating area were generally unknown unless we possessed the coded chart. Over a period of time, we could laborously reconstruct portions of the chart from U-boat attack and sinking reports and HF/DF fixes. The capture of those newly issued charts in *U-505* were therefore of inestimable value to the British and us.

While "Ultra Intelligence" gave us an advantage over the U-boat that no technical skill could surmount, there were frequent lapses when no "Ultra" was forthcoming, in some cases of several months' duration. We did, however, receive on a regular basis from Winn reports of U-boat arrivals and departures to and from their French and Norwegian bases, as well as new U-boats departing the Baltic. These gave us a continuing and reliable count of U-boats at sea, and usually their individual indentities. During the gaps in "Ultra Intelligence," we relied on operational patterns developed from previous "Ultra," and, when these grew dim in time, we leaned heavily on HF/DF fixes. As I recall, we had some thirty to thirty-five reporting stations extending from South Africa to Iceland and around to Brazil on the western periphery. Normally, we received by facsimile a preliminary fix on three to five bearings within thirty minutes of the U-boat's transmission, and a more precise fix of perhaps eight to twelve bearings within the hour. The fixes were designated as to accuracy, the best being characterized as "within fifty miles." Perhaps 15 to 20 percent came within this degree of accuracy.

Historians generally consider that the turning point in the Battle of the Atlantic came after the summer of 1943 following the sinking of some ninety U-boats. The spring had been disastrous for us in ship losses, with tonnage exceeding any previous period. The U-boat fleet was at its prime, while we had not yet attained necessary strength in aircraft and surface escorts and carriers. Also "Ultra Intelligence" had been exceedingly sparse. After that period we certainly had the distinct edge, especially since the Germans had lost so many of their experienced U-boat captains. However, in the background was emerging a whole new situation: a fleet working up of highly sophisticated Type XXI 1600-tonners and smaller Type XXIII U-boats, with new Schnorkels permitting underwater speeds exceeding most of our escorts. Once these boats became operational, it would be touch-and-go all over again.

In addition to these technical advances, including a new high-speed acoustical torpedo, the Germans were improving their surface radar and radar-detection, and introducing a revolutionary communication method of flash transmission which would send an entire message of fifty groups in perhaps ten seconds. Such brief radio transmissions would have literally undermined our whole system of HF/DF bearings and fixes, and could have cut seriously into the interception of U-boat radio traffic—the very grist of our "Ultra" mill.

It was imperative, therefore, that we crush German seapower before these ominous developments could become operational. Here is where "Ultra Intelligence" did, indeed, do yeoman service, for it enabled us to so weaken the German Navy after 1943 that we could hasten the European victory while there was still time. I cannot emphasize too strongly the crucial importance of this time factor. It was providential that the periscope/Schnorkel vibration problem of the new U-boats so delayed their

447

working up that but one Type XXI 1600-tonner became operational by the time of the German surrender.

Both the British and ourselves used "Ultra Intelligence" for defensive as well as offensive operations. Our primary defensive operations were concerned with routing convoys and the "Queens" liners which, because of their high speed, operated independently. In combat intelligence, we were in constant touch with the convoy and routing watch officers. A change in U-boat dispositions, such as the German "wolf packs," would immediately be noted and routing changes made. When the Germans started reading our convoy despatches, they became suspicious of these route changes just when a new "wolf pack" line was established. So there was always the danger in using "Ultra Intelligence" in operations that the Germans would change their cipher system, and they did begin changing their "Enigma" keys every few hours instead of once a day. We were more aggressive in our use of "Ultra Intelligence" than the British and got more mileage from it, but then they had so much more to lose. Perhaps it is fair to say that the British were more clever in its use, we, more daring. The teamwork between us was superb, and we were ever grateful for their more experienced counsel and advice.

Yet, in spite of every safeguard, there were occasional disasters. The one that still haunts my memory concerns the first convoy of aviation gasoline tankers en route from Trinidad to the Mediterranean, designated TM-1. We had routed it south of the Azores to by-pass a U-boat "wolf pack" which was generally north of the Azores. However, the short-legged escorts needed refueling when they got to that general area, so the escort commander chose the northern lee of the Azores for refueling to avoid the heavy weather farther south. By the time we received his change of route signal, it was too late. The "wolf pack" hit hard over several days and nights, and it only took one torpedo hit on a tanker for her to become a flaming holocaust. As I recall, only two tankers reached port. The irony of this disaster was that the escort commander had just come from a tour of duty in the British convoy and routing section!

One factor, often overlooked in the breaking of the "Enigma" cipher, was the sheer volume of U-boat radio traffic stemming from Dönitz's direct control of U-boat tactics, especially those involving U-boat attack concentrations, such as the "wolf packs." He not only insisted on complete information from his commanders, but also would himself personally direct individual U-boat tactics. No such volume of radio traffic—so urgently needed by cryptanalysts—would have been available in normal submarine operations. But then, Dönitz's methods almost succeeded!

A final observation about "Ultra Intelligence": I gather the impression from existing books and articles—and I note parenthetically that I have not yet seen the excellent book by Patrick Beesly—that the British not only succeeded in breaking the German U-boat cipher, with the acquisition of an "Enigma" machine and the capture of the U-boat location chart, but continued to break the cipher and sort of spoon-feed the Americans with its tremendous benefits throughout the Battle of the Atlantic. Not having played any part in that cryptographic wizardry, I can only speak indirectly, but it is my distinct impression that, once we got into the war, the American contribution to "Ultra" was at least equal to the British effort.

FOOTNOTE

[1] As a minor footnote to history, because of a pressing deadline I prepared this paper without references other than memory, over a long and pleasant weekend aboard my sloop while anchored in Dun Cove on the beautiful Eastern Shore of the Chesapeake. May it bear up under closer scrutiny than I could give it.

CHAPTER 36

U.S. Naval Forces in the Vietnam War: the Advisory Mission, 1961-1965

Oscar P. Fitzgerald

U.S. Naval Historical Center

The Naval Advisory Group in South Vietnam could point to major achievements during the eventful years from 1961 to 1965. Its members had helped to implement President John F. Kennedy's decision in November 1961 to greatly expand the military aid and advisory effort to the South Vietnamese. Under this program, the number of Navy advisors increased from 53 in the Military Assistance Advisory Group in 1961, working mainly at the headquarters level and the naval school at Nha Trang, to 215 advisors in 1965 assigned to every major component of the South Vietnamese Navy. The growth in the South Vietnamese Navy was equally dramatic. The number of Vietnamese naval personnel burgeoned from 3,000 to 8,000, and another 4,000 were deployed in a new paramilitary Coastal Force which consisted of 644 junks. The number of ships in the Sea Force had more than doubled from 21 to 48 and the River Force had increased from 5 River Assault Groups and 100 boats to 7 RAGs and 150 boats. U.S. naval advisors worked not only to expand the operational arms of the Navy, but also the essential supporting activities such as training, maintenance, repair, and supply facilities. In addition U.S. advisors took well-deserved credit for establishing an intelligence gathering system in the South Vietnamese Navy and for completely renovating and enlarging the naval communications network.[1]

In retrospect, these five years of rapid expansion built a necessary base for the continued growth of the South Vietnamese Navy. But in 1965 U.S. policymakers reached the conclusion that the South Vietnamese Navy's coastal surveillance and river operations were largely ineffective and ordered U.S. naval forces to take over many of their assignments. The discovery of a Communist trawler which had slipped undetected into Vung

Ro Bay in early 1965 and the results of aerial surveillance which revealed many supposedly patrolling South Vietnamese ships at anchor supported this decision.[2] While the American aid and advisory program could take credit for Vietnamese successes it also shared at least part of the responsibility for their failures.

The lavish growth of the Navy during the 1961 to 1965 period, which resulted from Washington-level decisions, caused some of the problems. With the exception of a destroyer, which U.S. advisors declared would be "strictly for window dressing," the South Vietnamese received virtually all the ships they requested. In fact, Captain William H. Hardcastle, Chief of the Naval Advisory Group in 1964 and 1965, compared the Vietnamese to pack rats who would take everything they could get whether they could immediately use it or not.[3]

The United States easily provided large quantities of hardware but training competent officers and crews to man the new equipment proved much more difficult. Leadership suffered as less capable Vietnamese officers were recruited to fill rapidly expanding billets. Just when more training was needed schools became overcrowded and courses were shortened to meet the increased demands. For example, at the Naval Academy in Nha Trang U.S. advisors approved an increase in the number of midshipmen entering in August 1962 from 50 to 100 and a reduction in their schooling from two years to 18 months. Specialized training in other parts of the Navy experienced similar expansion of students and contraction of instruction time. Even on-the-job training was limited, partially by U.S. pressure for more and more intensive operations to meet immediate commitments. It was no wonder that Hardcastle stated that during this period the South Vietnamese Navy "suffered from growing pains. . . ."[4]

Next to leadership and technical training the most obvious deficiency in the South Vietnamese Navy was the poor material condition of its ships. Lack of technical knowledge, initiative, and supervision on the part of many South Vietnamese naval officers obviously contributed to the problem, but the old age of most of their equipment discouraged all but the most diligent.

The South Vietnamese Navy was a young force which commissioned its first boats in 1953 but all of these units had already seen heavy use in the French-Indochina War.[5] After the end of fighting in 1954 the Navy received surplus French equipment and World War II-vintage American ships and craft. A survey at the end of 1961 found one-third of the Sea Force and River Force ships and craft in an unsatisfactory material condition, but the U.S. had only old units to give to the South Vietnamese. For example, the sixth River Assault Group, created in 1962, was equipped with reconditioned boats already in South Vietnam and World War II landing craft since the American Navy lacked craft that were specially designed for river patrol. In the Sea Force, of the 31 ships received between 1961 and 1965, only 12 patrol motor gunboats were new. A study submitted by Hardcastle in early 1965 summed up the situation in these words:

> Most MAP ships in foreign hands are of World War II construction. In many cases the maintenance problems of keeping these ships even marginally operational have become an excessive burden to the limited ship repair facilities available.[6]

Naval advisors recognized the problem and encouraged the development of new and specialized boats and craft for the Vietnamese. One such boat, a 36-foot river patrol craft, was designed by the Bureau of Ships to replace the French-built STCAN in the seventh RAG funded in the fiscal 1964 Military Assistance Program. However, the new boat was poorly conceived with a flat bottom, rather than the V-shaped hull of the STCAN, which made it highly vulnerable to mines. Furthermore, the quality control during construction in the United States was poor and many of them arrived with faulty equipment. Lieutenant Commander T. F. Wootten, the River Force Advisor in 1964, stated flatly that "we would rather have had more STCANs."[7] In July 1965, Hardcastle concurred with South Vietnamese recommendations to correct the most serious deficiencies of the new river patrol craft, including a proposal to modify the hull, but the work required was so extensive that authorities finally decided to phase out these boats altogether in December 1966 after receiving 27 of them.

In addition to a good river boat the Vietnamese needed a skip appropriate for coastal patrol. To accomplish this mission the South Vietnamese originally received an assortment of submarine chasers and minesweepers, then the most suitable units available in the U.S. Navy's inventory. However, they were far from ideal for South Vietnamese purposes, especially since they lacked a good long-range radar which was essential for coastal surveillance. In this period only one South Vietnamese Sea Force ship had a radar with an effective range of 10 miles. The gear on other ships could pick up suspected infiltrators at a maximum of only five miles.

The minesweepers and submarine chasers were useful in light of American contingency planning for Southeast Asia which called for the Vietnamese to maintain a limited capability to defend against external aggression from North Vietnam and Communist China. Even though there was no threat from Viet Cong ocean mines or submarines, other powers might deploy these weapons, so from time to time U.S. advisors insisted that the ships exercise the function for which they were originally designed. Such exercises took precious time away from their primary mission of interdicting coastal infiltration. Finally, in 1965 with ASW-equipped U.S. ships on the scene, the Vietnamese, with American approval, removed their sonar equipment which had been absorbing a great deal of scarce technical talent.[8]

Not until 1963 when the first increment of 12 PGMs began to arrive did the South Vietnamese receive a craft of recent construction specially designed for coastal operations. These ships had been developed in the late 1950's especially for the Military Assistance Program in developing nations. The 100-foot PGM with a small crew, simple design, and high reliability was the ideal ship for the South Vietnamese, but obtaining spare parts for the foreign-made Mercedez-Benz engines proved troublesome. As early as November 1961 Captain Henry M. Easterling, Chief of the Navy Section of the Military Assistance Group at that time, questioned the use of foreign engines in the PGM. The Bureau of Ships assured Easterling that spares would not be a problem and declared that, in any case, no U.S. made engine could meet the size, horsepower, and delivery requirements. Captain Joseph B. Drachnik, Easterling's relief, also expressed doubts about the foreign engines but the Bureau of Ships could offer no alternative power plants.[9]

The PGMs had been operating less than a year when the spare parts trouble feared by Dranchnik and Easterling began to occur. The engines performed well, but when something broke down parts were not readily available. By the end of 1963 less than half the spares requested had been received. Finally, American advisors obtained parts from the Navy purchasing office in London, a tactic which reduced to tolerable levels the previous four to six month lead time for receiving them.

Even with 12 new PGMs the Sea Force could not hope to effectively control the 1,000 mile coastline of South Vietnam. In 1965 the U.S. initially deployed 84 newly built, 50-foot, Swift boats, 26 Coast Guard cutters, and a squadron of patrol aircraft to do the job. American naval advisors recognized that the South Vietnamese had neither the trained manpower nor the resources to deploy such a force, but they thought that the South Vietnamese idea of a separate, paramilitary Coastal Force would make up in numbers what it lacked in sophisticated ships and equipment.

As the Naval Attaché saw it in 1960, the problem was that "there is too much coastline, too many junks, too few patrol craft, and inadequate authority to prevent the junks from doing almost as they please."[10] Commander Ho Tan Queyen, head of the South Vietnamese Navy, had long held that controlling Communist sea infiltration was essential to controlling guerrilla and terrorist activity. In April 1960 President Ngo Dinh Diem approved his plan for the establishment of a coastal surveillance force of 500 junks manned by locally recruited fishermen. It soon became apparent that most fishermen would not sell their junks to the government and refused to serve in the force because of the low pay. Consequently, the government contracted with private shipyards to build the junks and recruited personnel mostly from North Vietnamese refugee camps around Danang. By March 1961, 80 of the projected 500 junks were operating in coastal waters near the Demilitarized Zone.

During this period, the Kennedy administration sought ways to fight the Communists on their own terms among the Vietnamese peasantry. Counterinsurgency, coupled military with political, economic, and psychological measures, seemed to Washington to be the answer. While American leaders debated counterinsurgency doctrine, the South Vietnamese had developed in the junk force a means to control enemy movements at sea while at the same time maintaining government influence and control along the coast through the establishment of bases inhabited by the loyal junkmen and their families.

Once Saigon deployed this force, the United States quickly recognized its potential as an effective counterinsurgency operation. The limited military program for South Vietnam which President Kennedy approved in May 1961, included some support for the Coastal Force. The presidential decision in November resulted in U.S. funding of an expanded fleet of 644 junks. Most of the junks were eventually built under U.S. contract at private shipyards in South Vietnam and deployed by the summer of 1963.

Despite a promising start, the familiar results of rapid growth and maintenance difficulties soon severely reduced the effectiveness of the force. The 1962 South Vietnamese budget had funded only seven divisions but during the year the U.S. expanded the force to 28. In order to pay for the increase in junks and personnel, Coastal Force money was diverted from repairs, material, and equipment. The lack of repair resources came at a time when the original boats deployed in 1960 were sorely in need of repairs. The wooden hulls were highly susceptible to damage by marine borers and a lack of preventative maintenance by the South Vietnamese aggravated the situation.

Another basic cause of the readiness problem was the condition of the U.S. contracted boats. President Diem had expressed concern about the quality of the junks the U.S. was buying. Drachnik investigated at the end of 1962 and reported that:

> the U.S. contract junks under construction are of high quality. They are unquestionably superior to those being constructed under GVN contract. They are, in fact superior to all other junks COMNAVSEC has seen in or around Vietnam.[11]

The boats performed well in the beginning but in time the shortcomings of the U.S. directed construction program began to take their toll. Captain Hardcastle, who relieved Drachnik early in 1964, explained:

> These had been built on a crash program by, to say the least, incompetent house carpenters. They were built of green wood and after the wood dried out I've seen junks with seams open that were about 3/4th of an inch. It was terrible. . . .[12]

As a result, at the start of 1964 hull damage had laid up almost one-third of the Coastal Force junks.

One of Hardcastle's first projects was to rebuild the junk fleet. He chose the Yabuta junk, named after a Japanese technician who designed the boat at the Saigon Naval Shipyard. Ninety of these 57-foot, diesel-powered junks with fiberglassed, wooden hulls were added to the Military Assitance Program, and construction began in October 1964 at the Saigon Naval Shipyard. Hardcastle took particular pains to involve the Vietnamese with the planning and execution. "Let them have a part in it and if they believe in it they're going to succeed and they are capable," he said.[13] The Yabuta became the backbone of the junk fleet.

The Coastal Force had been designed to deter seaborne infiltration, but at least before 1965 evidence appeared to indicate that the Communists depended primarily on land routes. In mid-1961 U.S. observers agreed that the North Vietnamese had available less than 20 junks for infiltration which they used to transport high-level cadre or small amounts of critical supplies into the South. In addition, intra-coastal traffic carried Communist agents and supplies from province to province.[14] This limited activity undoubtedly expanded but Drachnik concluded in March 1964, "I sincerely doubt that there is any significant infiltration into Vietnam by sea."[15] Hardcastle believed that even in 1965 "about 90% of the infiltration of men and materials came in over the land routes."[16]

In view of the predictably meager patrol results, it was not surprising that junk commanders favored independent raids, which, as the Naval Attaché in 1963 admitted, offered "the best opportunity for notoriety, praise, and material results," though often at the expense of surveillance operations.[17] In 1962 and 1963, to support the raiding mission, American Mobile Training Teams trained 120 Biet Hai commandoes who were then assigned to some of the Coastal Divisions. The Vietnamese wanted commandoes with all of the divisions, but Drachnik rejected the idea fearing that it would detract from patrolling. Nevertheless, raids on coastal bases might have been more productive, a conclusion that U.S. advisors later reached in a 1967 study of the Coastal Force.

While naval advisors insisted on patrol as the major military mission of the junk force they were emphasizing amphibious operations as the primary task for the River Force in the Mekong Delta. The concept was a good one based on similar operations during the French-Indochina War but with one difference. The South Vietnamese Navy had no troops under their exclusive control and therefore depended upon the Army, which also exercised operational control over the RAGs, to mount operations. Unfortunately, Army officers exhibited little interest in or appreciation for the capabilities of the River Force. Only infrequently were naval officers included in planning for operations in which their boats took part. Lieutenant Commander Richard Chesebrough, the River Force advisor in 1963, declared that "the River Force is well aware of the extremely wasteful employment of its craft by the

ARVN which had operational control."[18] After priority efforts by U.S. advisors, operational control of the RAGs was finally transferred to the Navy in September 1963 but the troops still had to come from the Army and the force continued to be under-used.

In view of the difficulties with joint operations and the potential for Viet Cong use of the waterways, naval advisors might have given more emphasis to the secondary patrol mission of the River Force. When Secretary of Defense Robert McNamara raised the issue in 1963, Drachnik noted that he had little evidence of extensive Viet Cong use of the rivers in the Delta and predicted that a massive interdiction effort would yield only meager results.[19] However, the Viet Cong, like everyone else in the Delta, did depend upon the myriad canals and waterways for transportation. That the force could effectively interdict Communist traffic was proven in June 1963. After intelligence reports indicated major Communist resupply missions coming across the Cambodian border the River Force deployed a 15-boat patrol there with good results.

Contributing to the overall problem of building an effective South Vietnamese Navy was the difficulty in obtaining exceptional American officers for the advisory program. The naval advisor's job was extremely difficult. He was dealing with a type of inshore and coastal warfare with which the American Navy had little modern experience. Further, the advisors lacked command authority and could only influence their Vietnamese counterparts through persuasion and example. Overeager officers who pushed too hard or tried to circumvent the South Vietnamese found their effectiveness sharply reduced.[20]

Not surprisingly, most officers did not consider the job of advisor to be choice duty. For example, when he was informed that he would relieve Drachnik, Hardcastle worried that "it certainly sounded like a dead end job. I would go as a loyal naval officer but I certainly didn't see any future in that."[21] Drachnik reported that there was:

> a need for improvement in the caliber of advisors of LCDR rank and above. Despite the requirements directed by SECDEF, the quality of LCDRs and above in Navy Section, with few exceptions, continues to be inadequate. MAAG Vietnam probably gets the best of those made available for MAAG assignments, but I am convinced that this is after all of the top officers have been first assigned to prestige staffs and ships.[22]

Drachnik concluded that the caliber of personnel assigned to his command indicated "a distinct lack of interest in the naval effort in Vietnam."[23] Although there obviously were a number of highly competent officers serving in South Vietnam, the selection of suitable advisors continued to be a concern until the major American buildup began in 1965.

Other factors reduced the advisor's effectiveness. Few officers in the years before 1965 received even a brief instruction in the culture and customs of the country, much less the language. Advisors and members of special training teams returning from Vietnam consistently lamented the absence of such training.[24] Advisors could develop a rapport with the Vietnamese but lack of language training complicated an already difficult task. Commander J. L. Ashcroft, the Coastal Force advisor in 1963, expressed the frustrations of most U.S. advisors when he commented after a visit to a district headquarters: "No one speaks English so it is very hard to find out just what is going on and what their problems are."[25]

At best it took an average of six to eight months for an advisor to learn his role and understand the Vietnamese system.[26] But, early in 1962 tour lengths for officers serving in the field were reduced to 12 months. Advisors uniformly believed that the effectiveness of their effort would be substantially increased by lengthening tours. However, the effects on American morale and public opinion had outweighed the loss of valuable experience of only a one-year tour. The problem was compounded since tours did not often overlap to allow for even a short turn-over period between advisors.

At the beginning of 1965 it was easy to criticize the Vietnamese for not doing their job and much of the criticism was justified. But a close look at the advisory program revealed that at least some of the blame for poor Vietnamese performance rested with U.S. policymakers. As a result of decisions in Washington, the Navy's advisory effort in Vietnam was called upon to do a job for which it had little recent experience. U.S. advisors tried to build a South Vietnamese Navy to maintain a coastal blockade and to operate on the rivers and canals of the Mekong Delta. These missions the U.S. Navy had not performed on a large scale since the Civil War. But, despite its shortcomings, the U.S. advisory program laid a basis from which further progress could be made toward the ultimate goal of self-sufficiency for the South Vietnamese Navy.

FOOTNOTES

[1] Naval Advisory Group, "Summary of VNN and VNMC Improvements Attributable to Advisory Assistance, Mid-1961 to Mid-1964," no date.

[2] Naval Advisory Group, Monthly Report, March 1965, p. 2.

[3] Interview, Oscar P. Fitzgerald with Captain William H. Hardcastle, 22 April 1975. Transcript in Naval History Division. Hereafter, Hardcastle Interview.

[4] *Ibid.*

[5] See Edwin Bickford Hooper, Dean C. Allard, and Oscar P. Fitzgerald, *The United States Navy and the Vietnam Conflict*, Vol. I, *The Setting of the Stage to 1959* (Washington, D.C.: GPO, 1977), for background on the early days of the Vietnamese Navy.

[6] Staff Study, Naval Advisory Group, "Naval Craft Requirements in a Counterinsurgency Environment," 1 February 1965, p. 10.

[7] Interview, Oscar P. Fitzgerald with Lieutenant Commander T. F. Wootten, 23 April 1975. Transcript in Naval History Division.

[8] Naval Advisory Group, Monthly Report, March 1965, p. 10.

[9] Chief Navy Section MAAG to Bureau of Ships, ser 081 of 27 November 1961; Chief Bureau of Ships to Chief Navy Section MAAG, ser 009083, no date; Chief Navy Section MAAG to Bureau of Ships, ser 0011 of 18 January 1962.

[10] Naval Attaché, Saigon, Report 45-60 of 8 March 1960.

[11] Chief Navy Section MAAG to Commander Vietnamese Navy, 24 October, 1962.

[12] Hardcastle Interview.

[13] *Ibid.*

[14] Naval Attaché, Saigon, Reports, 170-61 of 10 August 1961; 164-61 of 31 July 1961; 82-S-62 of 25 September 1962.

[15] Captain Joseph B. Drachnik to Admiral Claude V. Ricketts, Report of Experiences as Chief Navy Section, MAAG, Vietnam, Dec. 1961-Jan. 1964, of 13 March 1964, p. 9. Hereafter Drachnik Report.

[16] Hardcastle Interview.

[17] Naval Attaché, Saigon, Report, 130-63 of 8 October 1963.

[18] River Force Advisor to Chief Navy Section, 23 July 1962.

[19] Drachnik Report, p. 11.

[20] This sentiment is reflected in a number of interviews with both Vietnamese and U.S. officers. See for example, Interview, Oscar P. Fitzgerald with Commodore Bank Cao Thang, 21 August 1975. Transcript in Naval History Division.

[21] Hardcastle Interview.

[22] Drachnik Report, p. 6.

[23] *Ibid.*, p. 12.

[24] G. C. Hickey, "The American Military Advisor and His Foreign Counterpart: The Case of Vietnam" (Santa Monica: Rand Corporation, 1965), pp. 19-20, 30-33.

[25] Senior Coastal Force Advisor, Weekly Situation Report, of May 1963.

[26] Hickey, "The American Military Advisory," p. 43.

CHAPTER 37

The U.S. Marine Corps in Vietnam: the Advisory Mission, 1961-1965

Lane Rogers

U.S. Marine Corps Historical Center

United States Marine advisors in Vietnam during 1961-1965 were assigned to three separate advisory missions.[1] The Marine Advisory Unit (MAU), under the Naval Advisory Group of the Military Assistance Command Vietnam (NAG, MACV), was assigned to advise the Vietnamese Marine Corps (VNMC). A second advisory mission evolved in September 1964. As MACV advisory billets increased in I Corps, the northern corps area of South Vietnam, the U.S. Marine Corps agreed to augment the U.S. Army's advisory effort there. Sixty Marine billets were assigned; these Marines advised Vietnamese Army units in I Corps. They had little or no contact with the Marine Advisory Unit Marines; they reported to MACV through the predominantly U.S. Army-staffed I Corps Advisory Group. A third, and lesser known, Marine advisory effort was initiated during the summer of 1964, the Rung Sat Special Zone Advisory Unit, a U.S. Marine- and Navy-manned unit which advised the units in the Vietnamese Navy controlled special zone southeast of Saigon. The Rung Sat advisors reported to NAG, MACV, much the same as the MAU Marines, but the two units had only infrequent contact.

This paper is devoted to the Marine Advisory Unit, primarily because of its unique task—that of Marines advising Marines and, secondly, because of the diversity of accomplishments attributable to this small group of U.S. Marines. The period 1961-65 is especially significant for two reasons: the war changed from "it's the only one we've got" into a conflict unequalled in American experience, and the Vietnamese Marine Corps emerged as a true fighting force. To tell the story of the U.S. Marine Advisory Unit is to tell the story of the Vietnamese Marine Corps.

459

The Vietnamese Marine Corps, or *Thuy Quan Luc Chien*, came into being on 13 October 1954 when Premier Ngo Dinh Diem signed a decree which stated, retroactively:

> Effective 1 October 1954 there is created within the Naval Establishment a corps of infantry specializing in the surveillance of waterways and amphibious operations on the coast and rivers. . . .[2]

With this decree, a heterogenious collection of commando units, both army and navy, was placed under the command of the Vietnamese Marine Corps. Most of these troops had seen action with the French, and later Vietnamese, *dinassauts* (literally: division, naval, assault).[3]

The first informal headquarters of the 2,400-man corps was established at the French naval training base at Nha Trang. The only battalion, the 1st Marine Landing Battalion, was organized there under French supervision.[4] The rest of the Marine Corps—six riverboat companies, five light combat support companies (true naval infantry), and a small training flotilla, was spread from Hue to the Mekong Delta.[5] The first "commandant," titled Senior Marine Officer, was former Vietnamese Army Major Le Quang Trong, but his command was restricted to Nha Trang and vicinity; French officers still filled command billets.[6]

Confrontations with dissatisfied Binh Xuyen, Cao Dai, and Hoa Hao factions in South Vietnam saved the young corps from extinction. National demobilization was scheduled for 1955, but Premier Diem ordered his marines to attack the dissidents in their strongholds. The 1st Marine Landing Battalion distinguished itself, and Diem rewarded his loyal Marine Corps by removing the French officers from command.[7]

While these events were taking place, the first U.S. Marine advisor, Lieutenant Colonel Victor J. Croizat, began to organize what was to become the Marine Advisory Unit. Croizat arrived in Vietnam in August 1954, and first served on the General Commission for Refugees, but in 1955 he was assigned to the U.S. Military Assistance Advisory Group's Naval Section and then to the Franco-American Training Relations Instruction Mission (TRIM). Croizat's tenure as solo Marine advisor was short; in September two more Marines, Captain James T. Breckinridge and Technical Sergeant Jackson E. Tracy, were assigned to TRIM.[8]

During the closing months of 1955, Croizat, his two assistants, and the Vietnamese Marine staff completed plans for a comprehensive reorganization of the corps. On 21 December 1955 the plans were approved *in toto* by the Joint General Staff and, on 18 January 1956, the head of the Marine planning staff, Major Phan Van Lieu, was appointed to the position of Senior Marine Officer.[9]

When the 1st Landing Battalion returned to Nha Trang in Februay 1956, the approved reorganization was accomplished. Within the restriction of a

1,837-man ceiling, the 2d Marine Landing Battalion was formed, as well as a headquarters and service company, and a heavy mortar company. To do this, the riverboat assault companies and the light combat support companies were disbanded.[10]

In 1956 the French withdrew and TRIM was disbanded. Lieutenant Colonel William N. Wilkes, Jr., relieved Lieutenant Colonel Croizat in June, and in August President Diem appointed a new Senior Marine Officer, Captain Bui Pho Chi, the former commander of the 1st Landing Battalion during the 1955 uprisings. In October, Chi was replaced by Major Le Nhu Hung, the fourth in the succession of Senior Marine Officers.[11]

Lieutenant Colonel Wilkes was relieved by Lieutenant Colonel Frank R. Wilkinson, Jr., in June 1958. During this period, a stimulating program for Vietnamese Marine leaders was initiated. Selected Vietnamese Marine officers were sent to the basic and intermediate level officers courses at Marine Corps Schools, Quantico. One early Junior School (intermediate level) attendee, Captain Le Nguyen Khang, established an academic record which was unsurpassed by any other foreign student for many years. Khang was to serve as the fifth and seventh Commandant of the Vietnamese Marines, while fellow Junior School student, Captain Bui The Lan, was to become the eighth and last commandant.[12]

During 1958, terrorism was the primary expression of the growing communist insurgency, but the Viet Cong began to pose a more serious threat as they began to appear in tactical formations. Consequently, as 1958 ended, Diem ordered his armed forces to go after the Viet Cong. The 1st and 2d Marine Battalions began operations near Bien Hoa.[13]

The marine battalions experienced varying degrees of success during 1959. The 1st and 2d Landing Battalions conducted operations in An Xuyen (Camau) and Vinh Binh Provinces. Unfortunately, the U.S. Marine advisors were unable to evaluate the battalions' combat effectiveness; U.S. State Department policy prohibited advisors from accompanying Vietnamese troops on combat operations.[14]

The first of June 1959 was a memorable date for both the Vietnamese Marine Corps and the advisors. On that day the 3d Landing Battalion was formed, the corps, authorized strength was raised to 2,276, and the 1st and 2d Battalions were reorganized. The most significant development associated with 1 June was a Joint General Staff decision to designate the Marine Corps and the ARVN airborne brigade as the nation's general reserve. As such, the marines were directly responsible to the Joint General Staff.[15]

The greatest advisory triumph of 1959 was the result of Lieutenant Colonel Wilkinson's tenacious quest for permission to allow his advisors to accompany their units in the field. Lieutenant General Samuel T. Williams, USA, the MAG Chief, finally granted Wilkinson's request, but with the

461

tacit admonition that the marines were to ". . . act strictly as nonpar-
ticipation observers."[16] The U.S. Marine advisors, thus, became the first U.S.
servicemen to witness ground combat against the Viet Cong.[17]

In May 1960, Major Hung was relieved as Senior Marine Officer by
Major Le Nguyen Khang, an officer who had already established a reputa-
tion for decisive action and sound leadership. The next month, Lieutenant
Colonel Clifford J. Robichaud, a seasoned commander, relieved Lieutenant
Colonel Wilkinson as Senior Marine Advisor.[18]

During the latter months of 1960, the Vietnamese Marine Corps began
task force-size operations, but their campaign was interrupted by an abortive coup attempt the night of 10-11 November. Fortuitously the U.S.
Marine advisors were spared the possible embarrassment of involvement.
The coup attempt coincided with the U.S. Marines' traditional birthday
celebration; all of the advisors were at a party at Robichaud's quarters.[19]

For the Vietnamese Marines, the years 1954-1960 were characterized by
transition from French dominion to autonomous independence. The sect
uprisings of 1955 and the growing communist insurgency provided a harsh
school of experience. The untiring efforts of a few U.S. Marine advisors, 12 in
number, had nurtured the fledgling corps.[20] The real test was about to begin.

By the summer of 1961, the Vietnamese armed forces were preparing to
add 20,000 men; 1,045 were to be Marines, bringing the authorized strength
to 3,321. In July, the 4th Marine Battalion was formed and stationed at
Vung Tau, the "Riviera" of Vietnam, 58 kilometers southeast of Saigon.
The resort town was also the site of the presidential refuge, so the 4th
Battalion was charged with the mission of presidential security. The 4th
Battalion's idyllic tour would last less than four years.[21]

In August 1961, Lieutenant Colonel Robert E. Brown relieved Lieutenant Colonel Robichaud. Brown's indoctrination included the implementation of the authorized expansion, but while he was occupied with the
manpower increase, a two-battalion Marine task force undertook an ambitious amphibious operation. Under orders from JGS, the 1st and 3d Battalions, with Marine advisors Captains Michael J. Gott and James S. G.
Turner, embarked on amphibious ships at Saigon and sailed south, destination: the U Minh Forest on the west coast of the Ca Mau Peninsula, the
general area of Marine operations during 1958 and 1959. The operation was
a flop; no Viet Cong were found, but valuable lessons were learned. Poor
maps, inexperienced navy crews, lack of observation, and difficult terrain
compounded the marines' problems.[22]

Undaunted, the marine task force went back again the next month, but
results were the same: nothing. Frustrating though these operations were,
the Vietnamese Marines were, at least, practicing their trade: amphibious
warfare. Frustration from another source was to overshadow the unpro-
ductive Ca Mau landings.[23]

When not deployed, the Marine battalions were held in their camps, ready to respond to JGS general reserve missions; but in 1961 the Joint General Staff began a practice that caused the advisors to reconsider the general reserve role. The direct link to JGS was not as promising as originally surmised. To keep the Marine battalions busy while in garrison, they were assigned to static security missions such as guarding bridges and installations. The advisors objected that that these tasks detracted from readiness, and that valuable training time was being lost. Their pleas fell on deaf ears; JGS continued the practice.[24]

One tangible result was derived from the extended garrison periods. The advisors were able to make more frequent inspections and, to their delight, discovered that appreciable progress was being made in logistic procedures and materiel upkeep.[25]

Concurrently, beginning in May 1961, Fleet Marine Force Pacific, in conjunction with MAAG, initiated an On-the-Job Training (OJT) Program for U.S. Marines in the Pacific commands. Small groups of Marine officers and NCOs were sent to Vietnam as observers for two-week periods. The dividends of the OJT Program were not fully realized until 1965 when regular Marine formations landed in Vietnam. Some of the 1965 small unit commanders and senior NCOs were OJT veterans; for them Vietnam was not a new experience. For the Marine advisors, the OJT Program was an interesting challenge. As advisors, they were resident experts and often middlemen between the OJTs and the Vietnamese. With the exception of a few misfits, the Marine advisors found the OJTs to be eager—at times too much so—receptive, and appreciative.[26]

In October 1961, retired Army General Maxwell D. Taylor was sent to Vietnam on a fact-finding mission as President John F. Kennedy's special military advisor. The results of Taylor's mission were to have far-reaching consequences, but one immediate product was his recommendation that American helicopter units be sent to Vietnam. The Vietnamese Marines would soon learn airmobile tactics.[27]

On 1 January 1962, the marine organization was redesignated Vietnamese Marine Brigade and authorized strength was raised to 5,483. Two new battalions were added: an artillery battalion of three firing batteries and an amphibious support battalion. The amphibious support battalion of 1,038 Marines provided reconnaissance communications, motor transport, engineer, training, and medical support for the Marine Brigade.[28]

On 8 February, the U.S. Military Assistance Command, Vietnam (MACV) replaced the MAAG, which then became a subordinate command under MACV. Reorganization and restructuring of the MAAG resulted in the creation of a new Marine advisory organization, the Marine Advisory Division (MAD), staffed with 18 marines.[29]

During the year the Vietnamese Marine Corps participated in 23 combat operations, 12 of which were amphibious landings. Eight operations involved the new tactic of helicopter assault. One of the helicopter operations was the first combined U.S. Marine/Vietnamese Marine tactical operation of the war. Marine Medium Helicopter Squadron 362 (HMM-362), in Vietnam as part of the American helicopter augmentation program, Marine Operation SHUFLY, airlifted a Vietnamese Marine Company for an outpost relief mission south of Ca Mau city.[30]

The JGS-imposed static security missions were still being tasked, but the Marines were spending more time in the field. Although they fought no major engagements, at the end of the year the Vietnamese Marines claimed 192 VC killed and 158 taken prisoner. Their advisors, using the Australian verification method "If yer can step on 'is bleedin' 'ead, 'e's dead," reported that 98 dead VC would be closer to the truth, by their count.[31]

The 4th Battalion became operational during the middle of the year and, with the enlarged artillery battalion, provided new flexibility to the marines' operational commitments. The Marine Artillery Battalion, advised by Major Alfred J. Croft and Gunnery Sergeant William A. Loyko, spent most of the year training, but two batteries saw some action. In the future, the attachment of one of the marine batteries to each marine task force would become common practice.[32]

In October, Lieutenant Colonel Clarence G. "Griff" Moody, Jr. (USNA '45), a Navy Cross winner at the Chosin Reservoir, relieved Brown. The Brown/Moody advisory years brought the Vietnamese Marines to a new level of professional skill. Amphibious techniques improved, and helicopter operations became a way of life.[33]

Moody concentrated on two issues: the Marines should have their own "boot camp," and Vietnamese Marine NCOs should be sent to U.S. Marine recruit training depots to learn recruit handling methods. Previously, all recruit training had been handled by the army. Before leaving in October, Moody was able to convince Commandant Khang that these two innovations were vital; and by the end of 1963 the JGS had approved the transfer of marine recruit training to the marines. Concurrently, the Vietnamese Marine engineers, advised by Captain Robert C. Jones, began construction of a basic training camp at Thu Duc. Moody's second project, sending NCOs to the United States for training, was not approved until 1964; then a select few were sent to Marine Corps Recruit Depot, San Diego.[34]

Tactically, the Vietnamese Marines were on the move. The Marine Artillery Battalion became fully operational in January. The task force once more became the marines' primary field formation, in part caused by the creation of the 4th Battalion, and, in part the result of Moody's insistance that the Vietnamese Marines perfect brigade headquarters field functioning.[35]

The year 1963 started with an ambitious amphibious operation: Khang and Moody; a provisional brigade headquarters; the 2d Battalion, Captain Richard B. Taylor, Senior Marine Advisor (SMA); and the 4th Battalion, SMA Captain Don R. Christensen (USNA '53) embarked at Saigon. Destination: Ca Mau, again. This time the plan was to land, seize, and hold, hold by building a fortified hamlet using Marine engineers to do the fortification work. The operation had been compromised from the start; no one, friend or enemy, was at the landing site, but the marines carried out the original plan. When the operation finally ended, 11 April, the marines had killed 11 VC.[36]

At the end of April, JGS ordered Khang's provisional brigade to go after the Viet Cong in the Do Xa, the former Viet Minh stronghold in the rugged highlands where the provinces of Kontum, Quang Ngai, and Quang Tin joined. If nothing else, the operation was an excellent logistic exercise. Other than demonstrating that the Do Xa could be penetrated, again, results were disappointing.[37]

In September, colonel selectee Wesley G. Noren arrived as Moody's October relief. Their extended contact relief time was fortuitous. Noren was in for a rough start.[38]

In mid-October the Vietnamese Marines formed a provisional regiment to conduct operations in Gia Dinh Province, only 32 kilometers northeast of Saigon. The provisional regiment, commanded by now Lieutenant Colonel Khang, consisted of the 1st Battalion, SMA Captain Willem Van Hemert; the 3d Battalion, SMA Captain James P. McWilliams, Jr.; the 4th Battalion, SMA Captain Donald E. Koelper; a composite artillery battery; and the Marine Reconnaissance Company from the Amphibious Support Battalion. This large operation, conducted with units of the Vietnamese Army, Navy, and Air Force, accomplished little. The marines killed six VC and found some tunnels and caves, but there was a surprise aftermath. Lieutenant Colonel Khang was already in Saigon when the operation ended, but when the battalions left the field they did not go back to their barracks.[39]

The Vietnamese Marines were key figures in still another coup. The provisional regiment moved into the capital, and as the 2d Marine Battalion blocked the road to Bien Hoa, the other Marine battalions seized key positions in Saigon. Their advisors had no indication that the marines would be involved in a coup. Noren ordered his staff to go to their quarters and await further instructions. As in 1960, as soon as the coup was over, the advisors went back to work, but this time there were some unsettling repercussions.[40]

The year ended on a sour note. Lieutenant Colonel Khang, a Diem appointee, had not participated in the coup, but also he had done nothing to prevent it. The new provisional government, headed by General Duong

Van "Big" Minh, could not abide Khang's uncommitted power position as marine commander. Consequently, Khang was promoted to colonel and sent to the Philippines as the South Vietnamese Armed Forces Attaché; he could do no harm there, but politically agile Khang would be back sooner than expected. Meanwhile, Lieutenant Colonel Nguyen Ba Lien was appointed as the new commander of the Vietnamese Marine Corps.[41]

Lieutenant Colonel Lien's burden was not easy. National strife and extended combat operations had left their mark. The desertion rate was on the upswing.

Early 1964 was marked by tragedy for the Marine Advisory Division. The first U.S. Marine to die as the result of enemy action was killed by a Viet Cong satchel charge in a Saigon theater. On 14 February 1964, Captain Donald E. Koelper, the 4th Battalion advisor, was killed while trying to warn the occupants of the theater. Koelper's was the first of 13,020 U.S. Marine combat deaths in Vietnam.[43]

On 30 January, Major General Nguyen Khanh had overthrown the "Big" Minh government, charging that Minh and his following were members of a French-led conspiracy to neutralize South Vietnam. In February, shortly after the bloodless coup, self-appointed Premier Khanh recalled Khang from the Philippines to take over the Vietnamese Marine Corps. Lien was out, Khang was in; in the process Khang was promoted to brigadier general.[44]

In mid-May the MAAG was abolished and the Naval Section, MAAG was redesignated Naval Advisory Group (NAG), MACV. The former Marine Advisory Division was renamed Marine Advisory Unit (MAU), NAG, MACV; authorized strength was 11 officers and nine enlisted.[45]

Operationally, the Vietnamese Marines started a prolonged task force campaign in Long An and Go Cong Provinces south of Saigon. As part of the Saigon area HOP TAC pacification program, two Marine battalions swept the two provinces for 9 months, finally leaving Go Cong Province in September. Another Marine task force conducted sweeps in Tay Ninh and An Xuyen Provinces.[46]

Internally, improvements continued to be made in the Vietnamese Marine Corps. Two permanent task force headquarters elements, ALPHA and BRAVO, were established. In July a fifth infantry battalion was authorized. The artillery battalion was reorganized to include one 75mm battery and two 105mm batteries. The Training Company was deleted from the Amphibious Support Battalion and absorbed by the Thu Duc Marine Recruit Training Center which opened in July.[47]

In September, Noren's relief, Colonel William P. Nesbit, arrived. One of his first duties was to implement an augmentation of nine new MAU officers, five of whom became much needed assistant infantry battalion advisors. All new advisors had had some Vietnamese-language training, and Nesbit would witness the result of improved communications.[48]

The year 1964 was characterized by larger, sustained marine operations. Marines were at work in three of the four corps areas. When the marine battalions left Go Cong Province in September the province was well on the way to being pacified, but the Viet Cong were far from idle.[49]

On 24 December a VC bomb killed two Americans and wounded 63 in the Brink BOQ in Saigon. One of the wounded was the Assistant Senior Marine Advisor, Lieutenant Colonel Raymond C. Damm (USNA '45).[50]

Viet Cong activity on the remote Isle de Phu Quoc, next to Cambodia, resulted in the dispatch of a two-company Marine element from the 3d Battalion to the island. I was the advisor. The Marine force was much too small for the task; at least a battalion of Viet Cong was in the hills around the island capital of Duong Dong. On 31 December I hitched a ride on a visiting Army plane and went back to Saigon with hopes of convincing Nesbit that Phu Quoc was just what the Vietnamese Marines needed: an ideal amphibious target, plenty of VC, and no place for them to run; but other Viet Cong activity cancelled all thoughts of Phu Quoc, and the two Marine companies there were quickly withdrawn.[51]

On 27 December 1964, a large VC formation seized the Catholic resettlement village of Binh Gia, 35 kilometers northeast of Vung Tau. The ARVN 30th Ranger Battalion and the 4th Marine Battalion, SMA Captain Franklin P. Eller (USNA '55), were ordered to retake the town. The ARVN 33d Ranger Battalion had tried but had been driven off with heavy casualties.[52]

Landing by helicopter on the morning of the 30th, the 4th Battalion reoccupied Binh Gia with no opposition. The combined force of the 30th and 33d Rangers, and the 4th Marine Battalion was ordered to hold the town. At 1400 a large VC force was spotted and attacked by U.S. Army armed helicopters about three kilometers east of Binh Gia. Another strike was made at 1800; the lead helicopter was shot down.[53]

At 0730 the next morning—31 December—the 2d Company, 4th Battalion was sent out to find the crashed helicopter. The crash site was found at 1045 and 15 minutes later the 2d Company was fighting for its life. As the company tried to break out, the rest of the 4th Battalion moved in to help. By 1545 the battalion found the main VC position in the rubber plantation east of Binh Gia, but the VC had fixed the 4th Battalion. The Viet Cong attacked at 1745 and by 1915 the battle was over. The 4th Battalion commander, Major Nguyen Van Nho, and 28 other battalion officers were dead, 83 enlisted Marines were dead, 13 more were missing; Captain Eller was wounded and evacuated, and wounded OJT Captain Donald G. Cook had been captured.[54]

The 4th Marine Battalion had ceased to exist as a fighting unit. Both ranger battalions had been badly mauled. For the next 3 days stragglers came in to Binh Gia. The Viet Cong were gone, but the impact of Binh Gia was not.[55]

The Vietnamese and American commands were dumbfounded. The Viet Cong had never operated in this strength before. Eventually, intelligence sources were able to piece together the enemy order of battle at Binh Gia; the marines had fought two regiments of the *9th Viet Cong Division.*[56]

The JGS ordered the national reserve, the airborne brigade and the marines, to find and destroy the VC formation that had won at Binh Gia. The marine operation, Operation NGUYEN VAN NHO, found nothing, save some rice stores, and finally was cancelled 7 February 1965.[57]

In mid-February the Amphibious Support Battalion Advisor, Captain Sterling W. Carter, was sent on a mission which was to result in a major U.S. Navy commitment in Vietnam. Vietnamese planes had damaged a suspicious ship which had beached in Vung Ro Bay, about 50 miles north of Cam Ranh Bay. Carter was sent along to advise the ARVN landing party and place demolitions. The VC were inshore defending the beached ship, but the South Vietnamese displayed a reluctance bordering on cowardice when faced with the prospect of landing. At Carter's insistence the landing finally was made. An ARVN battalion moved overland and secured the beach area; and the North Vietnamese cargo was seized, the largest arms cargo seized thus far in the war. As a direct result, Operation MARKET TIME, the U.S./South Vietnamese naval patrol of Vietnamese waters was initiated.[58]

In February, JGS ordered Marine Task Force ALPHA-Colonel Nguyen Thanh Yen and SMA William G. Leftwich, Jr. (USNA '53), to Bong Son in threatened Binh Dinh Province. The communists had almost cut the republic in two in this region.[59]

On 9 March, Vietnamese Marine Task Force ALPHA accomplished a classic counter-ambush south of Bon Son; 63 dead VC were left on the field. Only four Marines were killed, but one of them was Assistant Marine Advisor First Lieutenant Dempsey H. Williams, the second U.S. Marine to die as the result of enemy action. Task Force Advisor Major Leftwich was among the wounded.[60]

A month later, 7 April, the 2d Battalion (SMA Captain Franklin A. Hart, Jr.) operating under Task Force ALPHA was attacked by elements of the *93d, 95th,* and *97th VC Battalions.* Fifty-nine VC bodies were left behind at the cost of only four Vietnamese Marines killed. The 2d Battalion was awarded the U.S. Presidential Unit Citation for this action.[61]

On the 18th of April the 3d Marine Battalion (SMA, the author), originally sent to Da Nang in February to protect the base while U.S. aircraft struck North Vietnam, was committed to a three task force 2d ARVN Division sweep northwest of Tam Ky. The 3d Marine Battalion, the point battalion of the entire force, was in contact by 1145 on 18 April with what was later determined to have been the *60th VC Battalion.* In a sharp afternoon action, two prisoners were taken and the VC left 22 bodies behind when the marines carried the communist position with a bayonet assault.

After a quiet night, the attack continued on the 19th. Light contact continued through the day; progress was slow. At dusk, as it started to drizzle, the 4th Armored Battalion commander, the task force commander, insisted that the force move against the village of Chiem Son (3) to the west. All advisors and the 3d Battalion Commander, Major Nguyen Thi Luong, objected violently. It was getting dark, spotter planes had gone home, and the VC were in Chiem Son (3). The attack went in anyway. As the battalion's lead elements neared the village, the VC, later identified as the *1st VC Regiment*, struck with mortars, rockets, and heavy machine guns. The ARVN task force commander lost control, communications broke down, the armored personnel carrier drivers panicked, all semblance of order vanished. My assistant advisor, Captain Paul S. Marcani, Jr., was wounded. The 39th Rangers, on the left, broke and fled in disorder. Small groups of marines fought desperately in the rain and dark. Order was finally restored about 2130 on a line three kilometers to the rear, but 19 were dead and 18 more were missing. We learned a lot about the *1st VC Regiment* that night, but Chiem Son (3) also caused serious doubts about ARVN, and to a lesser extent marine, command, control, and leadership qualities.[62]

To the south, Colonel Yen's Task Force ALPHA remained in II Corps, rotating battalions between Saigon and Bon Son on a regular basis. The 5th Battalion was ready for combat in June and was blooded with the task force. On 8 August the task force, then including the 2d Battalion (SMA Captain Donald C. Pease) and the 5th Battalion (SMA Captain Francis X. Frey) was sent to the aid of the Special Forces garrison at Duc Co, west of Pleiku on the Cambodian border. On the 9th, as the force moved west on Route 19, it ran into a strong blocking force. As the head of the column broke through the block, the enemy attacked the rear of the column. After a violent nightlong action, the enemy unit, the *32d North Vietnamese Army Regiment*, withdrew. Marine advisors reported a conservative count of 155 dead communists; the official Vietnamese figure was 411; only 28 Marines were killed. The next day the Marines moved into Duc Co.[63]

On 7 September the 3d Battalion participated in combined Operation PIRANA/LIEN KET 8 with the 1st and 2d Battalions, U.S. 7th Marines and the 2d Battalion, 4th ARVN Regiment. It was the beginning of a lengthy association between the 3d Battalion and the 7th Marines.

Colonel John A. MacNeil relieved Nesbit as Senior Marine Advisor in September. The 3d Battalion's participation in November on Operation BLUE MARLIN with the 2d Battalion, 7th Marines, was the direct result of a visit to III MAF by Commandant Khang on 15 October; MacNeil was instrumental in arranging the meeting. Although BLUE MARLIN did not produce significant tactical results, battalion commander Luong remarked to his counterpart, Captain Paul D. Slack (USNA '55) that the operation was like "sending my battalion to Okinawa for on the job training."[64]

As the year ended, MacNeil could look forward to the formation of the 6th Marine Battalion. On 31 December 1965 the Marine Advisory Unit consisted of 24 officers, 1 warrant officer, and 4 enlisted Marines, a far cry from 1961 when there were only three Marine advisors.[65]

Were the Marine advisors effective? Can that judgment be made, even at this stage? Only 10 years later the Republic of Vietnam—beaten—ceased to exist. The fact remains that a small group of U.S. Marines was a vital part of the brief but cataclysmic history of the Vietnamese Marine Corps, a corps which remained in the forefront of its nation's destiny.

FOOTNOTES

[1] Much of the material in this paper is derived from the author's personal recollections as the Senior Marine Advisor to the 3d Vietnamese Marine Battalion from June 1964 until June 1965. Some additional material is in the author's personal collection of papers, memoranda, letters, clippings and notes accumulated during and after the 1964-65 tour with the Vietnamese Marines. Documentation reference to the above sources is noted as Rogers Collection.

[2] Captain Robert H. Whitlow, USMCR, *U.S. Marines in Vietnam: The Advisory and Combat Assistance Era, 1954-1964* (Washington, D.C.: Government Printing Office, 1977), p. 16

[3] Interview with Lieutenant General Le Nguyen Khang, Vietnamese Marine Corps, U.S. Marine Corps Oral History Collection, 30 September 1975

[4] Ibid.

[5] Whitlow, *U.S. Marines in Vietnam*, p. 17

[6] Khang interview

[7] Ibid.

[8] Whitlow, *U.S. Marines in Vietnam*, pp. 16, 19-20

[9] Ibid., pp. 20-21

[10] Ibid., pp. 21-22

[11] Ibid., pp. 22-33

[12] Ibid., p. 23; and Rogers Collection

[13] Whitlow, *U.S. Marines in Vietnam*, p. 31

[14] Ibid., p. 31

[15] Ibid., p. 32

[16] Interview with Colonel Frank R. Wilkinson, USMC, U.S. Marine Corps Oral History Collection, 14 July 1974

[17] Ibid.

[18] Whitlow, *U.S. Marines in Vietnam*, p. 35

[19] Ibid., Khang interview, and Rogers Collection

[20] Lt. Col. Victor J. Croizat, SMA 1954-56; Capt. James T. Breckinridge, AA 1955-57; TSgt Jackson E. Tracy, AA 1955-56; Lt Col William N. Wilkes, Jr., SMA 1956-58; Capt Frank G. Perrin, AA 1956-57; Capt. Cecil J. Bennett, AA 1957; Capt Dale W. Davis, AA 1957-59; Lt Col Frank R. Wilkinson, Jr., SMA 1958-60; Capt Gary Wilder, AA 1958-60; Capt Michael J. Gott, AA 1959-61; Capt James S. G. Turner, AA 1960-61; Lt Col Clifford J. Robichaud, Jr., SMA 1960-61

[21] Rogers Collection
[22] Whitlow, *U.S. Marines in Vietnam*, pp. 35-37
[23] Ibid., pp. 35-37
[24] Ibid., p. 39
[25] Ibid.
[26] Ibid., and Rogers Collection
[27] Whitlow, *U.S. Marines in Vietnam*, p. 43
[28] Ibid., p. 49
[29] Ibid., pp. 47-48
[30] Ibid., p. 65
[31] Ibid., p. 53; and Rogers Collection
[32] Whitlow, *U.S. Marines in Vietnam*, p. 49
[33] Ibid., p. 48
[34] Ibid., p. 100
[35] Ibid., pp. 100-101
[36] Ibid., pp. 101-102
[37] Ibid., pp. 103-105
[38] Ibid., p. 105
[39] Ibid., Khang interview, and Rogers Collection
[40] Rogers Collection
[41] Khang interview
[42] Rogers Collection
[43] Casualty Section, Headquarters, U.S. Marine Corps
[44] Khang interview
[45] Whitlow, *U.S. Marines in Vietnam*, p. 131
[46] Ibid., pp. 132-134
[47] Ibid., p. 136
[48] Ibid., p. 131; and Rogers Collection
[49] Rogers Collection
[50] Ibid.
[51] Ibid.
[52] Senior Marine Advisor's After Action Report (SMAAR) File, 1964-65 (Washington, D.C.: U.S. Marine Corps History and Museum Division Archives)
[53] Ibid.
[54] Ibid. Cook died in a Viet Cong prison camp in South Vietnam in 1967.
[55] Rogers Collection
[56] Ibid.
[57] Ibid.
[58] SMAAR file
[59] Rogers Collection
[60] SMAAR File
[61] Ibid.
[62] Ibid.
[63] Ibid.
[64] Ibid.
[65] Ibid.